T0364820

Citroën C5
Owners Workshop Manual

Martynn Randall

Models covered

(4745 - 10AR1 - 400)

Hatchback & Estate, including special/limited editions
Petrol: 1.8 litre (1749cc) & 2.0 litre (1997cc)
Turbo-diesel: 1.6 litre (1560cc) & 2.0 litre (1997cc)

Does NOT cover models with 3.0 litre V6 petrol engine or 2.2 litre diesel engine
Does NOT cover revised range introduced April 2008

© Haynes Group Limited 2012

ABCDE
FGHIJ
K

A book in the **Haynes Owners Workshop Manual Series**

ISBN 978 1 78521 349 6

British Library Cataloguing in Publication Data
A catalogue record for this book is available from the British Library.

Printed in India

Haynes Group Limited
Sparkford, Yeovil, Somerset BA22 7JJ, England

Haynes North America, Inc
2801 Townsgate Road, Suite 340, Thousand Oaks, CA 91361

Disclaimer

There are risks associated with automotive repairs. The ability to make repairs depends on the individual's skill, experience and proper tools. Individuals should act with due care and acknowledge and assume the risk of performing automotive repairs.

The purpose of this manual is to provide comprehensive, useful and accessible automotive repair information, to help you get the best value from your vehicle. However, this manual is not a substitute for a professional certified technician or mechanic.

This repair manual is produced by a third party and is not associated with an individual vehicle manufacturer. If there is any doubt or discrepancy between this manual and the owner's manual or the factory service manual, please refer to the factory service manual or seek assistance from a professional certified technician or mechanic.

Even though we have prepared this manual with extreme care and every attempt is made to ensure that the information in this manual is correct, neither the publisher nor the author can accept responsibility for loss, damage or injury caused by any errors in, or omissions from, the information given.

Contents

Contents

The Citroën C5 was introduced into the UK in April 2001 to replace the popular Xantia model. At its launch, the C5 was offered with a choice of 1.8 (1749cc) and 2.0 litre (1997cc) petrol engines or 2.0 litre (1997cc) turbo-diesel engines. In September 2004 the range was facelifted, and a range of new, high-output, low-emission engines offered.

The engines fitted to the C5 range are all development of the well-proven units which have appeared in many Citroën/Peugeot vehicles over the years, with the exception of the 1.6 litre diesel engine, newly developed in a joint-venture with the Ford Motor Co.

The engine is mounted transversely at the front of vehicle, with the transmission mounted on its left-hand end. All engines are fitted with a manual transmission as standard (an automatic transmission is available on certain engines).

All models have fully-independent front and rear suspension, incorporating Citroën's unique self-levelling hydropneumatic system. The braking system incorporates discs at the front and the rear.

A wide range of standard and optional equipment is available within the range to suit most tastes, including central locking, electric windows and front, side and curtain airbags. An air conditioning system is available on all models.

Provided that regular servicing is carried out in accordance with the manufacturer's recommendations, the vehicle should prove reliable and economical. The engine compartment is well-designed, and most of the items requiring frequent attention are easily accessible.

Your Citroën C5 manual

The aim of this manual is to help you get the best value from your vehicle. It can do so in several ways. It can help you decide what work must be done (even should you choose to get it done by a garage). It will also provide information on routine maintenance and servicing, and give a logical course of action and diagnosis when random faults occur. However, it is hoped that you will use the manual by tackling the work yourself. On simpler jobs it may even be quicker than booking the car into a garage and going there twice, to leave and collect it. Perhaps most important, a lot of money can be saved by avoiding the costs a garage must charge to cover its labour and overheads.

The manual has drawings and descriptions to show the function of the various components so that their layout can be understood. Tasks are described and photographed in a clear step-by-step sequence.

References to the 'left' and 'right' of the vehicle are in the sense of a person in the driver's seat facing forward.

Acknowledgements

Thanks are due to Draper tools Limited, who provided some of the workshop tools, and to all those people at Sparkford who helped in the production of this manual.

We take great pride in the accuracy of information given in this manual, but vehicle manufacturers make alterations and design changes during the production run of a particular vehicle of which they do not inform us. No liability can be accepted by the authors or publishers for loss, damage or injury caused by any errors in, or omissions from, the information given

Working on your car can be dangerous. This page shows just some of the potential risks and hazards, with the aim of creating a safety-conscious attitude.

General hazards

Scalding

• Don't remove the radiator or expansion tank cap while the engine is hot.
• Engine oil, transmission fluid or power steering fluid may also be dangerously hot if the engine has recently been running.

Burning

• Beware of burns from the exhaust system and from any part of the engine. Brake discs and drums can also be extremely hot immediately after use.

Crushing

• When working under or near a raised vehicle, always supplement the jack with axle stands, or use drive-on ramps.
Never venture under a car which is only supported by a jack.
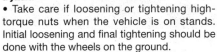
• Take care if loosening or tightening high-torque nuts when the vehicle is on stands. Initial loosening and final tightening should be done with the wheels on the ground.

Fire

• Fuel is highly flammable; fuel vapour is explosive.
• Don't let fuel spill onto a hot engine.
• Do not smoke or allow naked lights (including pilot lights) anywhere near a vehicle being worked on. Also beware of creating sparks (electrically or by use of tools).
• Fuel vapour is heavier than air, so don't work on the fuel system with the vehicle over an inspection pit.
• Another cause of fire is an electrical overload or short-circuit. Take care when repairing or modifying the vehicle wiring.
• Keep a fire extinguisher handy, of a type suitable for use on fuel and electrical fires.

Electric shock

• Ignition HT and Xenon headlight voltages can be dangerous, especially to people with heart problems or a pacemaker. Don't work on or near these systems with the engine running or the ignition switched on.

• Mains voltage is also dangerous. Make sure that any mains-operated equipment is correctly earthed. Mains power points should be protected by a residual current device (RCD) circuit breaker.

Fume or gas intoxication

• Exhaust fumes are poisonous; they can contain carbon monoxide, which is rapidly fatal if inhaled. Never run the engine in a confined space such as a garage with the doors shut.
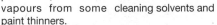
• Fuel vapour is also poisonous, as are the vapours from some cleaning solvents and paint thinners.

Poisonous or irritant substances

• Avoid skin contact with battery acid and with any fuel, fluid or lubricant, especially antifreeze, brake hydraulic fluid and Diesel fuel. Don't syphon them by mouth. If such a substance is swallowed or gets into the eyes, seek medical advice.
• Prolonged contact with used engine oil can cause skin cancer. Wear gloves or use a barrier cream if necessary. Change out of oil-soaked clothes and do not keep oily rags in your pocket.
• Air conditioning refrigerant forms a poisonous gas if exposed to a naked flame (including a cigarette). It can also cause skin burns on contact.

Asbestos

• Asbestos dust can cause cancer if inhaled or swallowed. Asbestos may be found in gaskets and in brake and clutch linings. When dealing with such components it is safest to assume that they contain asbestos.

Special hazards

Hydrofluoric acid

• This extremely corrosive acid is formed when certain types of synthetic rubber, found in some O-rings, oil seals, fuel hoses etc, are exposed to temperatures above 4000C. The rubber changes into a charred or sticky substance containing the acid. *Once formed, the acid remains dangerous for years. If it gets onto the skin, it may be necessary to amputate the limb concerned.*
• When dealing with a vehicle which has suffered a fire, or with components salvaged from such a vehicle, wear protective gloves and discard them after use.

The battery

• Batteries contain sulphuric acid, which attacks clothing, eyes and skin. Take care when topping-up or carrying the battery.
• The hydrogen gas given off by the battery is highly explosive. Never cause a spark or allow a naked light nearby. Be careful when connecting and disconnecting battery chargers or jump leads.

Air bags

• Air bags can cause injury if they go off accidentally. Take care when removing the steering wheel and trim panels. Special storage instructions may apply.

Diesel injection equipment

• Diesel injection pumps supply fuel at very high pressure. Take care when working on the fuel injectors and fuel pipes.

⚠ *Warning: Never expose the hands, face or any other part of the body to injector spray; the fuel can penetrate the skin with potentially fatal results.*

Remember...

DO
• Do use eye protection when using power tools, and when working under the vehicle.

• Do wear gloves or use barrier cream to protect your hands when necessary.

• Do get someone to check periodically that all is well when working alone on the vehicle.

• Do keep loose clothing and long hair well out of the way of moving mechanical parts.

• Do remove rings, wristwatch etc, before working on the vehicle – especially the electrical system.

• Do ensure that any lifting or jacking equipment has a safe working load rating adequate for the job.

DON'T
• Don't attempt to lift a heavy component which may be beyond your capability – get assistance.

• Don't rush to finish a job, or take unverified short cuts.

• Don't use ill-fitting tools which may slip and cause injury.

• Don't leave tools or parts lying around where someone can trip over them. Mop up oil and fuel spills at once.

• Don't allow children or pets to play in or near a vehicle being worked on.

The following pages are intended to help in dealing with common roadside emergencies and breakdowns. You will find more detailed fault finding information at the back of the manual, and repair information in the main chapters.

If your car won't start and the starter motor doesn't turn

- ☐ If it's a model with automatic transmission, make sure the selector is in P or N.
- ☐ Open the bonnet and make sure that the battery terminals are clean and tight.
- ☐ Switch on the headlights and try to start the engine. If the headlights go very dim when you're trying to start, the battery is probably flat. Get out of trouble by jump starting (see next page) using a friend's car.

If your car won't start even though the starter motor turns as normal

- ☐ Is there fuel in the tank?
- ☐ Is there moisture on electrical components under the bonnet? Switch off the ignition, then wipe off any obvious dampness with a dry cloth. Spray a water-repellent aerosol product (WD-40 or equivalent) on ignition and fuel system electrical connectors like those shown in the photos. (Note that diesel engines don't usually suffer from damp).

A Remove the plastic cover and check the condition and security of the battery connections.

B Check that the fuel/ignition system (as applicable) wiring connectors are securely connected (2.0 litre diesel model shown).

C Check that the alternator wiring connectors are securely connected.

D Check that all fuses on the top are still in good condition and none have blown, then release the clips (arrowed) . . .

. . . lift the fusebox and check the fuses at the front face.

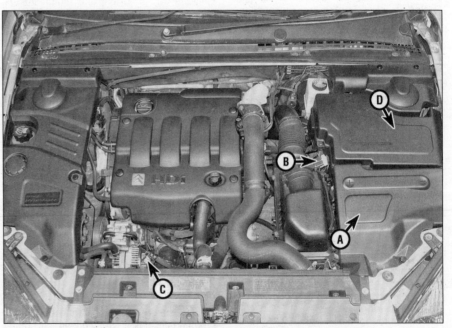

Check that electrical connections are secure (with the ignition switched off) and spray them with a water-dispersant spray like WD-40 if you suspect a problem due to damp

Jump starting

Jump starting will get you out of trouble, but you must correct whatever made the battery go flat in the first place. There are three possibilities:

1 *The battery has been drained by repeated attempts to start, or by leaving the lights on.*

2 *The charging system is not working properly (alternator drivebelt slack or broken, alternator wiring fault or alternator itself faulty).*

3 *The battery itself is at fault (electrolyte low, or battery worn out).*

When jump-starting a car, observe the following precautions:

✓ Before connecting the booster battery, make sure that the ignition is switched off.

Caution: Remove the key in case the central locking engages when the jump leads are connected

✓ Ensure that all electrical equipment (lights, heater, wipers, etc) is switched off.

✓ Take note of any special precautions printed on the battery case.

✓ Make sure that the booster battery is the same voltage as the discharged one in the vehicle.

✓ If the battery is being jump-started from the battery in another vehicle, the two vehicles MUST NOT TOUCH each other.

✓ Make sure that the transmission is in neutral (or PARK, in the case of automatic transmission).

Budget jump leads can be a false economy, as they often do not pass enough current to start large capacity or diesel engines. They can also get hot.

1 Connect one end of the red jump lead to the positive (+) terminal of the flat battery

2 Connect the other end of the red lead to the positive (+) terminal of the booster battery.

3 Connect one end of the black jump lead to the negative (-) terminal of the booster battery

4 Connect the other end of the black jump lead to a bolt or bracket on the engine block, well away from the battery, on the vehicle to be started.

5 Make sure that the jump leads will not come into contact with the fan, drive-belts or other moving parts of the engine.

6 Start the engine using the booster battery and run it at idle speed. Switch on the lights, rear window demister and heater blower motor, then disconnect the jump leads in the reverse order of connection. Turn off the lights etc.

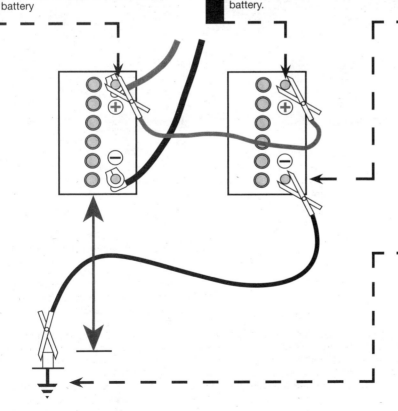

Wheel changing

⚠ *Warning: Do not change a wheel in a situation where you risk being hit by other traffic. On busy roads, try to stop in a lay-by or a gateway. Be wary of passing traffic while changing the wheel – it is easy to become distracted by the job in hand.*

Preparation

☐ When a puncture occurs, stop as soon as it is safe to do so.

☐ Park on firm level ground, if possible, and well out of the way of other traffic.

☐ If you have one, use a warning triangle to alert other drivers of your presence.

☐ Use hazard warning lights if necessary.

☐ Apply the handbrake and engage first or reverse gear (or Park on models with automatic transmission).

☐ If the ground is soft, use a flat piece of wood to spread the load under the jack.

☐ Chock the wheel diagonally opposite the one being removed – a couple of large stones will do for this.

☐ Start the engine, set the suspension height at maximum, and wait for the vehicle to raise fully. Turn off the engine.

Changing the wheel

1 The spare wheel and tools are stored in the luggage compartment. Lift up the floor panel and remove the tool kit and jack from the centre of the spare wheel. Lift out the spare wheel.

2 Remove the wheel trim (where fitted) using the tool provided in the tool kit.

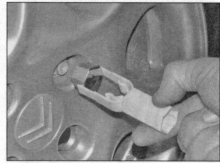

3 Where fitted, pull off the plastic covers from the wheel nuts using the special tool provided.

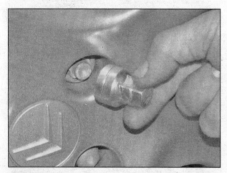

4 With the vehicle on the ground, slacken each wheel bolt by half a turn. On models with alloy wheels, use the special tool to undo the locking wheel nuts.

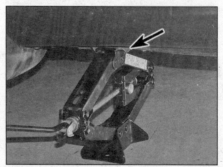

5 Make sure the jack is located on firm ground, and engage the jack head correctly with the sill, indicated by a raised section of the sill. Then raise the jack until the wheel is raised clear of the ground.

6 Unscrew the wheel bolts and remove the wheel. Fit the spare wheel and screw in the bolts. Lightly tighten the bolts with the wheelbrace then lower the car to the ground.

Finally . . .

☐ Remove the wheel chocks.

☐ Set the vehicle suspension height back at Normal.

☐ Check the tyre pressure on the wheel just fitted. If it is low, or if you don't have a pressure gauge with you, drive slowly to the nearest garage and inflate the tyre to the correct pressure.

☐ The wheel bolts should be slackened and retightened to the specified torque at the earliest possible opportunity (see Chapter 1A or 1B).

☐ Have the damaged tyre or wheel repaired as soon as possible.

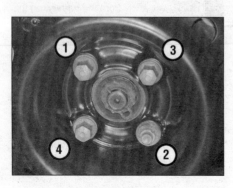

7 Securely tighten the wheel bolts in a diagonal sequence then refit the wheel trim/hub cap/wheel bolt covers (as applicable). Stow the punctured wheel and tools back in the boot, and secure them in position.

Identifying leaks

Puddles on the garage floor or drive, or obvious wetness under the bonnet or underneath the car, suggest a leak that needs investigating. It can sometimes be difficult to decide where the leak is coming from, especially if an engine undershield is fitted. Leaking oil or fluid can also be blown rearwards by the passage of air under the car, giving a false impression of where the problem lies.

 Warning: Most automotive oils and fluids are poisonous. Wash them off skin, and change out of contaminated clothing, without delay.

 The smell of a fluid leaking from the car may provide a clue to what's leaking. Some fluids are distinctively coloured. It may help to remove the engine undershield, clean the car carefully and to park it over some clean paper overnight as an aid to locating the source of the leak.
Remember that some leaks may only occur while the engine is running.

Sump oil

Engine oil may leak from the drain plug...

Oil from filter

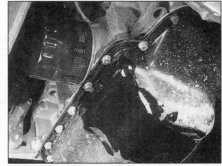

...or from the base of the oil filter.

Gearbox oil

Gearbox oil can leak from the seals at the inboard ends of the driveshafts.

Antifreeze

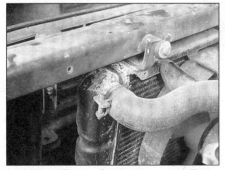

Leaking antifreeze often leaves a crystalline deposit like this.

Brake fluid

A leak occurring at a wheel is almost certainly brake fluid.

Power steering fluid

Power steering fluid may leak from the pipe connectors on the steering rack.

Towing

When all else fails, you may find yourself having to get a tow home – or of course you may be helping somebody else. Long-distance recovery should only be done by a garage or breakdown service. For shorter distances, DIY towing using another car is easy enough, but observe the following points:

☐ Use a proper tow-rope – they are not expensive. The vehicle being towed must display an ON TOW sign in its rear window.

☐ Always turn the ignition key to the 'on' position when the vehicle is being towed, so that the steering lock is released, and the direction indicator and brake lights work.

☐ The towing eye is kept inside the spare wheel (see *Wheel changing*). To fit the eye, unclip the access cover from the relevant bumper and screw the eye firmly into position **(see illustration)**.

☐ The vehicle must not be towed with the suspension in the 'minimum' or 'maximum' height position.

☐ Before being towed, release the handbrake and select neutral on the transmission.

Caution: On models with automatic transmission, do not exceed 30 mph and do not tow for more than 30 miles. If in doubt, do not tow, or transmission damage may result.

☐ Note that greater-than-usual pedal pressure will be required to operate the brakes, since the vacuum servo unit is only operational with the engine running.

☐ On models with power steering, greater-than-usual steering effort will also be required.

☐ The driver of the car being towed must keep the tow-rope taut at all times to avoid snatching.

☐ Only ever tow the vehicle with all four wheels on the ground..

☐ Make sure that both drivers know the route before setting off.

☐ Only drive at moderate speeds and keep the distance towed to a minimum. Drive smoothly and allow plenty of time for slowing down at junctions.

Screw the towing eye firmly into position

Introduction

There are some very simple checks which need only take a few minutes to carry out, but which could save you a lot of inconvenience and expense.

These *Weekly checks* require no great skill or special tools, and the small amount of time they take to perform could prove to be very well spent, for example:

☐ Keeping an eye on tyre condition and pressures, will not only help to stop them wearing out prematurely, but could also save your life.

☐ Many breakdowns are caused by electrical problems. Battery-related faults are particularly common, and a quick check on a regular basis will often prevent the majority of these.

☐ If your car develops a brake fluid leak, the first time you might know about it is when your brakes don't work properly. Checking the level regularly will give advance warning of this kind of problem.

☐ If the oil or coolant levels run low, the cost of repairing any engine damage will be far greater than fixing the leak, for example.

Underbonnet check points

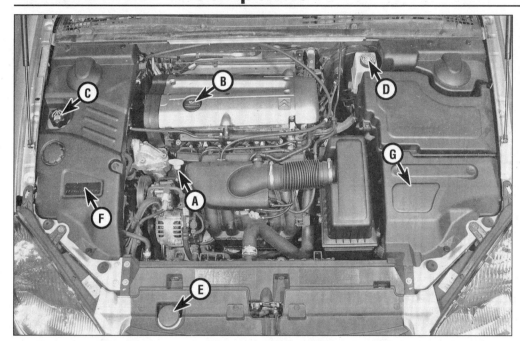

◄ 1.8 litre petrol (2.0 litre similar)

A *Engine oil level dipstick*

B *Engine oil filler cap*

C *Coolant expansion tank*

D *Brake/clutch fluid reservoir*

E *Screen washer fluid reservoir*

F *LDS suspension/steering fluid reservoir*

G *Battery*

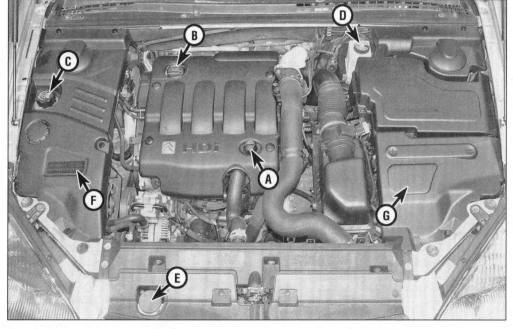

◄ 2.0 litre SOHC diesel

A *Engine oil level dipstick*

B *Engine oil filler cap*

C *Coolant expansion tank*

D *Brake/clutch fluid reservoir*

E *Screen washer fluid reservoir*

F *LDS suspension/steering fluid reservoir*

G *Battery*

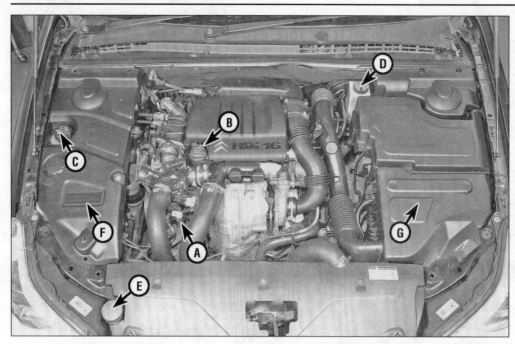

A *Engine oil level dipstick*
B *Engine oil filler cap*
C *Coolant expansion tank*
D *Brake/clutch fluid reservoir*
E *Screen washer fluid reservoir*
F *LDS suspension/steering fluid reservoir*
G *Battery*

Engine oil level

Before you start

✔ Make sure that the car is on level ground.
✔ Check the oil level before the car is driven, or at least 5 minutes after the engine has been switched off.

If the oil is checked immediately after driving the vehicle, some of the oil will remain in the upper engine components, resulting in an inaccurate reading on the dipstick.

The correct oil

Modern engines place great demands on their oil. It is very important that the correct oil for your car is used (see *Lubricants and fluids*).

Car care

● If you have to add oil frequently, you should check whether you have any oil leaks. Place some clean paper under the car overnight, and check for stains in the morning. If there are no leaks, then the engine may be burning oil.
● Always maintain the level between the upper and lower dipstick marks (see photo 2). If the level is too low, severe engine damage may occur. Oil seal failure may result if the engine is overfilled by adding too much oil.

1 The dipstick is located at the front of the engine (see *Underbonnet check points* for exact location); The dipstick is often brightly-coloured or has a picture of an oil can on the top for easy identification. Withdraw the dipstick, and wipe it clean.

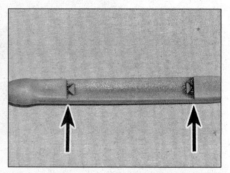

2 Insert the clean dipstick into the tube as far as it will go, then withdraw it again. Note the oil level on the end of the dipstick, which should be between the upper and lower mark.

3 Oil is added through the filler cap. Unscrew the cap and top-up the level; a funnel may help to reduce spillage.

4 Add the oil slowly, checking the level on the dipstick often. Don't overfill (see *Car care*). Approximately 1.5 litres of oil will raise the level from the lower mark to the upper mark.

Coolant level

 Warning: Do not attempt to remove the expansion tank pressure cap when the engine is hot, as there is a very great risk of scalding. Do not leave open containers of coolant about, as it is poisonous.

Car care

● With a sealed-type cooling system, adding coolant should not be necessary on a regular basis. If frequent topping-up is required, it is likely there is a leak. Check the radiator, all hoses and joint faces for signs of staining or wetness, and rectify as necessary.

● It is important that antifreeze is used in the cooling system all year round, not just during the winter months. Don't top up with water alone, as the antifreeze will become diluted.

1 The coolant level must be checked with the engine cold. Prise up the centre pins from the plastic rivets, then lift the plastic cover from the coolant expansion tank. Unscrew the coolant expansion tank cap (see **Warning**).

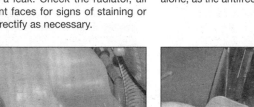

2 The coolant level should be between the MAX and MIN marks on the expansion tank neck insert.

3 If topping-up is necessary, add a mixture of water and antifreeze to the expansion tank until the coolant level is between the level marks. Once the level is correct, securely refit the cap.

Brake and clutch fluid level

Before you start

✔ Make sure that the car is on level ground.

✔ Cleanliness is of great importance when dealing with the braking system, so take care to clean around the reservoir cap before topping-up. Use only clean brake fluid.

Safety first!

● If the reservoir requires repeated topping-up, this is an indication of a fluid leak somewhere in the system, which should be investigated immediately.

● If a leak is suspected, the car should not be driven until the braking system has been checked. Never take any risks where brakes are concerned.

 Warning: Brake fluid can harm your eyes and damage painted surfaces, so use extreme caution when handling and pouring it. Do not use fluid which has been standing open for some time, as it absorbs moisture from the air, which can cause a dangerous loss of braking effectiveness.

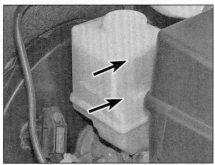

1 The upper (MAX) and lower (DANGER) fluid level markings are on the side of the reservoir, which is located in the left-hand rear corner of the engine compartment. The fluid level must always be kept between these two marks.

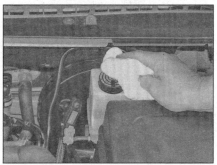

2 If topping-up is necessary, first wipe clean the area around the filler cap with a clean cloth, then unscrew the cap and remove it along with the rubber diaphragm.

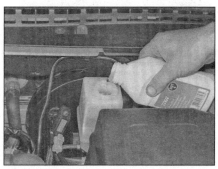

3 Carefully add fluid, avoiding spilling it on the surrounding paintwork. Use only the specified hydraulic fluid. After filling the correct level, refit the cap and diaphragm and tighten it securely. Wipe off any spilt fluid.

Tyre condition and pressure

It is very important that tyres are in good condition, and at the correct pressure - having a tyre failure at any speed is highly dangerous. Tyre wear is influenced by driving style - harsh braking and acceleration, or fast cornering, will all produce more rapid tyre wear. As a general rule, the front tyres wear out faster than the rears. Interchanging the tyres from front to rear ("rotating" the tyres) may result in more even wear. However, if this is completely effective, you may have the expense of replacing all four tyres at once! Remove any nails or stones embedded in the tread before they penetrate the tyre to cause deflation. If removal of a nail does reveal that the tyre has been punctured, refit the nail so that its point of penetration is marked. Then immediately change the wheel, and have the tyre repaired by a tyre dealer.

Regularly check the tyres for damage in the form of cuts or bulges, especially in the sidewalls. Periodically remove the wheels, and clean any dirt or mud from the inside and outside surfaces. Examine the wheel rims for signs of rusting, corrosion or other damage. Light alloy wheels are easily damaged by "kerbing" whilst parking; steel wheels may also become dented or buckled. A new wheel is very often the only way to overcome severe damage.

New tyres should be balanced when they are fitted, but it may become necessary to re-balance them as they wear, or if the balance weights fitted to the wheel rim should fall off. Unbalanced tyres will wear more quickly, as will the steering and suspension components. Wheel imbalance is normally signified by vibration, particularly at a certain speed (typically around 50 mph). If this vibration is felt only through the steering, then it is likely that just the front wheels need balancing. If, however, the vibration is felt through the whole car, the rear wheels could be out of balance. Wheel balancing should be carried out by a tyre dealer or garage.

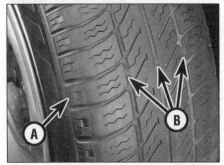

1 *Tread Depth - visual check*
The original tyres have tread wear safety bands (B), which will appear when the tread depth reaches approximately 1.6 mm. The band positions are indicated by a triangular mark on the tyre sidewall (A).

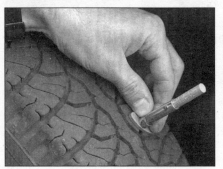

2 *Tread Depth - manual check*
Alternatively, tread wear can be monitored with a simple, inexpensive device known as a tread depth indicator gauge.

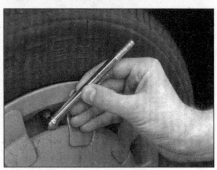

3 *Tyre Pressure Check*
Check the tyre pressures regularly with the tyres cold. Do not adjust the tyre pressures immediately after the vehicle has been used, or an inaccurate setting will result.

Tyre tread wear patterns

Shoulder Wear

Underinflation (wear on both sides)
Under-inflation will cause overheating of the tyre, because the tyre will flex too much, and the tread will not sit correctly on the road surface. This will cause a loss of grip and excessive wear, not to mention the danger of sudden tyre failure due to heat build-up.
Check and adjust pressures
Incorrect wheel camber (wear on one side)
Repair or renew suspension parts
Hard cornering
Reduce speed!

Centre Wear

Overinflation
Over-inflation will cause rapid wear of the centre part of the tyre tread, coupled with reduced grip, harsher ride, and the danger of shock damage occurring in the tyre casing.
Check and adjust pressures

If you sometimes have to inflate your car's tyres to the higher pressures specified for maximum load or sustained high speed, don't forget to reduce the pressures to normal afterwards.

Uneven Wear

Front tyres may wear unevenly as a result of wheel misalignment. Most tyre dealers and garages can check and adjust the wheel alignment (or "tracking") for a modest charge.
Incorrect camber or castor
Repair or renew suspension parts
Malfunctioning suspension
Repair or renew suspension parts
Unbalanced wheel
Balance tyres
Incorrect toe setting
Adjust front wheel alignment
Note: *The feathered edge of the tread which typifies toe wear is best checked by feel.*

Screen washer fluid level

● Screenwash additives not only keep the windscreen clean during bad weather, they also prevent the washer system freezing in cold weather – which is when you are likely to need it most. Don't top-up using plain water, as the screenwash will become diluted, and will freeze in cold weather.

 Warning: On no account use engine coolant antifreeze in the screen washer system – this may damage the paintwork.

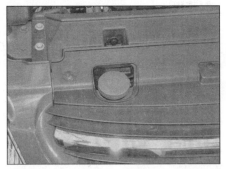

1 The washer fluid reservoir is located in the right-hand front corner of the engine compartment. To check the fluid level, open the cap and look down the filler neck.

2 If topping-up is necessary, add water and a screenwash additive in the quantities recommended on the bottle.

Wiper blades

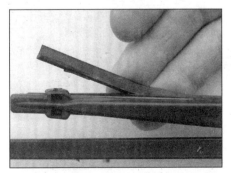

1 Check the condition of the wiper blades: if they are cracked or show signs of deterioration, or if the glass swept area is smeared, renew them. For maximum clarity of vision, wiper blades should be renewed annually.

2 To remove a windscreen wiper blade, on early models, raise the wiper arm slightly away from the screen, then lift the arm locking clip. Slide the blade from the wiper arm and remove it from the vehicle, taking care not to allow the arm to damage the windscreen.

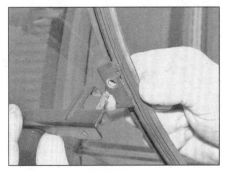

3 On later models, lift the arm, rotate the blade 90°, and pull it from the mounting pin.

Battery

Caution: Before carrying out any work on the vehicle battery, read the precautions given in 'Safety first!' at the start of this manual.

✔ Make sure that the battery tray is in good condition, and that the clamp is tight. Corrosion on the tray, retaining clamp and the battery itself can be removed with a solution of water and baking soda. Thoroughly rinse all cleaned areas with water. Any metal parts damaged by corrosion should be covered with a zinc-based primer, then painted.

✔ Periodically (approximately every three months), check the charge condition of the battery as described in Chapter 5A.

✔ If the battery is flat, and you need to jump start your vehicle, see *Roadside Repairs*.

 Battery corrosion can be kept to a minimum by applying a layer of petroleum jelly to the clamps and terminals after they are reconnected.

1 Prise up the centre pin of the clip on the front edge . . .

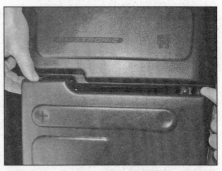

2 . . . then release the clips at the rear, and remove the plastic cover to gain access to the battery, which is located at the front left-hand corner of the engine compartment. The exterior of the battery should be inspected periodically for damage such as a cracked case or cover.

3 Check the battery lead clamps for tightness to ensure good electrical connections, and check the leads for signs of damage.

4 If corrosion (white, fluffy deposits) is evident, remove the cables from the battery terminals, clean them with a small wire brush, then refit them. Automotive stores sell a tool for cleaning the battery post . . .

5 . . . as well as the battery cable clamps.

Bulbs and fuses

✔ Check all external lights and the horn. Refer to the appropriate Sections of Chapter 12 for details if any of the circuits are found to be inoperative.

✔ Visually check all accessible wiring connectors, harnesses and retaining clips for security, and for signs of chafing or damage.

 If you need to check your brake lights and indicators unaided, back up to a wall or garage door and operate the lights. The reflected light should show if they are working properly.

1 If a single indicator light, stop-light, sidelight or headlight has failed, it is likely that a bulb has blown, and will need to be renewed. Refer to Chapter 12 for details. If both stop-lights have failed, it is possible that the switch has failed (see Chapter 9).

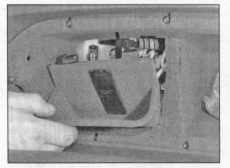

2 If more than one indicator light or tail light has failed, it is likely that either a fuse has blown or that there is a fault in the circuit (see Chapter 12). Fuses are located behind the cover in the passenger's glovebox, release the three retaining clips and lower the cover. Additional fuses and relays are located in the left-hand side of the engine compartment fusebox.

3 To renew a blown fuse, simply pull it out using the tweezers provided and fit a new fuse of the correct rating (see Chapter 12). If the fuse blows again, it is important that you find out why – a complete checking procedure is given in Chapter 12.

Lubricants and fluids

Engine (petrol).	Multigrade engine oil 5W30 to 10W40 to specification ACEA A3/A5, API SL/CF or better Total Quartz or Esso Ultra/Ultron
Engine (diesel).	Multigrade 5W40 engine oil to ACEA B3, API CF or better* Esso Ultron diesel or Total Quartz
Cooling system.	Citroën antifreeze Gurit Essex Revkogel 2000 or BASF Glysantin G33
Manual transmission	SAE 75W-80W to API GL5 Total Transmission BV
Automatic transmission:	
AL4	Citroën fluid No 9736 22
AM6.	Citroën fluid No 9980 D4
Braking and clutch system	Hydraulic fluid to DOT 4
Power steering/suspension.	Total fluide LDS (note that LDS fluid cannot be mixed with LHM fluid)

Note that engines fitted with a particulate filter must use 5W40 fully synthetic oil to ACEA B5 (Total Quartz 9000)

Tyre pressures (cold)

Note 1: *The make of tyres, the sizes and the pressures for each specific vehicle are given on a label attached to the driver's door A-pillar. On models with a space-saver spare wheel (family estates), a separate pressure is given for the spare tyre, and care must be taken not to misread the sticker; the space-saver wheel is inflated to a lot higher pressure than the standard tyres (typically 60 psi). On models with a space-saver spare wheel, note that the spare is for temporary use only; whilst the spare is fitted, the vehicle should not be driven at speeds in excess of 50 mph.*
Note 2: *Pressures on the label apply to original-equipment tyres listed, and may vary if any other make or type of tyre is fitted; check with the tyre manufacturer or supplier for correct pressures if necessary.*
Note 3: *Tyre pressures must always be checked with the tyres cold to ensure accuracy.*

Chapter 1 Part A:
Routine maintenance and servicing – petrol models

Contents

Degrees of difficulty

| Easy, suitable for novice with little experience | 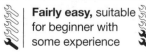 | Fairly easy, suitable for beginner with some experience | | Fairly difficult, suitable for competent DIY mechanic | | Difficult, suitable for experienced DIY mechanic | 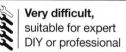 | Very difficult, suitable for expert DIY or professional | |

Engine identification

Indirect injection:
Designation:
1.8 litre EW7J4
2.0 litre EW10J4
Engine code:
1.8 litre 6FZ
2.0 litre . . . . RFN
Direct injection:
Designation:
2.0 litre EW10D
Engine code . . . . RLZ

Lubricants and fluids

See end of *Weekly checks* on page 0•17

Capacities

Engine oil
Drain and refill, with filter change. . . . . 4.25 litres
Between dipstick MAX and MIN markings. 1.7 litres
Cooling system . . . . 8.8 litres

Transmission
Manual (drain and refill) . . . . 1.8 litres
Automatic:
Drain and refill. . . . . 4.5 litres
Total capacity (including torque converter). . . . . 6.0 litres

Fuel tank
All models (approximately) . . . . 66.0 litres

Cooling system

Antifreeze mixture*:
50% antifreeze . . . . Protection down to -37°C
55% antifreeze . . . . Protection down to -45°C
* Note: *Refer to antifreeze manufacturer for latest recommendations.*

Ignition system

Firing order . . . . 1 – 3 – 4 – 2

Spark plugs:	**Type**	**Electrode gap**
EW7J4 engines.	Eyquem RFN52HZ	0.9 to 1.0 mm
	or Champion REC9YCL	0.9 to 1.0 mm
EW10J4	Eyquem RFN52HZ	0.9 to 1.0 mm
	or Champion REC9YCL	0.9 to 1.0 mm
EW10D	Bosch ZR8TPP15	1.0 mm

Brakes

Front brake pad friction material minimum thickness . . . . 2.5 mm
Rear brake pad friction material minimum thickness. . . . . 3.0 mm
Front disc minimum thickness:
1.8 litre Hatchback . . . . 20.0 mm
1.8 litre Estate and 2.0 litre. . . . . 24.0 mm
Rear disc minimum thickness . . . . 12.0 mm

Remote control battery

Type CR1620

Tyre pressures

Refer to the end of *Weekly checks* on page 0•17

Torque wrench settings	Nm	lbf ft
Automatic transmission filler plug	24	18
Automatic transmission level plug	24	18
Manual transmission level/filler plug	20	15
Spark plugs:		
EW7J4 and EW10J4 engines	25	18
EW10D	22	17
Sump engine oil drain plug.	30	22
Wheel bolts.	90	66

The maintenance intervals in this manual are provided with the assumption that you will be carrying out the work yourself. These are the minimum maintenance intervals recommended by the manufacturer for vehicles driven daily. If you wish to keep your vehicle in peak condition at all times, you may wish to perform some of these procedures more often. We encourage frequent maintenance, because it enhances the efficiency, performance and resale value of your vehicle.

If the vehicle is driven in dusty areas, used to tow a trailer, or driven frequently at slow speeds (idling in traffic) or on short journeys, more frequent maintenance intervals are recommended.

When the vehicle is new, it should be serviced by a dealer service department (or other workshop recognised by the vehicle manufacturer as providing the same standard of service) in order to preserve the warranty. The vehicle manufacturer may reject warranty claims if you are unable to prove that servicing has been carried out as and when specified, using only original equipment parts or parts certified to be of equivalent quality.

All Citroën models are equipped with a service indicator function incorporated into the mileage recorder, which will indicate the mileage until the next service is due. However, Citroën point out that, 'due to the relationship between time and mileage, some operating conditions will make annual service more suitable'.

Every 250 miles or weekly
- [ ] Refer to *Weekly checks*

Every 6000 miles or 6 months
- [ ] Engine oil and filter – renewal (Section 3)

Note: *Citroën recommend that the engine oil and filter are changed every 18 000 miles. However, oil and filter changes are good for the engine and we recommend that the oil and filter are renewed more frequently, especially if the vehicle is used on a lot of short journeys.*

Every 12 000 miles or 12 months
Note: *The 12 000 mile intervals start at 18 000 miles, ie, at 18 000 miles, 30 000 miles, 42 000 miles, 54 000 miles, etc.*
- [ ] Service indicator – resetting (Section 4)
- [ ] Hoses and fluids – leak check (Section 5)
- [ ] Steering and suspension components – check (Section 6)
- [ ] Brake pad wear and disc check (Section 7)
- [ ] Handbrake – check and adjustment (Section 8)
- [ ] Seat belt condition – check (Section 9)
- [ ] Airbag system – check (Section 10)
- [ ] Headlight beam alignment – check (Section 11)
- [ ] LDS fluid level – check (Section 12)
- [ ] Road test (Section 13)
- [ ] Coolant antifreeze concentration – check (Section 14)
- [ ] Driveshaft joints and gaiters – check (Section 15)
- [ ] Exhaust system – check (Section 16)
- [ ] Hinges and locks – lubrication (Section 17)
- [ ] Lane wandering warning system sensor – clean (Section 18)
- [ ] Auxiliary drivebelt condition – check (Section 19)

Every 24 000 miles or 2 years (whichever occurs first)
- [ ] Pollen filter – renewal (Section 20)
- [ ] Spark plugs – renewal (Section 21)

Note: *EW10D engine only*

Every 36 000 miles
- [ ] Spark plugs – renewal (Section 21)

Note: *All except EW10D engine*
- [ ] Air filter element – renewal (Section 22)
- [ ] Manual transmission fluid level – check (Section 23)
- [ ] Automatic transmission fluid level – check (Section 24)

Every 80 000 miles or 10 years (whichever occurs first)
- [ ] Timing belt – renewal (Section 25)

Note: *This is the interval recommended by Citroën. However, It is strongly recommended that the interval is reduced on vehicles which are subjected to intensive use, ie, mainly short journeys or a lot of stop-start driving. The actual belt renewal interval is very much up to the individual owner, but bear in mind that severe engine damage will result if the belt breaks.*

Every 2 years
- [ ] Coolant – renewal (Section 26)

Note: *This work is not included in the Citroën schedule, and should not be required if the recommended Citroën antifreeze/inhibitor is used.*
- [ ] Brake fluid – renewal (Section 27)
- [ ] Remote control battery – renewal (Section 28)

Every 10 years
- [ ] Renew the airbags – models up to September 2004 (pre-facelift) (Section 29)

Every 15 years
- [ ] Renew the airbags – models from September 2004 (post-facelift) (Section 29)

Underbonnet view of a 1.8 litre model – others similar

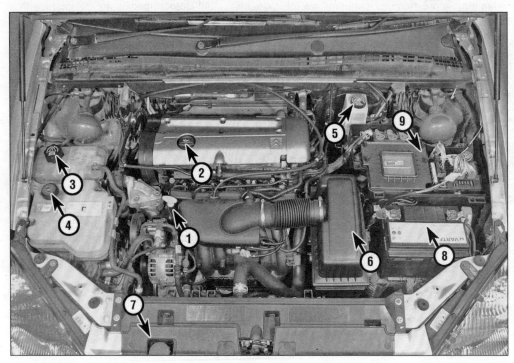

1 Oil level dipstick
2 Oil filler cap
3 Coolant expansion tank cap
4 LDS fluid reservoir
5 Brake/clutch fluid reservoir
6 Air filter cover
7 Washer fluid reservoir cap
8 Battery
9 ECM/fusebox

Front underbody view – 1.8 litre model

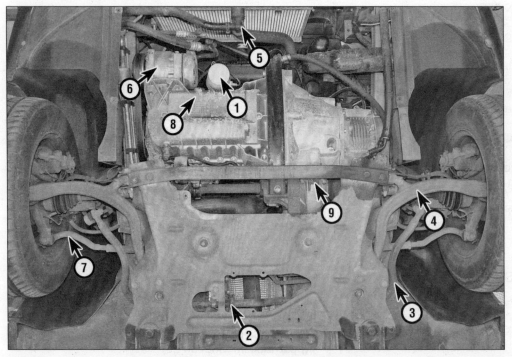

1 Oil filter
2 Height sensor
3 Anti-roll bar
4 Lower suspension arm
5 Radiator lower hose connection
6 Air conditioning compressor
7 Steering track rod end
8 Engine oil drain plug
9 Transmission oil drain plug

Rear underbody view

1 Fuel tank
2 Rear suspension sphere
3 Trailing arm
4 Rear anti-roll bar
5 Rear height sensor
6 Exhaust tailbox
7 Suspension strut

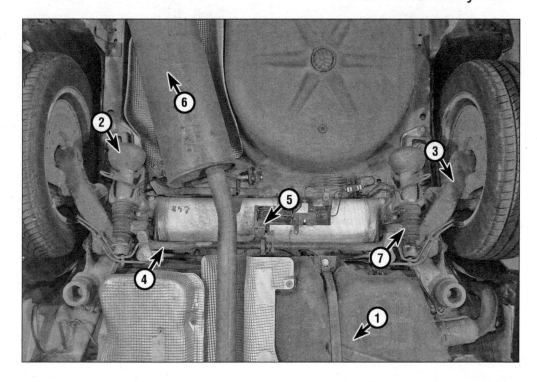

Maintenance procedures

1 General information

This Chapter is designed to help the home mechanic maintain his/her vehicle for safety, economy, long life and peak performance.

The Chapter contains a master maintenance schedule, followed by Sections dealing specifically with each task in the schedule. Visual checks, adjustments, component renewal and other helpful items are included. Refer to the accompanying illustrations of the engine compartment and the underside of the vehicle for the locations of the various components.

Servicing your vehicle in accordance with the mileage/time maintenance schedule and the following Sections will provide a planned maintenance programme, which should result in a long and reliable service life. This is a comprehensive plan, so maintaining some items, but not others, at the specified service intervals will not produce the same results.

As you service your vehicle, you will discover that many of the procedures can – and should – be grouped together, because of the particular procedure being performed, or because of the close proximity of two otherwise-unrelated components to one another. For example, if the vehicle is raised for any reason, the exhaust system could be inspected at the same time as the suspension and steering components.

The first step in this maintenance programme is to prepare yourself before the actual work begins. Read through all the Sections relevant to the work to be carried out, then make a list and gather together all the parts and tools required. If a problem is encountered, seek advice from a parts specialist, or a dealer service department.

2 Regular maintenance

If, from the time the vehicle is new, the routine maintenance schedule is followed closely, and frequent checks are made of fluid levels and high-wear items, as suggested throughout this manual, the engine will be kept in relatively good running condition, and the need for additional work will be minimised.

It is possible that there will be times when the engine is running poorly due to the lack of regular maintenance. This is even more likely if a used vehicle, which has not received regular and frequent maintenance checks, is purchased. In such cases, additional work may need to be carried out, outside of the regular maintenance intervals.

If engine wear is suspected, a compression test (refer to Chapter 2A or 2B) will provide valuable information regarding the overall performance of the main internal components. Such a test can be used as a basis to decide on the extent of the work to be carried out. If, for example, a compression test indicates serious internal engine wear, conventional maintenance as described in this Chapter will not greatly improve the performance of the engine, and may prove a waste of time and money, unless extensive overhaul work (Chapter 2F) is carried out first.

The following series of operations are those most often required to improve the performance of a generally poor-running engine:

Primary operations

a) Clean, inspect and test the battery ('Weekly checks' and Chapter 5A)
b) Check all the engine-related fluids ('Weekly checks').
c) Check the condition and tension of the auxiliary drivebelt (Section 19).
d) Renew the spark plugs (Section 21).
e) Check the condition of the air filter element, and renew if necessary (Section 22).
f) Check the condition of all hoses, and check for fluid leaks (Section 5).

If the above operations do not prove fully effective, carry out the following secondary operations:

Secondary operations

a) Check the charging system (Chapter 5A).
b) Check the ignition system (Chapter 5B).
c) Check the fuel system (Chapter 4A).

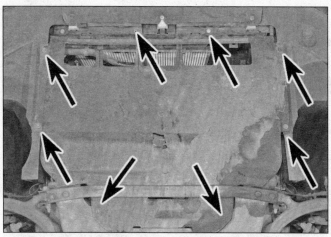

3.3 Undershield fasteners (arrowed)

3.4 Slacken the engine oil sump drain plug (arrowed)

Every 6000 miles or 6 months

3 Engine oil and filter – renewal

1 Frequent oil changes are the most important preventative maintenance the DIY home

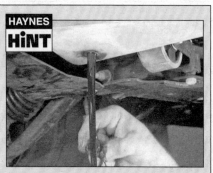

As the drain plug releases from the threads, move it away sharply so the stream of oil runs into the container and not up your sleeve.

mechanic can give the engine, because ageing oil becomes diluted and contaminated, which leads to premature engine wear.

2 Before starting this procedure, gather together all the necessary tools and materials. Also make sure that you have plenty of clean rags and newspapers handy, to mop-up any spills. Ideally, the engine oil should be warm, as it will drain better, and more built-up sludge will be removed with it. Take care, however, not to touch the exhaust or any other hot parts of the engine when working under the vehicle. To avoid any possibility of scalding, and to protect yourself from possible skin irritants and other harmful contaminants in used engine oils, it is advisable to wear gloves when carrying out this work.

3 Access to the filter and drain plug will be greatly improved if the front of the vehicle is raised and support securely on axle stands (see *Jacking and vehicle support*). Undo the fasteners and remove the engine undershield (where fitted) **(see illustration)**.

4 Slacken the plug about half a turn **(see illustration)**. Position the draining container

under the drain plug, then remove the plug completely – recover the sealing washer **(see Haynes Hint)**.

5 Allow some time for the old oil to drain, noting that it may be necessary to reposition the container as the oil flow slows to a trickle.

6 After all the oil has drained, wipe off the drain plug with a clean rag. Clean the area around the drain plug opening, and refit the plug with a new sealing washer **(see illustration)**. Tighten the plug securely.

7 Two different types of oil filter may be fitted. On some models, the oil filter is of the disposable metal cartridge type, whilst on others, the oil filter consists of a separate disposable paper element contained in a plastic cap, screwed in the housing on the front of the cylinder block. Proceed as follows according to the filter type.

Metal canister type filter

8 Use a filter removal tool to unscrew the filter cartridge from the housing **(see illustration)**. Empty the old oil into the container.

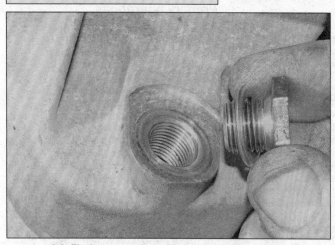

3.6 Fit the sump plug with a new sealing washer

3.8 Use a tool to remove the oil filter

9 Use a clean rag to remove all oil, dirt and sludge from the filter housing mating face. Check the old filter to ensure the rubber sealing ring hasn't stuck to the housing. If it has, carefully remove it.

10 Apply a light coating of clean engine oil to the sealing ring on the new filter, then screw it into position on the engine. Tighten the filter firmly by hand only – do not use any tools **(see illustrations)**.

Paper element type filter

11 Using a socket or spanner, slacken the oil filter cap initially, then unscrew it by hand the rest of the way **(see illustration)**.

12 Lift the filter cap away, and remove the paper element, and the O-ring seal from the cap.

13 Use a clean rag to remove all oil and dirt from inside the filter cap and housing.

14 Fit a new O-ring seal to the cap, and fit the new paper element to the cap. Lightly lubricate the O-ring seal with clean engine oil.

15 Screw the cap into place, and tighten it securely.

All filter types

16 Lower the vehicle to the ground, then remove the oil filler cap and withdraw the level dipstick from the tube. Fill the engine, using the correct oil (see *Lubricants and fluids*). An oil can spout or funnel may help to reduce spillage. Pour in half the specified quantity of oil first, then wait a few minutes for the oil to run to the sump. Continue adding oil a small quantity at a time until the level is up to the lower mark on the dipstick. Adding a further 1.7 litres will bring the level up to the upper mark on the dipstick. Insert the dipstick, and refit the filler cap **(see illustration)**.

3.10a Apply clean engine oil to the filter seal . . .

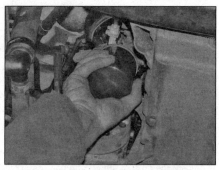

3.10b . . . then screw it into position by hand

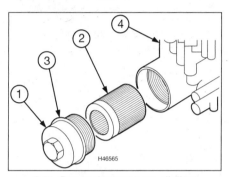

3.11 Paper element type oil filter

1 Filter cap   3 O-ring seal
2 Paper element 4 Oil filter housing

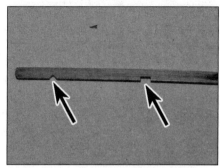

3.16 Oil level dipstick maximum and minimum marks (arrowed)

17 Start the engine and run it for a few minutes; check for leaks around the oil filter seal and the sump drain plug. Note that there may be a delay of a few seconds before the oil pressure warning light goes out when the engine is first started, as the oil circulates through the engine oil galleries and the new oil filter, before the pressure builds-up.

18 Switch off the engine, and wait a few minutes for the oil to settle in the sump once more. With the new oil circulated and the filter completely full, recheck the level on the dipstick, and add more oil as necessary.

19 Dispose of the used engine oil safely, in accordance with the guidance given in *General repair procedures*.

Every 12 000 miles or 12 months

4 Service indicator – resetting

1 The instrument cluster mileage recorder incorporates a service interval indicator. When the vehicle is started, the unit displays the mileage until the next service, or the mileage covered since the service was due. The service indicator is manually reset to zero after the vehicle has been serviced. The indicator can also be reset at any time using the Citroën diagnostic tool.

2 Switch off the ignition, then on the instrument panel, press and hold down the reset button.

3 Switch on the ignition – the distance remaining until (or covered since) the next service is due will flash in the display. Keep the button pressed until the display resets to zero and the maintenance 'key' disappears. Release the knob.

5 Hoses and fluids – leak check

Cooling system

⚠️ *Warning: Refer to the safety information given in 'Safety first!' and Chapter 3 before disturbing any of the cooling system components.*

1 Carefully check the radiator and heater coolant hoses along their entire length. Renew any hose which is cracked, swollen or which shows signs of deterioration. Cracks will show up better if the hose is squeezed. Pay close attention to the clips that secure the hoses to the cooling system components. Hose clips that have been overtightened can pinch and puncture hoses, resulting in cooling system leaks.

2 Inspect all the cooling system components (hoses, joint faces, etc) for leaks. Where any

problems of this nature are found on system components, renew the component or gasket with reference to Chapter 3 **(see Haynes hint)**.

A leak in the cooling system will usually show-up as white- or antifreeze-coloured deposits on the area adjoining the leak.

Fuel system

Warning: Refer to the safety information given in 'Safety first!' and Chapter 4A before disturbing any of the fuel system components.

3 Petrol leaks can be difficult to pinpoint, unless the leakage is significant and hence easily visible. Fuel tends to evaporate quickly once it comes into contact with air, especially in a hot engine bay. Small drips can disappear before you get a chance to identify the point of leakage. If you suspect that there is a fuel leak from the area of the engine bay, leave the vehicle overnight then start the engine from cold, with the bonnet open. Metal components tend to shrink when they are cold, and rubber seals and hoses tend to harden, so any leaks will be more apparent whilst the engine is warming-up from a cold start.

4 Check all fuel lines at their connections to the fuel rail, fuel pressure regulator and fuel filter (where fitted). Examine each rubber fuel hose along its length for splits or cracks. Check for leakage from the crimped joints between rubber and metal fuel lines. Examine the unions between the metal fuel lines and the fuel filter housing. Also check the area around the fuel injectors for signs of O-ring leakage.

5 To identify fuel leaks between the fuel tank and the engine bay, the vehicle should be raised and securely supported on axle stands (see *Jacking and vehicle support*). Inspect the petrol tank and filler neck for punctures, cracks and other damage. The connection between the filler neck and tank is especially critical. Sometimes a rubber filler neck or connecting hose will leak due to loose retaining clamps or deteriorated rubber.

6 Carefully check all rubber hoses and metal fuel lines leading away from the petrol tank. Check for loose connections, deteriorated hoses, kinked lines, and other damage. Pay particular attention to the vent pipes and hoses, which often loop up around the filler neck and can become blocked or kinked, making tank filling difficult. Follow the fuel supply and return lines to the front of the vehicle, carefully inspecting them all the way for signs of damage or corrosion. Renew damaged sections as necessary.

Engine oil

7 Inspect the area around the camshaft cover, cylinder head, oil filter and sump joint faces. Bear in mind that, over a period of time, some very slight seepage from these areas is to be expected – what you are really looking for is any indication of a serious leak caused by gasket failure. Engine oil seeping from the base of the timing belt cover or the transmission bellhousing may be an indication of crankshaft or transmission input shaft oil seal failure. Should a leak be found, renew the failed gasket or oil seal by referring to the appropriate Chapters in this manual.

Automatic transmission fluid

8 Where applicable, check the hoses leading to the transmission fluid cooler at the front of the engine bay for leakage. Look for deterioration caused by corrosion and damage from grounding, or debris thrown up from the road surface. Automatic transmission fluid is a thin oil and is usually red in colour.

LDS fluid

9 Examine the hose running between the fluid reservoir and the power steering pump, the return hose running from the steering rack to the fluid reservoir, and the various suspension pipes. Also examine the high-pressure supply hose between the pump and the steering rack.

10 Check the condition of each hose/pipe carefully. Look for deterioration caused by corrosion and damage from grounding, or debris thrown up from the road surface.

11 Pay particular attention to crimped unions, and the area surrounding the hoses that are secured with adjustable worm-drive clips. LDS fluid is a thin oil, and is orange in colour.

Air conditioning refrigerant

Warning: Refer to the safety information given in 'Safety first!' and Chapter 3 regarding the dangers of disturbing any of the air conditioning system components.

12 The air conditioning system is filled with a liquid refrigerant, which is retained under high pressure. If the air conditioning system is opened and depressurised without the aid of specialised equipment the refrigerant will immediately turn into gas and escape into the atmosphere. If the liquid comes into contact with your skin, it can cause severe frostbite. In addition, the refrigerant contains substances which are environmentally damaging; for this reason, it should not be allowed to escape into the atmosphere in an uncontrolled fashion.

13 Any suspected air conditioning system leaks should be immediately referred to a Citroën dealer or air conditioning specialist. Leakage will be shown up as a steady drop in the level of refrigerant in the system.

14 Note that water may drip from the condenser drain pipe, underneath the car, immediately after the air conditioning system has been in use. This is normal, and should not be cause for concern.

Brake/clutch fluid

Warning: Refer to the safety information given in 'Safety first!' and Chapter 9 regarding the dangers of handling brake fluid.

15 With reference to Chapter 9, examine the area surrounding the brake/clutch pipe unions at the master cylinder for signs of leakage. Check the area around the base of fluid reservoir, for signs of leakage caused by seal failure. Also examine the brake pipe unions at the ABS hydraulic unit.

16 If fluid loss is evident, but the leak cannot be pinpointed in the engine bay, the brake calipers and underbody brake lines should be carefully checked with the vehicle raised and supported on axle stands (see *Jacking and vehicle support*). Leakage of fluid from the braking system is a serious fault that must be rectified immediately.

17 Brake/clutch hydraulic fluid is a toxic substance with a watery consistency. New fluid is almost colourless, but it becomes darker with age and use.

Unidentified fluid leaks

18 If there are signs that a fluid of some description is leaking from the vehicle, but you cannot identify the type of fluid or its exact origin, park the vehicle overnight and slide a large piece of card underneath it. Providing that the card is positioned in roughly the right location, even the smallest leak will show up on the card. Not only will this help you to pinpoint the exact location of the leak, it should be easier to identify the fluid from its colour. Bear in mind, though, that the leak may only be occurring when the engine is running!

Vacuum hoses

19 Although the braking system is hydraulically-operated, the brake servo unit amplifies the effort applied at the brake pedal by making use of the vacuum in the inlet manifold generated by the engine. Vacuum is ported to the servo by means of a large-bore hose. Any leaks that develop in this hose will reduce the effectiveness of the braking system, and may affect the running of the engine.

20 In addition, a number of the underbonnet components, particularly the emission control components, are driven by vacuum supplied from the inlet manifold via narrow-bore hoses. A leak in a vacuum hose means that air is being drawn into the hose (rather than escaping from it) and this makes leakage very difficult to detect. One method is to use an old length of vacuum hose as a kind of stethoscope – hold one end close to (but not in!) your ear and use the other end to probe the area around the suspected leak. When the end of the hose is directly over a vacuum leak, a hissing sound will be heard clearly through the hose. Care must be taken to avoid contacting hot or moving components, as the engine must be running, when testing in this manner. Renew any vacuum hoses that are found to be defective.

---

6   Steering and suspension components – check

Front suspension and steering

1 Raise the front of the vehicle, and securely support it on axle stands (see *Jacking and vehicle support*).

2 Visually inspect the balljoint dust covers and the steering rack-and-pinion gaiters for splits, chafing or deterioration. Any wear of these components will cause loss of lubricant,

together with dirt and water entry, resulting in rapid deterioration of the balljoints or steering gear.

3 Check the power steering fluid hoses for chafing or deterioration, and the pipe and hose unions for fluid leaks. Also check for signs of fluid leakage under pressure from the steering gear rubber gaiters, which would indicate failed fluid seals within the steering gear.

4 Grasp the roadwheel at the 12 o'clock and 6 o'clock positions, and try to rock it **(see illustration)**. Very slight free play may be felt, but if the movement is appreciable, further investigation is necessary to determine the source. Continue rocking the wheel while an assistant depresses the footbrake. If the movement is now eliminated or significantly reduced, it is likely that the hub bearings are at fault. If the free play is still evident with the footbrake depressed, then there is wear in the suspension joints or mountings.

5 Now grasp the wheel at the 9 o'clock and 3 o'clock positions, and try to rock it as before. Any movement felt now may again be caused by wear in the hub bearings or the steering track rod balljoints. If the outer balljoint is worn, the visual movement will be obvious. If the inner joint is suspect, it can be felt by placing a hand over the rack-and-pinion rubber gaiter and gripping the track rod. If the wheel is now rocked, movement will be felt at the inner joint if wear has taken place.

6 Using a large screwdriver or flat bar, check for wear in the suspension mounting bushes by levering between the relevant suspension component and its attachment point. Some movement is to be expected, as the mountings are made of rubber, but excessive wear should be obvious. Also check the condition of any visible rubber bushes, looking for splits, cracks or contamination of the rubber.

7 With the car standing on its wheels, have an assistant turn the steering wheel back-and-forth, about an eighth of a turn each way. There should be very little, if any, lost movement between the steering wheel and roadwheels. If this is not the case, closely observe the joints and mountings previously described. In addition, check the steering column universal joints for wear, and also check the rack-and-pinion steering gear itself.

8 The front suspension mountings should be checked for tightness.

Rear suspension

9 Chock the front wheels, then jack up the rear of the vehicle and support securely on axle stands (see *Jacking and vehicle support*).

10 Working as described previously for the front suspension, check the rear hub bearings, the suspension bushes and the strut or shock absorber mountings (as applicable) for wear.

11 The rear suspension mountings should be checked for tightness.

Shock absorber

12 Check for any signs of fluid leakage around the shock absorber bodies, or from the rubber gaiters around the piston rods. Should any fluid be noticed, the shock absorber is defective internally, or the rubber gaiter is split, and may need renewing. **Note:** *Shock absorbers should always be renewed in pairs on the same axle.*

13 The shock absorbency of the unit is provided by the nitrogen-filled sphere. Should the sphere leak, the suspension will become very hard. Citroën insist that the spheres cannot be recharged, so renewal would appear to be the only option (see Chapter 10).

7 Brake pad wear and disc check

1 The work described in this Section should be carried out at the specified intervals, or whenever a defect is suspected in the braking system. Any of the following symptoms could indicate a potential brake system defect:

   a) *The vehicle pulls to one side when the brake pedal is depressed.*
   b) *The brakes make squealing, scraping or dragging noises when applied.*
   c) *Brake pedal travel is excessive, or pedal feel is poor.*
   d) *The brake fluid requires repeated topping-up. Note that, because the hydraulic clutch shares the same fluid as the braking system (see Chapter 6), this problem could be due to a leak in the clutch system.*

Front disc brakes

2 Chock the rear wheels then loosen the front wheel bolts. Jack up the front of the vehicle, and support it on axle stands (see *Jacking and vehicle support*).

3 For better access to the brake calipers, remove the wheels.

4 Look through the inspection window in the caliper, and check that the thickness of the friction lining material on each of the pads is not less than the recommended minimum thickness given in the Specifications **(see Haynes Hint)**. Bear in mind that the lining material is normally bonded to a metal backing plate. To differentiate between the metal and the lining material, it is helpful to turn the disc slowly at first – the edge of the disc can then be identified, with the lining material on each pad either side of it, and the backing plates behind.

5 If it is difficult to determine the exact thickness of the pad linings, or if you are at all concerned about the condition of the pads, then remove them from the calipers for further inspection (refer to Chapter 9).

6 Check the other caliper in the same way.

7 If any one of the brake pads has worn down to, or below, the specified limit, *all four* pads at that end of the car must be renewed as a set. If the pads on one side are significantly more worn than the other, this may indicate

6.4 Check for wear in the hub bearings by grasping the wheel and trying to rock it

that the caliper pistons have partially seized – refer to the brake pad renewal procedure in Chapter 9, and push the pistons back into the caliper to free them.

8 Measure the thickness of the discs with a micrometer, if available, to make sure that they still have service life remaining. Do not be fooled by the lip of rust which often forms on the outer edge of the disc, which may make the disc appear thicker than it really is – scrape off the loose rust if necessary, without scoring the disc friction (shiny) surface.

9 If any disc is thinner than the specified minimum thickness, renew both (refer to Chapter 9).

10 Check the general condition of the discs. Look for excessive scoring and discolouration caused by overheating. If these conditions exist, remove the relevant disc and have it resurfaced or renewed (refer to Chapter 9).

11 Make sure that the transmission is in neutral. Spin the wheel, and check that the brake is not binding. Some drag is normal with a disc brake, but it should not require any great effort to turn the wheel – also, do not confuse brake drag with resistance from the transmission. Abnormal effort may indicate that the handbrake needs adjusting – see Chapter 9.

12 Before refitting the wheels, check all brake lines and hoses (refer to Chapter 9). In particular, check the flexible hoses in the vicinity of the calipers, where they are subjected to most movement. Bend them

HAYNES HiNT

For a quick check, the thickness of the friction material on each brake pad can be measured through the aperture in the caliper body.

between the fingers (but do not actually bend them double, or the casing may be damaged) and check that this does not reveal previously-hidden cracks, cuts or splits.

13 On completion, refit the wheels and lower the car to the ground. Tighten the wheel bolts to the specified torque.

Rear disc brakes

14 Loosen the rear wheel bolts then chock the front wheels. Jack up the rear of the car, and support it on axle stands. Release the handbrake and remove the rear wheels.

15 The procedure for checking the rear brakes is much the same as described in paragraphs 2 to 13 above. Check that the rear brakes are not binding, noting that transmission resistance is not a factor on the rear wheels.

8 Handbrake – check and adjustment
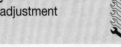

1 Chock the rear wheels then jack up the front of the vehicle and support on axle stands (see *Jacking and vehicle support*).

2 Fully apply and release the handbrake 5 times.

3 Ensure the caliper lever arms are resting against the stops, then check that the distance between the handbrake cable hook and the caliper arm lever is between 0.1 and 1.0 mm **(see illustration)**. If not, adjust the handbrake as described in Chapter 9.

4 Fully apply the handbrake lever, and check that both front wheels are locked when attempting to turn them by hand.

5 Lower the vehicle to the ground.

9 Seat belt condition – check
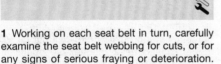

1 Working on each seat belt in turn, carefully examine the seat belt webbing for cuts, or for any signs of serious fraying or deterioration. Pull the belt all the way out, and examine the full extent of the webbing.

2 Fasten and unfasten the belt, ensuring that the locking mechanism holds securely,

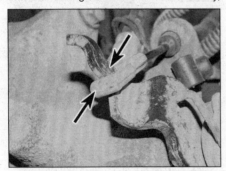

8.3 The clearance between the cable end fitting and the caliper operating lever must be 0.1 to 1.0 mm (arrowed)

and releases properly when intended. Check also that the retracting mechanism operates correctly when the belt is released.

3 Check the security of all seat belt mountings and attachments which are accessible from inside the vehicle without removing any trim or other components.

4 Check the function of the seat belt reminder lamp.

10 Airbag system – check

1 The following work can be carried out by the home mechanic, however, if an electronic fault is apparent, it will be necessary to take the car to a Citroën dealer or specialist, who will have the necessary diagnostic equipment to extract fault codes from the system.

2 Turn the ignition switch to the drive position (ignition warning lights on), and check that the airbag warning light is illuminated for approximately 6 seconds. After this period the light should go out, indicating that the system has been checked and is functioning correctly.

3 If the warning light remains on or refuses to light, have the system checked by a Citroën dealer or specialist.

4 Visually examine the steering wheel centre pad, knee airbag and the passenger airbag modules for external damage. Also check the exterior of the front seats around the side airbag locations. If damage is evident, consult a Citroën dealer or specialist.

5 In the interests of safety, make sure that there are no loose items inside the car which could be thrown onto the airbag modules in the event of an accident.

11 Headlight beam alignment – check

Refer to Chapter 12 for details

12 LDS fluid level – check

Checking, and if necessary, topping-up the LDS fluid level is described in Chapter 10, Section 16.

13 Road test

Instruments and electrical equipment

1 Check the operation of all instruments and electrical equipment.

2 Make sure that all instruments read correctly,

and switch on all electrical equipment in turn to check that it functions properly. Check the function of the heating, air conditioning and automatic climate control systems.

Steering and suspension

3 Check for any abnormalities in the steering, suspension, handling or road 'feel'.

4 Drive the vehicle, and check that there are no unusual vibrations or noises.

5 Check that the steering feels positive, with no excessive 'sloppiness', or roughness, and check for any suspension noises when cornering, or when driving over bumps. Check that the power steering system operates correctly.

Drivetrain

6 Check the performance of the engine, clutch (manual transmission), transmission and driveshafts.

7 Listen for any unusual noises from the engine, clutch (manual transmission) and transmission.

8 Make sure that the engine runs smoothly when idling, and that there is no hesitation when accelerating.

9 On manual transmission models, check that the clutch action is smooth and progressive, that the drive is taken up smoothly, and that the pedal travel is correct. Also listen for any noises when the clutch pedal is depressed. Check that all gears can be engaged smoothly, without noise, and that the gear lever action is smooth and not abnormally vague or 'notchy'.

10 On automatic transmission models, make sure that all gearchanges occur smoothly without snatching, and without an increase in engine speed between changes. Check that all the gear positions can be selected with the vehicle at rest. If any problems are found, they should be referred to a Citroën dealer.

11 Listen for a metallic clicking sound from the front of the vehicle, as the vehicle is driven slowly in a circle with the steering on full lock. Carry out this check in both directions. If a clicking noise is heard, this indicates wear in a driveshaft joint, in which case, refer to Chapter 8.

Braking system

12 Make sure that the vehicle does not pull to one side when braking, and that the wheels do not lock when braking hard.

13 Check that there is no vibration through the steering when braking.

14 Check that the handbrake operates correctly, without excessive movement of the lever, and that it holds the vehicle stationary on a slope.

15 Test the operation of the brake servo unit as follows. With the engine off, depress the footbrake four or five times to exhaust the vacuum, then start the engine while holding the brake pedal depressed. As the engine starts, there should be a noticeable 'give' in the brake pedal as vacuum builds-up. Allow the engine to run for at least two minutes, and then switch it off. If the brake pedal is now depressed again, it should be possible to detect a 'hiss' from the servo as the pedal is depressed. After about four or five applications, no further sound should be heard, and the pedal should feel considerably harder.

14 Coolant antifreeze concentration – check

1 The cooling system should be filled with the recommended antifreeze and corrosion protection fluid. Over a period of time, the concentration of fluid may be reduced due to topping-up (this can be avoided by topping-up with the correct antifreeze mixture) or fluid loss. If loss of coolant has been evident, it is important to make the necessary repair before adding fresh fluid. The exact mixture of antifreeze-to-water which you should use depends on the relative weather conditions. The mixture should contain at least 40% antifreeze, but not more than 70%. Consult the mixture ratio chart on the antifreeze container before adding coolant. Hydrometers are available at most automotive accessory shops to test the coolant. Use antifreeze which meets the vehicle manufacturer's specifications.
2 With the engine cold, carefully remove the cap from the expansion tank. If the engine is not completely cold, place a cloth rag over the cap before removing it, and remove it slowly to allow any pressure to escape.
3 Antifreeze checkers are available from car accessory shops. Draw some coolant from the expansion tank and observe how many plastic balls are floating in the checker (see illustration). Usually, 2 or 3 balls must be floating for the correct concentration of antifreeze, but follow the manufacturer's instructions.
4 If the concentration is incorrect, it will be necessary to either withdraw some coolant and add antifreeze, or alternatively drain the old coolant and add fresh coolant of the correct concentration.

15 Driveshaft joints and gaiters – check

1 With the front of the vehicle raised and securely supported on stands, turn the steering onto full lock then slowly rotate the roadwheel. Inspect the condition of the outer constant velocity (CV) joint rubber gaiters while squeezing the gaiters to open out the folds (see illustration). Check for signs of cracking, splits or deterioration of the rubber which may allow the grease to escape and lead to water and grit entry into the joint. Also check the security and condition of the retaining clips. Repeat these checks on the inner CV joints. If any damage or deterioration is found, the

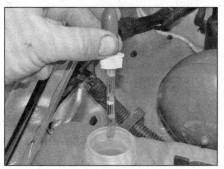

14.3 Check the antifreeze concentration using a hydrometer

gaiters should be renewed as described in Chapter 8.
2 At the same time check the general condition of the CV joints themselves by first holding the driveshaft and attempting to rotate the wheel. Repeat this check by holding the inner joint and attempting to rotate the driveshaft. Any appreciable movement indicates wear in the joints, wear in the driveshaft splines or a loose driveshaft retaining nut.

16 Exhaust system – check

1 With the engine cold, check the complete exhaust system, from its starting point at the engine to the end of the tailpipe. If necessary, raise the front and rear of the vehicle and support it on axle stands (see Jacking and vehicle support). Remove any engine undershields as necessary for full access to the exhaust system.
2 Check the exhaust pipes and connections for evidence of leaks, severe corrosion, and damage. Make sure that all brackets and mountings are in good condition and that all relevant nuts and bolts are tight (see illustration). Leakage at any of the joints or in other parts of the system will usually show up as a black sooty stain in the vicinity of the leak.
3 Rattles and other noises can often be traced to the exhaust system, especially the brackets and rubber mountings. Try to move the pipes and silencers. If the components are able to come into contact with the body or suspension parts, secure the system with new mountings. Otherwise separate the joints (if possible) and twist the pipes as necessary to provide additional clearance.

17 Hinges and locks – lubrication

1 Work around the vehicle and lubricate the hinges of the bonnet, doors and tailgate with a light machine oil.
2 Lightly lubricate the two bonnet release locks with a smear of grease.
3 Check carefully the security and operation

15.1 Check the CV joint gaiters for cracks or splits

of all hinges, latches and locks. Check that the central locking system operates correctly.
4 Check the condition and operation of the bonnet and tailgate struts, renewing them if either is leaking or no longer able to support the bonnet/tailgate.

18 Lane wandering warning system sensor – clean

1 The sensors are located under the front bumper, 3 on each side. In order for them to function correctly, traffic/road dirt must be cleared from the lenses.
2 Chock the rear wheels, raise the front of the vehicle and support it securely on axle stands (see Jacking and vehicle support).
3 The sensors can be cleaned without removing them, using clean soapy water, and a soft sponge. Take care not to scratch the lenses. Dry the sensors with soft, clean, lint-free cloth.
4 Lower the vehicle to the ground.

19 Auxiliary drivebelt condition – check

1 On all engines, a single, multi-grooved auxiliary drivebelt is used to transmit drive from the crankshaft pulley to the alternator and the refrigerant compressor. The drivebelt is tensioned automatically by a spring-loaded tensioner pulley.

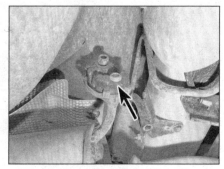

16.2 Check the condition of the exhaust rubber mountings

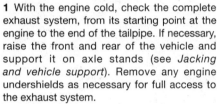

2 For better access to the drivebelt, chock the rear wheels then jack up the front of the car and support it on axle stands (see *Jacking and vehicle support*). Remove the right-hand front roadwheel, then remove the plastic liner from under the right-hand wheel arch to expose the crankshaft pulley.

3 Using a socket and extension bar fitted to the crankshaft pulley bolt, rotate the crankshaft so that the entire length of the drivebelt(s) can be examined. Examine the drivebelt for cracks, splitting, fraying, or other damage. Check also for signs of glazing (shiny patches) and for separation of the belt plies. Renew the belt if worn or damaged, as described in Chapter 5A.

Every 24 000 miles or 2 years

20 Pollen air filter – renew

1 Undo the fasteners and remove the facia panel above the passenger's footwell **(see illustration)**.

2 Undo the 2 retaining screws **(see illustration)**.

3 Note which way around it's fitted, then pull the filter from the housing **(see illustration)**.

4 Fit the new element using a reversal of the removal procedure.

21 Spark plugs – renewal

1 The correct functioning of the spark plugs is vital for the correct running and efficiency of the engine. It is essential that the plugs fitted are appropriate for the engine. If this type is used and the engine is in good condition, the spark plugs should not need attention between scheduled renewal intervals.

2 Remove the ignition coil assembly as described in Chapter 5B.

3 If they did not come away with the coils, remove the HT extenders from the top of the spark plugs **(see illustration)**.

4 It is advisable to remove the dirt from the spark plug recesses using a clean brush, vacuum cleaner or compressed air before removing the plugs, to prevent dirt dropping into the cylinders.

5 Unscrew the plugs using a spark plug spanner, suitable box spanner or a deep socket and extension bar **(see illustration)**. Keep the socket aligned with the spark plug – if it is forcibly moved to one side, the ceramic insulator may be broken off. As each plug is removed,

20.1 Remove the scrivet and the fastener (arrowed)

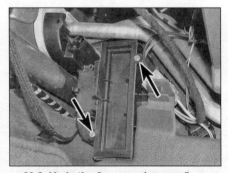

20.2 Undo the 2 screws (arrowed) . . .

20.3 . . . and pull the pollen filter from place

21.3 The HT extenders should come away with the ignition coil assembly

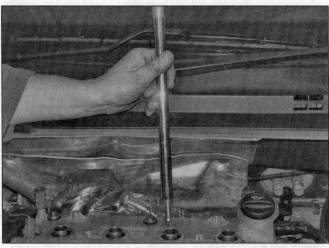

21.5 On 2.0 litre EW10D engines, a 12-sided socket and long extension are required to reach the deeply recessed spark plugs

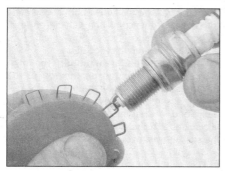

21.10a Measure the gap with a wire gauge . . .

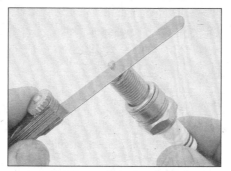

21.10b . . . or feeler gauge

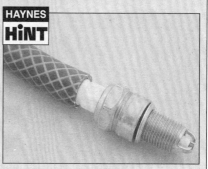

It's often difficult to insert spark plugs into their holes without cross-threading them. To avoid this possibility, fit a length of rubber hose over the end of the spark plug. The flexible hose acts as a universal joint, to help align the plug with the plug hole. Should the plug begin to cross-thread, the hose will slip on the spark plug, preventing thread damage.

examine it as follows. **Note:** *The spark plugs on the EW10D engine are deeply recessed, and a bi-hexagon (12-sided) 14 mm spark plug socket and extension at least 150 mm long will be needed. Citroën tool No (C).0189.P may be available.*

6 Examination of the spark plugs will give a good indication of the condition of the engine. If the insulator nose of the spark plug is clean and white, with no deposits, this is indicative of a weak mixture or too hot a plug (a hot plug transfers heat away from the electrode slowly, a cold plug transfers heat away quickly).

7 If the tip and insulator nose are covered with hard black-looking deposits, then this is indicative that the mixture is too rich. Should the plug be black and oily, then it is likely that the engine is fairly worn, as well as the mixture being too rich.

8 If the insulator nose is covered with light tan to greyish-brown deposits, then the mixture is correct, and it is likely that the engine is in good condition.

9 The electrode gap is of considerable importance as, if it is too large or too small, the size of the spark and its efficiency will be seriously impaired. The gap should be set to the value given in the Specifications.

10 To set the gap, measure it with a feeler blade or wire gauge and then bend open, or closed, the outer plug electrode until the correct gap is achieved. The centre electrode should never be bent, as this will crack the insulator and cause plug failure, if nothing worse. If using feeler blades, the gap is correct when the appropriate-size blade is a firm sliding fit. Note that some models may be fitted with multi-electrode spark plugs – no attempt to adjust the electrode gap should be made on this type of spark plug **(see illustrations)**.

11 Special spark plug electrode gap adjusting tools are available from most motor accessory shops, or from some spark plug manufacturers.

12 Before fitting the spark plugs, check that

the threaded connector sleeves are tight, and that the plug exterior surfaces and threads are clean. It is very often difficult to insert spark plugs into their holes without cross-threading them. To avoid this possibility, fit a short length of hose over the end of the spark plug **(see Haynes Hint)**.

13 Remove the rubber hose (if used), and tighten the plug to the specified torque (see Specifications) using the spark plug socket and a torque wrench. Refit the remaining plugs in the same way.

14 Refit the ignition coil assembly as described in Chapter 5B.

Every 36 000 miles

22 Air filter element – renewal

1 The air cleaner is located on the left-hand side of the engine compartment, and the air

inlet is taken from the front of the car behind the radiator grille area.

2 Release the clamp and disconnect the outlet hose from the air filter cover **(see illustration)**.

3 Undo the screws and remove the air filter cover **(see illustration)**.

4 Lift out the air cleaner filter element, noting which way round it is fitted **(see illustration)**.

5 Wipe clean the inner surfaces of the cover and main housing, then locate the new element in the housing, making sure that the sealing lip is correctly engaged with the edge of the housing.

6 Refit the cover, and secure with the screws.

7 Reconnect the air outlet hose and secure it by tightening the hose clip.

22.2 Slacken the clamp (arrowed) and disconnect the outlet hose

22.3 Undo the screws and remove the filter cover (arrowed)

22.4 Lift the element from the housing

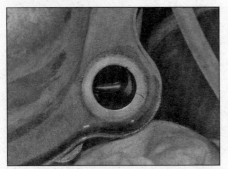

23.3a The fluid should be up to the bottom of the filler/level plug hole

23.3b If necessary, top-up the transmission fluid

24.2 Unscrew the transmission filler plug (arrowed)

24.5 Unscrew the level plug (arrowed) from the centre of the drain plug

23 Manual transmission fluid – level check

1 Take the car on a short journey to warm the transmission up to normal operating temperature. Position the car over an inspection pit, or alternatively jack up the front and rear of the car and support on axle stands (see *Jacking and vehicle support*). Whichever method is used, make sure that the car is level for checking the fluid level later.
2 Position a suitable container beneath the transmission, then unscrew the filler/level plug located on the left-hand side of the transmission casing.
3 The fluid level should be up to the bottom of the filler/level plug hole. If necessary, add the specified fluid until it begins to run out of the hole **(see illustrations)**.
4 Refit the filler/level plug and tighten it to the specified torque.
5 Lower the vehicle to the ground.

24 Automatic transmission fluid – level check

1 Take the vehicle on a short journey, to warm the transmission up to normal operating temperature, then park the vehicle on level ground. Firmly apply the handbrake and place the selector lever in the P position.
2 Wipe clean the area around the filler plug, which is situated on the top of the transmission, directly beneath the air cleaner assembly. Remove the air cleaner as described in Chapter 4A, then unscrew the filler plug from the transmission and recover the sealing washer **(see illustration)**.
3 Carefully add 0.5 litre of the specified type of fluid to the transmission via the filler plug aperture. Fit a new sealing washer to the filler plug then refit the plug, tightening it to the specified torque.
4 Undo the screws and remove the engine undershield – where fitted **(see illustration 3.3)**.
5 Position a suitable container under the drain/level plug arrangement, situated on the base of the transmission. The level plug is the smaller plug fitted to the centre of the larger drain plug **(see illustration)**.
Caution: Do not remove the drain plug by mistake.
6 Start the engine and allow it to idle. With the engine running, retain the drain plug then slacken and remove the level plug and sealing washer.

 Warning: The fluid will be hot, take precautions against scalding.

7 If there is sufficient fluid in the transmission unit, fluid should trickle out the centre of the drain plug before slowing to a drip. **Note:** *If no fluid trickles out, or just a few drips appear when the plug is removed, the fluid level is too low. Refit the level plug then switch off the engine. Add a further 0.5 litre of fluid to the transmission then refit the filler plug and repeat the check (see paragraphs 4 to 7).*
8 Once the flow of fluid stops, the level is correct. Fit a new sealing washer to the level plug then refit the plug and tighten it to the specified torque. Switch off the engine.

Every 80 000 miles or 10 years

25 Timing belt – renewal

Refer to Chapter 2A or 2B as applicable.

Every 2 years

26 Coolant – renewal

Note: *This work is not included in the Citroën schedule, and should not be required if the recommended Citroën antifreeze/inhibitor is used.*

⚠ *Warning: Do not allow antifreeze to come in contact with your skin or painted surfaces of the vehicle. Flush contaminated areas immediately with plenty of water. Don't store new coolant, or leave old coolant lying around, where it's accessible to children or pets – they're attracted by its sweet smell. Ingestion of even a small amount of coolant can be fatal.*

Wipe up garage-floor and drip-pan spills immediately. Keep antifreeze containers covered, and repair cooling system leaks as soon as they're noticed.

⚠ *Warning: Never remove the expansion tank filler cap when the engine is running, or has just been switched off, as the cooling system will be hot, and the consequent escaping steam*

26.4a Bleed screw on the top of the radiator (arrowed) . . .

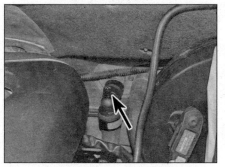

26.4b . . . on the heater hoses (arrowed) . . .

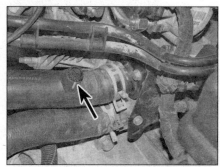

26.4c . . . on the top hose at the coolant junction (arrowed) . . .

and scalding coolant could cause serious injury.

 Warning: Wait until the engine is cold before starting these procedures.

Cooling system draining

1 With the engine completely cold, remove the expansion tank filler cap. Turn the cap anti-clockwise, wait until any pressure remaining in the system is released, then unscrew it and lift it off.

2 Chock the rear wheels, raise the front of the vehicle and support it on axle stands (see *Jacking and vehicle support*).

3 Undo the screws and remove the undershield beneath the radiator. Note the retaining screws in the wheel arch liner.

4 Bleed screws may be fitted in several different locations: top of the radiator, heater hoses at the bulkhead, top hose at the coolant junction at the left-hand end of the cylinder head, and on the coolant junction itself **(see illustrations)**. Open the bleed screws.

5 Attach a hose to the drain plug (where fitted) at the base of the radiator, and position the other end of the hose in a suitable container. Slacken the drain plug and allow the coolant to drain into the container. On models without a drain plug, prise out the clips and disconnect the radiator lower hose to drain the coolant **(see illustrations)**.

6 When the flow of coolant stops, tighten the drain plug, remove the hose, or reconnect the lower hose as applicable, and refit the undershield. Lower the vehicle to the ground.

7 If the coolant has been drained for a reason other than renewal, then provided it is clean and less than two years old, it can be re-used, though this is not recommended.

Cooling system flushing

8 If coolant renewal has been neglected, or if the antifreeze mixture has become diluted, then in time the cooling system may gradually lose efficiency, as the coolant passages become restricted due to rust, scale deposits and other sediment. The cooling system efficiency can be restored by flushing the system clean.

9 The radiator should be flushed independently of the engine, to avoid unnecessary contamination.

26.4d . . . and on the coolant junction itself (arrowed) – 2.0 litre EW10D engine . . .

Radiator flushing

10 Disconnect the top and bottom hoses and any other relevant hoses from the radiator, with reference to Chapter 3.

11 Insert a garden hose into the radiator top inlet. Direct a flow of clean water through the radiator, and continue flushing until clean water emerges from the radiator bottom outlet.

12 If after a reasonable period, the water still does not run clear, the radiator can be flushed with a good proprietary cleaning agent. It is important that the manufacturer's instructions are followed carefully. If the contamination is particularly bad, remove the radiator and insert the hose in the bottom outlet, and reverse-flush the radiator, then refit it.

Engine flushing

13 Remove the thermostat as described in Chapter 3. If the radiator top hose has been disconnected, temporarily reconnect the hose.

26.5a Prise up the retaining clip . . .

26.4e . . . or 1.8 and 2.0 litre EW7J4 and EW10J4 engines (arrowed)

14 With the top and bottom hoses disconnected from the radiator, insert a garden hose into the radiator top hose. Direct a clean flow of water through the engine, and continue flushing until clean water emerges from the radiator bottom hose.

15 On completion of flushing, refit the thermostat and reconnect the hoses with reference to Chapter 3.

Cooling system filling

16 Before attempting to fill the cooling system, make sure that all hoses and clips are in good condition, and that the clips are tight. Note that an antifreeze mixture must be used all year round, to prevent corrosion of the engine components.

17 Make sure that the air conditioning (A/C) or automatic climate control (ACC) is switched off. This is to prevent the air conditioning system starting the radiator cooling fan before

26.5b . . . and pull the bottom hose junction from the radiator

Cut the bottom off an old antifreeze container to make a 'header tank' for use when refitting the cooling system. The seal at the point arrowed should be as tight as possible – use an O-ring if available, or seal the joint by some other means.

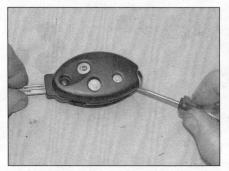

28.1 Use a small screwdriver to separate the two halves of the remote control

28.3 Slide in the new battery, positive side up

the engine is at normal temperature when refilling the system.

18 Ensure the bleed screws are open (see paragraph 4).

19 To provide the required 'head' of coolant necessary to force all trapped air from the system, a 'header tank' must be used by refitting. Although Citroën dealers use a special header tank, the same effect can be achieved by using a suitable bottle, with a seal between the bottle and the expansion tank **(see Haynes Hint)**.

20 Fit the 'header tank' to the expansion tank, and slowly fill the system. Coolant will emerge from the bleed screws, starting with the lowest screw. As soon as coolant free from air bubbles emerges from the bleed screw, tighten it, and watch the next bleed screw in the system. Repeat the procedure until the coolant is emerging from the highest bleed screw in the cooling system and all bleed screws are securely tightened.

21 Ensure the header tank is full (at least 0.5 litres of coolant). Start the engine, and run it at a fast idle speed (do not exceed 2000 rpm) until the cooling fan cuts in, and then cuts out 3 times. Stop the engine.

22 Stop the engine, and allow it to cool, then remove the 'header tank'. Recheck the coolant level with reference to *Weekly checks*. Top-up the level if necessary and refit the expansion tank filler cap.

Antifreeze mixture

23 Always use an ethylene-glycol based antifreeze which is suitable for use in mixed-metal cooling systems. The quantity of antifreeze and levels of protection are given in the Specifications.

24 Before adding antifreeze, the cooling system should be completely drained, preferably flushed, and all hoses checked for condition and security.

25 After filling with antifreeze, a label should be attached to the expansion tank, stating the type and concentration of antifreeze used, and the date installed. Any subsequent topping-up should be made with the same type and concentration of antifreeze.

Caution: Do not use engine antifreeze in the windscreen/tailgate washer system, as it will cause damage to the vehicle paintwork. A screenwash additive should be added to the washer system in the quantities stated on the bottle.

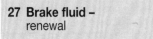

27 Brake fluid –
renewal

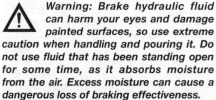

⚠️ *Warning: Brake hydraulic fluid can harm your eyes and damage painted surfaces, so use extreme caution when handling and pouring it. Do not use fluid that has been standing open for some time, as it absorbs moisture from the air. Excess moisture can cause a dangerous loss of braking effectiveness.*

1 The procedure is similar to that for the bleeding of the hydraulic system as described in Chapter 9.

2 Working as described in Chapter 9, open the first bleed screw in the sequence, and pump the brake pedal gently until nearly all the old fluid has been emptied from the master cylinder reservoir. Top-up to the MAX

level with new fluid, and continue pumping until only the new fluid remains in the reservoir, and new fluid can be seen emerging from the bleed screw. Tighten the screw, and top the reservoir level up to the MAX level line.

3 Work through all the remaining bleed screws in the sequence until new fluid can be seen at all of them. Be careful to keep the master cylinder reservoir topped-up to above the MIN level at all times, or air may enter the system and greatly increase the length of the task.

4 When the operation is complete, check that all bleed screws are securely tightened, and that their dust caps are refitted. Wash off all traces of spilt fluid, and recheck the master cylinder reservoir fluid level.

5 Check the operation of the brakes before taking the car on the road.

28 Remote control battery –
renewal

1 Insert a small screwdriver, then twist it to separate the 2 halves of the control **(see illustration)**.

2 Note how it's fitted, then remove the battery from the control. **Note:** *Avoid touching the battery contacts or remote control circuitry with bare fingers.*

3 Insert the new battery (positive side up), and clip together the two halves of the control **(see illustration)**.

4 It is now necessary to synchronise the control with the receiver, by inserting the key into the ignition switch, turning the ignition on, then immediately pressing the 'locking' button, and holding it down until the locks actuate.

Every 10 years

29 Airbags –
renewal

Renewal of the airbags is described in Chapter 12.

Chapter 1 Part B:
Routine maintenance and servicing – diesel models

Contents

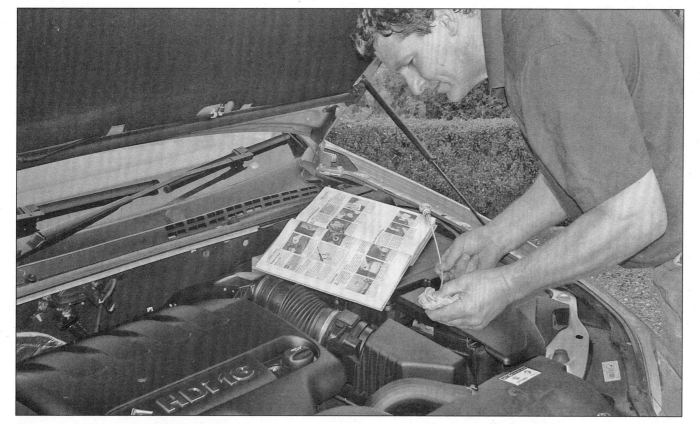

Degrees of difficulty

Easy, suitable for novice with little experience	Fairly easy, suitable for beginner with some experience	Fairly difficult, suitable for competent DIY mechanic	Difficult, suitable for experienced DIY mechanic	Very difficult, suitable for expert DIY or professional

Engine identification

1.6 litre:

Designation. DV6TED4

Engine codes . . . . 9HY or 9HZ

2.0 litre SOHC:

Designation. . . . . DW10TD or DW10ATED

Engine codes:

DW10TD . . . . RHY

DW10ATED . . . . RHZ

2.0 litre DOHC:

Designation. DW10BTED4

Engine code . . . . RHR

Lubricants and fluids. . . . . See end of *Weekly checks* on page 0•17

Capacities

Note: *All values are approximate.*

Engine oil

Drain and refill, with filter change:

1.6 litre engine . . . . 3.75 litres

2.0 litre SOHC engine. . . . . 4.5 litres

2.0 litre DOHC engine. . . . . 4.9 litres

Between dipstick MAX and MIN markings. . . . . 1.5 litres

Cooling system

1.6 litre engine . . . . 6.5 litres

2.0 litre engines . . . . 10.7 litres

Transmission

Manual (drain and refill):

BE4R transmission . . . . 1.8 litres

ML5T And ML5C transmission. . . . . 2.1 litres

ML6C transmission:

Without cooling fins on the gearbox casing . . . . 1.9 litres

With cooling fins on the gearbox casing . . . . 2.6 litres

Automatic:	AL4	AM6
Drain and refill.	4.5 litres	3.0 litres
Total capacity (including torque converter).	6.0 litres	7.0 litres

Fuel tank (all models approximately). 68.0 litres

Cooling system

Antifreeze mixture*:

50% antifreeze . . . . Protection down to -37°C

55% antifreeze . . . . Protection down to -45°C

* Note: *Refer to antifreeze manufacturer for latest recommendations.*

Brakes

Front brake pad friction material minimum thickness . . . . 2.5 mm

Rear brake pad friction material minimum thickness. . . . . 3.0 mm

Front disc minimum thickness . . . . 24.0 mm

Rear disc minimum thickness . . . . 12.0 mm

Remote control battery

Type CR1620

Tyre pressures . . . . Refer to the end of *Weekly checks* on page 0•17

Torque wrench settings

	Nm	lbf ft
Automatic transmission level plug	24	28
Automatic transmission filler plug:		
AL4	24	18
AM6	40	30
Engine oil sump drain plug:		
1.6 litre engines	25	18
2.0 litre engines	34	25
Manual transmission level/filler plug	20	15
Oil filter cap (paper element type – see text)	24	18
Wheel bolts.	90	66

The maintenance intervals in this manual are provided with the assumption that you will be carrying out the work yourself. These are the minimum maintenance intervals recommended by ourselves for vehicles driven daily, based on the schedule produced by the manufacturer. If you wish to keep your vehicle in peak condition at all times, you may wish to perform some of these procedures more often. We encourage frequent maintenance, because it enhances the efficiency, performance and resale value of your vehicle.

If the vehicle is driven in dusty areas, used to tow a trailer, or driven frequently at slow speeds (idling in traffic) or on short journeys, more frequent maintenance intervals are recommended.

When the vehicle is new, it should be serviced by a dealer service department (or other workshop recognised by the vehicle manufacturer as providing the same standard of service) in order to preserve the warranty. The vehicle manufacturer may reject warranty claims if you are unable to prove that servicing has been carried out as and when specified, using only original equipment parts or parts certified to be of equivalent quality.

All Citroën models are equipped with a service indicator function incorporated into the mileage recorder, which will indicate the mileage until the next service is due. However, Citroën point out that, 'due to the relationship between time and mileage, some operating conditions will make annual service more suitable'.

Every 250 miles or weekly
- [ ] Refer to *Weekly checks*

Every 6000 miles or 6 months
- [ ] Engine oil and filter – renewal (Section 3)

Note: *Citroën recommend that the engine oil and filter are changed every 12 500 miles. However, oil and filter changes are good for the engine and we recommend that the oil and filter are renewed more frequently, especially if the vehicle is used on a lot of short journeys.*

Every 12 000 miles or 12 months
Note: *The 12 000 mile intervals start at 18 000 miles, ie, at 18 000 miles, 30 000 miles, 42 000 miles, 54 000 miles, etc.*
- [ ] Service indicator – resetting (Section 4)
- [ ] Hoses and fluids – leak check (Section 5)
- [ ] Steering and suspension components – check (Section 6)
- [ ] Brake pad wear and disc check (Section 7)
- [ ] Handbrake – check and adjustment (Section 8)
- [ ] Seat belt condition – check (Section 9)
- [ ] Airbag system – check (Section 10)
- [ ] Headlight beam alignment – check (Section 11)
- [ ] LDS fluid level – check (Section 12)
- [ ] Road test (Section 13)
- [ ] Coolant antifreeze concentration – check (Section 14)
- [ ] Driveshaft joints and gaiters – check (Section 15)
- [ ] Exhaust system – check (Section 16)
- [ ] Hinges and locks – lubrication (Section 17)
- [ ] Fuel filter – drain (Section 18)
- [ ] Lane wandering warning system sensor – clean (Section 19)
- [ ] Auxiliary drivebelt condition – check (Section 20)

Every 24 000 miles or 2 years (whichever occurs first)
- [ ] Fuel filter – renewal (Section 18)

Note: *Vehicles up to September 2004 (pre-facelift)*
- [ ] Pollen filter – renewal (Section 21)

Every 40 000 miles
- [ ] Air filter element – renewal (Section 22)
- [ ] Manual transmission fluid – level check (Section 23)
- [ ] Automatic transmission fluid – level check (Section 24)
- [ ] Fuel filter – renewal (Section 18)

Note: *Vehicles from September 2004 (post-facelift)*

Every 50 000 miles
- [ ] Eolys fluid – check (Section 25)

Note: *Vehicles up to September 2004 (pre-facelift)*

Every 62 500 miles
- [ ] Particulate filter – renewal (Section 26)

Note: *1.6 litre engine*

Every 75 000 miles
- [ ] Eolys fluid – check (Section 25)

Note: *Vehicles from September 2004 (post-facelift)*

Every 120 000 miles
- [ ] Particulate filter – renewal (Section 26)

Note: *2.0 litre engines*

Every 150 000 miles or 10 years (whichever occurs first)
- [ ] Timing belt – renewal (Section 27)

Note: *This is the interval recommended by Citroën. However, It is strongly recommended that the interval is reduced on vehicles which are subjected to intensive use, ie, mainly short journeys or a lot of stop-start driving. The actual belt renewal interval is very much up to the individual owner, but bear in mind that severe engine damage will result if the belt breaks.*

Every 2 years
- [ ] Brake fluid – renewal (Section 28)
- [ ] Remote control battery – renewal (Section 29)
- [ ] Coolant – renewal (Section 30)

Note: *This work is not included in the Citroën schedule, and should not be required if the recommended Citroën antifreeze/inhibitor is used.*

Every 10 years
- [ ] Renew the airbags (Section 31)

Note: *Models up to September 2004 (pre-facelift)*

Every 15 years
- [ ] Renew the airbags (Section 31)

Note: *Models from September 2004 (post-facelift)*

Underbonnet view – 1.6 litre

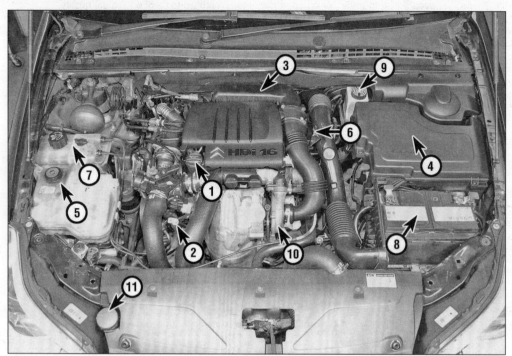

1 Engine oil filler cap
2 Engine oil level dipstick
3 Air filter
4 Engine fusebox/ECM box
5 LDS fluid reservoir
6 Fuel filter
7 Coolant expansion tank
8 Battery
9 Brake/clutch fluid reservoir
10 Turbocharger
11 Windscreen washer reservoir

Underbonnet view – 2.0 litre SOHC

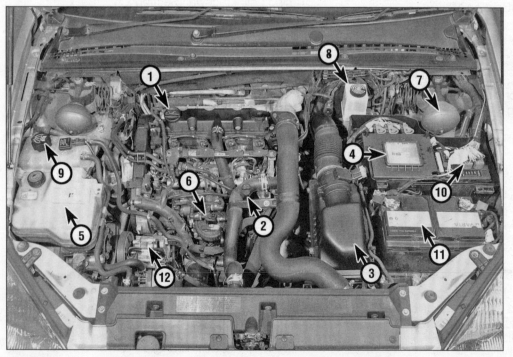

1 Engine oil filler cap
2 Engine oil level dipstick
3 Air filter
4 Engine management ECM
5 LDS fluid reservoir
6 Fuel filter
7 Suspension sphere
8 Brake/clutch fluid reservoir
9 Coolant expansion tank
10 Fusebox
11 Battery
12 Power steering pump

Front underbody view – 2.0 litre SOHC

1 Engine oil drain plug
2 Engine oil filter
3 Transmission drain plug
4 Anti-roll bar
5 Steering track rod end
6 Intercooler
7 Charge air pipe
8 Air conditioning compressor
9 Suspension lower arm
10 Front subframe

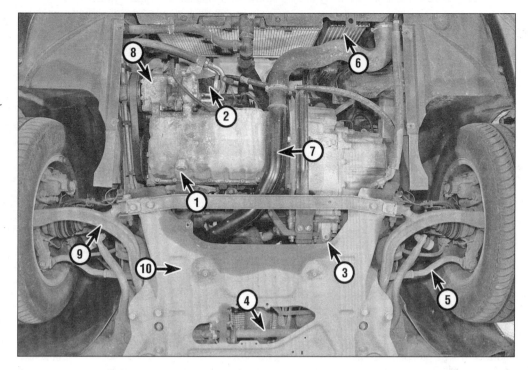

Rear underbody view

1 Fuel tank
2 Rear suspension sphere
3 Trailing arm
4 Rear anti-roll bar
5 Rear height sensor
6 Exhaust tailbox
7 Suspension strut

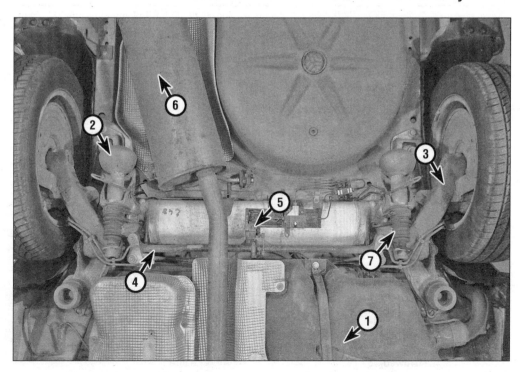

Maintenance procedures

1 General information

This Chapter is designed to help the home mechanic maintain his/her vehicle for safety, economy, long life and peak performance.

The Chapter contains a master maintenance schedule, followed by Sections dealing specifically with each task in the schedule. Visual checks, adjustments, component renewal and other helpful items are included. Refer to the accompanying illustrations of the engine compartment and the underside of the vehicle for the locations of the various components.

Servicing your vehicle in accordance with the mileage/time maintenance schedule and the following Sections will provide a planned maintenance programme, which should result in a long and reliable service life. This is a comprehensive plan, so maintaining some items, but not others, at the specified service intervals will not produce the same results.

As you service your vehicle, you will discover that many of the procedures can – and should – be grouped together, because of the particular procedure being performed, or because of the close proximity of two otherwise-unrelated components to one another. For example, if the vehicle is raised for any reason, the exhaust system could be inspected at the same time as the suspension and steering components.

The first step in this maintenance programme is to prepare yourself before the actual work begins. Read through all the Sections relevant to the work to be carried out, then make a list and gather together all the parts and tools required. If a problem is encountered, seek advice from a parts specialist, or a dealer service department.

2 Regular maintenance

If, from the time the vehicle is new, the routine maintenance schedule is followed closely, and frequent checks are made of fluid levels and high-wear items, as suggested throughout this manual, the engine will be kept in relatively good running condition, and the need for additional work will be minimised.

It is possible that there will be times when the engine is running poorly due to the lack of regular maintenance. This is even more likely if a used vehicle, which has not received regular and frequent maintenance checks, is purchased. In such cases, additional work may need to be carried out, outside of the regular maintenance intervals.

If engine wear is suspected, a compression test (refer to Chapter 2C, 2D or 2E) will provide valuable information regarding the overall performance of the main internal components. Such a test can be used as a basis to decide on the extent of the work to be carried out. If, for example, a compression test indicates serious internal engine wear, conventional maintenance as described in this Chapter will not greatly improve the performance of the engine, and may prove a waste of time and money, unless extensive overhaul work (Chapter 2F) is carried out first.

The following series of operations are those most often required to improve the performance of a generally poor-running engine:

Primary operations

a) Clean, inspect and test the battery ('Weekly checks' and Chapter 5A)
b) Check all the engine-related fluids ('Weekly checks').
c) Check the condition and tension of the auxiliary drivebelt (Section 20).
d) Check the condition of the air filter element, and renew if necessary (Section 22).
e) Check the condition of all hoses, and check for fluid leaks (Section 5).

If the above operations do not prove fully effective, carry out the following secondary operations:

Secondary operations

a) Check the charging system (Chapter 5A).
b) Check the fuel system (Chapter 4B).

Every 6000 miles or 6 months

3 Engine oil and filter – renewal

1 Frequent oil changes are the most important preventative maintenance the DIY home mechanic can give the engine, because ageing oil becomes diluted and contaminated, which leads to premature engine wear.
2 Before starting this procedure, gather together all the necessary tools and materials.

Also make sure that you have plenty of clean rags and newspapers handy, to mop-up any spills. Ideally, the engine oil should be warm, as it will drain better, and more built-up sludge will be removed with it. Take care, however, not to touch the exhaust or any other hot parts of the engine when working under the vehicle. To avoid any possibility of scalding, and to protect yourself from possible skin irritants and other harmful contaminants in used engine oils, it is advisable to wear gloves when carrying out this work.

3 Access to the filter and drain plug will be greatly improved if the front of the vehicle is raised and support securely on axle stands (see *Jacking and vehicle support*).
4 Undo the fasteners and remove the engine undershield **(see illustration)**.
5 Slacken the plug about half a turn **(see illustrations)**. Position the draining container under the drain plug, then remove the plug completely – recover the sealing washer **(see Haynes Hint)**.
6 Allow some time for the old oil to drain,

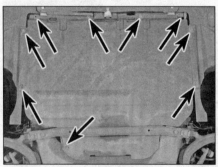

3.4 Engine undershield fasteners (arrowed)

3.5a Engine sump drain plug (arrowed) – 1.6 litre . . .

3.5b . . . 2.0 litre SOHC (arrowed) . . .

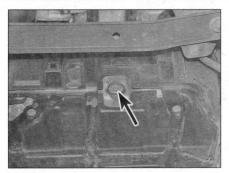

3.5c . . . and 2.0 litre DOHC (arrowed)

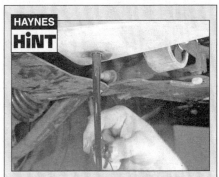

HAYNES HiNT

As the drain plug releases from the threads, move it away sharply so the stream of oil runs into the container and not up your sleeve.

3.7 Fit a new sealing washer to the oil drain plug

noting that it may be necessary to reposition the container as the oil flow slows to a trickle. On models with a paper element type filter (see later in this Section), slacken the oil filter cap a couple of turns to allow the oil in the filter housing to drain into the sump.

7 After all the oil has drained, wipe off the drain plug with a clean rag. Clean the area around the drain plug opening, and refit the plug with a new sealing washer **(see illustration)**. Tighten the plug to the specified torque.

8 Two different types of oil filter may be fitted. On some models, the oil filter is of the disposable metal cartridge type, whilst on others, the oil filter consists of a separate disposable paper element contained in a plastic cap, screwed in the housing on the front of the cylinder block. Proceed as follows according to the filter type.

Metal canister type filter

9 Use a filter removal tool to unscrew the filter cartridge from the housing **(see illustration)**. Empty the old oil into the container.

10 Use a clean rag to remove all oil, dirt and sludge from the filter housing mating face. Check the old filter to ensure the rubber sealing ring hasn't stuck to the housing. If it has, carefully remove it.

11 Apply a light coating of clean engine oil to the sealing ring on the new filter, then screw it into position on the engine. Tighten the filter firmly by hand only – do not use any tools **(see illustration)**.

Paper element type filter

12 Using a socket or spanner, slacken the oil filter cap initially, then unscrew it by hand the rest of the way. On 1.6 litre engines, undo the screw and manoeuvre the air intake ducting from the air filter housing to access the oil filter cap **(see illustrations)**.

13 Lift the filter cap away, remove the paper element from the filter housing, and the O-ring seal from the cap **(see illustration)**.

14 Use a clean rag to remove all oil and dirt from inside the filter cap and housing.

15 Fit a new O-ring seal to the cap, and on 2.0 litre engines, fit the new paper element to the cap. On 1.6 litre engines, fit the element to the housing, ensuring the lug on the base of the element locates correctly in the corresponding hole in the housing. Lightly

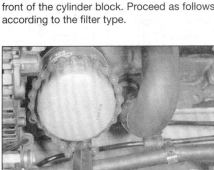

3.9 Use a filter removal tool to slacken the oil filter

3.11 Apply clean engine oil to the filter rubber seal

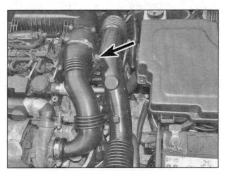

3.12a Undo the screw (arrowed) and remove the air intake ducting . . .

3.12b . . . for access to the oil filter cap (arrowed) – 1.6 litre engines

3.12c Oil filter location (arrowed) – 2.0 litre DOHC engines

3.13 Remove the cap and lift the element from the housing

3.15a Renew the O-ring seal . . .

3.15b . . . insert the new filter element into the cap . . .

3.15c . . . then apply a little clean engine oil to the seal

3.15d Ensure the lug on the base of the filter engages with the hole in the housing (arrowed) – 1.6 litre engines

lubricate the O-ring seal with clean engine oil **(see illustrations)**.

16 Screw the cap into place, and tighten it to the specified torque.

All filter types

17 Lower the vehicle to the ground, then

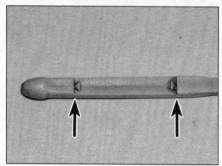

3.17 Upper and lower dipstick marks (arrowed)

remove the oil filler cap and withdraw the level dipstick from the tube. Fill the engine, using the correct oil (see *Lubricants and fluids*). An oil can spout or funnel may help to reduce spillage. Pour in half the specified quantity of oil first, then wait a few minutes for the oil to run to the sump. Continue adding oil a small

quantity at a time until the level is up to the lower mark on the dipstick. Adding a further 1.5 litres (see Specifications) will bring the level up to the upper mark on the dipstick. Insert the dipstick, and refit the filler cap **(see illustration)**.

18 Refit the engine undershield.

19 Start the engine and run it for a few minutes; check for leaks around the oil filter seal and the sump drain plug. Note that there may be a delay of a few seconds before the oil pressure warning light goes out when the engine is first started, as the oil circulates through the engine oil galleries and the new oil filter before the pressure builds-up.

20 Switch off the engine, and wait a few minutes for the oil to settle in the sump once more. With the new oil circulated and the filter completely full, recheck the level on the dipstick, and add more oil as necessary.

21 Dispose of the used engine oil safely, in accordance with the guidance given in *General repair procedures*.

Every 12 000 miles or 12 months

4 Service indicator – resetting

1 The instrument cluster mileage recorder incorporates a service interval indicator. When the vehicle is started, the unit displays the mileage until the next service, or the mileage covered since the service was due. The service indicator is manually reset to zero after the vehicle has been serviced. The indicator can also be reset at any time using the Citroën diagnostic tool.

2 Switch off the ignition, then on the instrument panel, press and hold down the reset button.

3 Switch on the ignition – the distance remaining until (or covered since) the next service is due will flash in the display. Keep the button pressed until the display resets to zero and the maintenance 'key' disappears. Release the knob.

5 Hoses and fluids – leak check

Cooling system

⚠️ *Warning: Refer to the safety information given in 'Safety first!' and Chapter 3 before disturbing any of the cooling system components.*

1 Carefully check the radiator and heater coolant hoses along their entire length. Renew any hose which is cracked, swollen or which shows signs of deterioration. Cracks will show up better if the hose is squeezed. Pay close attention to the clips that secure the hoses to the cooling system components. Hose clips that have been overtightened can pinch and puncture hoses, resulting in cooling system leaks.

2 Inspect all the cooling system components (hoses, joint faces, etc) for leaks. Where any

problems of this nature are found on system components, renew the component or gasket with reference to Chapter 3 **(see Haynes hint)**.

HAYNES HiNT

A leak in the cooling system will usually show-up as white- or antifreeze-coloured deposits on the area adjoining the leak.

Fuel system

 Warning: Refer to the safety information given in 'Safety first!' and Chapter 4B before disturbing any of the fuel system components.

3 Diesel leaks are easier to spot than petrol, but can be difficult to pinpoint unless the leakage is significant and hence easily visible. Fuel tends to spread, especially in a hot engine bay. Small drips can spread before you get a chance to identify the point of leakage. If you suspect that there is a fuel leak from the area of the engine bay, leave the vehicle overnight then start the engine from cold, with the bonnet open. Metal components tend to shrink when they are cold, and rubber seals and hoses tend to harden, so any leaks will be more apparent whilst the engine is warming-up from a cold start.

4 Check all fuel lines at their connections to the fuel rail, fuel pressure regulator, fuel filter, fuel cooler and especially the return hoses on top of the injectors. Examine each rubber fuel hose along its length for splits or cracks. Check for leakage from the crimped joints between rubber and metal fuel lines. Examine the unions between the metal fuel lines and the fuel filter housing. Also check the area around the fuel injectors for signs of O-ring leakage.

5 To identify fuel leaks between the fuel tank and the engine bay, the vehicle should be raised and securely supported on axle stands (see *Jacking and vehicle support*). Inspect the fuel tank and filler neck for punctures, cracks and other damage. The connection between the filler neck and tank is especially critical. Sometimes a rubber filler neck or connecting hose will leak due to loose retaining clamps or deteriorated rubber.

6 Carefully check all rubber hoses and metal fuel lines leading away from the fuel tank. Check for loose connections, deteriorated hoses, kinked lines, and other damage. Pay particular attention to the vent pipes and hoses, which often loop up around the filler neck and can become blocked or kinked, making tank filling difficult. Follow the fuel supply and return lines to the front of the vehicle, carefully inspecting them all the way for signs of damage or corrosion. Renew damaged sections as necessary.

Engine oil

7 Inspect the area around the camshaft cover, cylinder head, oil filter and sump joint faces. Bear in mind that, over a period of time, some very slight seepage from these areas is to be expected – what you are really looking for is any indication of a serious leak caused by gasket failure. Engine oil seeping from the base of the timing belt cover or the transmission bellhousing may be an indication of crankshaft or transmission input shaft oil seal failure. Should a leak be found, renew the failed gasket or oil seal by referring to the appropriate Chapters in this manual.

Automatic transmission fluid

8 Where applicable, check the hoses leading to the transmission fluid cooler at the front of the engine bay for leakage. Look for deterioration caused by corrosion and damage from grounding, or debris thrown up from the road surface. Automatic transmission fluid is a thin oil and is usually red in colour.

LDS fluid

9 Examine the hose running between the fluid reservoir and the power steering pump, the return hose running from the steering rack to the fluid reservoir, and the various suspension pipes. Also examine the high-pressure supply hose between the pump and the steering rack.

10 Check the condition of each hose/pipe carefully. Look for deterioration caused by corrosion and damage from grounding, or debris thrown up from the road surface.

11 Pay particular attention to crimped unions, and the area surrounding the hoses that are secured with adjustable worm-drive clips. LDS fluid is a thin oil, and is orange in colour.

Air conditioning refrigerant

 Warning: Refer to the safety information given in 'Safety first!' and Chapter 3 regarding the dangers of disturbing any of the air conditioning system components.

12 The air conditioning system is filled with a liquid refrigerant, which is retained under high pressure. If the air conditioning system is opened and depressurised without the aid of specialised equipment the refrigerant will immediately turn into gas and escape into the atmosphere. If the liquid comes into contact with your skin, it can cause severe frostbite. In addition, the refrigerant contains substances which are environmentally damaging; for this reason, it should not be allowed to escape into the atmosphere in an uncontrolled fashion.

13 Any suspected air conditioning system leaks should be immediately referred to a Citroën dealer or air conditioning specialist. Leakage will be shown up as a steady drop in the level of refrigerant in the system.

14 Note that water may drip from the condenser drain pipe, underneath the car, immediately after the air conditioning system has been in use. This is normal, and should not be cause for concern.

Brake/clutch fluid

 Warning: Refer to the safety information given in 'Safety first!' and Chapter 9 regarding the dangers of handling brake fluid.

15 With reference to Chapter 9, examine the area surrounding the brake/clutch pipe unions at the master cylinder for signs of leakage. Check the area around the base of fluid reservoir, for signs of leakage caused by seal failure. Also examine the brake pipe unions at the ABS hydraulic unit.

16 If fluid loss is evident, but the leak cannot be pinpointed in the engine bay, the brake calipers and underbody brake lines should be carefully checked with the vehicle raised and supported on axle stands (see *Jacking and vehicle support*). Leakage of fluid from the braking system is a serious fault that must be rectified immediately.

17 Brake/clutch hydraulic fluid is a toxic substance with a watery consistency. New fluid is almost colourless, but it becomes darker with age and use.

Unidentified fluid leaks

18 If there are signs that a fluid of some description is leaking from the vehicle, but you cannot identify the type of fluid or its exact origin, park the vehicle overnight and slide a large piece of card underneath it. Providing that the card is positioned in roughly the right location, even the smallest leak will show up on the card. Not only will this help you to pinpoint the exact location of the leak, it should be easier to identify the fluid from its colour. Bear in mind, though, that the leak may only be occurring when the engine is running!

Vacuum hoses

19 Although the braking system is hydraulically-operated, the brake servo unit amplifies the effort applied at the brake pedal by making use of the vacuum supplied by the vacuum pump, driven by the engine. Vacuum is ported to the servo by means of a large-bore hose. Any leaks that develop in this hose will reduce the effectiveness of the braking system, and may affect the running of the engine.

20 In addition, a number of the underbonnet components, particularly the turbocharger control components, are driven by vacuum supplied from the vacuum pump via narrow-bore hoses. A leak in a vacuum hose means that air is being drawn into the hose (rather than escaping from it) and this makes leakage very difficult to detect. One method is to use an old length of vacuum hose as a kind of stethoscope – hold one end close to (but not in!) your ear and use the other end to probe the area around the suspected leak. When the end of the hose is directly over a vacuum leak, a hissing sound will be heard clearly through the hose. Care must be taken to avoid contacting hot or moving components, as the engine must be running, when testing in this manner. Renew any vacuum hoses that are found to be defective.

6 Steering and suspension components – check

Front suspension and steering

1 Raise the front of the vehicle, and securely support it on axle stands (see *Jacking and vehicle support*).

2 Visually inspect the balljoint dust covers

6.4 Check for wear in the hub bearings by grasping the wheel and trying to rock it

and the steering rack-and-pinion gaiters for splits, chafing or deterioration. Any wear of these components will cause loss of lubricant, together with dirt and water entry, resulting in rapid deterioration of the balljoints or steering gear.

3 Check the power steering fluid hoses for chafing or deterioration, and the pipe and hose unions for fluid leaks. Also check for signs of fluid leakage under pressure from the steering gear rubber gaiters, which would indicate failed fluid seals within the steering gear.

4 Grasp the roadwheel at the 12 o'clock and 6 o'clock positions, and try to rock it **(see illustration)**. Very slight free play may be felt, but if the movement is appreciable, further investigation is necessary to determine the source. Continue rocking the wheel while an assistant depresses the footbrake. If the movement is now eliminated or significantly reduced, it is likely that the hub bearings are at fault. If the free play is still evident with the footbrake depressed, then there is wear in the suspension joints or mountings.

5 Now grasp the wheel at the 9 o'clock and 3 o'clock positions, and try to rock it as before. Any movement felt now may again be caused by wear in the hub bearings or the steering track rod balljoints. If the outer balljoint is worn, the visual movement will be obvious. If the inner joint is suspect, it can be felt by placing a hand over the rack-and-pinion

For a quick check, the thickness of the friction material on each brake pad can be measured through the aperture in the caliper body.

rubber gaiter and gripping the track rod. If the wheel is now rocked, movement will be felt at the inner joint if wear has taken place.

6 Using a large screwdriver or flat bar, check for wear in the suspension mounting bushes by levering between the relevant suspension component and its attachment point. Some movement is to be expected, as the mountings are made of rubber, but excessive wear should be obvious. Also check the condition of any visible rubber bushes, looking for splits, cracks or contamination of the rubber.

7 With the car standing on its wheels, have an assistant turn the steering wheel back-and-forth, about an eighth of a turn each way. There should be very little, if any, lost movement between the steering wheel and roadwheels. If this is not the case, closely observe the joints and mountings previously described. In addition, check the steering column universal joints for wear, and also check the rack-and-pinion steering gear itself.

8 The front suspension mountings should be checked for tightness.

Rear suspension

9 Chock the front wheels, then jack up the rear of the vehicle and support securely on axle stands (see *Jacking and vehicle support*).

10 Working as described previously for the front suspension, check the rear hub bearings, the suspension bushes and the strut or shock absorber mountings (as applicable) for wear.

11 The rear suspension mountings should be checked for tightness.

Shock absorber

12 Check for any signs of fluid leakage around the shock absorber bodies, or from the rubber gaiters around the piston rods. Should any fluid be noticed, the shock absorber is defective internally, or the rubber gaiter is split, and may need renewing. **Note:** *Shock absorbers should always be renewed in pairs on the same axle.*

13 The shock absorbency of the unit is provided by the nitrogen-filled sphere. Should the sphere leak, the suspension will become very hard. Citroën insist that the spheres cannot be recharged, so renewal would appear to be the only option (see Chapter 10).

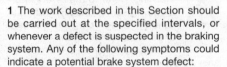

7 Brake pad wear and disc check

1 The work described in this Section should be carried out at the specified intervals, or whenever a defect is suspected in the braking system. Any of the following symptoms could indicate a potential brake system defect:
  a) *The vehicle pulls to one side when the brake pedal is depressed.*
  b) *The brakes make squealing, scraping or dragging noises when applied.*
  c) *Brake pedal travel is excessive, or pedal feel is poor.*

  d) *The brake fluid requires repeated topping-up. Note that, because the hydraulic clutch shares the same fluid as the braking system (see Chapter 6), this problem could be due to a leak in the clutch system.*

Front disc brakes

2 Chock the rear wheels then loosen the front wheel bolts. Jack up the front of the vehicle, and support it on axle stands (see *Jacking and vehicle support*).

3 For better access to the brake calipers, remove the wheels.

4 Look through the inspection window in the caliper, and check that the thickness of the friction lining material on each of the pads is not less than the recommended minimum thickness given in the Specifications **(see Haynes hint)**. Bear in mind that the lining material is normally bonded to a metal backing plate. To differentiate between the metal and the lining material, it is helpful to turn the disc slowly at first – the edge of the disc can then be identified, with the lining material on each pad either side of it, and the backing plates behind.

5 If it is difficult to determine the exact thickness of the pad linings, or if you are at all concerned about the condition of the pads, then remove them from the calipers for further inspection (refer to Chapter 9).

6 Check the other caliper in the same way.

7 If any one of the brake pads has worn down to, or below, the specified limit, *all four* pads at that end of the car must be renewed as a set. If the pads on one side are significantly more worn than the other, this may indicate that the caliper pistons have partially seized – refer to the brake pad renewal procedure in Chapter 9, and push the pistons back into the caliper to free them.

8 Measure the thickness of the discs with a micrometer, if available, to make sure that they still have service life remaining. Do not be fooled by the lip of rust which often forms on the outer edge of the disc, which may make the disc appear thicker than it really is – scrape off the loose rust if necessary, without scoring the disc friction (shiny) surface.

9 If any disc is thinner than the specified minimum thickness, renew both (refer to Chapter 9).

10 Check the general condition of the discs. Look for excessive scoring and discolouration caused by overheating. If these conditions exist, remove the relevant disc and have it resurfaced or renewed (refer to Chapter 9).

11 Make sure that the the transmission is in neutral. Spin the wheel, and check that the brake is not binding. Some drag is normal with a disc brake, but it should not require any great effort to turn the wheel – also, do not confuse brake drag with resistance from the transmission. Abnormal effort may indicate that the handbrake needs adjusting – see Chapter 9.

12 Before refitting the wheels, check all brake lines and hoses (refer to Chapter 9). In particular, check the flexible hoses in the vicinity of the calipers, where they are subjected to most movement. Bend them between the fingers (but do not actually bend them double, or the casing may be damaged) and check that this does not reveal previously-hidden cracks, cuts or splits.

13 On completion, refit the wheels and lower the car to the ground. Tighten the wheel bolts to the specified torque.

Rear disc brakes

14 Loosen the rear wheel bolts then chock the front wheels. Jack up the rear of the car, and support it on axle stands. Release the handbrake and remove the rear wheels.

15 The procedure for checking the rear brakes is much the same as described in paragraphs 2 to 13 above. Check that the rear brakes are not binding, noting that transmission resistance is not a factor on the rear wheels.

8 Handbrake – check and adjustment

1 Chock the rear wheels, then jack up the front of the vehicle and support on axle stands (see *Jacking and vehicle support*).

2 Fully apply and release the handbrake 5 times.

3 Ensure the caliper lever arms are resting against the stops, then check that the distance between the handbrake cable hook and the caliper arm lever is between 0.1 and 1.0 mm **(see illustration)**. If not, adjust the handbrake as described in Chapter 9.

4 Fully apply the handbrake lever, and check that both front wheels are locked when attempting to turn them by hand.

5 Lower the vehicle to the ground.

9 Seat belt condition – check

1 Working on each seat belt in turn, carefully examine the seat belt webbing for cuts, or for any signs of serious fraying or deterioration. Pull the belt all the way out, and examine the full extent of the webbing.

2 Fasten and unfasten the belt, ensuring that the locking mechanism holds securely, and releases properly when intended. Check also that the retracting mechanism operates correctly when the belt is released.

3 Check the security of all seat belt mountings and attachments which are accessible from inside the vehicle without removing any trim or other components.

4 Check the function of the seat belt reminder lamp.

10 Airbag system – check

1 The following work can be carried out by the home mechanic, however, if an electronic fault is apparent, it will be necessary to take the car to a Citroën dealer or specialist, who will have the necessary diagnostic equipment to extract fault codes from the system.

2 Turn the ignition switch to the drive position (ignition warning lights on), and check that the airbag warning light is illuminated for approximately 6 seconds. After this period the light should go out, indicating that the system has been checked and is functioning correctly.

3 If the warning light remains on or refuses to light, have the system checked by a Citroën dealer or specialist.

4 Visually examine the steering wheel centre pad, knee airbag and the passenger airbag modules for external damage. Also check the exterior of the front seats around the side airbag locations. If damage is evident, consult a Citroën dealer or specialist.

5 In the interests of safety, make sure that there are no loose items inside the car which could be thrown onto the airbag modules in the event of an accident.

11 Headlight beam alignment – check

Refer to Chapter 12 for details

12 LDS fluid level – check

Checking, and if necessary, topping-up the LDS fluid level is described in Chapter 10, Section 16.

13 Road test

Instruments and electrical equipment

1 Check the operation of all instruments and electrical equipment.

2 Make sure that all instruments read correctly, and switch on all electrical equipment in turn to check that it functions properly. Check the function of the heating, air conditioning and automatic climate control systems.

Steering and suspension

3 Check for any abnormalities in the steering, suspension, handling or road 'feel'.

4 Drive the vehicle, and check that there are no unusual vibrations or noises.

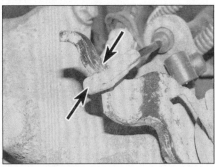

8.3 The clearance between the cable end fitting and the caliper operating lever must be 0.1 to 1.0 mm (arrowed)

5 Check that the steering feels positive, with no excessive 'sloppiness', or roughness, and check for any suspension noises when cornering, or when driving over bumps. Check that the power steering system operates correctly.

Drivetrain

6 Check the performance of the engine, clutch (manual transmission), transmission and driveshafts.

7 Listen for any unusual noises from the engine, clutch (manual transmission) and transmission.

8 Make sure that the engine runs smoothly when idling, and that there is no hesitation when accelerating.

9 On manual transmission models, check that the clutch action is smooth and progressive, that the drive is taken up smoothly, and that the pedal travel is correct. Also listen for any noises when the clutch pedal is depressed. Check that all gears can be engaged smoothly, without noise, and that the gear lever action is smooth and not abnormally vague or 'notchy'.

10 On automatic transmission models, make sure that all gearchanges occur smoothly without snatching, and without an increase in engine speed between changes. Check that all the gear positions can be selected with the vehicle at rest. If any problems are found, they should be referred to a Citroën dealer.

11 Listen for a metallic clicking sound from the front of the vehicle, as the vehicle is driven slowly in a circle with the steering on full lock. Carry out this check in both directions. If a clicking noise is heard, this indicates wear in a driveshaft joint, in which case, refer to Chapter 8.

Braking system

12 Make sure that the vehicle does not pull to one side when braking, and that the wheels do not lock when braking hard.

13 Check that there is no vibration through the steering when braking.

14 Check that the handbrake operates correctly, without excessive movement of the lever, and that it holds the vehicle stationary on a slope.

15 Test the operation of the brake servo unit as follows. With the engine off, depress the

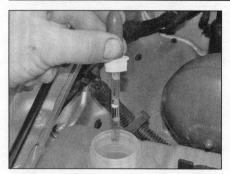

14.3 Check the antifreeze concentration using a hydrometer

footbrake four or five times to exhaust the vacuum, then start the engine while holding the brake pedal depressed. As the engine starts, there should be a noticeable 'give' in the brake pedal as vacuum builds-up. Allow the engine to run for at least two minutes, and then switch it off. If the brake pedal is now depressed again, it should be possible to detect a 'hiss' from the servo as the pedal is depressed. After about four or five applications, no further sound should be heard, and the pedal should feel considerably harder.

14 Coolant antifreeze concentration – check

1 The cooling system should be filled with the recommended antifreeze and corrosion protection fluid. Over a period of time, the concentration of fluid may be reduced due to topping-up (this can be avoided by topping-up with the correct antifreeze mixture) or fluid loss. If loss of coolant has been evident, it is important to make the necessary repair before adding fresh fluid. The exact mixture of antifreeze-to-water which you should use depends on the relative weather conditions. The mixture should contain at least 40% anti-freeze, but not more than 70%. Consult the mixture ratio chart on the antifreeze container before adding coolant. Hydrometers are available at most automotive accessory shops to test the coolant. Use antifreeze which meets the vehicle manufacturer's specifications.

15.1 Check the CV joint gaiters for cracks or splits

2 With the engine cold, carefully remove the cap from the expansion tank. If the engine is not completely cold, place a cloth rag over the cap before removing it, and remove it slowly to allow any pressure to escape.
3 Antifreeze checkers are available from car accessory shops. Draw some coolant from the expansion tank and observe how many plastic balls are floating in the checker (see illustration). Usually, 2 or 3 balls must be floating for the correct concentration of antifreeze, but follow the manufacturer's instructions.
4 If the concentration is incorrect, it will be necessary to either withdraw some coolant and add antifreeze, or alternatively drain the old coolant and add fresh coolant of the correct concentration.

15 Driveshaft joints and gaiters – check

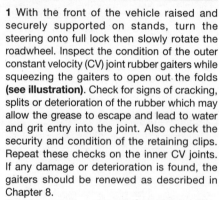

1 With the front of the vehicle raised and securely supported on stands, turn the steering onto full lock then slowly rotate the roadwheel. Inspect the condition of the outer constant velocity (CV) joint rubber gaiters while squeezing the gaiters to open out the folds (see illustration). Check for signs of cracking, splits or deterioration of the rubber which may allow the grease to escape and lead to water and grit entry into the joint. Also check the security and condition of the retaining clips. Repeat these checks on the inner CV joints. If any damage or deterioration is found, the gaiters should be renewed as described in Chapter 8.
2 At the same time check the general condition of the CV joints themselves by first holding the driveshaft and attempting to rotate the wheel. Repeat this check by holding the inner joint and attempting to rotate the driveshaft. Any appreciable movement indicates wear in the joints, wear in the driveshaft splines or a loose driveshaft retaining nut.

16 Exhaust system – check

1 With the engine cold, check the complete exhaust system, from its starting point at the engine to the end of the tailpipe. If necessary, raise the front and rear of the vehicle and support it on axle stands (see *Jacking and vehicle support*). Remove any engine undershields as necessary for full access to the exhaust system.
2 Check the exhaust pipes and connections for evidence of leaks, severe corrosion, and damage. Make sure that all brackets and mountings are in good condition and that all relevant nuts and bolts are tight (see illustration). Leakage at any of the joints or in other parts of the system will usually show

up as a black sooty stain in the vicinity of the leak.
3 Rattles and other noises can often be traced to the exhaust system, especially the brackets and rubber mountings. Try to move the pipes and silencers. If the components are able to come into contact with the body or suspension parts, secure the system with new mountings. Otherwise separate the joints (if possible) and twist the pipes as necessary to provide additional clearance.

17 Hinges and locks – lubrication

1 Work around the vehicle and lubricate the hinges of the bonnet, doors and tailgate with a light machine oil.
2 Lightly lubricate the two bonnet release locks with a smear of grease.
3 Check carefully the security and operation of all hinges, latches and locks. Check that the central locking system operates correctly.
4 Check the condition and operation of the bonnet and tailgate struts, renewing them if either is leaking or no longer able to support the bonnet/tailgate.

18 Fuel filter – draining and renewal

Draining

1 The purpose of this operation is to purge the filter assembly of any accumulated water. Remove the plastic cover on the top of the engine. On 1.6 litre engines, undo the screw and remove the intake air ducting from the front of the engine compartment to the air cleaner housing (see illustration 3.12a).
2 Place a container underneath the filter, then slacken the fuel filter bleed screw, and operate the hand priming pump a few times until all water or impurities cease to run out (see illustrations). Tighten the bleed screw.
3 Start the engine and run it at a fast idle speed (less than 2000 rpm) for 30 seconds. Refit the engine cover.

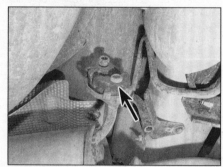

16.2 Check the condition of the exhaust rubber mountings (arrowed)

18.2a Fuel filter bleed screw (arrowed) – 1.6 litre engines

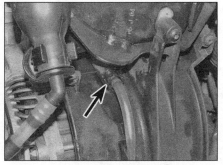

18.2b Fuel filter bleed screw (arrowed) – 2.0 litre engines

18.7a Depress the release button (arrowed) . . .

18.7b . . . then disconnect the pipes from the fuel filter

18.8 Release the clip and slide the filter upwards

18.9a Release the clip (arrowed) . . .

Renewal – 1.6 litre engine

4 Disconnect the battery negative lead (see Chapter 5A), then remove the plastic cover from the top of the engine.

5 Undo the screw and remove the intake air ducting from the front of the engine compartment to the air cleaner housing **(see illustration 3.12a)**.

6 Undo the screws securing the air filter cover, disconnect the mass airflow sensor wiring plug, then slacken the clamp securing the intake pipe to the turbocharger, and manoeuvre the cover/ducting assembly from place **(see illustrations 22.2a, 22.2b, 22.2c and 22.2d)**.

7 Note their fitted positions and disconnect the pipes and wiring plug from the fuel filter assembly **(see illustrations)**. Plug the openings to prevent contamination.

8 Release the retaining clip and lift the filter from place **(see illustrations)**.

9 Release the clip and detach the fuel heater from the side of the filter assembly **(see illustrations)**.

10 Clip the fuel heater into place on the new filter. Fit the new filter into place, remove the plugs and reconnect the pipes, and the wiring plug.

11 Refit the air pipes.

Renewal – 2.0 litre SOHC engine

12 Disconnect the battery negative lead (see Chapter 5A), then remove the plastic cover from the top of the engine.

13 Undo the fasteners and remove the engine undershield **(see illustration 3.4)**.

14 Position a container beneath then slacken the bleed screw and allow the filter to drain **(see illustration 18.2b)**.

15 Thoroughly clean the area around the fuel pipe connectors, then disconnect the pipes and wiring connector (where applicable) at the top of the filter assembly. Plug the openings to prevent contamination.

Filter with serrated collar

16 Using a strap wrench or large water pump pliers, unscrew the serrated collar at the top of the filter assembly **(see illustration)**.

17 Remove the filter head, followed by the filter element, and the seal.

18 Thoroughly clean the filter housing chamber using clean, lint-free rags.

19 Fit the new filter element, then lubricate the new seal and fit it in place.

20 Refit the filter head and tighten the serrated collar until the marks align.

21 Reconnect the fuel pipes, and wiring plug, then refit the engine undershield.

Filter with hexagonal section

22 Using a 22 mm socket on the filter head, rotate the filter head 90° anti-clockwise.

23 Lift the filter head, followed by the washer, filter element and seal **(see illustrations)**.

18.9b . . . and slide the heater from the filter body

18.16 Unscrew the top of the filter using a strap wrench

18.23a Remove the filter housing cover, followed by the metal sealing ring, and O-ring seal . . .

18.23b . . . then lift out the filter element

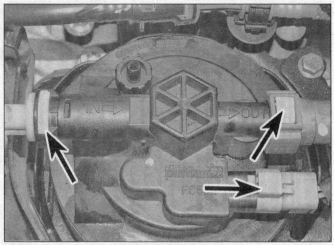

18.30 Depress the release buttons, disconnect the fuel pipes, and the wiring plug (arrowed)

24 Thoroughly clean the filter housing chamber using clean, lint-free rags.

25 Fit the new filter element into the housing, followed by the washer, then lubricate the new seal using clean fuel, and fit it in place.

26 Refit the filter head and tighten it 90° clockwise. Remove the plugs, reconnect the fuel pipes, and refit the engine undershield.

Renewal – 2.0 litre DOHC engine

27 Disconnect the battery negative lead (see Chapter 5A), then remove the plastic cover from the top of the engine.

28 Undo the fasteners and remove the engine undershield (see illustration 3.4).

29 Slacken the bleed screw at the base of the filter and allow the filter to drain (see illustration 18.2b).

30 Thoroughly clean the area around the fuel pipe connectors, then disconnect the pipes and wiring connector (where applicable) at the top of the filter assembly (see illustration). Plug the openings to prevent contamination.

31 Using a 27 mm socket, unscrew the filter head (see illustration).

32 Lift the filter head, and extract the filter element. Discard the seal on the filter head – a new one must be fitted.

33 Thoroughly clean the filter housing chamber using clean, lint-free rags.

34 Fit the new filter element into the filter head, then lubricate the new seal using clean fuel, and fit it in place on the filter head (see illustrations).

35 Refit the filter head and tighten it until the filter head touches the stop (see illustration).

36 Remove the plugs, reconnect the fuel pipes/wiring plug, and refit the engine undershield.

All engines

37 Reconnect the battery negative lead as described in Chapter 5A.

38 Bleed the fuel system as described in Chapter 4B, Section 3.

19 Lane wandering warning system sensor – clean

1 The sensors are located under the front bumper, 3 on each side. In order for them to function correctly, traffic/road dirt must be cleared from the lenses.

2 Chock the rear wheels, raise the front of the vehicle and support it securely on axle stands (see *Jacking and vehicle support*).

3 The sensors can be cleaned without removing them, using clean soapy water, and a soft sponge. Take care not to scratch the lenses. Dry the sensors with soft, clean, lint-free cloth.

4 Lower the vehicle to the ground.

20 Auxiliary drivebelt condition – check

1 On all engines, a single, multi-grooved auxiliary drivebelt is used to transmit drive from the crankshaft pulley to the alternator and the refrigerant compressor. The drivebelt is tensioned automatically by a spring-loaded tensioner pulley.

2 For better access to the drivebelt, chock the

18.31 Use a 27 mm socket to unscrew the filter head

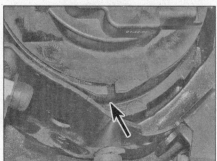

18.34a Renew the O-ring seal . . .

18.34b . . . and fit the new element into the filter head

18.35 Tighten the filter head until it touches the stop (arrowed)

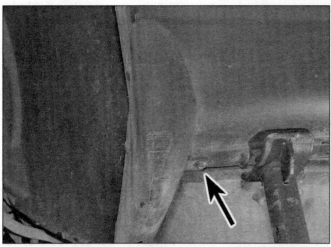

20.2a Remove the front mudflap (fastener arrowed) to access the liner fasteners

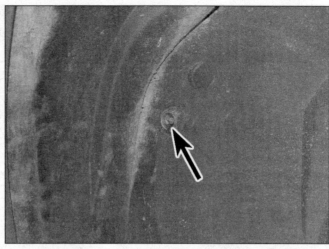

20.2b The wheel arch liner is secured by plastic nuts (arrowed) . . .

rear wheels then jack up the front of the car and support it on axle stands (see *Jacking and vehicle support*). Remove the right-hand front roadwheel, then remove the plastic liner from under the right-hand wheel arch to expose the crankshaft pulley **(see illustrations)**.

3 Using a suitable socket and extension bar fitted to the crankshaft pulley bolt, rotate the crankshaft so that the entire length of the drivebelt(s) can be examined. Examine the drivebelt for cracks, splitting, fraying, or other damage. Check also for signs of glazing (shiny patches) and for separation of the belt plies. Renew the belt if worn or damaged, as described in Chapter 5A.

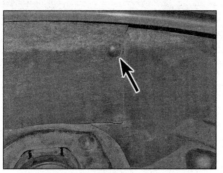

20.2c . . . plastic push-in clips (arrowed) . . .

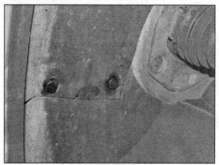

20.2d . . . and plastic rivets (prise up the centre pins)

Every 24 000 miles or 2 years

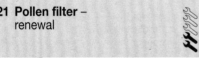

21 Pollen filter – renewal

1 Undo the fasteners and remove the facia panel above the passenger's footwell **(see illustration)**.

2 Undo the 2 retaining screws **(see illustration)**.

3 Note which way around it's fitted, then pull the filter from the housing **(see illustration)**.

4 Fit the new element using a reversal of the removal procedure.

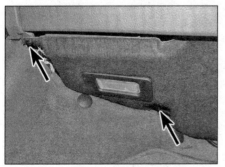

21.1 Remove the scrivet and the fastener (arrowed)

21.2 Undo the 2 screws (arrowed) . . .

21.3 . . . and pull the pollen filter from place

22.2a Undo the cover screws (arrowed) . . .

22.2b . . . disconnect the pipe from the turbocharger . . .

22.2c . . . release the clips and disconnect the breather tube (arrowed) . . .

22.2d . . . then remove the ducting/cover assembly

22.3 Lift the filter element from the housing

22.8 Disconnect the mass airflow sensor wiring plug (arrowed)

Every 40 000 miles

22 Air filter element – renewal

1.6 litre engine

1 Pull the plastic cover upwards from the top of the engine.

2 Disconnect the mass airflow meter wiring plug, undo the air filter cleaner cover screws, slacken the clamp securing the air intake ducting to the turbocharger, release the breather tube clips and remove the air ducting/cover assembly **(see illustrations)**.

3 Note which way round it's fitted, and lift the air filter element from the housing **(see illustration)**.

4 Wipe clean the inner surfaces of the cover and main housing, then locate the new element in the housing, making sure that the sealing lip is correctly engaged with the edge of the housing.

5 Refit the filter cover/intake ducting assembly, ensuring the rear edge of the cover engages correctly with the rear of the filter housing.

6 Refit the plastic cover to the top of the engine.

2.0 litre SOHC engine

7 The air cleaner is located on the left-hand side of the engine compartment, and the air inlet is taken from the front of the car behind the radiator grille area.

8 Disconnect the mass airflow sensor wiring plug **(see illustration)**.

9 Release the clamp and disconnect the outlet hose from the mass airflow sensor **(see illustration)**.

10 Undo the Torx bolts and remove the air filter cover **(see illustration)**.

11 Lift out the air cleaner filter element, noting which way round it is fitted **(see illustration)**.

12 Wipe clean the inner surfaces of the cover and main housing, then locate the new element in the housing, making sure that the sealing lip is correctly engaged with the edge of the housing.

13 Refit the cover, and secure with the screws.

14 Reconnect the air outlet hose and secure it by tightening the hose clip.

15 Reconnect the mass airflow sensor wiring plug.

22.9 Slacken the hose clamp (arrowed)

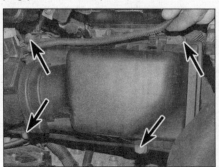

22.10 Undo the Torx bolts (arrowed)

22.11 Lift out the filter element

22.16 Disconnect the mass airflow sensor wiring plug (arrowed) . . .

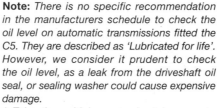

22.17 . . . undo the 4 screws (arrowed) . . .

22.18 . . . lift the cover and remove the filter element

2.0 litre DOHC engine

16 Disconnect the mass airflow sensor wiring plug **(see illustration)**.
17 Undo the 4 retaining screws, and lift the cover from place **(see illustration)**.
18 Lift the air filter element from place, noting which way around it's fitted **(see illustration)**.
19 Wipe clean the inner surfaces of the cover and main housing, then locate the new element in the housing, making sure that the sealing lip is correctly engaged with the edge of the housing.
20 Refit the cover, and secure it with the screws.
21 Reconnect the mass airflow sensor wiring plug.

23 Manual transmission fluid – level check

Note: *There is no specific recommendation in the manufacturers schedule to check the oil level on ML5T, ML5C and ML6C transmissions. They are described as 'Lubricated for life'. However, we consider it prudent to check the oil level, as a leak from the driveshaft oil seal, or sealing washer could cause expensive damage. On the ML5C and ML6C transmissions, there is also no level plug. If it is suspected the oil level is low, drain and refill the transmission as described in Chapter 7A. The following information applies only to the BE4R and ML5T transmissions.*

1 Take the car on a short journey to warm the transmission up to normal operating temperature. Position the car over an inspection pit, or alternatively jack up the front and rear of the car and support on axle stands (see *Jacking and vehicle support*). Whichever method is used, make sure that the car is level for checking the fluid level later.
2 Position a suitable container beneath the transmission, then unscrew the filler/level plug located on the left-hand side of the transmission casing **(see illustrations)**.
3 The fluid level should be up to the bottom of the filler/level plug hole. If necessary, add the specified fluid until it begins to run out of the hole.
4 Refit the filler/level plug and tighten it to the specified torque.
5 Lower the vehicle to the ground.

24 Automatic transmission fluid – level check

Note: *There is no specific recommendation in the manufacturers schedule to check the oil level on automatic transmissions fitted the C5. They are described as 'Lubricated for life'. However, we consider it prudent to check the oil level, as a leak from the driveshaft oil seal, or sealing washer could cause expensive damage.*

1 Take the vehicle on a short journey, to warm the transmission up to normal operating temperature, then park the vehicle on level ground. Firmly apply the handbrake and place the selector lever in the P position.
2 Wipe clean the area around the filler plug, which is situated on the top of the transmission, directly beneath the air cleaner assembly. Remove the air cleaner assembly as described in Chapter 4B, then unscrew the filler plug from the transmission and recover the sealing washer **(see illustration)**.
3 Carefully add 0.5 litre of the specified type of fluid to the transmission via the filler plug aperture. Fit a new sealing washer to the filler plug then refit the plug, tightening it to the specified torque.
4 Undo the screws and remove the engine undershield – where fitted **(see illustration 3.4)**.
5 Position a suitable container under the drain/level plug arrangement, situated on the base of the transmission. The level plug is the smaller plug fitted to the centre of the larger drain plug **(see illustration)**.
Caution: Do not remove the drain plug by mistake.
6 Start the engine and allow it to idle. With the engine running, retain the drain plug then

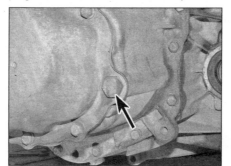

23.2a Fluid level plug (arrowed) – BE4R transmission . . .

23.2b . . . and ML5T transmission

24.2 Unscrew the transmission filler plug (arrowed)

24.5 Unscrew the level plug (arrowed) from the centre of the drain plug

slacken and remove the level plug and sealing washer.

> **Warning: The fluid will be hot, take precautions against scalding.**

7 If there is sufficient fluid in the transmission unit, fluid should trickle out the centre of the drain plug before slowing to a drip. **Note:** *If no fluid trickles out, or just a few drips appear when the plug is removed, the fluid level is too low. Refit the level plug then switch off the engine. Add a further 0.5 litre of fluid to the transmission then refit the filler plug and repeat the check (see paragraphs 5 to 7).*
8 Once the flow of fluid stops, the level is correct. Fit a new sealing washer to the level plug then refit the plug and tighten it to the specified torque. Switch off the engine.

Every 50 000 miles

25 Eolys fluid – check

1 Eolys fluid is an additive used on vehicles equipped with a particulate filter incorporated into the exhaust system. Over a period of time, the soot produced by the engine will clog the filter. When the filter requires cleaning, the engine management system injects a small quantity of fuel into the combustion chamber after combustion has taken place. The unburnt fuel enters the exhaust system, where it ignites, and burns the soot deposits from the particulate filter. In order to lower the temperature at which the soot is burnt, Eolys fluid is added to the fuel in the tank. The fluid is stored in a separate tank adjacent to the fuel tank, and added to the main fuel tank. Every time the fuel tank is replenished, the system computes how much Eolys fluid to add. Eventually the level of fluid will fall below a minimum level and a warning light will illuminate on the instrument cluster. If the system runs out of fluid, the particulate filter will be unable to purge, causing its blockage, and premature failure. Unfortunately, the process of checking the level, replenishing the Eolys fluid tank and resetting the engine management values requires access to Citroën diagnostic equipment, and therefore must be entrusted to a Citroën dealer or suitably-equipped specialist. Failure to reset the ECM values will prevent the filter cleaning process from occurring.

Every 62 500 miles

26 Particulate filter – renewal

Renewal of the particulate filter is described in Chapter 4B, Section 19.

Every 150 000 miles or 10 years

27 Timing belt – renewal

Refer to Chapter 2C, 2D or 2E as applicable.

Every 2 years

28 Brake fluid – renewal

> **Warning: Brake hydraulic fluid can harm your eyes and damage painted surfaces, so use extreme caution when handling and pouring it. Do not use fluid that has been standing open for some time, as it absorbs moisture from the air. Excess moisture can cause a dangerous loss of braking effectiveness.**

1 The procedure is similar to that for the bleeding of the hydraulic system as described in Chapter 9.
2 Working as described in Chapter 9, open the first bleed screw in the sequence, and pump the brake pedal gently until nearly all the old fluid has been emptied from the master cylinder reservoir. Top-up to the MAX level with new fluid, and continue pumping until only the new fluid remains in the reservoir, and new fluid can be seen emerging from the bleed screw. Tighten the screw, and top the reservoir level up to the MAX level line.
3 Work through all the remaining bleed screws in the sequence until new fluid can be seen at all of them. Be careful to keep the master cylinder reservoir topped-up to above the MIN level at all times, or air may enter the system and greatly increase the length of the task.
4 When the operation is complete, check that all bleed screws are securely tightened, and that their dust caps are refitted. Wash off all traces of spilt fluid, and recheck the master cylinder reservoir fluid level.
5 Check the operation of the brakes before taking the car on the road.

29 Remote control battery – renewal

1 Insert a small screwdriver, then twist it to separate the 2 halves of the control (**see illustration**).
2 Lift out the printed circuit board, and slide

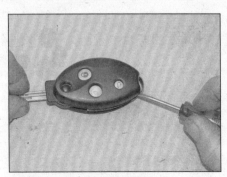

29.1 Use a small screwdriver to separate the two halves of the remote control

29.3 Slide in the new battery, positive side up

the battery from place. **Note:** *Avoid touching the battery contacts or remote control circuitry with bare fingers.*

3 Insert the new battery as shown, refit the circuit board, and clip together the two halves of the control **(see illustration)**.

4 It is now necessary to synchronise the control with the receiver, by inserting the key into the ignition switch, turning the ignition on, then immediately pressing the 'locking' button, and holding it down until the locks actuate.

30 Coolant – renewal

Note: *This work is not included in the Citroën schedule, and should not be required if the recommended Citroën antifreeze/inhibitor is used.*

> ⚠️ **Warning: Do not allow antifreeze to come in contact with your skin or painted surfaces of the vehicle. Flush contaminated areas immediately with plenty of water. Don't store new coolant, or leave old coolant lying around, where it's accessible to children or pets – they're attracted by its sweet smell. Ingestion of even a small amount of coolant can be fatal. Wipe up garage-floor and drip-pan spills immediately. Keep antifreeze containers covered, and repair cooling system leaks as soon as they're noticed.**

> ⚠️ **Warning: Never remove the expansion tank filler cap when the engine is running, or has just been switched off, as the cooling system will be hot, and the consequent escaping steam and scalding coolant could cause serious injury.**

> ⚠️ **Warning: Wait until the engine is cold before starting these procedures.**

Cooling system draining

1 With the engine completely cold, remove the expansion tank filler cap. Turn the cap anticlockwise, wait until any pressure remaining in the system is released, then unscrew it and lift it off.

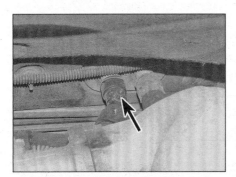

30.10a Undo the bleed screw at the bulkhead (arrowed) . . .

30.3 Prise out the clip (arrowed) and pull the coolant drain plug at the rear of the engine

2 Chock the rear wheels, raise the front of the vehicle and support it on axle stands (see *Jacking and vehicle support*).

1.6 litre engine

3 Position a container under the rear of the engine, then pull out the retaining clip and remove the plug from the coolant pipe **(see illustration)**.

4 Open the bleed screw of the heater matrix hose at the engine compartment bulkhead **(see illustration)**.

5 Disconnect the bottom hose from the radiator **(see illustration)**.

6 Once the coolant has finished draining, refit the plug, and reconnect the bottom hose. If the coolant has been drained for a reason other than renewal, then provided it is clean and less than two years old, it can be re-used, though this is not recommended.

2.0 litre SOHC engine

7 Undo the screws and remove the undershield beneath the radiator. Note the retaining screws in the wheel arch liner.

8 Detach the bottom hose from the radiator and allow the coolant to drain into a container.

9 Move the container, undo the cylinder block drain plug, and drain the block.

10 Open the bleed screws on the heater hoses (at the bulkhead), the coolant outlet housing and the top of the radiator **(see illustrations)**.

11 When the flow of coolant stops, refit the

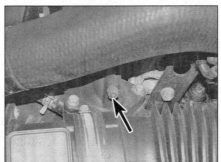

30.10b . . . and the one on the top of the coolant outlet housing (arrowed)

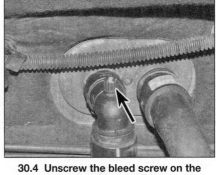

30.4 Unscrew the bleed screw on the heater hose (arrowed)

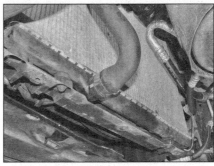

30.5 Release the clamp and disconnect the radiator bottom hose

hose, and refit the undershield. Lower the vehicle to the ground.

12 If the coolant has been drained for a reason other than renewal, then provided it is clean and less than two years old, it can be re-used, though this is not recommended.

2.0 litre DOHC engine

13 Undo the screws and remove the undershield beneath the radiator. Note the retaining screws in the wheel arch liner.

14 Detach the bottom hose from the radiator, and drain the coolant into a container **(see illustration)**.

15 Although a cylinder block drain plug is fitted, access to the plug is extremely limited, and we found it impossible to undo the plug with the engine fitted **(see illustration)**.

16 Open the bleed screws at each hose

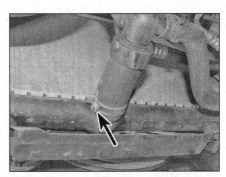

30.14 Disconnect the radiator lower hose (arrowed)

30.15 Access to the cylinder block drain plug (arrowed) is extremely limited

30.16 Undo the bleed screws on the EGR cooler (arrowed)

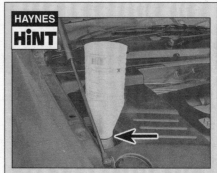

Cut the bottom off an old antifreeze container to make a 'header tank' for use when refitting the cooling system. The seal at the point arrowed should be as tight as possible – use an O-ring if available, or seal the joint by some other means.

attached to the EGR cooler at the back of the cylinder head **(see illustration)**.

17 When the flow of coolant stops, refit the coolant hose, and refit the undershield. Lower the vehicle to the ground.

18 If the coolant has been drained for a reason other than renewal, then provided it is clean and less than two years old, it can be re-used, though this is not recommended.

Cooling system flushing

19 If coolant renewal has been neglected, or if the antifreeze mixture has become diluted, then in time the cooling system may gradually lose efficiency, as the coolant passages become restricted due to rust, scale deposits and other sediment. The cooling system efficiency can be restored by flushing the system clean.

20 The radiator should be flushed independently of the engine, to avoid unnecessary contamination.

Radiator flushing

21 Disconnect the top and bottom hoses and any other relevant hoses from the radiator, with reference to Chapter 3.

22 Insert a garden hose into the radiator top inlet. Direct a flow of clean water through the radiator, and continue flushing until clean water emerges from the radiator bottom outlet.

23 If after a reasonable period, the water still does not run clear, the radiator can be flushed with a good proprietary cleaning agent. It is important that the manufacturer's instructions are followed carefully. If the contamination is particularly bad, remove the radiator and insert the hose in the bottom outlet, and reverse-flush the radiator, then refit it.

Engine flushing

24 Remove the thermostat as described in Chapter 3. If the radiator top hose has been

disconnected, temporarily reconnect the hose.

25 With the top and bottom hoses disconnected from the radiator, insert a garden hose into the radiator top hose. Direct a clean flow of water through the engine, and continue flushing until clean water emerges from the radiator bottom hose.

26 On completion of flushing, refit the thermostat and reconnect the hoses with reference to Chapter 3.

Cooling system filling

27 Before attempting to fill the cooling system, make sure that all hoses and clips are in good condition, and that the clips are tight. Note that an antifreeze mixture must be used all year round, to prevent corrosion of the engine components.

28 Make sure that the air conditioning (A/C) or automatic climate control (ACC) is switched off. This is to prevent the air conditioning system starting the radiator cooling fan before the engine is at normal temperature when refilling the system.

29 Ensure the bleed screws are open (see paragraphs 4, 10 or 16 as applicable).

30 To provide the required 'head' of coolant necessary to force al trapped air from the system, a 'header tank' must be used by refitting. Although Citroën dealers use a special header tank, the same effect can be achieved by using a suitable bottle, with a seal between the bottle and the expansion tank **(see Haynes hint)**.

31 Fit the 'header tank' to the expansion tank, and slowly fill the system. Coolant will emerge from the bleed screws, starting with the lowest screw. As soon as coolant free from air bubbles emerges from the bleed screw, tighten it, and watch the next bleed screw in the system. Repeat the procedure until the coolant is emerging from the highest bleed

screw in the cooling system and all bleed screws are securely tightened.

32 Ensure the header tank is full (at least 0.5 litres of coolant). Start the engine, and run it at a fast idle speed (do not exceed 2000 rpm) until the cooling fan cuts in, and then cuts out 3 times. Stop the engine.

33 Stop the engine, and allow it to cool, then remove the 'header tank'. Recheck the coolant level with reference to *Weekly checks*. Top-up the level if necessary and refit the expansion tank filler cap.

Antifreeze mixture

34 Always use an ethylene-glycol based antifreeze which is suitable for use in mixed-metal cooling systems. The quantity of antifreeze and levels of protection are given in the Specifications.

35 Before adding antifreeze, the cooling system should be completely drained, preferably flushed, and all hoses checked for condition and security.

36 After filling with antifreeze, a label should be attached to the expansion tank, stating the type and concentration of antifreeze used, and the date installed. Any subsequent topping-up should be made with the same type and concentration of antifreeze.

Caution: Do not use engine antifreeze in the windscreen/tailgate washer system, as it will cause damage to the vehicle paintwork. A screenwash additive should be added to the washer system in the quantities stated on the bottle.

Every 10 years

31 Airbags – renewal

Renewal of the airbags is described in Chapter 12.

Chapter 2 Part A:
Indirect injection petrol engine in-car repair procedures

Contents

Degrees of difficulty

Easy, suitable for novice with little experience	Fairly easy, suitable for beginner with some experience	Fairly difficult, suitable for competent DIY mechanic	Difficult, suitable for experienced DIY mechanic	Very difficult, suitable for expert DIY or professional

Specifications

Engine (general)

Designation:
   1.8 litre EW7J4
   2.0 litre EW10J4
Engine code*:
   1.8 litre 6FZ
   2.0 litre . . . . RFN
Capacity:
   1.8 litre . . . . 1749 cc
   2.0 litre . . . . 1997 cc
Bore:
   1.8 litre . . . . 82.7 mm
   2.0 litre . . . . 85.0 mm
Stroke:
   1.8 litre . . . . 81.4 mm
   2.0 litre . . . . 88.0 mm
Output:
   Torque:
      1.8 litre . . . . 160 Nm @ 4000 rpm
      2.0 litre . . . . 190 Nm @ 4100 rpm
   Power:
      1.8 litre . . . . 85 kW @ 5500 rpm
      2.0 litre . . . . 99 kW @ 6000 rpm
Direction of crankshaft rotation . . . . Clockwise (viewed from the right-hand side of vehicle)
No 1 cylinder location . . . . At the transmission end of block
Compression ratio . . . . 10.8 : 1

* *The engine code is stamped onto the right-hand front face of the cylinder block, adjacent to the engine mounting bracket.*

Camshafts

Drive . . . . Toothed belt
No of bearings 5

Cylinder head bolts

Maximum bolt length (see text):
   Up to vehicle No RPO 09653 . . . . 147.0 mm
   From vehicle No RPO 09653 . . . . 143.0 mm

Lubrication system

Oil pump type . . . .   Rotor-type, driven directly off the crankshaft

Minimum oil pressure at 80°C:

    At 1000 rpm . . . .   1.5 bar

    At 3000 rpm . . . .   5.0 bar

Torque wrench settings

	Nm	lbf ft
Ancillary components mounting bracket	19	14
Auxiliary drivebelt tensioner pulley bolt	20	15
Auxiliary drivebelt idler pulley	35	26
Big-end bearing cap bolts*:		
Stage 1	10	7
Stage 2	Slacken by 180°	
Stage 3	23	17
Stage 4	Angle-tighten a further 46°	
Camshaft bearing cap housing bolts:		
Stage 1	5	4
Stage 2	10	7
Camshaft sprocket retaining bolt:		
Stage 1	30	22
Stage 2	85	63
Crankshaft main bearing cap housing:		
Stage 1:		
M11 bolts	10	7
M6 bolts	2	1
Stage 2:		
M11 bolts	Fully slacken	
Stage 3:		
M11 bolts	20	15
Stage 4:		
M11 bolts	Angle-tighten a further 70°	
Stage 5:		
M6 bolts	10	7
Crankshaft pulley-to-sprocket retaining bolts:		
Stage 1	15	11
Stage 2	20	15
Crankshaft sprocket centre bolt:		
Stage 1	40	30
Stage 2	Angle-tighten a further 40°	
Cylinder head bolts:		
Stage 1	15	11
Stage 2	50	37
Stage 3	Slacken by 360°	
Stage 4	20	15
Stage 5	Angle-tighten a further 285°	
Cylinder head cover bolts:		
Stage 1	5	4
Stage 2	11	8
Driveplate retaining bolts*:		
Stage 1	25	18
Stage 2	Fully slacken	
Stage 3	8	6
Stage 4	20	15
Stage 5	Angle-tighten a further 21°	
Engine-to-transmission fixing bolts	50	37
Engine/transmission left-hand mounting:		
Mounting bracket-to-transmission bolts	45	33
Rubber mounting centre nut	65	48
Rubber mounting-to-bracket nuts	27	20
Engine/transmission rear mounting:		
Connecting link-to-mounting bracket bolt	50	37
Connecting link-to-subframe bolt	50	37
Mounting bracket-to-cylinder block bolts	45	33
Engine/transmission right-hand mounting:		
Connecting link to body	50	37
Connecting link to engine mounting	50	37
Upper mounting bracket-to-lower (engine) bracket nuts	61	45

Torque wrench settings (continued)

	Nm	lbf ft
Flywheel retaining bolts*:		
Stage 1	25	18
Stage 2	Fully slacken	
Stage 3	8	6
Stage 4	20	15
Stage 5	Angle-tighten a further 21°	
Oil pump retaining bolts	8	6
Sump retaining bolts	8	6
Timing belt idler pulley bolt	35	26
Timing belt tensioner pulley bolt	20	15
* New nuts/bolts must be used.		

1 General information

Using this Chapter

This Part of Chapter 2 is devoted to in-car repair procedures for the 1.8 litre and 2.0 litre petrol engines with indirect injection. All procedures concerning engine removal and refitting, and engine block/cylinder head overhaul for petrol and diesel engines can be found in Chapter 2F.

Most of the operations included in Chapter 2A are based on the assumption that the engine is still installed in the car. Therefore, if this information is being used during a complete engine overhaul, with the engine already removed, many of the steps included here will not apply.

EW series engine description

The EW series engine is of the DOHC 16-valve, in-line four-cylinder type, mounted transversely at the front of the car with the clutch and transmission attached to its left-hand end.

The aluminium alloy cylinder block/ crankcase is of modular construction consisting of three sections – the cylinder block itself, the crankshaft bearing cap housing and the sump. The cylinder block incorporates four cast iron dry cylinder liners which are cast into the block and cannot be renewed.

The crankshaft is supported in five shell-type main bearings with thrustwashers fitted to No 2 main bearing, to control crankshaft endfloat.

The connecting rods are attached to the crankshaft by horizontally-split shell-type big-end bearings, and to the pistons by gudgeon pins which are an interference fit in the connecting rod small-end eyes. The aluminium alloy pistons are of the slipper type, and are fitted with three piston rings – two compression rings and a scraper-type oil control ring.

The cylinder head is of the crossflow type, the inlet ports being at the front of the engine and the exhaust ports at the rear. The camshafts run in plain bearings integral with the cylinder head and with the two camshaft bearing cap housings. The inlet and exhaust valves are each closed by single coil springs, and operate in guides pressed into the cylinder head. Valve actuation is by self-adjusting hydraulic tappets acted upon directly by the camshaft lobes.

Drive to the camshafts is by a toothed timing belt and sprockets, and incorporates an automatic tensioning mechanism. The timing belt also drives the coolant pump. All accessories are driven from the crankshaft pulley by a single multi-ribbed auxiliary drivebelt.

The lubrication system is of the full-flow, pressure-feed type. Oil is drawn from the sump by a rotor type pump, driven directly from the end of the crankshaft. The pump draws oil through a strainer located in the sump and then forces it through an externally-mounted filter into galleries in the cylinder block. From there, the oil is distributed to the crankshaft (main bearings) and camshafts. The big-end bearings are supplied with oil via internal drillings in the crankshaft; the camshaft bearings also receive a pressurised supply. The camshaft lobes and valves are lubricated by splash, as are all other engine components.

Throughout this manual, it is often necessary to identify the engines not only by their capacity, but also by their engine code which is incorporated in the engine number. This can be found stamped onto the right-hand front face of the cylinder block, adjacent to the engine mounting bracket. The first part of the engine number gives the engine code – eg, 6FZ.

Operations with engine in vehicle

The following work can be carried out with the engine in the vehicle:
a) *Compression pressure – testing.*
b) *Cylinder head covers – removal and refitting.*
c) *Crankshaft pulley – removal and refitting.*
d) *Timing belt covers – removal and refitting.*
e) *Timing belt – removal, refitting and adjustment.*
f) *Timing belt tensioner and sprockets – removal and refitting.*
g) *Camshaft oil seals – renewal.*
h) *Camshafts and tappets – removal, inspection and refitting.*
i) *Cylinder head – removal and refitting.*
j) *Cylinder head and pistons – decarbonising.*
k) *Sump – removal and refitting.*
l) *Crankshaft oil seals – renewal.*
m) *Engine/transmission mountings – inspection and renewal.*
n) *Flywheel – removal, inspection and refitting.*

2 Compression test – description and interpretation

1 When engine performance is down, or if misfiring occurs which cannot be attributed to the ignition or fuel systems, a compression test can provide diagnostic clues as to the engine's condition. If the test is performed regularly, it can give warning of trouble before any other symptoms become apparent.

2 The engine must be fully warmed-up to normal operating temperature, the battery must be fully-charged. The aid of an assistant will also be required.

3 Remove the ignition HT coil assembly (see Chapter 5B) then remove the spark plugs (see Chapter 1A).

4 Fit a compression tester to the No 1 cylinder spark plug hole – the type of tester which screws into the plug thread is to be preferred.

5 Crank the engine on the starter motor; after one or two revolutions, the compression pressure should build-up to a maximum figure, and then stabilise. Record the highest reading obtained.

6 Repeat the test on the remaining cylinders, recording the pressure in each.

7 All cylinders should produce very similar pressures; a difference of more than 2 bars between any two cylinders indicates a fault. Note that the compression should build-up quickly in a healthy engine; low compression on the first stroke, followed by gradually-increasing pressure on successive strokes, indicates worn piston rings. A low compression reading on the first stroke, which does not build-up during successive strokes, indicates leaking valves or a blown head gasket (a cracked head could also be the cause). Deposits on the undersides of the valve heads can also cause low compression.

8 Although Citroën do not specify exact compression pressures, as a guide, any cylinder pressure of below 10 bars can be considered as less than healthy. Refer to a Citroën dealer or other specialist if in doubt

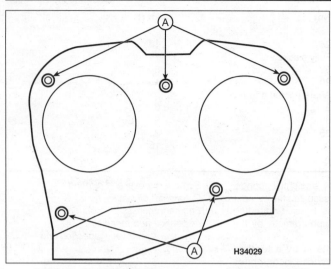

3.2 Undo the timing belt upper cover retaining bolts (A)

3.4 Insert an 8.0 mm drill bit/rod through the crankshaft pulley/ endplate and into the corresponding hole in the oil pump housing

as to whether a particular pressure reading is acceptable.

9 If the pressure in any cylinder is low, carry out the following test to isolate the cause. Introduce a teaspoonful of clean oil into that cylinder through its spark plug hole, and repeat the test.

10 If the addition of oil temporarily improves the compression pressure, this indicates that bore or piston wear is responsible for the pressure loss. No improvement suggests that leaking or burnt valves, or a blown head gasket, may be to blame.

11 A low reading from two adjacent cylinders is almost certainly due to the head gasket having blown between them; the presence of coolant in the engine oil will confirm this.

12 If one cylinder is about 20 percent lower than the others and the engine has a slightly rough idle, a worn camshaft lobe could be the cause.

13 If the compression reading is unusually high, the combustion chambers are probably coated with carbon deposits. If this is the

case, the cylinder head should be removed and decarbonised.

14 On completion of the test, refit the spark plugs and ignition HT coil (see Chapters 1A and 5B).

3 Engine assembly/ valve timing holes – general information and usage

Vehicles up to RPO 9440 (approximately October 2002)

Note 1: *The following procedure entails the use of Citroën special tool (-).0189.A (camshaft setting rods). If the Citroën tool is not available, details for fabricating suitable alternatives are given in the text.*

Note 2: *Do not attempt to rotate the engine whilst the crankshaft/camshafts are locked in position. If the engine is to be left in this state for a long period of time, it is a good idea to place suitable warning notices inside the vehicle, and in the engine compartment. This will reduce the possibility of the engine being accidentally cranked on the starter motor, which is likely to cause damage with the locking pins in place.*

1 Timing holes are drilled in the crankshaft sprocket endplate and in the two camshaft sprockets. The holes are used to ensure that the crankshaft and camshafts are correctly positioned when assembling the engine (to prevent the possibility of the valves contacting the pistons when refitting the cylinder head), or refitting the timing belt. When the timing holes are aligned with corresponding holes in the cylinder head and oil pump housing, suitable diameter pins or bolts can be inserted to lock both the camshafts and crankshaft in position, preventing them from rotating. To set the engine in the timing position, proceed as follows.

2 Undo the bolts and remove the timing belt upper cover **(see illustration)**.

3 Using a socket and extension bar fitted to the crankshaft sprocket centre bolt, turn the crankshaft in the normal direction of rotation until the timing holes in both camshaft sprockets are aligned with their corresponding holes in the cylinder head. The holes are aligned when the inlet camshaft sprocket hole is in approximately the 5 o'clock position and the exhaust camshaft sprocket hole is in approximately the 7 o'clock position, when viewed from the right-hand end of the engine. Use a small mirror to accurately observe the position of the holes.

4 With the camshaft sprocket holes correctly positioned, insert an 8.0 mm diameter drill bit or bolt through the timing hole in the crankshaft pulley/endplate, and locate it in the corresponding hole in the oil pump housing **(see illustration)**.

5 The camshaft sprockets can now be locked in position using the Citroën camshaft setting rods, or suitable home-made alternatives **(see Tool Tip)**. With the crankshaft locked in position, insert the Citroën special tools, or alternatives, through the timing hole in each camshaft sprocket and locate it in the corresponding hole in the cylinder head **(see illustration)**.

6 The crankshaft and camshafts are now

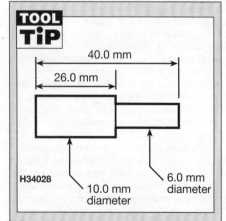

TOOL TIP

40.0 mm

26.0 mm

H34028 10.0 mm diameter 6.0 mm diameter

Camshaft sprocket locking tools can be made from 10.0 mm diameter steel bar, fabricated to the dimensions shown.

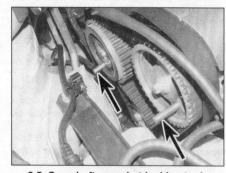

3.5 Camshaft sprocket locking tools (arrowed) inserted through the timing hole in each sprocket

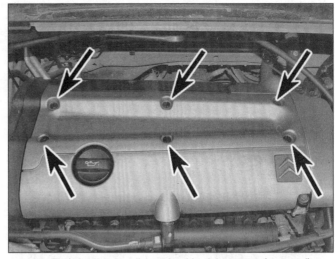

3.10 Flywheel locking tool – from approximately November 2002

4.1 The plastic cover is retained by 6 fasteners (arrowed)

locked in position, preventing rotation. In this position the crankshaft is at 90° BTDC and all the pistons are positioned half-way down their cylinder bores.

Vehicles from RPO 9441 (approximately November 2002)

Note 1: *The following procedure entails the use of Citroën special tool (-).0189.A (camshaft setting rods) and (-).0189.R (crankshaft setting tool). If the Citroën tool is not available, details for fabricating suitable alternatives are given in the text.*

Note 2: *Do not attempt to rotate the engine whilst the crankshaft/camshafts are locked in position. If the engine is to be left in this state for a long period of time, it is a good idea to place suitable warning notices inside the vehicle, and in the engine compartment. This will reduce the possibility of the engine being accidentally cranked on the starter motor, which is likely to cause damage with the locking rods/tool in place.*

7 Timing holes are drilled in the flywheel/ cylinder block and in the two camshaft sprockets. The holes are used to ensure that the crankshaft and camshafts are correctly positioned when assembling the engine (to prevent the possibility of the valves contacting the pistons when refitting the cylinder head),

or refitting the timing belt. When the timing holes are aligned with corresponding holes in the cylinder head and flywheel, suitable diameter pins or bolts can be inserted to lock both the camshafts and crankshaft in position, preventing them from rotating. To set the engine in the timing position, proceed as follows.

8 Undo the bolts and remove the timing belt upper cover **(see illustration 3.2)**.

9 Using a socket and extension bar fitted to the crankshaft sprocket centre bolt, turn the crankshaft in the normal direction of rotation until the timing holes in both camshaft sprockets are aligned with their corresponding holes in the cylinder head. The holes are aligned when the inlet camshaft sprocket hole is in approximately the 5 o'clock position and the exhaust camshaft sprocket hole is in approximately the 7 o'clock position, when viewed from the right-hand end of the engine. Use a small mirror to accurately observe the position of the holes.

10 With the camshaft sprocket holes correctly positioned, insert Citroën tool (-).0189.R, or home-made equivalent, through the timing cylinder block transmission flange, and locate it in the corresponding hole in the flywheel **(see illustration)**.

11 The camshaft sprockets can now be locked

in position using the Citroën camshaft setting rods, or suitable home-made alternatives **(see Tool Tip in this Section)**. With the crankshaft locked in position, insert the Citroën special tools, or alternatives, through the timing hole in each camshaft sprocket and locate it in the corresponding hole in the cylinder head **(see illustration 3.5)**.

12 The crankshaft and camshafts are now locked in position, preventing rotation. In this position the crankshaft is at 90° BTDC and all the pistons are positioned half-way down their cylinder bores.

4 Cylinder head covers – removal and refitting

Removal

1 Rotate the 6 fasteners 90° anti-clockwise and lift off the engine cover **(see illustration)**.

2 Disconnect the crankcase breather hose at the quick-fit connector on the rear cylinder head cover **(see illustration)**.

3 Disconnect the wiring connector at the camshaft position sensor, then undo the bolt and remove the sensor from the rear cylinder head cover **(see illustrations)**.

4.2 Disconnect the breather hose from the rear cylinder head cover

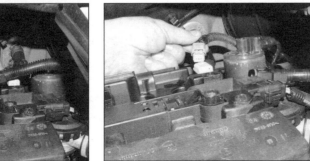

4.3a Disconnect the wiring plug . . .

4.3b . . . then undo the bolt and remove the camshaft position sensor

4.5a Lift off the front . . .

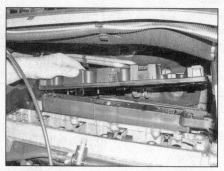

4.5b . . . and rear cylinder head covers

4.7 Ensure the new seal is correctly located in the groove

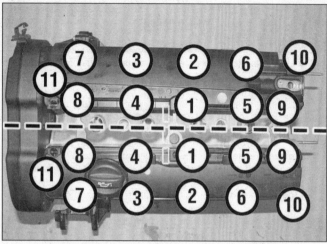

4.9 Cylinder head cover bolt tightening sequence

5.2a Undo the 4 retaining bolts . . .

4 Working in the **reverse** sequence to that shown in illustration 4.9, progressively slacken then remove the eleven retaining bolts from each cylinder head cover.

5 Lift off each cover in turn and remove it **(see illustrations)**. The cover seal should remain attached as the cover is removed – do not try to remove it, unless it is obviously damaged.

Refitting

6 Clean the cylinder head and cylinder head cover mating surfaces, and remove all traces of oil.

7 Check the condition of the rubber seal attached to each cover. The seal is designed to be re-usable, and so should not automatically be renewed unless its condition is suspect. If renewal is necessary, locate the seal in the cover groove, ensuring that it is fully seated along its entire length **(see illustration)**.

8 Carefully refit the cylinder head cover(s) to the engine.

9 Refit the cover retaining bolts and, working in sequence, tighten them to the specified torque in the two Stages given in the Specifications **(see illustration)**.

10 Check the condition of the O-ring seal on the camshaft position sensor and renew the seal if it is in any way suspect.

11 Refit the camshaft position sensor and secure with the retaining bolt. Reconnect the sensor wiring connector.

12 Reconnect the breather hoses to the rear cover.

13 Refit the engine cover.

5 Crankshaft pulley – removal and refitting

Removal

Vehicles up to RPO 9440 (approximately October 2002)

1 Remove the auxiliary drivebelt as described in Chapter 5A.

2 Undo the four crankshaft pulley retaining

5.2b . . . and lift away the crankshaft pulley

bolts and remove the pulley from the crankshaft sprocket endplate **(see illustrations)**.

Vehicles from RPO 9441 (approximately November 2002)

3 One these engines, the pulley can only be removed after the crankshaft sprocket bolt. Removal of this bolt is only possible once the camshafts and crankshaft are locked in the reference position, as described in Section 3. Removal of the pulley is therefore described in the timing belt removal procedure – see Section 6.

Refitting

Vehicles up to RPO 9440

4 Locate the pulley on the crankshaft sprocket endplate, refit the four retaining bolts and tighten them to the specified torque.

5 Refit and tension the auxiliary drivebelt as described in Chapter 5A.

6 Timing belt – general information, removal and refitting

General information

1 The timing belt drives the camshafts and coolant pump from a toothed sprocket on the right-hand end of the crankshaft. If the belt breaks or slips in service, the pistons are likely to hit the valve heads, resulting in extensive (and expensive) damage.

2 The timing belt should be renewed at the specified intervals (see Chapter 1A), or earlier if it is contaminated with oil or if it is at all noisy in operation (a 'scraping' noise due to uneven wear).

3 If the timing belt is being removed, it is a wise precaution to check the condition of the coolant pump at the same time (check for signs of coolant leakage). This may avoid the need to remove the timing belt again at a later stage should the coolant pump fail.

4 On vehicles up to RPO 9440 (approximately October 2002), the crankshaft sprocket is a two-piece assembly consisting of the toothed sprocket itself and an outer endplate. The endplate is locked to the crankshaft by means of a conventional Woodruff key. When the sprocket retaining bolt is slackened, the sprocket is free to turn on the crankshaft within the limits afforded by an additional keyway within the endplate. When the sprocket retaining bolt is tightened the complete assembly is locked to the crankshaft. This arrangement allows accurate tensioning of the timing belt when refitting, provided that the procedures contained in this Section are strictly adhered to.

5 On vehicles from RPO 9441 (approximately November 2002) the crankshaft sprocket is a one-piece assembly with integral flange. Once the pulley retaining bolt is slackened, the sprocket is free to revolve on the crankshaft. Again, this arrangement allows accurate tensioning of the timing belt when refitting, provided that the procedures contained in this Section are strictly adhered to.

Removal

6 On vehicles up to RPO 9440 (approximately October 2002) undo the 4 bolts and detach the auxiliary drivebelt pulley from the crankshaft sprocket as described in Section 5.

7 Align the engine assembly/valve timing holes as described in Section 3, and lock the crankshaft sprocket and camshaft sprockets in position. *Do not* attempt to rotate the engine whilst the locking tools are in position.

8 On vehicles from RPO 9441 (approximately November 2002), slacken and remove the crankshaft sprocket bolt.

9 Undo the bolts and remove the timing belt lower cover **(see illustration)**.

Vehicles up to RPO 9440 (approximately October 2002)

10 Loosen the timing belt tensioner pulley retaining bolt. Using an Allen key in the hole provided on the front of the pulley, rotate the pulley in a clockwise direction, to relieve the tension from the timing belt **(see illustration)**. Retighten the tensioner pulley retaining bolt to secure it in the slackened position.

Vehicles from RPO 9441 (approximately November 2002)

11 Slacken the timing belt tensioner pulley

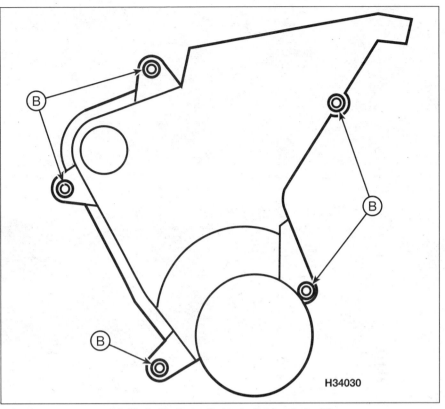

6.9 Undo the lower timing belt cover bolts (B)

retaining bolt. Rotate the tensioner roller clockwise.

All vehicles

12 If the timing belt is to be re-used, use white paint or chalk to mark the direction of rotation on the belt (if markings do not already exist), then slip the belt off the sprockets and pulleys. Note that the crankshaft must not be rotated whilst the belt is removed.

13 Check the timing belt carefully for any signs of uneven wear, splitting, or oil contamination. Pay particular attention to the roots of the teeth. Renew it if there is the slightest doubt about its condition. If the engine is undergoing an overhaul, it is advisable to renew the belt as a matter of course, regardless of its apparent condition. The cost of a new belt is nothing compared with the cost of repairs, should the belt break

in service. If signs of oil contamination are found, trace the source of the oil leak and rectify it. Wash down the engine timing belt area and all related components, to remove all traces of oil.

Refitting

14 Before refitting, thoroughly clean the timing belt sprockets. Check that the tensioner and idler pulleys rotate freely, without any sign of roughness. If necessary, renew the relevant pulley as described in Section 7.

15 Ensure that the crankshaft and camshaft sprocket locking tools are still in position.

16 Locate the timing belt on the crankshaft sprocket, ensuring that any arrows on the belt are pointing in the direction of rotation (clockwise when viewed from the right-hand end of the engine) **(see illustration)**.

6.10 Use an Allen key in the hole provided (arrowed)

6.16 Ensure that any arrows on the timing belt point in the direction of rotation

6.17a Retain the belt on the crankshaft sprocket, and feed it over the idler pulley . . .

6.17b . . . inlet camshaft sprocket . . .

6.17c . . . exhaust camshaft sprocket . . .

6.17c . . . coolant pump and tensioner pulley

6.19a Rotate the tensioner anti-clockwise . . .

17 Retain the timing belt on the crankshaft sprocket then, keeping it taut, feed the belt over the remaining sprockets and pulleys in the following order, ensuring the belt is as flush as possible with the outer faces of the sprockets/rollers **(see illustrations)**:

  a) Idler pulley.
  b) Inlet camshaft.
  c) Exhaust camshaft.
  d) Coolant pump.
  e) Tensioner pulley.

Note that there is a special Citroën tool available (-).0189.K which clips over the belt, retaining it on the crankshaft sprocket. The use of this tool is not essential.

18 Remove the locking tool from the exhaust camshaft sprocket, and (where applicable) the clip securing the timing belt to the crankshaft sprocket.

Vehicles up to RPO 9440

19 Slacken the tensioner retaining bolt, and using an 8 mm Allen key, rotate the pulley hub clockwise until the tensioner index is positioned 10° below the notch in the backplate **(see illustrations)**. Note that if the index will not attain a position of at least 10° past the notch, then the tensioner pulley, or both the tensioner pulley and belt, must be renewed.

20 Now rotate the hub clockwise until the index aligns with the notch in the backplate **(see illustration)**. If the index is allowed to go past the notch, repeat the tensioning procedure.

21 Tighten the tensioning pulley retaining bolt to the specified torque, without allowing the pulley hub to rotate. With the belt tensioned and the retaining bolt tightened, the Allen key slot should be just below the cylinder head gasket level. If not, renew the tensioner, or both the tensioner and belt.

22 Remove the camshaft and crankshaft locking tools, and rotate the crankshaft 10 complete revolutions clockwise (viewed from the right-hand end of the engine). Realign the engine assembly/valve timing holes and refit the inlet camshaft sprocket locking tool.

23 Check that the tensioner pulley index pointer is still aligned with the slot in the backing plate. If not repeat the tensioning operation from paragraph 19 onward.

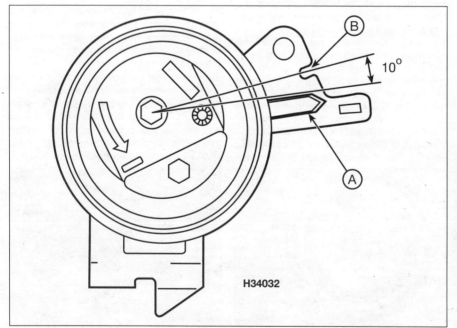

H34032

6.19b . . . until the upper edge of the index pointer (A) is positioned approximately 10° past the slot (B) in the backing plate

6.20 Now rotate the tensioner clockwise until the index pointer is exactly aligned with the slot in the backing plate

To make a sprocket holding tool, obtain two lengths of steel strip about 6.0 mm thick by about 30 mm wide or similar, one 600 mm long, the other 200 mm long (all dimensions approximate). Bolt the two strips together to form a forked end, leaving the bolt slack so that the shorter strip can pivot freely. At the other end of each 'prong' of the fork, drill a suitable hole and fit a nut and bolt to engage with the spokes or holes in the sprocket. The same tool can be used to hold both the camshaft and crankshaft sprockets.

24 With the inlet camshaft sprocket locking tool in place, it should now also be possible to fit the crankshaft sprocket locking tool. If so, continue with the refitting procedure from paragraph 30 onward. If the crankshaft sprocket locking tool will not engage, then the crankshaft sprocket endplate must be repositioned as follows.

25 Slacken the crankshaft sprocket retaining bolt while holding the sprocket endplate stationary using Citroën special tool 6310-T or a suitable home-made alternative **(see Tool Tip).** *Do not* attempt to use only the sprocket locking tools inserted in the engine assembly/valve timing holes to prevent rotation whilst the bolt is slackened.

26 With the sprocket retaining bolt slackened, turn the endplate until the sprocket locking tool can be fully inserted through the endplate and into the hole in the oil pump housing.

27 Hold the endplate with the holding tool and tighten the sprocket retaining bolt to the specified torque, then through the specified angle **(see illustrations).**

28 Remove the camshaft and crankshaft locking tools and refit the lower and upper (outer) timing belt covers, tightening the retaining bolts securely.

29 Refit the crankshaft pulley as described in Section 5.

Vehicles from RPO 9441

30 Refit the lower timing belt cover, and tighten the retaining bolts securely.

31 Using an Allen key, rotate the belt tensioner hub anti-clockwise until the tensioner index is positioned at least 10° below the notch in the backplate **(see illustration 6.19b).** Note that if the index will not attain a position of at least

6.27a Hold the crankshaft sprocket endplate with the holding tool and tighten the bolt to the specified torque . . .

10° past the notch, then the tensioner pulley, or both the tensioner pulley and belt must be renewed.

32 Now rotate the tensioner hub clockwise until the index is aligned with the notch in the backplate **(see illustration 6.20).** If the index is allowed to go past the notch, repeat the tensioning procedure.

33 Tighten the tensioning pulley retaining bolt to the specified torque, without allowing the pulley hub to rotate. With the belt tensioned and the retaining bolt tightened, the Allen key slot should be approximately 15° below the cylinder head gasket level. If not, renew the tensioner, or both the tensioner and belt.

34 Refit the crankshaft sprocket, and tighten the retaining bolt to the specified torque.

35 Remove the camshaft and crankshaft locking tools, and rotate the crankshaft 10 complete revolutions clockwise (viewed from the right-hand end of the engine). Realign the engine assembly/valve timing holes and refit the inlet camshaft sprocket locking tool.

36 Check that the tensioner pulley index pointer is still aligned with the slot in the backing plate. If not repeat the tensioning operation from paragraph 31 onward.

37 Remove the inlet camshaft sprocket locking tool, then refit the upper timing belt cover, and the auxiliary drivebelt (see Chapter 5A).

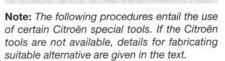

7 Timing belt tensioner and sprockets – removal, inspection and refitting

Note: *The following procedures entail the use of certain Citroën special tools. If the Citroën tools are not available, details for fabricating suitable alternative are given in the text.*

Camshaft sprockets removal

1 Remove the timing belt as described in Section 6.

2 The camshafts must now be prevented from rotating to allow the sprocket retaining bolts to be slackened. If working on the exhaust camshaft sprocket, it will be necessary to remove the rear cylinder head cover (see Section 4) to allow a spanner to be engaged with a square section of the camshaft,

6.27b . . . then through the specified angle

provided for this purpose. This is because the sprocket contains a rubber vibration damper incorporated into the sprocket hub. If the sprocket itself is held as the bolt is slackened, the rubber hub will be damaged. The inlet camshaft sprocket is conventional and can be held using Citroën tool 6016-T, or an acceptable substitute can be fabricated at home **(see Tool Tip in Section 6).** Alternatively, remove the front cylinder head cover and hold the camshaft with a spanner as described for the exhaust camshaft. *Do not* attempt to use the engine assembly/valve timing hole locking tools to prevent the sprockets from rotating whilst the bolts are slackened.

3 Remove the engine assembly/valve timing hole locking tool from the relevant sprocket, then slacken the centre retaining bolt. If a spanner is being used to prevent camshaft rotation, the spanner should be engaged with the square section of the camshaft adjacent to No 8 cam lobe **(see illustration).**

4 Remove the previously-slackened sprocket retaining bolt and washer, and withdraw the relevant sprocket from the end of the camshaft **(see illustrations).**

Crankshaft sprocket removal

5 Remove the timing belt as described in Section 6.

Vehicles up to RPO 9440 (approximately October 2002)

6 Remove the crankshaft sprocket locking tool and slacken the crankshaft sprocket

7.3 The camshafts can be held with a spanner engaged with the square section adjacent to the No 8 cam lobe

7.4a Remove the previously-slackened sprocket retaining bolt and washer . . .

7.4b . . . and withdraw the sprocket from the end of the camshaft

7.6 Hold the crankshaft sprocket endplate stationary using the home-made tool

7.7a Withdraw the endplate . . .

7.7b . . . and the sprocket itself

7.7c Remove the Woodruff key from the end of the crankshaft

retaining bolt. Prevent the crankshaft from turning while the bolt is slackened using Citroën special tool 6310-T or a suitable home-made alternative bolted to the sprocket endplate **(see illustration)**. *Do not* attempt to use only the sprocket locking tools inserted in the engine assembly/valve timing holes to prevent rotation whilst the bolt is slackened.

7 Unscrew the retaining bolt and slide the sprocket endplate and the sprocket itself off the end of the crankshaft. If loose, remove the Woodruff key from the crankshaft, and store it with the sprocket components for safe-keeping **(see illustrations)**.

8 Examine the crankshaft oil seal for signs of oil leakage and, if necessary, renew it as described in Section 13.

Vehicles from RPO 9441 (approximately November 2002)

9 Slide the sprocket from the crankshaft.

10 Examine the crankshaft oil seal for signs

of oil leakage and, if necessary, renew it as described in Section 13.

Tensioner and idler pulleys removal

11 Remove the timing belt as described in Section 6.

12 Undo the tensioner and idler pulley retaining bolts and remove the relevant pulley from the engine **(see illustrations)**.

Inspection

13 Clean the camshaft/crankshaft sprockets thoroughly, and renew any that show signs of wear, damage or cracks. Check the condition of the rubber vibration damper in the exhaust camshaft sprocket and renew the sprocket if there is any sign of deterioration of the rubber.

14 Clean the tensioner/idler pulleys, but do not use any strong solvent which may enter the pulley bearings. Check that the pulleys

rotate freely, with no sign of stiffness or free play. Renew them if there is any doubt about their condition, or if there are any obvious signs of wear or damage.

Camshaft sprockets refitting

15 Locate the relevant sprocket on the end of the camshaft, engaging the lug in the sprocket hub with the slot in the end of the camshaft.

16 Refit the sprocket retaining bolt and washer, and tighten it to the specified torque. Prevent the sprocket from turning as the bolt is tightened using the method employed for removal.

17 Realign the hole in the camshaft sprocket with the corresponding hole in the cylinder head, and refit the locking tool. Check that the crankshaft pulley locking tool is still in position.

18 Where removed, refit the cylinder head cover(s) as described in Section 4.

19 Refit and tension the timing belt as described in Section 6.

Crankshaft sprocket refitting

Vehicles up to RPO 9440

20 Refit the Woodruff key (if removed) to its slot in the crankshaft end.

21 Slide on the crankshaft sprocket followed by the sprocket endplate, then refit the retaining bolt.

22 Hold the endplate with the holding tool and tighten the sprocket retaining bolt to the specified torque, then through the specified angle.

23 Realign the hole in the sprocket endplate

7.12a Remove the timing belt tensioner . . .

7.12b . . . and idler pulley

7.27 Ensure the slot on the tensioner pulley body (arrowed) engages with the cylinder block web

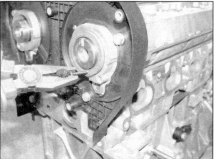

8.3 Use pliers and a self-tapping screw to extract the camshaft seal

8.5 Locate the new oil seal in position with the seal lips facing inwards

with the corresponding hole in the oil pump housing, and refit the locking tool. Check that the camshaft sprocket locking tools are still in position.
24 Refit and tension the timing belt as described in Section 6.

Vehicles from RPO 9441

25 Slide the sprocket onto the crankshaft.
26 Refit the timing belt as described in Section 6.

Tensioner and idler pulleys refitting

27 Refit the tensioner and idler pulleys, ensuring that the slot on the tensioner pulley body correctly engages with the projecting web on the cylinder block **(see illustration)**.
28 Secure the pulleys with the retaining bolts tightened to the specified torque.
29 Refit and tension the timing belt as described in Section 6.

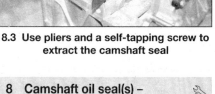

8 Camshaft oil seal(s) – renewal

1 Remove the timing belt as described in Section 6.
2 Remove the camshaft sprocket(s) as described in Section 7.
3 Punch or drill a small hole in the face of the oil seal. Screw a self-tapping screw into the hole, and pull on the screw with pliers to extract the seal **(see illustration)**.
4 Clean the seal housing, and polish off any burrs or raised edges, which may have caused the seal to fail in the first place.
5 Lubricate the lips of the new seal with clean engine oil, and locate it in position with the seal lips facing inwards **(see illustration)**.
6 Using a block of wood, tap the seal into place initially, then finish using a suitable drift

until the seal is fully seated. Take care not to damage the seal lips during fitting.
7 Refit the camshaft sprocket(s) as described in Section 7.
8 Refit and tension the timing belt as described in Section 6.

9 Camshafts and tappets – removal, inspection and refitting

Removal

1 Remove both cylinder head covers as described in Section 4.
2 Refer to Section 7 and remove both camshaft sprockets.
3 Undo the bolts and remove the timing belt upper (inner) cover **(see illustration)**.
4 Progressively slacken, by a few turns at a time, the twelve bolts securing each camshaft bearing cap housing to the cylinder head. Release the bearing cap housings from their dowels and cylinder head locations. When each housing is free, remove the bolts completely, and lift off the housings **(see illustration)**.
5 As both camshafts are visually identical, suitably mark them inlet and exhaust, or front and rear before removal.
6 Tilt the camshafts by pressing them down at their transmission end to release the centralising bearing at the timing belt end. Carefully lift the camshafts up and out of

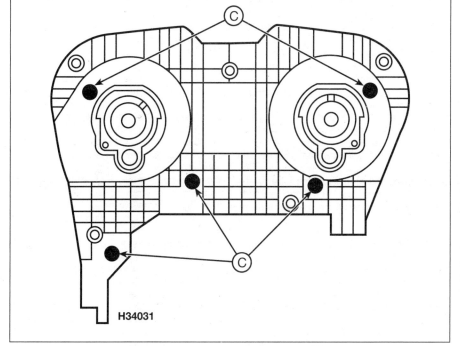

9.3 Upper timing belt (inner) cover bolts (C)

9.4 Progressively slacken and remove the bolts, then lift off the camshaft bearing cap housing(s)

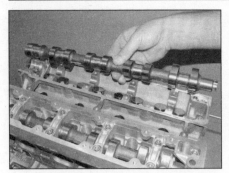

9.6 Lift the camshaft(s) from their locations

9.7 Use a rubber sucker to withdraw the hydraulic tappets

9.12a Lubricate the hydraulic tappets and bores . . .

9.12b . . . then refit the tappets into their original locations

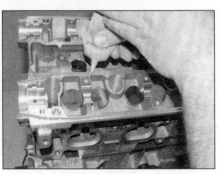

9.14 Apply a bead of sealant around the perimeter of the cylinder head mating surface

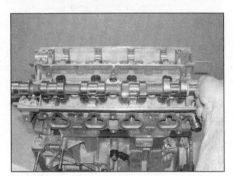

9.15 Liberally oil the camshaft bearings and lobes, then lay the camshafts in the cylinder head

their locations and slide the oil seal off each camshaft end **(see illustration)**.

7 Obtain sixteen small, clean plastic containers, and number them inlet 1 to 8 and exhaust 1 to 8; alternatively, divide a larger container into sixteen compartments and number each compartment accordingly. Using a rubber sucker, withdraw each hydraulic tappet in turn, and place it in its respective container **(see illustration)**. Do not interchange the tappets, or the rate of wear will be much increased.

Inspection

8 Thoroughly clean the sealant from the mating surfaces of the cylinder head and bearing cap housings. Use a suitable liquid gasket dissolving agent (available from Citroën dealers) together with a soft putty knife; do not use a metal scraper or the faces will be

9.16 Carefully locate the bearing cap housings over the camshafts

damaged. As there is no conventional gasket used, the cleanliness of the mating faces is of the utmost importance.

9 Examine the camshaft bearing surfaces and cam lobes for signs of wear ridges and scoring. Renew the camshaft if any of these conditions are apparent. Examine the condition of the bearing surfaces, both on the camshaft journals and in the cylinder head/ bearing cap housings. If the head bearing surfaces are worn excessively, the cylinder head will need to be renewed. If suitable measuring equipment is available, camshaft bearing journal wear can be checked by direct measurement, noting that No 1 journal is at the transmission end of the head.

10 Examine the hydraulic tappet bearing surfaces which contact the camshaft lobes for wear ridges and scoring. Renew any tappet on which these conditions are apparent. If a tappet bearing surface is badly scored, also examine the corresponding lobe on the camshaft for wear, as it is likely that both will be worn. Renew worn components as necessary.

Refitting

11 Prior to refitting, remove all traces of oil from the bearing cap housing retaining bolt holes in the cylinder head, using a clean rag. Also ensure that both the cylinder head and bearing cap housing mating faces are clean and free from oil.

12 Liberally oil the cylinder head hydraulic tappet bores and the tappets. Carefully refit the tappets to the cylinder head, ensuring

that each tappet is refitted to its original bore **(see illustrations)**. Some care will be required to enter the tappets squarely into their bores. Check that each tappet rotates freely in its bore.

13 Ensure that the four locating dowels are in position, one at each corner of the cylinder head.

14 Apply a bead of anaerobic jointing compoundv around the perimeter of the cylinder head mating faces **(see illustration)**.

15 Liberally oil the camshaft bearings in the cylinder head and the camshaft lobes, then lay the camshafts in the cylinder head, ensuring that they are in their correct locations **(see illustration)**. Turn the camshafts so that the cam lobes are in the best position to facilitate the seating of the bearing cap housings.

16 Liberally oil the camshaft bearings and carefully locate the bearing cap housings over the camshafts **(see illustration)**. Refit the retaining bolts and progressively tighten them finger tight only at this stage.

17 Working in sequence, progressively tighten the bearing cap housing retaining bolts to the Stage 1 torque setting then to the Stage 2 setting **(see illustration 4.9)**.

18 Refit the timing belt upper (inner) cover as and tighten the bolts securely.

19 Fit a new oil seal to each camshaft, using the information given in Section 8, then refit the camshaft sprockets as described in Section 7.

20 Refit the cylinder head covers as described in Section 4.

10.9 Disconnect the air inlet hose from the secondary air injection valve

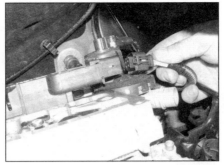

10.10 Disconnect the ignition coil unit wiring plug

10.11a Disconnect the wiring plug from the EGR valve . . .

10.11b . . . and the coolant temperature sensor

10.13 Prise out the clips (arrowed) and disconnect the heater hoses

10.14 Remove the bolt and horseshoe-shaped clamp plate securing the coolant hose to the outlet housing

10 Cylinder head – removal and refitting

Removal

1 Disconnect the battery negative terminal (refer to *Disconnecting the battery* in the Reference Chapter).

2 Drain the cooling system as described in Chapter 1A.

3 Remove the timing belt as described in Section 6.

4 Remove the cylinder head covers as described in Section 4.

5 Remove the air cleaner assembly and inlet ducting as described in Chapter 4A.

6 Remove the inlet manifold as described in Chapter 4A.

7 Working as described in Chapter 4A, disconnect the catalytic converter from the exhaust manifold. Where necessary, disconnect or release the lambda sensor wiring, so that it is not strained by the weight of the exhaust.

8 Disconnect the radiator hoses from the coolant outlet housing and thermostat cover.

9 Disconnect the air inlet hose from the secondary air injection valve at the left-hand end of the cylinder head (where applicable) **(see illustration)**.

10 Disconnect the wiring connector from the left-hand end of the ignition coil unit **(see illustration)**.

11 Disconnect the wiring connectors from the EGR valve and coolant temperature sensor **(see illustrations)**.

12 Undo the nuts securing the wiring harness support bracket to the studs on the coolant outlet housing. Release any additional cable ties and clips then move the support bracket, wiring harness and hoses clear of the cylinder head.

13 Disconnect the two heater hose from the heater matrix pipes **(see illustration)**.

14 Undo the bolt and remove the horseshoe-shaped clamp plate securing the coolant pipe to the rear of the coolant outlet housing **(see illustration)**. Withdraw the coolant pipe from the housing and recover the sealing O-ring.

15 Undo the bolt securing the lower (engine) mounting bracket to the cylinder head **(see illustration)**. Ensure that the bolt is fully unscrewed but note that there is insufficient clearance to completely remove the bolt from its location.

16 Check that all vacuum/breather hoses, pipes and electrical connectors likely to

impede removal have been disconnected from the cylinder head.

17 Working in the **reverse** of the sequence shown in illustration 10.36, progressively slacken the ten cylinder head bolts by half a turn at a time, until all bolts can be unscrewed by hand. Remove the bolts along with their washers.

18 Connect an engine hoist or suitable lifting gear to the two lifting brackets on the cylinder head.

19 Release the joint between the cylinder head and gasket using two L-shaped metal bars which fit into the cylinder head bolt holes. Using the bars, gently 'rock' the cylinder head free towards the front of the vehicle. *Do not* try to swivel the head on the cylinder block as it is located by dowels.

20 When the joint is broken, obtain the help of an assistant and slowly raise the hoist to lift the cylinder head off the block **(see illustration)**.

10.15 Undo the bolt securing the lower mounting bracket to the cylinder head

10.20 Lift the cylinder head from the block

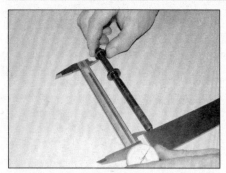

10.29 Measure the length of the cylinder head bolts from the underside of the head to the end of the bolt

10.31a Check the locating dowels are still in position (arrowed) . . .

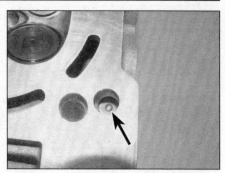

10.31b . . . and the camshaft oil supply non-return valve (arrowed) is in place in the cylinder head

At the same time, support the head at the rear as it will tend to tip backwards due to the offset position of the lifting brackets. Take care as the head is lifted as it is very easy to break the lower rear projecting corner of the upper (inner) timing belt cover. Try to keep the head as level as possible until it is raised sufficiently to clear the cylinder block.

21 During removal, check that the camshaft oil supply non-return valve (located in the underside of the cylinder head at the timing belt end) does not drop out; it is easily lost if it does.

22 When sufficient clearance exists, move the hoist forward, raise it further and lift the cylinder head out of the engine compartment.

23 Remove the gasket from the top of the block, noting the two locating dowels. If the locating dowels are a loose fit, remove them and store them with the head for safe-keeping. Do not discard the gasket; it may be needed for identification purposes.

24 If the cylinder head is to be dismantled for overhaul, refer to Part F of this Chapter.

Preparation for refitting

25 The mating faces of the cylinder head and cylinder block must be perfectly clean before refitting the head. Citroën recommend the use of a scouring agent for this purpose, but acceptable results can be achieved by using a hard plastic or wood scraper to remove all traces of gasket and carbon. The same method can also be used to clean the piston crowns. Take particular care to avoid scoring or gouging the cylinder head/cylinder block mating surfaces during the cleaning operations, as aluminium alloy is

easily damaged. Make sure that the carbon is not allowed to enter the oil and water passages – this is particularly important for the lubrication system, as carbon could block the oil supply to the engine's components. Using adhesive tape and paper, seal the water, oil and bolt holes in the cylinder block. To prevent carbon entering the gap between the pistons and bores, smear a little grease in the gap. After cleaning each piston, use a small brush to remove all traces of grease and carbon from the gap, then wipe away the remainder with a clean rag.

26 Check the mating surfaces of the cylinder block and the cylinder head for nicks, deep scratches and other damage. If slight, they may be removed carefully with a file, but if excessive, machining may be the only alternative to renewal. If warpage of the cylinder head gasket surface is suspected, use a straight-edge to check it for distortion. Refer to Part F of this Chapter if necessary.

27 Thoroughly clean the threads of the cylinder head bolt holes in the cylinder block. Ensure that the bolts run freely in their threads, and that all traces of oil and water are removed from each bolt hole.

28 When purchasing a new cylinder head gasket, it is essential that a gasket of the correct thickness is obtained. At the time of writing, there are two different thicknesses available – the standard gasket which is fitted at the factory, and a slightly thicker 'repair' gasket (+ 0.3 mm), for use once the head gasket face has been machined. If the cylinder head has been machined, it should be marked '-0.3' on the upper corner, on the inlet manifold side,

at the timing belt end. Note that modifications to the cylinder head gasket material, type, and manufacturer are constantly taking place; seek the advice of a Citroën dealer as to the latest recommendations.

29 Check the condition of the cylinder head bolts, and particularly their threads, whenever they are removed. Wash the bolts in a suitable solvent, and wipe them dry. Check each bolt for any sign of visible wear or damage, renewing them if necessary. Measure the length of each bolt from the underside of its head (not the washer) to the end of the bolt **(see illustration)**. When new, the bolt length is 144.5 mm (up to vehicle No RPO 09653) or 140.5 mm (from vehicle No RPO 9653). The bolts may be re-used if their length does not exceed 147.0 mm or 143.0 mm respectively.

30 If any one bolt is longer than the specified length, *all* of the bolts should be renewed as a complete set. Considering the stress which the cylinder head bolts are under, it is highly recommended that they are renewed, regardless of their apparent condition.

Refitting

31 Wipe clean the mating surfaces of the cylinder head and cylinder block and check that the two locating dowels are in position at each diagonally opposite end of the block. Check also that the camshaft oil supply non-return valve is in place in the oil feed bore at the timing belt end of the cylinder head **(see illustrations)**.

32 Position a new gasket on the cylinder block surface, with the word TOP uppermost and toward the oil filter side of the block **(see illustration)**.

33 Check that the crankshaft pulley and camshaft sprockets are still locked in position with their respective locking tools. With the aid of an assistant, carefully refit the cylinder head assembly to the block, aligning it with the locating dowels.

34 Apply a smear of grease to the threads, and to the underside of the heads, of the cylinder head bolts. Citroën recommend the use of Molykote G Rapid Plus for this purpose.

35 Carefully enter each bolt and washer into its relevant hole (*do not drop it in*) and screw it in finger-tight.

36 Working in sequence, tighten all the

10.32 Position the cylinder head gasket with the word TOP uppermost and towards the oil filter side of the block

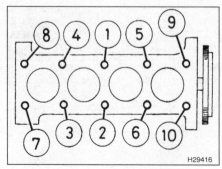

10.36 Cylinder head bolt tightening sequence

cylinder head bolts first to their Stage 1 torque setting, then to their Stage 2 torque setting using a torque wrench and a suitable socket **(see illustration)**.

37 Once all the bolts have been tightened to their Stage 2 torque setting, slacken all the head bolts by one complete turn, working in the **reverse** of the tightening sequence. Once the bolts are loose, and again working in sequence, tighten all the bolts to the Stage 4 torque setting.

38 When all the bolts have been tightened to the Stage 4 torque setting, tighten each bolt in sequence through the specified Stage 5 angle, using a socket and extension bar. It is recommended that an angle-measuring gauge is used during this stage of tightening, to ensure accuracy.

39 The remainder of the refitting procedure is a reversal of removal, noting the following points:

 a) *Fit new O-ring seals to all applicable components.*
 b) *Ensure that all wiring is correctly routed, and that all connectors are securely reconnected to the correct components.*
 c) *Ensure that all coolant, vacuum and breather hoses are correctly reconnected, and that their retaining clips are securely tightened, where applicable.*
 d) *Refit and tension the timing belt as described in Section 6.*
 e) *Refit the cylinder head covers as described in Section 4.*
 f) *Reconnect the catalytic converter to the exhaust manifold, refit the inlet manifold, air cleaner assembly and inlet ducting as described in Chapter 4A.*
 g) *On completion, refill the cooling system as described in Chapter 1A, and reconnect the battery.*

11 Sump –
removal and refitting

Removal

1 Chock the rear wheels then jack up the front of the vehicle and support it on axle stands (see *Jacking and vehicle support*). Undo the fasteners and remove the engine undershield (where fitted).

2 Drain the engine oil, then clean and refit the engine oil drain plug, tightening it securely. If the engine is nearing its service interval when the oil and filter are due for renewal, it is recommended that the filter is also removed, and a new one fitted. After reassembly, the engine can then be refilled with fresh oil. Refer to Chapter 1A for further information.

3 Withdraw the engine oil dipstick from the guide tube.

4 Undo the bolt securing the upper end of the dipstick guide tube to the ancillary components mounting bracket. Undo the bolt securing the base of the guide tube to the sump and remove the guide tube **(see illustration)**. Collect the two O-rings from the base of the guide tube, noting that new O-rings will be required for refitting.

5 Release the retaining clamps securing the power steering fluid pipes to the sump. Move the pipes as far as possible towards the transmission and suitably retain them in this position.

6 Where fitted, disconnect the wiring connector from the oil temperature sender unit, which is screwed into the rear of the sump.

7 Undo the lower centre bolt securing the sump to the transmission bellhousing.

8 Progressively slacken and remove all the sump retaining bolts noting that there are nineteen short bolts and seven long bolts.

9 Carefully insert a putty knife or similar between the sump and cylinder block. Ease the knife along the joint to break the seal, carefully levering down at the same time. When the sump is released, lower it straight down from its location and remove it from under the vehicle.

10 If access to the crankshaft components is required, undo the bolt and two nuts and remove the oil pump pick-up tube and gasket. Similarly, undo the four bolts and remove the crankcase baffle plate **(see illustrations)**.

Refitting

11 Thoroughly clean all the removed components ensuring that all traces of sealant and gasket are removed from the mating surfaces of the sump, cylinder block, oil pump and oil pump pick-up tube, as applicable. Use a suitable liquid gasket dissolving agent

11.4 Undo the upper and lower retaining bolts, then remove the dipstick guide tube

(available from Citroën dealers) together with a soft putty knife; do not use a metal scraper or the faces will be damaged. As there is no conventional gasket used between the sump and cylinder block, the cleanliness of the mating faces is of the utmost importance.

12 If removed, locate the splash plate in position and secure with the four bolts tightened securely.

13 If the oil pump pick-up tube was removed, locate a new gasket over the oil pump studs then place the tube in position. Fit the retaining nuts and bolt and tighten them securely.

14 Ensure that the sump and cylinder block mating faces are clean and dry, then apply a thin bead of RTV sealant to the sump mating surface **(see illustration)**. Citroën recommend the use of Loctite Autojoint Noir for this purpose.

15 Check that the centring dowel is in place in the cylinder block then locate the sump in position. Refit the retaining bolts noting that four of the long bolts are fitted at the transmission end, and three at the timing belt end on the oil filter side of the engine **(see illustrations)**. Tighten the bolts finger tight only at this stage.

16 If the engine is in the vehicle with the transmission attached, refit the lower centre bolt securing the sump to the transmission bellhousing and tighten it sufficiently to hold the sump in contact with the bellhousing face. Tighten the sump to cylinder block retaining bolts evenly and progressively to the specified torque setting. When the sump retaining bolts have been tightened, tighten the sump to bellhousing bolt to the specified torque.

11.10a Oil pump pick-up tube retaining nuts and bolt (arrowed)

11.10b Crankcase baffle plate bolts (arrowed)

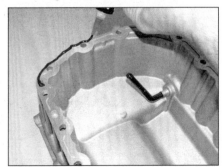

11.14 Apply a thin bead of sealant to the sump mating surface

11.15a 4 long bolts are fitted at the transmission end of the sump . . .

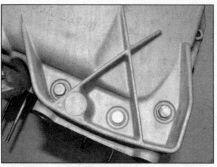

11.15b . . . and 3 at the timing belt end on the oil filter side

11.17 Use a straight-edge to ensure the faces of the sump and cylinder block are flush

17 If the engine is out of the vehicle or the transmission has been removed, use a straight-edge to ensure that the faces of the cylinder block and sump are flush **(see illustration)**. Hold the sump in this position and tighten the retaining bolts evenly and progressively to the specified torque setting.
18 Lubricate the two new O-rings and locate them on the end of the dipstick guide tube. Engage the guide tube with the sump and fit the upper and lower retaining bolts. Tighten the bolts securely, then refit the dipstick.
19 Move the power steering fluid pipes back into position under the sump and secure with the retaining clamps.
20 Where fitted, reconnect the wiring connector to the oil temperature sender unit at the rear of the sump.
21 Refit the engine undershield, lower the vehicle to the ground, then refill the engine with oil as described in Chapter 1A.

12 Oil pump – removal, inspection and refitting

Removal

1 Remove the sump as described in the previous Section.
2 Remove the crankshaft sprocket as described in Section 7.

3 Undo the bolts and pull the pump assembly from the cylinder block **(see illustration)**.
4 Slide the oil pump drive collar off the end of the crankshaft and collect the O-ring located behind the collar **(see illustrations)**.
5 With the oil pump removed, note the fitted depth of the crankshaft oil seal, then drive it from the oil pump housing. A new oil seal must be obtained for refitting.

Inspection

6 At the time of writing, checking specifications for the oil pump were not available. However, if the oil pump is to be re-used, the internal gears should be cleaned. To do this, unbolt the cover, then mark the gears for location

12.3 Oil pump housing retaining bolts (arrowed)

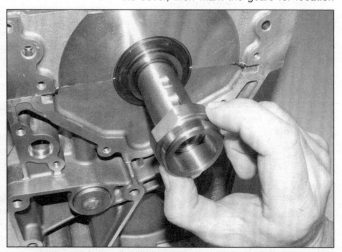

12.4a Slide the pump drive collar from the crankshaft . . .

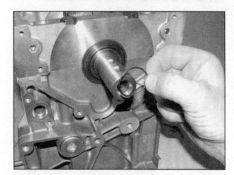

12.4b . . . and recover the O-ring located behind the collar

12.6a Undo the screws and lift off the pump rear cover

12.6b Remove the inner rotor . . .

12.6c . . . and outer rotor from the pump housing

12.9 Locate a new O-ring seal over the pump outlet stub

12.10 Apply a thin layer of RTV sealant to the oil pump mating surface

12.13 Fit a new O-ring over the end of the crankshaft

12.14 Carefully fit the seal over the oil pump drive collar

12.15 Slide the drive collar onto the crank-shaft and engage it with the inner rotor

and remove them (see illustrations). Clean the gears and inspect them for damage and excessive wear.

7 Lubricate the gears with clean engine oil, then refit them into their locations noted during removal. Refit the cover and tighten the screws securely.

8 Thoroughly clean the oil pump strainer with a suitable solvent, and check it for clogging or splitting.

Refitting

9 Clean the mating surfaces of the oil pump and main bearing ladder/cylinder block. Check the locating dowels are in place, then locate a new O-ring over the oil pump outlet stub (see illustration).

10 Apply a thin layer of suitable sealant (available from Citroën dealers or motor factors) to the mating face of the pump (see illustration).

11 Prime the pump by injecting clean engine oil into the outlet stub, then place the pump in position on the cylinder block, engaging the locating dowels.

12 Apply thread-locking compound to the retaining bolts, then refit and tighten them to the specified torque.

13 Position a new O-ring on the end of the crankshaft (see illustration).

14 Lubricate the sealing lips of the new crankshaft right-hand oil seal and carefully fit the seal over the oil pump drive collar (see illustration). Note that the open part of the seal must be towards the shoulder of the drive collar.

15 Slide the drive collar over the end of the

crankshaft and engage it with the oil pump inner rotor (see illustration). As the collar engages with the pump inner rotor, push the oil seal initially into place in the oil pump housing. Tap the seal fully into position using a suitable tubular drift.

16 Refit the pick-up/strainer and sump as described in Section 11, and the crankshaft sprocket and timing belt as described in Sections 7 and 6.

13 Crankshaft oil seals – renewal

Right-hand oil seal

1 Remove the crankshaft sprocket as described in Section 7.

2 Make a note of the correct fitted depth of

13.5 Tap the crankshaft right-hand oil seal into position using a suitable drift

the seal in the oil pump housing, then punch or drill a small hole in the face of the seal. Screw a self-tapping screw into the hole and pull on the screw with pliers to extract the seal. Alternatively, the seal can be levered out of position. Use a flat-bladed screwdriver, and take great care not to damage the oil pump drive flange or seal housing.

3 Clean the seal housing, and polish off any burrs or raised edges on the pump drive flange, which may have caused the seal to fail in the first place.

4 Lubricate the lips of the new seal with clean engine oil, and carefully locate the seal over the oil pump drive flange. Note that its sealing lip must be facing inwards. Take care not to damage the seal lips during fitting.

5 Tap the seal into position, using a suitable drift, to the same depth in the housing as the original was prior to removal (see illustration).

6 Wash off any traces of oil, then refit the crankshaft sprocket as described in Section 7.

Left-hand oil seal

7 Remove the flywheel as described in Section 14. Make a note of the correct fitted depth of the seal in its location.

8 Punch or drill two small holes opposite each other in the seal. Screw a self-tapping screw into each, and pull on the screws with pliers to extract the seal.

9 Clean the seal housing, and polish off any burrs or raised edges on the crankshaft, which may have caused the seal to fail in the first place.

13.10 Lubricate the crankshaft left-hand oil seal fitting sleeve and locate it over the end of the crankshaft

13.11 Slide the oil seal over the fitting sleeve and onto the crankshaft

15 Engine/transmission mountings –
inspection and renewal

10 The new seal will normally be supplied with a plastic fitting sleeve to protect the seal lips as the seal is fitted. If so, lubricate the fitting sleeve and locate it over the end of the crankshaft **(see illustration)**.
11 Lubricate the lips of the new seal with clean engine oil, and carefully locate the seal over the fitting sleeve and onto the end of the crankshaft **(see illustration)**.
12 Drive the seal into position, using a suitable tubular drift, to the same depth in the housing as the original was prior to removal.
13 Remove the fitting sleeve, wash off any traces of oil, then refit the flywheel as described in Section 14.

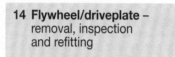

14 Flywheel/driveplate –
removal, inspection and refitting

Note: *This is the procedure for the flywheel. The driveplate is similar.*

Removal

1 Remove the transmission as described in Chapter 7A, then remove the clutch assembly as described in Chapter 6.
2 Prevent the flywheel from turning using a sturdy screwdriver inserted between the ring gear teeth and the cylinder block. Alternatively, bolt a strap between one of the clutch pressure plate mounting bolt holes and an adjacent hole on the cylinder block end face. *Do not* attempt to lock the flywheel in position using the crankshaft pulley locking tool described in Section 3.
3 Slacken and remove the flywheel retaining bolts, and remove the flywheel from the end of the crankshaft. Be careful not to drop it; it is heavy. If the flywheel locating dowel is a loose fit in the crankshaft end, remove it and store it with the flywheel for safe-keeping. Discard the flywheel bolts; new ones must be used on refitting.

Inspection

4 Examine the flywheel for scoring of the clutch face, and for wear or chipping of the ring gear teeth. If the clutch face is scored, the flywheel may be surface-ground, but renewal is preferable. Seek the advice of a Citroën

dealer or engine reconditioning specialist to see if machining is possible. If the ring gear is worn or damaged, the flywheel must be renewed, as it is not possible to renew the ring gear separately.

Refitting

5 Clean the mating surfaces of the flywheel and crankshaft. Remove any remaining locking compound from the threads of the crankshaft holes, using the correct size of tap, if available.

> **HAYNES HINT** *If a suitable tap is not available, cut two slots along the threads of one of the old flywheel bolts, and use the bolt to remove the locking compound from the threads.*

6 If the new flywheel retaining bolts are not supplied with their threads already precoated, apply a suitable thread-locking compound to the threads of each bolt prior to fitting.
7 Ensure that the locating dowel is in position. Offer up the flywheel, locating it on the dowel, and fit the new retaining bolts.
8 Lock the flywheel using the method employed on removal, and tighten the retaining bolts to the specified torque and through the specified angle, in the stages given in the Specifications.
9 Refit the clutch as described in Chapter 6. Remove the flywheel locking tool, and refit the transmission as described in Chapter 7A.

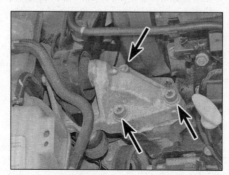

15.7 Right-hand engine mounting bracket Torx bolts (arrowed)

Inspection

1 If improved access is required, chock the rear wheels then jack up the front of the vehicle and support it securely on axle stands (see *Jacking and vehicle support*). Remove the engine undershield.
2 Check the mounting rubbers to see if they are cracked, hardened or separated from the metal at any point; renew the mounting if any such damage or deterioration is evident.
3 Check that all the mountings' fasteners are securely tightened; use a torque wrench to check if possible.
4 Using a large screwdriver or a crowbar, check for wear in each mounting by carefully levering against it to check for free play. Where this is not possible, enlist the aid of an assistant to move the engine/transmission back-and-forth, or from side-to-side, while you watch the mounting. While some free play is to be expected even from new components, excessive wear should be obvious. If excessive free play is found, check first that the fasteners are correctly secured, then renew any worn components as described below.

Renewal

Right-hand mounting

5 Release all the relevant hoses and wiring from their retaining clips, and position them clear of the mounting so that they do not hinder the removal procedure.
6 Place a jack beneath the engine, with a block of wood on the jack head. Raise the jack until it is supporting the weight of the engine.
7 Slacken and remove the three bolts, securing the upper mounting bracket to the lower (engine) bracket **(see illustration)**.
8 Undo the bolt securing the connecting link to the engine mounting bracket, and the bolt securing the link to the vehicle body. Remove the link.
9 Check all components carefully for signs of wear or damage, and renew them where necessary.
10 On reassembly, screw the mounting into the vehicle body, and tighten it securely.
11 Refit the rubber buffer plate to the rubber mounting stud, and install the upper mounting bracket. Tighten the retaining nuts/bolts to the specified torque setting.
12 Secure all disturbed hoses and wiring in their relevant retaining clips.
13 Remove the jack from underneath the engine.

Left-hand mounting

14 Remove the air cleaner assembly and inlet ducting as described in Chapter 4A.
15 Remove the engine management ECM and module box as described in Chapter 4A.
16 Place a jack beneath the transmission,

with a block of wood on the jack head. Raise the jack until it is supporting the weight of the transmission.

17 Slacken and remove the centre nut and washer from the left-hand mounting, then undo the nuts securing the mounting to the mounting bracket. Lift off the mounting and remove it from the engine compartment.

18 If necessary, slide the spacer (where fitted) off the mounting stud, then unscrew the stud from the top of the transmission housing, and remove it along with its washer. If the mounting stud is tight, a universal stud extractor can be used to unscrew it.

19 Check all components carefully for signs of wear or damage, and renew as necessary.

20 Clean the threads of the mounting stud, and apply a coat of thread-locking compound to its threads. Refit the stud and washer to the top of the transmission, and tighten it to the specified torque setting.

21 Slide the spacer (where fitted) onto the mounting stud, then refit the rubber mounting. Tighten both the mounting-to-bracket nuts and the mounting centre nut to their specified torque settings, and remove the jack from underneath the transmission.

22 Refit the ECM and module box as described in Chapter 4A.

23 Refit the air cleaner assembly and inlet ducting as described in Chapter 4A.

Rear mounting

24 If not already done, chock the rear wheels then jack up the front of the vehicle and support it securely on axle stands (see *Jacking and vehicle support*). Remove the engine undershield.

25 Unscrew and remove the bolt securing the rear mounting connecting link to the mounting bracket on the rear of the cylinder block.

26 Remove the bolt securing the connecting link to the bracket on the subframe and withdraw the link.

27 To remove the mounting assembly it will first be necessary to remove the right-hand driveshaft as described in Chapter 8.

28 With the driveshaft removed, undo the retaining bolts and remove the mounting from the rear of the cylinder block.

29 Check carefully for signs of wear or damage on all components, and renew them where necessary.

30 On reassembly, fit the rear mounting assembly to the rear of the cylinder block, and tighten its retaining bolts to the specified torque. Refit the driveshaft as described in Chapter 8.

31 Refit the rear mounting connecting link, and tighten both its bolts to their specified torque settings.

32 Lower the vehicle to the ground.

Notes

Chapter 2 Part B:
Direct injection petrol engine in-car repair procedures

Contents

Degrees of difficulty

Easy, suitable for novice with little experience	**Fairly easy,** suitable for beginner with some experience	**Fairly difficult,** suitable for competent DIY mechanic	**Difficult,** suitable for experienced DIY mechanic	**Very difficult,** suitable for expert DIY or professional

Specifications

Engine (general)

Designation	EW10D
Engine code*	RLZ
Capacity	1997 cc
Bore	85.0 mm
Stroke	88.0 mm
Output:	
Torque	192 Nm @ 4250 rpm
Power	103 kW @ 5500 rpm
Direction of crankshaft rotation	Clockwise (viewed from the right-hand side of vehicle)
No 1 cylinder location	At the transmission end of block
Compression ratio	11.4 : 1

* The engine code is stamped onto the right-hand front face of the cylinder block, adjacent to the engine mounting bracket

Camshafts

Drive	Toothed belt
No of bearings	5

Lubrication system

Oil pump type	Rotor-type, driven directly off the crankshaft
Minimum oil pressure at 80ºC:	
At 1000 rpm	1.5 bar
At 3000 rpm	5.0 bar

Torque wrench settings

	Nm	lbf ft
Ancillary components mounting bracket	19	14
Auxiliary drivebelt tensioner pulley bolt	20	15
Auxiliary drivebelt idler pulley	35	26
Big-end bearing cap bolts*:		
Stage 1	10	7
Stage 2	23	17
Stage 3	Angle-tighten a further 46°	
Camshaft bearing cap housing bolts	10	7
Camshaft sprocket retaining bolt:		
Exhaust:		
Stage 1	30	22
Stage 2	85	63
Inlet*:		
Stage 1	30	22
Stage 2	55	41
Sprocket-to-hub	9	7
Crankshaft bearing cap housing:		
Stage 1:		
M11 bolts	10	7
M6 bolts	2	1
Stage 2:		
M11 bolts	Fully slacken	
Stage 3:		
M11 bolts	20	15
Stage 4:		
M11 bolts	Angle-tighten a further 70°	
Stage 5:		
M6 bolts	10	7
Crankshaft pulley-to-sprocket retaining bolts (early engines only):		
Stage 1	15	11
Stage 2	20	15
Crankshaft sprocket centre bolt:		
Stage 1	40	30
Stage 2:		
2-piece hub and pulley (up to approximately November 2002)	Angle-tighten a further 40°	
1-piece hub and pulley (from approximately November 2002)	Angle-tighten a further 53°	
Cylinder head bolts:		
Stage 1	15	11
Stage 2	50	37
Stage 3	Slacken by 360°	
Stage 4	20	15
Stage 5	Angle-tighten a further 285°	
Cylinder head cover bolts:		
Stage 1	5	4
Stage 2	11	8
Driveplate retaining bolts*:		
Stage 1	25	18
Stage 2	Slacken 360°	
Stage 3	20	15
Stage 4	Angle-tighten a further 21°	
Engine-to-transmission fixing bolts	50	37
Engine/transmission left-hand mounting:		
Mounting bracket-to-transmission bolts	45	33
Rubber mounting centre nut	65	48
Rubber mounting-to-bracket nuts	27	20
Engine/transmission rear mounting:		
Connecting link-to-mounting bracket bolt	50	37
Connecting link-to-subframe bolt	50	37
Mounting bracket-to-cylinder block bolts	45	33
Engine/transmission right-hand mounting:		
Connecting link to mounting bracket	50	37
Connecting link to body	50	37
Upper mounting bracket-to-lower (engine) bracket Torx bolts	61	45
Lower mounting bracket to cylinder block	45	33

Torque wrench settings (continued)

	Nm	lbf ft
Flywheel retaining bolts*:		
Stage 1	25	18
Stage 2	Slacken 360°	
Stage 3	20	15
Stage 4	Angle-tighten a further 21°	
Oil pump retaining bolts	8	6
Sump retaining bolts	8	6
Timing belt guide roller	37	27
Timing belt tensioner pulley bolt	20	15

New nuts/bolts must be used.

1 General information

Using this Chapter

This Part of Chapter 2 is devoted to in-car repair procedures for the 2.0 litre petrol engine with direct injection. All procedures concerning engine removal and refitting, and engine block/cylinder head overhaul for petrol and diesel engines can be found in Chapter 2F.

Most of the operations included in Chapter 2B are based on the assumption that the engine is still installed in the car. Therefore, if this information is being used during a complete engine overhaul, with the engine already removed, many of the steps included here will not apply.

EW series engine description

The EW series engine is of the DOHC 16-valve, in-line four-cylinder type, mounted transversely at the front of the car with the clutch and transmission attached to its left-hand end.

The aluminium alloy cylinder block/crankcase is of modular construction consisting of three sections – the cylinder block itself, the crankshaft bearing cap housing and the sump. The cylinder block incorporates four cast iron dry cylinder liners which are cast into the block and cannot be renewed.

The crankshaft is supported in five shell-type main bearings with thrustwashers fitted to No 2 main bearing, to control crankshaft endfloat.

The connecting rods are attached to the crankshaft by horizontally-split shell-type big-end bearings, and to the pistons by gudgeon pins which are an interference fit in the connecting rod small-end eyes. The aluminium alloy pistons are of the slipper type, and are fitted with three piston rings – two compression rings and a scraper-type oil control ring.

The cylinder head is of the crossflow type, the inlet ports being at the front of the engine and the exhaust ports at the rear. The camshafts run in plain bearings integral with the cylinder head and with the two camshaft bearing cap housings. The inlet and exhaust valves are each closed by single coil springs, and operate in guides pressed into the cylinder head. Valve actuation is by self-adjusting hydraulic tappets acted upon directly by the camshaft lobes.

Drive to the camshafts is by a toothed timing belt and sprockets, and incorporates an automatic tensioning mechanism. The timing belt also drives the coolant pump. All accessories are driven from the crankshaft pulley by a single multi-ribbed auxiliary drivebelt. The direct injection EW series of engines are equipped with variable inlet camshaft timing, achieved by a 'dephaser' hub fitted to the end of the camshaft. The engine management ECM controls the flow of pressurised oil to the hub, which responds by rotating up to 20° independently of the camshaft. As the timing belt acts upon the hub, the timing of the camshaft is altered accordingly. This results in improved performance, and a reduction in exhaust emissions.

The lubrication system is of the full-flow, pressure-feed type. Oil is drawn from the sump by a rotor type pump, driven directly from the end of the crankshaft. The pump draws oil through a strainer located in the sump and then forces it through an externally-mounted filter into galleries in the cylinder block. From there, the oil is distributed to the crankshaft (main bearings) and camshafts. The big-end bearings are supplied with oil via internal drillings in the crankshaft; the camshaft bearings also receive a pressurised supply. The camshaft lobes and valves are lubricated by splash, as are all other engine components.

These engines differ from those in Chapter 2A in that the fuel is injected directly into the combustion chamber in order to increase fuel efficiency and performance, whilst reducing exhaust emissions.

Throughout this manual, it is often necessary to identify the engines not only by their capacity, but also by their engine code which is incorporated in the engine number. This can be found stamped onto the right-hand front face of the cylinder block, adjacent to the engine mounting bracket. The first part of the engine number gives the engine code – eg, RLZ.

Operations with engine in vehicle

The following work can be carried out with the engine in the vehicle:

a) Compression pressure – testing.
b) Cylinder head covers – removal and refitting.
c) Crankshaft pulley – removal and refitting.
d) Timing belt covers – removal and refitting.
e) Timing belt – removal, refitting and adjustment.
f) Timing belt tensioner and sprockets – removal and refitting.
g) Camshaft oil seals – renewal.
h) Camshafts and tappets – removal, inspection and refitting.
i) Cylinder head – removal and refitting.
j) Cylinder head and pistons – decarbonising.
k) Sump – removal and refitting.
l) Crankshaft oil seals – renewal.
m) Engine/transmission mountings – inspection and renewal.
n) Flywheel – removal, inspection and refitting.

2 Compression test – description and interpretation

1 When engine performance is down, or if misfiring occurs which cannot be attributed to the ignition or fuel systems, a compression test can provide diagnostic clues as to the engine's condition. If the test is performed regularly, it can give warning of trouble before any other symptoms become apparent.

2 The engine must be fully warmed-up to normal operating temperature, the battery must be fully-charged. The aid of an assistant will also be required.

3 Remove the ignition HT coil assembly (see Chapter 5B) then remove the spark plugs (see Chapter 1A).

4 Fit a compression tester to the No 1 cylinder spark plug hole – the type of tester which screws into the plug thread is to be preferred.

5 Crank the engine on the starter motor; after one or two revolutions, the compression pressure should build-up to a maximum figure, and then stabilise. Record the highest reading obtained.

6 Repeat the test on the remaining cylinders, recording the pressure in each.

7 All cylinders should produce very similar pressures; a difference of more than 2 bars between any two cylinders indicates a fault. Note that the compression should build-up quickly in a healthy engine; low compression on the first stroke, followed by gradually-increasing pressure on successive strokes, indicates worn piston rings. A low

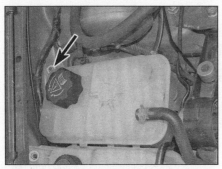

3.3a Undo the coolant expansion tank retaining nut (arrowed)

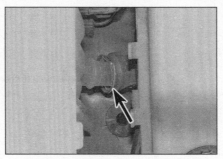

3.3b Prise out the clip (arrowed) and disconnect the hose as the tank is withdrawn

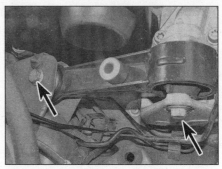

3.4 Undo the 2 bolts (arrowed) and remove the upper torque arm

compression reading on the first stroke, which does not build-up during successive strokes, indicates leaking valves or a blown head gasket (a cracked head could also be the cause). Deposits on the undersides of the valve heads can also cause low compression.

8 Although Citroën do not specify exact compression pressures, as a guide, any cylinder pressure of below 10 bars can be considered as less than healthy. Refer to a Citroën dealer or other specialist if in doubt as to whether a particular pressure reading is acceptable.

9 If the pressure in any cylinder is low, carry out the following test to isolate the cause. Introduce a teaspoonful of clean oil into that cylinder through its spark plug hole, and repeat the test.

10 If the addition of oil temporarily improves the compression pressure, this indicates that bore or piston wear is responsible for the pressure loss. No improvement suggests that leaking or burnt valves, or a blown head gasket, may be to blame.

11 A low reading from two adjacent cylinders is almost certainly due to the head gasket having blown between them; the presence of coolant in the engine oil will confirm this.

12 If one cylinder is about 20 percent lower than the others and the engine has a slightly rough idle, a worn camshaft lobe could be the cause.

13 If the compression reading is unusually high, the combustion chambers are probably coated with carbon deposits. If this is the case, the cylinder head should be removed and decarbonised.

14 On completion of the test, refit the spark plugs and ignition HT coil (see Chapters 1A and 5B).

3 Engine assembly/ valve timing holes – general information and usage

1 Jack up the front of the vehicle and support it securely on axle stands (see *Jacking and vehicle support*). Remove the right-hand front roadwheel and wheel arch liner. Drain the cooling system as described in Chapter 1A.

Up to approx October 2002

Note 1: *The following procedure entails the use of Citroën special tools (-).0189.A and (-).0189.L (camshaft setting rods). If the Citroën tools are not available, details for fabricating suitable alternatives are given in the text.*

Note 2: *Do not attempt to rotate the engine whilst the crankshaft/camshafts are locked in position. If the engine is to be left in this state for a long period of time, it is a good idea to place suitable warning notices inside the vehicle, and in the engine compartment. This will reduce the possibility of the engine being accidentally cranked on the starter motor, which is likely to cause damage with the locking pins in place.*

2 Timing holes are drilled in the crankshaft sprocket endplate and in the two camshaft sprockets. The holes are used to ensure that the crankshaft and camshafts are correctly positioned when assembling the engine (to prevent the possibility of the valves contacting

the pistons when refitting the cylinder head), or refitting the timing belt. When the timing holes are aligned with corresponding holes in the cylinder head and oil pump housing, suitable diameter pins or bolts can be inserted to lock both the camshafts and crankshaft in position, preventing them from rotating. To set the engine in the timing position, proceed as follows.

3 Undo the nut and pull the coolant expansion tank upwards, disconnecting the hoses as it's withdrawn **(see illustrations)**.

4 Undo the 2 bolts and remove the right-hand engine mounting upper torque arm **(see illustration)**.

5 Undo the 4 Allen screws, release the 2 clips at the top edge and remove the timing belt upper cover **(see illustrations)**.

6 Using a socket and extension bar fitted to the crankshaft sprocket centre bolt, turn the crankshaft in the normal direction of rotation (clockwise) until the timing holes in both camshaft sprockets are aligned with their corresponding holes in the cylinder head. The holes are aligned when the inlet camshaft sprocket hole is in approximately the 5 o'clock position and the exhaust camshaft sprocket hole is in approximately the 7 o'clock position, when viewed from the right-hand end of the engine. Use a small mirror to accurately observe the position of the holes.

7 With the camshaft sprocket holes correctly positioned, insert an 8.0 mm diameter drill bit or bolt through the timing hole in the crankshaft pulley/endplate, and locate it in the corresponding hole in the oil pump housing **(see illustration)**.

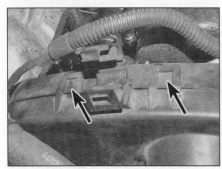

3.5a Release the 2 clips (arrowed) . . .

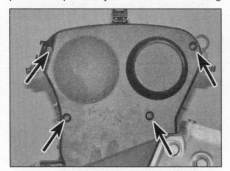

3.5b . . . and undo the 4 Allen screws (arrowed)

3.7 Insert an 8.0 mm drill bit or rod through the hole in pulley plate

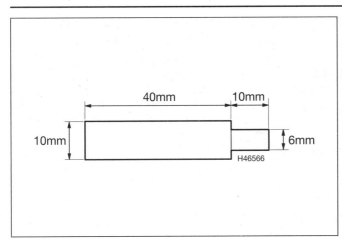

3.8a Camshaft sprocket locking tool dimensions

3.8b Insert the locking tools though the holes in the sprockets (arrowed)

8 The camshaft sprockets can now be locked in position using the Citroën camshaft setting rods, or suitable home-made alternatives **(see illustration)**. Note that if using the Citroën tools, (-).0189.L is used to lock the inlet camshaft. With the crankshaft locked in position, insert the Citroën special tools, or alternatives, through the timing hole in each camshaft sprocket and locate it in the corresponding hole in the cylinder head **(see illustration)**.

9 The crankshaft and camshafts are now locked in position, preventing rotation. In this position the crankshaft is at 90° BTDC and all the pistons are positioned half-way down their cylinder bores.

From approx November 2002

Note 1: *The following procedure entails the use of Citroën special tools (-).0189.A and (-).0189.L (camshaft setting rods) and (-).0189.R (crankshaft setting tool). If the Citroën tools are not available, details for fabricating suitable alternatives are given in the text.*

Note 2: *Do not attempt to rotate the engine whilst the crankshaft/camshafts are locked in position. If the engine is to be left in this state for a long period of time, it is a good idea to place suitable warning notices inside the vehicle, and in the engine compartment. This will reduce the possibility of the engine being accidentally cranked on the starter motor, which is likely to cause damage with the locking rods/tool in place.*

10 Timing holes are drilled in the flywheel/cylinder block and in the two camshaft sprockets. The holes are used to ensure that the crankshaft and camshafts are correctly positioned when assembling the engine (to prevent the possibility of the valves contacting the pistons when refitting the cylinder head), or refitting the timing belt. When the timing holes are aligned with corresponding holes in the cylinder head and flywheel, suitable diameter pins or bolts can be inserted to lock both the camshafts and crankshaft in position, preventing them from rotating. To set

the engine in the timing position, proceed as follows.

11 Undo the bolts, release the clips and remove the timing belt upper cover **(see illustration 3.5a and 3.5b)**.

12 Using a socket and extension bar fitted to the crankshaft sprocket centre bolt, turn the crankshaft in the normal direction of rotation until the timing holes in both camshaft sprockets are aligned with their corresponding holes in the cylinder head. The holes are aligned when the inlet camshaft sprocket hole is in approximately the 5 o'clock position and the exhaust camshaft sprocket hole is in approximately the 7 o'clock position, when viewed from the right-hand end of the engine. Use a small mirror to accurately observe the position of the holes.

13 With the camshaft sprocket holes correctly positioned, insert Citroën tool (-).0189.R, or home-made equivalent, through the timing cylinder block transmission flange, and locate it in the corresponding hole in the flywheel **(see illustration)**.

14 The camshaft sprockets can now be

locked in position using the Citroën camshaft setting rods, or suitable home-made alternatives **(see illustration 3.8a)**. Note that if using the Citroën tools, (-).0189.L is used to lock the inlet camshaft. With the crankshaft locked in position, insert the Citroën special tools, or alternatives, through the timing hole in each camshaft sprocket and locate it in the corresponding hole in the cylinder head **(see illustration 3.8b)**.

15 The crankshaft and camshafts are now locked in position, preventing rotation. In this position the crankshaft is at 90° BTDC and all the pistons are positioned half-way down their cylinder bores.

4 Cylinder head cover – removal and refitting

Removal

1 Remove the plastic cover from the top of the engine (where fitted) by pulling it straight up from its rubber mountings.

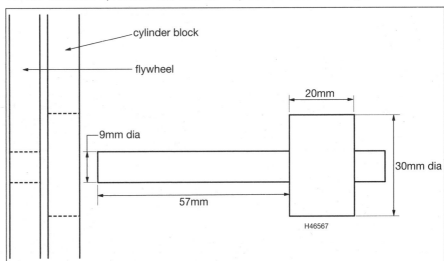

3.13 Flywheel locking tool – from approximately November 2002

4.5 Squeeze together the clips and disconnect the breather hose

4.6 Undo the cylinder head cover bolts (arrowed)

4.9a Fit a new seal into the cover groove . . .

4.9b . . . use a socket to push in the spark plug well seals

2 Remove the inlet manifold as described in Chapter 4A.

3 Remove the EGR valve as described in Chapter 4C (where not already done as part of the inlet manifold removal).

4 Remove the ignition coil as described in Chapter 5B.

5 Release the clips and disconnect the breather hose from the left-hand end of the cover **(see illustration)**.

6 Progressively slacken, then remove the retaining bolts from the cylinder head cover **(see illustration)**.

7 Lift off the cover and remove it. The cover seals should remain attached as the cover is removed – do not try to remove them unless they're obviously damaged.

Refitting

8 Clean the cylinder head and cylinder head cover mating surfaces, and remove all traces of oil.

9 Check the condition of the rubber seal attached to the cover. The seals are designed to be re-usable, and so should not automatically be renewed unless their condition is suspect, eg, hardened or perished. If renewal is necessary, locate the seal in the cover groove, ensuring that it is fully seated along its entire length, then fit the new spark plug well seals **(see illustrations)**.

10 Carefully refit the cylinder head cover to the engine.

11 Refit the cover retaining bolts, and tighten them to the specified torque given in the Specifications.

12 Reconnect the breather hose.

13 Refit the ignition coil as described in Chapter 5A.

14 Refit the EGR valve as described in Chapter 4C.

15 Refit the inlet manifold as described in Chapter 4A.

16 Refit the engine cover.

5 Crankshaft pulley – removal and refitting

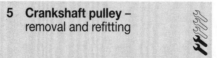

Removal

Up to approx October 2002

1 Remove the auxiliary drivebelt as described in Chapter 5A.

2 Undo the four crankshaft pulley retaining bolts and remove the pulley from the crankshaft sprocket endplate **(see illustration)**.

5.2 Undo the 4 outer bolts and remove the crankshaft pulley

From approx November 2002

3 On these engines, the pulley can only be removed once the crankshaft sprocket bolt has been removed. Removal of this bolt is only possible once the camshafts and crankshaft are locked in the reference position, as described in Section 3. Removal of the pulley is therefore described in the timing belt removal procedure – see Section 6.

Refitting

Up to approx October 2002

4 Locate the pulley on the crankshaft sprocket endplate, refit the four retaining bolts and tighten them to the specified torque.

5 Refit and tension the auxiliary drivebelt as described in Chapter 5A.

6 Timing belt – general information, removal and refitting

General information

1 The timing belt drives the camshafts and coolant pump from a toothed sprocket on the right-hand end of the crankshaft. If the belt breaks or slips in service, the pistons are likely to hit the valve heads, resulting in extensive (and expensive) damage.

2 The timing belt should be renewed at the specified intervals (see Chapter 1A), or earlier if it is contaminated with oil or if it is at all noisy in operation (a 'scraping' noise due to uneven wear).

3 If the timing belt is being removed, it is a wise precaution to check the condition of the coolant pump at the same time (check for signs of coolant leakage). This may avoid the need to remove the timing belt again at a later stage should the coolant pump fail.

4 On vehicles up to approximately October 2002, the crankshaft sprocket is a two-piece assembly consisting of the toothed sprocket itself and an outer endplate. The endplate is locked to the crankshaft by means of a conventional Woodruff key. When the sprocket retaining bolt is slackened, the sprocket is free to turn on the crankshaft within the limits afforded by an additional keyway within the endplate. When the sprocket retaining bolt is tightened the complete assembly is locked to the crankshaft. This arrangement allows accurate tensioning of the timing belt when refitting, provided that the procedures contained in this Section are strictly adhered to.

5 On vehicles from approximately November 2002 the crankshaft sprocket is a one-piece assembly with integral flange. Once the pulley retaining bolt is slackened, the sprocket is free to revolve on the crankshaft. Again, this arrangement allows accurate tensioning of the timing belt when refitting, provided that the procedures contained in this Section are strictly adhered to.

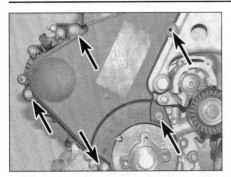

6.9 Lower timing cover bolts (arrowed)

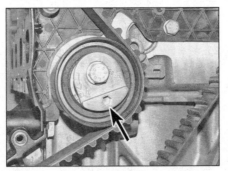

6.10 Insert an Allen key into the tensioner hub (arrowed)

6.18 Timing belt routing

Removal

6 On vehicles up to approximately October 2002 undo the 4 bolts and detach the auxiliary drivebelt pulley from the crankshaft sprocket as described in Section 5.

7 Align the engine assembly/valve timing holes as described in Section 3, and lock the crankshaft sprocket and camshaft sprockets in position. *Do not* attempt to rotate the engine whilst the locking tools are in position.

8 On vehicles from approximately November 2002, slacken and remove the crankshaft sprocket bolt.

9 Undo the bolts and remove the timing belt lower cover **(see illustration)**.

10 Loosen the timing belt tensioner pulley retaining bolt. Using an Allen key in the hole provided on the front of the pulley, rotate the pulley in a clockwise direction to relieve the tension from the timing belt **(see illustration)**. Retighten the tensioner pulley retaining bolt to secure it in the slackened position.

11 If the timing belt is to be re-used, use white paint or chalk to mark the direction of rotation on the belt (if markings do not already exist), then slip the belt off the sprockets and pulleys. Note that the crankshaft must not be rotated whilst the belt is removed.

12 Check the timing belt carefully for any signs of uneven wear, splitting, or oil contamination. Pay particular attention to the roots of the teeth. Renew it if there is the slightest doubt about its condition. If the engine is undergoing an overhaul, it is advisable to renew the belt as a matter of course, regardless of its apparent condition. The cost of a new belt is nothing compared

with the cost of repairs should the belt break in service. If signs of oil contamination are found, trace the source of the oil leak and rectify it. Wash down the engine timing belt area and all related components to remove all traces of oil.

Refitting

13 Before refitting, thoroughly clean the timing belt sprockets.

14 Check that the tensioner and idler pulleys rotate freely, without any sign of roughness. If necessary, renew the relevant pulley as described in Section 7.

15 Ensure that the crankshaft and camshaft sprocket locking tools are still in position.

From approx November 2002

16 Fit Citroën tool (-).0189.S1 over the tensioner roller, rotate the tensioner clockwise until the tensioner index passes the notch, then lock the index in place using Citroën tool (-). 0189.S2. Remove the tensioner rotating tool (-).0189.S1.

All vehicles

17 Locate the timing belt on the crankshaft sprocket, ensuring that any arrows on the belt are pointing in the direction of rotation (clockwise when viewed from the right-hand end of the engine).

18 Retain the timing belt on the crankshaft sprocket then, keeping it taut, feed the belt over the remaining sprockets and pulleys in the following order, ensuring the belt is as flush as possible with the outer faces of the sprockets/rollers **(see illustration)**:

  a) *Idler pulley.*

  b) *Inlet camshaft.*

  c) *Exhaust camshaft.*

  d) *Coolant pump.*

  e) *Tensioner pulley.*

Note that there is a special Citroën tool available (-).0189.K which clips over the belt, retaining it on the crankshaft sprocket. The use of this tool is not essential.

19 Remove the locking tool from the exhaust camshaft sprocket, the tool locking the tensioner index (where applicable), and (where applicable) the clip securing the timing belt to the crankshaft sprocket.

Up to approx October 2002

20 Slacken the tensioner retaining bolt, and using an 8 mm Allen key, rotate the pulley hub anti-clockwise until the tensioner index is positioned 10° below the notch in the backplate **(see illustrations)**. Note that if the index will not attain a position of at least 10° past the notch, then the tensioner pulley, or both the tensioner pulley and belt must be renewed.

21 Now rotate the hub clockwise until the index aligns with the notch in the backplate **(see illustration)**. If the index is allowed to go past the notch, repeat the tensioning procedure.

22 Tighten the tensioning pulley retaining bolt to the specified torque, without allowing the pulley hub to rotate. With the belt tensioned and the retaining bolt tightened, the Allen key slot should be approximately 15° below the cylinder head gasket level. If not, renew the tensioner, or both the tensioner and belt **(see illustration)**.

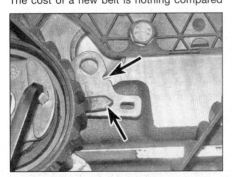

6.20 The index must be 10° below the notch (arrowed)

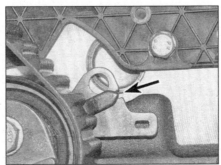

6.21 Align the index with the notch (arrowed)

6.22 The Allen key hole in the tensioner hub should be just below the level of the cylinder head gasket as shown

To make a sprocket holding tool, obtain two lengths of steel strip about 6.0 mm thick by about 30 mm wide or similar, one 600 mm long, the other 200 mm long (all dimensions approximate). Bolt the two strips together to form a forked end, leaving the bolt slack so that the shorter strip can pivot freely. At the other end of each 'prong' of the fork, drill a suitable hole and fit a nut and bolt to engage with the spokes or holes in the sprocket. The same tool can be used to hold both the camshaft and crankshaft sprockets.

23 Remove the camshaft and crankshaft locking tools, and rotate the crankshaft 10 complete revolutions clockwise (viewed from the right-hand end of the engine). Realign the engine assembly/valve timing holes and refit the inlet camshaft sprocket locking tool.

24 Check that the tensioner pulley index

pointer is still aligned with the slot in the backing plate. If not repeat the tensioning operation from paragraph 20 onward.

25 With the inlet camshaft sprocket locking tool in place, it should now also be possible to fit the crankshaft sprocket locking tool. If so, continue with the refitting procedure from paragraph 29 onward. If the crankshaft sprocket locking tool will not engage, then the crankshaft sprocket endplate must be repositioned as follows.

26 Slacken the crankshaft sprocket retaining bolt while holding the sprocket endplate stationary using Citroën special tool 6310-T or a suitable home-made alternative **(see Tool Tip)**. *Do not* attempt to use only the sprocket locking tools inserted in the engine assembly/valve timing holes to prevent rotation whilst the bolt is slackened.

27 With the sprocket retaining bolt slackened, turn the endplate until the sprocket locking tool can be fully inserted through the endplate and into the hole in the oil pump housing.

28 Hold the endplate with the holding tool and tighten the sprocket retaining bolt to the specified torque, then through the specified angle.

29 Remove the camshaft and crankshaft locking tools and refit the lower and upper (outer) timing belt covers, tightening the retaining bolts securely.

30 Refit the crankshaft pulley as described in Section 5.

From approx November 2002

31 Refit the lower timing belt cover, and tighten the retaining bolts securely.

7.3 Jam the old timing belt between the sprockets to prevent them from rotating

7.4 Unscrew the cap from the inlet camshaft dephaser unit

7.5 Undo the dephaser Torx bolt

7.6 Undo the exhaust camshaft sprocket Torx bolt

32 Refit the crankshaft sprocket, and tighten the retaining bolt to the specified torque.

33 Using an Allen key, rotate the belt tensioner hub anti-clockwise until the tensioner index is positioned at least 10° below the notch in the backplate **(see illustration 6.20)**. Note that if the index will not attain a position of at least 10° past the notch, then the tensioner pulley, or both the tensioner pulley and belt must be renewed.

34 Now rotate the tensioner hub clockwise until the index is aligned with the notch in the backplate **(see illustration 6.21)**. If the index is allowed to go past the notch, repeat the tensioning procedure.

35 Tighten the tensioning pulley retaining bolt to the specified torque, without allowing the pulley hub to rotate. With the belt tensioned and the retaining bolt tightened, the Allen key slot should be approximately 15° below the cylinder head gasket level **(see illustration 6.22)**. If not, renew the tensioner, or both the tensioner and belt.

36 Remove the camshaft and crankshaft locking tools, and rotate the crankshaft 10 complete revolutions clockwise (viewed from the right-hand end of the engine). Realign the engine assembly/valve timing holes and refit the inlet camshaft sprocket locking tool.

37 Check that the tensioner pulley index pointer is still aligned with the slot in the backing plate. If not repeat the tensioning operation from paragraph 33 onward.

38 Remove the inlet camshaft sprocket locking tool, then refit the upper timing belt cover, and the auxiliary drivebelt (see Chapter 5A).

7 Timing belt tensioner and sprockets – removal, inspection and refitting

Note: *The following procedures entail the use of certain Citroën special tools. If the Citroën tools are not available, details for fabricating suitable alternative are given in the text.*

Camshaft sprockets removal

1 Remove the timing belt as described in Section 6.

2 Remove the air cleaner assembly and high-pressure injection pump as described in Chapter 4A.

3 Lock the inlet camshaft in position using Citroën tool no. (-).0189.M. Alternatively, jam the old timing belt between the two sprockets **(see illustration)**.

4 Undo the cap screw from the inlet camshaft sprocket dephaser unit **(see illustration)**. Recover the O-ring seal.

5 Undo the Torx bolt securing the dephaser unit to the camshaft **(see illustration)**.

6 Hold the exhaust camshaft sprocket stationary by jamming the old timing belt between the sprockets, and undo the sprocket retaining bolt **(see illustration)**. Remove both sprockets.

Crankshaft sprocket removal

Up to approx October 2002

7 Remove the timing belt as described in Section 6.

8 Remove the crankshaft sprocket locking tool and slacken the crankshaft sprocket retaining bolt. Prevent the crankshaft from turning while the bolt is slackened using Citroën special tool 6310-T or a suitable home-made alternative bolted to the sprocket endplate **(see Tool Tip in Section 6)**. *Do not attempt to use only the sprocket locking tools inserted in the engine assembly/valve timing holes to prevent rotation whilst the bolt is slackened.*

9 Unscrew the retaining bolt and slide the sprocket endplate and the sprocket itself off the end of the crankshaft. If loose, remove the Woodruff key from the crankshaft, and store it with the sprocket components for safe-keeping **(see illustrations)**.

10 Examine the crankshaft oil seal for signs of oil leakage and, if necessary, renew it as described in Section 13.

From approx November 2002

11 Remove the timing belt as described in Section 6.

12 Slide the crankshaft sprocket from place.

13 Examine the crankshaft oil seal for signs of oil leakage and, if necessary, renew it as described in Section 13.

Tensioner and idler pulleys removal

14 Remove the timing belt as described in Section 6.

15 Undo the tensioner and idler pulley retaining bolts and remove the relevant pulley from the engine **(see illustration)**.

Inspection

16 Clean the camshaft/crankshaft sprockets thoroughly, and renew any that show signs of wear, damage or cracks.

17 Clean the tensioner/idler pulleys, but do

7.9a Remove the sprocket endplate . . .

7.9b . . . followed by the sprocket . . .

7.9c . . . and the Woodruff key

7.15 Timing belt idler pulley

not use any strong solvent which may enter the pulley bearings. Check that the pulleys rotate freely, with no sign of stiffness or free play. Renew them if there is any doubt about their condition, or if there are any obvious signs of wear or damage.

Camshaft sprockets refitting

18 Locate the relevant sprocket on the end of the camshaft, engaging the lug in the sprocket hub with the slot in the end of the camshaft.

19 Retain the inlet camshaft using Citroën tool No. 0189.M or home-made equivalent **(see illustrations)**. Fit the new sprocket

retaining bolt, and tighten it to the specified torque.

20 Remove the inlet camshaft locking tool, then refit the exhaust camshaft sprocket and tighten the bolt to the specified torque. Prevent the sprocket from turning as the bolt is tightened using a length of old timing belt jammed between the sprockets.

21 Realign the holes in the camshaft sprockets with the corresponding holes in the cylinder head, and refit the locking tools. Check that the crankshaft pulley locking tool is still in position.

22 Slacken the 3 inlet camshaft dephaser hub retaining bolts, and rotate the sprocket

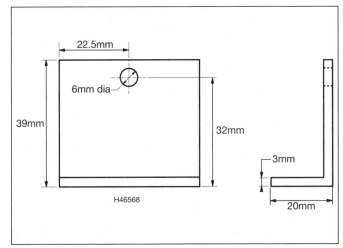

7.19a Inlet camshaft locking tool dimensions – use steel angle iron

H46568

7.19b Fit the locking tool over one of the high-pressure pump mounting studs, and into the slot in the end of the camshaft. Fit some spacers over the stud and retaining the tool with a washer and nut

7.22 With the dephaser hub bolts slackened, it should only be possible to rotate the sprocket a very small amount until it jams against the alignment tool

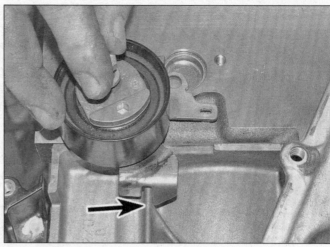

7.32 Ensure the tensioner body engages with the projecting web (arrowed) on the cylinder block

fully anti-clockwise. Tighten the bolts to the specified torque **(see illustration)**. If the position is already correct, the sprocket will not rotate at all. **Note:** *Ensure the sprocket/ hub locking tool is a good fit in the head/ sprocket/hub. If not, it will be possible to rotate the sprocket on the hub far more than intended.*

23 Refit the high-pressure injection pump and air cleaner assembly as described in Chapter 4A.

24 Refit and tension the timing belt as described in Section 6.

Crankshaft sprocket refitting

Up to approx October 2002

25 Refit the Woodruff key (if removed) to its slot in the crankshaft end.

26 Slide on the crankshaft sprocket followed by the sprocket endplate, then refit the retaining bolt.

27 Hold the endplate with the holding tool and tighten the sprocket retaining bolt to both the specified torque and angle.

28 Realign the hole in the sprocket endplate with the corresponding hole in the oil pump housing, and refit the locking tool. Check that

the camshaft sprocket locking tools are still in position.

29 Refit and tension the timing belt as described in Section 6.

From approx November 2002

30 Slide the crankshaft sprocket into place.

31 Refit the timing belt as described in Section 6.

Tensioner & idler pulleys refitting

32 Refit the tensioner and idler pulleys, ensuring that the slot on the tensioner pulley body correctly engages with the projecting web on the cylinder block **(see illustration)**.

33 Secure the pulleys with the retaining bolts tightened to the specified torque.

34 Refit and tension the timing belt as described in Section 6.

8.2 Insert a self-tapping screw and pull the oil seal using pliers

8.4 Fit the oil seal over the end of the camshaft

8.5a Drive the seal into position using a socket which bears only on the hard outer part of the seal . . .

8.5b . . . until the seal is level with the bottom of the chamfer in the housing

---

8 Camshaft oil seal(s) – renewal

1 Remove the camshaft sprocket(s) as described in Section 7.

2 Punch or drill a small hole in the face of the oil seal. Screw a self-tapping screw into the hole, and pull on the screw with pliers to extract the seal **(see illustration)**.

3 Clean the seal housing, and polish off any burrs or raised edges, which may have caused the seal to fail in the first place.

4 Lubricate the lips of the new seal with clean engine oil, and locate it in position with the seal lips facing inwards **(see illustration)**.

5 Using a block of wood, tap the seal into place initially, then finish using a suitable drift until the seal is level with the bottom of the chamfer of the hole in the housing **(see illustrations)**. Take care not to damage the seal lips during fitting.

6 Refit the camshaft sprocket(s) as described in Section 7.

7 Refit and tension the timing belt as described in Section 6.

9.4 Rear housing retaining bolts (arrowed)

9.5 Unscrew the dephaser solenoid

9.8 The rocker arms are clipped to the top of the hydraulic tappets – lift them out as one

9 Camshafts and tappets – removal, inspection and refitting

Removal

1 Disconnect the battery negative terminal.
2 Remove the cylinder head cover as described in Section 4.
3 Refer to Section 7 and remove both camshaft sprockets.
4 Undo the 3 bolts and remove the timing belt rear plastic housing **(see illustration)**.
5 Disconnect the wiring plug, then unscrew the camshaft dephaser solenoid valve **(see illustration)**. Recover the O-ring on the base of the solenoid body.
6 Disconnect the wiring plug from the camshaft position sensor at the left-hand rear corner of the cylinder head.
7 Progressively slacken, by a few turns at a time, the 23 bolts securing the camshaft bearing cap housing to the cylinder head. Release the bearing cap housing from the dowels and cylinder head locations. When the housing is free, remove the bolts completely, and lift off the housing.
8 Carefully lift the camshafts up and out of their locations and slide the oil seal off each camshaft end **(see illustration)**. Note that the exhaust camshaft incorporates the signal wheel for the position sensor.
9 Obtain sixteen small, clean plastic containers, and number them inlet 1 to 8 and exhaust 1 to 8; alternatively, divide a

larger container into sixteen compartments and number each compartment accordingly. Withdraw each hydraulic tappet in turn, and place it in its respective container. Do not interchange the tappets, or the rate of wear will be much increased.

Inspection

10 Thoroughly clean the sealant from the mating surfaces of the cylinder head and bearing cap housings. Use a suitable liquid gasket dissolving agent (available from Citroën dealers) together with a soft putty knife; do not use a metal scraper or the faces will be damaged. As there is no conventional gasket used, the cleanliness of the mating faces is of the utmost importance.
11 Examine the camshaft bearing surfaces and cam lobes for signs of wear ridges and scoring. Renew the camshaft if any of these conditions are apparent. Examine the condition of the bearing surfaces, both on the camshaft journals and in the cylinder head/bearing cap housings. If the head bearing surfaces are worn excessively, the cylinder head will need to be renewed. If suitable measuring equipment is available, camshaft bearing journal wear can be checked by direct measurement, noting that No 1 journal is at the transmission end of the head.
12 Examine the hydraulic tappet bearing surfaces which contact the camshaft lobes for wear ridges and scoring. Renew any tappet on which these conditions are apparent. If a tappet bearing surface is badly scored, also examine the corresponding lobe on the

camshaft for wear, as it is likely that both will be worn. Renew worn components as necessary.

Refitting

13 Prior to refitting, remove all traces of oil from the bearing cap housing retaining bolt holes in the cylinder head, using a clean rag. Also ensure that both the cylinder head and bearing cap housing mating faces are clean and free from oil.
14 Liberally oil the cylinder head hydraulic tappet bores and the tappets. Carefully refit the tappets to the cylinder head, ensuring that each tappet is refitted to its original bore **(see illustration)**. Some care will be required to enter the tappets squarely into their bores. Check that each tappet rotates freely in its bore. Note that the rocker arms should still be clipped to the top of the tappets.
15 Ensure that the two locating dowels are in position at each end of the cylinder head cover.
16 Apply a thin bead of silicone sealant jointing compound around the perimeter of the cylinder head cover mating face, and the around the spark plug tube apertures **(see illustration)**.
17 Liberally oil the camshaft bearings in the cylinder head and the camshaft lobes, then lay the camshafts in the cylinder head, ensuring that they are in their correct locations. Turn the camshafts so that the cam lobes above No 1 cylinder (flywheel end) are in the upright position (approximately) **(see illustrations)**.
18 Liberally oil the camshaft bearings and

9.14 Refit the tappets/rocker arms to their original locations

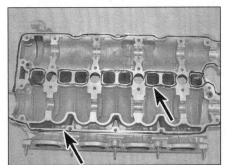

9.16 Apply sealant to the to the cover at the outer edges and central apertures (arrowed)

9.17a Refit the camshafts . . .

9.17b . . . with the No 1 cylinder lobes pointing upwards (arrowed)

9.18 Locate the housing over the camshafts

10 Cylinder head –
removal and refitting

Removal

1 Disconnect the battery negative terminal.
2 Drain the cooling system as described in Chapter 1A.
3 Remove the camshafts as described in Section 9, but fully unscrew the retaining bolt and remove the timing belt tensioner assembly.
4 Disconnect the wiring plugs from the following components:
a) *Exhaust gas temperature sensor (unclip from bracket – left-hand end of the cylinder head).*
b) *Pre-catalytic converter oxygen sensor (unclip from bracket – left-hand end of the cylinder head).*
c) *Fuel injectors.*
d) *Pressure regulator and sensor (on the fuel rail).*
5 Depressurise the fuel system as described in Chapter 4A (if not already done so).
6 Disconnect the fuel hose from the fuel rail and the fuel damper **(see illustrations)**. Plug or cover the openings to prevent contamination. Pull the damper upwards from position, then remove the sound insulation from over the fuel rail **(see illustration)**.
7 Working as described in Chapter 4A, disconnect the front exhaust pipe from the pre-catalyser attached to the exhaust manifold. Undo the 3 bolts securing the support bracket to the cylinder block and pre-catalyser.
8 Disconnect the left-hand heater matrix hose from the coolant outlet housing.
9 Undo the screw and detach the coolant pipe from the rear of the coolant outlet housing **(see illustration)**. If the pipe is reluctant to release, use a lever between the pipe and the cylinder head. Recover the O-ring seals.
10 Disconnect the wiring connector from the coolant temperature sensor located on the top of the coolant outlet housing at the left-hand end of the cylinder head.
11 Release the clips and disconnect the

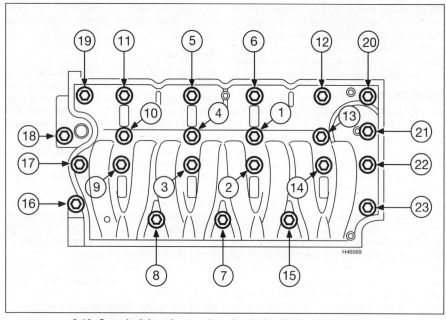

9.19 Camshaft bearing cap housing bolts tightening sequence

carefully locate the bearing cap housing over the camshafts **(see illustration)**. Refit the retaining bolts and progressively tighten them finger tight only at this stage.
19 Working in the order shown, progressively tighten the bearing cap housing retaining bolts to the specified torque setting **(see illustration)**.
20 Refit the camshaft dephaser solenoid valve, and reconnect the position sensor wiring plug.

21 Refit the timing belt rear plastic housing, apply a little thread-locking compound, then tighten the retaining bolts securely.
22 Fit a new oil seal to each camshaft, using the information given in Section 8, then refit the camshaft sprockets as described in Section 7.
23 Refit the cylinder head cover as described in Section 4.

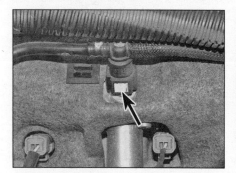

10.6a Depress the release button (arrowed) and disconnect the fuel hose from the rail . . .

10.6b . . . then lift up the damper assembly (arrowed)

10.6c Unclip the sound insulation from the fuel rail

10.9 Undo the bolts and pull the coolant pipe from the outlet housing and coolant pump housing

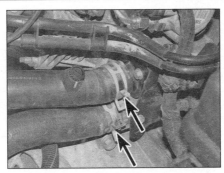

10.11 Release the clips and disconnect the radiator hoses from the coolant outlet housing (arrowed)

10.13 Unscrew as far as possible the lower engine mounting bracket bolt (arrowed)

radiator upper and lower hoses from the front of the coolant outlet housing **(see illustration)**.

12 Undo the nuts securing the wiring harness support bracket to the studs on the coolant outlet housing (if not already done so). Release any additional cable ties and clips then move the support bracket, wiring harness and hoses clear of the cylinder head.

13 Unscrew as far as possible the bolt securing the lower (engine) mounting bracket to the right-hand end of the cylinder head **(see illustration)**. Note that there is insufficient clearance to completely remove the bolt from its location.

14 Check that all vacuum/breather hoses, pipes, and electrical connectors likely to impede removal have been disconnected from the cylinder head.

15 Working in the **reverse** of the sequence shown in illustration 10.32, progressively slacken the ten cylinder head bolts by half a turn at a time using an E14 Torx socket, until all bolts can be unscrewed by hand. Remove the bolts along with their integral washers.

16 Connect an engine hoist or suitable lifting gear to the two lifting brackets on the cylinder head.

17 Release the joint between the cylinder head and gasket using two L-shaped metal bars which fit into the cylinder head bolt holes. Using the bars, gently 'rock' the cylinder head free towards the front of the vehicle. *Do not* try to swivel the head on the cylinder block as dowels locate it.

18 When the joint is broken, obtain the help of an assistant and slowly raise the hoist to lift the cylinder head off the block. At the same time, support the head at the rear as it will tend to tip backwards due to the offset position of the lifting brackets. Try to keep the head as level as possible until it is raised sufficiently to clear the cylinder block.

19 When sufficient clearance exists, move the hoist forward, raise it further and lift the cylinder head out of the engine compartment.

20 Remove the gasket from the top of the block, noting the two locating dowels. If the locating dowels are a loose fit, remove them and store them with the head for safe-keeping. Do not discard the gasket; it may be needed for identification purposes.

21 If the cylinder head is to be dismantled for overhaul, refer to Part F of this Chapter.

Preparation for refitting

22 The mating faces of the cylinder head and cylinder block must be perfectly clean before refitting the head. Citroën recommend the use of a scouring agent for this purpose, but acceptable results can be achieved by using a hard plastic or wood scraper to remove all traces of gasket and carbon. The same method can also be used to clean the piston crowns. Take particular care to avoid scoring or gouging the cylinder head/cylinder block mating surfaces during the cleaning operations, as aluminium alloy is easily damaged. Make sure that the carbon is not allowed to enter the oil and water passages – this is particularly important for the lubrication system, as carbon could block the oil supply to the engine's components. Using adhesive tape and paper, seal the water, oil and bolt holes in the cylinder block. To prevent carbon entering the gap between the pistons and bores, smear a little grease in the gap. After cleaning each piston, use a small brush to remove all traces of grease and carbon from the gap, then wipe away the remainder with a clean rag.

23 Check the mating surfaces of the cylinder block and the cylinder head for nicks, deep scratches and other damage. If slight, they may be removed carefully with a file, but if excessive, machining may be the only alternative to renewal. If warpage of the cylinder head gasket surface is suspected,

use a straight-edge to check it for distortion. Refer to Part F of this Chapter if necessary.

24 Thoroughly clean the threads of the cylinder head bolt holes in the cylinder block. Ensure that the bolts run freely in their threads, and that all traces of oil and water are removed from each bolt hole.

25 Check the condition of the cylinder head bolts, and particularly their threads, whenever they are removed. Wash the bolts in a suitable solvent, and wipe them dry. Check each bolt for any sign of visible wear or damage, renewing them if necessary. Measure the length of each bolt from the underside of its head (not the washer) to the end of the bolt **(see illustration)**. When new, the bolt length is 144.5 mm. The bolts may be re-used if their length does not exceed 147.0 mm

26 If any one bolt is longer than the specified length, *all* of the bolts should be renewed as a complete set. Considering the stress which the cylinder head bolts are under, it is highly recommended that they are renewed, regardless of their apparent condition.

Refitting

27 Wipe clean the mating surfaces of the cylinder head and cylinder block and check that the two locating dowels are in position at each diagonally opposite end of the block **(see illustration)**.

28 Position a new gasket on the cylinder block surface, with the word TOP uppermost and toward the oil filter side of the block **(see illustration)**.

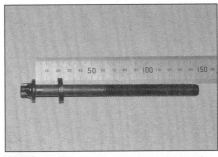

10.25 Measure from the underside of the bolt head to the end of the bolt – maximum length is 147.0 mm

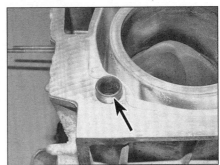

10.27 Ensure the dowels are in position at each end of the block (arrowed)

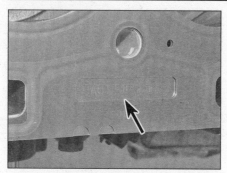

10.28 The word TOP must be uppermost (arrowed)

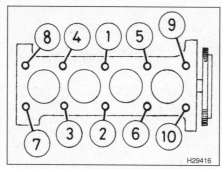

10.32 Cylinder head bolt tightening sequence

29 Check that the crankshaft pulley/flywheel is still locked in position with their respective locking tools. With the aid of an assistant, carefully refit the cylinder head assembly to the block, aligning it with the locating dowels.

30 Apply a smear of grease to the threads, and to the underside of the heads, of the cylinder head bolts. Citroën recommend the use of Molykote G Rapid Plus for this purpose.

31 Carefully enter each bolt and washer into its relevant hole (*do not drop it in*) and screw it in finger-tight.

32 Working in sequence, tighten all the cylinder head bolts first to their Stage 1 torque setting, then to their Stage 2 torque setting using a torque wrench and a suitable E14 socket **(see illustration)**.

33 Once all the bolts have been tightened to their Stage 2 torque setting, slacken all the head bolts by one complete turn, working in

the **reverse** of the tightening sequence. Once the bolts are loose, and again working in sequence, tighten all the bolts to the Stage 4 torque setting.

34 When all the bolts have been tightened to the Stage 4 torque setting, tighten each bolt in sequence through the specified Stage 5 angle, using a socket and extension bar. It is recommended that an angle-measuring gauge is used during this stage of tightening, to ensure accuracy.

35 The remainder of the refitting procedure is a reversal of removal, noting the following points:

a) Fit new O-ring seals to all applicable components.

b) Ensure that all wiring is correctly routed, and that all connectors are securely reconnected to the correct components.

c) Ensure that all coolant, vacuum and breather hoses are correctly reconnected,

and that their retaining clips are securely tightened, where applicable.

d) Refit the camshafts as described in Section 9.

e) Refit and tension the timing belt as described in Section 6.

f) Reconnect the front exhaust pipe to the pre-catalyser, refit the inlet manifold, air cleaner assembly and inlet ducting as described in Chapter 4A.

g) On completion, refill the cooling system as described in Chapter 1A, and reconnect the battery.

11 Sump – removal and refitting

Removal

1 Chock the rear wheels then jack up the front of the vehicle and support it on axle stands (see *Jacking and vehicle support*). Undo the fasteners and remove the engine undershield.

2 Drain the engine oil, then clean and refit the engine oil drain plug, tightening it securely. If the engine is nearing its service interval when the oil and filter are due for renewal, it is recommended that the filter is also removed, and a new one fitted. After reassembly, the engine can then be refilled with fresh oil. Refer to Chapter 1A for further information.

3 Withdraw the engine oil dipstick from the guide tube.

4 Undo the bolt securing the upper end of the dipstick guide tube to the ancillary components mounting bracket. Undo the bolt securing the base of the guide tube to the sump and remove the guide tube **(see illustrations)**. Collect the two O-rings from the base of the guide tube, noting that new O-rings will be required for refitting.

5 Release the retaining clamps securing the power steering fluid pipes to the sump. Move the pipes as far as possible towards the transmission and suitably retain them in this position.

6 Where fitted, disconnect the wiring connector from the oil temperature sender unit, which is screwed into the rear of the sump.

7 Undo the bolts securing the sump to the transmission bellhousing.

8 Progressively slacken and remove all the sump retaining bolts noting that there are nineteen short bolts and seven long bolts.

9 Carefully insert a putty knife or similar between the sump and cylinder block. Ease the knife along the joint to break the seal, carefully levering down at the same time. When the sump is released, lower it straight down from its location and remove it from under the vehicle.

10 If access to the crankshaft components is required, undo the bolt and two nuts and remove the oil pump pick-up tube and gasket. Similarly, undo the four bolts and remove the crankcase baffle plate **(see illustrations)**.

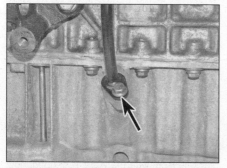

11.4a Oil level dipstick guide tube lower retaining bolt (arrowed)

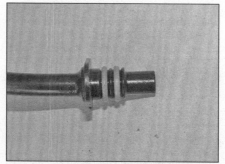

11.4b Renew the 2 O-ring seals at the base of the guide tube

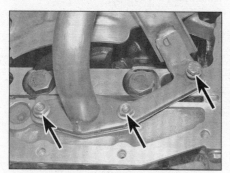

11.10a Undo the oil pump pick-up pipe bolt and 2 nuts (arrowed)

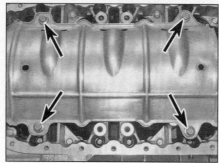

11.10b Baffle plate bolts (arrowed)

Refitting

11 Thoroughly clean all the removed components ensuring that all traces of sealant and gasket are removed from the mating surfaces of the sump, cylinder block, oil pump and oil pump pick-up tube, as applicable. Use a suitable liquid gasket dissolving agent (available from Citroën dealers) together with a soft putty knife; do not use a metal scraper or the faces will be damaged. As there is no conventional gasket used between the sump and cylinder block, the cleanliness of the mating faces is of the utmost importance.

12 If removed, locate the baffle plate in position and secure with the four bolts securely tightened.

13 If the oil pump pick-up tube was removed, locate a new gasket over the oil pump studs then place the tube in position. Fit the retaining nuts and bolt and tighten them securely **(see illustration)**.

14 Ensure that the sump and cylinder block mating faces are clean and dry, then apply a thin bead of RTV sealant to the sump mating surface **(see illustration)**. Citroën recommend the use of Loctite Autojoint Noir for this purpose.

15 Check that the centring dowel is in place in the cylinder block then locate the sump in position. Refit the retaining bolts noting that four of the long bolts are fitted at the transmission end, and three at the timing belt end on the oil filter side of the engine **(see illustrations)**. Tighten the bolts finger-tight only at this stage.

16 If the engine is in the vehicle with the transmission attached, refit the lower centre bolt securing the sump to the transmission bellhousing and tighten it sufficiently to hold the sump in contact with the bellhousing face. Tighten the sump-to-cylinder block retaining bolts evenly and progressively to the specified torque setting. When the sump retaining bolts have been tightened, tighten the sump-to-bellhousing bolt to the specified torque.

17 If the engine is out of the vehicle or the transmission has been removed, use a straight-edge to ensure that the faces of

11.13 Fit a new oil pump pick-up pipe gasket

11.15a Four long bolts are fitted at the transmission end . . .

the cylinder block and sump are flush **(see illustration)**. Hold the sump in this position and tighten the retaining bolts evenly and progressively to the specified torque setting.

18 Lubricate the two new O-rings and locate them on the end of the dipstick guide tube. Engage the guide tube with the sump and fit the upper and lower retaining bolts. Tighten the bolts securely, then refit the dipstick.

19 Move the power steering fluid pipes back into position under the sump and secure with the retaining clamps.

20 Where fitted, reconnect the wiring connector to the oil temperature sender unit at the rear of the sump.

21 Refit the engine undershield, lower the

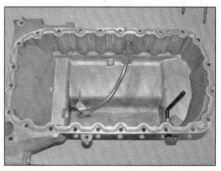

11.14 Apply sealant to the sump mating face

11.15b . . . and at the timing belt end (arrowed)

vehicle to the ground, then refill the engine with oil as described in Chapter 1A.

12 Oil pump – removal, inspection and refitting

Removal

1 Remove the sump as described in the previous Section.

2 Remove the crankshaft sprocket as described in Section 7.

3 Undo the bolts and pull the pump assembly from the cylinder block **(see illustration)**.

11.17 Ensure the faces of the sump and block are flush

12.3 Oil pump housing retaining bolts (arrowed)

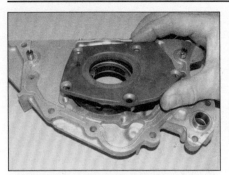

12.6a Undo the screws and lift off the oil pump cover

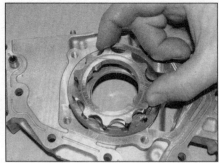

12.6b Remove the inner rotor . . .

12.6c . . . and outer rotor from the pump housing

12.9 Fit a new O-ring seal over the pump outlet stub

12.10 Apply a thin bead of sealant to the pump mating surface

12.13 Carefully fit the new seal over the oil pump drive collar

4 Slide the oil pump drive collar off the end of the crankshaft and collect the O-ring located behind the collar.

5 With the oil pump removed, note the fitted depth of the crankshaft oil seal, then drive it from the oil pump housing. A new oil seal must be obtained for refitting.

Inspection

6 At the time of writing, checking specifications for the oil pump were not available. However, if the oil pump is to be re-used, the internal gears should be cleaned. To do this, unbolt the cover, then mark the gears for location and remove them **(see illustrations)**. Clean the gears and inspect them for damage and excessive wear.

7 Lubricate the gears with clean engine oil, then refit them into their locations noted during removal. Refit the cover and tighten the screws securely.

8 Thoroughly clean the oil pump strainer with a suitable solvent, and check it for clogging or splitting.

Refitting

9 Clean the mating surfaces of the oil pump and main bearing ladder/cylinder block. Check the locating dowels are in place, then locate a new O-ring over the oil pump outlet stub **(see illustration)**.

10 Apply a thin layer of suitable sealant such as Loctite Autojoint Noir (available from Citroën dealers or motor factors) to the mating face of the pump **(see illustration)**.

11 Prime the pump by injecting clean engine oil into the outlet stub, then place the pump in position on the cylinder block, engaging the locating dowels.

12 Apply thread-locking compound to the retaining bolts, then refit and tighten them to the specified torque.

13 Lubricate the sealing lips of the new crankshaft right-hand oil seal and carefully fit the seal over the oil pump drive collar **(see illustration)**. Note that the open part of the seal must be towards the shoulder of the drive collar.

14 Slide the O-ring and drive collar over the end of the crankshaft and engage the flats of the flange with the oil pump inner rotor **(see illustrations)**.

15 Refit the pick-up/strainer and sump as described in Section 11, and the crankshaft sprocket and timing belt as described in Sections 7 and 6.

13 Crankshaft oil seals – renewal

Right-hand oil seal

1 Remove the crankshaft sprocket as described in Section 7.

2 Make a note of the correct fitted depth of the seal in the oil pump housing, then punch or drill a small hole in the face of the seal. Screw a self-tapping screw into the hole and pull on the screw with pliers to extract the seal **(see illustration)**. Alternatively, the seal can be levered out of position. Use a flat-bladed screwdriver, and take great care not to damage the oil pump drive flange or seal housing.

3 Clean the seal housing, and polish off any burrs or raised edges on the pump drive flange, which may have caused the seal to fail in the first place.

12.14a Fit a new O-ring seal over the end of the crankshaft . . .

12.14b . . . then slide the drive collar into place and engage it with the oil pump inner rotor

13.2 Pull the self-tapping screw and seal from place

4 Lubricate the lips of the new seal with clean engine oil, position the fitting guide sleeve supplied with the seal, and carefully locate the seal over the oil pump drive flange. Note that its sealing lip must be facing inwards. Take care not to damage the seal lips during fitting.
5 Tap the seal into position, using a suitable drift, to the same depth in the housing as the original was prior to removal **(see illustration)**.
6 Wash off any traces of oil, then refit the crankshaft sprocket as described in Section 7.

Left-hand oil seal

7 Remove the flywheel as described in Section 14. Make a note of the correct fitted depth of the seal in its location.
8 Punch or drill two small holes opposite each other in the seal. Screw a self-tapping screw into each, and pull on the screws with pliers to extract the seal.
9 Clean the seal housing, and polish off any burrs or raised edges on the crankshaft, which may have caused the seal to fail in the first place.
10 The new seal will normally be supplied with a plastic fitting sleeve to protect the seal lips as the seal is fitted. If so, lubricate the fitting sleeve and locate it over the end of the crankshaft.
11 Lubricate the lips of the new seal with clean engine oil, and carefully locate the seal over the fitting sleeve and onto the end of the crankshaft. Ensure the inner lips of the seal are not damaged by the crankshaft shoulder.
12 Drive the seal into position, using a suitable tubular drift, to the same depth in the housing as the original was prior to removal **(see illustration)**.
13 Remove the fitting sleeve, wash off any traces of oil, then refit the flywheel as described in Section 14.

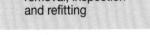

14 Flywheel/driveplate – removal, inspection and refitting

Note: *This is the procedure for the flywheel. The driveplate is similar.*

Removal

1 Remove the transmission as described in

13.5 Tap the new seal into place until it's flush with the oil pump housing

Chapter 7A, then remove the clutch assembly as described in Chapter 6.
2 Prevent the flywheel from turning using a sturdy screwdriver inserted between the ring gear teeth and the cylinder block. Alternatively, bolt a strap between one of the clutch pressure plate mounting bolt holes and an adjacent hole on the cylinder block end face. *Do not* attempt to lock the flywheel in position using the crankshaft pulley locking tool described in Section 3.
3 Slacken and remove the flywheel retaining bolts, and remove the flywheel from the end of the crankshaft. Be careful not to drop it; it is heavy. If the flywheel locating dowel is a loose fit in the crankshaft end, remove it and store it with the flywheel for safe-keeping. Discard the flywheel bolts; new ones must be used on refitting.

Inspection

4 Examine the flywheel for scoring of the clutch face, and for wear or chipping of the ring gear teeth. If the clutch face is scored, the flywheel may be surface-ground, but renewal is preferable. Seek the advice of a Citroën dealer or engine reconditioning specialist to see if machining is possible. If the ring gear is worn or damaged, the flywheel must be renewed, as it is not possible to renew the ring gear separately.

Refitting

5 Clean the mating surfaces of the flywheel and crankshaft. Remove any remaining locking compound from the threads of the crankshaft holes, using the correct size of tap, if available.

 HAYNES HINT *If a suitable tap is not available, cut two slots along the threads of one of the old flywheel bolts, and use the bolt to remove the locking compound from the threads.*

6 If the new flywheel retaining bolts are not supplied with their threads already precoated, apply a suitable thread-locking compound to the threads of each bolt prior to fitting.
7 Ensure that the locating dowel is in position.

13.12 Tap the new crankshaft seal into place

Offer up the flywheel, locating it on the dowel, and fit the new retaining bolts.
8 Lock the flywheel using the method employed on removal, and tighten the retaining bolts to the specified torque and through the specified angle, in the stages given in the Specifications.
9 Refit the clutch as described in Chapter 6. Remove the flywheel locking tool, and refit the transmission as described in Chapter 7A.

15 Engine/transmission mountings – inspection and renewal

Inspection

1 If improved access is required, chock the rear wheels then jack up the front of the vehicle and support it securely on axle stands (see *Jacking and vehicle support*). Undo the fasteners and remove the engine undershield.
2 Check the mounting rubbers to see if they are cracked, hardened or separated from the metal at any point; renew the mounting if any such damage or deterioration is evident.
3 Check that all the mountings' fasteners are securely tightened; use a torque wrench to check if possible.
4 Using a large screwdriver or a crowbar, check for wear in each mounting by carefully levering against it to check for free play. Where this is not possible, enlist the aid of an assistant to move the engine/transmission back-and-forth, or from side-to-side, while you watch the mounting. While some free play is to be expected even from new components, excessive wear should be obvious. If excessive free play is found, check first that the fasteners are correctly secured, then renew any worn components as described below.

Renewal

Right-hand mounting

5 Release all the relevant hoses and wiring from their retaining clips, and position them clear of the mounting so that they do not hinder the removal procedure.
6 Place a jack beneath the engine, with a block of wood on the jack head. Raise the jack until it is supporting the weight of the engine.
7 Slacken and remove the three Torx bolts

15.7 Upper mounting bracket Torx bolts (arrowed)

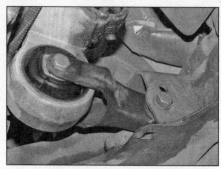

15.25 Rear mounting connecting link

securing the upper mounting bracket to the lower (engine) bracket **(see illustration)**. Remove the single nut securing the upper bracket to the connecting link, and lift off the bracket.

8 Undo the bolt securing the connecting link to the body, and remove it from the vehicle.

9 Check all components carefully for signs of wear or damage, and renew them where necessary.

10 On reassembly, refit the connecting link, and tighten the retaining bolts/nuts to the specified torque.

11 Secure all disturbed hoses and wiring in their relevant retaining clips.

12 Remove the jack from underneath the engine.

Left-hand mounting

13 Remove the air cleaner assembly and inlet ducting as described in Chapter 4A.

14 Remove the engine management ECM and module box as described in Chapter 4A.

15 Withdraw the engine management ECM from its location on the support tray and move it to one side.

16 Place a jack beneath the transmission, with a block of wood on the jack head. Raise the jack until it is supporting the weight of the transmission.

17 Slacken and remove the centre nut and washer from the left-hand mounting, then undo the nuts securing the mounting to the mounting bracket. Lift off the mounting and remove it from the engine compartment.

18 If necessary, slide the spacer (where fitted) off the mounting stud, then unscrew the stud from the top of the transmission housing, and remove it along with its washer. If the mounting stud is tight, a universal stud extractor can be used to unscrew it.

19 Check all components carefully for signs of wear or damage, and renew as necessary.

20 Clean the threads of the mounting stud, and apply a coat of thread-locking compound to its threads. Refit the stud and washer to the top of the transmission, and tighten it to the specified torque setting.

21 Slide the spacer (where fitted) onto the mounting stud, then refit the rubber mounting. Tighten both the mounting-to-bracket nuts

and the mounting centre nut to their specified torque settings, and remove the jack from underneath the transmission.

22 Refit the ECM and module box as described in Chapter 4A.

23 Refit the air cleaner assembly and inlet ducting as described in Chapter 4A, then reconnect the battery negative terminal.

Rear mounting

24 If not already done, chock the rear wheels then jack up the front of the vehicle and support it securely on axle stands (see *Jacking and vehicle support*). Remove the engine undershield.

25 Unscrew and remove the bolt securing the rear mounting connecting link to the mounting bracket on the rear of the cylinder block **(see illustration)**.

26 Remove the bolt securing the connecting link to the bracket on the subframe and withdraw the link.

27 To remove the mounting assembly it will first be necessary to remove the right-hand driveshaft as described in Chapter 8.

28 With the driveshaft removed, undo the retaining bolts and remove the mounting from the rear of the cylinder block.

29 Check carefully for signs of wear or damage on all components, and renew them where necessary.

30 On reassembly, fit the rear mounting assembly to the rear of the cylinder block, and tighten its retaining bolts to the specified torque. Refit the driveshaft as described in Chapter 8.

31 Refit the rear mounting connecting link, and tighten both its bolts to their specified torque settings.

32 Refit the engine undershield and lower the vehicle to the ground.

Chapter 2 Part C:
1.6 litre diesel engine in-car repair procedures

Contents

Degrees of difficulty

Easy, suitable for novice with little experience	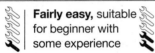	Fairly easy, suitable for beginner with some experience		Fairly difficult, suitable for competent DIY mechanic		Difficult, suitable for experienced DIY mechanic		Very difficult, suitable for expert DIY or professional	

Specifications

General

Designation	DV6TED4
Engine codes*	9HY or 9HZ
Capacity.	1560 cc
Bore	75.0 mm
Stroke.	88.3 mm
Direction of crankshaft rotation	Clockwise (viewed from the right-hand side of vehicle)
No 1cylinder location	At the transmission end of block
Maximum power output.	80 kW @ 4000 rpm
Maximum torque output.	245 Nm @ 2000 rpm
Compression ratio	18.0 :1

* The engine code is stamped on a plate attached to the front of the cylinder block, next to the oil filter

Compression pressures (engine hot, at cranking speed)

Normal	20 ± 5 bar
Minimum.	15 bar
Maximum difference between any two cylinders.	5 bar

Camshaft

Drive.	Toothed belt

Lubrication system

Oil pump type.	Gear-type, driven directly by the right-hand end of the crankshaft, by two flats machined along the crankshaft journal.

Minimum oil pressure at 80°C:

1000 rpm	1.3 bar
4000 rpm	3.5 bar

Torque wrench settings

	Nm	lbf ft
Ancillary drivebelt tensioner roller	20	15
Big-end bolts*:		
Stage 1	10	7
Stage 2	Slacken 180°	
Stage 3	30	22
Stage 4	Angle-tighten a further 140°	
Camshaft bearing caps	10	7
Camshaft cover/bearing ladder:		
Studs	10	7
Bolts	10	7
Camshaft position sensor bolt	5	4
Camshaft sprocket:		
Stage 1	20	15
Stage 2	Angle-tighten a further 50°	
Coolant outlet housing bolts	7	5
Crankshaft position/speed sensor bolt	5	4
Crankshaft pulley/sprocket bolt*:		
Stage 1	35	27
Stage 2	Angle-tighten a further 190 °	
Cylinder head bolts:		
Stage 1	20	15
Stage 2	40	30
Stage 3	Angle-tighten a further 230°	
Cylinder head cover/manifold	10	7
EGR valve	10	7
Engine-to-transmission fixing bolts	60	44
Flywheel bolt*:		
Dual mass flywheel:		
Stage 1	25	18
Stage 2	Fully slacken	
Stage 3	8	6
Stage 4	30	22
Stage 5	Angle-tighten a further 90°	
Normal flywheel:		
Stage 1	25	18
Stage 2	Fully slacken	
Stage 3	8	6
Stage 4	17	2
Stage 5	Angle-tighten a further 75°	
Fuel pump sprocket	50	37
Left-hand engine/transmission mounting:		
Mounting bracket to transmission	55	41
Mounting to bracket	60	44
Main bearing ladder outer seam bolts:		
Stage 1	5	4
Stage 2	10	7
Main bearing ladder to cylinder block:		
Stage 1	10	7
Stage 2	Slacken 180°	
Stage 3	30	22
Stage 4	Angle-tighten a further 140°	
Piston oil jet spray tube bolt	20	15
Oil filter cover	25	18
Oil pick-up pipe	10	7
Oil pressure switch	32	24
Oil pump to cylinder block	10	7
Rear engine/transmission mounting:		
Connecting link to mounting assembly	60	44
Connecting link-to-subframe nut/bolt	60	44
Mounting to engine	60	44
Right-hand engine mounting:		
Mounting to body	60	44
Mounting to support bracket	60	44
Support bracket to engine	55	41
Sump drain plug	25	18
Sump bolts/nuts	12	9

Torque wrench settings (continued)

	Nm	lbf ft
Timing belt idler pulley	35	26
Timing belt tensioner pulley	25	18
Timing chain tensioner	10	7
Vacuum pump:		
Stage 1	18	13
Stage 2	Angle-tighten a further 5°	

* Do not re-use

1 General information

How to use this Chapter

This Part of Chapter 2 describes the repair procedures that can reasonably be carried out on the engine while it remains in the vehicle. If the engine has been removed from the vehicle and is being dismantled as described in Part F, any preliminary dismantling procedures can be ignored.

Note that, while it may be possible physically to overhaul items such as the piston/connecting rod assemblies while the engine is in the car, such tasks are not usually carried out as separate operations. Usually, several additional procedures are required (not to mention the cleaning of components and oil ways); for this reason, all such tasks are classed as major overhaul procedures, and are described in Part F of this Chapter.

Part F describes the removal of the engine/transmission from the car, and the full overhaul procedures that can then be carried out.

DV series engines

The 1.6 litre DV series engine is the result of development collaboration between Citroën/Peugeot and Ford. The engine is of double overhead camshaft (DOHC) 16-valve design. The direct injection, turbocharged, four-cylinder engine is mounted transversely, with the transmission mounted on the left-hand side.

A toothed timing belt drives the inlet camshaft, high-pressure fuel pump and coolant pump. The inlet camshaft drives the exhaust camshaft via a chain. The camshafts operate the inlet and exhaust valves via rocker arms which are supported at their pivot ends by hydraulic self-adjusting tappets. The camshafts are supported by bearings machined directly in the cylinder head and camshaft bearing housing.

The high-pressure fuel pump supplies fuel to the fuel rail, and subsequently to the electronically-controlled injectors which inject the fuel direct into the combustion chambers. This design differs from the previous type where an injection pump supplies the fuel at high-pressure to each injector. The earlier, conventional type injection pump required fine calibration and timing, and these functions are now completed by the high-pressure pump, electronic injectors and engine management ECM.

The crankshaft runs in five main bearings of the usual shell type. Endfloat is controlled by thrustwashers either side of No 2 main bearing.

The pistons are selected to be of matching weight, and incorporate fully-floating gudgeon pins retained by circlips.

Repair operations precaution

The engine is a complex unit with numerous accessories and ancillary components. The design of the engine compartment is such that every conceivable space has been utilised, and access to virtually all of the engine components is extremely limited. In many cases, ancillary components will have to be removed, or moved to one side, and wiring, pipes and hoses will have to be disconnected or removed from various cable clips and support brackets.

When working on this engine, read through the entire procedure first, look at the car and engine at the same time, and establish whether you have the necessary tools, equipment, skill and patience to proceed. Allow considerable time for any operation, and be prepared for the unexpected.

Because of the limited access, many of the engine photographs appearing in this Chapter were, by necessity, taken with the engine removed from the vehicle.

⚠️ **Warning: It is essential to observe strict precautions when working on the fuel system components of the engine, particularly the high-pressure side of the system. Before carrying out any engine operations that entail working on, or near, any part of the fuel system, refer to the special information given in Chapter 4B.**

Operations with engine in vehicle

a) Compression pressure – testing.
b) Cylinder head cover – removal and refitting.
c) Crankshaft pulley – removal and refitting.
d) Timing belt covers – removal and refitting.
e) Timing belt – removal, refitting and adjustment.
f) Timing belt tensioner and sprockets – removal and refitting.
g) Camshaft oil seal – renewal.
h) Camshaft, rocker arms and hydraulic tappets – removal, inspection and refitting.
i) Sump – removal and refitting.
j) Oil pump – removal and refitting.
k) Crankshaft oil seals – renewal.
l) Engine/transmission mountings – inspection and renewal.
m) Flywheel – removal, inspection and refitting.

2 Compression and leakdown tests – description and interpretation

Compression test

Note: A compression tester specifically designed for diesel engines must be used for this test.

1 When engine performance is down, or if misfiring occurs which cannot be attributed to the fuel system, a compression test can provide diagnostic clues as to the engine's condition. If the test is performed regularly, it can give warning of trouble before any other symptoms become apparent.

2 A compression tester specifically intended for diesel engines must be used, because of the higher pressures involved. The tester is connected to an adapter which screws into the glow plug or injector hole. On this engine, an adapter suitable for use in the glow plug holes will be required, so as not to disturb the fuel system components. It is unlikely to be worthwhile buying such a tester for occasional use, but it may be possible to borrow or hire one – if not, have the test performed by a garage.

3 Unless specific instructions to the contrary are supplied with the tester, observe the following points:

a) The battery must be in a good state of charge, the air filter must be clean, and the engine should be at normal operating temperature.
b) All the glow plugs should be removed as described in Chapter 5A before starting the test.
c) The wiring connectors on the engine management system ECM (located in the plastic box behind the battery) must be disconnected.

4 The compression pressures measured are not so important as the balance between cylinders. Values are given in the Specifications.

5 The cause of poor compression is less easy to establish on a diesel engine than on a petrol one. The effect of introducing oil into the cylinders ('wet' testing) is not conclusive, because there is a risk that the oil will sit in the swirl chamber or in the recess on the piston crown instead of passing to the rings. However, the following can be used as a rough guide to diagnosis.

6 All cylinders should produce very similar pressures; any difference greater than

3.9 Insert a 5.0 mm drill bit/bolt through the round hole in the sprocket flange, into the hole in the oil pump housing (lower timing belt cover removed for clarity)

3.10 Insert an 8.0 mm drill bit/bolt through the hole in the camshaft sprocket into the corresponding hole in the cylinder head

that specified indicates the existence of a fault. Note that the compression should build-up quickly in a healthy engine; low compression on the first stroke, followed by gradually-increasing pressure on successive strokes, indicates worn piston rings. A low compression reading on the first stroke, which does not build-up during successive strokes, indicates leaking valves or a blown head gasket (a cracked head could also be the cause). Deposits on the undersides of the valve heads can also cause low compression.

7 A low reading from two adjacent cylinders is almost certainly due to the head gasket having blown between them; the presence of coolant in the engine oil will confirm this.

8 If the compression reading is unusually high, the cylinder head surfaces, valves and pistons are probably coated with carbon deposits. If this is the case, the cylinder head should be removed and decarbonised (see Part F).

Leakdown test

9 A leakdown test measures the rate at which compressed air fed into the cylinder is lost. It is an alternative to a compression test, and in many ways it is better, since the escaping air provides easy identification of where pressure loss is occurring (piston rings, valves or head gasket).

10 The equipment needed for leakdown testing is unlikely to be available to the home mechanic. If poor compression is suspected, have the test performed by a suitably-equipped garage.

3 Engine assembly/ valve timing holes – general information and usage

Note: *Do not attempt to rotate the engine whilst the crankshaft and camshaft are locked in position. If the engine is to be left in this state for a long period of time, it is a good idea to place suitable warning notices inside the vehicle, and in the engine compartment.*

This will reduce the possibility of the engine being accidentally cranked on the starter motor, which is likely to cause damage with the locking pins in place.

1 Timing holes or slots are located only in the crankshaft pulley flange and camshaft sprocket hub. The holes/slots are used to position the pistons halfway up the cylinder bores. This will ensure that the valve timing is maintained during operations that require removal and refitting of the timing belt. When the holes/slots are aligned with their corresponding holes in the cylinder block and cylinder head, suitable diameter bolts/pins can be inserted to lock the crankshaft and camshaft in position, preventing rotation.

2 Note that the HDi type fuel system used on these engines does not have a conventional diesel injection pump, but instead uses a high-pressure fuel pump that does not have to be timed. The alignment of the fuel pump sprocket (and hence the fuel pump itself) with respect to crankshaft and camshaft position, is therefore irrelevant.

3 To align the engine assembly/valve timing holes, proceed as follows.

4 Chock the rear wheels then jack up the front of the vehicle and support it on axle stands (see *Jacking and vehicle support*). Remove the right-hand front roadwheel.

5 To gain access to the crankshaft pulley, to enable the engine to be turned, the wheel arch plastic liner must be removed. The liner is secured by several plastic expanding rivets/nut/screws. To remove the rivets, push in the centre pins a little, then prise the clips from place. Remove the liner from under the front wing. The crankshaft can then be turned using a suitable socket and extension bar fitted to the pulley bolt.

6 Remove the upper and lower timing belt covers as described in Section 6.

7 Temporarily refit the crankshaft pulley bolt, remove the crankshaft locking tool, then turn the crankshaft until the timing hole in the camshaft sprocket hub is aligned with the corresponding hole in the cylinder head. Note

that the crankshaft must always be turned in a clockwise direction (viewed from the right-hand side of vehicle). Use a small mirror so that the position of the sprocket hub timing slot can be observed. When the slot is aligned with the corresponding hole in the cylinder head, the camshaft is positioned correctly.

8 Remove the crankshaft drivebelt pulley as described in Section 5.

9 Insert a 5 mm diameter bolt, rod or drill through the hole in crankshaft sprocket flange and into the corresponding hole in the oil pump **(see illustration)**, if necessary, carefully turn the crankshaft either way until the rod enters the timing hole in the block.

10 Insert an 8 mm bolt, rod or drill through the hole in the camshaft sprocket hub and into engagement with the cylinder head **(see illustration)**.

11 The crankshaft and camshaft are now locked in position, preventing unnecessary rotation.

4 Cylinder head cover/ manifold – removal and refitting

Removal

1 Pull the plastic cover upwards from the top of the engine **(see illustration)**

4.1 Pull the plastic cover upwards to release the rubber mountings

4.2 Release the clip (arrowed) and disconnect the mass airflow meter wiring plug

4.3a Undo the screw (arrowed) and remove the inlet ducting

4.3b Disconnect the hose to the turbocharger . . .

4.3c . . . release the clips (arrowed) and disconnect the breather hose . . .

4.4a . . . then undo the cover screws (arrowed) . . .

4.4b . . . and remove the ducting/cover assembly

2 Disconnect the mass airflow meter wiring plug **(see illustration)**.

3 Remove the inlet and outlet air ducting from the air filter housing **(see illustrations)**.

4 Unscrew the air filter housing cover bolts, then remove the cover and filter element – refer to Chapter 4B **(see illustrations)**. Pull the air filter housing from its mountings.

5 Disconnect the wiring plugs from the top of each injector, undo the guide bolts, then make sure all wiring harnesses are freed from any retaining brackets on the cylinder head cover/inlet manifold **(see illustration)**. Disconnect any vacuum pipes as necessary, having first noted their fitted positions.

6 Remove the EGR cooler as described in Chapter 4C.

7 Depress the release buttons and disconnect the fuel feed and return hoses at the right-hand end of the cylinder head, then disconnect the fuel temperature sensor wiring plug, and move the pipe/priming bulb assembly to the rear **(see illustrations)**.

8 Release the clamps, undo the bolts and remove the inlet ducting between the turbocharger and the inlet manifold. Make a note of their fitted positions, then disconnect the various wiring plugs as the assembly is withdrawn **(see illustrations)**.

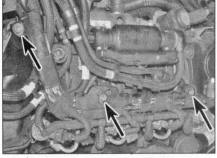

4.5 Undo the Allen screws (arrowed) and position the wiring harness/guide to one side

4.7a Depress the release buttons (arrowed) and disconnect the fuel feed and return hoses

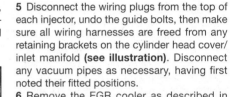
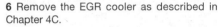

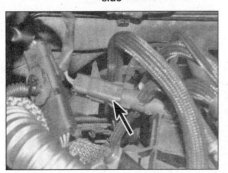

4.7b Disconnect the fuel temperature sensor wiring plug (arrowed) . . .

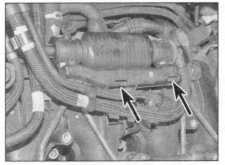

4.7c . . . then unclip the fuel priming bulb/pipes (arrowed)

4.8a Slacken the left-hand turbocharger outlet hose bolt, undo the right-hand bolt (arrowed) . . .

4.8b . . . then slacken the hose clamps (arrowed), disconnect the wiring plugs . . .

4.8c . . . undo the bolt on the end (arrowed) . . .

4.8d . . . and the 2 at the front (arrowed), then remove the assembly

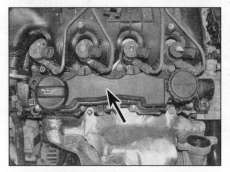

4.9 Undo the bolts and remove the oil separator (arrowed)

4.10a Prise out the clip and pull the return hose from the top of each injector

4.10b Use a second spanner to hold the injector port whilst slackening the fuel pipe unions

9 Undo the retaining bolts and remove the oil separator from the top of the cylinder head **(see illustration)**. Recover the rubber seal.
10 Prise out the retaining clips and disconnect the fuel return pipes from the injectors, then undo the unions and remove the high-pressure fuel pipes from the injectors and the common fuel rail at the rear of the cylinder head – counterhold the unions with a second spanner **(see illustrations)**. Plug the openings to prevent dirt ingress.
11 Undo the 2 bolts securing the cylinder head cover/inlet manifold. Lift the assembly away **(see illustration)**. Recover the manifold rubber seals.

Refitting

12 Refitting is a reversal of removal, bearing in mind the following points:
a) Examine the seals for signs of damage

and deterioration, and renew if necessary. Smear a little clean engine oil on the manifold seals.
b) Renew the fuel injector high-pressure pipes – see Chapter 4B.

5 Crankshaft pulley – removal and refitting

Removal

1 Remove the auxiliary drivebelt as described in Chapter 5A.
2 To lock the crankshaft, working underneath the engine, insert Citroën tool No 0194-C into the hole in the right-hand face of the engine block casting over the lower section of the flywheel. Rotate the crankshaft until the tool engages in the corresponding hole in the

flywheel. In the absence of the Citroën tool, insert a 12 mm rod or drill into the hole **(see illustration)**. **Note:** *The hole in the casting and the hole in the flywheel are provided purely to lock the crankshaft whilst the pulley bolt is undone, it does <u>not</u> position the crankshaft at TDC.*
3 Using a suitable socket and extension bar, unscrew the retaining bolt, remove the washer, then slide the pulley off the end of the crankshaft **(see illustration)**. If the pulley is tight fit, it can be drawn off the crankshaft using a suitable puller. If a puller is being used, refit the pulley retaining bolt without the washer to avoid damaging the crankshaft as the puller is tightened.
Caution: Do not touch the outer magnetic sensor ring of the sprocket with your fingers, or allow metallic particles to come into contact with it.

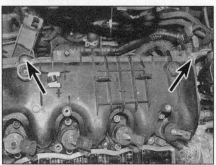

4.11 Undo the 2 remaining bolts (arrowed) and pull the cover/manifold upwards

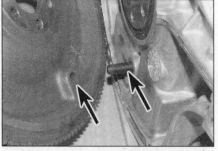

5.2 The locking pin/bolt (arrowed) must locate in the hole in the flywheel (arrowed) to prevent rotation

5.3 Undo the crankshaft pulley retaining bolt (arrowed)

Refitting

4 Refit the pulley to the end of the crankshaft.

5 Thoroughly clean the threads of the pulley retaining bolt, then apply a coat of locking compound to the bolt threads. Citroën recommend the use of Loctite (available from your Citroën dealer); in the absence of this, any good-quality locking compound may be used.

6 Refit the crankshaft pulley retaining bolt and washer. Tighten the bolt to the specified torque, then through the specified angle, preventing the crankshaft from turning using the method employed on removal.

7 Refit and tension the auxiliary drivebelt as described in Chapter 5A.

6 Timing belt covers – removal and refitting

⚠️ **Warning: Refer to the precautionary information contained in Section 1 before proceeding.**

Removal

Upper cover

1 Remove the plastic cover from the top of the engine.

2 Release the wiring harness and fuel pipes from the upper cover **(see illustrations)**.

3 Undo the five screws and remove the timing belt upper cover **(see illustration)**.

Lower cover

4 Remove the upper cover as described previously.

5 Remove the crankshaft pulley as described in Section 5.

6 Remove the auxiliary drivebelt tensioner locking tool (where applicable), then undo the five bolts and remove the lower cover **(see illustration)**.

Refitting

7 Refitting of all the covers is a reversal of the relevant removal procedure, ensuring that each cover section is correctly located, and that the cover retaining bolts are securely tightened. Ensure that all disturbed hoses are reconnected and retained by their relevant clips.

7 Timing belt – removal, inspection, refitting and tensioning

General

1 The timing belt drives the inlet camshaft, high-pressure fuel pump, and coolant pump from a toothed sprocket on the end of the crankshaft. If the belt breaks or slips in service, the pistons are likely to hit the valve heads, resulting in expensive damage.

2 The timing belt should be renewed at the

6.2a Unclip the fuel pipes (arrowed) . . .

6.3 Upper timing belt cover screws (arrowed)

specified intervals, or earlier if it is contaminated with oil, or at all noisy in operation (a 'scraping' noise due to uneven wear).

3 If the timing belt is being removed, it is a wise precaution to check the condition of the coolant pump at the same time (check for signs of coolant leakage). This may avoid the need to remove the timing belt again at a later stage should the coolant pump fail.

Removal

4 Chock the rear wheels then jack up the front of the vehicle and support it on axle stands (see *Jacking and vehicle support*). Remove the front right-hand roadwheel, wheel arch liner (to expose the crankshaft pulley), and the engine undershield. The wheel arch liner is secured by several plastic expanding rivets/nuts/plastic clips. Push the centre pins in a little then prise the rivets from place. The engine undershield is retained by several screws.

7.10 Undo the bolt (arrowed) and remove the crankshaft position sensor

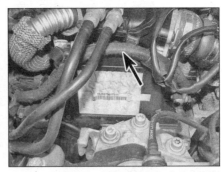

6.2b . . . and the wiring harness (arrowed) from the timing belt upper cover

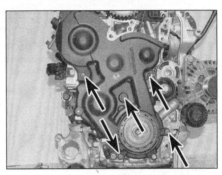

6.6 Lower timing belt cover screws (arrowed)

5 Remove the auxiliary drivebelt as described in Chapter 5A.

6 Remove the upper and lower timing belt covers, as described in Section 6.

7 Refer to Chapter 4B and disconnect the front exhaust pipe at the flexible section.

8 Position a trolley jack under the engine, and using a block of wood on the jack head, take the weight of the engine.

9 Undo the bolts/nut and remove the right-hand engine mounting and support bracket – see Section 17.

10 Undo the screw and remove the crankshaft position sensor adjacent to the crankshaft sprocket flange, and move it to one side **(see illustration)**.

11 Undo the retaining screw and remove the timing belt protection bracket, again adjacent to the crankshaft sprocket flange **(see illustration)**.

12 Lock the crankshaft and camshaft in the

7.11 Remove the timing belt protection bracket

7.13 Slacken the bolt and allow the tensioner to rotate, relieving the tension on the belt

7.17 Timing belt routing

7.19 The index arm must align with the lug (arrowed)

correct position as described in Section 3. If necessary, temporarily refit the crankshaft pulley bolt to enable the crankshaft to be rotated.

13 Insert a hexagon key into the belt tensioner pulley centre, slacken the pulley bolt, and allow the tensioner to rotate, relieving the belt tension (see illustration). With belt slack, temporarily tighten the pulley bolt.

14 Note its routing, then remove the timing belt from the sprockets.

Tool Tip 1: A sprocket holding tool can be made from two lengths of steel strip bolted together to form a forked end. Drill holes and insert bolts in the ends of the fork to engage with the sprocket spokes.

Inspection

15 Renew the belt as a matter of course, regardless of its apparent condition. The cost of a new belt is nothing compared with the cost of repairs should the belt break in service. If signs of oil contamination are found, trace the source of the oil leak and rectify it. Wash down the engine timing belt area and all related components, to remove all traces of oil. Check that the tensioner and idler pulleys rotate freely without any sign of roughness, and also check that the coolant pump pulley rotates freely. If necessary, renew these items.

Refitting and tensioning

16 Commence refitting by ensuring that the crankshaft and camshaft timing pins are still in position correctly.

17 Locate the timing belt on the crankshaft sprocket, then keeping it taut, locate it around the idler pulley, camshaft sprocket, high-pressure pump sprocket, coolant pump sprocket, and the tensioner pulley (see illustration).

18 Refit the timing belt protection bracket and tighten the retaining bolt securely.

19 Slacken the tensioner pulley bolt, and using a hexagonal key, rotate the tensioner anti-clockwise, which moves the index arm clockwise, until the index arm is aligned as shown (see illustration).

20 Remove the camshaft and crankshaft timing pins and, using a socket on the crankshaft pulley bolt, crankshaft clockwise 10 complete revolutions. Refit the crankshaft and camshaft locking pins.

21 Check that the tensioner index arm is still aligned between the edges of the area shown (see illustration 7.19). If it is not, remove and belt and begin the refitting process again, starting at Paragraph 19.

22 The remainder of refitting is a reversal of removal. Tighten all fasteners to the specified torque where given.

8 Timing belt sprockets and tensioner – removal and refitting

Camshaft sprocket

Removal

1 Remove the timing belt as described in Section 7.

2 Remove the locking tool from the camshaft sprocket/hub. Slacken the sprocket hub retaining bolt. To prevent the camshaft rotating as the bolt is slackened, a sprocket holding tool will be required. In the absence of the special Citroën tool, an acceptable substitute can be fabricated at home (see Tool Tip 1). *Do not* attempt to use the engine assembly/valve timing locking tool to prevent the sprocket from rotating whilst the bolt is slackened.

3 Remove the sprocket hub retaining bolt, and slide the sprocket and hub off the end of the camshaft.

4 Clean the camshaft sprocket thoroughly, and renew it if there are any signs of wear, damage or cracks.

Refitting

5 Refit the camshaft sprocket to the camshaft (see illustration).

6 Refit the sprocket hub retaining bolt. Tighten the bolt to the specified torque, preventing the camshaft from turning as during removal.

7 Align the engine assembly/valve timing slot in the camshaft sprocket hub with the hole in the cylinder head and refit the timing pin to lock the camshaft in position.

8 Fit the timing belt around the pump sprocket and camshaft sprocket, and tension the timing belt as described in Section 7.

Crankshaft sprocket

Removal

9 Remove the timing belt as described in Section 7.

8.5 Ensure the lug on the sprocket hub engages with the slot on the end of the camshaft (arrowed)

10 Check that the engine assembly/valve timing holes are still aligned as described in Section 3, and the camshaft sprocket and flywheel are locked in position.

11 Slide the sprocket off the end of the crankshaft and collect the Woodruff key **(see illustrations)**.

12 Examine the crankshaft oil seal for signs of oil leakage and, if necessary, renew it as described in Section 14.

13 Clean the crankshaft sprocket thoroughly, and renew it if there are any signs of wear, damage or cracks. Recover the crankshaft locating key.

Refitting

14 Refit the key to the end of the crankshaft, then refit the crankshaft sprocket (with the flange facing the crankshaft pulley).

15 Fit the timing belt around the crankshaft sprocket, and tension the timing belt as described in Section 7.

Fuel pump sprocket

Removal

16 Remove the timing belt as described in Section 7.

17 Using a suitable socket, undo the pump sprocket retaining nut. The sprocket can be held stationary by inserting a suitably sized locking pin, drill or rod through the hole in the sprocket, and into the corresponding hole in the backplate **(see illustration)**, or by using a suitable forked tool engaged with the holes in the sprocket **(see Tool Tip 1)**.

18 The pump sprocket is a taper fit on the

8.17 Insert a suitable drill bit through the sprocket into the hole in the backplate

8.11a Slide the sprocket from the crankshaft . . .

pump shaft and it will be necessary to make up another tool to release it from the taper **(see Tool Tip 2)**.

19 Partially unscrew the sprocket retaining nut, fit the home-made tool, and secure it to the sprocket with two suitable bolts. Prevent the sprocket from rotating as before, and unscrew the sprocket retaining nut. The nut will bear against the tool as it is undone, forcing the sprocket off the shaft taper. Once the taper is released, remove the tool, unscrew the nut fully, and remove the sprocket from the pump shaft.

20 Clean the sprocket thoroughly, and renew it if there are any signs of wear, damage or cracks.

Refitting

21 Refit the pump sprocket and retaining nut, and tighten the nut to the specified torque. Prevent the sprocket rotating as the nut is tightened using the sprocket holding tool.

22 Fit the timing belt around the pump sprocket, and tension the timing belt as described in Section 7.

Coolant pump sprocket

23 The coolant pump sprocket is integral with the pump, and cannot be removed. Coolant pump removal is described in Chapter 3.

Tool Tip 2: Make a sprocket releasing tool from a short strip of steel. Drill two holes in the strip to correspond with the two holes in the sprocket. Drill a third hole just large enough to accept the flats of the sprocket retaining nut.

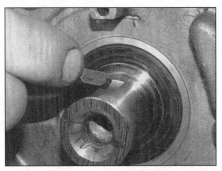

8.11b . . . and recover the Woodruff key

Tensioner pulley

Removal

24 Remove the timing belt as described in Section 7.

25 Remove the tensioner pulley retaining bolt, and slide the pulley off its mounting stud.

26 Clean the tensioner pulley, but do not use any strong solvent which may enter the pulley bearings. Check that the pulley rotates freely, with no sign of stiffness or free play. Renew the pulley if there is any doubt about its condition, or if there are any obvious signs of wear or damage.

27 Examine the pulley mounting stud for signs of damage and if necessary, renew it.

Refitting

28 Refit the tensioner pulley to its mounting stud, and fit the retaining bolt.

29 Refit the timing belt as described in Section 7.

Idler pulley

Removal

30 Remove the timing belt as described in Section 7.

31 Undo the retaining bolt/nut and withdraw the idler pulley from the engine **(see illustration)**.

32 Clean the idler pulley, but do not use any strong solvent which may enter the bearings. Check that the pulley rotates freely, with no sign of stiffness or free play. Renew the idler pulley if there is any doubt about its condition, or if there are any obvious signs of wear or damage.

8.31 Timing belt idler pulley retaining nut (arrowed)

9.5 Vacuum pump bolts (arrowed)

9.7 Timing belt inner, upper cover bolts (arrowed)

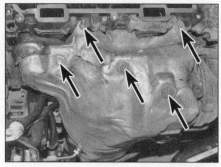

9.9a Undo the bolts (arrowed) and remove the rear section of the heat shield

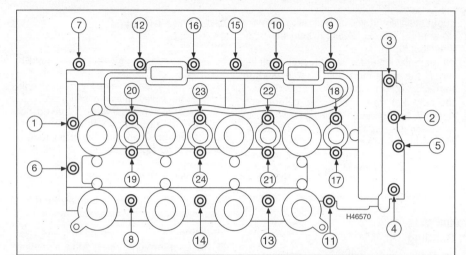

9.9b Camshaft cover/bearing ladder bolt slackening sequence

the 3 bolts and remove the timing belt inner, upper cover **(see illustration)**.

8 Disconnect the wiring plug, unscrew the retaining bolt, and remove the camshaft position sensor from the camshaft cover/bearing ladder.

9 Undo the 5 bolts and remove the upper rear section of the turbocharger heat shield, then working gradually and evenly, slacken and remove the bolts securing the camshaft cover/bearing ladder to the cylinder head in sequence **(see illustrations)**. Lift the cover/ladder from position complete with the camshafts.

10 Undo the retaining bolts and remove the bearing caps. Note their fitted positions, as they must be refitted into their original positions **(see illustration)**. Note that the bearing caps are marked A for inlet, and E for exhaust, and 1 to 4 from the flywheel end of the cylinder head.

11 Undo the bolts securing the chain tensioner assembly to the camshaft cover/bearing ladder, then lift the camshafts, chain and tensioner from place **(see illustrations)**. Discard the camshaft oil seal.

12 Obtain 16 small, clean plastic containers, and number them 1 to 8 inlet and 1 to 8 exhaust; alternatively, divide a larger container into 16 compartments.

13 Lift out each rocker arm. Place the rocker arms in their respective positions in the box or containers.

14 A compartmentalised container filled with engine oil is now required to retain the hydraulic tappets while they are removed from

Refitting

33 Locate the idler pulley on the engine, and fit the retaining bolt/nut. Tighten the bolt/nut to the specified torque.

34 Refit the timing belt (see Section 7).

9 Camshafts, rocker arms and hydraulic tappets – removal, inspection and refitting

Removal

1 Remove the cylinder head cover/manifold as described in Section 4.

2 Remove the injectors as described in Chapter 4B.

3 Remove the camshaft sprocket as described in Section 8.

4 Refit the right-hand engine mounting, but only tighten the bolts moderately; this will keep the engine supported during the camshaft removal.

5 Undo the bolts and remove the vacuum pump. Recover the pump O-ring seals **(see illustration)**.

6 Remove the fuel filter (see Chapter 1B), then undo the bolts and remove the fuel filter mounting bracket.

7 Release the wiring harness clips, then undo

9.10 The camshaft bearing caps are numbered 1 to 4 from the flywheel end – A for inlet, and E for exhaust (arrowed)

9.11a Undo the tensioner bolts (arrowed) . . .

9.11b . . . then lift the camshafts, chain and tensioner from place

9.21 Refit the hydraulic tappets . . .

9.22 . . . and rocker arms to their original locations

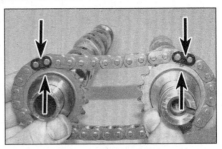

9.23 Align the marks on the sprockets with the centre of the black-coloured chain links (arrowed). There must be 12 link pins between the sprocket marks

the cylinder head. Withdraw each hydraulic follower and place it in the container, keeping them each identified for correct refitting. The tappets must be totally submerged in the oil to prevent air entering them.

Inspection

15 Inspect the cam lobes and the camshaft bearing journals for scoring or other visible evidence of wear. Once the surface hardening of the cam lobes has been eroded, wear will occur at an accelerated rate. **Note:** *If these symptoms are visible on the tips of the camshaft lobes, check the corresponding rocker arm, as it will probably be worn as well.*
16 Examine the condition of the bearing surfaces in the cylinder head and camshaft bearing housing. If wear is evident, the cylinder head and bearing housing will both have to be renewed, as they are a matched assembly.
17 Inspect the rocker arms and tappets for scuffing, cracking or other damage and renew any components as necessary. Also check the condition of the tappet bores in the cylinder head. As with the camshafts, any wear in this area will necessitate cylinder head renewal.

Refitting

18 Thoroughly clean the sealant from the mating surfaces of the cylinder head and camshaft bearing housing. Use a suitable liquid gasket dissolving agent (available from Citroën dealers) together with a soft putty knife; do not use a metal scraper or the faces will be damaged. As there is no conventional gasket used, the cleanliness of the mating faces is of the utmost importance. Prise out the oil injector oil seals from the camshaft bearing housing.
19 Clean off any oil, dirt or grease from both components and dry with a clean lint-free cloth. Ensure that all the oilways are completely clean.
20 Liberally lubricate the hydraulic tappet bores in the cylinder head with clean engine oil.
21 Insert the hydraulic tappets into their original bores in the cylinder head unless they have been renewed **(see illustration)**.
22 Lubricate the rocker arms and place them over their respective tappets and valve stems **(see illustration)**.

9.24a Assemble the chain tensioner between the upper and lower runs of the chain . . .

23 Engage the timing chain around the camshaft sprockets, aligning the black-coloured links with the marked teeth on the camshaft sprockets **(see illustration)**. If the black colouring has been lost, there must be 12 chain link pins between the marks on the sprockets.
24 Fit the chain tensioner between the upper and lower runs of the chain, then lubricate the bearing surfaces with clean engine oil, and fit the camshafts into position on the underside of the camshaft cover/bearing ladder. Refit the bearing caps to their original positions and tighten the retaining bolts to the specified torque **(see illustrations)**. Tighten the tensioner retaining bolts to the specified torque.

9.24b . . . and lower the camshafts, chain and tensioner into position

25 Apply a thin bead of sealant to the mating surface of the camshaft cover/bearing ladder as shown. Citroën recommend the use of Autojoint Noir **(see illustration)**. Do not allow the sealant to obstruct the oil channels for the hydraulic chain tensioner.
26 Check that the black-coloured links on the chain are still aligned with the marks on the camshaft sprockets, then refit the camshaft cover/bearing ladder, and gradually and evenly tighten the retaining bolts until the cover/ladder is in contact with the cylinder head, then tighten the bolts to the specified torque in sequence **(see illustration)**. **Note:** *Ensure the cover/ladder is correctly located by checking the bores of the vacuum pump and camshaft oil seal at each end of the cover/ladder.*

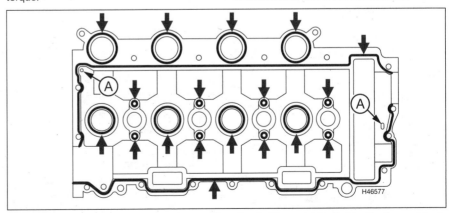

9.25 Apply sealant to the camshaft cover/bearing ladder as indicated by the heavy black lines. Ensure sealant does not enter the tensioner oil holes – marked A

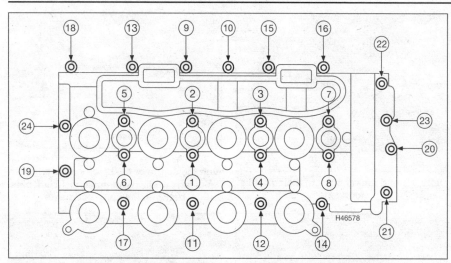

9.26 Camshaft cover/bearing ladder bolt tightening sequence

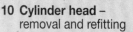

10 Cylinder head – removal and refitting

Removal

1 Chock the rear wheels then jack up the front of the vehicle and support it on axle stands (see *Jacking and vehicle support*). Remove the front right-hand roadwheel, the engine undershield, and the front wheel arch liner. The undershield is secured by several screws, and the wheel arch liner is secured by several plastic expanding rivets/nuts/plastic clips. Push the centre pins in a little, then prise the rivet from place.
2 Disconnect the battery negative lead as described in Chapter 5A.
3 Drain the cooling system as described in Chapter 1B.
4 Remove the camshafts, rocker arms and hydraulic tappets as described in Section 9.
5 Remove the turbocharger as described in Chapter 4B.
6 Remove the glow plugs as described in Chapter 5A.
7 Undo the 3 mounting bolts and move the power steering pump to one side (there's no need to disconnect the hoses).
8 Undo the upper mounting bolts, and pivot the alternator away from the engine, undo the oil dipstick guide tube bolt, then undo the bolts securing the alternator/power steering pump mounting bracket to the cylinder head/block **(see illustration)**.
9 Undo the coolant outlet housing (left-hand end of the cylinder head) retaining bolts, slacken the two bolts securing the housing support bracket to the top of the transmission bellhousing, and move the outlet housing away from the cylinder head a little **(see illustration)**. There is no need to disconnect the hoses.
10 Disconnect the high-pressure fuel pipe from the common rail to the pump, and disconnect the fuel supply and return hoses.

9.32a Fit the new seal around a 20 mm outside diameter socket . . .

9.32b . . . and push it into place

27 Fit a new camshaft oil seal as described in Section 14.
28 Refit the camshaft sprocket, and tighten the retaining bolt finger tight.
29 Using a spanner on the camshaft sprocket bolt, rotate the camshafts approximately 40 complete revolutions clockwise. Check the black-coloured links on the chain still align with the marks on the camshaft sprockets.
30 If the marks still align, refit the camshaft sprocket as described in Section 8.

31 Refit and adjust the camshaft position sensor as described in Chapter 4B.
32 Press the new oil seals into the bearing housing, using a tube/socket of approximately 20 mm outside diameter, ensuring the inner lip of the seal fits around the injector guide tube **(see illustrations)**. Refit the injectors as described in Chapter 4B.
33 Refit the cylinder head cover/manifold as described in Section 4.

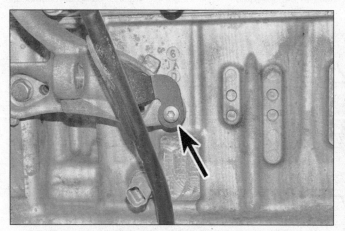

10.8 The engine oil level dipstick is secured to the alternator bracket by a Torx bolt (arrowed)

10.9 Undo the bolts (arrowed) and pull the coolant outlet housing from the left-hand end of the cylinder head

10.10a Remove the high-pressure pipe (arrowed) . . .

10.10b . . . and the bracket (arrowed)

10.10c Pump mounting bracket upper nut and lower mounting bolt (arrowed)

Remove the bracket at the rear of the pump, then undo the bolt/nut and remove the pump and mounting bracket as an assembly (see illustrations). Note that a new high-pressure pipe must be fitted – see Chapter 4B.

11 Working in the reverse of the sequence shown (see illustration 10.32) undo the cylinder head bolts.

12 Release the cylinder head from the cylinder block and location dowels by rocking it. The Citroën tool for doing this consists simply of two metal rods with 90-degree angled ends (see illustration). Do not prise between the mating faces of the cylinder head and block, as this may damage the gasket faces.

13 Lift the cylinder head from the block, and recover the gasket.

14 If necessary, remove the exhaust manifold with reference to Chapter 4B.

Preparation for refitting

15 The mating faces of the cylinder head and cylinder block must be perfectly clean before refitting the head. Citroën recommend the use of a scouring agent for this purpose, but acceptable results can be achieved by using a hard plastic or wood scraper to remove all traces of gasket and carbon. The same method can be used to clean the piston crowns. Take particular care to avoid scoring or gouging the cylinder head/cylinder block mating surfaces during the cleaning operations, as aluminium alloy is easily damaged. Make sure that the carbon is not allowed to enter the oil and water passages – this is particularly important for the lubrication system, as carbon could block the

oil supply to the engine's components. Using adhesive tape and paper, seal the water, oil and bolt holes in the cylinder block. To prevent carbon entering the gap between the pistons and bores, smear a little grease in the gap. After cleaning each piston, use a small brush to remove all traces of grease and carbon from the gap, then wipe away the remainder with a clean rag.

16 Check the mating surfaces of the cylinder block and the cylinder head for nicks, deep scratches and other damage. If slight, they may be removed carefully with a file, but if excessive, machining may be the only alternative to renewal. If warpage of the cylinder head gasket surface is suspected, use a straight-edge to check it for distortion. Refer to Part F of this Chapter if necessary.

17 Thoroughly clean the threads of the cylinder head bolt holes in the cylinder block. Ensure that the bolts run freely in their threads, and that all traces of oil and water are removed from each bolt hole. If required, pull the oil feed non-return valve from the cylinder head, and check the ball moves freely. Push a new valve into place if necessary (see illustrations).

Gasket selection

18 Remove the crankshaft timing pin, then turn the crankshaft until pistons 1 and 4 are at TDC (Top Dead Centre). Position a dial test indicator (dial gauge) on the cylinder block adjacent to the rear of No 1 piston, and zero it on the block face. Transfer the probe to the crown of No 1 piston (10.0 mm in from the

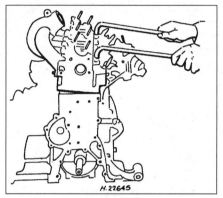

10.12 Free the cylinder head using angled rods

rear edge), then slowly turn the crankshaft back-and-forth past TDC, noting the highest reading on the indicator. Record this reading as protrusion A.

19 Repeat the check described in paragraph 18, this time 10.0 mm in from the front edge of the No 1 piston crown. Record this reading as protrusion B.

20 Add protrusion A to protrusion B, then divide the result by 2 to obtain an average reading for piston No 1.

21 Repeat the procedure described in paragraphs 18 to 20 on piston 4, then turn the crankshaft through 180° and carry out the procedure on the piston Nos 2 and 3 (see illustration). Check that there is a maximum difference of 0.07 mm protrusion between any two pistons.

10.17a Pull the non-return valve from the cylinder head . . .

10.17b . . . and push a new one into place

10.21 Measure the piston protrusion using a DTI gauge

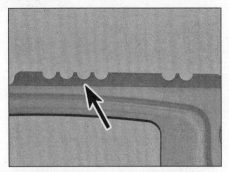

10.23 Cylinder head gasket thickness identification notches (arrowed)

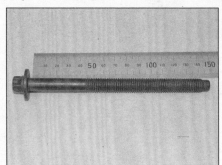

10.24 Measure the length from under the bolt head to its end

10.27 Ensure the gasket locates over the dowels (arrowed)

22 If a dial test indicator is not available, piston protrusion may be measured using a straight-edge and feeler blades or Vernier calipers. However, this is much less accurate, and cannot therefore be recommended.

23 Note the greatest piston protrusion measurement, and use this to determine the correct cylinder head gasket from the following table. The series of notches/holes on the side of the gasket are used for thickness identification **(see illustration)**.

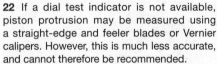

Piston protrusion	Gasket identification
0.6115 to 0.720 mm	2 notches
0.721 to 0.770 mm	3 notches
0.771 to 0.820 mm	1 notches
0.821 to 0.870 mm	4 notches
0.871 to 0.977 mm	5 notches

Head bolt examination

24 Carefully examine the cylinder head bolts for signs of damage to the threads or head, and for any sign of corrosion. If the bolts are in a satisfactory condition, measure the length of each bolt from the underside of the head to the end of the shank. The bolts may be re-used providing that the measured length does not exceed 149.0 mm **(see illustration)**. **Note:** *Considering the stress to which the cylinder head bolts are subjected, it is highly recommended that they are all renewed, regardless of their apparent condition.*

Refitting

25 Turn the crankshaft and position Nos 1 and 4 pistons at TDC, then turn the crankshaft a quarter turn (90°) anti-clockwise.

26 Thoroughly clean the surfaces of the cylinder head and block.

27 Make sure that the locating dowels are in place, then fit the correct gasket the right way round on the cylinder block **(see illustration)**.

28 If necessary, refit the exhaust manifold to the cylinder head as described in Chapter 4B.

29 Carefully lower the cylinder head onto the gasket and block, making sure that it locates correctly onto the dowels.

30 Apply a smear of grease to the threads, and to the underside of the heads, of the cylinder head bolts. Citroën recommend the use of Molykote G Rapid Plus (available from your Citroën dealer); in the absence of the specified grease, any good-quality high melting-point grease may be used.

31 Carefully insert the cylinder head bolts into their holes (*do not drop them in*) and initially finger-tighten them.

32 Working progressively and in sequence, tighten the cylinder head bolts to their Stage 1 torque setting, using a torque wrench and suitable socket **(see illustration)**.

33 Once all the bolts have been tightened to their Stage 1 torque setting, working again in the specified sequence, tighten each

bolt to the specified Stage 2 setting. Finally, angle-tighten the bolts through the specified Stage 3 angle. It is recommended that an angle-measuring gauge is used during this stage of tightening, to ensure accuracy. **Note:** *Retightening of the cylinder head bolts after running the engine is not required.*

34 Refit the hydraulic tappets, rocker arms, and camshaft housing (complete with camshafts) as described in Section 9.

35 Refit the timing belt as described in Section 7.

36 The remainder of refitting is a reversal of removal, noting the following points.

a) *Use a new seal when refitting the coolant outlet housing.*

b) *When refitting a cylinder head, it is good practice to renew the thermostat.*

c) *Refit the camshaft position sensor and set the air gap with reference to Chapter 4B.*

d) *Tighten all fasteners to the specified torque where given.*

e) *Refill the cooling system as described in Chapter 1B.*

f) *The engine may run erratically for the first few miles, until the engine management ECM relearns its stored values.*

11 Sump –
removal and refitting

Removal

1 Drain the engine oil, then clean and refit the engine oil drain plug, tightening it securely. If the engine is nearing the service interval when the oil and filter are due for renewal, it is recommended that the filter is also removed, and a new one fitted. After reassembly, the engine can then be refilled with fresh oil. Refer to Chapter 1B for further information.

2 Chock the rear wheels then jack up the front of the vehicle and support it on axle stands (see *Jacking and vehicle support*). Undo the screws and remove the engine undershield.

3 Remove the exhaust front pipe as described in Chapter 4B.

4 Where necessary, disconnect the wiring connector from the oil temperature sender unit, which is screwed into the sump.

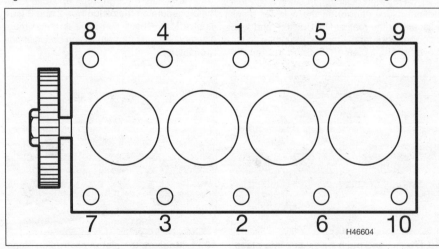

10.32 Cylinder head bolt tightening sequence

11.8 Apply a bead of sealant to the sump or crankcase mating surface. Ensure the sealant is applied on the inside of the retaining bolt holes

11.9 Refit the sump and tighten the bolts

5 Progressively slacken and remove all the sump retaining bolts/nuts. Since the sump bolts vary in length, remove each bolt in turn, and store it in its correct fitted order by pushing it through a clearly-marked cardboard template. This will avoid the possibility of installing the bolts in the wrong locations on refitting.

6 Try to break the joint by striking the sump with the palm of your hand, then lower and withdraw the sump from under the car. If the sump is stuck (which is quite likely) use a putty knife or similar, carefully inserted between the sump and block. Ease the knife along the joint until the sump is released. While the sump is removed, take the opportunity to check the oil pump pick-up/strainer for signs of clogging or splitting. If necessary, remove the pump as described in Section 12, and clean or renew the strainer.

Refitting

7 Clean all traces of sealant from the mating surfaces of the cylinder block/crankcase and sump, then use a clean rag to wipe out the sump and the engine's interior.

8 On engines where the sump was fitted without a gasket, ensure that the sump mating surfaces are clean and dry, then apply a thin coating of suitable sealant to the sump or crankcase mating surface **(see illustration)**.

9 Offer up the sump to the cylinder block/crankcase. Refit its retaining bolts/nuts, ensuring that each bolt is screwed into its original location. Tighten the bolts evenly and progressively to the specified torque setting **(see illustration)**.

10 Where necessary, align the air conditioning compressor with its mountings on the sump, and insert the retaining bolts. Securely tighten the compressor retaining bolts, then refit the drivebelt as described in Chapter 5A.

11 Reconnect the wiring connector to the oil temperature sensor (where fitted).

12 Lower the vehicle to the ground, then refill the engine with oil as described in Chapter 1B.

12 Oil pump –
removal, inspection and refitting

Removal

1 Remove the sump as described in Section 11.

2 Remove the crankshaft sprocket as described in Section 8. Recover the locating key from the crankshaft.

3 Disconnect the wiring plug, undo the bolts and remove the crankshaft position sensor, located on the right-hand end of the cylinder block.

4 Undo the three Allen screws and remove the oil pump pick-up tube from the pump/block **(see illustration)**. Discard the oil seal, a new one must be fitted.

5 Undo the 8 bolts, and remove the oil pump **(see illustration)**.

12.4 Oil pick-up tube Allen screws (arrowed)

12.5 Oil pump retaining bolts (arrowed)

12.6 Undo the Torx bolts and remove the pump cover

12.7a Remove the circlip . . .

12.7b . . . cap . . .

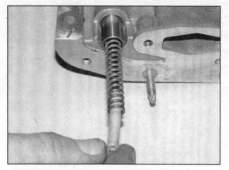

12.7c . . . spring . . .

12.7d . . . and piston

12.11 Apply a bead of sealant to the cylinder block mating surface

Inspection

6 Undo and remove the Torx bolts securing the cover to the oil pump **(see illustration)**. Examine the pump rotors and body for signs of wear and damage. If worn, the complete pump must be renewed.

7 Remove the circlip, and extract the cap, valve piston and spring, noting which way around they are fitted **(see illustrations)**. The condition of the relief valve spring can only be measured by comparing it with a new one; if there is any doubt about its condition, it should also be renewed.

8 Refit the relief valve piston and spring, then secure them in place with the circlip.

9 Refit the cover to the oil pump, and tighten the Torx bolts securely.

Refitting

10 Remove all traces of sealant, and thoroughly clean the mating surfaces of the oil pump and cylinder block.

11 Apply a 4 mm wide bead of silicone sealant to the mating face of the cylinder block **(see illustration)**. Ensure that no sealant enters any of the holes in the block.

12 With a new oil seal fitted, refit the oil pump over the end of the crankshaft, aligning the flats in the pump drivegear with the flats machined in the crankshaft **(see illustrations)**. Note that new oil pumps are supplied with the oil seal already fitted, and a seal protector sleeve. The sleeve fits over the end of the crankshaft to protect the seal as the pump is fitted.

13 Install the oil pump bolts and tighten them to the specified torque.

14 Refit the oil pick-up tube to the pump/ cylinder block using a new O-ring seal. Ensure the oil dipstick guide tube is correctly refitted.

15 Refit the woodruff key to the crankshaft, and slide the crankshaft sprocket into place.

16 The remainder of refitting is a reversal of removal.

13 Oil cooler –
removal and refitting

Removal

1 Chock the rear wheels then jack up the front of the vehicle and support it on axle stands (see *Jacking and vehicle support*). Undo the screws and remove the engine undershield.

2 The oil cooler is fitted to the front of the oil filter housing. Drain the coolant as described in Chapter 1B.

3 Drain the engine oil as described in Chapter 1B, or be prepared for fluid spillage.

12.12a Fit a new seal . . .

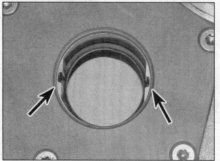

12.12b . . . align the pump gear flats (arrowed) . . .

12.12c . . . with those of the crankshaft (arrowed)

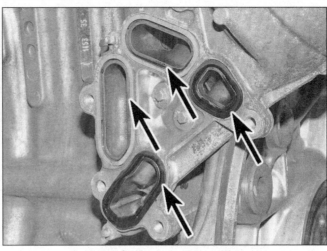

13.4a Undo the oil cooler bolts/stud (arrowed)

13.4b Renew the O-ring seals (arrowed)

4 Undo the 5 bolts/stud and remove the oil cooler. Recover the O-ring seals **(see illustrations)**.

Refitting

5 Fit new O-ring seals into the recesses in the oil filter housing, and refit the cooler. Tighten the bolts securely.

6 Refill or top-up the cooling system and engine oil level as described in Chapter 1B or *Weekly Checks* (as applicable). Start the engine, and check the oil cooler for signs of leakage.

14 Oil seals – renewal

Crankshaft

Right-hand oil seal

1 Remove the crankshaft sprocket and Woodruff key as described in Section 8.

2 Measure and note the fitted depth of the oil seal.

3 Pull the oil seal from the housing using a screwdriver. Alternatively, drill a small hole in the oil seal, and use a self-tapping screw and a pair of pliers to remove it **(see illustration)**.

4 Clean the oil seal housing and the crankshaft sealing surface.

5 The seal has a Teflon lip and must not be oiled or marked. The new seal should be supplied with a protector sleeve, which fits over the end of the crankshaft to prevent any damage to the seal lip. With the sleeve in place, press the seal (open end first) into the pump to the previously-noted depth, using a suitable tube or socket **(see illustrations)**.

6 Where applicable, remove the plastic sleeve from the end of the crankshaft.

7 Refit the timing belt crankshaft sprocket as described in Section 8.

Left-hand oil seal

8 Remove the flywheel, as described in Section 16.

9 Measure and note the fitted depth of the oil seal.

10 Pull the oil seal from the housing using a screwdriver. Alternatively, drill a small hole in the oil seal, and use a self-tapping screw and a pair of pliers to remove it **(see illustration 14.3)**.

11 Clean the oil seal housing and the crank-shaft sealing surface.

12 The seal has a Teflon lip and must not be oiled or marked. The new seal should be supplied with a protector sleeve, which fits over the end of the crankshaft to prevent any damage to the seal lip **(see illustration)**. With the sleeve in place, press the seal (open end first) into the housing to the previously-noted depth, using a suitable tube or socket.

13 Where applicable, remove the plastic sleeve from the end of the crankshaft.

14 Refit the flywheel, as described in Section 16.

Camshaft

15 Remove the camshaft sprocket as described in Section 8. In principle there is no need to remove the timing belt completely, but remember that if the belt has been contaminated with oil, it must be renewed.

16 Pull the oil seal from the housing using a hooked instrument. Alternatively, drill a small hole in the oil seal and use a self-tapping screw and a pair of pliers to remove it **(see illustration)**.

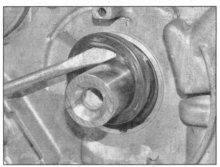

14.3 Take great care not to mark the crankshaft whilst levering out the oil seal

14.5a Slide the seal and protective sleeve over the end of the crankshaft . . .

14.5b . . . and press the seal into place

14.12 Slide the seal and protective sleeve over the left-hand end of the crankshaft

14.16 Drill a hole, insert a self-tapping screw, and pull the seal from place using pliers

17 Clean the oil seal housing and the camshaft sealing surface.

18 The seal has a Teflon lip and must not be oiled or marked. The new seal should be supplied with a protector sleeve. which fits over the end of the camshaft to prevent any damage to the seal lip **(see illustration)**. With the sleeve in place, press the seal (open end first) into the housing, using a suitable tube or socket which bears only of the outer edge of the seal.

19 Refit the camshaft sprocket as described in Section 8.

20 Where necessary, fit a new timing belt with reference to Section 7.

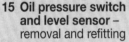

15 Oil pressure switch and level sensor – removal and refitting

Removal

Oil pressure switch

1 The oil pressure switch is located at the front of the cylinder block, adjacent to the oil dipstick guide tube. Note that on some models, access to the switch may be improved if the vehicle is jacked up and supported on axle stands, then undo the screws and remove the engine undershield so that the switch can be reached from underneath (see *Jacking and vehicle support*).

2 Remove the protective sleeve from the wiring plug (where applicable), then disconnect the wiring from the switch.

15.3 The oil pressure switch is located on the front face of the cylinder block (arrowed)

14.18 Fit the protective sleeve and seal over the end of the camshaft

3 Unscrew the switch from the cylinder block, and recover the sealing washer **(see illustration)**. Be prepared for oil spillage, and if the switch is to be left removed from the engine for any length of time, plug the hole in the cylinder block.

Oil level sensor

4 The oil level sensor is located at the rear of the cylinder block. Jack up the front of the vehicle and support it securely on axle stands (see *Jacking and vehicle support*). Undo the screws and remove the engine undershield.

5 Reach up between the driveshaft and the cylinder block and disconnect the sensor wiring plug **(see illustration)**.

6 Using an open-ended spanner, unscrew the sensor and withdraw it from position.

Refitting

Oil pressure switch

7 Examine the sealing washer for any signs of damage or deterioration, and if necessary renew.

8 Refit the switch, complete with washer, and tighten it to the specified torque.

9 Refit the engine undershield, and lower the vehicle to the ground.

Oil level sensor

10 Smear a little silicone sealant on the threads and refit the sensor to the cylinder block, tightening it securely.

11 Reconnect the sensor wiring plug.

12 Refit the engine undershield, and lower the vehicle to the ground.

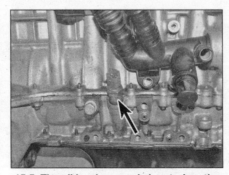

15.5 The oil level sensor is located on the rear face of the cylinder block (arrowed)

16 Flywheel – removal, inspection and refitting

Removal

1 Remove the transmission as described in Chapter 7A, then remove the clutch assembly as described in Chapter 6.

2 Prevent the flywheel from turning by locking the ring gear teeth **(see illustration 5.2)**. Alternatively, bolt a strap between the flywheel and the cylinder block/crankcase. *Do not* attempt to lock the flywheel in position using the crankshaft pulley locking tool described in Section 3. Insert a 12 mm diameter rod or drill bit through the hole in the flywheel cover casting, and into a slot in the flywheel.

3 Make alignment marks between the flywheel and crankshaft to aid refitment. Slacken and remove the flywheel retaining bolts, and remove the flywheel from the end of the crankshaft. Be careful not to drop it; it is heavy. If the flywheel locating dowel (where fitted) is a loose fit in the crankshaft end, remove it and store it with the flywheel for safe-keeping. Discard the flywheel bolts; new ones must be used on refitting.

Inspection

4 Examine the flywheel for scoring of the clutch face, and for wear or chipping of the ring gear teeth. If the clutch face is scored, the flywheel may be surface-ground, but renewal is preferable. Seek the advice of a Citroën dealer or engine reconditioning specialist to see if machining is possible. If the ring gear is worn or damaged, the flywheel must be renewed, as it is not possible to renew the ring gear separately.

Refitting

5 Clean the mating surfaces of the flywheel and crankshaft. Remove any remaining locking compound from the threads of the crankshaft holes, using the correct size of tap, if available.

> **HAYNES HINT** *If a suitable tap is not available, cut two slots along the threads of one of the old flywheel bolts, and use the bolt to remove the locking compound from the threads.*

6 If the new flywheel retaining bolts are not supplied with their threads already pre-coated, apply a suitable thread-locking compound to the threads of each bolt.

7 Ensure that the locating dowel is in position. Offer up the flywheel, locating it on the dowel (where fitted), and fit the new retaining bolts. Where no locating dowel is fitted, align the previously-made marks to ensure the flywheel is refitted in its original position.

8 Lock the flywheel using the method

employed on dismantling, and tighten the retaining bolts to the specified torque (see illustration).

9 Refit the clutch as described in Chapter 6. Remove the flywheel locking tool, and refit the transmission as described in Chapter 7A.

17 Engine/transmission mountings – inspection and renewal

Inspection

1 If improved access is required, chock the rear wheels then jack up the front of the car and support it on axle stands (see *Jacking and vehicle support*). Undo the screws and remove the engine undershield.

2 Check the mounting rubbers to see if they are cracked, hardened or separated from the metal at any point; renew the mounting if any such damage or deterioration is evident.

3 Check that all the mountings' fasteners are securely tightened; use a torque wrench to check if possible.

4 Using a large screwdriver or a crowbar, check for wear in each mounting by carefully levering against it to check for free play. Where this is not possible, enlist the aid of an assistant to move the engine/transmission back-and-forth, or from side-to-side, while you watch the mounting. While some free play is to be expected even from new components, excessive wear should be obvious. If excessive free play is found, check first that the fasteners are correctly secured, then renew any worn components as described below.

Renewal

Right-hand mounting

5 Release all the relevant hoses and wiring from their retaining clips. Place the hoses/wiring clear of the mounting so that the removal procedure is not hindered. Undo the screws and remove the engine undershield.

6 Place a jack beneath the engine, with a block of wood on the jack head. Raise the jack until it is supporting the weight of the engine.

7 Undo the bolts/nut securing the engine mounting to the body and the support bracket (see illustration).

8 If required, undo the bolts/nuts securing the support bracket to the cylinder head/cylinder block.

9 Check all components carefully for signs of wear or damage, and renew as necessary.

10 Where removed, refit the support bracket to the cylinder head, and tighten the bolts securely.

16.8 Flywheel retaining Torx bolts

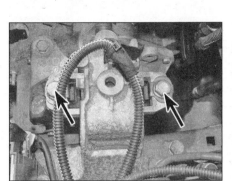
17.15 Left-hand engine/transmission mounting bolts (arrowed)

11 Refit the mount to the body and support bracket, then tighten the bolts to the specified torque.

12 Remove the jack from underneath the engine.

Left-hand mounting

13 Remove the engine management ECM and module box as described in Chapter 4B.

14 Undo the screws and remove the engine undershield, then place a jack beneath the transmission, with a block of wood on the jack head. Raise the jack until it is supporting the weight of the transmission.

15 Slacken and remove the bolts securing the mounting to the support bracket and vehicle body. If required, undo the bolts/nut and remove the support bracket (see illustration).

16 Check all components carefully for signs of wear or damage, and renew as necessary.

17 Refit the mounting, tighten the bolts to the specified torque settings, and remove the jack from underneath the transmission.

18 Refit the module box and ECM as described in Chapter 4B.

Lower engine torque rod

19 If not already done, chock the rear wheels, then jack up the front of the vehicle and support it securely on axle stands (see *Jacking*

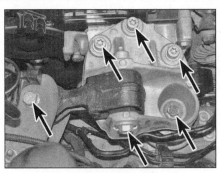
17.7 Undo the right-hand engine mounting bolts/nut (arrowed)

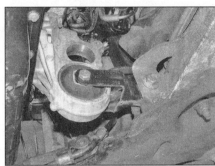
17.20 Lower engine torque rod

and *vehicle support*). Undo the screws and remove the engine undershield.

20 Unscrew and remove the bolt securing the movement limiter link to the driveshaft intermediate bearing housing (see illustration).

21 Remove the bolt securing the link to the subframe. Withdraw the link.

22 To remove the intermediate bearing housing assembly it will first be necessary to remove the right-hand driveshaft as described in Chapter 8.

23 With the driveshaft removed, undo the retaining bolts and remove the bearing housing from the rear of the cylinder block.

24 Check carefully for signs of wear or damage on all components, and renew them where necessary. The rubber bush fitted to the bearing housing is available as a separate item (at the time of writing), and can be pressed out of, and back into place.

25 On reassembly, fit the bearing housing assembly to the rear of the cylinder block, and tighten its retaining bolts securely. Refit the driveshaft as described in Chapter 8.

26 Refit the movement limiter link, and tighten both its bolts to their specified torque settings. Refit the engine undershield.

27 Lower the vehicle to the ground.

Notes

Chapter 2 Part D:
2.0 litre SOHC diesel engine in-car repair procedures

Contents

Degrees of difficulty

Easy, suitable for novice with little experience 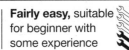	**Fairly easy,** suitable for beginner with some experience 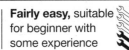	**Fairly difficult,** suitable for competent DIY mechanic 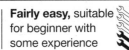
Difficult, suitable for experienced DIY mechanic	**Very difficult,** suitable for expert DIY or professional	

Specifications

General

Designation:	
2.0 litre (1997 cc engine)	DW10TD or DW10ATED
Engine codes*:	
DW10TD.	RHY
DW10ATED.	RHZ
Bore	85.00 mm
Stroke	88.00 mm
Direction of crankshaft rotation	Clockwise (viewed from the right-hand side of vehicle)
No 1 cylinder location.	At the transmission end of block
Maximum power output:	
Code RHY.	66 kW @ 4000 rpm
Code RHZ.	80 kW @ 4000 rpm
Maximum torque output:	
Code RHY.	213 Nm @ 1900 rpm
Code RHZ.	260 Nm @ 1750 rpm
Compression ratio	17.6 : 1

* The engine code is stamped on a plate attached to the front of the cylinder block, next to the oil filter.

Compression pressures (engine hot, at cranking speed)

Normal	20 ± 5 bar
Maximum difference between any two cylinders.	5 bar

Timing belt

Tension setting (see text – Section 7):
Initial setting . . . . 98 ± 2 SEEM units
Final setting . . . . 54 ± 3 SEEM units

Camshaft

Drive . . . . Toothed belt

Lubrication system

Oil pump type . . . . Gear-type, chain-driven off the crankshaft right-hand end
Minimum oil pressure @ 80°C:
1000 rpm . . . . 2.0 bar
4000 rpm . . . . 4.0 bar
Oil pressure warning switch operating pressure . . . . 0.8 bar

Torque wrench settings

	Nm	lbf ft
Big-end bearing cap nuts*:		
Stage 1	20	15
Stage 2	Angle-tighten a further 70°	
Camshaft bearing housing bolts	10	7
Camshaft sprocket hub-to-camshaft bolt	43	32
Camshaft sprocket-to-hub bolts:		
Up to RPO 9128 (approximately March 2002)	20	15
Coolant outlet manifold:		
Stage 1 – studs	25	18
Stage 2 – stud nuts	20	15
Stage 3 – 3 bolts	20	15
Crankshaft pulley bolt:		
Up to RPO 08630 (approximately Jan 2002 – see Section 7):		
Stage 1	40	30
Stage 2	Angle-tighten a further 51°	
From RPO 08631 (approximately Jan 2002 – see Section 7):		
Stage 1	50	37
Stage 2	Angle-tighten a further 62°	
Crankshaft right-hand oil seal housing bolts	14	10
Cylinder head bolts:		
Stage 1	22	16
Stage 2	60	44
Stage 3	Angle-tighten a further 220° ± 5°	
Cylinder head cover bolts	10	7
Engine-to-transmission fixing bolts	45	33
Flywheel/driveplate bolts*	50	37
High-pressure fuel pump sprocket nut	50	37
Left-hand engine/transmission mounting:		
Bracket-to-transmission bolts	45	33
Mounting to bracket	27	20
Rubber mounting centre nut	65	48
Main bearing cap bolts:		
Stage 1	25	18
Stage 2	Angle-tighten a further 60°	
Oil pump mounting bolts	13	10
Piston oil jet spray tube bolt	10	7
Rear engine mounting/torque rod:		
Torque rod to mounting assembly	50	37
Torque rod-to-subframe nut/bolt	50	37
Mounting to engine	45	33
Right-hand engine mounting:		
Connecting link to body	50	37
Connecting link to bracket	50	37
Mounting to bracket	45	33
Bracket to engine bracket	60	44
Engine bracket to engine:		
Upper bolts	21	15
Lower bolts	45	33
Sump bolts	16	12
Sump oil drain plug	34	25
Timing belt idler pulley bolt	25	18
Timing belt tensioner	25	18

* Do not re-use.

1 General information

How to use this Chapter

This Part of Chapter 2 describes the repair procedures that can reasonably be carried out on the engine while it remains in the vehicle. If the engine has been removed from the vehicle and is being dismantled as described in Part F, any preliminary dismantling procedures can be ignored.

Note that, while it may be possible physically to overhaul items such as the piston/connecting rod assemblies while the engine is in the car, such tasks are not usually carried out as separate operations. Usually, several additional procedures are required (not to mention the cleaning of components and oil ways); for this reason, all such tasks are classed as major overhaul procedures, and are described in Part F of this Chapter.

Part F describes the removal of the engine/transmission from the car, and the full overhaul procedures that can then be carried out.

DW series engines

The DW series engine is based on the well-proven XUD series engine which has appeared in many Peugeot and Citroën vehicles. In particular, the cylinder block components are very similar to the XUD, however, the remainder of the engine has been completely redesigned. The engine is of single overhead camshaft 8-valve design. The turbocharged, four-cylinder engine is mounted transversely, with the transmission mounted on the left-hand side.

A toothed timing belt drives the camshaft, high-pressure fuel pump and coolant pump. The camshaft operates the inlet and exhaust valves via rocker arms which are supported at their pivot ends by hydraulic self-adjusting tappets. The camshaft is supported by bearings machined directly in the cylinder head and camshaft bearing housing.

The high-pressure fuel pump supplies fuel to the fuel rail, and subsequently to the electronically-controlled injectors which inject the fuel direct into the combustion chambers. This design differs from the previous type where an injection pump supplies the fuel at high-pressure to each injector. The earlier conventional type injection pump required fine calibration and timing, and these functions are now completed by the high-pressure pump, electronic injectors and engine management ECM.

The crankshaft runs in five main bearings of the usual shell type. Endfloat is controlled by thrustwashers either side of No 2 main bearing.

The pistons are selected to be of matching weight, and incorporate fully-floating gudgeon pins retained by circlips.

The oil pump is chain-driven from the right-hand end of the crankshaft.

Throughout the manual it is often necessary to identify the engines not only by their cubic capacity, but also by their engine code. The engine code, consists of three letters (eg, RHZ). The code is stamped on a plate attached to the front of the cylinder block.

Repair operations precaution

The engine is a complex unit with numerous accessories and ancillary components. The design of the engine compartment is such that every conceivable space has been utilised, and access to virtually all of the engine components is extremely limited. In many cases, ancillary components will have to be removed, or moved to one side, and wiring, pipes and hoses will have to be disconnected or removed from various cable clips and support brackets.

When working on this engine, read through the entire procedure first, look at the car and engine at the same time, and establish whether you have the necessary tools, equipment, skill and patience to proceed. Allow considerable time for any operation, and be prepared for the unexpected. Any major work on these engines is not for the faint-hearted!

Because of the limited access, many of the engine photographs appearing in this Chapter were, by necessity, taken with the engine removed from the vehicle.

 Warning: It is essential to observe strict precautions when working on the fuel system components of the engine, particularly the high-pressure side of the system. Before carrying out any engine operations that entail working on, or near, any part of the fuel system, refer to the special information given in Chapter 4B, Section 2.

Operations with engine in vehicle

a) *Compression pressure – testing.*
b) *Cylinder head cover(s) – removal and refitting.*
c) *Crankshaft pulley – removal and refitting.*
d) *Timing belt covers – removal and refitting.*
e) *Timing belt – removal, refitting and adjustment.*
f) *Timing belt tensioner and sprockets – removal and refitting.*
g) *Camshaft oil seal – renewal.*
h) *Camshaft, rocker arms and hydraulic tappets – removal, inspection and refitting.*
i) *Sump – removal and refitting.*
j) *Oil pump – removal and refitting.*
k) *Crankshaft oil seals – renewal.*
l) *Engine/transmission mountings – inspection and renewal.*
m) *Flywheel/driveplate – removal, inspection and refitting.*

2 Compression and leakdown tests – description and interpretation

Compression test

Note: *A compression tester specifically designed for diesel engines must be used for this test.*

1 When engine performance is down, or if misfiring occurs which cannot be attributed to the fuel system, a compression test can provide diagnostic clues as to the engine's condition. If the test is performed regularly, it can give warning of trouble before any other symptoms become apparent.

2 A compression tester specifically intended for diesel engines must be used, because of the higher pressures involved. The tester is connected to an adapter which screws into the glow plug or injector hole. On these engines, an adapter suitable for use in the glow plug holes will be required, so as not to disturb the fuel system components. It is unlikely to be worthwhile buying such a tester for occasional use, but it may be possible to borrow or hire one – if not, have the test performed by a garage.

3 Unless specific instructions to the contrary are supplied with the tester, observe the following points:

a) *The battery must be in a good state of charge, the air filter must be clean, and the engine should be at normal operating temperature.*
b) *All the glow plugs should be removed as described in Chapter 5A before starting the test.*
c) *The wiring connector on the engine management system ECM (see Chapter 4B) must be disconnected.*

4 The compression pressures measured are not so important as the balance between cylinders. Values are given in the Specifications.

5 The cause of poor compression is less easy to establish on a diesel engine than on a petrol one. The effect of introducing oil into the cylinders ('wet' testing) is not conclusive, because there is a risk that the oil will sit in the swirl chamber or in the recess on the piston crown instead of passing to the rings. However, the following can be used as a rough guide to diagnosis.

6 All cylinders should produce very similar pressures; any difference greater than that specified indicates the existence of a fault. Note that the compression should build-up quickly in a healthy engine; low compression on the first stroke, followed by gradually-increasing pressure on successive strokes, indicates worn piston rings. A low compression reading on the first stroke, which does not build-up during successive strokes, indicates leaking valves or a blown head gasket (a cracked head could also be the cause). Deposits on the undersides of the valve heads can also cause low compression.

3.7a Use a small mirror to observe the camshaft sprocket/
cylinder head timing holes on later engines . . .

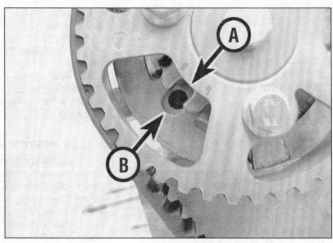

3.7b . . . and early engines

A Timing slot

B Timing hole in cylinder head

7 A low reading from two adjacent cylinders is almost certainly due to the head gasket having blown between them; the presence of coolant in the engine oil will confirm this.

8 If the compression reading is unusually high, the cylinder head surfaces, valves and pistons are probably coated with carbon deposits. If this is the case, the cylinder head should be removed and decarbonised (see Part F).

Leakdown test

9 A leakdown test measures the rate at which compressed air fed into the cylinder is lost. It is an alternative to a compression test, and in many ways it is better, since the escaping air provides easy identification of where pressure loss is occurring (piston rings, valves or head gasket).

10 The equipment needed for leakdown testing is unlikely to be available to the home mechanic. If poor compression is suspected, have the test performed by a suitably-equipped garage.

3 Engine assembly/ valve timing holes – general information and usage

Note: *Do not attempt to rotate the engine whilst the crankshaft and camshaft are locked*

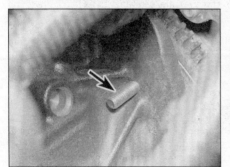

3.8 Crankshaft/flywheel locking pin (arrowed)

in position. If the engine is to be left in this state for a long period of time, it is a good idea to place suitable warning notices inside the vehicle, and in the engine compartment. This will reduce the possibility of the engine being accidentally cranked on the starter motor, which is likely to cause damage with the locking pins in place.

1 Timing holes or slots are located only in the flywheel/driveplate and camshaft sprocket hub. The holes/slots are used to align the crankshaft and camshaft at the TDC position for Nos 1 and 4. This will ensure that the valve timing is maintained during operations that require removal and refitting of the timing belt. When the holes/slots are aligned with their corresponding holes in the cylinder block and cylinder head, suitable diameter bolts/pins can be inserted to lock the crankshaft and camshaft in position, preventing rotation. Note that with the timing holes aligned, No 4 piston is at TDC on its compression stroke.

2 Note that the HDi type fuel system used on these engines does not have a conventional diesel injection pump, but instead uses a high-pressure fuel pump that does not have to be timed. The alignment of the fuel pump sprocket (and hence the fuel pump itself) with respect to crankshaft and camshaft position, is therefore irrelevant.

3.9 Insert an 8.0 mm bolt through the camshaft sprocket/hub into the cylinder head hole

3 To align the engine assembly/valve timing holes, proceed as follows.

4 Chock the rear wheels then jack up the front of the vehicle and support it on axle stands (see *Jacking and vehicle support*). Remove the right-hand front roadwheel.

5 To gain access to the crankshaft pulley, to enable the engine to be turned, the wheel arch plastic liner must be removed. The liner is secured by various plastic expanding rivets, plastic nuts and quick release fasteners. To remove the rivets, push in the centre pins a little, then prise the clips from place. Remove the liner from under the front wing. Where necessary, unclip the coolant hoses from under the wing to improve access further. The crankshaft can then be turned using a suitable socket and extension bar fitted to the pulley bolt.

6 Remove the upper and lower timing belt covers as described in Section 6.

7 Turn the crankshaft until the timing hole in the camshaft sprocket/hub is aligned with the corresponding hole in the cylinder head. Note that the crankshaft must always be turned in a clockwise direction (viewed from the right-hand side of vehicle). Use a small mirror so that the position of the sprocket/hub timing slot can be observed **(see illustrations)**. When the slot is aligned with the corresponding hole in the cylinder head, the camshaft is positioned correctly. On early vehicles (pre-March 2002) with a separate camshaft sprocket and hub, make sure that the centre part of the slot is aligned with the hole in the cylinder head, as it is possible to incorrectly align the area to each side of the slot.

8 Insert an 8 mm diameter bolt, rod or drill through the hole in the left-hand flange of the cylinder block by the starter motor; if necessary, carefully turn the crankshaft either way until the rod enters the timing hole in the flywheel/driveplate **(see illustration)**.

9 Insert an 8 mm bolt, or rod, approximately 50 mm long through the hole in the camshaft sprocket hub and into engagement with the cylinder head **(see illustration)**.

10 The crankshaft and camshaft are now locked in position, preventing unnecessary rotation.

4 Cylinder head cover – removal and refitting

Removal

1 Remove the plastic cover from the top of the engine. The cover is retained by four fasteners – rotate them 90° anti-clockwise and lift off the cover.
2 Remove the timing belt upper cover, as described in Section 6.
3 As applicable, slacken or release the clips securing the crankcase ventilation hoses to the cylinder cover and disconnect the hoses.
4 Undo the bolts and move the engine cover and cable guide support bracket clear of the right-hand end of the cylinder head cover.
5 Disconnect the camshaft position sensor wiring connector.
6 Release the wiring harness from the clip on the cylinder head cover and move the harness to one side.
7 Progressively unscrew the bolts securing the cylinder head cover to the camshaft carrier and collect the washers.
8 Carefully lift off the cover taking care not to damage the camshaft position sensor as the cover is removed. Recover the seal from the cover.

Refitting

9 Refitting is a reversal of removal, bearing in mind the following points:
 a) Examine the cover seal(s) for signs of damage and deterioration, and renew if necessary.
 b) Tighten the cylinder head cover bolts to the specified torque.
 c) Before refitting the timing belt upper cover, adjust the camshaft position sensor air gap as described in Chapter 4B, Section 13.

5 Crankshaft pulley – removal and refitting

Removal

1 Remove the auxiliary drivebelt as described in Chapter 5A. Turn the tensioner anti-clockwise and insert a pin or drill to hold it away from the drivebelt (see illustration).
2 To prevent crankshaft turning whilst the pulley retaining bolt is being slackened the flywheel/driveplate ring gear can be locked using a suitable tool made from steel angle (see illustration). Remove the cover plate from the base of the transmission bellhousing and bolt the tool to the bellhousing flange so it engages with the ring gear teeth. Do not attempt to lock the pulley by inserting a

5.1 Rotate the tensioner anti-clockwise and insert a pin or drill bit to hold it away from the drivebelt

bolt/drill through the timing hole. If the timing hole bolt/drill is in position from a previous operation, temporarily remove it prior to slackening the pulley bolt, then refit it once the bolt has been slackened. **Note:** On later engines (see Section 7), it is essential that the crankshaft and camshaft timing pins are in place as described in Section 3. This is because on these engines, the crankshaft sprocket has a wider key way, to allow it to rotate a little independently of the crankshaft. Failure to lock the crankshaft and camshaft could result in the timing being lost.
3 Using a suitable socket and extension bar, unscrew the retaining bolt, remove the washer, then slide the pulley off the end of the crankshaft (see illustration). If the pulley is tight fit, it can be drawn off the crankshaft using a suitable puller. If a puller is being used, refit the pulley retaining bolt without the washer, to avoid damaging the crankshaft as the puller is tightened.
4 If the pulley locating key is a loose fit, remove it and store it with the pulley for safe-keeping.

Refitting

5 Ensure that the key is correctly located in its crankshaft groove, then refit the pulley to the end of the crankshaft.
6 Thoroughly clean the threads of the pulley retaining bolt, then apply a coat of locking compound to the bolt threads. Citroën recommend the use of Loctite (available from your Citroën dealer); in the absence of this, any good-quality locking compound may be used.

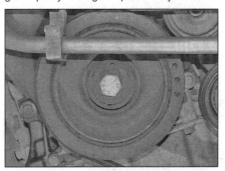

5.3 Undo the crankshaft pulley retaining bolt

5.2 Use a fabricated tool similar to this to lock the flywheel ring gear and prevent crankshaft rotation

7 Refit the crankshaft pulley retaining bolt and washer (see illustration). Tighten the bolt to the specified torque, then through the specified angle, preventing the crankshaft from turning using the method employed on removal.
8 Refit and tension the auxiliary drivebelt as described in Chapter 5A.

6 Timing belt covers – removal and refitting

> ⚠ Warning: Refer to the pre-cautionary information contained in Section 1 before proceeding.

Removal

Upper cover

1 Remove the plastic covers from the top of the engine, then undo the screws and remove the engine undershield. The cover over the engine is release by rotating the four fasteners anti-clockwise whist gently pulling up the cover.
2 Position a trolley jack under the engine, and using a piece of wood on the jack head, support the weight of the engine.
3 Undo the bolts and remove the right-hand engine mounting and support bracket – see Section 17.
4 At the connections above the fuel pump, disconnect the fuel supply and return hose quick-release fittings using a small screwdriver to press down and release the locking clip

5.7 Refit the crankshaft pulley bolt and washer

6.4 Depress the release buttons and disconnect the fuel hoses (arrowed)

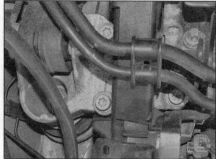

6.5 Release the hoses from the clip on the timing cover

(see illustration). Cover the open unions to prevent dirt entry, using small plastic bags, or fingers cut from clean rubber gloves.

5 Release the two hoses from the retaining clips on the upper timing belt cover and move them to one side **(see illustration)**.

6 Undo the bolt securing the upper cover to the cylinder head cover **(see illustration)**.

7 Undo the upper bolt on the edge of the cover nearest to the engine compartment bulkhead.

8 Undo the lower bolt on the bulkhead side of the cover, at the join between the upper and lower covers. Note that this bolt also retains the coolant pump. To avoid coolant leakage after the upper cover is removed, refit the bolt fitted with a 17.0 mm spacer, and tighten it securely.

9 Undo the remaining bolt in the centre of the cover.

10 Disengage the upper cover from the intermediate cover and manipulate the upper cover from its location.

Intermediate cover

11 Remove the upper cover as described previously.

12 Undo the upper bolt on the top edge of the intermediate cover.

13 Undo the two remaining bolts at the join between the intermediate cover and lower cover, then manipulate the intermediate cover from its location.

Lower cover

14 Remove the upper and intermediate covers as described previously.

15 Remove the crankshaft pulley as described in Section 5.

16 Undo the two remaining bolts on the edge of the cover, one on either side of the crankshaft pulley location.

17 Lift the cover off the front of the engine.

Refitting

18 Refitting of all the covers is a reversal of the relevant removal procedure, ensuring that each cover section is correctly located, and that the cover retaining bolts are securely tightened. Ensure that all disturbed hoses are reconnected and retained by their relevant clips.

7 Timing belt – removal, inspection, refitting and tensioning

Note: *Citroën specify the use of an electronic belt tension checking tool (SEEM CTG 105.5M) to correctly set the timing belt tension. The following procedure assumes that this equipment (or suitable alternative equipment calibrated to display belt tension in SEEM units) is available. Accurate tensioning of the timing belt is essential, and if the electronic equipment is not available, it is recommended that the work is entrusted to a Citroën dealer or suitably-equipped garage.*

General

1 The timing belt drives the camshaft, high-pressure fuel pump, and coolant pump from a toothed sprocket on the end of the crankshaft. If the belt breaks or slips in service, the pistons are likely to hit the valve heads, resulting in expensive damage.

2 The timing belt should be renewed at the specified intervals, or earlier if it is contaminated with oil, or at all noisy in operation (a 'scraping' noise due to uneven wear).

3 If the timing belt is being removed, it is a wise precaution to check the condition of the coolant pump at the same time (check for signs of coolant leakage). This may avoid the need to remove the timing belt again at a later stage, should the coolant pump fail.

Removal

4 Chock the rear wheels then jack up the front of the vehicle and support it on axle stands (see *Jacking and vehicle support*). Remove the front right-hand roadwheel, wheel arch liner (to expose the crankshaft pulley), and the engine undershield. The wheel arch liner is secured by various plastic expanding rivets, plastic nuts and quick release fasteners. Push the centre pins in a little then prise the rivet from place. The engine undershield is retained by several screw fasteners.

5 Remove the auxiliary drivebelt as described in Chapter 5A.

6 Unbolt the closure plate from the bottom of the clutch housing.

7 Using a suitable tool, lock the flywheel/driveplate, then loosen the crankshaft pulley bolt. Citroën technicians use a tool which engages the teeth of the starter ring gear and is bolted to the clutch bellhousing (188.F). A similar tool may be made out of a length of angle-iron, bent to engage the teeth, or

6.6 Timing belt cover retaining bolt locations (arrowed)

1 *Upper cover*   2 *Intermediate cover*   3 *Lower cover*

H34018

A square section tool to fit the timing belt tensioner pulley can be made from a length of standard 8.0 mm door handle rod (A), obtained from a DIY shop, and then cut to size. Once the rod has been fitted to the tensioner, then timing belt can be tensioned by turning the rod with an 8.0 mm spanner (B).

alternatively an assistant may restrain the starter ring gear with a wide-blade screwdriver.

8 Remove the crankshaft pulley as described in Section 5.

9 Unbolt the rear engine mounting connecting link/torque arm – see Section 17.

10 An 8.0 mm diameter flywheel/driveplate locking pin is now required, and may be obtained from a Citroën dealer (part No 0188.X) or car accessory shop. Alternatively, use an 8.0 mm diameter bolt or drill bit.

11 Temporarily refit the crankshaft pulley bolt, then turn the engine until the TDC hole in the flywheel/driveplate is aligned with the hole in the front engine flange (next to the transmission bellhousing – see Section 3). Insert the locking pin to lock the engine.

12 Remove the upper, intermediate and lower timing belt covers as described in the previous Section.

13 As a precaution against damage to the radiator, place a card or piece of hardboard over it on the engine side.

14 Insert a suitable drill or metal dowel through the TDC hole in the camshaft sprocket/hub, and into the cylinder head (see Section 3).

15 Loosen the bolt on the tensioner roller, and turn the tensioner clockwise to release

7.19 Slacken the 3 camshaft sprocket-to-hub retaining bolts – early engines only

the tension on the timing belt. If available, use an 8.0 mm square drive extension in the hole provided to turn the tensioner bracket against the spring tension **(see Tool Tip)**. Retighten the bolt sufficiently to hold the tensioner in its released position; do not fully tighten the bolt in this position.

16 Mark the timing belt with an arrow to indicate its running direction, if it is to be re-used. Remove the belt from the sprockets.

Inspection

17 Renew the belt as a matter of course, regardless of its apparent condition. The cost of a new belt is nothing compared with the cost of repairs should the belt break in service. If signs of oil contamination are found, trace the source of the oil leak and rectify it. Wash down the engine timing belt area and all related components, to remove all traces of oil. Check that the tensioner and idler pulleys rotate freely without any sign of roughness, and also check that the coolant pump pulley rotates freely. If necessary, renew these items. **Note:** *Citroën recommend that the tensioner and idler pulleys should not be re-used, regardless of apparent condition.*

Refitting and tensioning

18 Commence refitting by ensuring that the crankshaft and camshaft timing pins are still in position correctly.

Up to RPO 9127 (approx March 2002)

19 Early models are identified by three bolts securing the camshaft sprocket to the hub. Loosen the three bolts securing the camshaft

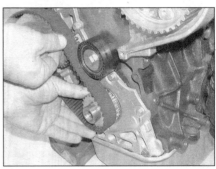

7.21a Retain the belt on the crankshaft sprocket and feed it around the idler roller . . .

sprocket to the camshaft, so that the sprocket can be turned on its hub **(see illustration)**. To do this, either use a tool engaged with the holes in the sprocket, or alternatively, hold the sprocket with an old timing belt.

20 Finger-tighten the sprocket bolts, then slacken each bolt by one sixth of a turn. Turn the sprocket clockwise to the end of the slots.

21 Locate the timing belt on the crankshaft sprocket splines, then, keeping it taut, locate it around the idler pulley and onto the high-pressure pump sprocket **(see illustrations)**. Peugeot technicians use a plastic clip to retain the belt on the crankshaft pulley; if necessary, use a plastic cable tie to hold it.

22 Locate the belt onto the camshaft sprocket splines. If the teeth do not align correctly, turn the camshaft sprocket slightly anti-clockwise until the belt engages. **Note:** *Do not turn the pulley anti-clockwise more than one tooth space.*

23 Continue to locate the belt onto the tensioner pulley and coolant pump splines, then loosen the bolt and turn the tensioner *anti-clockwise* to tension the belt moderately. Pretighten the bolt to 1.0 Nm, then remove the holding clip or cable tie.

24 A timing belt tension setting tool is now required to apply the correct tension. A tool which checks SEEM units is necessary, and should be fitted to the belt run between the camshaft sprocket and high-pressure pump sprocket.

25 Loosen the bolt, then turn the tensioner *anti-clockwise* until 98.0 ± 2.0 SEEM units

7.21c . . . camshaft sprocket . . .

7.21d . . . coolant pump and tensioner pulley

7.21b . . . high-pressure fuel pump sprocket . . .

7.25a Pivot the tensioner pulley anti-clockwise, then tighten the retaining bolt . . .

7.25b . . . when the specified tension value is shown on the measuring equipment

is read on the tool **(see illustrations)**. At this point, tighten the tensioner bolt to the specified torque.

26 Temporarily remove one of the three bolts securing the sprocket to the camshaft, and check that the bolts are not at the anti-clockwise limit of their slots. If they are, repeat the refitting procedure.

27 Tighten the camshaft sprocket bolts to the specified torque.

28 Remove the crankshaft and camshaft TDC setting pins. Also remove the tensioning tool.

29 Turn the engine clockwise 8 times. Do not turn the engine anti-clockwise during this operation.

30 Refit the crankshaft and camshaft TDC setting pins.

31 Loosen the camshaft sprocket bolts again, then finger-tighten them, and loosen each by one sixth of a turn.

32 Refit the tensioning tool midway between the camshaft and high-pressure pump sprocket.

33 Loosen the tensioner bolt, then turn the tensioner anti-clockwise until the tool reads 54.0 ± 2.0 SEEM units. With the tensioner held in this position, tighten the bolt to the specified torque. It is important to apply the correct tension to the timing belt, otherwise the belt may be noisy in operation, or worse still, may break.

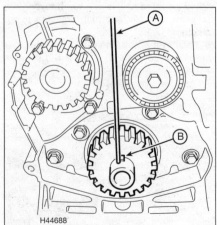

7.43 Insert a 2.0 mm rod (A) on the left-hand side of the Woodruff key (B)

34 Tighten the camshaft sprocket bolts to the specified torque.

35 Remove the tensioning tool to release its internal forces, then refit it and check the tension of the belt is between 51.0 and 57.0 SEEM units. If necessary, repeat the tensioning procedure.

36 Remove the tensioning tool and TDC setting pins.

37 Turn the engine clockwise 2 times. Do not turn the engine anti-clockwise during this operation.

38 Refit the crankshaft and camshaft TDC setting/locking pins.

39 Visually check that the offset between the camshaft hub hole and the corresponding setting hole does not exceed 1.0 mm.

40 Remove the TDC setting/locking pins.

41 The remainder of refitting is a reversal of removal. Tighten all fasteners to the specifies torque where given.

From RPO 9128 (approx March 2002)

42 Later engines are identified by the camshaft sprocket being retained by one central bolt.

43 Set the crankshaft sprocket by inserting a 2 mm diameter rod on the left-hand side of the Woodruff key **(see illustration)**. Check the flywheel and camshaft timing pins are still in place.

44 Locate the timing belt on the camshaft sprocket splines, then, keeping it taut, locate it around the high-pressure pump pulley, idler pulley, crankshaft sprocket, coolant pump sprocket and tensioner pulley. Citroën technicians use a plastic clip to retain the belt on the camshaft sprocket; if necessary, use a plastic cable tie to hold it.

45 Loosen the bolt and turn the tensioner *anti-clockwise* to tension the belt moderately. Pretighten the bolt to 1.0 Nm, then remove the holding clip or cable tie. Remove the 2 mm diameter rod from alongside the crankshaft sprocket key.

46 A timing belt tension setting tool is now required to apply the correct tension. A tool which checks SEEM units is necessary, and should be fitted to the belt run between the camshaft sprocket and high-pressure pump sprocket.

47 Loosen the bolt, then turn the tensioner *anti-*

clockwise until 98.0 ± 2.0 SEEM units is read on the tool **(see illustrations 7.25a and 7.25b)**. At this point, tighten the tensioner bolt to the specified torque.

48 Immobilise the flywheel as described in paragraph 7, then refit the auxiliary belt pulley, and tighten its retaining bolt to 70 Nm (52 lbf ft).

49 Remove the crankshaft and camshaft timing pins, and the flywheel locking tool.

50 Turn the engine clockwise 8 times. Do not turn the engine anti-clockwise during this operation.

51 Refit the crankshaft and camshaft TDC setting pins, then lock the flywheel as described in Paragraph 7.

52 Undo the bolt and remove the auxiliary drivebelt pulley.

53 Refit the tensioning tool midway between the camshaft and high-pressure pump sprocket.

54 Loosen the tensioner bolt, then turn the tensioner anti-clockwise until the tool reads 54.0 ± 2.0 SEEM units. With the tensioner held in this position, tighten the bolt to the specified torque. It is important to apply the correct tension to the timing belt, otherwise the belt may be noisy in operation, or worse still, may break.

55 Remove the tensioning tool to release its internal forces, then refit it and check the tension of the belt is between 51.0 and 57.0 SEEM units. If necessary, repeat the tensioning procedure.

56 Remove the crankshaft and camshaft timing pins, and the flywheel locking tool.

57 The remainder of refitting is a reversal of removal, noting the following points.

a) *Ensure the timing covers engage correctly with each other.*

b) *When refitting the auxiliary drivebelt pulley, apply a few drops of thread-locking compound to the pulley bolt.*

c) *Tighten all fasteners to the specified torque where given.*

8 Timing belt sprockets and tensioner – removal and refitting

Camshaft sprocket

Removal

1 Remove the timing belt as described in Section 7.

2 Remove the locking tool from the camshaft sprocket/hub. Slacken the sprocket hub retaining bolt, and the three sprocket-to-hub retaining bolts (where applicable). To prevent the camshaft rotating as the bolt(s) s are slackened, a sprocket holding tool will be required. In the absence of the special Citroën tool, an acceptable substitute can be fabricated at home **(see Tool Tip 1)**. *Do not attempt to use the engine assembly/valve timing locking tool to prevent the sprocket from rotating whilst the bolt is slackened.*

3 Remove the sprocket hub retaining bolt and

Tool Tip 1: *A sprocket holding tool can be made from 2 lengths of steel strip bolted together to form a forked end. Bend the end of the strip through 90° to form the fork 'prongs'.*

8.13a Slide the sprocket from the end of the crankshaft . . .

8.13b . . . and collect the Woodruff key

washer (where fitted), and slide the sprocket and hub off the end of the camshaft. If the Woodruff key is a loose fit in the camshaft, remove it for safe-keeping. Examine the camshaft oil seal for signs of oil leakage and, if necessary, renew it as described in Section 14.

4 If necessary on early engines, the sprocket can be separated from the hub after removing the three retaining bolts.

5 Clean the camshaft sprocket thoroughly, and renew it if there are any signs of wear, damage or cracks.

Refitting

6 If removed on early engines, refit the sprocket to the hub and secure with the three retaining bolts, tightened finger-tight only at this stage.

7 Where applicable, refit the Woodruff key to the end of the camshaft, then refit the camshaft sprocket and hub.

8 Refit the sprocket hub retaining bolt and washer. Tighten the bolt to the specified torque, preventing the camshaft from turning as during removal.

9 Align the engine assembly/valve timing slot in the camshaft sprocket hub with the hole in the cylinder head and refit the timing pin to lock the camshaft in position.

10 Fit the timing belt around the pump sprocket and camshaft sprocket, and tension the timing belt as described in Section 7.

Crankshaft sprocket

Removal

11 Remove the timing belt as described in Section 7.

12 Check that the engine assembly/valve timing holes are still aligned as described in Section 3, and the camshaft sprocket/hub and flywheel/driveplate are locked in position.

13 Slide the sprocket off the end of the crankshaft and collect the Woodruff key **(see illustrations)**.

14 Examine the crankshaft oil seal for signs of oil leakage and, if necessary, renew it as described in Section 14.

15 Clean the crankshaft sprocket thoroughly,

and renew it if there are any signs of wear, damage or cracks. Recover the crankshaft locating key.

Refitting

16 Refit the key to the end of the crankshaft, then refit the crankshaft sprocket (with the flange nearest the cylinder block).

17 Fit the timing belt around the crankshaft sprocket, and tension the timing belt as described in Section 7.

Fuel pump sprocket

Removal

18 Remove the timing belt as described in Section 7.

19 Using a suitable socket, undo the pump sprocket retaining nut. The sprocket can be held stationary by using a suitable forked tool engaged with the holes in the sprocket **(see Tool Tip 1)**.

20 The pump sprocket is a taper fit on the pump shaft and it will be necessary to make up another tool to release it from the taper **(see Tool Tip 2)**.

21 Partially unscrew the sprocket retaining nut, fit the home-made tool, and secure it to the sprocket with two suitable bolts. Prevent the sprocket from rotating as before, and unscrew the sprocket retaining nut **(see illustration)**. The nut will bear against the tool

Tool Tip 2: *Make a sprocket releasing tool from a short strip of steel. Drill two holes in the strip to correspond with the two holes in the sprocket. Drill a third hole just large enough to accept the slats of the sprocket retaining nut.*

as it is undone, forcing the sprocket off the shaft taper. Once the taper is released, remove the tool, unscrew the nut fully, and remove the sprocket from the pump shaft.

22 Clean the sprocket thoroughly, and renew it if there are any signs of wear, damage or cracks.

Refitting

23 Refit the pump sprocket and retaining nut, and tighten the nut to the specified torque. Prevent the sprocket rotating as the nut is tightened using the sprocket holding tool.

24 Fit the timing belt around the pump sprocket, and tension the timing belt as described in Section 7.

Coolant pump sprocket

25 The coolant pump sprocket is integral with the pump, and cannot be removed. Coolant pump removal is described in Chapter 3.

Tensioner pulley

Removal

26 Remove the timing belt as described in Section 7.

27 Remove the tensioner pulley retaining bolt, and slide the pulley off its mounting stud.

28 Clean the tensioner pulley, but do not use any strong solvent which may enter the pulley bearings. Check that the pulley rotates freely, with no sign of stiffness or free play. Renew the pulley if there is any doubt about its condition, or if there are any obvious signs of wear or damage.

29 Examine the pulley mounting stud for signs of damage and if necessary, renew it.

8.21 Use the home-made tools to remove the fuel pump sprocket

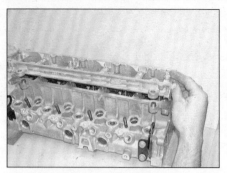

9.9 Remove the camshaft bearing housing from the cylinder head . . .

Refitting

30 Refit the tensioner pulley to its mounting stud, and fit the retaining bolt.

31 Refit the timing belt as described in Section 7.

Idler pulley

Removal

32 Remove the timing belt as described in Section 7.

33 Undo the retaining bolt/nut and withdraw the idler pulley from the engine.

34 Clean the idler pulley, but do not use any strong solvent which may enter the bearings. Check that the pulley rotates freely, with no sign of stiffness or free play. Renew the idler pulley if there is any doubt about its condition, or if there are any obvious signs of wear or damage.

Refitting

35 Locate the idler pulley on the engine, and fit the retaining bolt/nut. Tighten the bolt/nut to the specified torque.

36 Refit the timing belt as described in Section 7.

---

9 **Camshaft, rocker arms and hydraulic tappets** – removal, inspection and refitting

---

Removal

1 Remove the cylinder head cover as described in Section 4.

2 Remove the camshaft sprocket as described in Section 8.

9.13a . . . followed by the hydraulic tappets . . .

3 Slacken the retaining clamps and disconnect the air inlet hose from the left-hand end of the cylinder head. On the DW10ATED engine, remove the intercooler air duct from the left-hand end of the cylinder head.

4 Remove the air cleaner assembly as described in Chapter 4B.

5 Refit the right-hand engine mounting, but only tighten the bolts moderately; this will keep the engine supported during the camshaft removal.

6 Disconnect the vacuum pipe from the brake vacuum pump on the left-hand end of the cylinder head.

7 Remove the vacuum pump from the cylinder head with reference to Chapter 9.

8 Working in a spiral pattern from the outside-in, progressively loosen the camshaft bearing cap housing bolts until they can be removed.

9 Withdraw the bearing cap housing from the cylinder head. The housing is likely to be initially tight to release as it is located by two dowels on the forward facing side of the cylinder head. If necessary, very carefully prise up the housing using a screwdriver inserted in the slotted lug adjacent to each dowel location. Once the bearing housing is free, lift it squarely from the cylinder head **(see illustration)**. The camshaft will rise up slightly under the pressure of the valve springs – be careful it doesn't tilt and jam in the cylinder head or bearing housing section.

10 Carefully lift the camshaft from its location and remove the oil seal **(see illustration)**. Discard the seal, a new one should be used on refitting.

11 Obtain eight small, clean plastic containers,

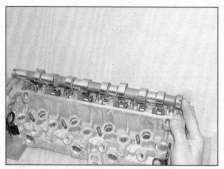

9.10 . . . then lift out the camshaft

9.13b . . . and place of the components in their respective positions in a box

9.12 Lift out the rocker arms . . .

and number them 1 to 8; alternatively, divide a larger container into eight compartments.

12 Lift out each rocker arm and release it from the spring clip on the tappet. Place the rocker arms in their respective positions in the box or containers **(see illustration)**.

13 A compartmentalised container filled with engine oil is now required to retain the hydraulic tappets while they are removed from the cylinder head. Withdraw each hydraulic follower and place it in the container, keeping them each identified for correct refitting **(see illustrations)**. The tappets must be totally submerged in the oil to prevent air entering them.

Inspection

14 Inspect the cam lobes and the camshaft bearing journals for scoring or other visible evidence of wear. Once the surface hardening of the cam lobes has been eroded, wear will occur at an accelerated rate. **Note:** *If these symptoms are visible on the tips of the camshaft lobes, check the corresponding rocker arm, as it will probably be worn as well.*

15 Examine the condition of the bearing surfaces in the cylinder head and camshaft bearing housing. If wear is evident, the cylinder head and bearing housing will both have to be renewed, as they are a matched assembly.

16 Inspect the rocker arms and tappets for scuffing, cracking or other damage and renew any components as necessary. Also check the condition of the tappet bores in the cylinder head. As with the camshafts, any wear in this area will necessitate cylinder head renewal.

Refitting

17 Thoroughly clean the sealant from the mating surfaces of the cylinder head and camshaft bearing housing. Use a suitable liquid gasket dissolving agent (available from Citroën dealers) together with a soft putty knife; do not use a metal scraper or the faces will be damaged. As there is no conventional gasket used, the cleanliness of the mating faces is of the utmost importance.

18 Clean off any oil, dirt or grease from both components and dry with a clean lint-free cloth. Ensure that all the oilways are completely clean.

19 To prevent any possibility of the valves contacting the pistons as the camshaft is

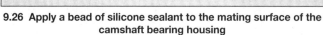

9.26 Apply a bead of silicone sealant to the mating surface of the camshaft bearing housing

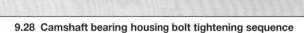

9.28 Camshaft bearing housing bolt tightening sequence

refitted, remove the locking pin/drill from the flywheel/driveplate and turn the crankshaft a quarter turn in the *opposite* direction to normal rotation (ie, anti-clockwise), to position all the pistons at mid-stroke.

20 Liberally lubricate the hydraulic tappet bores in the cylinder head with clean engine oil.

21 Insert the hydraulic tappets into their original bores in the cylinder head unless they have been renewed.

22 Lubricate the rocker arms and place them over their respective tappets and valve stems. Ensure that the ends of the rocker arms engage with the spring clips on the tappets.

23 Lubricate the camshaft bearing journals in the cylinder head sparingly with oil, taking care not to allow the oil to spill over onto the camshaft bearing housing contact areas.

24 Lay the camshaft in the cylinder head. On early engines position the camshaft so that the engine assembly/valve timing slot in the sprocket hub is approximately aligned with the timing hole in the cylinder head.

25 Ensure that the mating faces of the cylinder head and camshaft bearing housing are clean and free of any oil or grease.

26 Sparingly apply a bead of silicone sealant to the mating face of the camshaft bearing housing, taking care not to allow the product to contaminate the camshaft bearing journal areas **(see illustration)**.

27 Locate the bearing housing over the camshaft and into position on the cylinder head.

28 Insert all the bearing housing retaining bolts and *progressively* tighten them to the specified torque, in sequence **(see illustration)**.

29 Fit a new camshaft oil seal as described in Section 14.

30 Refit the camshaft hub and/or sprocket as described in Section 8.

31 Rotate the crankshaft clockwise until the timing rod can be re-inserted through the hole in the block and into the flywheel/driveplate (see Section 3).

32 Refit the timing belt as described in Section 7.

33 The remainder of refitting is a reversal of removal.

10 Cylinder head – removal and refitting

Note: *This is an involved procedure, and it is suggested that the Section is read thoroughly before starting work. To aid refitting, make notes on the locations of all relevant brackets and the routing of hoses and cables before removal.*

Removal

1 Chock the rear wheels then jack up the front of the vehicle and support it on axle stands (see *Jacking and vehicle support*). Remove the front right-hand roadwheel, the engine undershield, and the front wheel arch liner. The undershield is secured by several screws, and the wheel arch liner is secured by several plastic expanding rivets. Push the centre pins in a little, then prise the rivet from place.

2 Remove the battery (see Chapter 5A).

3 Drain the cooling system as described in Chapter 1B. For improved general access, remove the bonnet as described in Chapter 11.

4 Remove the air cleaner assembly, airflow meter and inlet air ducts, fuel injectors, common fuel rail, fuel filter/bracket, and turbocharger as described in Chapter 4B.

5 Remove the EGR valve with reference to Chapter 4C.

6 Remove the timing belt as described in Section 7.

7 Temporarily refit the right-hand engine mounting to support the engine whilst the cylinder head is removed.

8 Note their fitted positions and routing, then disconnect all coolant and vacuum hoses from the cylinder head.

9 Unscrew the nuts on the two studs securing the coolant outlet manifold to the left-hand end of the cylinder head, then unscrew and remove the studs. Use a stud extractor or alternatively tighten two nuts together on the stud before unscrewing it. Note the location of brackets on the studs for correct refitting **(see illustrations)**.

10 Without disconnecting the hoses, unscrew the mounting bolts and move the coolant outlet manifold away from the left-hand end of the cylinder head **(see illustrations)**. If necessary, tie it to one side. Recover the seal.

Note: *At the time of writing, the coolant outlet manifold seal was not available separately. If damaged, the complete outlet manifold must be replaced. Check with a Citroën dealer.*

11 Disconnect the wiring from the camshaft

10.9a Unscrew the nuts . . .

10.9b . . . then remove the studs from the coolant outlet manifold

10.10a Unscrew the bolts . . .

10.10b . . . and move the coolant outlet manifold away from the cylinder head

10.11 Remove the camshaft position sensor

position sensor then undo the screw and remove the sensor (see illustration). Check that all relevant wiring is disconnected from the sensors on the cylinder head, then move the wiring harness to one side.

12 Remove the cylinder head cover as described in Section 4.

13 Progressively slacken the cylinder head bolts, in the reverse order to that shown for tightening (see illustration 10.35). A Torx socket will be required for this.

14 When all the bolts are loose, unscrew them fully and remove them from the cylinder head.

15 Release the cylinder head from the cylinder block and location dowels by rocking it. The Citroën tool for doing this consists simply of two metal rods with 90-degree angled ends (see illustration). Do not prise between the mating faces of the cylinder head and block, as this may damage the gasket faces.

16 Lift the cylinder head from the block, and recover the gasket.

17 If necessary, remove the manifolds (if not already done so) with reference to Chapter 4B.

Preparation for refitting

18 The mating faces of the cylinder head and cylinder block must be perfectly clean before refitting the head. Citroën recommend the use of a scouring agent for this purpose, but acceptable results can be achieved by using a hard plastic or wood scraper to remove all traces of gasket and carbon. The same method

can be used to clean the piston crowns. Take particular care to avoid scoring or gouging the cylinder head/cylinder block mating surfaces during the cleaning operations, as aluminium alloy is easily damaged. Make sure that the carbon is not allowed to enter the oil and water passages – this is particularly important for the lubrication system, as carbon could block the oil supply to the engine's components. Using adhesive tape and paper, seal the water, oil and bolt holes in the cylinder block. To prevent carbon entering the gap between the pistons and bores, smear a little grease in the gap. After cleaning each piston, use a small brush to remove all traces of grease and carbon from the gap, then wipe away the remainder with a clean rag.

19 Check the mating surfaces of the cylinder block and the cylinder head for nicks, deep scratches and other damage. If slight, they may be removed carefully with a file, but if excessive, machining may be the only alternative to renewal. If warpage of the cylinder head gasket surface is suspected, use a straight-edge to check it for distortion. Refer to Part F of this Chapter if necessary.

20 Thoroughly clean the threads of the cylinder head bolt holes in the cylinder block. Ensure that the bolts run freely in their threads, and that all traces of oil and water are removed from each bolt hole.

Gasket selection

21 Remove the crankshaft timing pin, then turn the crankshaft until pistons 1 and 4 are at TDC (Top Dead Centre). Position a dial test indicator (dial gauge) on the cylinder block adjacent

to the rear of No 1 piston, and zero it on the block face. Transfer the probe to the crown of No 1 piston (10.0 mm in from the rear edge), then slowly turn the crankshaft back-and-forth past TDC, noting the highest reading on the indicator. Record this reading as protrusion A.

22 Repeat the check described in paragraph 21, this time 10.0 mm in from the front edge of the No 1 piston crown. Record this reading as protrusion B.

23 Add protrusion A to protrusion B, then divide the result by 2 to obtain an average reading for piston No 1.

24 Repeat the procedure described in paragraphs 21 to 23 on piston 4, then turn the crankshaft through 180° and carry out the procedure on the piston Nos 2 and 3 (see illustration). Check that there is a maximum difference of 0.07 mm protrusion between any two pistons.

25 If a dial test indicator is not available, piston protrusion may be measured using a straight-edge and feeler blades or Vernier calipers. However, this is much less accurate, and cannot therefore be recommended.

26 Note the greatest piston protrusion measurement, and use this to determine the correct cylinder head gasket from the following table. The series of notches/holes on the side of the gasket are used for thickness identification (see illustration).

Piston protrusion	Gasket identification
0.470 to 0.604 mm	1 notch
0.605 to 0.654 mm	2 notches
0.655 to 0.704 mm	3 notches
0.705 to 0.754 mm	4 notches
0.755 to 0.830 mm	5 notches

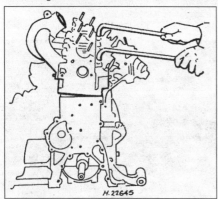

10.15 Free the cylinder head using angled rods

10.24 Measure the piston protrusion using a DTI gauge

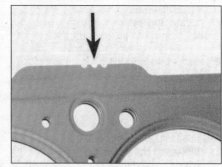

10.26 Cylinder head gasket thickness indication notches (arrowed)

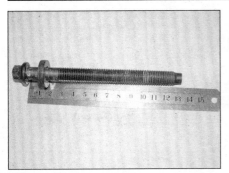

10.27 Measure the length of the bolt from under the bolt head, not the washer

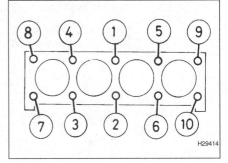

10.30 Ensure the gasket locates correctly over the dowels

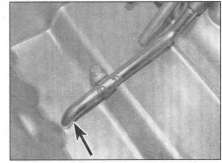

10.35 Cylinder head bolt tightening sequence

Head bolt examination

27 Carefully examine the cylinder head bolts for signs of damage to the threads or head, and for any sign of corrosion. If the bolts are in a satisfactory condition, measure the length of each bolt from the underside of the head, to the end of the shank. The bolts may be re-used providing that the measured length does not exceed 133.3 mm **(see illustration)**. **Note:** *Considering the stress to which the cylinder head bolts are subjected, it is highly recommended that they are all renewed, regardless of their apparent condition.*

Refitting

28 Turn the crankshaft and position Nos 1 and 4 pistons at TDC, then turn the crankshaft a quarter turn (90°) anti-clockwise.
29 Thoroughly clean the surfaces of the cylinder head and block.
30 Make sure that the locating dowels are in place, then fit the correct gasket the right way round on the cylinder block **(see illustration)**.
31 If necessary, refit the inlet and exhaust manifolds with reference to Chapter 4B.
32 Check that the camshaft TDC timing pin is in position, then carefully lower the cylinder head onto the gasket and block, making sure that it locates correctly onto the dowels.
33 Apply a smear of grease to the threads, and to the underside of the heads, of the cylinder head bolts. Citroën recommend the use of Molykote G Rapid Plus (available from your Citroën dealer); in the absence of the specified grease, any good-quality high-melting-point grease may be used.
34 Carefully insert the cylinder head bolts into their holes *(do not drop them in)* and initially finger-tighten them.
35 Working progressively and in sequence, tighten the cylinder head bolts to their Stage 1 torque setting, using a torque wrench and suitable socket **(see illustration)**.
36 Once all the bolts have been tightened to their Stage 1 torque setting, working again in the specified sequence, tighten each bolt to the specified Stage 2 setting. Finally, angle-tighten the bolts through the specified Stage 3 angle. It is recommended that an angle-measuring gauge is used during this stage of tightening, to ensure accuracy. **Note:** *Retightening of the cylinder*

head bolts after running the engine is not required.
37 Refit the cylinder head cover with reference to Section 4.
38 Refit the timing belt as described in Section 7.
39 The remainder of refitting is a reversal of removal, noting the following points.
 a) *Use a new seal when refitting the coolant outlet housing.*
 b) *When refitting a cylinder head, it is good practice to renew the thermostat.*
 c) *Refit the camshaft position sensor and set the air gap with reference to Chapter 4B.*
 d) *Tighten all fasteners to the specified torque where given.*
 e) *Refill the cooling system as described in Chapter 1B.*
 f) *The engine may run erratically for the first few miles, until the engine management ECM relearns its stored values.*

11 Sump –
removal and refitting

Removal

1 Drain the engine oil, then clean and refit the engine oil drain plug, tightening it securely. If the engine is nearing its service interval when the oil and filter are due for renewal, it is recommended that the filter is also removed, and a new one fitted. After reassembly, the engine can then be refilled with fresh oil. Refer to Chapter 1B for further information.
2 Chock the rear wheels then jack up the front of the vehicle and support it on axle stands (see *Jacking and vehicle support*). Undo the screws and remove the engine undershield.
3 On models with air conditioning, where the compressor is mounted onto the side of the sump, remove the drivebelt as described in Chapter 5A. Unbolt the compressor, and position it clear of the sump. Support the weight of the compressor by tying it to the vehicle, to prevent any excess strain being placed on the compressor lines. Do not disconnect the refrigerant lines from the compressor (refer to the warnings given in Chapter 3).

4 Where necessary, disconnect the wiring connector from the oil temperature sender unit, which is screwed into the sump.
5 Progressively slacken and remove all the sump retaining bolts/nuts. Since the sump bolts vary in length, remove each bolt in turn, and store it in its correct fitted order by pushing it through a clearly-marked cardboard template. This will avoid the possibility of installing the bolts in the wrong locations on refitting.
6 Try to break the joint by striking the sump with the palm of your hand, then lower and withdraw the sump from under the car. If the sump is stuck (which is quite likely) use a putty knife or similar, carefully inserted between the sump and block. Ease the knife along the joint until the sump is released. While the sump is removed, take the opportunity to check the oil pump pick-up/strainer for signs of clogging or splitting. If necessary, remove the pump as described in Section 12, and clean or renew the strainer. Note that on some models, the oil dipstick tube extends to the bottom of the sump in order to allow the oil to sucked out of the tube using special equipment **(see illustration)**.

Refitting

7 Clean all traces of sealant/gasket from the mating surfaces of the cylinder block/crankcase and sump, then use a clean rag to wipe out the sump and the engine's interior.
8 On engines where the sump was fitted without a gasket, ensure that the sump mating surfaces are clean and dry, then

11.6 On later engines, the dipstick guide tube extends to the bottom of the sump (arrowed)

11.8 Apply sealant to the crankcase mating surface

11.9a Fitting the sump

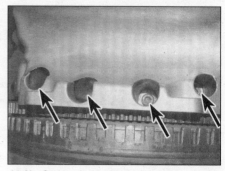

11.9b Concealed bolts at the transmission end of the sump (arrowed)

apply a thin coating of suitable sealant to the sump or crankcase mating surface **(see illustration)**.

9 Offer up the sump to the cylinder block/crankcase. Refit its retaining bolts/nuts, ensuring that each bolt is screwed into its original location. Tighten the bolts evenly and progressively to the specified torque setting. Note the concealed bolts at one end of the sump **(see illustrations)**.

10 Where necessary, align the air conditioning compressor with its mountings on the sump, and insert the retaining bolts. Securely tighten the compressor retaining bolts, then refit the drivebelt as described in Chapter 5A.

11 Reconnect the wiring connector to the oil temperature sensor (where fitted).

12 Lower the vehicle to the ground, then refill the engine with oil as described in Chapter 1B.

12 Oil pump – removal, inspection and refitting

Removal

1 Remove the sump as described in Section 11.

2 Unscrew and remove the bolts securing the oil pump to the base of the cylinder block/crankcase.

3 Disengage the pump sprocket from the chain, and remove the oil pump **(see illustration)**. Where necessary, also remove the spacer plate which is fitted behind the oil pump.

Inspection

4 Examine the oil pump sprocket for signs

of damage and wear, such as chipped or missing teeth. If the sprocket is worn, the pump assembly must be renewed, since the sprocket is not available separately. It is also recommended that the chain and drive sprocket, fitted to the crankshaft, be renewed at the same time. To renew the chain and drive sprocket, first remove the crankshaft timing belt sprocket, then unbolt the oil seal carrier from the cylinder block. The sprocket, spacer (where fitted) and chain can then be slid off the end of the crankshaft.

5 Unscrew and remove the bolts (along with the baffle plate, where fitted) securing the strainer cover to the pump body. Lift off the strainer cover, and take off the relief valve piston and spring, noting which way round they are fitted **(see illustrations)**.

6 Examine the pump rotors and body for signs of wear ridges or scoring. If worn, the complete pump assembly must be renewed.

7 Examine the relief valve piston for signs of wear or damage, and renew if necessary. The condition of the relief valve spring can only be measured by comparing it with a new one; if there is any doubt about its condition, it should also be renewed. Both the piston and spring are available individually.

8 Thoroughly clean the oil pump strainer with a suitable solvent, and check it for signs of clogging or splitting. If the strainer is damaged, the strainer and cover assembly must be renewed.

9 Locate the relief valve spring and piston in the strainer cover. Refit the cover to the pump body, aligning the relief valve piston with its bore in the pump. Refit the baffle plate (where fitted) and the cover retaining bolts, and tighten them securely.

10 Prime the pump by filling it with clean engine oil before refitting.

Refitting

11 Offer up the spacer plate (where fitted), then engage the pump sprocket with its drive chain, and seat the pump on the base of the cylinder block/crankcase. Refit the pump retaining bolts, and tighten them to the specified torque setting.

12 Refit the sump as described in Section 11.

12.3 Disengage the chain and remove the pump

12.5a Remove the oil pump cover bolts . . .

12.5b . . . then lift off the cover and remove the spring . . .

12.5c . . . and relief valve piston, noting which way round it's fitted

13 Oil cooler –
removal and refitting

Removal

1 Chock the rear wheels then jack up the front of the vehicle and support it on axle stands (see *Jacking and vehicle support*). Undo the screws and remove the engine undershield.
2 Drain the cooling system as described in Chapter 1B. Alternatively, clamp the oil cooler coolant hoses directly above the cooler, and be prepared for some coolant loss as the hoses are disconnected.
3 Position a suitable container beneath the oil filter on the front of the engine. Unscrew the filter using an oil filter removal tool if necessary, and drain the oil into the container. If the oil filter is damaged or distorted during removal, it must be renewed. Given the low cost of a new oil filter relative to the cost of repairing the damage which could result if a re-used filter leaks, it is probably a good idea to renew the filter in any case.
4 Release the hose clips, and disconnect the coolant hoses from the oil cooler.
5 Unscrew the oil cooler/oil filter mounting bolt/stud from the cylinder block, and withdraw the cooler. Note the locating notch in the cooler flange, which fits over the lug on the cylinder block (see illustration). Discard the oil cooler sealing ring; a new one must be used on refitting.

Refitting

6 Fit a new sealing ring to the recess in the rear of the cooler, then offer the cooler to the cylinder block.
7 Ensure that the locating notch in the cooler flange is correctly engaged with the lug on the cylinder block. Apply locking fluid to the threads of the mounting bolt/stud, then insert it through the oil cooler and tighten securely.
8 Fit the oil filter, then lower the vehicle to the ground.
9 Refill or top-up the cooling system and engine oil level as described in Chapter 1B or *Weekly Checks* (as applicable). Start the engine, and check the oil cooler for signs of leakage.

14 Oil seals –
renewal

Crankshaft

Right-hand oil seal

1 Remove the crankshaft sprocket as described in Section 8.
2 Measure and note the fitted depth of the oil seal.
3 Pull the oil seal from the housing using a hooked instrument. Alternatively, drill a small hole in the oil seal, and use a self-tapping

13.5 Oil cooler/oil filter mounting bolt (A) and locating notch (B)

screw and a pair of pliers to remove it (see illustration).
4 Clean the oil seal housing and the crankshaft sealing surface.
5 Dip the new oil seal in clean engine oil, and press it into the housing (open end first) to the previously-noted depth, using a suitable tube or socket. A piece of thin plastic or tape wound around the front of the crankshaft is useful to prevent damage to the oil seal as it is fitted.
6 Where applicable, remove the plastic or tape from the end of the crankshaft.
7 Refit the timing belt crankshaft sprocket as described in Section 8.

Left-hand oil seal

8 Remove the flywheel/driveplate, as described in Section 16.
9 Measure and note the fitted depth of the oil seal.
10 Pull the oil seal from the housing using a hooked instrument. Alternatively, drill a small hole in the oil seal, and use a self-tapping screw and a pair of pliers to remove it (see illustration 14.3).
11 Clean the oil seal housing and the crankshaft sealing surface.
12 Dip the new oil seal in clean engine oil, and press it into the housing (open end first) to the previously-noted depth, using a suitable tube or socket. A piece of thin plastic or tape wound around the end of the crankshaft is useful to prevent damage to the oil seal as it is fitted.
13 Where applicable, remove the plastic or tape from the end of the crankshaft.

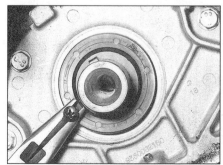

14.3 Use a self-tapping screw and pliers to remove the oil seal

14 Refit the flywheel/driveplate, as described in Section 16.

Camshaft

Right-hand oil seal

15 Remove the camshaft sprocket (and hub where applicable) as described in Section 8. In principle there is no need to remove the timing belt completely, but remember that if the belt has been contaminated with oil, it must be renewed.
16 Pull the oil seal from the housing using a hooked instrument. Alternatively, drill a small hole in the oil seal and use a self-tapping screw and a pair of pliers to remove it (see illustration 14.3).
17 Clean the oil seal housing and the camshaft sealing surface.
18 Smear the new oil seal with clean engine oil, then fit it over the end of the camshaft, open end first (see illustration). A piece of thin plastic or tape wound around the front of the camshaft is useful to prevent damage to the oil seal as it is fitted.
19 Press the seal into the housing until it is flush with the end face of the cylinder head. Use an M10 bolt (screwed into the end of the camshaft), washers and a suitable tube or socket that bears only on the outer edge of the seal to press it into position.
20 Refit the camshaft sprocket (and hub where applicable) as described in Section 8.
21 Where necessary, fit a new timing belt with reference to Section 7.

Left-hand oil seal

22 No oil seal is fitted to the left-hand end of the camshaft. The sealing is provided by an O-ring fitted to the endplate flange. The O-ring can be renewed after unbolting the plate from the cylinder head.

15 Oil pressure switch
and level sensor –
removal and refitting

Removal

Oil pressure switch

1 The oil pressure switch is located at the front of the cylinder block, above the oil filter mounting.

14.18 Locate the new seal in the cylinder head

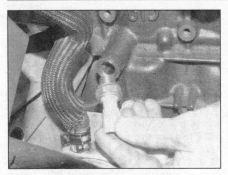

15.3 Oil pressure switch

Note that on some models, access to the switch may be improved if the vehicle is jacked up and supported on axle stands, then undo the screws and remove the engine undershield so that the switch can be reached from underneath (see *Jacking and vehicle support*).

2 Remove the protective sleeve from the wiring plug (where applicable), then disconnect the wiring from the switch.

3 Unscrew the switch from the cylinder block, and recover the sealing washer **(see illustration)**. Be prepared for oil spillage, and if the switch is to be left removed from the engine for any length of time, plug the hole in the cylinder block.

Oil level sensor

4 The oil level sensor is located at the rear of the cylinder block. Jack up the front of the vehicle and support it securely on axle stands (see *Jacking and vehicle support*). Undo the screws and remove the engine undershield.

5 Reach up between the driveshaft and the cylinder block and disconnect the sensor wiring plug **(see illustration)**.

6 Using an open-ended spanner, unscrew the sensor and withdraw it from position. Discard the sealing washer, a new one must be fitted.

Refitting

Oil pressure switch

7 Examine the sealing washer for any signs of damage or deterioration, and if necessary renew.

8 Refit the switch, complete with washer, and tighten it securely.

16.10 If the new bolts are not supplied with their threads precoated, apply thread-locking compound to them . . .

15.5 Oil level sensor (arrowed)

9 Refit the engine undershield, and lower the vehicle to the ground.

Oil level sensor

10 Smear a little silicone sealant on the threads and refit the sensor to the cylinder block, tightening it securely. Renew the sealing washer prior to refitting the sensor.

11 Reconnect the sensor wiring plug.

12 Refit the engine undershield, and lower the vehicle to the ground.

16 Flywheel/driveplate – removal, inspection and refitting

Removal

Flywheel

1 Remove the transmission as described in Chapter 7A, then remove the clutch assembly as described in Chapter 6.

2 Prevent the flywheel from turning by locking the ring gear teeth **(see illustration 5.2)**. Alternatively, bolt a strap between the flywheel and the cylinder block/crankcase. *Do not* attempt to lock the flywheel in position using the crankshaft pulley locking tool described in Section 3.

3 Make alignment marks between the flywheel and crankshaft to aid refitment. Slacken and remove the flywheel retaining bolts, and remove the flywheel from the end of the crankshaft. Be careful not to drop it; it is heavy. If the flywheel locating dowel (where

16.12 . . . then refit the flywheel and tighten the bolts to the specified torque

fitted) is a loose fit in the crankshaft end, remove it and store it with the flywheel for safe-keeping. Discard the flywheel bolts; new ones must be used on refitting.

Driveplate

4 Remove the transmission as described in Chapter 7B. Lock the driveplate as described in paragraph 2 of this Section. Mark the relationship between the torque converter plate and the driveplate, and slacken all the driveplate retaining bolts.

5 Remove the retaining bolts, along with the torque converter plate and the two shims (one fitted on each side of the torque converter plate). Note that the shims are of different thickness, the thicker one being on the outside of the torque converter plate. Discard the driveplate retaining bolts; new ones must be used on refitting.

6 Remove the driveplate from the end of the crankshaft. If the locating dowel is a loose fit in the crankshaft end, remove it and store it with the driveplate for safe-keeping.

Inspection

7 On models with manual transmission, examine the flywheel for scoring of the clutch face, and for wear or chipping of the ring gear teeth. If the clutch face is scored, the flywheel may be surface-ground, but renewal is preferable. Seek the advice of a Citroën dealer or engine reconditioning specialist to see if machining is possible. If the ring gear is worn or damaged, the flywheel must be renewed, as it is not possible to renew the ring gear separately.

8 On models with automatic transmission, check the torque converter driveplate carefully for signs of distortion. Look for any hairline cracks around the bolt holes or radiating outwards from the centre, and inspect the ring gear teeth for signs of wear or chipping. If any sign of wear or damage is found, the driveplate must be renewed.

Refitting flywheel

9 Clean the mating surfaces of the flywheel and crankshaft. Remove any remaining locking compound from the threads of the crankshaft holes, using the correct size of tap, if available.

If a suitable tap is not available, cut two slots along the threads of one of the old flywheel bolts, and use the bolt to remove the locking compound from the threads.

10 If the new flywheel retaining bolts are not supplied with their threads already precoated, apply a suitable thread-locking compound to the threads of each bolt **(see illustration)**.

All except DW10ATED engine with dual mass flywheel

11 Ensure that the locating dowel is in

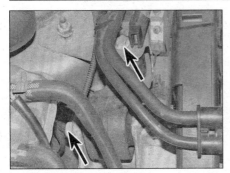

17.7 Connecting link/torque arm bolts (arrowed)

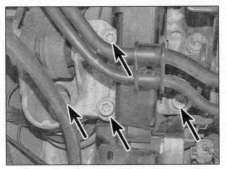

17.8 Engine mounting bracket Torx bolts/ nut (arrowed)

17.24 Remove engine torque rod/ connecting link

position. Offer up the flywheel, locating it on the dowel (where fitted), and fit the new retaining bolts. Where no locating dowel is fitted, align the previously-made marks to ensure the flywheel is refitted in its original position.

12 Lock the flywheel using the method employed on dismantling, and tighten the retaining bolts to the specified torque (see illustration).

DW10ATED engine with dual mass flywheel

13 The dual mass flywheel is designed to reduce harshness and vibration in the action of the engine, clutch and transmission. With this type of flywheel, two flywheel centralising tools are needed (0216-L – available from Citroën dealers). These are screwed into two opposite flywheel bolt holes in the crankshaft. As the tools are screwed down, their conical shape centralises the flywheel with regard to the crankshaft.

14 With the flywheel centralised, fit the new bolts into the remaining flywheel holes, then lock the flywheel using the same method employed on dismantling, and tighten the bolts to the specified torque.

15 Remove the two centralising tools, fit the new bolts and tighten them to the specified torque.

All models

16 Refit the clutch as described in Chapter 6. Remove the flywheel locking tool, and refit the transmission as described in Chapter 7A.

Refitting driveplate

17 Carry out the operations described above in paragraphs 9 and 10, substituting 'driveplate' for all references to the flywheel.

18 Locate the driveplate on its locating dowel.

19 Offer up the torque converter plate, with the thinner shim positioned behind the plate and the thicker shim on the outside, and align the marks made prior to removal.

20 Fit the new retaining bolts, then lock the driveplate using the method employed on dismantling. Tighten the retaining bolts to the specified torque wrench setting.

21 Remove the driveplate locking tool, and refit the transmission (see Chapter 7B).

17 Engine/transmission mountings – inspection and renewal

Inspection

1 If improved access is required, chock the rear wheels then jack up the front of the car and support it on axle stands (see *Jacking and vehicle support*). Undo the screws and remove the engine undershield.

2 Check the mounting rubbers to see if they are cracked, hardened or separated from the metal at any point; renew the mounting if any such damage or deterioration is evident.

3 Check that all the mountings' fasteners are securely tightened; use a torque wrench to check if possible.

4 Using a large screwdriver or a crowbar, check for wear in each mounting by carefully levering against it to check for free play. Where this is not possible, enlist the aid of an assistant to move the engine/transmission back-and-forth, or from side-to-side, while you watch the mounting. While some free play is to be expected even from new components, excessive wear should be obvious. If excessive free play is found, check first that the fasteners are correctly secured, then renew any worn components as described below.

Renewal

Right-hand mounting

5 Release all the relevant hoses and wiring from their retaining clips. Place the hoses/ wiring clear of the mounting so that the removal procedure is not hindered. Undo the screws and remove the engine undershield.

6 Place a jack beneath the engine, with a block of wood on the jack head. Raise the jack until it is supporting the weight of the engine.

7 Undo the bolts and remove the torque arm/ connecting link (see illustration).

8 Undo the bolts/nuts securing the engine mounting to the body and the support bracket (see illustration).

9 If required, undo the bolts/nuts securing the support bracket to the cylinder head/cylinder block.

10 Check all components carefully for signs

of wear or damage, and renew as necessary.

11 Where removed, refit the support bracket to the cylinder head, and tighten the bolts securely.

12 Refit the mount to the body and support bracket, then tighten the bolts to the specified torque.

13 Refit the connecting link/torque arm and tighten the bolts to the specified torque.

14 Remove the jack from underneath the engine.

Left-hand mounting

15 Remove the battery and battery tray (see Chapter 5A). Undo the screws and remove the engine undershield.

16 Remove the diesel engine management ECM and module box as described in Chapter 4B.

17 Place a jack beneath the transmission, with a block of wood on the jack head. Raise the jack until it is supporting the weight of the transmission.

18 Undo the fasteners and remove the mounting assembly. If required, undo the bolts/nut and remove the support bracket.

19 Check all components carefully for signs of wear or damage, and renew as necessary.

20 Clean the threads of the mounting stud (where applicable), and apply a coat of thread-locking compound to its threads.

21 Refit the support bracket and mounting, tightening the bolts/nuts to the specified torque.

22 The remainder of refitting is a reversal of removal.

Rear engine torque rod

23 If not already done, chock the rear wheels, then jack up the front of the vehicle and support it securely on axle stands (see *Jacking and vehicle support*). Undo the screws and remove the engine undershield.

24 Unscrew and remove the bolt securing the torque rod to the driveshaft intermediate bearing housing (see illustration).

25 Remove the bolt securing the torque rod to the subframe. Withdraw the torque rod.

26 To remove the intermediate bearing housing assembly it will first be necessary to remove the right-hand driveshaft as described in Chapter 8.

27 With the driveshaft removed, undo the

retaining bolts and remove the bearing housing from the rear of the cylinder block.
28 Check carefully for signs of wear or damage on all components, and renew them where necessary. The rubber bush fitted to the bearing housing is available as a separate item (at the time of writing), and can be pressed out of, and back into place.
29 On reassembly, fit the bearing housing assembly to the rear of the cylinder block, and tighten its retaining bolts securely. Refit the driveshaft as described in Chapter 8.

30 Refit the torque rod, and tighten both its bolts to their specified torque settings. Refit the engine undershield.
31 Lower the vehicle to the ground.

Chapter 2 Part E:
2.0 litre DOHC diesel engine in-car repair procedures

Contents

Degrees of difficulty

Easy, suitable for novice with little experience	Fairly easy, suitable for beginner with some experience	Fairly difficult, suitable for competent DIY mechanic	Difficult, suitable for experienced DIY mechanic	Very difficult, suitable for expert DIY or professional

Specifications

General

Designation:
  2.0 litre (1997 cc) DW10BTED4
Engine code* . . . . RHR
Bore . . . . 85.00 mm
Stroke. . . . . 88.00 mm
Direction of crankshaft rotation . . . . Clockwise (viewed from the right-hand side of vehicle)
No 1 cylinder location. . . . . At the transmission end of block
Maximum power output. . . . . 100 kW @ 4000 rpm
Maximum torque output. . . . . 320 Nm @ 2000 rpm
Compression ratio . . . . 18.0 : 1

*The engine code is stamped on a plate attached to the front of the cylinder block, next to the oil filter.

Compression pressures (engine hot, at cranking speed)
Normal . . . .   20 ± 5 bar
Maximum difference between any two cylinders . . . .   5 bar

Camshaft
Drive . . . .   Toothed belt

Lubrication system
Oil pump type . . . .   Gear-type, chain-driven off the crankshaft right-hand end
Minimum oil pressure @ 80°C:
  1000 rpm . . . .   1.9 bar
  4000 rpm . . . .   4.0 bar
Oil pressure warning switch operating pressure . . . .   0.8 bar

Torque wrench settings

	Nm	lbf ft
Big-end bearing cap nuts*:		
Stage 1	20	15
Stage 2	Angle-tighten a further 70°	
Camshaft bearing housing bolts	10	7
Camshaft position sensor bolt	6	4
Camshaft sprocket bolt:		
Stage 1	20	15
Stage 2	Angle-tighten a further 60°	
Clutch bellhousing closure plate	18	13
Coolant outlet housing	18	13
Crankshaft pulley bolt:		
Stage 1	70	52
Stage 2	Angle-tighten a further 60°	
Crankshaft right-hand oil seal housing bolts	14	10
Crankshaft sensor bolt	7	5
Cylinder head bolts:		
Stage 1	15	11
Stage 2	60	44
Stage 3	Angle-tighten a further 220° ± 5°	
Cylinder head cover bolts	10	7
Driveplate bolts*:		
Stage 1	20	15
Stage 2	66	49
Engine-to-transmission fixing bolts	45	33
Exhaust manifold nuts	25	18
Flywheel bolts*	50	37
High-pressure fuel pump bolts	20	15
Left-hand engine/transmission mounting:		
Bracket-to-transmission bolts	60	44
Bracket-to-transmission nut	55	41
Mounting to body/bracket	60	44
Main bearing cap bolts:		
Stage 1	25	18
Stage 2	Angle-tighten a further 60°	
Oil filter cap	25	18
Oil pressure switch	20	15
Oil pump mounting bolts	16	12
Piston oil jet spray tube bolt	10	7
Rear engine mounting/torque rod:		
Torque rod to mounting assembly	50	37
Torque rod-to-subframe nut/bolt	50	37
Mounting-to-engine	60	44
Right-hand engine mounting:		
Connecting link to body	50	37
Connecting link to bracket	50	37
Bracket to mounting (nut)	45	33
Bracket to engine bracket (Torx)	60	44
Engine bracket to engine	56	41
Sump bolts	16	12
Sump drain plug	34	25
Timing belt idler pulley bolt	56	41
Timing belt tensioner	21	15
Timing chain tensioner bolts	6	4

* Do not re-use.

1 General information

How to use this Chapter

This Part of Chapter 2 describes the repair procedures that can reasonably be carried out on the engine while it remains in the vehicle. If the engine has been removed from the vehicle and is being dismantled as described in Part F, any preliminary dismantling procedures can be ignored.

Note that, while it may be possible physically to overhaul items such as the piston/connecting rod assemblies while the engine is in the car, such tasks are not usually carried out as separate operations. Usually, several additional procedures are required (not to mention the cleaning of components and oilways); for this reason, all such tasks are classed as major overhaul procedures, and are described in Part F of this Chapter.

Part F describes the removal of the engine/transmission from the car, and the full overhaul procedures that can then be carried out.

DW10BTED4 engines

This engine is based on the well-proven DW10 SOHC direct injection engine which has appeared in many Peugeot and Citroën vehicles. In particular, the cylinder block components are very similar but the remainder of the engine has been completely redesigned. The engine is of double overhead camshaft (DOHC) 16-valve design. The turbocharged, four-cylinder engine is mounted transversely, with the transmission mounted on the left-hand side.

A toothed timing belt drives the exhaust camshaft, and coolant pump. The exhaust camshaft drives the inlet camshaft via a chain at the timing belt end. The camshafts operate the inlet and exhaust valves via rocker arms which are supported at their pivot ends by hydraulic self-adjusting tappets. The camshafts are supported by bearings machined directly in the cylinder head and camshaft bearing housing.

The high-pressure fuel pump is driven from the left-hand end of the exhaust camshaft. The high-pressure fuel pump supplies fuel to the fuel rail, and subsequently to the electronically-controlled injectors which inject the fuel direct into the combustion chambers. This design differs from the previous type where an injection pump supplies the fuel at high-pressure to each injector. The earlier conventional type injection pump required fine calibration and timing, and these functions are now completed by the high-pressure pump, electronic injectors and engine management ECM.

The crankshaft runs in five main bearings of the usual shell type. Endfloat is controlled by thrustwashers either side of No 2 main bearing.

The pistons are selected to be of matching weight, and incorporate fully-floating gudgeon pins retained by circlips.

The oil pump is chain-driven from the right-hand end of the crankshaft.

Throughout the manual it is often necessary to identify the engines not only by their cubic capacity, but also by their engine code. The engine code, consists of three letters (eg, RHR). The code is stamped on a plate attached to the front of the cylinder block.

Repair operations precaution

The engine is a complex unit with numerous accessories and ancillary components. The design of the engine compartment is such that every conceivable space has been utilised, and access to virtually all of the engine components is extremely limited. In many cases, ancillary components will have to be removed, or moved to one side, and wiring, pipes and hoses will have to be disconnected or removed from various cable clips and support brackets.

When working on this engine, read through the entire procedure first, look at the car and engine at the same time, and establish whether you have the necessary tools, equipment, skill and patience to proceed. Allow considerable time for any operation, and be prepared for the unexpected. Any major work on these engines is not for the faint-hearted!

Because of the limited access, many of the engine photographs appearing in this Chapter were, by necessity, taken with the engine removed from the vehicle.

⚠ **Warning: It is essential to observe strict precautions when working on the fuel system components of the engine, particularly the high-pressure side of the system. Before carrying out any engine operations that entail working on, or near, any part of the fuel system, refer to the special information given in Chapter 4B, Section 2.**

Operations with engine in vehicle

a) Compression pressure – testing.
b) Cylinder head cover(s) – removal and refitting.
c) Crankshaft pulley – removal and refitting.
d) Timing belt covers – removal and refitting.
e) Timing belt/chain – removal, refitting and adjustment.
f) Timing belt tensioner and sprockets – removal and refitting.
g) Camshaft oil seal – renewal.
h) Camshafts, rocker arms and hydraulic tappets – removal, inspection and refitting.
i) Sump – removal and refitting.
j) Oil pump – removal and refitting.
k) Crankshaft oil seals – renewal.
l) Engine/transmission mountings – inspection and renewal.
m) Flywheel/driveplate – removal, inspection and refitting.

2 Compression and leakdown tests – description and interpretation

Compression test

Note: *A compression tester specifically designed for diesel engines must be used for this test.*

1 When engine performance is down, or if misfiring occurs which cannot be attributed to the fuel system, a compression test can provide diagnostic clues as to the engine's condition. If the test is performed regularly, it can give warning of trouble before any other symptoms become apparent.

2 A compression tester specifically intended for diesel engines must be used, because of the higher pressures involved. The tester is connected to an adapter which screws into the glow plug or injector hole. On these engines, an adapter suitable for use in the glow plug holes will be required, so as not to disturb the fuel system components. It is unlikely to be worthwhile buying such a tester for occasional use, but it may be possible to borrow or hire one – if not, have the test performed by a garage.

3 Unless specific instructions to the contrary are supplied with the tester, observe the following points:
   a) The battery must be in a good state of charge, the air filter must be clean, and the engine should be at normal operating temperature.
   b) All the glow plugs should be removed as described in Chapter 5A before starting the test.
   c) The wiring connector on the engine management system ECM (see Chapter 4B) must be disconnected.

4 The compression pressures measured are not so important as the balance between cylinders. Values are given in the Specifications.

5 The cause of poor compression is less easy to establish on a diesel engine than on a petrol one. The effect of introducing oil into the cylinders ('wet' testing) is not conclusive, because there is a risk that the oil will sit in the swirl chamber or in the recess on the piston crown instead of passing to the rings. However, the following can be used as a rough guide to diagnosis.

6 All cylinders should produce very similar pressures; any difference greater than that specified indicates the existence of a fault. Note that the compression should build-up quickly in a healthy engine; low compression on the first stroke, followed by gradually-increasing pressure on successive strokes, indicates worn piston rings. A low compression reading on the first stroke, which does not build-up during successive strokes, indicates leaking valves or a blown head gasket (a cracked head could also be the cause). Deposits on the undersides of the valve heads can also cause low compression.

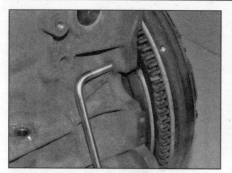

3.7a The tool fits through the hole in the cylinder block flange . . .

3.7b . . . and into a hole in the rear of the flywheel

3.8 Fit the tool through the hole in the exhaust camshaft sprocket, into the timing hole in the cylinder head

7 A low reading from two adjacent cylinders is almost certainly due to the head gasket having blown between them; the presence of coolant in the engine oil will confirm this.

8 If the compression reading is unusually high, the cylinder head surfaces, valves and pistons are probably coated with carbon deposits. If this is the case, the cylinder head should be removed and decarbonised (see Part F).

Leakdown test

9 A leakdown test measures the rate at which compressed air fed into the cylinder is lost. It is an alternative to a compression test, and in many ways it is better, since the escaping air provides easy identification of where pressure loss is occurring (piston rings, valves or head gasket).

10 The equipment needed for leakdown testing is unlikely to be available to the home mechanic. If poor compression is suspected, have the test performed by a suitably-equipped garage.

3 Engine assembly/ valve timing holes – general information and usage

Note: *Do not attempt to rotate the engine whilst the crankshaft and camshaft are locked in position. If the engine is to be left in this state for a long period of time, it is a good idea to place suitable warning notices inside the vehicle, and in the engine compartment. This will reduce the possibility of the engine*

4.3 Undo the bolt and remove the camshaft position sensor (arrowed)

being accidentally cranked on the starter motor, which is likely to cause damage with the locking pins in place.

1 Timing holes or slots are located only in the flywheel/driveplate and camshaft sprocket hub. The holes/slots are used to align the crankshaft and camshaft at the TDC position for Nos 1 and 4. This will ensure that the valve timing is maintained during operations that require removal and refitting of the timing belt. When the holes/slots are aligned with their corresponding holes in the cylinder block and cylinder head, suitable diameter bolts/pins can be inserted to lock the crankshaft and camshaft in position, preventing rotation. Note that with the timing holes aligned, No 4 piston is at TDC on its compression stroke.

2 To align the engine assembly/valve timing holes, proceed as follows.

3 Chock the rear wheels then jack up the front of the vehicle and support it on axle stands (see *Jacking and vehicle support*). Remove the right-hand front roadwheel.

4 To gain access to the crankshaft pulley, to enable the engine to be turned, the wheel arch plastic liner must be removed. The liner is secured by several plastic expanding rivets. To remove the rivets, push in the centre pins a little, then prise the clips from place. Remove the liner from under the front wing. Where necessary, unclip the coolant hoses from under the wing to improve access further. The crankshaft can then be turned using a suitable socket and extension bar fitted to the pulley bolt.

5 Remove the upper timing belt cover as described in Section 6.

4.5 Release the clips (arrowed) and detach the injector wiring harness duct

6 Turn the crankshaft until the timing hole in the camshaft sprocket is aligned with the corresponding hole in the cylinder head. Note that the crankshaft must always be turned in a clockwise direction (viewed from the right-hand side of vehicle). Use a small mirror so that the position of the sprocket timing slot can be observed. When the slot is aligned with the corresponding hole in the cylinder head, the camshaft is positioned correctly.

7 Insert Citroën tool No. (-).0188.X or an 8 mm diameter bolt, rod or drill through the hole in the left-hand flange of the cylinder block by the starter motor; if necessary, carefully turn the crankshaft either way until the rod enters the timing hole in the flywheel/driveplate **(see illustrations)**. Note that if an 8.0 mm bolt/rod/drill bit is used, it must be flat (not tapered at all) at the end. If improved access is required, remove the starter motor as described in Chapter 5A.

8 Insert an 8 mm bolt, rod or drill through the hole in the camshaft sprocket hub and into engagement with the cylinder head **(see illustration)**.

9 The crankshaft and camshaft are now locked in position, preventing unnecessary rotation.

4 Cylinder head cover – removal and refitting

Removal

1 Remove the plastic cover from the top of the engine. The cover simply pulls up from its rubber mountings.

2 The cylinder head cover is integral with the inlet manifold. Begin by releasing the wiring harness from the timing belt upper cover.

3 Disconnect the wiring plug, then unscrew the camshaft position sensor from the cover **(see illustration)**.

4 Undo the bolts securing the upper timing belt cover to the cylinder head cover/inlet manifold.

5 Disconnect the injectors' wiring plugs, then detach the harness duct from the inlet manifold/cover and position it to one side **(see illustration)**.

4.6a Release the clamps and disconnect the breather hose (arrowed) from the cylinder head cover . . .

4.6b . . . the EGR pipe from the inlet manifold . . .

4.6c . . . then slide out the locking clip and disconnect the breather hose from the rear of the cylinder head cover

6 Disconnect the crankcase ventilation hoses from the inlet manifold/cover, then release the clamp and disconnect the EGR pipe from the inlet manifold **(see illustrations)**.

7 Release the glow plugs' wiring harness from the 2 clips on the cover.

8 Slacken the clamps and disconnect the inlet hoses from the manifold.

9 Unclip the fuel temperature sensor from the underside of the manifold.

10 Undo the manifold/cover retaining bolts in the **reverse** of the sequence shown in illustration 4.12. Discard the gaskets, new ones must be fitted.

Refitting

11 Clean the sealing surfaces of the manifold/cover and the cylinder head.

12 Fit the new seals to the inlet manifold/cover, then fit it to the cylinder head. Use a little petroleum jelly on the manifold O-rings to ease reassembly. Tighten the bolts to the specified torque in sequence **(see illustration)**.

13 The remainder of refitting is a reversal of removal, noting the following points:

a) *Tighten all fasteners to their specified torque.*

b) *Before refitting the timing belt upper cover, adjust the camshaft position sensor air gap as described in Chapter 4B, Section 13.*

5 Crankshaft pulley – removal and refitting

Removal

1 Remove the auxiliary drivebelt as described in Chapter 5A.

2 Position the camshaft and crankshaft at TDC for No 1 cylinder, as described in Section 3. **Note:** *It is essential that the crankshaft and camshaft timing pins are in place as described in Section 3. This is because on these engines, the crankshaft sprocket has a wider keyway, to allow it to rotate a little independently of the crankshaft during the belt tensioning procedure. Failure to lock the crankshaft and camshaft could result in the timing being lost.*

3 To prevent crankshaft turning whilst the

pulley retaining bolt is being slackened the flywheel/driveplate ring gear can be locked using (Citroën tool No. (-).0188.F) or a suitable tool made from steel angle. Remove the starter motor as described in Chapter 5A, and bolt the tool to the bellhousing flange so it engages with the ring gear teeth **(see illustration)**. *Do not attempt to lock the pulley by only inserting a bolt/drill through the timing hole.*

4 Using a suitable socket and extension bar, unscrew the retaining bolt, remove the washer, then slide the pulley off the end of the crankshaft **(see illustration)**. If the pulley is tight fit, it can be drawn off the crankshaft using a suitable puller. If a puller is being used, refit the pulley retaining bolt without the washer, to avoid damaging the crankshaft as the puller is tightened.

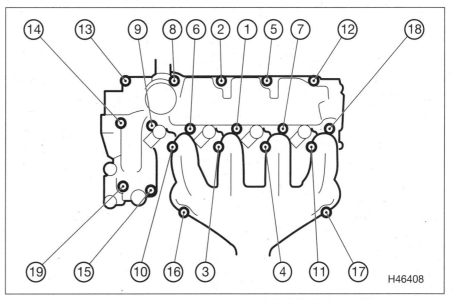

4.12 Inlet manifold/cylinder head cover bolt tightening sequence

Note that the 55 mm bolt is fitted in position 14, and the 70 mm bolts are fitted in positions 16 and 17

5.3 Use a fabricated tool similar to this to lock the flywheel ring gear and prevent crankshaft rotation

5.4 Undo the bolt and remove the crankshaft pulley

6.4 Depress the clips and disconnect the fuel pipes (arrowed)

Refitting

5 Ensure the camshaft and crankshaft are positioned at TDC as described previously, and the flywheel/driveplate ring gear is locked in position, as described in paragraph 3.

6 Thoroughly clean the threads of the pulley retaining bolt, then apply a coat of locking compound to the bolt threads. Citroën recommend the use of Loctite (available from your Citroën dealer); in the absence of this, any good-quality locking compound may be used.

7 Refit the crankshaft pulley retaining bolt and washer. Tighten the bolt to the specified torque, then through the specified angle.

8 Remove the crankshaft, camshaft and flywheel/driveplate locking tools.

9 Refit and tension the auxiliary drivebelt as described in Chapter 5A.

6 Timing belt covers – removal and refitting

⚠️ **Warning: Refer to the precautionary information contained in Section 1 before proceeding.**

Removal

Upper cover

1 Pull up the plastic cover from the top of the engine, then undo the screws and remove the engine undershield.

2 Position a trolley jack under the engine, and using a piece of wood on the jack head,

6.9 Crankshaft position sensor bolt (arrowed)

support the weight of the engine.

3 Undo the bolts and remove the right-hand engine mounting and support bracket – see Section 17.

4 At the connections at the right-hand end of the cylinder head, disconnect the fuel supply and return hose quick-release fittings using a small screwdriver to press down and release the locking clip **(see illustration)**. Cover the open unions to prevent dirt entry, using small plastic bags, or fingers cut from clean rubber gloves.

5 Release the two fuel hoses from the retaining clips at the right-hand end of the cylinder head.

6 Move the electrical harness to one side, then undo the screws/nut and remove the upper timing belt cover **(see illustration)**.

Lower cover

7 Remove the upper cover as described previously.

8 Remove the crankshaft pulley as described in Section 5.

9 Undo the bolt and position the crankshaft sensor to one side **(see illustration)**.

10 Carefully pull the crankshaft sensor signal disc from the crankshaft **(see illustration)**. If the disc is reluctant to move, screw in two 6.0 mm bolts into the threaded holes in the disc and force it from place.

11 Undo the bolts and remove the lower timing belt cover.

Refitting

12 Refitting of all the covers is a reversal of the relevant removal procedure, ensuring that each

6.10 Sensor signal disc

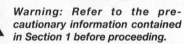

6.6 Upper timing belt fasteners (arrowed)

cover section is correctly located, and that the cover retaining bolts are securely tightened. Ensure that all disturbed hoses are reconnected and retained by their relevant clips.

7 Timing belt – removal, inspection, refitting and tensioning

General

1 The timing belt drives the camshaft and coolant pump from a toothed sprocket on the end of the crankshaft. If the belt breaks or slips in service, the pistons are likely to hit the valve heads, resulting in expensive damage.

2 The timing belt should be renewed at the specified intervals, or earlier if it is contaminated with oil, or at all noisy in operation (a 'scraping' noise due to uneven wear).

3 If the timing belt is being removed, it is a wise precaution to check the condition of the coolant pump at the same time (check for signs of coolant leakage). This may avoid the need to remove the timing belt again at a later stage should the coolant pump fail.

Removal

4 Chock the rear wheels then jack up the front of the vehicle and support it on axle stands (see *Jacking and vehicle support*). Remove the front right-hand roadwheel, wheel arch liner (to expose the crankshaft pulley), and the engine undershield. The wheel arch liner is secured by several plastic expanding rivets, or push-in clips. Push the centre pins in a little then prise the rivet from place. The engine undershield is retained by several screw fasteners. Rotate the fasteners 90 degrees anti-clockwise and remove them.

5 Remove the crankshaft pulley as described in Section 5, then use 6.0 mm bolts to draw the sensor disc from the end of the crankshaft **(see illustration 6.10)**.

6 Remove the upper and lower timing belt covers as described in the previous Section.

7 Ensure the engine is positioned at TDC as described in Section 3, with the camshaft and crankshaft locking tools described in place.

8 Loosen the bolt on the tensioner pulley, and turn the tensioner clockwise to release the tension on the timing belt. Use an Allen key in the hole provided, to turn the tensioner bracket against the spring tension. Retighten the bolt sufficiently to hold the tensioner in its released position; do not fully tighten the bolt in this position.

9 Mark the timing belt with an arrow to indicate its running direction if it is to be re-used. Remove the belt from the sprockets.

Inspection

10 Renew the belt as a matter of course, regardless of its apparent condition. The cost of a new belt is nothing compared with the cost of repairs should the belt break in service. If signs of oil contamination are found, trace the source of the oil leak and rectify it.

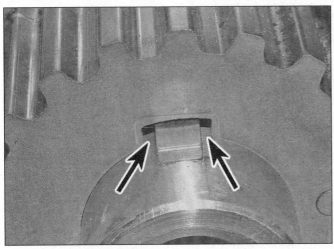

7.12 Position the crankshaft sprocket so that equal gaps exists each side of the key (arrowed)

7.14 Timing belt routing

Wash down the engine timing belt area and all related components, to remove all traces of oil. Check that the tensioner and idler pulleys rotate freely without any sign of roughness, and also check that the coolant pump rotates freely. If necessary, renew these items.

Refitting and tensioning

11 Commence refitting by ensuring that the TDC timing pins are still in position correctly.
12 Centre the crankshaft sprocket by inserting Citroën tool (-).0188.AH either side of the crankshaft key, and into the keyway in the sprocket. In the absence of the tool, position the sprocket centrally, ensuring a gap exists each side of the key **(see illustration)**.
13 Fit the timing belt to the camshaft sprocket. Citroën technicians use a clip to retain the belt on the sprocket; if necessary, use a plastic cable tie to hold it.
14 Continue to fit the belt in the following order, keeping the belt taut between as it's fitted around the idler pulley and the crankshaft sprocket **(see illustration)**:
 a) Idler pulley.
 b) Crankshaft sprocket.
 c) Coolant pump sprocket.
 d) Tensioner pulley.
15 Remove the tool/cable tie securing the belt to the camshaft sprocket, and the crankshaft sprocket centring tool.

16 Slacken the tensioner pulley retaining bolt, then using an Allen key, rotate the tensioner anti-clockwise until the index pointer is aligned with the lower, outside edge of the reference plate **(see illustrations)**. Tighten the tensioner pulley retaining bolt to the specified torque.
17 Ensure the crankshaft/flywheel ring gear locking tool is still in place, then refit the lower timing belt cover, sensor disc and crankshaft pulley, and tighten the retaining bolt to 70 Nm (52 lbf ft).
18 Remove the camshaft sprocket and crankshaft locking/timing tools.
19 Rotate the crankshaft 10 times in the normal direction of rotation, and refit the camshaft sprocket and crankshaft locking/timing tools.
20 With the flywheel ring gear locked, slacken the crankshaft pulley bolt.
21 Slacken the timing belt tensioner retaining bolt, then use an Allen key to rotate the tensioner clockwise until the index pointer aligns with the notch in the reference plate **(see illustration)**. Tighten the tensioner pulley bolt to the specified torque.
22 Tighten the crankshaft pulley bolt to 70 Nm (52 lbf ft).
23 Remove the camshaft sprocket, and crankshaft/flywheel ring gear locking/aligning tools, and rotate the crankshaft 2 complete revolutions in the normal direction of rotation (clockwise).
24 Check that the camshaft sprocket and

crankshaft/flywheel aligning tools can still be inserted, and that the tensioner index pointer is still aligned with the notch in the reference plate. If necessary, repeat the tensioning procedure until the pointer and notch align.
25 Lock the flywheel ring gear using the previously described tool, undo the crankshaft pulley bolt.
26 Refit the crankshaft sensor. Tighten the retaining bolt securely.
27 Apply a little thread-locking compound to the threads, then tighten the crankshaft pulley retaining bolt to the specified torque.
28 Remove the camshaft sprocket, and crankshaft/flywheel ring gear locking/aligning tools.
29 The remainder of refitting is a reversal of removal.

8 Timing belt sprockets and tensioner – removal and refitting

Camshaft sprocket

Removal

1 Remove the timing belt as described in Section 7.
2 Remove the locking tool from the camshaft sprocket, then slacken the sprocket retaining

7.16a Use an Allen key in the tensioner (arrowed)

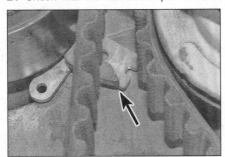

7.16b Rotate the tensioner anti-clockwise until the index pointer is aligned with the lower edge of the reference plate (arrowed)

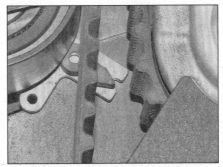

7.21 Align the index pointer with the notch in the reference plate

TOOL TiP

To make a sprocket holding tool, obtain two lengths of steel strip about 6.0 mm thick by about 30 mm wide or similar, one 600 mm long, the other 200 mm long (all dimensions approximate). Bolt the two strips together to form a forked end, leaving the bolt slack so that the shorter strip can pivot freely. At the other end of each 'prong' of the fork, drill a suitable hole and fit a nut and bolt to engage with the spokes or holes in the sprocket. It may be necessary to cut-off or grind the side slightly to allow them to fit in the sprocket holes.

bolt. To prevent the camshaft rotating as the bolt is slackened, Citroën technicians use tool No 6016-T. In the absence of this tool, fabricate a substitute as described (see Tool Tip). *Do not* attempt to use the camshaft sprocket locking tool to prevent the sprocket from rotating whilst the bolt is slackened. **Note:** *Take care not to damage the sensor signal disc integral with the sprocket.*

3 Remove the bolt, and slide the sprocket from the camshaft. If the Woodruff key is a loose fit in the camshaft, remove it for safe-keeping. Examine the camshaft oil seal for signs of oil leakage and, if necessary, renew it as described in Section 14.
4 Clean the camshaft sprocket thoroughly, and renew it if there are any signs of wear, damage or cracks.

Refitting

5 Where applicable, refit the Woodruff key to the end of the camshaft, then refit the camshaft sprocket and hub.
6 Refit the sprocket retaining bolt and washer. Tighten the bolt to the specified torque, preventing the camshaft from turning as during removal.
7 Align the timing slot in the camshaft sprocket with the hole in the cylinder head and refit the tool lock the camshaft in position.
8 Refit the timing belt as described in Section 7.

Crankshaft sprocket

Removal

9 Remove the timing belt as described in Section 7.
10 Slide the sprocket off the end of the crankshaft and collect the Woodruff key (see illustrations).

8.10a Slide off the crankshaft pulley . . .

11 Examine the crankshaft oil seal for signs of oil leakage and, if necessary, renew it as described in Section 14.
12 Clean the crankshaft sprocket thoroughly, and renew it if there are any signs of wear, damage or cracks.

Refitting

13 Refit the Woodruff key to the end of the crankshaft, then refit the crankshaft sprocket (with the flange nearest the cylinder block).
14 Refit the timing belt as described in Section 7.

Coolant pump sprocket

15 The coolant pump sprocket is integral with the pump, and cannot be removed.

Tensioner pulley

Removal

16 Remove the timing belt as described in Section 7.
17 Remove the tensioner pulley retaining bolt, and slide the pulley off its mounting stud.
18 Clean the tensioner pulley, but do not use any strong solvent which may enter the pulley bearings. Check that the pulley rotates freely, with no sign of stiffness or free play. Renew the pulley if there is any doubt about its condition, or if there are any obvious signs of wear or damage.

Refitting

19 Refit the tensioner pulley, and insert the retaining bolt.
20 Refit the timing belt as described in Section 7.

9.8 Lift up the upper chain guide rail and insert a 2.0 mm diameter rod/drill bit into the hole in the tensioner body

8.10b . . . and recover the Woodruff key

Idler pulley

Removal

21 Remove the timing belt as described in Section 7.
22 Undo the retaining bolt and withdraw the idler pulley from the engine.
23 Clean the idler pulley, but do not use any strong solvent which may enter the bearings. Check that the pulley rotates freely, with no sign of stiffness or free play. Renew the idler pulley if there is any doubt about its condition, or if there are any obvious signs of wear or damage.

Refitting

24 Locate the idler pulley on the engine, and fit the retaining bolt. Tighten the bolt to the specified torque.
25 Fit the timing belt around the idler pulley, and tension the timing belt as described in Section 7.

9 Camshaft, rocker arms and hydraulic tappets – removal, inspection and refitting

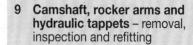

Removal

1 Remove the cylinder head cover as described in Section 4.
2 Remove the camshaft sprocket as described in Section 8.
3 Slacken the retaining clamps and disconnect the air inlet hose from the left-hand end of the cylinder head. Remove the intercooler air duct from the left-hand end of the cylinder head.
4 Remove the air cleaner assembly, high-pressure fuel pump, and fuel injectors as described in Chapter 4B.
5 Refit the right-hand engine mounting, but only tighten the bolts moderately; this will keep the engine supported during the camshaft removal.
6 Disconnect the vacuum pipe from the brake vacuum pump on the left-hand end of the cylinder head.
7 Remove the vacuum pump from the cylinder head with reference to Chapter 9.
8 Compress the timing chain tensioner and insert a 2.0 mm drill bit into the tensioner body to lock the piston in the compressed state (see illustration).

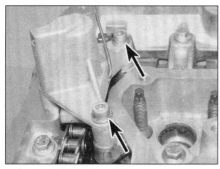

9.9 Undo the tensioner retaining bolts (arrowed)

9 Undo the bolts and remove the timing chain tensioner **(see illustration)**.

10 Working in a spiral pattern from the outside-in, progressively loosen the camshaft bearing cap housing bolts until they can be removed.

11 Withdraw the bearing cap housing from the cylinder head. The housing is likely to be initially tight to release as it is located by two dowels on the forward facing side of the cylinder head. If necessary, very carefully prise up the housing using a screwdriver inserted in the slotted lug adjacent to each dowel location. Once the bearing housing is free, lift it squarely from the cylinder head. The camshaft will rise up slightly under the pressure of the valve springs – be careful it doesn't tilt and jam in the cylinder head or bearing housing section.

12 Check that the camshafts and chain are marked in relation to each other – the chain should have two black or copper links which align with marks on the teeth. If necessary, mark the chain and teeth with dabs of paint. The marks on the teeth are the most important as they determine the valve timing, however the chain links can be marked as they are 7 links (inclusive) apart **(see illustrations)**.

13 Simultaneously, lift the camshafts and chain from the cylinder head. Release the camshafts from the chain.

14 Either get sixteen small, clean plastic containers, and number them 1 to 16, or divide a larger container into sixteen compartments.

15 Lift out each rocker arm and release it from the spring clip on the tappet **(see illustration)**. Place the rocker arms in their respective positions in the box or containers.

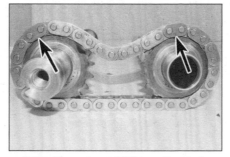

9.12a The coloured links on the chain (arrowed) align with the marks on the camshaft sprockets . . .

16 A compartmentalised container filled with engine oil is now required to retain the hydraulic tappets while they are removed from the cylinder head. Using a rubber sucker, withdraw each hydraulic follower and place it in the container, keeping them each identified for correct refitting. The tappets must be totally submerged in the oil to prevent air entering them.

Inspection

17 Inspect the cam lobes and the camshaft bearing journals for scoring or other visible evidence of wear. Once the surface hardening of the cam lobes has been eroded, wear will occur at an accelerated rate. **Note:** *If these symptoms are visible on the tips of the camshaft lobes, check the corresponding rocker arm, as it will probably be worn as well.*

18 Examine the condition of the bearing surfaces in the cylinder head and camshaft bearing housing. If wear is evident, the cylinder head and bearing housing will both have to be renewed, as they are a matched assembly.

19 Inspect the rocker arms and tappets for scuffing, cracking or other damage and renew any components as necessary. Also check the condition of the tappet bores in the cylinder head. As with the camshafts, any wear in this area will necessitate cylinder head renewal.

Refitting

20 Thoroughly clean the sealant from the mating surfaces of the cylinder head and camshaft bearing housing. Use a suitable liquid gasket dissolving agent (available from Citroën dealers) together with a soft putty

9.12b . . . the mark on the sprockets is a dot and a line

knife; do not use a metal scraper or the faces will be damaged. As there is no conventional gasket used, the cleanliness of the mating faces is of the utmost importance.

21 Clean off any oil, dirt or grease from both components and dry with a clean lint-free cloth. Ensure that all the oilways are completely clean.

22 To prevent any possibility of the valves contacting the pistons as the camshaft is refitted, remove the locking pin/drill from the flywheel/driveplate and turn the crankshaft a quarter turn in the *opposite* direction to normal rotation (ie, anti-clockwise), to position all the pistons at mid-stroke.

23 Liberally lubricate the hydraulic tappet bores in the cylinder head with clean engine oil.

24 Insert the hydraulic tappets into their original bores in the cylinder head unless they have been renewed **(see illustration)**.

25 Lubricate the rocker arms and place them over their respective tappets and valve stems. Ensure that the ends of the rocker arms engage with the spring clips on the tappets.

26 Lubricate the camshaft bearing journals in the cylinder head sparingly with oil, taking care not to allow the oil to spill over onto the camshaft bearing housing contact areas.

27 Engage the camshafts with the chain, making sure that the coloured links are aligned with the marked teeth, fit the tensioner between the chain runs, then lower them into position. The longer exhaust camshaft must go at the rear of the cylinder head. Rotate the camshaft so the mark on the inlet camshaft is in the 12 o'clock position **(see illustration)**.

9.15 Lift out the rocker arms with the hydraulic tappets

9.24 Insert the tappets and rocker arms into their original locations

9.27 Position the camshafts so the mark on the inlet camshaft (arrowed) is in the 12 o'clock position

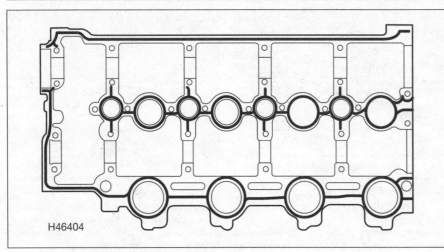

9.32a Apply a thin bead of sealant as indicated by the heavy black line

9.32b We inserted a tapered rod (arrowed) into the tensioner oil supply hole to prevent any sealant from entering

28 Fit a new camshaft oil seal as described in Section 14.

29 Refit the camshaft sprocket, lightly tighten the retaining bolt, then fit the camshaft sprocket locking tool.

30 Check the marks on the camshaft sprockets still align with the coloured links on the chain.

31 Ensure that the mating faces of the cylinder head and camshaft bearing housing are clean and free of any oil or grease.

32 Sparingly apply a bead of sealant (Loctite 518) to the mating face of the camshaft bearing housing, taking care not to allow the product to contaminate the camshaft bearing journal areas **(see illustrations)**.

33 Lower the housing into place, then insert and tighten the camshaft bearing housing bolts to the specified torque, in sequence **(see illustration)**.

34 Refit the chain tensioner, tighten the retaining bolts to the specified torque, then pull out the locking pin and allow the tensioner to act upon the chain.

35 The remainder of refitting is a reversal of removal.

10 Cylinder head –
removal and refitting

Note: *This is an involved procedure, and it is suggested that the Section is read thoroughly before starting work. To aid refitting, make notes on the locations of all relevant brackets and the routing of hoses and cables before removal.*

Removal

1 Chock the rear wheels then jack up the front of the vehicle and support it on axle stands (see *Jacking and vehicle support*). Remove the front right-hand roadwheel, the engine undershield, and the front wheel arch liner.

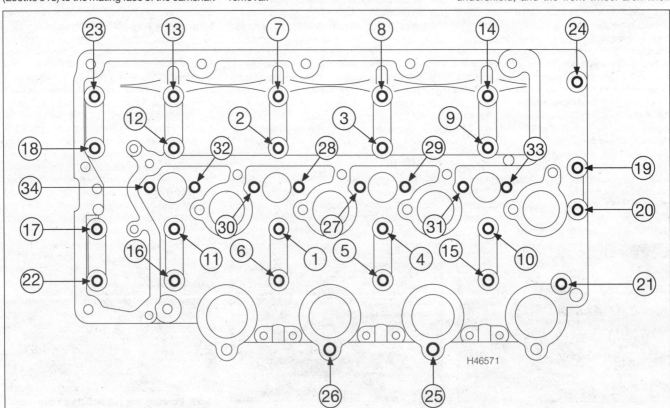

9.33 Camshaft bearing cap housing bolts tightening sequence

10.5 Remove the timing chain pad from the cylinder head

10.8 Undo the bracket upper bolt (arrowed)

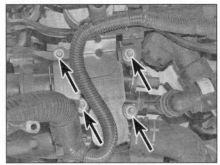

10.10 Undo the nuts (arrowed) and remove the coolant outlet housing

The undershield is secured by several screws, and the wheel arch liner is secured by several plastic expanding rivets. Push the centre pins in a little, then prise the rivet from place.
2 Remove the battery (see Chapter 5A).
3 Drain the cooling system as described in Chapter 1B.
4 Remove the camshafts, rocker arms and hydraulic tappets as described in Section 9.
5 Remove the timing chain pad at the right-hand side of the cylinder head **(see illustration)**.
6 Remove the fuel filter and bracket.
7 Remove the common (fuel) rail as described in Chapter 4B.
8 Remove the uppermost bolt securing the engine mounting support bracket to the right-hand end of the cylinder head **(see illustration)**, then temporarily refit the mounting to support the engine whilst the cylinder head is being removed.
9 Note their fitted positions and routing, then disconnect all coolant and vacuum hoses from the cylinder head.
10 Undo the bolts/studs securing the coolant outlet housing to the left-hand end of the cylinder head. Pull the housing away from the cylinder head **(see illustration)**.
11 Remove the turbocharger and exhaust manifold as described in Chapter 4B.
12 Progressively slacken the cylinder head bolts, in the **reverse** order to that shown for tightening **(see illustration 10.33)**. A Torx socket will be required for this.
13 When all the bolts are loose, unscrew them fully and remove them from the cylinder head.
14 Release the cylinder head from the cylinder block and location dowels by rocking it. The Citroën tool for doing this consists simply of two metal rods with 90-degree angled ends. Do not prise between the mating faces of the cylinder head and block, as this may damage the gasket faces.
15 Lift the cylinder head from the block, and recover the gasket.

Preparation for refitting

16 The mating faces of the cylinder head and cylinder block must be perfectly clean before refitting the head. Citroën recommend the use of a scouring agent for this purpose, but

acceptable results can be achieved by using a hard plastic or wood scraper to remove all traces of gasket and carbon. The same method can be used to clean the piston crowns. Take particular care to avoid scoring or gouging the cylinder head/cylinder block mating surfaces during the cleaning operations, as aluminium alloy is easily damaged. Make sure that the carbon is not allowed to enter the oil and water passages – this is particularly important for the lubrication system, as carbon could block the oil supply to the engine's components. Using adhesive tape and paper, seal the water, oil and bolt holes in the cylinder block. To prevent carbon entering the gap between the pistons and bores, smear a little grease in the gap. After cleaning each piston, use a small brush to remove all traces of grease and carbon from the gap, then wipe away the remainder with a clean rag.
17 Check the mating surfaces of the cylinder block and the cylinder head for nicks, deep scratches and other damage. If slight, they may be removed carefully with a file, but if excessive, machining may be the only alternative to renewal. If warpage of the cylinder head gasket surface is suspected, use a straight-edge to check it for distortion. Refer to Part F of this Chapter if necessary.
18 Thoroughly clean the threads of the cylinder head bolt holes in the cylinder block. Ensure that the bolts run freely in their threads, and that all traces of oil and water are removed from each bolt hole. If possible, use a M12 x 150 tap to clean out the threads.

10.19 Zero the DTI on the gasket face

Gasket selection

19 Turn the crankshaft until pistons 1 and 4 are at TDC (Top Dead Centre). Position a dial test indicator (dial gauge) on the cylinder block adjacent to the rear of No 1 piston, and zero it on the block face **(see illustration)**. Transfer the probe to the crown of No 1 piston (10.0 mm in from the rear edge), then slowly turn the crankshaft back-and-forth past TDC, noting the highest reading on the indicator. Record this reading as protrusion A.
20 Repeat the check described in paragraph 19, this time 10.0 mm in from the front edge of the No 1 piston crown. Record this reading as protrusion B.
21 Add protrusion A to protrusion B, then divide the result by 2 to obtain an average reading for piston No 1.
22 Repeat the procedure described in paragraphs 19 to 21 on piston 4, then turn the crankshaft through 180° and carry out the procedure on the piston Nos 2 and 3. Check that there is a maximum difference of 0.07 mm protrusion between any two pistons.
23 If a dial test indicator is not available, piston protrusion may be measured using a straight-edge and feeler blades or Vernier calipers. However, this is much less accurate, and cannot therefore be recommended.
24 Note the greatest piston protrusion measurement, and use this to determine the correct cylinder head gasket from the following table. The series of holes on the front side of the gasket are used for thickness identification.

Piston protrusion	Gasket identification
0.55 to 0.60 mm	1 hole
0.61 to 0.65 mm	2 holes
0.66 to 0.70 mm	3 holes
0.71 to 0.75 mm	4 holes

Head bolt examination

25 Carefully examine the cylinder head bolts for signs of damage to the threads or head, and for any sign of corrosion. If the bolts are in a satisfactory condition, measure the length of each bolt from the underside of the head, to the end of the shank. Two different types of bolts may be fitted. The older type do not have integral, captive washers; on these bolts, they may be re-used providing that the measured length from beneath the head to the very end of

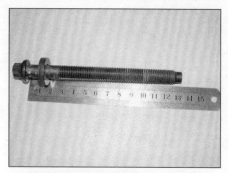

10.25 Measure the length of the cylinder head bolts from under the bolt head, not the washer

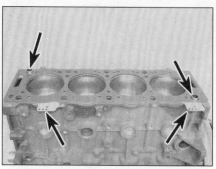

10.28 Fit the new gasket over the dowels, with the thickness identification holes at the front (arrowed)

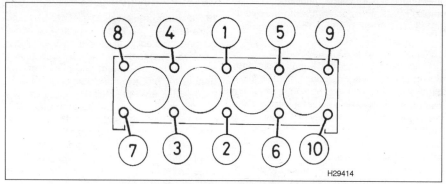

10.33 Cylinder head bolt tightening sequence

the bolt, does not exceed 129.0 mm ± 0.5 mm **(see illustration)**. On the later type of bolt, there is a washer which is captive under the head of the bolt; on these bolts, they may be re-used providing the measured length from beneath head (not the washer) to the end of the bolt, does not exceed 134.5 mm ± 0.05 mm. **Note:** *Considering the stress to which the cylinder head bolts are subjected, it is highly recommended that they are all renewed, regardless of their apparent condition.*

Refitting

26 Turn the crankshaft and position Nos 1 and 4 pistons at TDC, then turn the crankshaft a quarter turn (90°) anti-clockwise.
27 Thoroughly clean the surfaces of the cylinder head and block.
28 Make sure that the locating dowels are in

place, then fit the correct gasket the right way round on the cylinder block **(see illustration)**.
29 If necessary, refit the exhaust manifold with reference to Chapter 4B.
30 Carefully lower the cylinder head onto the gasket and block, making sure that it locates correctly onto the dowels.
31 Apply a light smear of grease to the threads, and to the underside of the heads, of the cylinder head bolts. Citroën recommend the use of Molykote G Rapid Plus (available from your Citroën dealer); in the absence of the specified grease, any good-quality high melting-point grease may be used.
32 Carefully insert the cylinder head bolts into their holes (*do not drop them in*) and initially finger-tighten them.
33 Working progressively and in sequence, tighten the cylinder head bolts to their Stage 1

torque setting, using a torque wrench and suitable socket **(see illustration)**.
34 Once all the bolts have been tightened to their Stage 1 torque setting, working again in the specified sequence, tighten each bolt to the specified Stage 2 setting. Finally, angle-tighten the bolts through the specified Stage 3 angle. It is recommended that an angle-measuring gauge is used during this stage of tightening, to ensure accuracy. **Note:** *Retightening of the cylinder head bolts after running the engine is not required.*
35 The remainder of refitting is a reversal of removal, noting the following points:
  a) *Use a new seal when refitting the coolant outlet housing.*
  b) *Refit the camshaft position sensor and set the air gap with reference to Chapter 4B.*
  c) *Tighten all fasteners to the specified torque where given.*
  d) *Refill the cooling system as described in Chapter 1B.*
  e) *The engine may run erratically for the first few miles, until the engine management ECM relearns its stored values.*

11 Sump –
removal and refitting

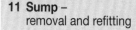

Removal

1 Drain the engine oil, then clean and refit the engine oil drain plug, tightening it securely. If the engine is nearing its service interval when the oil and filter are due for renewal, it is recommended that the filter is also removed, and a new one fitted. After reassembly, the engine can then be refilled with fresh oil. Refer to Chapter 1B for further information.
2 Chock the rear wheels then jack up the front of the vehicle and support it on axle stands (see *Jacking and vehicle support*). Undo the screws and remove the engine undershield.
3 On models with air conditioning, where the compressor is mounted onto the side of the sump, remove the drivebelt as described in Chapter 5A. Unbolt the compressor, and position it clear of the sump. Support the weight of the compressor by tying it to the vehicle, to prevent any excess strain being placed on the compressor lines. Do not disconnect the refrigerant lines from the compressor (refer to the warnings given in Chapter 3).
4 Undo the 4 Torx bolts, release the retaining clips and remove the sump shield (where fitted) **(see illustrations)**.
5 Slacken the clamps, undo the bolts and remove the charge air pipe from under the sump **(see illustration)**.
6 Where necessary, disconnect the wiring connector from the oil temperature sender unit, which is screwed into the sump.
7 Progressively slacken and remove all the sump retaining bolts **(see illustrations)**. Since the sump bolts vary in length, remove each

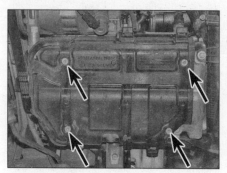

11.4a Undo the 4 Torx bolts (arrowed) . . .

11.4b . . . release the clips around the edge, and remove the sump shield

bolt in turn, and store it in its correct fitted order by pushing it through a clearly-marked cardboard template. This will avoid the possibility of installing the bolts in the wrong locations on refitting.

8 Try to break the joint by striking the sump with the palm of your hand, then lower and withdraw the sump from under the car. If the sump is stuck (which is quite likely) use a putty knife or similar, carefully inserted between the sump and block. Ease the knife along the joint until the sump is released. While the sump is removed, take the opportunity to check the oil pump pick-up/strainer for signs of clogging or splitting. If necessary, remove the pump as described in Section 12, and clean or renew the strainer.

Refitting

9 Clean all traces of sealant/gasket from the mating surfaces of the cylinder block/crankcase and sump, then use a clean rag to wipe out the sump and the engine's interior.

10 Ensure that the sump mating surfaces are clean and dry, then apply a thin coating of suitable sealant (E10 – available from Citroën dealers) to the sump or crankcase mating surface **(see illustration)**.

11 Offer up the sump to the cylinder block/crankcase. Refit its retaining bolts, ensuring that each bolt is screwed into its original location. Tighten the bolts evenly and progressively to the specified torque setting.

12 The remainder of refitting is a reversal of removal, remembering to refill the engine with oil as described in Chapter 1B.

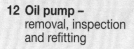

12 Oil pump – removal, inspection and refitting

Removal

1 Remove the timing belt as described in Section 7, then slide off the crankshaft sprocket. Recover the Woodruff key from the end of the crankshaft.

2 Remove the sump as described in Section 11.

3 Undo the retaining bolts and remove the front cover and crankshaft seal. Note the original locations of the cover screws – they are different lengths.

4 Undo the bolt securing the oil level pipe **(see illustration)**.

5 Pull out the key from the end of the crankshaft sprocket, then undo the pump mounting bolts, slide the pump, chain and crankshaft sprocket from the end of the engine **(see illustrations)**. Recover the O-ring between the sprocket and crankshaft.

Inspection

6 Examine the oil pump sprocket for signs of damage and wear, such as chipped or missing teeth. If the sprocket is worn, the pump assembly must be renewed, since the sprocket is not available separately. It is

11.5 Remove the charge air pipe (arrowed)

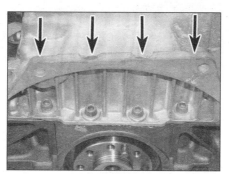

11.7b . . . access to the sump end bolts is through the holes (arrowed)

also recommended that the chain and drive sprocket, fitted to the crankshaft, be renewed at the same time.

7 Undo the retaining screws and remove the

11.7a Undo the 2 bolts securing the sump to the transmission (arrowed) . . .

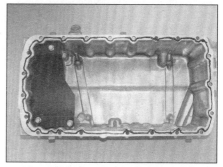

11.10 Apply a bead of sealant around the inside of the bolt holes

cover from the oil pump **(see illustration)**. Note the location of any identification marks on the inner and outer rotors for refitting.

8 Unscrew the plug and remove the pressure

12.4 Oil level pipe bracket bolt (arrowed)

12.5b . . . undo the pump mounting bolts (arrowed), slide the assembly from the crankshaft . . .

12.5a Remove the sprocket key . . .

12.5c . . . and recover the O-ring between the sprocket and the crankshaft (arrowed)

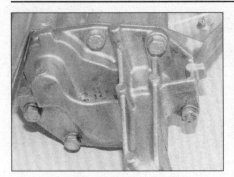

12.7 Oil pump cover screws

12.8 Oil pressure relief valve plug

12.15 Fit the O-ring to the end of the crankshaft

relief valve, spring and plunger, clean out and check the condition of the components **(see illustration)**.

9 Examine the pump rotors and body for signs of wear ridges or scoring. If worn, the complete pump assembly must be renewed.

10 Examine the relief valve piston for signs of wear or damage, and renew if necessary. The condition of the relief valve spring can only be measured by comparing it with a new one; if there is any doubt about its condition, it should also be renewed. Both the piston and spring are available individually.

11 Thoroughly clean the oil pump strainer with a suitable solvent, and check it for signs of clogging or splitting. If the strainer is damaged, the strainer and cover assembly must be renewed.

12 Locate the relief valve spring and piston in the strainer cover. Refit the cover to the pump body, aligning the relief valve plunger with its bore in the pump. Refit the baffle plate (where fitted) and the cover retaining bolts, and tighten them securely.

13 Prime the pump by filling it with clean engine oil before refitting.

Refitting

14 Before refitting the oil pump, ensure the mating faces of the pump and engine block are completely clean.

15 Fit the O-ring to the end of the crankshaft **(see illustration)**.

16 Engage the drive chain with the oil pump and crankshaft sprockets, then slide the crankshaft sprocket into place (aligning the slot in the sprocket with the keyway in the

crankshaft) as the pump is refitted. Refit the crankshaft key.

17 Refit the mounting bolts and tighten them to the specified torque. Note that the front, left-hand bolt is slightly longer than the others.

18 Apply a 3 mm bead of sealant to the oil seal housing flange. Refit the housing and tighten the bolts to the specified torque.

19 Fit a new oil seal to the carrier as described in Section 14.

20 Refit the bolt securing the oil level pipe.

21 The remainder of refitting is a reversal of removal.

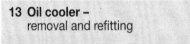

13 Oil cooler –
removal and refitting

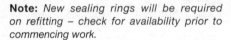

Note: *New sealing rings will be required on refitting – check for availability prior to commencing work.*

Removal

1 The cooler is fitted to the oil filter housing on the front of the cylinder block. Access is from under the vehicle. Undo the fasteners and remove the engine undershield. To further improve access, undo the mounting bolts and move the air conditioning compressor to one side. Suspend the compressor using wire or straps. There is no need to disconnect the refrigerant pipes.

2 Undo the 4 retaining bolts and detach the cooler from the housing **(see illustration)**. Recover the sealing rings and be prepared for coolant/oil spillage.

Refitting

3 Refitting is a reversal of removal, bearing in mind the following points:
  a) Use new sealing rings.
  b) Tighten the cooler mounting bolts securely.
  c) On completion lower the car to the ground. Check and if necessary top-up the oil and coolant levels, then start the engine and check for signs of oil or coolant leakage.

14 Oil seals –
renewal

Crankshaft

Right-hand oil seal

1 Remove the crankshaft sprocket as described in Section 8.

2 Measure and note the fitted depth of the oil seal.

3 Pull the oil seal from the housing using a hooked instrument. Alternatively, drill a small hole in the oil seal, and use a self-tapping screw and a pair of pliers to remove it **(see illustrations)**.

4 Clean the oil seal housing and the crankshaft sealing surface.

5 Press the new seal into the housing (open end first) to the previously-noted depth, using a suitable tube or socket. A piece of thin plastic or tape wound around the front of the crankshaft is useful to prevent damage to the

13.2 Oil cooler retaining bolts (arrowed)

14.3a Drill a small hole in the seal . . .

14.3b . . . insert a self-tapping screw and pull out the seal

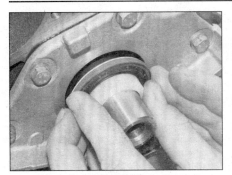

14.5a Locate the new seal and guide over the end of the crankshaft . . .

14.5b . . . then drive the seal home until it's flush with housing

14.10a Drill a hole in the seal . . .

14.10b . . . then insert a self-tapping screw and pull out the seal

14.19a Use a socket or similar to drive the seal into place . . .

14.19b . . . until it's flush with the casing surface

oil seal as it is fitted. Note that special tools to guide the seal onto the crankshaft and drive it into place may be available from Citroën **(see illustrations)**.

6 Where applicable, remove the plastic or tape from the end of the crankshaft.

7 Refit the timing belt crankshaft sprocket as described in Section 8.

Left-hand oil seal

8 Remove the flywheel/driveplate, as described in Section 16.

9 Measure and note the fitted depth of the oil seal.

10 Pull the oil seal from the housing using a hooked instrument. Alternatively, drill a small hole in the oil seal, and use a self-tapping screw and a pair of pliers to remove it **(see illustrations)**.

11 Clean the oil seal housing and the crankshaft sealing surface.

12 Press the new seal into the housing (open end first) to the previously-noted depth, using a suitable tube or socket. A piece of thin plastic or tape wound around the end of the crankshaft is useful to prevent damage to the oil seal as it is fitted.

13 Where applicable, remove the plastic or tape from the end of the crankshaft.

14 Refit the flywheel/driveplate, as described in Section 16.

Camshaft

Right-hand oil seal

15 Remove the camshaft sprocket as described in Section 8. In principle there is no need to remove the timing belt completely,

but remember that if the belt has been contaminated with oil, it must be renewed.

16 Pull the oil seal from the housing using a hooked instrument. Alternatively, drill a small hole in the oil seal and use a self-tapping screw and a pair of pliers to remove it **(see illustration 14.3b)**.

17 Clean the oil seal housing and the camshaft sealing surface.

18 Fit it over the end of the camshaft, open end first. Note that the seal must not be oiled prior to fitting. A piece of thin plastic or tape wound around the end of the camshaft is useful to prevent damage to the oil seal as it is fitted.

19 Press the seal into the housing until it is flush with the end face of the cylinder head. Use an M10 bolt (screwed into the end of the camshaft), washers and a suitable tube or socket that bears only on the outer edge of the seal to press it into position **(see illustrations)**.

15.1 Oil pressure warning light switch (arrowed)

20 Refit the camshaft sprocket as described in Section 8.

21 Where necessary, fit a new timing belt with reference to Section 7.

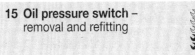

15 Oil pressure switch – removal and refitting

Removal

1 The switch is screwed into the oil filter housing **(see illustration)**. Access is from under the vehicle. Undo the fasteners and remove the engine undershield. To further improve access, undo the mounting bolts and move the air conditioning compressor to one side. Suspend the compressor from the radiator crossmember using wire or straps. There is no need to disconnect the refrigerant pipes.

2 Remove the protective sleeve from the wiring plug (where applicable), then disconnect the wiring from the switch.

3 Unscrew the switch from the cylinder block, and recover the sealing washer. Be prepared for oil spillage, and if the switch is to be left removed from the engine for any length of time, plug the hole in the cylinder block.

Refitting

4 Examine the sealing washer for any signs of damage or deterioration, and if necessary renew.

5 Refit the switch, complete with washer, and tighten it to the specified torque where given.

16.3 Flywheel retaining bolts

6 Refit all components removed for access to the switch.

7 Check the engine oil level, and top-up as required (see *Weekly checks*).

8 Check for correct operation of the warning light, and for signs of oil leaks once the engine has been started and warmed-up to normal operating temperature.

16 Flywheel/driveplate – removal, inspection and refitting

Removal

Flywheel

1 Remove the transmission as described in Chapter 7A, then remove the clutch assembly as described in Chapter 6.

2 Prevent the flywheel from turning by locking the ring gear teeth **(see illustration 5.3)**. Alternatively, bolt a strap between the flywheel and the cylinder block/crankcase. *Do not attempt to lock the flywheel in position using the crankshaft pulley locking tool described in Section 3.*

3 Slacken and remove the flywheel retaining bolts, and remove the flywheel from the end of the crankshaft **(see illustration)**. Be careful not to drop it; it is heavy. If the flywheel locating dowel is a loose fit in the crankshaft end, remove it and store it with the flywheel for safe-keeping. Discard the flywheel bolts; new ones must be used on refitting.

Driveplate

4 Remove the transmission as described in Chapter 7B. Lock the driveplate as described in paragraph 2 of this Section. Mark the relationship between the torque converter plate and the driveplate, and slacken all the driveplate retaining bolts.

5 Remove the retaining bolts, along with the torque converter plate and the two shims (one fitted on each side of the torque converter plate). Note that the shims are of different thickness, the thicker one being on the outside of the torque converter plate. Discard the driveplate retaining bolts; new ones must be used on refitting.

6 Remove the driveplate from the end of the crankshaft. If the locating dowel is a loose fit

16.11 Note the locating dowel and the corresponding hole (arrowed)

in the crankshaft end, remove it and store it with the driveplate for safe-keeping.

Inspection

7 On models with manual transmission, examine the flywheel for scoring of the clutch face, and for wear or chipping of the ring gear teeth. If the clutch face is scored, the flywheel may be surface-ground, but renewal is preferable. Seek the advice of a Citroën dealer or engine reconditioning specialist to see if machining is possible. If the ring gear is worn or damaged, the flywheel must be renewed, as it is not possible to renew the ring gear separately.

8 On models with automatic transmission, check the torque converter driveplate carefully for signs of distortion. Look for any hairline cracks around the bolt holes or radiating outwards from the centre, and inspect the ring gear teeth for signs of wear or chipping. If any sign of wear or damage is found, the driveplate must be renewed.

Refitting

Flywheel

9 Clean the mating surfaces of the flywheel and crankshaft. Remove any remaining locking compound from the threads of the crankshaft holes, using the correct size of tap, if available.

HAYNES HiNT *If a suitable tap is not available, cut two slots along the threads of one of the old flywheel bolts, and use the bolt to remove the locking compound from the threads.*

10 If the new flywheel retaining bolts are not supplied with their threads already precoated, apply a suitable thread-locking compound to the threads of each bolt.

11 Ensure that the locating dowel is in position. Offer up the flywheel, locating it on the dowel, and fit the new retaining bolts **(see illustration)**.

12 Lock the flywheel using the method employed on dismantling, and tighten the retaining bolts to the specified torque.

13 Refit the clutch as described in Chapter 6.

Remove the flywheel locking tool, and refit the transmission as described in Chapter 7A.

Driveplate

14 Carry out the operations described above in paragraphs 9 and 10, substituting 'driveplate' for all references to the flywheel.

15 Locate the driveplate on its locating dowel.

16 Offer up the torque converter plate, with the thinner shim positioned behind the plate and the thicker shim on the outside, and align the marks made prior to removal.

17 Fit the new retaining bolts, then lock the driveplate using the method employed on dismantling. Tighten the retaining bolts to the specified torque wrench setting.

18 Remove the driveplate locking tool, and refit the transmission (see Chapter 7B).

17 Engine/transmission mountings – inspection and renewal

Inspection

1 If improved access is required, chock the rear wheels then jack up the front of the car and support it on axle stands (see *Jacking and vehicle support*). Undo the screws and remove the engine undershield.

2 Check the mounting rubbers to see if they are cracked, hardened or separated from the metal at any point; renew the mounting if any such damage or deterioration is evident.

3 Check that all the mountings' fasteners are securely tightened; use a torque wrench to check if possible.

4 Using a large screwdriver or a crowbar, check for wear in each mounting by carefully levering against it to check for free play. Where this is not possible, enlist the aid of an assistant to move the engine/transmission back-and-forth, or from side-to-side, while you watch the mounting. While some free play is to be expected even from new components, excessive wear should be obvious. If excessive free play is found, check first that the fasteners are correctly secured, then renew any worn components as described below.

Renewal

Right-hand mounting

5 Release all the relevant hoses and wiring from their retaining clips. Place the hoses/wiring clear of the mounting so that the removal procedure is not hindered. Undo the screws and remove the engine undershield.

6 Place a jack beneath the engine, with a block of wood on the jack head. Raise the jack until it is supporting the weight of the engine.

7 Undo the bolts/nuts securing the engine mounting to the body and the support bracket **(see illustration)**.

8 If required, undo the bolts/nuts securing the support bracket to the cylinder head/cylinder block.

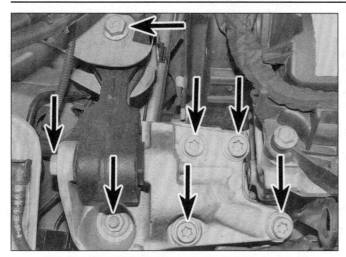

17.7 Right-hand engine mounting bolts/nuts (arrowed)

17.16 Left-hand engine/transmission mounting assembly

9 Check all components carefully for signs of wear or damage, and renew as necessary.
10 Where removed, refit the support bracket to the cylinder head, and tighten the bolts securely.
11 Refit the mount to the body and support bracket, then tighten the bolts to the specified torque.
12 Remove the jack from underneath the engine.

Left-hand mounting

13 Remove the battery (see Chapter 5A). Undo the screws and remove the engine undershield.
14 Remove the diesel engine management ECM and module box as described in Chapter 4B.
15 Place a jack beneath the transmission, with a block of wood on the jack head. Raise the jack until it is supporting the weight of the transmission.
16 Undo the nuts securing the mounting in position and remove it from the engine compartment (see illustration).
17 If required, undo the bolts/nut and remove the support bracket.
18 Check all components carefully for signs of wear or damage, and renew as necessary.

19 Clean the threads of the mounting stud (where applicable), and apply a coat of thread-locking compound to its threads.
20 Refit the support bracket and mounting, tightening the bolts/nuts to the specified torque.
21 The remainder of refitting is a reversal of removal.

Rear engine torque rod

22 If not already done, chock the rear wheels, then jack up the front of the vehicle and support it securely on axle stands (see Jacking and vehicle support). Undo the screws and remove the engine undershield.
23 Unscrew and remove the bolt securing the torque rod to the driveshaft intermediate bearing housing (see illustration).
24 Remove the bolt securing the torque rod to the subframe. Withdraw the torque rod.
25 To remove the intermediate bearing housing assembly it will first be necessary to remove the right-hand driveshaft as described in Chapter 8.
26 With the driveshaft removed, undo the retaining bolts and remove the bearing housing from the rear of the cylinder block.
27 Check carefully for signs of wear or damage on all components, and renew them

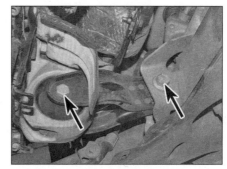

17.23 Rear engine torque rod mounting bolts (arrowed)

where necessary. The rubber bush fitted to the bearing housing is available as a separate item (at the time of writing), and can be pressed out of, and back into place.
28 On reassembly, fit the bearing housing assembly to the rear of the cylinder block, and tighten its retaining bolts securely. Refit the driveshaft as described in Chapter 8.
29 Refit the torque rod, and tighten both its bolts to their specified torque settings. Refit the engine undershield.
30 Lower the vehicle to the ground.

Chapter 2 Part F:
Engine removal and overhaul procedures

Contents

Degrees of difficulty

Easy, suitable for novice with little experience 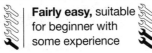	**Fairly easy,** suitable for beginner with some experience	**Fairly difficult,** suitable for competent DIY mechanic	**Difficult,** suitable for experienced DIY mechanic	**Very difficult,** suitable for expert DIY or professional

Specifications

Note: *At the time of writing, some specifications for certain engines were not available. Where the relevant specifications are not given here, refer to your Citroën dealer for further information.*

Engine identification

Petrol engines

Indirect injection:
  Designation:
    1.8 litre EW7J4
    2.0 litre EW10J4
  Engine code:
    1.8 litre 6FZ
    2.0 litre . . . .   RFN
Direct injection:
  Designation:
    2.0 litre EW10D
  Engine code . . . .   RLZ

Diesel engines

1.6 litre:
  Designation DV6TED4
  Engine codes . . . .   9HY or 9HZ
2.0 litre SOHC:
  Designation . . . .   DW10TD or DW10ATED
  Engine codes:
    DW10TD . . . .   RHY
    DW10ATED . . . .   RHZ
2.0 litre DOHC:
  Designation DW10BTED4
  Engine code . . . .   RHR

Cylinder head

Maximum gasket face distortion:
EW engines..	0.05 mm
DV engines..	0.05 mm
DW engines...	0.03 mm

Cylinder head height:

EW7J4 and EW10J4 engines:
Nominal..	137.00 ± 0.05 mm
Minimum (after grinding).........................	136.70 ± 0.05 mm

EW10D engines:
Nominal..	138.00 ± 0.05 mm
Minimum (after grinding).........................	137.70 ± 0.05 mm

DV6TED engines:
Nominal..	124.00 ± 0.05 mm
Minimum (after grinding).........................	Not available

DW10TD and ATED engines:
Nominal..	133.00 ± 0.05 mm
Minimum (after grinding).........................	132.8 mm

DW10BTED4 engines:
Nominal..	133.00 ± 0.05 mm
Minimum (after grinding).........................	132.60 mm

Valves

	Inlet	Exhaust
Valve stem diameter:		
EW engines..	5.985 +0.0, -0.015 mm	5.975 +0.0, -0.015 mm
DV6TED engines...................................	5.485 +0.0, -0.015 mm	5.475 +0.0, -0.015 mm
DW10TD and ATED engines.......................	5.978 ± 0.05 mm	5.973 ± 0.05 mm
DW10BTED4 engines..............................	5.978 ± 0.009 mm	5.968 ± 0.009 mm
Overall length:		
EW7 engines......................................	104.17 ± 0.1 mm	104.10 ± 0.1 mm
EW10J4 engines..................................	106.18 ± 0.3 mm	103.66 ± 0.1 mm
EW10D engines...................................	106.04 ± 0.35 mm	102.74 ± 0.2 mm
DV6TED engines..................................	96.43 ± 0.25 mm	96.65 ± 0.2 mm
DW10TD and ATED engines.......................	106.13 ± 0.15 mm	106.73 ± 0.15 mm
DW10BTED4 engines..............................	105.00 +0.20, -0.25 mm	105 +0.2, -0.25 mm

Cylinder block

Cylinder bore diameter (nominal):
EW7 engines.......................................	82.70 mm
EW10 engines......................................	85.00 mm
DV6TED engines (reboring not possible)	75.00 mm
DW10 engines	85.00 mm

Piston rings

End gaps:

EW engines:
Top compression ring.............................	0.2 +0.25, +0.0 mm
Second compression ring..........................	0.2 +0.25, +0.0 mm

DV6TED engines:
Top compression ring.............................	0.15 to 0.25 mm
Second compression ring..........................	0.30 to 0.50 mm
Oil control ring	0.35 to 0.55 mm

DW10 engines:
Top compression ring.............................	0.20 to 0.35 mm
Second compression ring..........................	0.80 to 1.00 mm
Oil control ring	0.25 to 0.50 mm

Crankshaft

Endfloat:
EW engines..	0.06 to 0.15 mm
DV6TED engines thrustwasher thickness....................	2.40 ± 0.05 mm
DW10 engines	0.07 to 0.32 mm
Maximum bearing journal out-of-round (all models)	0.007 mm

1 General information

Included in this Part of Chapter 2 are details of removing the engine/transmission from the car and general overhaul procedures for the cylinder head, cylinder block/crankcase and all other engine internal components.

The information given ranges from advice concerning preparation for an overhaul and the purchase of parts, to detailed step-by-step procedures covering removal, inspection, renovation and refitting of engine internal components.

After Section 6, all instructions are based on the assumption that the engine has been removed from the car. For information concerning in-car engine repair, as well as the removal and refitting of those external components necessary for full overhaul, refer to Part A, B, C, D or E of this Chapter (as applicable) and to Section 6. Ignore any preliminary dismantling operations described in Part A, B, C, D or E that are no longer relevant once the engine has been removed from the car.

Apart from torque wrench settings, which are given at the beginning of Part A, B, C, D or E (as applicable), all specifications relating to engine overhaul are at the beginning of this Part of Chapter 2.

2 Engine overhaul – general information

It is not always easy to determine when, or if, an engine should be completely overhauled, as a number of factors must be considered.

High mileage is not necessarily an indication that an overhaul is needed, while low mileage does not preclude the need for an overhaul. Frequency of servicing is probably the most important consideration. An engine which has had regular and frequent oil and filter changes, as well as other required maintenance, should give many thousands of miles of reliable service. Conversely, a neglected engine may require an overhaul very early in its life.

Excessive oil consumption is an indication that piston rings, valve seals and/or valve guides are in need of attention. Make sure that oil leaks are not responsible before deciding that the rings and/or guides are worn. Perform a compression test, as described in Part A or B (petrol engines) or C, D or E (diesel engines) of this Chapter, to determine the likely cause of the problem.

Check the oil pressure with a gauge fitted in place of the oil pressure switch, and compare it with that specified. If it is extremely low, the main and big-end bearings, and/or the oil pump, are probably worn out.

Loss of power, rough running, knocking or metallic engine noises, excessive valve gear noise, and high fuel consumption may also point to the need for an overhaul, especially if they are all present at the same time. If a complete service does not cure the situation, major mechanical work is the only solution.

An engine overhaul involves restoring all internal parts to the specification of a new engine. During an overhaul, the pistons and the piston rings are renewed. New main and big-end bearings are generally fitted; if necessary, the crankshaft may be renewed to restore the journals. The valves are also serviced as well, since they are usually in less-than-perfect condition at this point. While the engine is being overhauled, other components, such as the distributor, starter and alternator, can be overhauled as well. The end result should be an as-new engine that will give many trouble-free miles.

Note: *Critical cooling system components such as the hoses, thermostat and coolant pump should be renewed when an engine is overhauled. The radiator should be checked carefully, to ensure that it is not clogged or leaking. Also, it is a good idea to renew the oil pump whenever the engine is overhauled.*

Before beginning the engine overhaul, read through the entire procedure, to familiarise yourself with the scope and requirements of the job. Overhauling an engine is not difficult if you follow carefully all of the instructions, have the necessary tools and equipment, and pay close attention to all specifications. It can, however, be time-consuming. Plan on the car being off the road for a minimum of two weeks, especially if parts must be taken to an engineering works for repair or reconditioning. Check on the availability of parts and make sure that any necessary special tools and equipment are obtained in advance. Most work can be done with typical hand tools, although a number of precision measuring tools are required for inspecting parts to determine if they must be renewed. Often the engineering works will handle the inspection of parts and offer advice concerning reconditioning and renewal.

Always wait until the engine has been completely dismantled, and until all components (especially the cylinder block/crankcase and the crankshaft) have been inspected, before deciding what service and repair operations must be performed by an engineering works. The condition of these components will be the major factor to consider when determining whether to overhaul the original engine, or to buy a reconditioned unit. Do not, therefore, purchase parts or have overhaul work done on other components until they have been thoroughly inspected. As a general rule, time is the primary cost of an overhaul, so it does not pay to fit worn or sub-standard parts.

As a final note, to ensure maximum life and minimum trouble from a reconditioned engine, everything must be assembled with care, in a spotlessly-clean environment.

3 Engine/transmission removal – methods and precautions

If you have decided that the engine must be removed for overhaul or major repair work, several preliminary steps should be taken.

Engine/transmission removal is extremely complicated and involved on these vehicles. It must be stated, that unless the vehicle can be positioned on a ramp, or raised and supported on axle stands over an inspection pit, it will be very difficult to carry out the work involved.

Cleaning the engine compartment and engine/transmission before beginning the removal procedure will help keep tools clean and organised.

An engine hoist will also be necessary. Make sure the equipment is rated in excess of the combined weight of the engine and transmission. Safety is of primary importance, considering the potential hazards involved in removing the engine/transmission from the car.

The help of an assistant is essential. Apart from the safety aspects involved, there are many instances when one person cannot simultaneously perform all of the operations required during engine/transmission removal.

Plan the operation ahead of time. Before starting work, arrange for the hire of or obtain all of the tools and equipment you will need. Some of the equipment necessary to perform engine/transmission removal and installation safely (in addition to an engine hoist) is as follows: a heavy duty trolley jack, complete sets of spanners and sockets as described in the rear of this manual, wooden blocks, and plenty of rags and cleaning solvent for mopping-up spilled oil, coolant and fuel. If the hoist must be hired, make sure that you arrange for it in advance, and perform all of the operations possible without it beforehand. This will save you money and time.

Plan for the car to be out of use for quite a while. An engineering machine shop or engine reconditioning specialist will be required to perform some of the work which cannot be accomplished without special equipment. These places often have a busy schedule, so it would be a good idea to consult them before removing the engine, in order to accurately estimate the amount of time required to rebuild or repair components that may need work.

During the engine/transmission removal procedure, it is advisable to make notes of the locations of all brackets, cable ties, earthing points, etc, as well as how the wiring harnesses, hoses and electrical connections are attached and routed around the engine and engine compartment. An effective way of doing this is to take a series of photographs of the various components before they are disconnected or removed; the resulting photographs will prove invaluable when the engine/transmission is refitted.

Always be extremely careful when removing and refitting the engine/transmission. Serious

4.9 Undo the 2 bolts securing the accelerator cable potentiometer (arrowed)

injury can result from careless actions. Plan ahead and take your time, and a job of this nature, although major, can be accomplished successfully.

On all C5 models, the engine must be removed complete with the transmission as an assembly. There is insufficient clearance in the engine compartment to remove the engine leaving the transmission in the vehicle. The assembly is removed by raising the front of the vehicle, and lowering the assembly from the engine compartment.

4 Engine and manual transmission – removal, separation and refitting

Note: *Such is the complexity of the power unit arrangement on these vehicles, and the variations that may be encountered according*

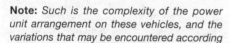

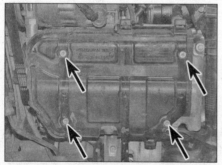

4.11a Undo the 4 Torx bolts (arrowed) . . .

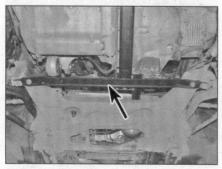

4.12 Undo the bolts and remove the tie bar (arrowed)

to model and optional equipment fitted, that the following should be regarded as a guide to the work involved, rather than a step-by-step procedure. Where differences are encountered, or additional component disconnection or removal is necessary, make notes of the work involved as an aid to refitting.
Note: *On diesel models with air conditioning, have the system discharged by a suitably-equipped specialist. It is necessary to completely remove the compressor during this procedure.*

Removal

1 Remove the battery and battery tray (see Chapter 5A).
2 Remove the engine management ECM and module box as described in Chapter 4A or 4B.
3 Chock the rear wheels then jack up the front of the vehicle and support it on axle stands (see *Jacking and vehicle support*). Remove both front roadwheels and wheel arch liners. Also remove the undershield from beneath the engine and transmission where fitted.
4 Remove the engine top cover. To improve access, remove the bonnet as described in Chapter 11.
5 Drain the cooling system with reference to Chapter 1A or 1B.
6 Drain the transmission oil as described in Chapter 7A. Refit the drain plug, and tighten it to the specified torque setting.
7 If the engine is to be dismantled, drain the engine oil and remove the oil filter as described in Chapter 1A or 1B. Clean and refit the drain plug, tightening it to the specified torque.

4.11b . . . and release the clips on the sides of the sump shield

4.18 Use a hose clamp to seal the fluid supply hose to the power steering pump

8 Refer to Chapter 8 and remove both front driveshafts.
9 Undo the 2 Torx bolts securing the accelerator cable potentiometer (where applicable) to the top of the transmission mounting **(see illustration)**. Move the assembly to one side – there's no need to disconnect the accelerator cable or wiring plug.
10 Refer to Chapter 5A and remove the auxiliary drivebelt.
11 Where fitted, undo the 4 Torx bolts, release the clips and remove the sump shield **(see illustrations)**.
12 Undo the bolts and remove the tie bar from the front of the subframe **(see illustration)**.
13 On diesel engines with an intercooler, remove the air duct leading from the turbocharger to the intercooler.
14 Remove the exhaust system with reference to Chapter 4A or 4B.
15 From underneath the vehicle, slacken and remove the nuts and bolts securing the rear engine mounting connecting link to the mounting assembly and subframe, and remove the connecting link. Refer to Chapter 2A, 2B, 2C, 2D or 2E.
16 On petrol models with air conditioning, refer to Chapter 3 and unbolt the compressor from the engine. **Do not** disconnect the refrigerant lines. Support or tie the compressor to one side. On diesel models, completely remove compressor as described in Chapter 3.
17 On some models, the power steering fluid pipe is attached to the left-hand end of the transmission. Undo the bolt and release the power steering fluid pipe from the transmission, then on all models, undo the bolt securing the power steering pipe to the left-hand side of the subframe.
18 On models with an engine-mounted power steering pump, use a hose clamp to seal the fluid supply hose, then disconnect it from the pump. Plug the openings to prevent contamination. Disconnect the wiring plug, unbolt the pump from its mounting, and move it to one side without disconnecting the pressure pipe **(see illustration)**. Place a rag over the alternator to prevent oil contamination.
19 On diesel engines with an intercooler, remove the air duct leading from the intercooler to the inlet manifold.
20 Refer to Chapter 4A or 4B and remove the air cleaner, and all remaining air inlet ducts.
21 On petrol models, remove the inlet manifold as described in Chapter 4A.
22 On diesel models, disconnect the fuel supply and return hoses at the right-hand side of the engine compartment. Plug/cover the openings to prevent contamination.
23 Refer to Chapter 3 and remove the radiator.
24 Remove the engine management ECM and module box as described in Chapter 4A or 4B. Note their fitted positions, then disconnect the engine/transmission harness wiring plugs and earth connections from the fusebox on the right-hand side of the engine compartment. Make a note of the harness routing. Also trace

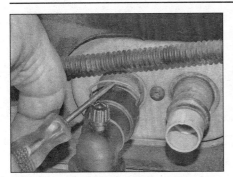

4.27 Prise up the clips and disconnect the hoses from the bulkhead

4.32 With the hoist attached to the lifting eyes, lower the assembly to the ground

4.46 The power steering rear bolt must be tightened last

the wiring connectors back to the transmission and disconnect all engine related wiring and earth leads in this area, including the earth lead on the top of the transmission casing. Check that all the relevant connectors have been disconnected, and that the harness is released from all the clips or ties. Move the harness to one side.

25 Remove the clutch slave cylinder and move it to one side (without disconnecting the hose) as described in Chapter 6, and disconnect the selector cables as described in Chapter 7A. Release the hose from the retaining clip.

26 On diesel models depress the release button and disconnect the brake vacuum pipe from the servo. Also disconnect the vacuum pipes from throttle bodies and swirl-control unit (where applicable).

27 At the bulkhead, disconnect the coolant hoses from the heater matrix **(see illustration)**.

28 Raise the front of the vehicle sufficiently high enough to be able to remove the engine/ transmission assembly from underneath it. Position a workshop trolley jack under the engine/transmission, or attach an engine lifting hoist. Take the weight of the engine.

29 Refer to Chapter 2A, 2B, 2C, 2D or 2E and unbolt the right-hand engine mounting connecting link/mounting.

30 Unscrew and remove the left-hand engine/transmission mounting, then remove the bracket from the top of the transmission.

31 Make a final check that any components which would prevent the removal of the engine/transmission from the car have been removed or disconnected. Ensure that components such as the gearchange selector cables are secured so that they cannot be damaged on removal.

32 Carefully lower the assembly to the ground, making sure it clears the surrounding engine compartment components **(see illustration)**.

Separation

33 With the engine/transmission assembly removed, support the assembly on suitable blocks of wood on a workbench (or failing that, on a clean area of the workshop floor).

34 Undo the retaining bolts, and remove the flywheel lower cover plate(s) and lower brace (where fitted) from the transmission.

35 Slacken and remove the retaining bolts,

and remove the starter motor from the transmission.

36 Ensure that both engine and transmission are adequately supported, then slacken and remove the remaining bolts securing the transmission housing to the engine. Note the correct fitted positions of each bolt (and the relevant brackets) as they are removed, to use as a reference on refitting.

37 Carefully withdraw the transmission from the engine, ensuring that the weight of the transmission is not allowed to hang on the input shaft while it is engaged with the clutch friction disc. On models with the 'pull-type' clutch, make sure that the release fork disengages fully from the release bearing.

38 If they are loose, remove the locating dowels from the engine or transmission, and keep them in a safe place.

Refitting

39 If the engine and transmission have not been separated, perform the operations described below from paragraph 46 onwards.

40 On ML6 gearboxes, apply a smear of high melting-point grease (Citroën recommend the use of Molykote BR2 plus – available from your Citroën dealer) to the splines of the transmission input shaft. Do not apply too much, otherwise there is a possibility of the grease contaminating the clutch friction disc. On all other gearboxes, Citroën insist no grease is applied.

41 On models with the 'pull-type' clutch, fit the release bearing to the release fork with reference to Chapter 6, ensuring that the snap-ring is correctly in position in its groove.

42 Ensure that the locating dowels are correctly positioned in the engine or transmission.

43 Carefully offer the transmission to the engine, until the locating dowels are engaged. Ensure that the weight of the transmission is not allowed to hang on the input shaft as it is engaged with the clutch friction disc.

44 Refit the transmission housing-to-engine bolts, ensuring that all the necessary brackets are correctly positioned, and tighten them securely.

45 On models with the 'pull-type' clutch, use the special tool described in Chapter 6 to pull the release fork in order to force the release bearing through the friction disc.

46 The remainder of the refitting procedure is a direct reversal of the removal sequence, with reference to the relevant chapters and noting the following points:

a) *Ensure that the wiring loom is correctly routed and retained by all the relevant retaining clips; all connectors should be correctly and securely reconnected.*

b) *Prior to refitting the driveshafts to the transmission, renew the driveshaft oil seals as described in Chapter 7A.*

c) *Refer to Chapter 10 when refitting the power steering pump; the rear mounting bolt must be tightened last* **(see illustration)**.

d) *Ensure that all coolant hoses are correctly reconnected, and securely retained by their retaining clips.*

e) *Refill the engine and transmission with the correct quantity and type of lubricant, as described in Chapters 1A or 1B, and 7A.*

f) *Refill the cooling system as described in Chapter 1A or 1B.*

g) *Bleed the power steering system as described in Chapter 10.*

h) *Have the air conditioning system recharged (where applicable) by a suitably-equipped specialist.*

5 Engine and automatic transmission – removal, separation and refitting

Note: *Such is the complexity of the power unit arrangement on these vehicles, and the variations that may be encountered according to model and optional equipment fitted, that the following should be regarded as a guide to the work involved, rather than a step-by-step procedure. Where differences are encountered, or additional component disconnection or removal is necessary, make notes of the work involved as an aid to refitting.*

Removal

1 The procedure is essentially the same as described in Section 4, but carry out the following operations with reference to Chapter 7B.

a) *Carefully prise the selector cable balljoint from the selector lever on the transmission multifunction switch. Extract the horseshoe-shaped clip securing the*

cable to the mounting bracket on the transmission.
b) Trace the wiring back from the multifunction switch to the wiring connector. Release the connector from the support bracket and disconnect it. Release the switch wiring from the support clip on the transmission.
c) Using hose clamps or similar, clamp both the fluid cooler coolant hoses to minimise coolant loss during subsequent operations.
d) Disconnect both coolant hoses from the fluid cooler being prepared for some coolant spillage. Wash off any spilt coolant immediately with cold water, and dry the surrounding area before proceeding further.
e) Unclip the wiring connector from the support bracket located just above the fluid cooler, then remove the support bracket.
f) Disconnect the earth cable from the stud on the transmission.
g) Remove the wiring harness bracket and the hose support bracket from the transmission.
h) Disconnect the wiring from the speedometer transducer (speedometer drive) and crankshaft (RPM) sensor, then remove the sensor from the bellhousing.
i) Remove the starter motor.
j) Label and disconnect any remaining wiring connectors and support brackets connected to the transmission.

Separation

2 With the engine/transmission assembly removed, support the assembly on suitable blocks of wood, on a workbench (or failing that, on a clean area of the workshop floor).
3 Locate the access hole at the lower of the cylinder block, then turn the crankshaft, by means of a socket on the crankshaft pulley bolt, until one of the torque converter retaining bolts is accessible through the access hole.
4 Undo the accessible torque converter bolt then turn the crankshaft as necessary and undo the remaining two bolts.
5 Slacken and remove the bolts securing the transmission housing to the engine. Note the correct fitted positions of each bolt and brackets, as they are removed, to use as a reference on refitting. Make a final check that all components have been disconnected, and are positioned clear of the transmission so that they will not hinder the removal procedure.
6 With the bolts removed, pull the transmission off the engine, to free it from its locating dowels. Once the transmission is free, and sufficient clearance exists, insert a bolt with a suitable washer through the crankshaft (RPM) sensor hole in the transmission bellhousing, to retain the torque converter on the transmission.

Preparation for reconnection

7 Prior to reconnection it is necessary to make a simple tool to align the torque converter

with the driveplate as the transmission is refitted. To make the tool, obtain a bolt of the same size as the torque converter retaining bolts, but long enough to extend through the access hole in the cylinder block when the transmission is refitted.
8 Cut the head off the bolt and cut a slot (to enable it to be unscrewed) in the plain end. Check that the tool will slide easily through the torque converter retaining bolt hole in the driveplate.
9 Turn the engine crankshaft so that one of the torque converter retaining bolt holes in the driveplate, is aligned with the access hole in the cylinder block. Screw the alignment tool (finger-tight only) into one of the retaining bolt holes in the torque converter. Turn the torque converter so that the alignment tool is in approximately the correct position, relative to the cylinder block access hole. As the transmission is refitted, the alignment tool will pass through the retaining bolt hole in the driveplate and through the access hole. It can then be unscrewed with a screwdriver and the first torque converter retaining bolt fitted in its place.
10 Check that the torque converter support bush fitted to the centre of the crankshaft is in good condition, and in place.
11 Ensure that the engine/transmission locating dowels are correctly positioned prior to installation.

Reconnection

12 The transmission is reconnected by a reversal of the removal procedure, bearing in mind the following points:
a) Guide the transmission into position ensuring that the alignment tool passes through the driveplate and access hole.
b) Remove the bolt used to retain the torque converter in place, just before the transmission engages with the engine.
c) Once the transmission is bolted to the engine, remove the alignment tool and fit the first torque converter retaining bolt. Turn the crankshaft as necessary and fit the other two bolts.

Refitting

13 Refit the starter motor, and securely tighten its retaining bolts.
14 Refit the engine/transmission unit to the vehicle as described in the relevant refitting paragraphs of Section 4.
15 The remainder of the refitting procedure is a reversal of the removal sequence, noting the following points:
a) Ensure that the wiring loom is correctly routed, and retained by all the relevant retaining clips; all connectors should be correctly and securely reconnected.
b) Prior to refitting the driveshafts to the transmission, renew the driveshaft oil seals as described in Chapter 7B.
c) Ensure that all coolant hoses are correctly reconnected, and securely retained by their retaining clips.

d) Adjust the accelerator cable as described in the appropriate part of Chapter 4B.
e) Refill the engine and transmission with correct quantity and type of lubricant, as described in Chapter 1B and 7B.
f) Refill the cooling system (se Chapter 1B).

6 Engine overhaul – dismantling sequence

1 It is much easier to dismantle and work on the engine if it is mounted on a portable engine stand. These stands can often be hired from a tool hire shop. Before the engine is mounted on a stand, the flywheel/driveplate should be removed, so that the stand bolts can be tightened into the end of the cylinder block/crankcase.
2 If a stand is not available, it is possible to dismantle the engine with it blocked up on a sturdy workbench, or on the floor. Be extra careful not to tip or drop the engine when working without a stand.
3 If you are going to obtain a reconditioned engine, all the external components must be removed first, to be transferred to the new engine (just as they will if you are doing a complete engine overhaul yourself). These components include the following:
a) Engine wiring harness and support brackets.
b) Alternator, power steering pump and air conditioning compressor mounting brackets (as applicable).
c) Coolant inlet and outlet housings.
d) Dipstick tube.
e) Fuel system components.
f) All electrical switches and sensors.
g) Inlet and exhaust manifolds and, where fitted, the turbocharger.
h) Oil filter and oil cooler.
i) Flywheel/driveplate.
Note: When removing the external components from the engine, pay close attention to details that may be helpful or important during refitting. Note the fitted position of gaskets, seals, spacers, pins, washers, bolts, and other small items.
4 If you are obtaining a 'short' engine (which consists of the engine cylinder block/ crankcase, crankshaft, pistons and connecting rods all assembled), then the cylinder head, sump, oil pump, and timing belt will have to be removed also.
5 If you are planning a complete overhaul, the engine can be dismantled, and the internal components removed, in the order given below, referring to Part A, B, C, D or E of this Chapter unless otherwise stated.
a) Inlet and exhaust manifolds (Chapter 4A or 4B).
b) Timing belt, sprockets and tensioner.
c) Coolant pump (Chapter 3).
d) Cylinder head.
e) Flywheel/driveplate.
f) Sump.

g) *Oil pump.*
h) *Pistons/connecting rods (Section 10 of this Chapter).*
i) *Crankshaft (Section 11 of this Chapter).*

6 Before beginning the dismantling and overhaul procedures, make sure that you have all of the correct tools necessary. See *Tools and working facilities* for further information.

7 Cylinder head – dismantling

Note: *New and reconditioned cylinder heads are available from the manufacturer, and from engine overhaul specialists. Be aware that some specialist tools are required for the dismantling and inspection procedures, and new components may not be readily available. It may therefore be more practical and economical for the home mechanic to purchase a reconditioned head, rather than dismantle, inspect and recondition the original head.*

1 Remove the cylinder head as described in Part A, B, C, D or E of this Chapter (as applicable).

2 If not already done, remove the inlet and exhaust manifolds with reference to Chapter 4A or 4B. Remove any remaining brackets or housings as required.

3 Remove the camshaft(s), hydraulic tappets and rockers (as applicable) as described in Part A, B, C, D or E of this Chapter. On the 2.0 litre DOHC diesel engines, remove the camshaft drive chain guide from the cylinder head **(see illustration)**.

4 If not already done on petrol models, remove the spark plugs as described in Chapter 1A.

5 If not already done on diesel models, remove the glow plugs as described in Chapter 5A.

6 On all models, using a valve spring compressor, compress each valve spring in turn until the split collets can be removed. Release the compressor, and lift off the spring retainer, spring and, where fitted, the spring seat. Using a pair of pliers, carefully extract the valve stem oil seal from the top of the guide. On 16-valve engines, the valve stem oil seal also forms the spring seat and is deeply recessed in the cylinder head. It is also a tight fit on the valve guide making it difficult

7.3 Remove the camshaft drive chain guide – 2.0 litre DOHC diesel

7.6b . . . then extract the collets and release the spring compressor

to remove with pliers or a conventional valve stem oil seal removal tool. It can be easily removed, however, using a self-locking nut of suitable diameter screwed onto the end of a bolt and locked with a second nut. Push the nut down onto the top of the seal; the locking

7.6d . . . followed by the valve spring . . .

7.6f Remove the valve stem oil seal using a pair of pliers

7.6g Metal tube adapter for access to the valve collets

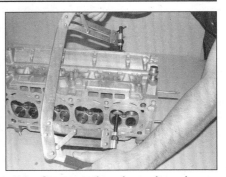

7.6a Compress the valve spring using a spring compressor . . .

7.6c Remove the spring retainer . . .

portion of the nut will grip the seal allowing it to be withdrawn from the top of the valve guide. Access to the valves is limited, and it may be necessary to make up an adapter out of metal tube – cut out a 'window' so that the valve collets can be removed **(see illustrations)**.

7.6e . . . and the spring seat (not all models)

7.6h Secure a self-locking nut of suitable diameter to a long bolt, then use the tool to remove the valve stem oil seal

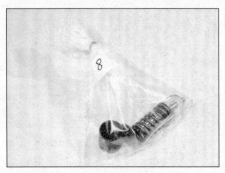

7.9 Place each valve and its associated components in a labelled bag

7 If, when the valve spring compressor is screwed down, the spring retainer refuses to free and expose the split collets, gently tap the top of the tool, directly over the retainer, with a light hammer. This will free the retainer.

8 Withdraw the valve from the combustion chamber. Remove the valve stem oil seal from the top of the guide, then lift out the spring seat where fitted.

9 It is essential that each valve is stored together with its collets, retainer, spring, and spring seat. The valves should also be kept in their correct sequence, unless they are so badly worn that they are to be renewed. If they are going to be kept and used again, place each valve assembly in a labelled polythene bag or similar small container **(see illustration)**. Note that No 1 valve is nearest to the transmission (flywheel/driveplate) end of the engine.

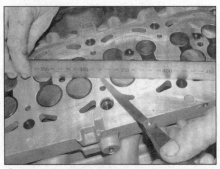

8.5 Check the cylinder head gasket surface for distortion

8.9b . . . and the camshaft oil supply non-return valve will be ejected from the underside of the cylinder head

8 Cylinder head and valves – cleaning and inspection

1 Thorough cleaning of the cylinder head and valve components, followed by a detailed inspection, will enable you to decide how much valve service work must be carried out during the engine overhaul. **Note:** *If the engine has been severely overheated, it is best to assume that the cylinder head is warped – check carefully for signs of this.*

Cleaning

2 Scrape away all traces of old gasket material from the cylinder head.

3 Scrape away the carbon from the combustion chambers and ports, then wash the cylinder head thoroughly with paraffin or a suitable solvent.

4 Scrape off any heavy carbon deposits that may have formed on the valves, then use a power-operated wire brush to remove deposits from the valve heads and stems.

Inspection

Note: *Be sure to perform all the following inspection procedures before concluding that the services of a machine shop or engine overhaul specialist are required. Make a list of all items that require attention.*

Cylinder head

5 Inspect the head very carefully for cracks, evidence of coolant leakage, and other damage. If cracks are found, a new cylinder

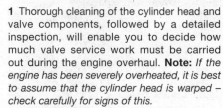

8.9a Apply compressed air to the oil feed bore of the intake camshaft, seal the bore in the exhaust camshaft with a rag . . .

8.11 Measure the valve stem diameter with a micrometer

head should be obtained. Use a straight-edge and feeler blade to check that the cylinder head gasket surface is not distorted **(see illustration)**. If it is, it may be possible to have it machined, provided that the cylinder head height is not significantly reduced.

6 Examine the valve seats in each of the combustion chambers. If they are severely pitted, cracked, or burned, they will need to be renewed or recut by an engine overhaul specialist. If they are only slightly pitted, this can be removed by grinding-in the valve heads and seats with fine valve-grinding compound, as described below. If in any doubt, have the cylinder head inspected by an engine overhaul specialist.

7 Check the valve guides for wear by inserting the relevant valve, and checking for side-to-side motion of the valve. A very small amount of movement is acceptable. If the movement seems excessive, remove the valve. Measure the valve stem diameter (see below), and renew the valve if it is worn. If the valve stem is not worn, the wear must be in the valve guide, and the guide must be renewed. The renewal of valve guides is best carried out by a Citroën dealer or engine overhaul specialist, who will have the necessary tools available.

8 If renewing the valve guides, the valve seats should be recut or reground only *after* the guides have been fitted.

9 Examine the camshaft oil supply non-return valve (where fitted) in the oil feed bore at the timing belt end of the cylinder head. Check that the valve is not loose in the cylinder head and that the ball is free to move within the valve body. If the valve is a loose fit in its bore, or if there is any doubt about its condition, it should be renewed. The non-return valve can be removed (assuming it is not loose), using compressed air, such as that generated by a tyre foot pump. Place the pump nozzle over the oil feed bore of the camshaft bearing journal and seal the corresponding oil feed bore with a rag. Apply the compressed air and the valve will be forced out of its location in the underside of the cylinder head **(see illustrations)**. Fit the new non-return valve to its bore on the underside of the head ensuring it is fitted the correct way. Oil should be able to pass upwards through the valve to the camshafts, but the ball in the valve should prevent the oil from returning back to the cylinder block. Use a thin socket or similar to push the valve fully into position.

Valves

10 Examine the head of each valve for pitting, burning, cracks, and general wear. Check the valve stem for scoring and wear ridges. Rotate the valve, and check for any obvious indication that it is bent. Look for pits or excessive wear on the tip of each valve stem. Renew any valve that shows any such signs of wear or damage.

11 If the valve appears satisfactory at this stage, measure the valve stem diameter at several points using a micrometer **(see illustration)**. Any

significant difference in the readings obtained indicates wear of the valve stem. Should any of these conditions be apparent, the valve must be renewed.

12 If the valves are in satisfactory condition, they should be ground (lapped) into their respective seats, to ensure a smooth, gas-tight seal. If the seat is only lightly pitted, or if it has been recut, fine grinding compound *only* should be used to produce the required finish. Coarse valve-grinding compound should *not* be used, unless a seat is badly burned or deeply pitted. If this is the case, the cylinder head and valves should be inspected by an expert, to decide whether seat recutting, or even the renewal of the valve or seat insert (where possible) is required.

13 Valve grinding is carried out as follows. Place the cylinder head upside-down on a bench.

14 Smear a trace of (the appropriate grade of) valve-grinding compound on the seat face, and press a suction grinding tool onto the valve head **(see illustration)**. With a semi-rotary action, grind the valve head to its seat, lifting the valve occasionally to redistribute the grinding compound. A light spring placed under the valve head will greatly ease this operation.

15 If coarse grinding compound is being used, work only until a dull, matt even surface is produced on both the valve seat and the valve, then wipe off the used compound, and repeat the process with fine compound. When a smooth unbroken ring of light grey matt finish is produced on both the valve and seat, the grinding operation is complete. *Do not* grind-in the valves any further than absolutely necessary, or the seat will be prematurely sunk into the cylinder head.

16 When all the valves have been ground-in, carefully wash off *all* traces of grinding compound using paraffin or a suitable solvent, before reassembling the cylinder head.

Valve components

17 Examine the valve springs for signs of damage and discoloration. No minimum free length is specified by Citroën, so the only way of judging valve spring wear is by comparison with a new component.

18 Stand each spring on a flat surface, and check it for squareness. If any of the springs are damaged, distorted or have lost their tension, obtain a complete new set of springs. It is normal to renew the valve springs as a matter of course if a major overhaul is being carried out.

19 Renew the valve stem oil seals regardless of their apparent condition.

9 Cylinder head – reassembly

1 Working on the first valve assembly, refit the spring seat then dip the new valve stem oil seal in fresh engine oil. Locate the seal

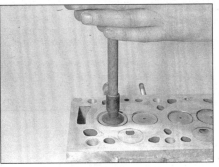

8.14 Grinding-in a valve

on the valve guide and press the seal firmly onto the guide using a suitable socket **(see illustrations)**.

2 Lubricate the stem of the first valve, and insert it in the guide **(see illustration)**.

3 Locate the valve spring on top of its seat, then refit the spring retainer. Note that on the EW petrol engines, the larger diameter of the spring must face the cylinder head.

4 Compress the valve spring, and locate the split collets in the recess in the valve stem. Release the compressor, then repeat the procedure on the remaining valves. Ensure that each valve is inserted into its original location. If new valves are being fitted, insert them into the locations to which they have been ground.

> **HAYNES HINT** *Use a little dab of grease to hold the collets in position on the valve stem while the spring compressor is released*

9.1a Locate the valve stem oil seal (arrowed) on the valve guide . . .

9.1c On some engines, the valve stem oil seal is integral with the spring seat

5 With all the valves installed, support the cylinder head and, using a hammer and interposed block of wood, tap the end of each valve stem to settle the components.

6 Refit the camshafts, hydraulic tappets and rocker arms (as applicable) as described in Part A, B, C, D or E of this Chapter.

7 Refit any remaining components using the reverse of the removal sequence and with new seals or gaskets as necessary.

8 The cylinder head can then be refitted as described in Part A, B, C, D or E of this Chapter.

10 Piston/connecting rod assembly – removal

1 Remove the cylinder head, sump and oil pump as described in Part A, B, C, D or E of this Chapter.

2 If there is a pronounced wear ridge at the top of any bore, it may be necessary to remove it with a scraper or ridge reamer, to avoid piston damage during removal. Such a ridge indicates excessive wear of the cylinder bore.

3 Using quick-drying paint, mark each connecting rod and big-end bearing cap with its respective cylinder number on the flat machined surface provided; if the engine has been dismantled before, note carefully any identifying marks made previously **(see illustration)**. Note that No 1 cylinder is at the transmission (flywheel) end of the engine.

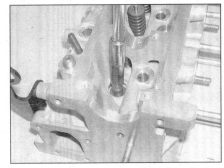

9.1b . . . and press the seal firmly onto the guide using a suitable socket

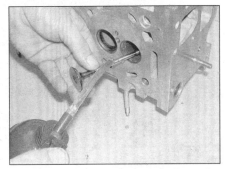

9.2 Lubricate the stem of the valve and insert it into the guide

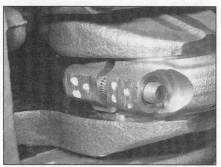

10.3 Connecting rod and big-end bearing cap identification marks (No 3 shown)

10.5 Remove the big-end bearing shell and cap

10.6 To protect the crankshaft journals, tape over the connecting rod stud threads

4 Turn the crankshaft to bring pistons 1 and 4 to BDC (bottom dead centre).

5 Unscrew the nuts or bolts, as applicable, from No 1 piston big-end bearing cap. Take off the cap, and recover the bottom half bearing

shell **(see illustration)**. If the bearing shells are to be re-used, tape the cap and the shell together.

6 Where applicable, to prevent the possibility of damage to the crankshaft bearing journals,

tape over the connecting rod stud threads **(see illustration)**.

7 Using a hammer handle, push the piston up through the bore, and remove it from the top of the cylinder block. Recover the bearing shell, and tape it to the connecting rod for safe-keeping.

8 Loosely refit the big-end cap to the connecting rod, and secure with the nuts/bolts – this will help to keep the components in their correct order.

9 Remove No 4 piston assembly in the same way.

10 Turn the crankshaft through 180° to bring pistons 2 and 3 to BDC (bottom dead centre), and remove them in the same way.

11.4 Remove the oil seal housing from the right-hand end of the cylinder block

11.5a Remove the oil pump drive chain . . .

11 Crankshaft – removal

1 Remove the crankshaft sprocket and the oil pump as described in Part A, B, C, D or E of this Chapter (as applicable).

2 Remove the pistons and connecting rods, as described in Section 10. If no work is to be done on the pistons and connecting rods, there is no need to remove the cylinder head, or to push the pistons out of the cylinder bores. The pistons should just be pushed far enough up the bores so that they are positioned clear of the crankshaft journals.

3 Check the crankshaft endfloat as described in Section 14, then proceed as follows.

DW engines

4 Slacken and remove the retaining bolts, and remove the oil seal housing from the timing belt end of the cylinder block, along with its gasket (where fitted) **(see illustration)**.

5 Remove the oil pump drive chain, and slide the drive sprocket and spacer (where fitted) off the end of the crankshaft. Remove the Woodruff key, and store it with the sprocket for safe-keeping **(see illustrations)**.

6 The main bearing caps should be numbered 1 to 5, starting from the transmission (flywheel/driveplate) end of the engine **(see illustration)**. If not, mark them accordingly using quick-drying paint. Also note the correct fitted depth of the crankshaft oil seal in the bearing cap.

11.5b . . . then slide off the drive sprocket . . .

11.5c . . . and remove the Woodruff key from the crankshaft

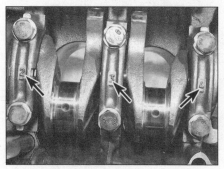

11.6 Main bearing cap identification markings (arrowed)

11.7 Note the thrustwasher fitted to the No 2 main bearing cap (arrowed)

7 On all engines, slacken and remove the main bearing cap retaining bolts/nuts, and lift off each bearing cap. Recover the lower bearing shells, and tape them to their respective caps for safe-keeping. Also recover the lower thrustwasher halves from the side of No 2 main bearing cap **(see illustration)**. Remove the rubber sealing strips from the sides of No 1 main bearing cap, and discard them.

8 Lift out the crankshaft, and discard the oil seal **(see illustration)**.

9 Recover the upper bearing shells from the cylinder block, and tape them to their respective caps for safe-keeping **(see illustration)**. Remove the upper thrustwasher halves from the side of No 2 main bearing, and store them with the lower halves.

EW and DV engines

10 Working around the inner periphery of the crankcase, unscrew the small bolts securing the crankshaft bearing cap housing to the base of the cylinder block. Note the correct fitted depth of the left-hand crankshaft oil seal in the cylinder block/bearing cap housing.

11 Working in the **reverse** of the tightening sequence, evenly and progressively slacken the ten large bearing cap housing retaining bolts by a turn at a time. Once all the bolts are loose, remove them from the housing. **Note:** *On 1.6 litre engines, prise up the flywheel end of the housing to expose the two end main bearing bolts* **(see illustration)**.

12 With all the retaining bolts removed, tap around the outer periphery of the bearing cap housing using a soft-faced mallet to break the seal between the housing and cylinder block. Once the seal is released and the housing is clear of the locating dowels, lift it up and off the crankshaft and cylinder block **(see illustration)**. Recover the lower main bearing shells, and tape them to their respective locations in the housing. If the two locating dowels are a loose fit, remove them and store them with the housing for safe-keeping.

13 Lift out the crankshaft, and collect the left-hand oil seal.

14 Recover the upper main bearing shells, and store them along with the relevant lower bearing shell. Also recover the two thrustwashers (one fitted either side of No 2 main bearing) from the cylinder block.

12 Cylinder block/crankcase – cleaning and inspection

Cleaning

1 Remove all external components and electrical switches/sensors from the block. For complete cleaning, the core plugs should ideally be removed **(see illustrations)**. Drill a small hole in the plugs, then insert a self-tapping screw into the hole. Pull out the plugs by pulling on the screw with a pair of grips, or by using a slide hammer.

11.8 Lift out the crankshaft

11.9 Remove the upper main bearing shells

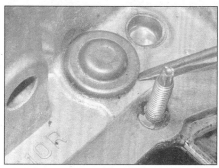

11.11 On 1.6 litre diesel engines, prise up the two caps to expose the main bearing bolts at the flywheel end

2 On aluminium block engines with wet liners, remove the liners, referring to paragraph 17.

3 Where applicable, undo the retaining bolts and remove the piston oil jet spray tubes from inside the cylinder block **(see illustration)**.

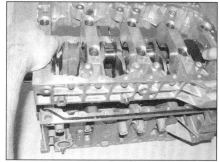

11.12 Remove the crankshaft bearing cap housing

4 Scrape all traces of gasket from the cylinder block/crankcase, and from the main bearing ladder (where fitted), taking care not to damage the gasket/sealing surfaces.

5 Remove all oil gallery plugs (where fitted).

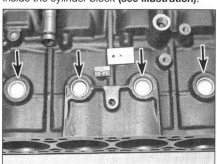

12.1a Cylinder block core plugs (arrowed)

12.1b Remove the air conditioning compressor bracket

12.1c Remove the crankcase ventilation/ oil separator box

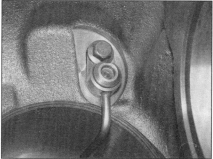

12.3 Piston cooling jets may be fitted to the base of each cylinder bore

12.17a Remove each liner . . .

12.17b . . . and recover the bottom O-ring seal (arrowed)

The plugs are usually very tight – they may have to be drilled out, and the holes retapped. Use new plugs when reassembling.

6 If any of the castings are extremely dirty, all should be steam-cleaned.

7 After the castings are returned, clean all oil holes and oil galleries one more time. Flush all internal passages with warm water until the water runs clear. Dry thoroughly, and apply a light film of oil to all mating surfaces, to prevent rusting. On cast-iron block engines, also oil the cylinder bores. If you have access to compressed air, use it to speed up the drying process, and to blow out all the oil holes and galleries.

 Warning: Wear eye protection when using compressed air.

8 If the castings are not very dirty, you can do an adequate cleaning job with hot (as hot as you can stand), soapy water and a stiff brush. Take plenty of time, and do a thorough job. Regardless of the cleaning method used, be sure to clean all oil holes and galleries very thoroughly, and to dry all components well. On cast-iron block engines, protect the cylinder bores as described above, to prevent rusting.

9 All threaded holes must be clean, to ensure accurate torque readings during reassembly. To clean the threads, run the correct-size tap into each of the holes to remove rust, corrosion, thread sealant or sludge, and to restore damaged threads. If possible, use compressed air to clear the holes of debris produced by this operation.

10 Apply suitable sealant to the new oil gallery plugs, and insert them into the holes

13.2 Remove the piston rings with the aid of feeler gauges

in the block. Tighten them securely. Apply suitable sealant to the new core plugs, and insert them into the holes in the block. Tap them into place with a close-fitting tube or socket.

11 Where applicable, clean the threads of the piston oil jet retaining bolt, and apply a drop of thread-locking compound to the bolt threads. Refit the piston oil jet spray tube to the cylinder block, and tighten its retaining bolt to the specified torque setting.

12 If the engine is not going to be reassembled right away, cover it with a large plastic bag to keep it clean; protect all mating surfaces and the cylinder bores as described above, to prevent rusting.

Inspection

Cast-iron cylinder block

13 Visually check the castings for cracks and corrosion. Look for stripped threads in the threaded holes. If there has been any history of internal water leakage, it may be worthwhile having an engine overhaul specialist check the cylinder block/crankcase with special equipment. If defects are found, have them repaired if possible, or renew the assembly.

14 Check each cylinder bore for scuffing and scoring. Check for signs of a wear ridge at the top of the cylinder, indicating that the bore is excessively worn.

15 If wear is suspected, have the cylinder bores measured by an automotive engineering workshop, who will be able to carry out the reboring, and supply suitable pistons/rings, etc, as applicable.

16 At the time of writing, it was not clear whether oversize pistons were available for all models. Consult your Citroën dealer for the latest information on piston availability. If oversize pistons are available, then it may be possible to have the cylinder bores rebored and oversize pistons fitted. If oversize pistons are not available, and the bores are worn, renewal of the block is the only option.

Aluminium cylinder block

17 Remove the liner clamps, then use a hard wood drift to tap out each liner from the inside of the cylinder block. When all the liners are released, tip the cylinder block/crankcase on its side and remove each liner from the top of the block. As each liner is removed, stick

masking tape on its left-hand (transmission side) face, and write the cylinder number on the tape. No 1 cylinder is at the transmission (flywheel/driveplate) end of the engine. Remove the O-ring from the base of each liner, and discard it **(see illustrations)**.

18 Check each cylinder liner for scuffing and scoring. Check for a wear ridge at the top of the liner, indicating that the bore is badly worn.

19 Have the cylinder bores inspected and measured by an automotive engineering workshop, who will be able to carry out any repairs, and supply suitable new parts as applicable.

13 Piston/connecting rod assembly – inspection

1 Before the inspection process can begin, the piston/connecting rod assemblies must be cleaned, and the original piston rings removed from the pistons.

2 Carefully expand the old rings over the top of the pistons. The use of two or three old feeler blades will be helpful in preventing the rings dropping into empty grooves **(see illustration)**. Be careful not to scratch the piston with the ends of the ring. The rings are brittle, and will snap if they are spread too far. They are also very sharp – protect your hands and fingers. Note that the third ring incorporates an expander. Always remove the rings from the top of the piston.

3 Scrape away all traces of carbon from the top of the piston. A hand-held wire brush (or a piece of fine emery cloth) can be used, once the majority of the deposits have been scraped away.

4 Remove the carbon from the ring grooves in the piston, using an old ring. Break the ring in half to do this. Be careful to remove only the carbon deposits – do not remove any metal, and do not nick or scratch the sides of the ring grooves.

5 Once the deposits have been removed, clean the piston/connecting rod assembly with paraffin or a suitable solvent, and dry thoroughly. Make sure that the oil return holes in the ring grooves are clear.

6 If the pistons and cylinder bores are not damaged or worn excessively, and if the cylinder block does not need to be rebored, the original pistons can be refitted. Normal piston wear shows up as even vertical wear on the piston thrust surfaces, and slight looseness of the top ring in its groove. New piston rings should always be used when the engine is reassembled.

7 Carefully inspect each piston for cracks around the skirt, around the gudgeon pin holes, and at the piston ring 'lands' (between the ring grooves).

8 Look for scoring and scuffing on the piston skirt, holes in the piston crown, and burned areas at the edge of the crown. If the skirt is scored or scuffed, the engine may have been suffering from overheating, and/or abnormal combustion which caused excessively high operating temperatures. The cooling and lubrication systems should be checked thoroughly. Scorch marks on the sides of the pistons show that blow-by has occurred. A hole in the piston crown, or burned areas at the edge of the piston crown, indicates that abnormal combustion (pre-ignition, knocking, or detonation) has been occurring. If any of the above problems exist, the causes must be investigated and corrected, or the damage will occur again.

9 Corrosion of the piston, in the form of pitting, indicates that coolant has been leaking into the combustion chamber and/or the crankcase. Again, the cause must be corrected, or the problem may persist in the rebuilt engine.

10 On aluminium-block engines with wet liners it is not possible to renew the pistons separately; pistons are only supplied with piston rings and a liner, as a part of a matched assembly. On iron-block engines, pistons can be purchased from a Citroën dealer.

11 Examine each connecting rod carefully for signs of damage, such as cracks around the big-end and small-end bearings. Check that the rod is not bent or distorted. Damage is highly unlikely, unless the engine has been seized or badly overheated. Detailed checking of the connecting rod assembly can only be carried out by a *Citroën* dealer or engine repair specialist with the necessary equipment.

12 The big-end cap bolts/nuts must be renewed as a complete set prior to refitting. This should be done after the big-end bearing running clearance check has been carried out.

Petrol engines

13 On petrol engines, the gudgeon pins are an interference fit in the connecting rod small-end bearing, therefore piston and/or connecting rod renewal should be entrusted to a Citroën dealer or engine repair specialist, who will have the necessary tooling to remove and install the gudgeon pins.

Diesel engines

14 On diesel engines, the gudgeon pins are of the floating type, secured in position by two circlips. On these engines, the pistons and connecting rods can be separated as described in the following paragraphs.

15 Before separating the piston and connecting rod, check the position of the valve recesses or markings on the piston crown in relation to the connecting rod big-end bearing shell cut-outs and make a note of the orientation.

16 Using a small flat-bladed screwdriver, prise out the circlips, and push out the gudgeon pin **(see illustrations)**. Hand pressure should be sufficient to remove the pin. Identify the piston and rod to ensure correct reassembly. Discard the circlips – new ones *must* be used on refitting.

13.16a Prise out the circlip . . .

17 Examine the gudgeon pin and connecting rod small-end bearing for signs of wear or damage. Wear can be cured by renewing both the pin and bush. Bush renewal, however, is a specialist job – press facilities are required, and the new bush must be reamed accurately.

18 The connecting rods themselves should not be in need of renewal, unless seizure or some other major mechanical failure has occurred. Check the alignment of the connecting rods visually, and if the rods are not straight, take them to an engine overhaul specialist for a more detailed check.

19 Examine all components, and obtain any new parts from your Citroën dealer. If new pistons are purchased, they will be supplied complete with gudgeon pins and circlips. Circlips can also be purchased individually.

20 Position the piston in relation to the connecting rod big-end bearing shell cut-outs as noted during separation.

21 Apply a smear of clean engine oil to the gudgeon pin and slide it into the piston and through the connecting rod small-end. Check that the piston pivots freely on the rod, then secure the gudgeon pin in position with two new circlips. Ensure that each circlip is correctly located in its groove in the piston.

14 Crankshaft – inspection

Checking endfloat

1 If the crankshaft endfloat is to be checked,

14.2 Check the crankshaft endfloat using a DTI gauge . . .

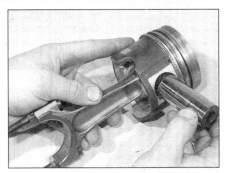
13.16b . . . and withdraw the gudgeon pin

this must be done when the crankshaft is installed in the cylinder block/crankcase, but is free to move.

2 Check the endfloat using a dial gauge in contact with the end of the crankshaft. Push the crankshaft fully one way, and then zero the gauge. Push the crankshaft fully the other way, and check the endfloat. The result can be compared with the specified amount, and will give an indication as to whether new thrustwashers are required **(see illustration)**.

3 If a dial gauge is not available, feeler gauges can be used. First push the crankshaft fully towards the flywheel end of the engine, then use feeler gauges to measure the gap between the web of No 2 crankpin and the thrustwasher **(see illustration)**.

Inspection

4 Clean the crankshaft using paraffin or a suitable solvent, and dry it, preferably with compressed air if available. Be sure to clean the oil holes with a pipe cleaner or similar probe, to ensure that they are not obstructed.

⚠️ *Warning: Wear eye protection when using compressed air.*

5 Check the main and big-end bearing journals for uneven wear, scoring, pitting and cracking.

6 Big-end bearing wear is accompanied by distinct metallic knocking when the engine is running (particularly noticeable when the engine is pulling from low speed) and by some loss of oil pressure.

7 Main bearing wear is accompanied by severe engine vibration and rumble – getting

14.3 . . . or with feeler gauges

progressively worse as engine speed increases – and again by loss of oil pressure.

8 Check the bearing journal for roughness by running a finger lightly over the bearing surface. Any roughness (which will be accompanied by obvious bearing wear) indicates that the crankshaft requires regrinding (where possible) or renewal.

9 If the crankshaft has been reground, check for burrs around the crankshaft oil holes (the holes are usually chamfered, so burrs should not be a problem unless regrinding has been carried out carelessly). Remove any burrs with a fine file or scraper, and thoroughly clean the oil holes as described previously.

10 Have the crankshaft inspected and measured by an automotive engineering workshop, who will be able to carry out any necessary repairs, and supply relevant parts.

11 Check the oil seal contact surfaces at each end of the crankshaft for wear and damage. If the seal has worn a deep groove in the surface of the crankshaft, consult an engine overhaul specialist; repair may be possible, but otherwise a new crankshaft will be required.

12 Citroën produce a set of undersize bearing shells for both the main and big-end bearings on most engines. Where the crankshaft journals have not already been reground, it may be possible to have the crankshaft reconditioned, and to fit undersize shells. If no undersize shells are available and the crankshaft has worn beyond the specified limits, the crankshaft will have to be renewed. Consult your Citroën dealer or engine specialist for further information on parts availability.

15 Main and big-end bearings – inspection

1 Even though the main and big-end bearings should be renewed during the engine overhaul, the old bearings should be retained for close examination, as they may reveal valuable information about the condition of the engine. The bearing shells are graded by thickness, the grade of each shell being indicated by the colour code marked on it.

2 Bearing failure can occur due to lack of lubrication, the presence of dirt or other foreign particles, overloading the engine, or corrosion **(see illustration)**. Regardless of the cause of bearing failure, the cause must be corrected (where applicable) before the engine is reassembled, to prevent it from happening again.

3 When examining the bearing shells, remove them from the cylinder block/crankcase, the main bearing ladder/caps (as appropriate), the connecting rods and the connecting rod big-end bearing caps. Lay them out on a clean surface in the same general position as their location in the engine. This will enable you to match any bearing problems with the corresponding crankshaft journal. *Do not*

touch any shell's bearing surface with your fingers while checking it, or the delicate surface may be scratched.

4 Dirt and other foreign matter gets into the engine in a variety of ways. It may be left in the engine during assembly, or it may pass through filters or the crankcase ventilation system. It may get into the oil, and from there into the bearings. Metal chips from machining operations and normal engine wear are often present. Abrasives are sometimes left in engine components after reconditioning, especially when parts are not thoroughly cleaned using the proper cleaning methods. Whatever the source, these foreign objects often end up embedded in the soft bearing material, and are easily recognised. Large particles will not embed in the bearing, and will score or gouge the bearing and journal. The best prevention for this cause of bearing failure is to clean all parts thoroughly, and keep everything spotlessly-clean during engine assembly. Frequent and regular engine oil and filter changes are also recommended.

5 Lack of lubrication (or lubrication breakdown) has a number of interrelated causes. Excessive heat (which thins the oil), overloading (which squeezes the oil from the bearing face) and oil leakage (from excessive bearing clearances, worn oil pump or high engine speeds) all contribute to lubrication breakdown. Blocked oil passages, which usually are the result of misaligned oil holes in a bearing shell, will also oil-starve a bearing, and destroy it. When lack of lubrication is the cause of bearing failure, the bearing material is wiped or extruded from the steel backing of the bearing. Temperatures may increase to the point where the steel backing turns blue from overheating.

6 Driving habits can have a definite effect on bearing life. Full-throttle, low-speed operation

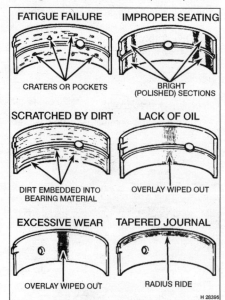

15.2 Typical bearing failures

(labouring the engine) puts very high loads on bearings, tending to squeeze out the oil film. These loads cause the bearings to flex, which produces fine cracks in the bearing face (fatigue failure). Eventually, the bearing material will loosen in pieces, and tear away from the steel backing.

7 Short-distance driving leads to corrosion of bearings, because insufficient engine heat is produced to drive off the condensed water and corrosive gases. These products collect in the engine oil, forming acid and sludge. As the oil is carried to the engine bearings, the acid attacks and corrodes the bearing material.

8 Incorrect bearing installation during engine assembly will lead to bearing failure as well. Tight-fitting bearings leave insufficient bearing running clearance, and will result in oil starvation. Dirt or foreign particles trapped behind a bearing shell result in high spots on the bearing, which lead to failure.

9 *Do not* touch any shell's bearing surface with your fingers during reassembly; there is a risk of scratching the delicate surface, or of depositing particles of dirt on it.

10 As mentioned at the beginning of this Section, the bearing shells should be renewed as a matter of course during engine overhaul; to do otherwise is false economy.

16 Engine overhaul – reassembly sequence

1 Before reassembly begins, ensure that all new parts have been obtained, and that all necessary tools are available. Read through the entire procedure to familiarise yourself with the work involved, and to ensure that all items necessary for reassembly of the engine are at hand. In addition to all normal tools and materials, thread-locking compound will be needed. A suitable tube of liquid sealant will also be required for the joint faces that are fitted without gaskets. It is recommended that Citroën's own products are used, which are specially formulated for this purpose; the relevant product names are quoted in the text of each Section where they are required.

2 In order to save time and avoid problems, engine reassembly can be carried out in the following order:

a) *Crankshaft (Section 18).*
b) *Piston/connecting rod assemblies (Section 19).*
c) *Oil pump (see Part A, B, C, D or E – as applicable).*
d) *Sump (see Part A, B, C, D or E – as applicable).*
e) *Flywheel (see Part A, B, C, D or E – as applicable).*
f) *Cylinder head (see Part A, B, C, D or E – as applicable).*
g) *Timing belt tensioner and sprockets, and timing belt (see Part A, B, C, D or E – as applicable).*
h) *Engine external components.*

3 At this stage, all engine components should be absolutely clean and dry, with all faults repaired. The components should be laid out (or in individual containers) on a completely clean work surface.

17 Piston rings – refitting

1 Before fitting new piston rings, the ring end gaps must be checked as follows.
2 Lay out the piston/connecting rod assemblies and the new piston ring sets, so that the ring sets will be matched with the same piston and cylinder during the end gap measurement and subsequent engine reassembly.
3 Insert the top ring into the first cylinder, and push it down the bore using the top of the piston. This will ensure that the ring remains square with the cylinder walls. Position the ring near the bottom of the cylinder bore, at the lower limit of ring travel. Note that the top and second compression rings are different. The second ring is easily identified by the step on its lower surface, and by the fact that its outer face is tapered.
4 Measure the end gap using feeler gauges.
5 Repeat the procedure with the ring at the top of the cylinder bore, at the upper limit of its travel, and compare the measurements with the figures given in the Specifications (see illustration). Where no figures are given, seek the advice of a Citroën dealer or engine reconditioning specialist.
6 If the gap is too small (unlikely if genuine Citroën parts are used), it must be enlarged, or the ring ends may contact each other during engine operation, causing serious damage. Ideally, new piston rings providing the correct end gap should be fitted. As a last resort, the end gap can be increased by filing the ring ends very carefully with a fine file. Mount the file in a vice equipped with soft jaws, slip the ring over the file with the ends contacting the file face, and slowly move the ring to remove material from the ends. Take care, as piston rings are sharp, and are easily broken.
7 With new piston rings, it is unlikely that the end gap will be too large. If the gaps are too large, check that you have the correct rings for your engine and for the particular cylinder bore size.
8 Repeat the checking procedure for each ring in the first cylinder, and then for the rings in the remaining cylinders. Remember to keep rings, pistons and cylinders matched up.
9 Once the ring end gaps have been checked and if necessary corrected, the rings can be fitted to the pistons.
10 Fit the piston rings using the same technique as for removal. Fit the bottom (oil control) ring first, and work up. When fitting the oil control ring, first insert the expander (where fitted), then fit the ring with its gap positioned 180° from the expander gap.

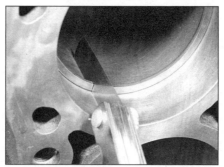
17.5 Measure the piston ring end gap with feeler gauges

Ensure that the second compression ring is fitted the correct way up, with its identification mark (either a dot of paint or the word TOP stamped on the ring surface) at the top, and the stepped surface at the bottom (see illustration). Arrange the gaps of the top and second compression rings 120° either side of the oil control ring gap. Note: Always follow any instructions supplied with the new piston ring sets – different manufacturers may specify different procedures. Do not mix up the top and second compression rings, as they have different cross-sections.

18 Crankshaft – refitting

New main bearing shells

1 To ensure that the main bearing running clearance is correct, the bearing shells are supplied in various thicknesses or grades. The grades are indicated by a colour-coding marked on the edge of each shell. The grade of the new bearing shells required (either standard size or undersize) is selected using the reference marks on the cylinder block and on the crankshaft. The cylinder block marks identify the diameter of the bearing bores in the block, and the crankshaft marks identify the diameter of the crankshaft journals.
2 Note that on the engines described in this Manual, the upper shells are all of the same size, and the running clearance is controlled by fitting a lower bearing shell of the required thickness.
3 Numerous grades of standard and oversize bearing shells are available, depending on the engine type, year of manufacture, and country of export. Using the cylinder block and crankshaft reference marks, together with the crankshaft journal diameter, a Citroën dealer or engine overhaul specialist will be able to supply the correct bearing shells to give the required bearing running clearance for each journal.

Final crankshaft refitting
DW engines
4 Using a little grease, stick the upper thrustwashers to each side of the No 2 main

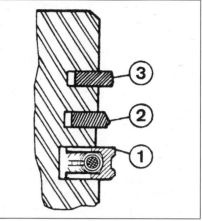
17.10 Piston rings (typical)
1   Oil control ring
2   Second compression ring
3   Top compression ring

bearing upper location. Ensure that the oilway grooves on each thrustwasher face outwards (away from the cylinder block) (see illustration).
5 Place the bearing shells in their locations. If new shells are being fitted, ensure that all traces of protective grease are cleaned off using paraffin. Wipe dry the shells and connecting rods with a lint-free cloth. Liberally lubricate each bearing shell in the cylinder block/crankcase and cap with clean engine oil.
6 Lower the crankshaft into position so that Nos 2 and 3 cylinder crankpins are at TDC; Nos 1 and 4 cylinder crankpins will be at BDC, ready for fitting No 1 piston. Check the crankshaft endfloat, referring to Section 14.
7 Lubricate the lower bearing shells in the main bearing caps with clean engine oil. Make sure that the locating lugs on the shells engage with the corresponding recesses in the caps.
8 Fit main bearing caps Nos 2 to 5 to their correct locations, ensuring that they are fitted the correct way round (the bearing shell tab recesses in the block and caps must be on the same side). Insert the bolts/nuts, tightening them only loosely at this stage.
9 Apply a small amount of sealant to the No 1

18.4 Ensure the oil grooves on each thrustwasher are facing outwards from the No 2 main bearing location

18.9 Apply sealant to the No 1 main bearing cap mating face on the cylinder block, around the sealing strip holes in the corners

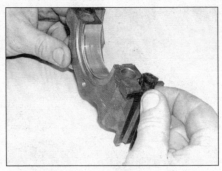

18.10 Fit the sealing strips to the No 1 main bearing cap

18.11 Use 2 metal strips (arrowed) to hold the sealing strips in place as the bearing cap is fitted

main bearing cap mating face on the cylinder block, around the sealing strip holes **(see illustration)**.

10 Locate the tab of each sealing strip over the pins on the base of No 1 bearing cap, and press the strips into the bearing cap grooves. It is now necessary to obtain two thin metal strips, of 0.25 mm thickness or less, in order to prevent the strips moving when the cap is being fitted. Citroën garages use the tool shown, which acts as a clamp. Metal strips (such as old feeler blades) can be used, provided all burrs which may damage the sealing strips are first removed **(see illustration)**.

11 Where applicable, oil both sides of the metal strips, and hold them on the sealing strips. Fit the No 1 main bearing cap, insert the bolts loosely, then carefully pull out the metal strips in a horizontal direction, using a pair of pliers **(see illustration)**.

12 Tighten all the main bearing cap bolts/nuts evenly to the specified torque. Using a sharp knife, trim off the ends of the No 1 bearing cap sealing strips, so that they protrude above the cylinder block/crankcase mating surface by approximately 1.0 mm **(see illustration)**.

13 Fit a new crankshaft left-hand oil seal as described in Part D or E of this Chapter (as applicable).

14 Refit the piston/connecting rod assemblies to the crankshaft as described in Section 19.

15 Refit the Woodruff key, then slide on the oil pump drive sprocket and spacer (where fitted), and locate the drive chain on the sprocket.

16 Ensure that the mating surfaces of the right-hand oil seal housing and cylinder block are clean and dry. Note the correct fitted depth of the oil seal then, lever or drive out the old seal from the housing. If preferred, a new

oil seal can be pressed into the housing at this stage **(see illustrations)**.

17 Apply a smear of suitable sealant to the oil seal housing mating surface. Ensure that the locating dowels are in position, then slide the housing over the end of the crankshaft and into position on the cylinder block **(see illustrations)**. Tighten the housing retaining bolts to the specified torque.

18 If not already done, fit a new crankshaft right-hand oil seal as described in Part D or E of this Chapter.

19 Ensuring that the drive chain is correctly located on the sprocket, refit the oil pump and sump as described in Part D or E of this Chapter.

20 Where removed, refit the cylinder head as described in Part D or E, of this Chapter.

EW and DV engines

21 Place the bearing shells in their locations. If new shells are being fitted, ensure that all traces of protective grease are cleaned off using paraffin. Wipe dry the shells with a lint-free cloth. On 1.6 litre diesel engines, the upper bearing shells all have a grooved surface, whereas the lower shells have a plain surface. On these engines, it's essential that the lower bearing shells are centrally located in the bearing cap housing/ladder. To ensure this use a Citroën tool positioned over the housing/ladder, and insert the bearing shells through the slots in the tool **(see illustration)**.

22 Liberally lubricate each bearing shell in the cylinder block with clean engine oil then lower the crankshaft into position.

18.12 Trim off the ends of the bearing cap sealing strips, so that they protrude by approximately 1.0 mm

18.16a Drive out the old oil seal . . .

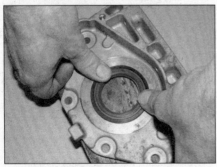

18.16b . . . then press in the new one to the previously-noted depth

18.17a Apply the sealant . . .

18.17b . . . and refit the oil seal housing

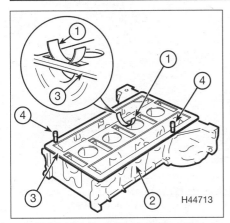

**18.21 Main bearing shell fitment –
1.6 litre diesel engine**

1 *Bearing shell*
2 *Main bearing
   ladder*
3 *Citroen tool
   No 0194-QZ*
4 *Aligning pins*

23 Insert the thrustwashers to either side of No 2 main bearing upper location and push them around the bearing journal until their edges are horizontal **(see illustration)**. Ensure that the oilway grooves on each thrustwasher face outwards (away from the bearing journal).

24 Thoroughly degrease the mating surfaces of the cylinder block and the crankshaft bearing cap housing. Apply a thin bead of RTV sealant to the bearing cap housing mating surface **(see illustration)**. Citroën recommend the use of Loctite Autojoint Noir for this purpose.

25 Lubricate the lower bearing shells with clean engine oil, then refit the bearing cap housing, ensuring that the shells are not displaced, and that the locating dowels engage correctly.

26 Install the ten large diameter and sixteen smaller diameter crankshaft bearing cap housing retaining bolts, and screw them in until they are just making contact with the housing.

**18.23 Place the thrustwashers each side
of the No 2 bearing upper location**

27 Working in the sequence shown, tighten the bolts to the torque settings given in the Specifications **(see illustrations)**.
28 With the bearing cap housing in place, check that the crankshaft rotates freely.
29 Refit the piston/connecting rod assemblies to the crankshaft as described in Section 19.
30 Refit the oil pump and sump.
31 Fit a new crankshaft left-hand oil seal, then refit the flywheel.
32 Where removed, refit the cylinder head, crankshaft sprocket and timing belt.

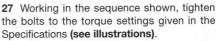

19 Pistons/connecting rods – refitting

Note: *New big-end cap nuts must be used on refitting.*

1 Note that the following procedure assumes that the cylinder liners (aluminium block petrol engines) are in position in the cylinder block/crankcase as described in Section 12, and that the crankshaft and main bearing ladder/caps are in place.
2 Clean the backs of the bearing shells, and the bearing locations in both the connecting rod and bearing cap.

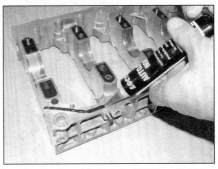

**18.24 Apply a thin bead of RTV sealant to
the bearing cap housing mating surface**

All engines except 1.6 litre diesel

3 Press the bearing shells into their locations, ensuring that the tab on each shell engages in the notch in the connecting rod and cap. Take care not to touch any shell's bearing surface with your fingers **(see illustration)**.

All engines

4 Lubricate the cylinder bores, the pistons, and piston rings, then lay out each piston/connecting rod assembly in its respective position.

5 Start with assembly No 1. Make sure that the piston rings are still spaced as described in Section 17, then clamp them in position with a piston ring compressor.

6 Insert the piston/connecting rod assembly into the top of cylinder/liner No 1, ensuring the piston is correctly positioned as follows.

a) *On petrol engines, ensure that the arrow
   on the piston crown is pointing towards
   the timing belt end of the engine.*
b) *On 1.6 litre diesel engines, ensure that the
   DIST mark or arrow on the piston crown is
   towards the timing belt end of the engine.*
c) *On 2.0 litre diesel engines, ensure that the
   valve recesses on the piston crown are
   towards the rear of the cylinder block.*

**18.27a Main bearing cap housing retaining bolt tightening
sequence – EW petrol engines**

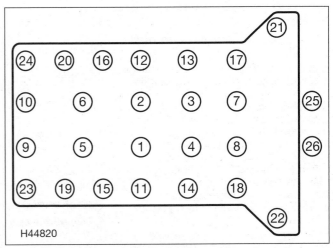

**18.27b Main bearing cap housing/ladder retaining bolt tightening
sequence – DV diesel engines**

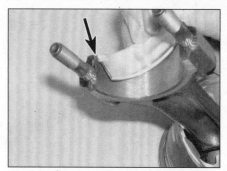

19.3 Ensure the bearing shell tab (arrowed) locates correctly in the cut-out

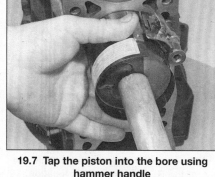

19.7 Tap the piston into the bore using hammer handle

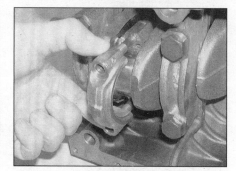

19.8 Fit the big-end bearing cap, ensuring it is fitted the right-way around, and screw on the new nuts

19.11 Big-end bearing shell positioning – 1.6 litre diesel engine

1 Citroen tool No 0194-P
2 Bearing shell in the cap

7 Once the piston is correctly positioned, using a block of wood or hammer handle against the piston crown, tap the assembly into the cylinder/liner until the piston crown is flush with the top of the cylinder/liner (see illustration).

All engines except 1.6 litre diesel

8 Ensure that the bearing shell is still correctly installed. Liberally lubricate the crankpin and both bearing shells. Taking care not to mark the cylinder/liner bores, pull the piston/connecting rod assembly down the bore and onto the crankpin. Refit the big-end bearing cap and fit the new nuts, tightening them finger-tight at first (see illustration). Note that the faces with the identification marks must match (which means that the bearing shell locating tabs abut each other).

9 Tighten the bearing cap retaining nuts evenly and progressively to the specified torque setting.

1.6 litre diesel engine

10 On these engines, the connecting rod is made in one piece, then the big-end bearing cap is 'cracked' off. This ensures that the cap fits onto the connecting rod only in one position, and with maximum rigidity. Consequently, there are no locating notches for the bearing shells to fit into.

11 To ensure that the big-end bearing shells are centrally located in the connecting rod and cap, two special tools are available from Citroën. These half-moon shaped tools are pressed in from either side of the rod/cap and locate the shell exactly in the centre (see illustration). Fit the shells into the connecting rods and big-end caps and lubricate them with plenty of clean engine oil.

12 Pull the connecting rods and pistons down the bores and onto the crankshaft journals. Fit the big-end caps – they will only fit properly one way round (see paragraph 10), and insert the new bolts.

13 Tighten the bolts to the specified torque settings.

All engines

14 Once the bearing cap retaining nuts have been correctly tightened, rotate the crankshaft. Check that it turns freely; some stiffness is to be expected if new components have been fitted, but there should be no signs of binding or tight spots.

15 Refit the cylinder head and oil pump as described in Part A, B, C, D or E of this Chapter (as applicable).

20 Engine – initial start-up after overhaul

1 With the engine refitted in the vehicle, double-check the engine oil and coolant levels. Make a final check that everything has been reconnected, and that there are no tools or rags left in the engine compartment.

Petrol engine models

2 Remove the spark plugs and disable the fuel system by disconnecting the wiring connectors from the fuel injectors, referring to Chapter 4A for further information.

3 Turn the engine on the starter until the oil pressure warning light goes out. Refit the spark plugs, and reconnect the wiring.

Diesel engine models

4 On the models covered in this Manual, the oil pressure warning light is linked to the STOP warning light, and is not illuminated when the ignition is initially switched on. Therefore it is not possible to check the oil pressure warning light when turning the engine on the starter motor.

5 Prime the fuel system (refer to Chapter 4B). Although the system is self-priming, it will help if the ignition is switched on and off several times before attempting to start the engine in order to purge air from the system.

6 Fully depress the accelerator pedal, turn the ignition key to position M, and wait for the preheating warning light to go out.

All models

7 Start the engine, noting that this may take a little longer than usual, due to the fuel system components having been disturbed.

8 While the engine is idling, check for fuel, water and oil leaks. Don't be alarmed if there are some odd smells and smoke from parts getting hot and burning off oil deposits.

9 Assuming all is well, keep the engine idling until hot water is felt circulating through the top hose, then switch off the engine.

10 After a few minutes, recheck the oil and coolant levels as described in *Weekly checks*, and top-up as necessary.

11 Note that there is no need to retighten the cylinder head bolts once the engine has first run after reassembly.

12 If new pistons, rings or crankshaft bearings have been fitted, the engine must be treated as new, and run-in for the first 500 miles. Do not operate the engine at full-throttle, or allow it to labour at low engine speeds in any gear. It is recommended that the oil and filter be changed at the end of this period.

Chapter 3
Cooling, heating and ventilation systems

Contents

Degrees of difficulty

Easy, suitable for novice with little experience	**Fairly easy,** suitable for beginner with some experience	**Fairly difficult,** suitable for competent DIY mechanic	**Difficult,** suitable for experienced DIY mechanic	**Very difficult,** suitable for expert DIY or professional

Specifications

General

Maximum system pressure	1.4 bars
Engine coolant temperature sensor resistance (approximately):	
All petrol engines:	
20°C	6100 ohms
80°C	620 ohms
1.6 litre diesel engine:	
60°C	1266 ohms
80°C	642 ohms
2.0 litre SOHC diesel engine:	
20°C	6200 ohms
30°C	1920 ohms
2.0 litre DOHC diesel engine:	
20°C	6200 ohms

Thermostat

Start of opening temperature:	
Petrol engine models	89°C
Diesel engine models	83°C

Air conditioning compressor oil

Quantity:	
All except 2.0 litre diesel engine..........................	135 cc
2.0 litre diesel engine	265 cc
Type:	
All except 2.0 litre diesel engine..........................	SP10
2.0 litre diesel engine	Planet Elf 488

Refrigerant

Quantity	625 ± 25 g
Type	R134a

Torque wrench settings

	Nm	lbf ft
Air conditioning compressor mounting bolts:		
Petrol engines	25	18
1.6 litre diesel engine	25	18
2.0 litre diesel engine	35	26
Coolant outlet housing	10	7
Coolant pump:		
Petrol engines......................................	14	10
1.6 litre diesel engine	10	7
2.0 litre diesel engine	16	12

1 General information and precautions

General information

1 The cooling system is of pressurised type, comprising a coolant pump driven by the timing belt, an aluminium radiator, an expansion tank, an electric cooling fan, a thermostat, a heater matrix, and all associated hoses and switches.

2 The system functions as follows. Cold coolant in the bottom of the radiator passes through the bottom hose to the coolant pump, where it is pumped around the cylinder block and head passages. After cooling the cylinder bores, combustion surfaces and valve seats, the coolant reaches the underside of the thermostat, which is initially closed. The coolant passes through the heater, and is returned via the cylinder block to the coolant pump.

3 When the engine is cold, the coolant circulates only through the cylinder block, cylinder head, and heater. When the coolant reaches a predetermined temperature, the thermostat opens, and the coolant passes through the top hose to the radiator. As the coolant passes down through the radiator, it is cooled by the inrush of air when the car is in forward motion. The airflow is supplemented by the action of the electric cooling fan when necessary. Upon reaching the bottom of the radiator, the coolant has now cooled, and the cycle is repeated.

4 On models with automatic transmission, a proportion of the coolant is recirculated through the transmission fluid cooler mounted on the transmission. On models fitted with an engine oil cooler, the coolant is also passed through the oil cooler.

5 The operation of the electric cooling fan is controlled by the engine management control unit.

Precautions

⚠️ *Warning: Do not attempt to remove the expansion tank filler cap, or to disturb any part of the cooling system, while the engine is hot, as there is a high risk of scalding. If the expansion tank filler cap must be removed before the engine and radiator have fully cooled (even though this is not recommended), the pressure in the cooling system must first be relieved. Cover the cap with a thick layer of cloth to avoid scalding, and slowly unscrew the filler cap until a hissing sound is heard. When the hissing has stopped, indicating that the pressure has reduced, slowly unscrew the filler cap until it can be removed; if more hissing sounds are heard, wait until they have stopped before unscrewing the cap. At all times keep well away from the filler cap opening, and protect your hands.*

⚠️ *Warning: Do not allow antifreeze to come into contact with your skin, or with the painted surfaces of the vehicle. Rinse off spills immediately, with plenty of water. Never leave antifreeze lying around in an open container, or in a puddle in the driveway or on the garage floor. Children and pets are attracted by its sweet smell, but antifreeze can be fatal if ingested.*

⚠️ *Warning: If the engine is hot, the electric cooling fan may start rotating even if the engine is not running. Be careful to keep your hands, hair, and any loose clothing well clear when working in the engine compartment.*

⚠️ *Warning: Refer to Section 11 for precautions to be observed when working on models equipped with air conditioning.*

2 Cooling system hoses – disconnection and renewal

Note: *Refer to the warnings given in Section 1 of this Chapter before proceeding. Hoses should only be disconnected once the engine has cooled sufficiently to avoid scalding.*

1 If the checks described in the *Hose and fluid leak check* Section in Chapter 1A or 1B reveal a faulty hose, it must be renewed as follows.

2 First drain the cooling system (see Chapter 1A or 1B). If the coolant is not due for renewal, it may be re-used, providing it is collected in a clean container.

3 To disconnect a hose, proceed as follows, according to the type of hose connection.

Conventional hose connections

4 On conventional connections, the clips used to secure the hoses in position may be either standard worm-drive clips, spring clips or disposable crimped types. The crimped type of clip is not designed to be re-used, so use a worm-drive type on reassembly.

5 To disconnect a hose, release the retaining clips and move them along the hose, clear of the relevant inlet/outlet. Carefully work the hose free. The hoses can be removed with relative ease when new – on an older car, they may have stuck **(see illustration)**.

6 If a hose proves to be difficult to remove, try to release it by rotating its ends before attempting to free it. Gently prise the end of the hose with a blunt instrument (such as a flat-bladed screwdriver), but do not apply too much force, and take care not to damage the pipe stubs or hoses. Note in particular that the radiator inlet stub is fragile; do not use excessive force when attempting to remove the hose. If all else fails, cut the hose with a sharp knife, then slit it so that it can be peeled off in two pieces. Although this may prove expensive if the hose is otherwise undamaged, it is preferable to buying a new radiator. Check first, however, that a new hose is readily available.

7 When fitting a hose, first slide the clips onto the hose, then work the hose into position. If crimped-type clips were originally fitted, use worm-drive clips when refitting the hose.

8 Work the hose into position, checking that it is correctly routed, then slide each clip back along the hose until it passes over the flared end of the relevant inlet/outlet, before tightening the clip securely.

> **HAYNES HiNT** *If the hose is stiff, use a little soapy water as a lubricant or soften the hose by soaking it in hot water. Do not use oil or grease as these may attack the rubber.*

9 Refill the cooling system (see Chapter 1A or 1B).

10 Check thoroughly for leaks as soon as possible after disturbing any part of the cooling system.

Click-fit connections

Note: *New sealing ring should be used when reconnecting the hose.*

11 On certain models, some cooling system hoses are secured in position with click-fit connectors where the hose is retained by a large circlip.

12 To disconnect this type of hose fitting, carefully prise the wire clip out of position then disconnect the hose connection **(see illustration)**. Once the hose has been

2.5 You can buy special tools specifically designed to release spring-type hose clips

2.12 Prise the wire clip up and disconnect the hose

2.13 Ensure the O-ring seal (arrowed) is in position

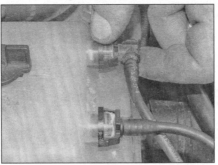

3.3 Squeeze together the collar and pull the hoses from the expansion tank

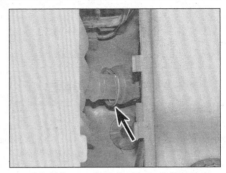

3.6 Prise up the clip (arrowed) and disconnect the hose as the tank is removed

disconnected, refit the wire clip to the hose union. Inspect the hose unit sealing ring for signs of damage or deterioration and renew if necessary.

13 On refitting, ensure that the sealing ring is in position and wire clip is correctly located in the groove in the union **(see illustration)**. Lubricate the sealing ring with a smear of soapy water, to ease installation, then push the hose into its union until it is heard to click into position.

14 Ensure the hose is securely retained by the wire clip then refill the cooling system as described in Chapter 1A or 1B.

15 Check thoroughly for leaks as soon as possible after disturbing any part of the cooling system.

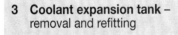

3 Coolant expansion tank – removal and refitting

Removal

1 Referring to Chapter 1A or 1B, drain the cooling system sufficiently to empty the contents of the expansion tank. Do not drain any more coolant than is necessary.

2 Remove the plastic cover from over the coolant and washer reservoirs. The cover is secured by two plastic expanding rivets. Push the centre pins in a little, then prise out the complete rivets.

3 Squeeze together the collar, then pull the plastic hoses from the expansion tank. On some models, the hoses may be secured by expanding clamps **(see illustration)**.

4 Disconnect the level sensor wiring plug – where fitted.

5 Unscrew the mounting bolt and free the tank from its mount. Take care not to lose the mounting rubber.

6 Release the clip and disconnect the remaining hose as the expansion tank is removed **(see illustration)**.

Refitting

7 Refitting is the reverse of removal, ensuring the hoses are securely reconnected. On completion, top-up the coolant level as described in *Weekly checks*.

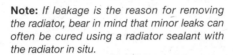

4 Radiator – removal, inspection and refitting

Note: *If leakage is the reason for removing the radiator, bear in mind that minor leaks can often be cured using a radiator sealant with the radiator in situ.*

Removal

1 Drain the cooling system (see Chapter 1A or 1B).

2 On post-facelift models (from September 2004), remove the 3 top fixings of the front bumper **(see illustration)**.

1.6 litre diesel models

3 Undo the bolt and move the pressure differential sensor and bracket rearwards a

4.2 Remove the top fixings of the front bumper (arrowed) – post-facelift models only

4.5a Undo the nuts and bolt (arrowed) . . .

little (located at the upper right-hand corner of the radiator) **(see illustration)**.

4 Slacken the clamps and disconnect the air hoses from the intercooler, intake manifold and turbocharger.

5 Undo the nut and bolt, then detach the air hose support bracket from the top of the radiator **(see illustrations)**.

All models

6 Remove the air ducts (where fitted) from the top of the radiator **(see illustrations)**.

7 Release the clamps and disconnect the upper and lower coolant hoses from the radiator. On automatic transmission models, release the clamp and disconnect the fluid cooler hose from the base of the radiator **(see illustration)**.

8 Release the clamp and disconnect the expansion hose from the top of the radiator

4.3 Undo the bolt (arrowed) and move the pressure differential sensor and bracket rearwards

4.5b . . . then remove the air hose support bracket assembly (arrowed)

4.6a Prise out the clip . . .

4.6b . . . and remove the air duct at the top of the radiator

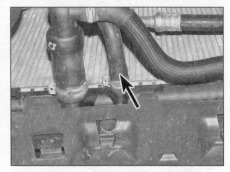

4.7 Disconnect the fluid cooler hose (arrowed) – automatic transmission models

4.8a Squeeze together the ends of the clip to release it . . .

4.8b . . . or press down the collar and pull the expansion hose from the radiator

(see illustrations). Unclip the expansion pipe from the top of the radiator (where applicable).

9 On pre-facelift models (up to September 2004), undo the 2 upper mounting bolts, depress the catches and carefully lift the radiator out of position, taking care not to damage the radiator fins. Recover the radiator lower mounting rubbers **(see illustrations)**.

10 On post-facelift models (from September 2004), use a small screwdriver to release the retaining clips and pull the top edge of the radiator rearwards **(see illustration)**. Lift the radiator upwards from its rubber mountings.

Inspection

11 If the radiator has been removed due to suspected blockage, reverse-flush it as described in Chapter 1A or 1B. Clean dirt and debris from the radiator fins, using an airline

(in which case, wear eye protection) or a soft brush. Be careful, as the fins are sharp, and easily damaged.

12 If necessary, a radiator specialist can perform a 'flow test' on the radiator, to establish whether an internal blockage exists.

13 A leaking radiator must be referred to a specialist for permanent repair. Do not attempt to weld or solder a leaking radiator, as damage to the plastic components may result.

14 Inspect the condition of the radiator mounting rubbers, and renew them if necessary.

Refitting

15 Refitting is a reversal of removal, bearing in mind the following points:

a) Ensure that the lower lugs on the radiator are correctly engaged with the mounting rubbers in the body panel.

b) Reconnect the hoses with reference to Section 2, using new sealing rings where applicable.

c) On completion, refill the cooling system as described in Chapter 1A or 1B.

---

5 Thermostat – removal, testing and refitting

Removal

1 Drain the cooling system (see Chapter 1A or 1B).

Petrol engines

2 The thermostat is fitted to the coolant housing on the left-hand end of the cylinder head. To improve access, remove the battery and battery tray as described in Chapter 5A.

3 Remove the plastic cover from the top of the engine. The cover is retained by 6 screws – rotate the screws 90° clockwise and lift the cover from place.

4 Disconnect the coolant hose from the front of the housing, then undo the two screws and remove the thermostat **(see illustrations)**. Recover the sealing ring.

5 Remove the plastic cover from the top of the engine. On all engines, the thermostat is fitted to the coolant housing at th left-hand end of the cylinder head.

Diesel engines – 1.6 litre and 2.0 litre DOHC from RPO No 10339

6 On theses engines, the thermostat is

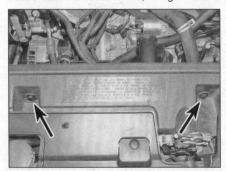

4.9a Undo the 2 upper mounting bolts (arrowed)

4.9b Press down the 2 catches (arrowed – shown with the mounting removed for clarity)

4.10 Release the clips and pull the radiator rearwards

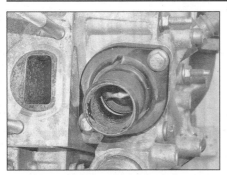

5.4a Undo the 2 bolts and remove the housing . . .

5.4b . . . then pull the thermostat from the housing

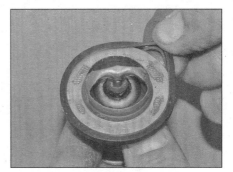

5.4c Renew the seal

5.7a Depress the release button (arrowed) and disconnect the hoses

5.7b Undo the bolts (arrowed) and detach the coolant outlet housing

integral with the coolant outlet housing at the left-hand end of the cylinder head. Begin by removing the air ducting at the that end of the cylinder head.

7 Disconnect the coolant hoses from the outlet housing, and the wiring plug from the coolant temperature sensor. Note that some of the hoses are disconnected after pressing down on the white-coloured release button. Undo the retaining bolts and remove the housing **(see illustrations)**.

Diesel engines – 2.0 litre SOHC and DOHC up to RPO No 10338

8 On these engines, although the thermostat is separate from the coolant outlet housing, at the left-hand end of the cylinder head, it is not available separately. Begin by removing the relevant air ducting from that end of the cylinder head.

9 Release the clamp and disconnect the radiator coolant hose from the thermostat housing, disconnect the wiring plug, then unscrew the retaining bolts and free the thermostat/housing from the outlet housing. Remove the thermostat/housing assembly from the housing, noting which way around it is fitted, and recover the sealing ring **(see illustrations)**.

Testing

10 A rough test of the thermostat may be made by suspending it with a piece of string in a container full of water. Heat the water to bring it to the boil – the thermostat must open by the time the water boils. If not, renew it.

11 If a thermometer is available, the precise opening temperature of the thermostat may be determined; compare with the figures given in the Specifications. The opening temperature is also marked on the thermostat.

12 A thermostat which fails to close as the water cools must also be renewed.

Refitting

13 Refitting is a reversal of removal, bearing in mind the following points.
a) *Examine the sealing ring for damage or deterioration, and if necessary, renew.*
b) *Where a separate thermostat is fitted, ensure that it is fitted the correct way round.*
c) *On completion, refill the cooling system as described in Chapter 1A or 1B.*

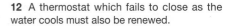

6 Electric cooling fan – removal and refitting

Removal

1 Remove the front bumper as described in Chapter 11.

2 Push in the centre pin, and detach the washer reservoir filler tube from the front panel **(see illustration)**. There's no need to remove the tube.

3 Slacken and remove the four bolts and washers securing the cooling fan to the front panel **(see illustration)**.

4 Release the wiring harness from the retaining clips, and disconnect the fan wiring plug. Manoeuvre the fan assembly out of position **(see illustrations)**.

5.9a On some diesel models, the thermostat is on top of the coolant housing (arrowed) . . .

5.9b . . . whilst on others, it's at the front of the housing (arrowed)

6.2 Press in the centre pin, prise out the plastic rivet securing the filler tube

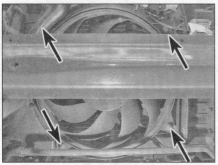

6.3 Undo the cooling fan mounting bolts (arrowed)

6.4a Disconnect the fan wiring plug (arrowed) . . .

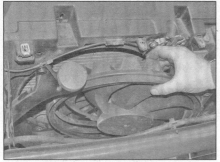

6.4b . . . and manoeuvre the fan from place

6.8 Cooling fan relays

Refitting

5 Refitting is a reversal of removal.

Cooling fan relays

6 The relays are fitted to the front panel and are located behind the cover on the left-hand side of the cooling fan.

7 To gain access to the relays, remove the front bumper as described in Chapter 11.

8 Release the clips and remove the cover from the front panel. The relays can then be removed (see illustration).

7 Cooling system electrical sensors – general information, removal and refitting

General information

1 There is only one coolant temperature

sensor on most models, which is fitted to the coolant outlet housing on the left-hand end of the cylinder head (see illustrations). The coolant temperature gauge and the cooling fan are all operated by the engine management ECM using the signal supplied by this sensor.

Removal

Note: Ensure the engine is cold before removing a temperature sensor.

2 Partially drain the cooling system to just below the level of the sensor (as described in Chapter 1A or 1B). Alternatively, have ready a suitable bung to plug the sensor aperture whilst the sensor is removed. If this method is used, take great care not to damage the switch aperture or use anything which will allow foreign matter to enter the cooling system. On diesel models, to improve

access, remove the battery as described in Chapter 5A.

3 Remove the air ducting as necessary from the left-hand end of the cylinder head, then disconnect the wiring connector from the sensor.

4 On some engines, the sensor is clipped in place. Prise out the sensor retaining circlip then remove the sensor and sealing ring from the housing (see illustration). If the system has not been drained, plug the sensor aperture to prevent further coolant loss.

5 On all other engines, unscrew the sensor and recover the sealing washer (where applicable). If the system has not been drained, plug the sensor aperture to prevent further coolant loss.

Refitting

6 Where the sensor was clipped in place, fit a new sealing ring to the sensor. Push the sensor firmly into the housing and secure it in position with the circlip, ensuring it is correctly located in the housing groove.

7 On all other engines, if the sensor was originally fitted using sealing compound, clean the sensor threads thoroughly, and coat them with fresh sealing compound. If the sensor was originally fitted using a sealing washer, use a new sealing washer. Fit the sensor and tighten securely.

8 Reconnect the wiring connector then refit any components removed from access.

9 Top-up the cooling system as described in Weekly checks.

8 Coolant pump – removal and refitting

Removal

1 Drain the cooling system (see Chapter 1A or 1B).

2 Remove the timing belt as described in Chapter 2A, 2B, 2C, 2D or 2E as applicable.

Diesel engines

3 Slacken and remove the retaining bolts and withdraw the pump assembly from the engine. Recover the pump sealing ring/gasket

7.1a Coolant temperature sensor (arrowed) – petrol engines

7.1b Coolant temperature sensor (arrowed) on the rear of the coolant housing – 2.0 litre DOHC diesel engine

7.4 Prise out the clip and remove the sensor

8.3a Undo the bolts (arrowed) and remove the coolant pump

8.3b Renew the coolant pump gasket

(as applicable) and discard it; a new one must be used on refitting **(see illustrations)**. Note that on some engines, the sealing ring is not available separately from the pump – check with your Citroën dealer.

Petrol engines

4 Remove the heat shield (where fitted) from the pump, then undo the bolts/nuts securing the pump to the cylinder block **(see illustration)**. Do not undo the bolts securing the two halves of the pump together. Withdraw the pump.

Refitting

5 Ensure that the pump and cylinder block/housing mating surfaces are clean and dry.
6 Fit the new sealing ring/gasket (as applicable) to the pump then refit the pump assembly, tightening its retaining bolts securely **(see illustration)**.
7 Refit the timing belt as described in Chapter 2A, 2B, 2C, 2D or 2E (as applicable).
8 Refill the cooling system as described in Chapter 1A or 1B (as applicable).

9 Heating and ventilation system – general information

Note: *Refer to Section 11 for information on the air conditioning side of the system.*

Manually-controlled heating/ventilation system

1 The heating/ventilation system consists of a multi-speed blower motor (housed behind the facia), face level vents in the centre and at each end of the facia, and air ducts to the front footwells.
2 The control unit is located in the facia, and the controls operate flap valves to deflect and mix the air flowing through the various parts of the heating/ventilation system. The flap valves are contained in the air distribution housing, which acts as a central distribution unit, passing air to the various ducts and vents.
3 Cold air enters the system through the grille in the scuttle. If required, the airflow is boosted by the blower, and then flows through the

various ducts, according to the settings of the controls. Stale air is expelled through ducts at the rear of the vehicle. If warm air is required, the cold air is passed over the heater matrix, which is heated by the engine coolant.
4 A recirculation lever enables the outside air supply to be closed off, while the air inside the vehicle is recirculated. This can be useful to prevent unpleasant odours entering from outside the vehicle, but should only be used briefly, as the recirculated air inside the vehicle will soon become stale.
5 On some diesel engine models an electric heater is fitted into the heater housing. When the coolant temperature is cold, the heater warms the air before it enters the heater matrix. This quickly increases the temperature of the heater matrix on cold starts, resulting in warm air being available to heat the vehicle interior soon after start-up.

Automatic climate control system

6 A fully-automatic electronic climate control system was offered as an option on most

8.4 Coolant pump retaining bolts/nuts (arrowed)

8.6 Renew the rubber seal

10.2a Push the switches from each side of the audio unit aperture . . .

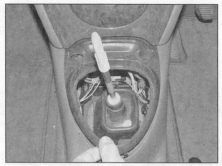

10.2b . . . and prise up the gear/selector lever surround trim panel

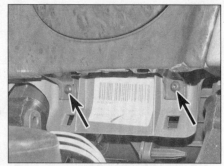

10.3a Undo the 2 Torx bolts (arrowed) . . .

10.3b . . . and carefully prise the centre panel from place

10.4a Depress the clips and release the outer cable . . .

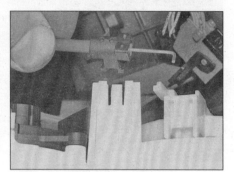

10.4b . . . then detach the operating cables from the control panel

models. The main components of the system are exactly the same as those described for the manual system, the only major difference being that the temperature and distribution flaps in the heating/ventilation housing are operated by electric motors rather than cables.

7 The operation of the system is controlled by the electronic control module (which is incorporated in the blower motor assembly) along with the following sensors.

a) The passenger compartment sensor – informs the control module of the temperature of the air inside the passenger compartment.

b) Evaporator temperature sensor – informs the control module of the evaporator temperature.

c) Heater matrix temperature sensor – informs the control module of the heater matrix temperature.

8 Using the information from the above sensors, the control module determines the appropriate settings for the heating/ventilation system housing flaps to maintain the passenger compartment at the desired setting on the control panel.

9 If the system develops a fault, the vehicle should be taken to a Citroën dealer. A complete test of the system can then be carried out, using a special electronic diagnostic test unit which is simply plugged into the system's diagnostic connector (located next to the fusebox).

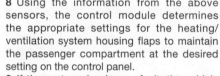

10 Heater/ventilation components –
removal and refitting

Control panel removal

1 Remove the facia-mounted audio unit as described in Chapter 12.

**Pre-facelift models
(up to September 2004)**

2 Push the switches each side of the audio aperture from place, and prise up the gear lever surround trim panel (see illustrations).

3 Undo the 2 Torx bolts at the lower edge of the centre panel, then carefully prise the centre panel from place (see illustrations).

4 On models with the manual control panel, it's necessary to release the retaining clips and disconnect the operating cables and wiring plugs before the panel can be manoeuvred from place (see illustrations).

5 Undo the 4 Torx bolts, release the clip each side, push the control panel forward, pull the lower part of the facia rearwards a little, then manoeuvre it from the console (see illustrations).

**Post-facelift models
(from September 2004)**

6 Pull the panel rearwards from position (see illustration).

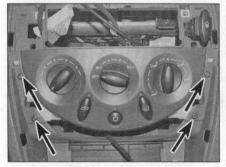

10.5a Undo the Torx bolts (arrowed) . . .

10.5b . . . release the clip each side . . .

10.5c . . . and manoeuvre the control panel from place

10.6 Pull the control panel from place

10.13 Prise up the clip and disconnect the heater hoses from the pipes

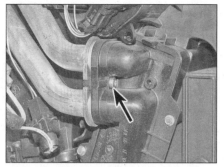

10.18 Undo the screw securing the matrix pipes (arrowed)

10.20a Remove the air distribution motor (arrowed) . . .

10.20b . . . then undo the screw, release the clips (arrowed) . . .

10.20c . . . and slide out the matrix

All models

7 On models with an automatic climate control system, disconnect the wiring connectors and remove the control panel from the vehicle.

Control panel refitting

8 Refitting is the reverse of removal. On models with a manual control panel ensure the control cables are correctly reconnected and securely held by the retaining clips; check the operation of the control knobs before securing the control panel to the facia.

Heater/ventilation control cables

Removal

9 Remove the facia as described in Chapter 11.
10 Release the retaining clip and detach the relevant cable from the rear of the control panel and the heating/ventilation housing (see illustration 10.4a and 10.4b). Remove the cable, noting its correct routing.

Refitting

11 Refitting is the reverse of removal, ensuring the cable is securely retained by its clips. Check the operation of the control panel and cables before refitting the facia (see Chapter 11).

Heater matrix removal

12 Disconnect the battery negative terminal as described in Chapter 5A.
13 Clamp the heater matrix coolant hoses at the engine compartment bulkhead to minimise coolant loss, then release the clips and pull the hoses from the pipes (see illustration).

14 Undo the Torx bolt and pull the pipe flange away from the bulkhead. Recover the seal.
15 Remove the facia as described in Chapter 11.

Pre-facelift models (up to September 2004)

16 On diesel models equipped with an additional electric heating element, undo the bolts, unplug the wiring connectors, and pull the element from the heater housing (see illustration 10.50b).
17 Position a container beneath the heater matrix pipe union on the left-hand side of the heating/ventilation housing to catch any spilt coolant.
18 Slacken and remove the screw securing the matrix pipes to the housing (see illustration).
19 Free the pipes from the matrix, catching the coolant in the container. Recover the sealing rings fitted to the pipe unions and

discard them; new ones should be used on refitting. Take care not to lose the bulkhead seal or retaining plate from the pipes.
20 Undo the screws, remove the air distribution motor above the matrix cover, then release the 3 retaining clips, undo the 2 screws, then slide the matrix out from the housing. Keep the matrix unions uppermost as the matrix is removed to prevent coolant spillage (see illustrations).

Post-facelift models (from September 2004)

21 Note their fitted positions, then disconnect the wiring plugs/earth connection beneath the matrix cover (see illustration).
22 Undo the screws and remove the matrix cover (see illustration).
23 Position a container beneath the matrix pipes, then use a hacksaw or rotary cutting tool to cut through the matrix pipes as shown (see illustration).

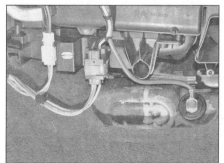

10.21 Disconnect the wiring plug and the earth connection beneath the matrix

10.22 Matrix cover screws (arrowed)

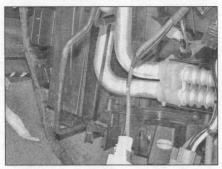

10.23 Cut through the matrix pipes at the bends

10.25 Retaining plate bolt (arrowed)

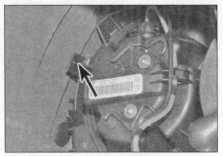

10.33 Pull the retaining tab rearwards a little, to release the blower motor (arrowed)

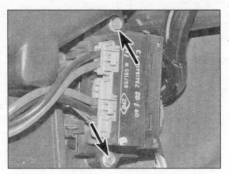

10.36 Heater blower motor resistor screws (arrowed)

24 With the pipes cut through, pull the matrix from the housing.

25 Undo the bolt, and remove the pipes, and retaining plate from the bulkhead/heater **(see illustration)**.

Heater matrix refitting

26 On post-facelift models, the new matrix is supplied with separate pipes, which are them clamped to the stubs from the matrix. Fit the new pipe assembly to the bulkhead.

10.42a Remove the bulkhead heat shield (where fitted) . . .

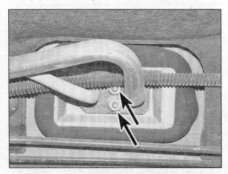

10.42b . . . then undo the 2 nuts securing the refrigerant pipes (arrowed)

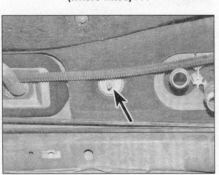

10.43a Undo the 2 nuts (arrowed) . . .

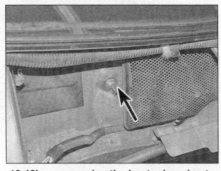

10.43b . . . securing the heater housing to the bulkhead

27 On both models, ease the matrix into the housing and secure it in position.

28 Ensure the bulkhead seal and retaining plate are correctly fitted to the matrix pipes and fit a new sealing ring to each of the pipe unions. Manoeuvre the pipe assembly into position and secure it to the matrix using the clamps provided.

29 The remainder of refitting is a reversal of removal.

Heater blower motor

Removal

30 The blower motor is fitted to the top of the heating/ventilation housing, on the left-hand side.

31 On left-hand drive models, remove the facia as described in Chapter 11, on right-hand drive models, remove the passenger's glovebox as described in Chapter 11.

32 Disconnect the wiring connector(s) from the blower motor, and release the wiring from the clips.

33 Release the retaining tab, rotate the motor anti-clockwise to free it from the housing then manoeuvre it out of position **(see illustration)**.

Refitting

34 Refitting is the reverse of removal.

Heater blower motor resistor

Removal

35 Remove the soundproofing panels under the driver's side of the facia.

36 Undo the 2 screws and remove the resistor. Disconnect the wiring connector and remove the resistor from the housing **(see illustration)**.

Refitting

37 Refitting is a reversal of removal.

Heating/ventilation housing

⚠️ **Warning: Refer to Section 11 for precautions to be observed when working on models equipped with air conditioning. Do not attempt the following procedure unless the system has been professionally discharged.**

Removal

38 On models with air conditioning, have the system discharged and evacuated by a suitably-equipped specialist.

39 Remove the facia as described in Chapter 11.

40 Working in the engine compartment, clamp the heater matrix coolant hoses to minimise coolant loss, then release the clips and disconnect the hoses at the bulkhead.

41 Slacken and remove the screw securing the heater matrix pipes to the bulkhead and remove the retaining plate and seal **(see illustrations 10.25)**.

42 Remove the heat shields from the engine compartment bulkhead, then undo the nuts securing the refrigerant pipes to the connection at the engine compartment bulkhead. Plug/cover the openings to prevent contamination/saturation. Recover and

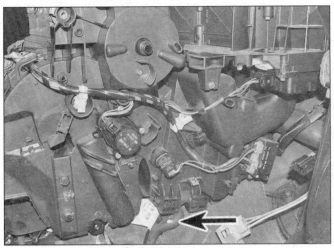

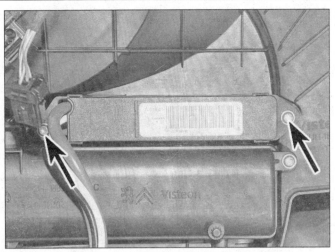

10.44 Disconnect the drain hose from the heater housing (arrowed)

10.50a Undo the 2 Torx bolts (arrowed) . . .

discard the O-ring seals – new ones must be fitted **(see illustrations)**.

⚠ *Warning: Failure to seal the refrigerant pipe unions will result in the receiver/drier becoming saturated, necessitating its renewal.*

43 Slacken and remove the nuts securing the heating/ventilation housing to the bulkhead **(see illustrations)**.
44 Where applicable, disconnect the evaporator drain hose from the base of the heater housing **(see illustration)**.
45 Detach the rear floor air vent ducts from the housing, then disconnect the wiring connector on the left-hand side of the housing then remove the housing assembly from the vehicle. Keep the heater matrix pipe unions uppermost as the assembly is removed to prevent coolant spillage.
46 Recover the seal and retaining plate from the heater matrix pipes, and the seal from the housing mounting. Renew the seals if they show signs of damage or deterioration.

Refitting

47 Refitting is the reverse of removal ensuring the seals are in position on the pipes and housing mounting. On completion, refill the cooling system (see Chapter 1A or 1B), and have the air conditioning system recharged (where applicable).

Additional heater (diesel models)

Removal

48 Remove the facia as described in Chapter 11.
49 Undo the bolt securing the heater earth connection.
50 Disconnect the heater wiring plug, then undo the bolts, and slide the heater from the housing **(see illustrations)**.

Refitting

51 Refitting is the reverse of removal.

Ambient temperature sensor

52 The ambient temperature sensor is located on the underside of the passenger's side exterior mirror. To remove the sensor, remove the mirror cover as described in Chapter 11.
53 Unclip the sensor from the mirror housing. To disconnect the wiring plug, it's necessary to remove the door trim panel as described in Chapter 11.

Sunlight/rain sensor

Mirror base-mounted sensor

54 Remove the interior mirror/sensor cover as described in Chapter 11.
55 Unclip the sensor from the mounting base, and disconnect the wiring plug **(see illustration)**.

56 Refitting is a reversal of removal.

Facia-mounted sunlight sensor

57 Carefully prise the sensor up from the centre of the facia **(see illustration)**.
58 Disconnect the wiring plug as the sensor is withdrawn.
59 Refitting is a reversal of removal.

11 Air conditioning system – general information and precautions

General information

1 An air conditioning system is available on certain models. It enables the temperature of incoming air to be lowered, and also dehumidifies the air, which makes for rapid demisting and increased comfort.
2 The cooling side of the system works in the same way as a domestic refrigerator. Refrigerant gas is drawn into a belt-driven compressor, and passes into a condenser mounted on the front of the radiator, where it loses heat and becomes liquid. The liquid passes through an expansion valve to an evaporator, where it changes from liquid under high pressure to gas under low pressure. This change is accompanied by a drop in

10.50b . . . and slide the heater from the housing

10.55 Unclip the rain or sunlight sensor from the mounting base

10.57 Prise the sunlight sensor from the facia

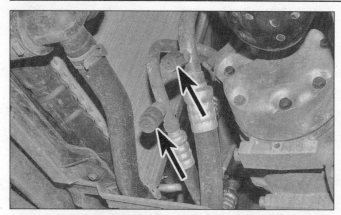

11.5a Air conditioning high and low-pressure circuits service ports (arrowed) under the vehicle . . .

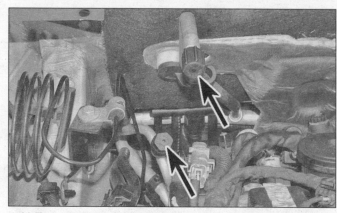

11.5b . . . or at the back of the engine compartment (arrowed)

temperature, which cools the evaporator. The refrigerant returns to the compressor, and the cycle begins again.

3 Air blown through the evaporator passes to the heating/ventilation housing, where it is mixed with hot air blown through the heater matrix to achieve the desired temperature in the passenger compartment.

4 The heating side of the system works in the same way as on models without air conditioning (see Section 9).

5 The operation of the system is controlled electronically by the ECM integral with the control panel. Any problems with the system should be referred to a Citroën dealer, or suitably-equipped specialist **(see illustrations)**.

Precautions

6 When an air conditioning system is fitted, it is necessary to observe special precautions whenever dealing with any part of the system, or its associated components. The refrigerant is potentially dangerous, and should only be handled by qualified persons. Uncontrolled discharging of the refrigerant is dangerous and damaging to the environment for the following reasons.

a) *If it is splashed onto the skin, it can cause frostbite.*

b) *The refrigerant is heavier then air and so displaces oxygen. In a confined space which is not adequately ventilated this could lead to a risk of suffocation. The gas is odourless and colourless so there is no warning of its presence in the atmosphere.*

c) *Although not poisonous, in the presence of a naked flame (including a cigarette) it forms a noxious gas which causes headaches, nausea, etc.*

⚠ *Warning: Never attempt to open any air conditioning system refrigerant pipe/hose union without first having the system fully-discharged by an air conditioning specialist. On completion of work, have the system recharged with the correct type and amount of fresh refrigerant.*

⚠ *Warning: Always seal disconnected refrigerant pipe/hose unions as soon as they are disconnected. Failure to form an air-tight seal on any union will result in the dehydrator reservoir become saturated, necessitating its renewal. Also renew all sealing rings disturbed.*
Caution: Do not operated the air conditioning system if it is known to be short of refrigerant as this could damage the compressor.

---

12 Air conditioning system components – removal and refitting 🔧

⚠ *Warning: Refer to the precautions given in Section 11 and have the system discharged by an air conditioning specialist before carrying out any work on the air conditioning system*

Compressor

Removal

1 Have the air conditioning system fully-discharged and evacuated by an air conditioning specialist.

2 Remove the auxiliary drivebelt as described in Chapter 5A.

3 Disconnect the compressor wiring connector from the engine harness.

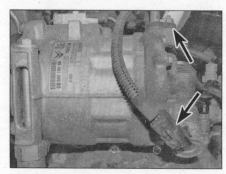

12.4 Compressor wiring plug and refrigerant pipes union nut (arrowed)

4 Unscrew the nuts securing the refrigerant pipe retaining plates to the compressor **(see illustration)**. Separate the pipes from the compressor and quickly seal the pipe and compressor unions to prevent the entry of moisture into the refrigerant circuit. Discard the sealing rings, new ones must be used on refitting.

⚠ *Warning: Failure to seal the refrigerant pipe unions will result in the dehydrator reservoir become saturated, necessitating its renewal.*

5 Unscrew the compressor mounting bolts and nuts then free the compressor from its mounting bracket and remove it from the engine. Take care not to lose the spacers from the compressor rear mountings (where fitted).

6 If the compressor is to be renewed, drain the refrigerant oil from the old compressor. The specialist who recharges the refrigerant system will need to add this amount of oil to the system.

Refitting

7 If a new compressor is being fitted, drain the refrigerant oil.

8 Ensure the spacers are correctly fitted to the rear mountings then manoeuvre the compressor into position and fit the mounting bolts and nuts. Tighten the compressor front (drivebelt pulley) end mounting bolts to the specified torque first then tighten the rear bolts.

9 Lubricate the new refrigerant pipe sealing rings with refrigerant oil. Remove the plugs and install the sealing rings then quickly fit the refrigerant pipes to the compressor. Ensure the refrigerant pipes are correctly joined then refit the retaining bolt, tighten it securely.

10 Reconnect the wiring connector then refit the auxiliary drivebelt (see Chapter 5A).

11 Have the air conditioning system recharged with the correct type and amount of refrigerant by a specialist before using the system. Remember to inform the specialist which components have been changed, so they can add the correct amount of oil.

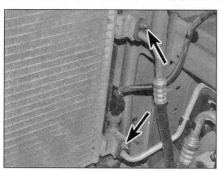

12.14 Undo the nuts (arrowed) and disconnect the refrigerant pipes

12.16 Ensure the condenser rubber mountings are correctly fitted

12.19a Undo the screw and remove the clip (arrowed) . . .

Condenser

Removal

12 Have the air conditioning system fully-discharged by an air conditioning specialist.
13 Remove the radiator as described in Section 4.
14 Undo the retaining nuts and disconnect the refrigerant pipes from the right-hand side of the condenser. Recover the O-ring seals **(see illustration)**.

 Warning: Failure to seal the refrigerant pipe unions will result in the dehydrator reservoir become saturated, necessitating its renewal.

15 Move the top of the condenser to the rear and remove it.

Refitting

16 Refitting is a reversal of removal. Noting the following points:
 a) *Ensure the upper and lower mounting rubbers are correctly fitted then seat the condenser in position in the front panel **(see illustration)**.*
 b) *Lubricate the sealing rings with compressor oil. Remove the plugs and install the sealing rings then quickly fit the refrigerant pipes to the condenser. Securely tighten the dehydrator pipe union nut and ensure the compressor pipe is correctly joined.*
 c) *Have the air conditioning system recharged with the correct type and amount of refrigerant by a specialist before using the system.*

12.19b . . . then unscrew the receiver/drier cartridge

Receiver/drier

Removal

17 The receiver/drier is located on the left-hand side of the condenser.
18 Remove the radiator as described in Section 4.
19 Undo the screw and remove the clip at the top then pull the top of the condenser rearwards slightly, and unscrew the receiver/drier cartridge using a Torx T70 bit. Take great care not to pull the condenser too far and damage the refrigerant pipes **(see illustrations)**.

 Warning: Prior to slackening the clamp, clean the dehydrator and wipe it dry, to avoid moisture/debris entering the air conditioning circuit.

Refitting

20 Refitting is a reversal of removal noting the following points:

12.19c Renew the cartridge seal

 a) *Lubricate the cartridge seals with compressor oil.*
 b) *Have the air conditioning system recharged with the correct type and amount of refrigerant by a specialist prior to using the system.*

Evaporator

Removal

21 Have the air conditioning system fully-discharged by an air conditioning specialist.
22 Remove the heating/ventilation housing as described in Section 10.
24 Note their fitted positions, then disconnect the wiring plugs and harness from the housing.
25 Release the retaining clips, undo the screws and separate the two halves of the heater housing **(see illustrations)**.
26 With the two halves of the housing separated, undo the 2 screws, remove the

12.25a Undo the various screws and clips around the housing (arrowed) . . .

12.25b . . . including the ones hidden at the sides (arrowed) . . .

12.25c . . . remove the base cover . . .

12.25d ... and separate the 2 halves of the housing

12.26a Undo the screws (arrowed), remove the pipe cover ...

12.26b ... then slide the evaporator from the housing

12.26c Ensure the nut plate is in place when refitting the evaporator

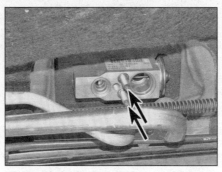

12.31a Undo the 2 studs (arrowed) using a Torx socket

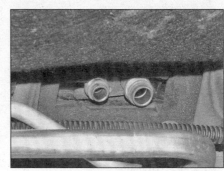

12.31b Renew the expansion valve seals on the pipes

pipe cover, then slide the evaporator from the housing **(see illustrations)**.

Refitting

27 Refitting is a reversal of removal.

Expansion valve

Removal

28 Have the air conditioning system fully-discharged by an air conditioning specialist.
29 Remove the sound insulation material/heat shield from the engine compartment bulkhead (where fitted).
30 Undo the nuts securing the refrigerant pipes to the connection at the engine compartment bulkhead. Plug/cover the openings to prevent contamination/saturation. Recover and discard the O-ring seals – new ones must be fitted **(see illustration 10.42a and 10.42b)**.

⚠ **Warning: Failure to seal the refrigerant pipe unions will result in the receiver/drier**

becoming saturated, necessitating its renewal.

31 Pull the seal from around the pipes connection at the bulkhead, then undo the 2 studs using a Torx socket, and remove the expansion valve **(see illustrations)**. Recover and discard the O-ring seals – new ones must be fitted.

Refitting

32 Refitting is a reversal of removal.

Chapter 4 Part A:
Fuel and exhaust system – petrol models

Contents

Degrees of difficulty

Easy, suitable for novice with little experience	**Fairly easy,** suitable for beginner with some experience	**Fairly difficult,** suitable for competent DIY mechanic	**Difficult,** suitable for experienced DIY mechanic	**Very difficult,** suitable for expert DIY or professional

Specifications

Engine identification

Indirect injection

Designation:
    1.8 litre engine EW7J4
    2.0 litre engine EW10J4
Engine code:
    1.8 litre engine 6FZ
    2.0 litre engine . . . . RFN

Direct injection

Designation:
    2.0 litre engine EW10D
Engine code . . . . RLZ

System type

1.8 litre engine . . . . Sagem S2000 MPI
2.0 litre engines:
    EW10J4 . . . . Magneti Marelli 48P or 6LP1
    EW10D . . . . Siemens Sirius 81

Fuel system data

Fuel pump type	Electric, immersed in tank
Fuel pump pressure:	
1.8 litre engine	3.5 bar
2.0 litre engines:	
EW10J4	3.5 bar
EW10D	5.0 bar
Fuel tank capacity	66 litres
Specified idle speed:	
1.8 litre engine	700 ± 50 rpm (not adjustable – controlled by ECM)
2.0 litre engines:	
EW10J4	700 ± 50 rpm (not adjustable – controlled by ECM)
EW10D	800 ± 50 rpm (not adjustable – controlled by ECM)
Injector resistance:	
1.8 litre engine	12.2 ohms
2.0 litre engines:	
EW10J4	12.2 ohms
EW10D	1.88 ohms
Crankshaft position sensor resistance:	
EW10J4 and EW7J4 engines	425 to 525 ohms
EW10D engine	500 ohms
Air temperature sensor resistance:	
2.0 litre engines:	
20°C	2500 ohms
80°C	310 ohms

Recommended fuel

Minimum octane rating	95 RON unleaded (UK unleaded premium)

Torque wrench settings

	Nm	lbf ft
Exhaust manifold nuts	35	26
Fuel rail bolts	10	7
High-pressure fuel pipe (pump to common rail)	26	19
High-pressure pump nuts	7	5
High-pressure fuel sensor	20	15
Inlet camshaft dephaser solenoid	7	5
Inlet manifold nuts:		
EW7J4 and EW10J4 engines	20	15
EW10D engines	9	7
Pre-catalyser to manifold (EW10D only)	25	18

1 General information and precautions

The fuel supply system consists of a fuel tank (which is mounted under the rear of the car, with an electric fuel pump immersed in it), a fuel filter, fuel feed and return lines. The fuel pump supplies fuel to the fuel rail, which acts as a reservoir for the four fuel injectors which inject fuel into the inlet tracts.

The 2.0 litre EW10D engine is equipped with a high-pressure direct injection system (HPI), where the fuel is injected directly into the combustion chamber, as opposed to the inlet tract behind the inlet valve. The injection point is accurately controlled to maximise engine output, whilst minimising emissions. The combustion process can be operated in three different modes: Stratified charge mode, Homogenous lean charge mode, and Homogenous (evenly spread) mode. At low-to-medium engine loads the engine operates in Stratified charge mode, where fuel is only injected into the area around the spark plug in the centre of the combustion chamber during the compression stroke, resulting in an extremely lean mixture of lambda 1.6 to 3.0. In this mode the fuel is injected towards the piston crown, which is shaped in such a way that the fuel is directed upwards to the spark plug. At high engine speeds and loads the engine runs in Homogenous charge mode, which is the traditional method of injecting fuel during the inlet piston stroke, and a resulting lambda value of 1.0. The transition zone between the two modes is known as Homogenous lean charge mode, where fuel is injected during the inlet stroke, but is regulated by the ECM in such a way that the lambda value is approximately 1.55. Although similar to the fuel supply system fitted to the other models covered, the HPI system has a high-pressure fuel pump driven from the left-hand end of the inlet camshaft. This pump supplies fuel at up to 100 bar to a common fuel rail mounted above each injector. Although more complex, the system ensures improved engine power and torque output, whilst lowering fuel consumption and exhaust emissions.

Refer to Section 6 for further information on the operation of each fuel injection system. Throughout this Chapter, it is also occasionally necessary to identify vehicles by their engine codes rather than by engine capacity alone. Refer to the relevant Part of Chapter 2 for further information on engine code identification.

⚠️ **Warning: Many of the procedures in this Chapter require the removal of fuel lines and connections, which may result in some fuel spillage. Before carrying out any operation on the fuel system, refer to the precautions given in 'Safety first!' at the beginning of this manual, and follow them implicitly. Petrol is a highly dangerous and volatile liquid, and the precautions necessary when handling it cannot be overstressed.**

Note: Residual pressure will remain in the fuel lines long after the vehicle was last used. When disconnecting any fuel line, first depressurise the fuel system (see Section 7).

2 Air cleaner – removal and refitting

Removal

1 Slacken the retaining clips and disconnect the inlet duct from the throttle housing and air cleaner housing lid.
2 Undo the screws securing the lid to the air cleaner housing body (see illustration). Lift off the lid and take out the filter element.
3 Release the retaining clip and lift the housing body upward to disengage it from the battery tray (see illustration). On some models, as the housing is lifted up, it will be necessary to disengage a small plastic retaining tag at the front securing the housing to the cold air inlet duct underneath.

Refitting

4 Refitting is a reversal of the removal procedure, ensuring that all hoses are properly reconnected, and that all ducts are correctly seated and securely held by their retaining clips.

3 Accelerator cable – removal, refitting and adjustment

Note: On some engines, no accelerator cable is fitted. On these models, an accelerator pedal position sensor is fitted, which informs the ECM of the pedal position and rate of change.

Removal

EW10D engine

1 Working in the engine compartment, remove the engine management ECM and mounting tray (see Section 13).
2 Free the accelerator inner cable from the cam on the position sensor, then pull the outer cable out from its mounting bracket. Remove the spring clip (see illustrations).

EW7J4 and EW10J4 engines

3 Undo the fasteners and remove the plastic cover from the top of the engine.

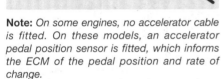

3.4 Free the cable end fitting from the cam on the throttle body

2.2 Undo the screws securing the air filter cover (arrowed)

4 Free the accelerator cable from the cam on the throttle body, then pull the outer cable from its mounting bracket. Remove the spring clip (see illustration).

All engines

5 Working back along the length of the cable, free it from any retaining clips or ties, noting its correct routing.
6 Working from inside the vehicle, remove the driver's side lower facia panel as described in Chapter 11.
7 Release the retaining clip, and detach the inner cable from the top of the accelerator pedal (see illustration).
8 Remove the clip securing the outer cable to the passenger's compartment bulkhead (see illustration). Recover the rubber washer.
9 Return to the engine compartment, and pull the cable through.

3.2a Free the cable end fitting from the cam . . .

3.7 Squeeze together the side of the clip and detach the cable from the pedal

2.3 Depress the clip and slide the air cleaner housing upwards from the battery tray

Refitting

10 Insert the end of the cable through the hole in the bulkhead, refit the rubber washer and refit the cable retaining clip.
11 Clip the inner cable to the top of the accelerator pedal, then refit the lower panel to the facia.
12 Insert the end of the cable into the bracket at the position sensor/throttle body, and engage the cable end fitting with the cam. Adjust the cable as described below.

Adjustment

13 Have an assistant fully depress the accelerator pedal, then rotate the position sensor to the full throttle position.
14 Pull the outer cable from the sensor bracket to the point where the all play is eliminated, then fit the spring clip to the nearest groove adjacent to the bracket (see

3.2b . . . and pull the outer cable from the mounting

3.8 Slide out the clip securing the outer cable

3.14 Refit the clip into the nearest groove adjacent to the bracket/grommet

illustration). When the clip is refitted and the outer cable is released, there should be only a small amount of free play in the inner cable.

15 Have an assistant depress the accelerator pedal, and check that the throttle cam opens fully and returns smoothly to its stop.

4 Accelerator pedal – removal and refitting

Removal

1 Disconnect the accelerator cable (where fitted) from the pedal as described in Section 3, or disconnect the wiring plug from the accelerator pedal position sensor.
2 According to type either remove the screws from the pedal mounting bracket, or unscrew the nuts securing the pedal assembly to the bulkhead (see illustration).

5.2 Depress the release button and disconnect the fuel supply pipe

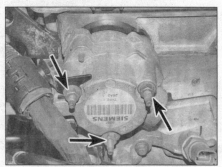

5.5a High-pressure fuel pump retaining nuts (arrowed)

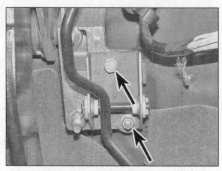

4.2 Accelerator pedal mounting screws/nuts (arrowed)

3 Remove the pedal. Note no further dismantling of the pedal assembly is recommended. The position sensor (where applicable) is not available separately from the pedal assembly.

Refitting

4 Refitting is a reversal of the removal procedure. On completion, adjust the accelerator cable as described in Section 3 (where applicable).

5 High-pressure fuel pump – removal and refitting

Note: *Only the 2.0 litre EW10D engine is fitted with this component.*

Removal

1 Remove the plastic cover from the top of

5.3 Undo the unions and remove the high-pressure pipe (arrowed)

5.5b Renew the O-ring seal

the engine, and depressurise the fuel system as described in Section 7.
2 Depress the release button and disconnect the fuel supply pipe from the pump (see illustration). Plug the openings to prevent contamination.
3 Slacken the unions and disconnect the high-pressure fuel pipe from the pump and the common rail (see illustration). Plug the openings to prevent contamination.
4 Note their fitted positions, then undo the nuts/bolts and move the wiring harness/vacuum pipe bracket away from the left-hand end of the cylinder head.
5 Undo the 3 retaining nuts and remove the high-pressure pump. Discard the seal – a new on must be fitted (see illustrations). No dismantling of the pump is recommended – at the time of writing, it would appear the pump is only available as a complete unit.

Refitting

6 Refitting is a reversal of removal, noting the following points:
   a) *Renew the pump O-ring seal.*
   b) *Renew the pump-to-common rail high-pressure pipe.*
   c) *Tighten the pump retaining nuts and pipe unions to the specified torque.*

6 Engine management systems – general information

Note: *The engine management ECM is of the 'self-learning' type, meaning that as it operates it also monitors and stores the settings which give optimum engine performance under all operating conditions. When the battery is disconnected, these settings are lost and the ECM reverts to the base settings programmed into its memory at the factory. On restarting, this may lead to the engine running/idling roughly for a short while, until the ECM has relearned the optimum settings. This process is best accomplished by taking the vehicle on a road test (for approximately 15 minutes), covering all engine speeds and loads, concentrating mainly in the 2500 to 3500 rpm region.*

On all engines, the fuel injection and ignition functions are combined into a single engine management system. The systems fitted are manufactured by Sagem, Siemens and Magneti Marelli, and are very similar to each other in most respects (see illustrations). Each system incorporates a closed-loop catalytic converter and an evaporative emission control system, and complies with the latest emission control standards. Refer to Chapter 5B for information on the ignition side of each system; the fuel side of the system operates as follows.

The fuel pump supplies fuel from the tank to the fuel rail, via a renewable cartridge filter mounted underneath the rear of the vehicle (vehicles marketed in dusty countries only).

The pump itself is mounted inside the fuel tank, permanently immersed in fuel to keep it cool. The fuel rail is mounted directly above the fuel injectors and acts as a fuel reservoir.

Fuel rail supply pressure is controlled by the pressure regulator integral with the tank pump.

The fuel injectors are electromagnetic valves, which spray atomised fuel into the inlet manifold tracts (EW7J4 and EW10J4), or directly into the combustion chamber (EW10D), under the control of the engine management system ECM. On the indirect injection systems (EW7J4 and EW10J4), there are four injectors, one per cylinder, mounted in the inlet manifold close to the cylinder head.

Each injector is mounted at an angle that allows it to spray fuel directly onto the back of the inlet valve(s). On the direct injection system (EW10D) the injector is mounted in the cylinder head, and sprays fuel directly onto the piston crown. Depending on the engine load, speed, etc, the fuel is injected as the piston falls on the induction stroke, or just before the piston reaches TDC on the compression stroke. On both systems, the ECM controls the volume of fuel injected by varying the length of time for which each injector is held open. On the Siemens direct injection system, the ECM also varies the volume by altering the pressure of the fuel injected.

The electrical control system consists of the ECM, along with the following sensors:
a) *Throttle potentiometer – informs the ECM of the throttle valve position, and the rate of throttle opening/closing (not all models).*
b) *Accelerator pedal position sensor – informs the ECM of the accelerator pedal position and rate of change (not all models)*
c) *Coolant temperature sensor – informs the ECM of engine coolant temperature.*
d) *Inlet air temperature sensor – informs the ECM of the temperature of the air passing through the throttle housing.*

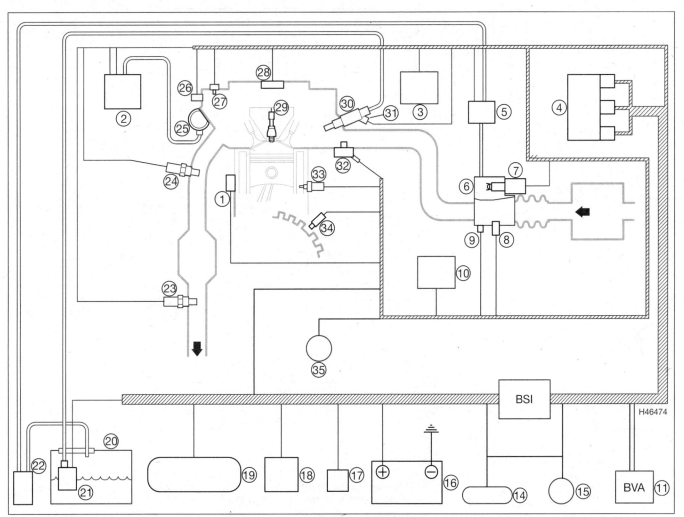

**6.1a Engine management system –
Sagem S2000 and Magneti-Marelli 48P**

1 Knock sensor
2 Air pump
3 Power steering pressure sensor
4 Engine management ECM
5 Canister purge valve
6 Throttle body/housing
7 Idle speed stepper motor
8 Inlet air temperature sensor
9 Throttle body heating element
10 Throttle position sensor
11 Automatic transmission
12 Built-in systems interface (BSI)
13 Transponder
14 Diagnostic socket
15 Instrument panel warning light
16 Battery
17 Immobiliser unit
18 Air conditioning
19 Instrument panel
20 Fuel tank
21 Fuel pump, gauge and filter assembly
22 Charcoal canister
23 Downstream oxygen sensor
24 Upstream oxygen sensor
25 Air inlet valve
26 EGR valve
27 Camshaft position sensor
28 Ignition coil
29 Spark plugs
30 Fuel rail
31 Injectors
32 Inlet air pressure sensor
33 Coolant temperature sensor
34 Crankshaft position sensor
35 Cooling fan unit

e) Engine oil temperature sensor – informs the ECM of the engine oil temperature (not all models).
f) High-pressure fuel sensor – informs the ECM of the fuel pressure (EW10D only).
g) Power steering pressure sensor – informs the ECM of the pressure in the power steering system.
h) Clutch and brake pedal position sensor – informs the ECM of the pedal positions (not all models).

i) Lambda sensors – informs the ECM of the oxygen content of the exhaust gases (explained in greater detail in Part C of this Chapter).
j) Manifold pressure sensor – informs the ECM of the load on the engine (expressed in terms of inlet manifold vacuum).
k) Crankshaft sensor – informs the ECM of engine speed and crankshaft angular position.
l) Knock sensor – informs the ECM of

pre-ignition (detonation) within the cylinders. Not all systems utilise this sensor.
m) Camshaft sensor – informs the ECM of camshaft position.

Signals from each of the sensors are compared by the ECM and, based on this information, the ECM selects the response appropriate to those values, and controls the fuel injectors (varying the pulse width – the length of time the injectors are held open – to

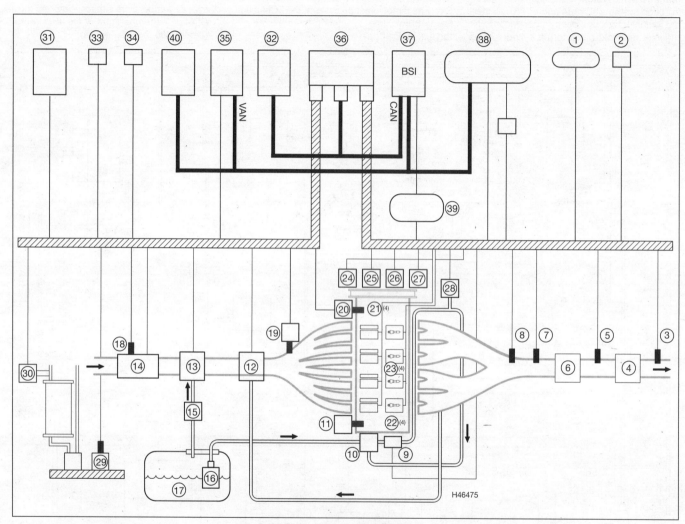

6.1b Engine management system –
Siemens Sirius 81 engine management components

1 Diagnostic socket	9 Fuel pressure regulator	18 Inlet air temperature sensor	26 Inlet camshaft variable timing control solenoid	33 Clutch pedal position sensor
2 Accelerator pedal position sensor	10 High-pressure fuel pump	19 Inlet air pressure sensor	27 Camshaft position sensor	34 Brake pedal position sensor
3 Downstream oxygen sensor	11 Knock sensor	20 Coolant temperature sensor	28 High-pressure fuel sensor	35 Air conditioning ECM
4 DeNOX catalyst	12 EGR valve	21 Spark plugs	29 Power steering pressure sensor	36 Engine management ECM
5 Downstream exhaust temperature sensor	13 Canister purge valve	22 Ignition coil block	30 Air conditioning refrigerant pressure sensor	37 Built-in systems interface (BSI)
6 3-way catalyst	14 Motorised throttle body	23 Injectors		38 Instrument panel
7 Pre-catalyst upstream oxygen sensor	15 Charcoal canister	24 Engine oil temperature sensor	31 Cooling fan unit	39 Coded anti-theft device
8 Upstream exhaust temperature sensor	16 Fuel pump and level sensor assembly	25 Crankshaft position/ speed sensor	32 ABS ECM	40 Cruise control
	17 Fuel tank			

provide a richer or weaker air/fuel mixture, as appropriate). The air/fuel mixture is constantly varied by the ECM, to provide the best settings for cranking, starting (with either a hot or cold engine) and engine warm-up, idle, cruising and acceleration.

The ECM also has full control over the engine idle speed. On models with indirect injection, this is achieved by a stepper motor fitted to the throttle housing. The stepper motor controls the amount of air passing through a bypass drilling at the side of the throttle. When the throttle valve is closed (accelerator pedal released), the ECM uses the motor to control the amount of air bypassing the throttle valve and so controlling the idle speed. On direct injection models, the ECM controls the position of the throttle butterfly valve by an electric motor connected directly to the valve – no accelerator cable is fitted. On all models, the ECM also carries out 'fine tuning' of the idle speed by varying the ignition timing to increase or reduce the torque of the engine as it is idling. This helps to stabilise the idle speed when electrical or mechanical loads (such as headlights, air conditioning, etc) are switched on and off.

The exhaust and evaporative loss emission control systems are described in more detail in Chapter 4C.

If there is any abnormality in any of the readings obtained from the sensors, the ECM may enter its 'back-up' mode. If this happens, the erroneous sensor signal is overridden, and the ECM assumes a pre-programmed 'back-up' value, which will allow the engine to continue running, albeit at reduced efficiency. If the ECM enters this mode, the warning lamp on the instrument panel will be illuminated, and the relevant fault code will be stored in the ECM memory.

If the warning light illuminates, the vehicle should be taken to a Citroën dealer or suitably-equipped repairer at the earliest opportunity. Once there, a complete test of the engine management system can be carried out, using a special electronic diagnostic test unit (scanner), which is plugged into the system's diagnostic connector **(see illustration)**.

7 Fuel injection system – depressurisation

Note: *Refer to the warning note in Section 1 before proceeding.*

⚠️ *Warning: The following procedure will merely relieve the pressure in the fuel system – remember that fuel will still be present in the system components and take precautions accordingly before disconnecting any of them.*

1 The fuel system referred to in this Section is defined as the tank-mounted fuel pump, the fuel injectors, the fuel rail, the high-pressure pump and the pressure regulator, and the metal pipes

6.9 The diagnostic plug (arrowed) is located in the passenger side glovebox

and flexible hoses of the fuel lines between these components (where applicable). All these contain fuel which will be under pressure while the engine is running, and/or while the ignition is switched on. The pressure will remain for some time after the ignition has been switched off, and must be relieved in a controlled fashion when any of these components are disturbed for servicing work.

2 Citroën technicians connect a special tube to the Schrader valve on the fuel rail or damper in order to depressurise the fuel system **(see illustrations)**. The tube incorporates a union nut which is screwed onto the valve, and an inner cable which is used to depress the valve core. If this tube is not available, cover the valve and surrounding area with cloth rag, and depress the valve with a screwdriver through the rag. Make sure that enough rag is used to soak up the fuel. Access to the valve is gained by first removing the engine top cover.

7.2a Depressurisation valve on the fuel rail (arrowed) . . .

8.3 Prise up the plastic access panel. Note the arrow at the front of the cover

3 With the pressure released, refit the cap to the valve.
4 Note that pressure may increase again in the fuel system due to an increase in ambient temperature, so any work required on the system should be started immediately after releasing the pressure.

8 Fuel pump – removal and refitting

Note: *Refer to the warning note in Section 1 before proceeding.*

Removal

1 Disconnect the battery negative lead (refer Chapter 5A). This is important, since any stray electrical discharge in the vicinity of the open fuel tank would be extremely dangerous.
2 For access to the fuel pump, remove the right-hand rear seat as described in Chapter 11.
3 Pull away the carpet, then remove the plastic access cover from the floor to expose the fuel pump **(see illustration)**.
4 Disconnect the wiring connector from the top of the fuel pump.
5 Mark the fuel supply hose (and, where applicable, the return hose) for identification purposes, then disconnect it from the top of the pump. Note that quick-release unions are fitted. The supply hose is usually indicated by an arrow on the top of the pump **(see illustration)**.
6 Noting the alignment arrows on the tank, locking ring and pump cover, unscrew the locking ring and remove it from the tank.

7.2b . . . or on the right-hand side inner wing (arrowed)

8.5 Depress the release tab (arrowed) and pull the hose from the pump

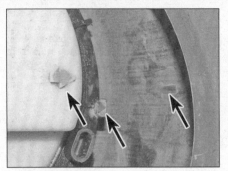

8.6a Note the collar, pump and tank alignment marks (arrowed)

8.6b Using a home-made tool to slacken the collar

8.6c Remove the collar from the top of the tank

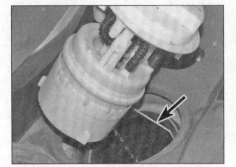

8.7a Take care not to damage the float arm (arrowed)

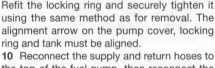

8.7b Renew the seal

Although Citroën recommend the use of tool 1607 to unscrew the locking ring, this can be accomplished by using a screwdriver on the raised studs of the locking ring. Carefully tap the screwdriver to turn the ring anti-clockwise and release it. Alternatively, a home-made tool may be fabricated out of metal rod, bent to locate on the studs (see illustrations).

7 Lift the fuel pump assembly out of the fuel tank, taking great care not to damage the float arm, or to spill fuel inside the car. Recover the seal from the assembly and discard it; a new one must be obtained for the refitting procedure (see illustrations).

8 Note that the fuel pump is only available as a complete assembly – no components are available separately.

Refitting

9 Wipe clean the contact surfaces of the pump/gauge and tank, then locate a new seal on the tank. Manoeuvre the assembly

into the fuel tank, ensuring that the lug on the pump locates with the notch on the tank rim. Refit the locking ring and securely tighten it using the same method as for removal. The alignment arrow on the pump cover, locking ring and tank must be aligned.

10 Reconnect the supply and return hoses to the top of the fuel pump, then reconnect the wiring.

11 Refit the plastic access cover with its arrow facing forwards, then refit the rear seat with reference to Chapter 11.

12 Reconnect the battery negative lead as describe in Chapter 5A.

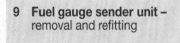

9 Fuel gauge sender unit –
removal and refitting

The fuel gauge sender unit is incorporated in the fuel pump – refer to Section 8.

At full deflection (empty tank), the sender unit resistance was 360 ohms (approximately), and at zero deflection (full tank) the resistance was 51 ohms (approximately).

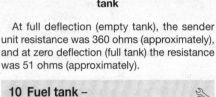

10 Fuel tank –
removal and refitting

Note: *Refer to the warning note in Section 1 before proceeding.*

Removal

1 Before removing the fuel tank, all fuel must be drained from the tank. Since a fuel tank drain plug is not provided, it is preferable to carry out the removal operation when the tank is nearly empty. If there is any fuel remaining in the fuel tank, it can be removed by disconnecting the fuel supply hose and connecting a suitable hose leading to a container outside the vehicle.

2 Disconnect the fuel pipes and wiring plugs from the fuel pump/gauge unit as described in Section 8.

3 Chock the front wheels then jack up the rear of the vehicle and support on axle stands (see *Jacking and vehicle support*). Remove the right-hand rear wheel and wheel arch liner.

4 Open the fuel filler flap, undo the nut securing the locking motor, remove the cap, release the clip and pushing from inside the wheel arch, remove the filler flap (see illustrations).

5 Undo the bolt securing the filler neck to the vehicle body (see illustration).

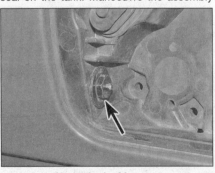

10.4a Undo the locking motor nut (arrowed)

10.4b Remove the filler flap assembly

10.5 Undo the filler neck bolt (arrowed)

6 Remove the section of the exhaust system that runs underneath the fuel tank.

7 Release the fasteners and remove the underbody protection panels beneath and adjoining the tank.

8 Unbolt and remove the exhaust heat shields from the underbody **(see illustrations)**.

9 Place a trolley jack with an interposed block of wood beneath the tank, then raise the jack until it is supporting the weight of the tank. Position the jack so as to allow room to remove the fuel tank cradle.

10 To improve access, undo the nuts and remove the exhaust mounting bracket from the front edge of the fuel tank.

11 Unscrew the fuel tank cradle mounting bolts and remove the cradle.

12 Unscrew the remaining tank retaining bolt, then lower the fuel tank approximately 15 cm.

13 Unclip the ABS sensor harness from the top of the tank, and move it one side.

14 Disconnect the fuel filler flap wiring harness, and move it to one side.

15 Lower the fuel tank and manoeuvre it from under the vehicle.

16 If the tank is contaminated with sediment or water, remove the fuel pump and swill the tank out with clean fuel. The tank is injection-moulded from a synthetic material – if seriously damaged, it should be renewed. However, in certain cases, it may be possible to have small leaks or minor damage repaired. Seek the advice of a specialist before attempting to repair the fuel tank.

Refitting

17 Refitting is the reverse of the removal procedure, noting the following points:
  a) *When lifting the tank back into position, take care to ensure none of the hoses get trapped between the tank and body.*
  b) *Ensure that all pipes and hoses are correctly routed, and securely held in position with their retaining clips.*
  c) *On completion, refill the tank with a small amount of fuel, and check for signs of leakage prior to taking the vehicle out on the road.*

11 Fuel injection system – testing

Testing

1 If a fault appears in the fuel injection/ engine management system, first ensure that all the system wiring connectors are securely connected and free of corrosion. Ensure that the fault is not due to poor maintenance; ie, check that the air cleaner filter element is clean, the spark plugs are in good condition and correctly gapped, the cylinder compression pressures are correct, and that the engine breather hoses are clear and undamaged, referring to the relevant

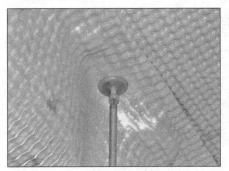
10.8a Undo the fasteners . . .

Parts of Chapters 1, 2 and 5 for further information.

2 If these checks fail to reveal the cause of the problem, the vehicle should be taken to a Citroën dealer or suitably-equipped garage for testing. A diagnostic socket is located adjacent to the passenger compartment fusebox in which a fault code reader or other suitable test equipment can be connected **(see illustration 6.2)**. By using the code reader or test equipment, the engine management ECM (and the various other vehicle system ECMs) can be interrogated, and any stored fault codes can be retrieved. This will allow the fault to be quickly and simply traced, alleviating the need to test all the system components individually, which is a time-consuming operation that carries a risk of damaging the ECM.

Adjustment

3 Experienced home mechanics with a considerable amount of skill and equipment (including a tachometer and an accurately calibrated exhaust gas analyser) may be able to check the exhaust CO level and the idle speed. However, if these are found to be outside the specified tolerance, the car must be taken to a suitably-equipped garage for further testing. Neither the mixture adjustment (exhaust gas CO level) nor the idle speed are adjustable, and should either be incorrect, a fault may be present in the engine management system.

12.2 Slacken the clamps (arrowed) and remove the air duct

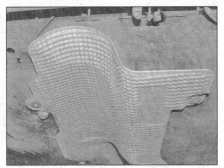
10.8b . . . and remove the heat shields beneath the fuel tank

12 Throttle housing/body – removal and refitting

EW7J4 and EW10J4 engines

Removal

1 Disconnect the battery negative lead (refer to Chapter 5A).

2 Slacken the clamps, and remove the air cleaner-to-throttle housing duct **(see illustration)**.

3 Insert a flat-bladed screwdriver through the access hole, slacken the clamp, and remove the plastic cover over the throttle body (where fitted) **(see illustration)**.

4 Disconnect the accelerator inner cable from the throttle cam then withdraw the outer cable from the mounting bracket along with its flat washer and spring clip. Where applicable, also disconnect the arm from the diaphragm canister **(see illustrations 3.2a and 3.2b)**.

5 Depress the retaining clips, and disconnect the wiring connectors from the throttle potentiometer, the electric heating element, the inlet air temperature sensor and idle speed control stepper motor (as applicable).

6 Release the retaining clips (where fitted), and disconnect all the relevant vacuum and breather hoses from the throttle housing. Make identification marks on the hoses, to ensure that they are connected correctly on refitting.

12.3 Insert a screwdriver through the access hole (arrowed) and slacken the clamp

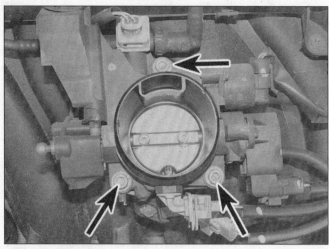

12.8 Throttle body retaining Allen screws (arrowed)

12.11 Slacken the clamps and remove the air duct (arrowed)

12.13 The throttle body is secured by Allen screws at the top, and nuts underneath (arrowed)

7 Where necessary, undo the bolts or screws and release the accelerator cable bracket and housing support bracket.

8 Slacken and remove the retaining screws, and remove the throttle housing from the inlet manifold (see illustration). Remove the O-ring from the manifold, and discard it – a new one must be used on refitting.

Refitting

9 Refitting is a reversal of the removal procedure, noting the following points:
 a) Fit a new O-ring to the manifold, then refit the throttle housing and securely tighten its retaining nuts or screws (as applicable).

13.2 Depress the release button and disconnect the fuel feed hose (arrowed)

 b) Ensure that all hoses are correctly reconnected and, where necessary, are securely held in position by the retaining clips.
 c) Ensure that all wiring is correctly routed, and that the connectors are securely reconnected.
 d) On completion, adjust the accelerator cable as described in Section 3.

EW10D engine

Removal

10 Disconnect the battery negative lead (refer to Chapter 5A).

11 Slacken the clamps and remove the air cleaner-to-throttle body duct (see illustration).

12 Note their fitted locations, and disconnect the throttle body wiring plugs.

13 Undo the bolts/nuts and remove the throttle body. Recover the gasket as the assembly is withdrawn (see illustration).

Refitting

14 Refitting is a reversal of removal, noting the following points:
 a) Fit a new gasket to the manifold, then refit the throttle body and securely tighten the retaining bolts/nuts.
 b) Ensure all wiring is correctly routed, and the connectors are securely reconnected.

13.4 Disconnect the injector wiring plugs (centre plugs arrowed)

13 Engine management electronic components – removal and refitting

Fuel rail and injectors

Note: *Refer to the warning note in Section 1 before proceeding. If a faulty injector is suspected, before condemning the injector, it is worth trying the effect of one of the proprietary injector-cleaning treatments which are available from car accessory shops.*

1 Disconnect the battery negative lead (refer to Chapter 5A).

EW7J4 and EW10J4 engines

2 Rotate the fasteners 90° anti-clockwise and remove the plastic cover over the engine. Bearing in mind the information given in Section 7, depress the catch on the fuel feed hose quick-release fitting, and disconnect the fuel feed (and return hoses, where applicable) from the fuel rail (see illustration). Suitably seal or plug the hose and the fuel rail union(s) after disconnection.

3 Open the retaining clips and release the wiring and hoses running along the front of the fuel rail (where applicable).

4 Depress the retaining tangs and disconnect the wiring connectors from the four injectors (see illustration).

5 Slacken and remove the fuel rail retaining bolts then carefully ease the fuel rail and injector assembly out from the inlet manifold and remove it from the engine (see illustration). Remove the O-rings from the end of each injector and discard them; they must be renewed whenever they are disturbed.

6 Slide out the retaining clip(s) and remove the relevant injector(s) from the fuel rail (see illustrations). Remove the upper O-ring from each disturbed injector and discard; all disturbed O-rings must be renewed.

7 Refitting is a reversal of the removal procedure, noting the following points.
 a) Fit new O-rings to all disturbed injector unions.

13.5 Fuel rail mounting bolts (arrowed)

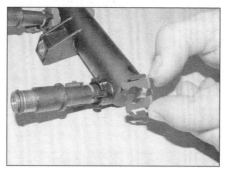

13.6a Slide out the retaining clip . . .

13.6b . . . and remove the injector from the fuel rail

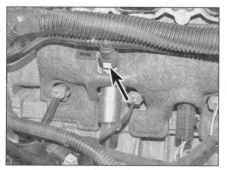

13.11 Depress the release button (arrowed) and disconnect the fuel supply hose from the fuel rail

13.12a Release the clip and disconnect the injector wiring plugs

13.12b Unclip the sound insulation from the fuel rail

b) *Apply a smear of engine oil to the O-rings to aid installation then ease the injectors and fuel rail into position ensuring that none of the O-rings are displaced.*
c) *On completion start the engine and check for fuel leaks.*

EW10D engine

8 Pull up the plastic cover over the top of the engine.
9 Depressurise the fuel system as described in Section 7.
10 Remove the inlet manifold as described in Section 14.
11 Press the release tab and disconnect the fuel supply hose from the fuel rail **(see illustration)**. Plug or cover the openings to prevent contamination.
12 Disconnect the injector wiring plugs, then unclip the soundproofing from above the fuel rail **(see illustrations)**.
13 Undo the union nuts, and remove the high-pressure pipe from the left-hand end of the fuel rail. Discard the pipe – a new one must be fitted.
14 Rotate each injector a little to break the carbon deposits between the cylinder head and the injector nozzles, then undo the retaining bolts and pull the fuel rail, complete with injectors, from the cylinder head **(see illustration)**. If the assembly is reluctant to move, use two screwdrivers and lever it from place.
15 Slide out the retaining clips and remove the injectors from the fuel rail **(see illustration)**. Citroën insist the retaining clips are renewed.

16 If the injectors are to be refitted, remove the seals from the injectors, taking care not to mark the injector stem, then use a paint brush and some suitable degreaser to carefully

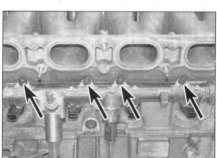

13.14 Fuel rail retaining bolts (arrowed)

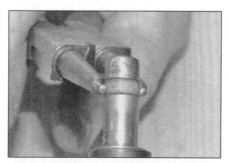

13.16a Use a pair of thin-nosed pliers to carefully break the old combustion seal from the injector

remove the carbon deposits from the injector nozzles **(see illustrations)**.
17 To renew the combustion seal, Citroën technicians use a number of special tools

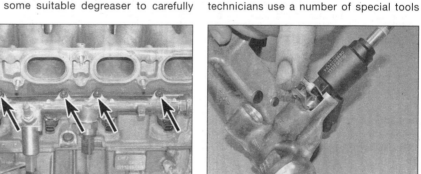

13.15 Prise out the retaining clip and pull the injector from the fuel rail

13.16b Remove all carbon deposits from the injector nozzles using degreaser

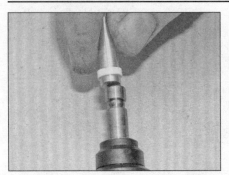

13.17a Butt the tool against the injector nozzle . . .

13.17b . . . and slide the new combustion seal into the groove on the injector . . .

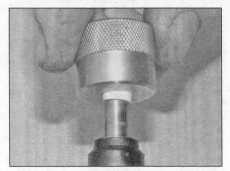

13.17c . . . then compress the seal into the groove

13.19 Renew the spiral seal and O-ring at the end of each injector

13.20 Insert the injector into the fuel rail and push the new clip into the groove (arrowed)

13.21 Note the shim (arrowed) fitted between the fuel rail and the cylinder head

(No (-).0189 N) which spreads the seal, pushes it into place, and compresses it into the groove afterwards. In the absence of these tools, it may be prudent to have the rings renewed by a Citroën dealer or specialist **(see illustrations)**. Note that the seal must not be lubricated. **Note:** *Citroën recommend that the injectors should be refitted to the fuel rail and cylinder head as soon as possible after the new combustion seals have been fitted and compressed on the injectors.*

18 Use a nylon brush and a vacuum cleaner to thoroughly clean out the injector holes in the cylinder head. Take care not to let any debris fall into the combustion chamber.

19 Renew the O-ring seals and spiral washers on the top of the injectors **(see illustration)**.

20 Fit the injectors into the fuel rail, and secure them with the new retaining clips **(see illustration)**.

21 Fit the assembly into place, then tighten the retaining bolts to the specified torque **(see illustration)**.

22 Refitting is a reversal of the removal procedure, noting the following points.

a) Renew the high-pressure pipe from the fuel rail to the fuel pump.

b) On completion start the engine and check for fuel leaks.

Fuel pressure regulator

EW10D engine only

Note: *On the EW7J4 and EW10J4 indirect injection engines, the pressure regulator is integral with the pump located in the fuel tank.*

23 Remove the inlet manifold as described in Section 14.

24 Disconnect the wiring plugs, then unclip the sound insulation material above the injectors.

25 Place some rags under the regulator, to catch any spilt fuel. Undo the retaining Allen screws and ease the regulator out from the fuel rail **(see illustration)**.

26 Refitting is a reversal of the removal procedure. Examine the regulator seal for signs of damage or deterioration and renew if necessary.

Throttle potentiometer

EW10J4 and EW7J4 engines

27 Slacken the clamp and remove the plastic cover over the throttle body (where fitted), then depress the retaining clip and disconnect the wiring connector from the throttle potentiometer located on the side of the throttle housing **(see illustration)**.

28 Slacken and remove the two retaining screws then disengage the potentiometer from the throttle valve spindle and remove it from the vehicle.

29 Refitting is a reverse of the removal procedure ensuring that the potentiometer is correctly engaged with the throttle valve spindle.

EW10D engine

30 Remove the ECM and module box as described in this Section.

31 Undo the 2 Torx bolts and remove the potentiometer **(see illustration)**. Disconnect the accelerator cable and wiring plug as the unit is withdrawn.

32 Refitting is a reversal of removal, but adjust the accelerator cable as described in Section 3.

13.25 Fuel pressure regulator

13.27 Throttle potentiometer wiring plug (arrowed)

Electronic Control Module

33 The ECM is located in a plastic box which is mounted on the left-hand front wheel arch.

34 Ensure that the ignition is switched off then rotate the fasteners 90° anti-clockwise lift off the ECM module box lid **(see illustration)**. On AL4 automatic transmission models there will be two ECMs in the box; the fuel injection/ignition ECM is the unit nearest to the engine.

35 Unscrew the Torx mounting bolts, then lift the ECM upwards and remove it from its location **(see illustration)**.

36 Release the wiring connectors by levering over the locking levers on top of the connector. Carefully withdraw the connectors from the ECM pins **(see illustration)**.

37 To remove the ECM module box, undo the bolt securing the battery connection, release the retaining clips, lift out the fusebox, and undo the 3 retaining bolts, then lift the box from place **(see illustrations)**.

38 Refitting is a reversal of removal. Note that if a new ECM has been fitted, it should be preconfigured by the selling agent, and the vehicle should be taken on an extensive road test. Initially, engine performance may be less than acceptable, but should improve as the ECM control circuitry adapts to the engine parameters.

Idle speed stepper motor

EW7J4 and EW10J4 engines only

39 The idle speed control stepper motor is located on the side of the throttle housing assembly. Slacken the clamp and remove the plastic cover from the top of the throttle body (where fitted) **(see illustration 12.3)**.

40 Release the retaining clip, and disconnect the wiring connector from the motor **(see illustration)**.

41 Slacken and remove the two retaining screws, and withdraw the motor from the throttle housing.

42 Refitting is a reversal of the removal procedure.

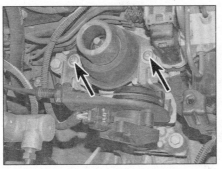
13.31 Throttle potentiometer Torx bolts (arrowed)

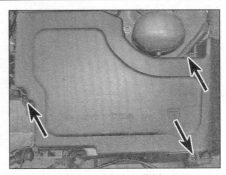
13.34 ECM module box lid fasteners (arrowed)

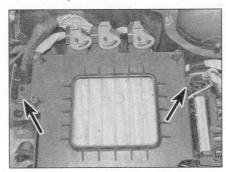
13.35 ECM Torx bolts (arrowed)

13.36 Lever over the locking catches and disconnect the wiring plugs

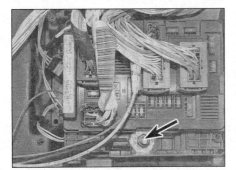
13.37a Undo the nut (arrowed) securing the battery connection

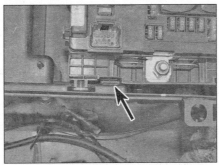
13.37b Release the clip at the front and rear of the fusebox (front clip arrowed) . . .

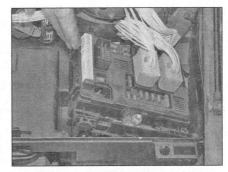
13.37c . . . and lift out the fusebox

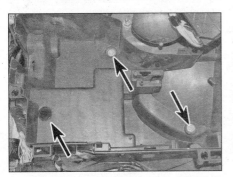
13.37d Undo the 3 mounting bolts (arrowed) . . .

13.37e . . . and remove the module box

13.40 Idle speed stepper motor wiring plug (arrowed)

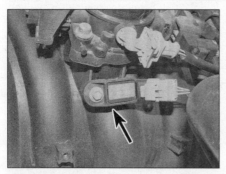

13.43a Inlet manifold pressure sensor on EW7J4 and EW10J4 engines (arrowed) . . .

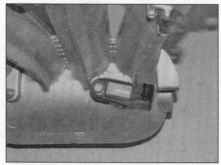

13.43b . . . and on EW10D engines

13.48 Inlet air temperature sensor

13.56a Camshaft position sensor (arrowed) – EW7J4 and EW10J4 engines

13.56b The camshaft position sensor is located at the left-hand rear end of the cylinder head, above the exhaust manifold (arrowed) – EW10D engines

Manifold absolute pressure sensor

43 The MAP sensor is situated on the underside of the inlet manifold on EW10D engines, and on the front of the manifold on EW7J4 and EW10J4 engines **(see illustrations)**.

44 Disconnect the wiring connector from the sensor.

45 Undo the securing screw, then pull the sensor out of the manifold.

46 Refitting is the reverse of the removal procedure.

Coolant temperature sensor

47 Refer to Chapter 3.

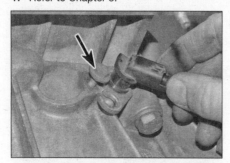

13.58 Slacken the bolt (arrowed) and remove the crankshaft position sensor from the clutch housing

Inlet air temperature sensor

48 The inlet air temperature sensor is located on the underside or front of the throttle housing **(see illustration)**. Note: *On EW10D direct injection engines, the sensor is integral with the throttle housing.*

49 Loosen the retaining clip, and release the air inlet duct from the throttle housing. Slacken the clamp and remove the plastic cover from the top of the throttle body **(see illustration 12.3)**.

50 Trace the wiring back from the sensor to its wiring connector on the throttle housing, and unplug the connector.

51 Release the clips and ease the sensor from the throttle body. Note that it is sealed in place, to prevent air leaks; a suitable sealant will be required for refitting.

52 Refitting is the reverse of removal.

Camshaft position sensor

53 The camshaft position sensor is located in the exhaust camshaft cylinder head cover.

54 On EW7J4 and EW10J4 engines, rotate the fasteners 90° anti-clockwise and remove the plastic cover over the top of the engine. On EW10D engines, the cover simply pulls up from place.

55 Disconnect the crankcase breather hose at the quick-fit connector on the rear cylinder head cover (EW7J4 and EW10J4 engines only).

56 Disconnect the wiring connector at the camshaft position sensor, then undo the bolt and remove the sensor from the cylinder head cover **(see illustrations)**.

57 Refitting is the reverse of removal but fit a new sealing O-ring to the sensor body.

Crankshaft sensor

58 The crankshaft sensor is situated on the top face of the transmission clutch housing **(see illustration)**.

59 Trace the wiring back from the sensor to the wiring connector and disconnect it from the main harness.

60 Undo the retaining bolt and withdraw the sensor from the transmission.

61 Refitting is the reverse of the removal procedure.

Vehicle speed sensor

62 The vehicle's speed information is provided by the ABS wheel sensors – see Chapter 9.

Knock sensor

63 Refer to Chapter 5B.

High-pressure fuel sensor

EW10D engine only

64 This sensor is fitted to the underside of

the fuel rail. To remove the sensor, remove the inlet manifold as described in Section 14, then disconnect the injector wiring plugs, and unclip the insulation material from the fuel rail **(see illustration 13.12a and 13.12b)**.

65 Disconnect the wiring plug, then unscrew the sensor from place **(see illustration)**. Plug or cover the openings to prevent contamination.

66 To refit the sensor, check the condition of the seal and renew if necessary. Tighten the sensor to the specified torque.

67 The remainder of refitting is a reversal of removal.

Inlet camshaft dephaser solenoid

EW10D engine only

68 The solenoid is located at the right-hand end of the cylinder head cover between the camshafts. Pull up the plastic cover on the of the engine.

69 Disconnect the wiring plug, then unscrew the solenoid from the camshaft cover **(see illustration)**. Examine the O-ring seal, and renew if necessary.

70 Refitting is a reversal of removal. Tighten the solenoid to the specified torque.

14 Inlet manifold – removal and refitting

Removal

1 Disconnect the battery negative lead (refer to Chapter 5A).

EW10J4 and EW7J4 engines

2 Remove the throttle housing as described in Section 12 and the fuel rail and injectors as described in Section 13.

3 Disconnect the braking system vacuum servo unit hose, and all the relevant vacuum/breather hoses, from the manifold **(see illustration)**. Where necessary, make identification marks on the hoses to ensure that they are correctly reconnected on refitting.

4 Where applicable, slacken and remove the bolt securing the dipstick tube to the side of the

14.6 Renew the manifold seals

13.65 Fuel pressure sensor (arrowed)

manifold, and also remove throttle diaphragm canister where fitted, and disconnect the EGR pipe **(see illustration)**.

5 Undo the nuts and bolts securing the manifold to the cylinder head, and remove the manifold from the engine compartment. Note the location of the engine top cover support bracket.

6 Recover the manifold gasket/seals, and discard them – new ones must be used on refitting **(see illustration)**.

EW10D engine

7 Remove the throttle body as described in Section 12, and the air cleaner housing as described in Section 2.

8 Note their fitted positions, then disconnect the various vacuum/emission hoses from the throttle body mounting flange **(see illustration)**. Note the hose connection on the underside of the manifold.

14.3 Disconnect the servo hose from beneath the throttle body

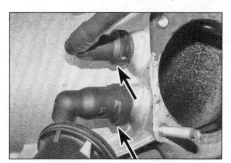
14.8 Depress the light-coloured release buttons and disconnect the hoses from the inlet manifold (arrowed)

13.69 Inlet camshaft dephaser solenoid

9 Undo the nuts/bolts and remove the manifold support bracket(s). On the left-hand upper bracket, hold the end of the stud with a Torx socket, undo the retaining nuts, then unscrew the studs from the captive nuts **(see illustration)**. Release the cooling hoses from the left-hand bracket.

10 Release the vacuum hoses from the clips, then undo the Torx bolt and detach the bracket from the left-hand end of the manifold **(see illustration)**.

11 Disconnect the wiring plug, then undo the 2 nuts securing the EGR valve to the cylinder head **(see illustration)**.

12 Disconnect the inlet manifold pressure sensor wiring plug from the right-hand underside end of the manifold, and release the harness from the cable ties **(see illustration)**.

13 Undo the nuts and detach the manifold from the cylinder head along with the EGR valve and pipe.

14.4 Release the locking clip and disconnect the EGR pipe

14.9 Counterhold the bolt with a Torx socket, then unscrew the manifold support bracket nuts

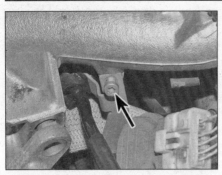

14.10 Undo the Torx bolt (arrowed) securing the bracket to the manifold

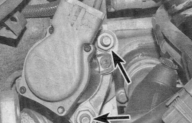

14.11 EGR valve retaining nuts (arrowed)

2 Remove the cylinder head cover as described in Chapter 2A.

3 Undo the retaining nuts securing the exhaust manifold to the cylinder head. Manoeuvre the manifold out of the engine compartment, and discard the manifold gaskets.

EW10D engine

4 Remove the pre-catalyser as described in Section 16.

5 Undo the nuts securing the manifold to the cylinder head **(see illustration)**.

6 Lower the manifold and heat shield/gasket from place **(see illustration)**.

Refitting

7 Refitting is the reverse of the removal procedure, noting the following points:

a) *Examine all the exhaust manifold studs for signs of damage and corrosion; remove all traces of corrosion, and repair or renew any damaged studs.*

b) *Ensure that the manifold and cylinder head sealing faces are clean and flat, and fit the new manifold gasket(s). Tighten the manifold retaining nuts to the specified torque setting.*

c) *Reconnect the catalyst to the manifold, using the information given in Section 16.*

14.12 Pressure sensor wiring plug (arrowed)

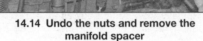

14.14 Undo the nuts and remove the manifold spacer

14 If required, undo the 5 nuts and remove the manifold rubber spacer **(see illustration)**.

Refitting

15 Refitting is a reverse of the relevant removal procedure, noting the following points:

a) *Ensure that the manifold and cylinder head mating surfaces are clean and dry, then locate the new gasket/seals on the manifold. Refit the manifold and tighten its retaining nuts and bolts to the specified torque setting.*

b) *Ensure that all relevant hoses are reconnected to their original positions and*

are securely held (where necessary) by the retaining clips.

c) *Adjust the accelerator cable (where applicable) as described in Section 3.*

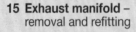

15 Exhaust manifold – removal and refitting

Removal

EW10J4 and EW7J4 engines

1 Slacken the clamp and disconnect the catalytic converter from the manifold.

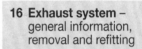

16 Exhaust system – general information, removal and refitting

General information

1 A multi-section exhaust system is fitted. The exhaust sections are joined by clamping rings or flanges, with a flexible section incorporated in the front pipe to cater for engine movement.

2 A catalytic converter is located on the front section of the exhaust. On EW10D engines, a pre-catalyser is fitted between the exhaust manifold and the front exhaust pipe. The system is suspended throughout its entire length by rubber mountings.

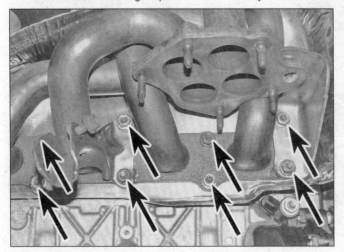

15.5 Undo the nuts (arrowed) and remove the exhaust manifold

15.6 Renew the exhaust manifold gasket/heat shield

16.6 Remove the tie-bar from the subframe (arrowed)

16.7a Unscrew the sensor from the left-hand end of the pre-catalyser (arrowed) . . .

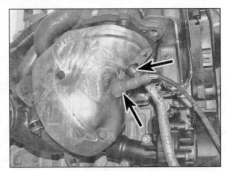

16.7b . . . and the two from the heat shield (arrowed)

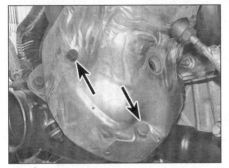

16.8 Heat shield retaining bolts (arrowed)

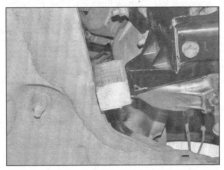

16.10 Wedge a block of wood between the engine and subframe

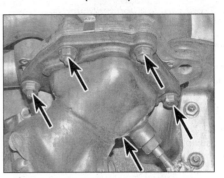

16.12 Pre-catalyser-to-manifold nuts (arrowed)

Removal

3 Each exhaust section can be removed individually, or the system can be removed complete, then separated after removal.
4 To remove part of the system, first jack up the front or rear of the car and support it on axle stands. Alternatively, position the car over an inspection pit or on car ramps.

Pre-catalyser

5 Remove the plastic cover from the top of the engine, and disconnect the battery negative lead as described in Chapter 5A.
6 Remove the right-hand driveshaft as described in Chapter 8, then undo the bolts and remove the tie-bar from the front of the subframe (see illustration).
7 Disconnect the pre-catalyser oxygen sensors, and temperature sensor wiring plugs, then unscrew the sensors from the heat shield, and the left-hand end of the pre-catalyser (see illustrations).
8 Undo the screws and remove the heat shield (see illustration).
9 Disconnect the exhaust pipe from the pre-catalyser.
10 Undo the lower, rear torque arm-to-sub-frame retaining bolt, then use a block of wood (approximately 40 mm thick) to wedge the engine from the subframe (see illustration).

11 Undo the 2 nuts securing the EGR pipe to the rear of the cylinder head.
12 Undo the nuts securing the pre-catalyser to the exhaust manifold (see illustration).
13 Undo the nuts/bolts securing the pre-catalyser support bracket in the order shown (see illustrations), then undo the bolts securing the lower bracket to the cylinder block, and manoeuvre the pre-catalyser downwards from place. Discard the gasket, a new one must be fitted. **Note:** *When refitting the catalyser, the nuts/bolts must be tightened in the* **reverse** *order to that shown.*

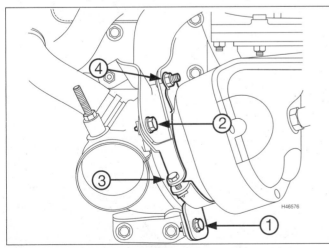

16.13a Pre-catalyser retaining bracket bolts/nuts tightening sequence

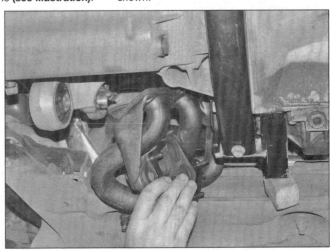

16.13b Lower the pre-catalyser from place

16.15 Flexible pipe-to-pre-catalyser clamp (arrowed)

Front pipe/catalytic converter

14 Trace the wiring back from the downstream lambda sensor to the wiring connector and disconnect the connector.

15 Unscrew the clamp bolt and release the ring, then separate the flexible exhaust pipe section from the exhaust manifold/pre-catalyser **(see illustration)**.

16 Loosen the clamp bolt securing the front pipe flange joint to the intermediate pipe/rear pipe and separate the joint. Withdraw the front pipe from underneath the vehicle, and recover the sealing ring. Where fitted, unscrew the rear oxygen sensor as the silencer is withdrawn.

Intermediate pipe and silencer

17 Slacken the clamping ring bolts and

16.17 Slacken the exhaust clamping ring (arrowed)

disengage the clamps from the front and rear flange joints. Note that there may be an earth strap attached to one of the clamp bolts **(see illustration)**.

18 Unhook the intermediate pipe and silencer from its mounting rubber and remove it from underneath the vehicle.

Tailpipe and silencer

19 Slacken the clamping ring bolt and disengage the clamp from the flange joint.

20 Unhook the tailpipe and silencer from its mounting rubbers and remove it from the car.

Complete system

21 Disconnect the lambda sensors wiring connectors from the main wiring harness.

22 Undo the nut and remove the through-bolt, then spread the clamping ring securing the front pipe flange joint to the exhaust manifold/pre-catalyser.

23 Free the system from all its mounting rubbers and lower it from under the vehicle.

Heat shield(s)

24 The heat shields are secured to the underbody by various nuts and bolts. Each shield can be removed once the relevant exhaust section has been removed. If a shield is being removed to gain access to a component located behind it, it may prove sufficient in some cases to remove the retaining nuts and/or bolts, and simply lower the shield, without disturbing the exhaust system.

Refitting

25 Each section is refitted by reversing the removal sequence, noting the following:

a) *Ensure that all traces of corrosion have been removed from the flanges.*

b) *Inspect the rubber mountings for damage or deterioration, and renew as necessary.*

c) *Prior to tightening the exhaust system fasteners, ensure that all rubber mountings are correctly located, and that there is adequate clearance between the exhaust system and vehicle underbody.*

d) *Ensure that the lambda sensors wiring is reconnected correctly and secured to the underbody by the relevant retaining clips.*

Chapter 4 Part B:
Fuel and exhaust systems – diesel models

Contents

Degrees of difficulty

Easy, suitable for novice with little experience	Fairly easy, suitable for beginner with some experience	Fairly difficult, suitable for competent DIY mechanic	Difficult, suitable for experienced DIY mechanic	Very difficult, suitable for expert DIY or professional

Specifications

Engine identification

1.6 litre engine:
Designation. DV6TED4
Engine codes . . . . 9HY or 9HZ
2.0 litre SOHC engine:
Designation. . . . . DW10TD or DW10ATED
Engine codes:
    DW10TD . . . . RHY
    DW10ATED . . . . RHZ
2.0 litre DOHC engine:
Designation. DW10BTED4
Engine code . . . . RHR

General

System type . . . . HDi (High-pressure Diesel injection) with full electronic control, direct injection and turbocharger
Designation:
    1.6 litre engine . . . . Bosch EDC 16 C34
    2.0 litre engines:
        SOHC . . . . Bosch EDC 15 C2
        DOHC . . . . Siemens SID 803
Firing order . . . . 1-3-4-2 (No 1 at flywheel end)
Fuel system operating pressure . . . . 200 to 1800 bars (according to engine speed)

Injectors

Type . . . . Electromagnetic or Piezo

Turbocharger

Type:
    1.6 litre engine . . . . Garrett GT1544V
    2.0 litre engines:
        SOHC . . . . KKK K03
        DOHC . . . . Garrett GT1749V
Boost pressure (approximate):
    1.6 litre engine . . . . 0.9 bar @ 3500 rpm
    2.0 litre engines:
        SOHC . . . . 1.2 bar @ 3000 rpm
        DOHC . . . . 1.0 bar @ 4000 rpm

Torque wrench settings

	Nm	lbf ft
Camshaft position sensor bolt	5	4
Common rail mounting bolts	23	17
Common rail-to-fuel injector fuel pipe unions:		
1.6 litre engine	25	18
2.0 litre engines	25	18
Exhaust manifold nuts	20	15
Exhaust system fasteners:		
Catalytic converter-to-manifold nuts	40	30
Clamping ring nuts	20	15
Fuel injector clamp bolts/nuts:		
1.6 litre engine:		
Stage 1	4	3
Stage 2	Angle-tighten a further 65°	
2.0 litre engines:		
SOHC	30	22
DOHC:		
Stage 1	4	3
Stage 2	Angle-tighten a further 65°	
Fuel pump-to-common rail fuel pipe unions:		
1.6 litre engine	25	18
2.0 litre engines:		
SOHC	20	15
DOHC	25	18
High-pressure fuel pump mounting bolts:		
1.6 litre engine	23	17
2.0 litre engines	20	15
High-pressure fuel pump rear mounting bolts/nut (8 mm)	17	13
High-pressure fuel pump sprocket nut	50	37
Inlet manifold bolts	10	7
Turbocharger mounting bolts/nuts	25	18
Turbocharger oil feed pipe banjo bolts:		
1.6 litre engine	30	20
2.0 litre engines:		
DOHC engine pipe to cylinder block	40	30
All other connections	25	18

1 General information and system operation

The fuel system consists of a rear-mounted fuel tank with an immersed fuel pump/level sensor, a fuel filter with integral water separator, a fuel cooler mounted under the car, and an electronically-controlled High-pressure Diesel injection (HDi) system, together with a single turbocharger.

The exhaust system is conventional, but to meet the latest emission levels an unregulated catalytic converter and an exhaust gas recirculation system are fitted to all models. On some models, an exhaust emission particulate filter is fitted – refer to Chapter 4C for further details.

The HDi system (generally known as a 'common rail' system) derives its name from the fact that a common rail, or fuel reservoir, is used to supply fuel to all the fuel injectors. Instead of an in-line or distributor type injection pump, which distributes the fuel directly to each injector, a high-pressure pump is used, which generates a very high fuel pressure (up to 1800 bar at high engine speed) in the common rail. The common rail stores fuel, and maintains a constant fuel pressure, with the aid of a pressure control valve. Each injector is supplied with high-pressure fuel from the common rail, and the injectors are individually controlled via signals from the system electronic control module (ECM). The injectors are electronically-operated.

In addition to the various sensors used on models with a conventional fuel injection pump, common rail systems also have a fuel pressure sensor. The fuel pressure sensor allows the ECM to maintain the required fuel pressure, via the pressure control valve.

System operation

For the purposes of describing the operation of a common rail injection system, the components can be divided into three sub-systems; the low-pressure fuel system, the high-pressure fuel system and the electronic control system.

Low-pressure fuel system

The low-pressure fuel system consists of the following components:
a) Fuel tank.
b) Fuel pump.
c) Fuel cooler.
d) Fuel heater (not all models).
e) Fuel filter/water trap.
f) Low-pressure fuel lines.

The low-pressure system (fuel supply system) is responsible for supplying clean fuel to the high-pressure fuel system.

High-pressure fuel system

The high-pressure fuel system consists of the following components:
a) High-pressure fuel pump with pressure control valve.
b) High-pressure fuel common rail.
c) Fuel injectors.
d) High-pressure fuel lines.

After passing through the fuel filter, the fuel reaches the high-pressure pump, which forces it into the common rail. As diesel fuel has a certain elasticity, the pressure in the common rail remains constant, even though fuel leaves the rail each time one of the injectors operates. Additionally, a pressure control valve mounted on the high-pressure pump ensures that the fuel pressure is maintained within preset limits.

The pressure control valve is operated by the ECM. When the valve is opened, fuel is returned from the high-pressure pump to the tank, via the fuel return lines, and the pressure in the common rail falls. To enable the ECM to trigger the pressure control valve correctly, the pressure in the common rail is measured by a fuel pressure sensor.

The electronically-controlled fuel injectors are operated individually, via signals from the ECM, and each injector injects fuel directly into the relevant combustion chamber. The fact that high fuel pressure is always available allows very precise and highly flexible injection in comparison to a conventional injection pump: for example combustion during the main injection process can be improved considerably by the pre-injection of a very small quantity of fuel.

Electronic control system

The electronic control system consists of the following components:

a) *Electronic control module (ECM).*
b) *Crankshaft speed/position sensor.*
c) *Camshaft position sensor.*
d) *Accelerator pedal position sensor.*
e) *Coolant temperature sensor.*
f) *Fuel temperature sensor.*
g) *Airflow meter.*
h) *Fuel pressure sensor.*
i) *Fuel injectors.*
j) *Fuel pressure control valve.*
k) *Preheating control unit.*
l) *EGR solenoid valve.*
m) *Air temperature sensor*
n) *Atmospheric pressure sensor – integral with the ECM (DV6TED4, DW10ATED and DW10BTED4 engines only).*
o) *Inlet manifold pressure sevnsor (DV6TED4 and DW10BTED4 engines only).*

The information from the various sensors is passed to the ECM, which evaluates the signals. The ECM contains electronic 'maps' which enable it to calculate the optimum quantity of fuel to inject, the appropriate start of injection, and even pre- and post-injection fuel quantities, for each individual engine cylinder under any given condition of engine operation.

Additionally, the ECM carries out monitoring and self-diagnostic functions. Any faults in the system are stored in the ECM memory, which enables quick and accurate fault diagnosis using appropriate diagnostic equipment (such as a suitable fault code reader).

2 High-pressure diesel injection system – special information

Warnings and precautions

1 It is essential to observe strict precautions when working on the fuel system components, particularly the high-pressure side of the system. Before carrying out any operations on the fuel system, refer to the precautions given in *Safety first!* at the beginning of this manual, and to the following additional information.

• Do not carry out any repair work on the high-pressure fuel system unless you are competent to do so, have all the necessary tools and equipment required, and are aware of the safety implications involved.

• Before starting any repair work on the fuel system, wait at least 30 seconds after switching off the engine to allow the fuel circuit pressure to reduce.

• Never work on the high-pressure fuel system with the engine running.

2.4 Typical plastic plug and cap set for sealing disconnected fuel pipes and components

• Keep well clear of any possible source of fuel leakage, particularly when starting the engine after carrying out repair work. A leak in the system could cause an extremely high-pressure jet of fuel to escape, which could result in severe personal injury.

• Never place your hands or any part of your body near to a leak in the high-pressure fuel system.

• Do not use steam cleaning equipment or compressed air to clean the engine or any of the fuel system components.

Procedures and information

2 Strict cleanliness must be observed at all times when working on any part of the fuel system. This applies to the working area in general, the person doing the work, and the components being worked on.

3 Before working on the fuel system components, they must be thoroughly cleaned with a suitable degreasing fluid. Specific cleaning products may be obtained from Citroën dealers. Alternatively, a suitable brake cleaning fluid may be used. Cleanliness is particularly important when working on the fuel system connections at the following components:

a) *Fuel filter.*
b) *High-pressure fuel pump.*
c) *Common rail.*
d) *Fuel injectors.*
e) *High-pressure fuel pipes.*

4 After disconnecting any fuel pipes or components, the open union or orifice must be immediately sealed to prevent the entry of dirt or foreign material. Plastic plugs and caps in various sizes are available in packs from motor factors and accessory outlets, and are particularly suitable for this application **(see illustration)**. Fingers cut from disposable rubber gloves should be used to protect components such as fuel pipes, fuel injectors and wiring connectors, and can be secured in place using elastic bands. Suitable gloves of this type are available at no cost from most petrol station forecourts.

5 Whenever any of the high-pressure fuel pipes are disconnected or removed, new pipes must be obtained for refitting.

6 On the completion of any repair on the high-pressure fuel system, Citroën recommend

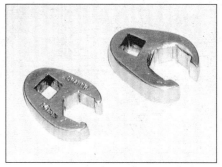

2.7 Two crow-foot adapters will be required for tightening the fuel pipe unions

the use of a leak-detecting compound. This is a powder which is applied to the fuel pipe unions and connections and turns white when dry. Any leak in the system will cause the product to darken indicating the source of the leak.

7 The torque wrench settings given in the Specifications must be strictly observed when tightening component mountings and connections. This is particularly important when tightening the high-pressure fuel pipe unions. To enable a torque wrench to be used on the fuel pipe unions, two Citroën crow-foot adapters are required. Suitable alternatives are available from motor factors and accessory outlets **(see illustration)**.

3 Fuel system – priming and bleeding

1 Should the fuel supply system be disconnected between the fuel tank and high pressure pump, it is necessary to prime the fuel system. This is achieved by connecting a suitable hose (if necessary, a special Citroën hose No 444-T may be available) from the fuel filter outlet pipe to the fuel return pipe and forcing fuel through the filter, into the return system. If the suitable hose is not available, it will suffice to connect a length of hose to the filter outlet, with the other end of the hose in a suitable container **(see illustration)**. The method of forcing the fuel through differs according to engine type:

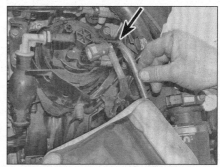

3.1 Attach a hose to the filter outlet (arrowed), and bleed the fuel into a container

4.2 Undo the screw (arrowed) and remove the inlet duct

4.3a Undo the air filter cover screws (arrowed) . . .

4.3b . . . disconnect the turbocharger inlet duct . . .

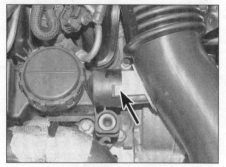

4.3c . . . release the clip (arrowed) and disconnect the breather . . .

4.3d . . . then remove the cover/duct assembly

DV6TED4 – Operate the hand priming pump for approximately 2 minutes.
DW10TD – Operate the hand priming pump for approximately 2 minutes.
DW10ATED – Turn the ignition key to

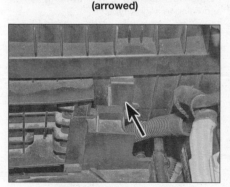

4.5 Slacken the air outlet hose clamp (arrowed)

*the ON position, allow the tank-mounted fuel pump to operate (it will only operate momentarily), then turn it **off**. Repeat a total of 10 times, then remove the by-pass hose, reconnect the normal fuel hoses, and turn the ignition key to the ON position. Allow the pump to operate, and turn the key OFF. Repeat the key ON-OFF procedure once more.*
DW10BTED4 – Operate the hand priming pump for approximately 1 minute.
2 Operate the starter until the engine starts.

4 Air cleaner assembly – removal and refitting

Removal

1 Pull the plastic engine cover up and remove it.

4.7b . . . and slide the air cleaner upwards

1.6 litre engine

2 Undo the screw and remove the air inlet ducting from the front of the engine compartment to the air filter housing **(see illustration)**.
3 Undo the two screws securing the air filter cover to the housing, disconnect the mass airflow sensor wiring plug, slacken the clamp securing the air inlet ducting to the turbocharger, release the clips securing the breather tube to the cylinder head cover, then manoeuvre the inlet ducting/filter cover assembly from position **(see illustrations)**.
4 Pull the air filter housing upwards from the rubber mounting grommets.

2.0 litre engines

5 Slacken the clamps and disconnect the air outlet hose from the airflow meter, and pull the air inlet hose upwards from the front of the air cleaner assembly **(see illustration)**.
6 Disconnect the airflow meter wiring plug.
7 Depress the retaining clip and lift the air cleaner upwards to release the mountings **(see illustrations)**.

Refitting

8 Refitting is a reverse of the removal procedure. Examine the condition of the seals and retaining clips and renew if necessary.

5 Accelerator cable – removal, refitting and adjustment

Note: *The accelerator cable is only fitted to some 2.0 litre models.*

Removal

1 Remove the engine management ECM and module box as described in Section 13 of this Chapter.
2 Rotate the accelerator pedal position sensor quadrant, and release the inner cable from the quadrant **(see illustration)**.
3 Withdraw the outer cable from the grommet in the pedal position sensor body, recover the flat washer from the end of the cable and remove the spring clip.
4 Release the cable from the remaining clips and brackets in the engine compartment, noting its routing.
5 Working in the passenger compartment,

4.7a Depress the clip (arrowed) . . .

5.2 The accelerator pedal position sensor is adjacent to the left-hand transmission mounting. Release the cable from the quadrant

reach up under the facia, depress the ends of the cable end fitting, and detach the inner cable from the top of the accelerator pedal.

6 Release the outer cable grommet from the pedal mounting bracket, then tie a length of string to the end of the cable.

7 Return to the engine compartment, release the cable grommet from the bulkhead and withdraw the cable. When the end of the cable appears, untie the string and leave it in position – it can then be used to draw the cable back into position on refitting.

Refitting

8 Refitting is a reversal of removal, but ensure that the cable is routed as noted before removal and, on completion, adjust the cable as follows.

Adjustment

9 Remove the spring clip from the accelerator outer cable **(see illustration)**. Ensuring that the pedal position sensor quadrant is against its stop, gently pull the cable out of its grommet until all free play is removed from the inner cable.

10 With the cable held in this position, refit the spring clip to the last exposed outer cable groove in front of the rubber grommet and washer. When the clip is refitted and the outer cable is released, there should be only a small amount of free play in the inner cable.

11 Have an assistant depress the accelerator pedal, and check that the pedal position sensor quadrant opens fully and returns smoothly to its stop.

12 Refit the engine cover on completion.

6 Accelerator pedal – removal and refitting

Refer to Chapter 4A.

7 Fuel lift pump – removal and refitting

The diesel fuel lift pump is located in the same position as the conventional fuel pump on petrol models, and the removal and refitting

procedures are virtually identical. Refer to Chapter 4A.

8 Fuel gauge sender unit – removal and refitting

The fuel gauge sender unit is integral with the fuel lift pump. Refer to Section 7.

9 Fuel tank and cooler – removal and refitting

Fuel tank

Refer to Chapter 4A.

Fuel cooler

Removal

1 The fuel cooler is located under the right-hand side of the vehicle. Jack up the rear of the vehicle, and support it on axle stands (see *Jacking and vehicle support*).

2 Undo the fasteners and remove the under-shield from the right-hand underside of the vehicle **(see illustration)**.

3 Working underneath the vehicle, undo the retaining nut, and release the cooler bracket from the locating holes **(see illustration)**.

4 Release the pipes from the clips on the vehicle underside, then depress the release buttons and disconnect the fuel feed and return hoses from the cooler. Be prepared

9.2 Rotate the undershield fasteners 90° anti-clockwise

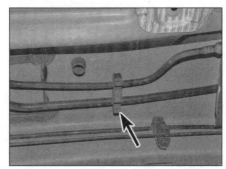

9.4a Release the pipes from the clips (arrowed) . . .

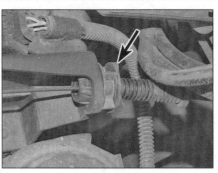

5.9 Outer cable clip (arrowed)

for fuel spillage, and plug the hose and cooler openings to prevent dirt ingress **(see illustrations)**.

Refitting

5 Refitting is a reversal of removal,

10 High-pressure fuel pump – removal and refitting

> **Warning: Refer to the information contained in Section 2 before proceeding.**

Note: *A new fuel pump-to-common rail high-pressure fuel pipe will be required for refitting.*

Removal

1.6 litre engine

1 Disconnect the battery (see Chapter 5A)

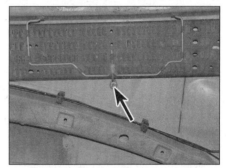

9.3 Undo the bracket retaining nut (arrowed)

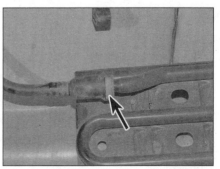

9.4b . . . then depress the release button (arrowed) and disconnect the pipes

10.4a Remove the air filter support bracket (arrowed) . . .

10.4b . . . and the brackets around the fuel pump (arrowed)

Tool Tip 1: Sprocket holding tool can be made from two lengths of steel strip bolted together to form a forked end. Bend the ends of the strip through 90° to form the 'prongs'.

Tool Tip 2: Make a sprocket releasing tool from a short strip of steel. Drill two holes in the strip to correspond with the two holes in the sprocket. Drill a third hole just large enough to accept the flats of the sprocket retaining nut.

and remove the timing belt as described in Chapter 2C. After removal of the timing belt, temporarily refit the right-hand engine mounting but do not fully tighten the bolts.

2 Remove the air filter assembly as described in Section 4.

3 Remove the EGR cooler as described in Chapter 4C.

4 Undo the bolts/nuts and remove the 3 support brackets above the fuel common rail and the high-pressure pump (see illustrations).

5 Undo the union nuts and remove the high-pressure fuel pipe between the fuel common rail and the high-pressure pump. Plug the openings to prevent contamination.

6 Disconnect the wiring plug from the high-pressure fuel pump.

7 Depress the release buttons and disconnect the fuel supply and return hoses from the pump. Note that the hoses may have a release button on each side of the fitting. Plug the openings to prevent contamination.

8 Hold the pump sprocket stationary, and loosen the centre nut securing it to the pump shaft (see Tool Tip 1).

9 The fuel pump sprocket is a taper fit on the pump shaft and it will be necessary to make up a tool to release it from the taper (see Tool Tip 2). Partially unscrew the sprocket retaining nut, fit the home-made tool, and secure it to the sprocket with two 7.0 mm bolts and nuts.

10.13 Unscrew the unions and remove the high-pressure fuel pipe

10.16 Use the home-made tools to remove the fuel pump sprocket

Prevent the sprocket from rotating as before, and screw down the nuts, forcing the sprocket off the shaft taper. Once the taper is released, remove the tool, unscrew the nut fully, and remove the sprocket from the pump shaft.

10 Undo the three bolts, and remove the pump from the mounting bracket.

Caution: The high-pressure fuel pump is manufactured to extremely close tolerances and must not be dismantled in any way. Do not unscrew the fuel pipe male union on the rear of the pump, or attempt to remove the sensor, piston de-activator switch, or the seal on the pump shaft. No parts for the pump are available separately and if the unit is in any way suspect, it must be renewed.

2.0 litre SOHC engine

11 Disconnect the battery (see Chapter 5A) and remove the timing belt as described in Chapter 2D. After removal of the timing belt, temporarily refit the right-hand engine mounting but do not fully tighten the bolts.

12 Remove the fuel filter as described in Chapter 1B, then undo the bolts and remove the fuel filter bracket.

13 Thoroughly clean the high-pressure fuel pipe unions on the fuel pump and common rail. Using an open-ended spanner, unscrew the union nuts securing the high-pressure fuel pipe to the fuel pump and common rail. Counterhold the unions on the pump and common rail with a second spanner, while unscrewing the union nuts. Withdraw the high-pressure fuel pipe and plug or cover the open unions to prevent dirt entry (see illustration). Note that a new high-pressure fuel pipe will be required for refitting. Note: *The fuel lines must be renewed every time they are removed, as it is possible for minute metal particles to enter them as a result of tightening the union nuts. If these particles enter the fuel injectors, fuel at high-pressure can enter the combustion chambers unrestricted.*

14 Disconnect the low pressure hoses from the fuel pump, then tape over the openings. Move the hoses to one side.

15 Disconnect the wiring connector at the pressure control valve on the rear of the fuel pump, and at the piston de-activator switch on the top of the pump.

16 Hold the pump pulley/sprocket stationary, and loosen the centre nut securing it to the pump shaft. The manufacturers recommend using a pin inserted through the pulley and into the cylinder head, however, a home-made forked tool engaged with the pulley holes can be used instead (see illustration and Tool Tip 1).

17 The fuel pump sprocket is a taper fit on the pump shaft and it will be necessary to make up a tool to release it from the taper (see Tool Tip 2). Partially unscrew the sprocket retaining nut, fit the home-made tool, and secure it to the sprocket with two 7.0 mm bolts. Prevent the sprocket from rotating as before, and unscrew the sprocket retaining nut. The nut

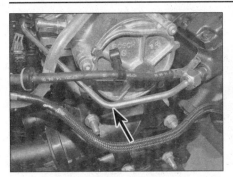

10.24 Remove the pipe (arrowed) between the pump and common rail

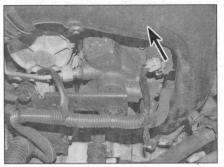

10.27 Move the inlet duct (arrowed) to one side

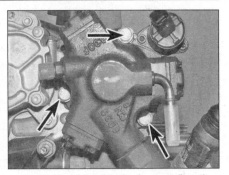

10.29 Undo the 3 bolts (arrowed) and remove the pump

will bear against the tool as it is undone, forcing the sprocket off the shaft taper. Once the taper is released, remove the tool, unscrew the nut fully, and remove the sprocket from the pump shaft.

Caution: The high-pressure fuel pump is manufactured to extremely close tolerances and must not be dismantled in any way. Do not unscrew the fuel pipe male union on the rear of the pump, or attempt to remove the pressure control valve, piston de-activator switch, or the seal on the pump shaft. No parts for the pump are available separately and if the unit is in any way suspect, it must be renewed.

18 Undo the bolts securing the bracket to the rear of the pump (where fitted), then undo the 3 bolts and pull the pump from the inner timing cover.

2.0 litre DOHC engine

19 Disconnect the battery negative lead as described in Chapter 5A.
20 Remove the plastic cover from the top of the engine.
21 Remove the air filter assembly as described in Section 4.
22 Slacken the clamps and detach the breather pipe from the left-hand end of the cylinder head cover.
23 Remove the ECM cover **(see illustration 13.5)**.
24 Thoroughly clean the high-pressure fuel pipe unions on the fuel pump and common rail. Using an open-ended spanner, unscrew the union nuts securing the high-pressure fuel pipe to the fuel pump and common rail. Counterhold the unions on the pump and common rail with a second spanner, while unscrewing the union nuts. Withdraw the high-pressure fuel pipe and plug or cover the open unions to prevent dirt entry **(see illustration)**. Note that a new high-pressure fuel pipe will be required for refitting. **Note:** *The fuel lines must be renewed every time they are removed, as it is possible for minute metal particles to enter them as a result of tightening the union nuts. If these particles enter the fuel injectors, fuel at high-pressure can enter the combustion chambers unrestricted.*
25 Disconnect the fuel supply and return hoses from the high-pressure pump. Plug the openings to prevent contamination.

26 Note their fitted positions, and disconnect the wiring plugs from the pump. Move the wiring harness to one side.
27 Undo the retaining bolt and move the turbocharger inlet duct to one side **(see illustration)**.
28 Undo the bolts/nuts and remove the support bracket from the pump.
29 Undo the 3 bolts and remove the pump **(see illustration)**.
Caution: The high-pressure fuel pump is manufactured to extremely close tolerances and must not be dismantled in any way. Do not unscrew the fuel pipe male union on the rear of the pump, or attempt to remove the pressure control valve, piston de-activator switch, or the seal on the pump shaft. No parts for the pump are available separately and if the unit is in any way suspect, it must be renewed.

Refitting

30 Refitting is a reversal of removal, noting the following points:
   a) *Always renew the pump-to-common rail high-pressure pipe.*
   b) *On engines with camshaft driven pumps, renew the drive seal.*
   c) *With everything reassembled and reconnected, and observing the precautions listed in Section 2, start the engine and allow it to idle. Check for leaks at the high-pressure fuel pipe unions with the engine idling. If satisfactory, increase the engine speed to 3000 rpm and check again for leaks.*
   d) *Take the car for a short road test and*

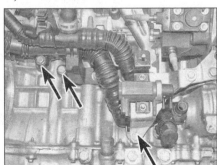

11.6 Undo the bolts (arrowed) and move the coolant pump outlet assembly aside

check for leaks once again on return. If any leaks are detected, obtain and fit another new high-pressure fuel pipe. Do not attempt to cure even the slightest leak by further tightening of the pipe unions.

11 Common rail –
removal and refitting

⚠️ **Warning: Refer to the information contained in Section 2 before proceeding.**
Note: *A complete new set of high-pressure fuel pipes will be required for refitting.*

Removal

1 Disconnect the battery (refer to Chapter 5A).
2 Remove the plastic cover from the top of the engine.

1.6 litre engine

3 Remove the cylinder head cover/inlet manifold as described in Chapter 2C.
4 Drain the cooling system as described in Chapter 1B.
5 Remove the EGR cooler as described in Chapter 4C.
6 Undo the 2 mounting bolts, slacken the clamps, and move the coolant pump outlet assembly aside **(see illustration)**.
7 Clean around the pipe, then undo the unions and remove the high-pressure pipe from the common rail to the high pressure pump. Plug the openings to prevent contamination.
8 Disconnect the pressure sensor wiring plug from the common rail **(see illustration)**.

11.8 The pressure sensor is located at the end of the common rail (arrowed)

11.9 Common rail mounting bolt/stud (arrowed)

11.10 Disconnect the wiring plugs at the fuel injectors

11.11 Undo the nuts and lift off the wiring harness guide

9 Unscrew the two rail mounting bolts and manoeuvre it from place (see illustration). **Note:** *Citroën insist that the fuel pressure sensor on the common rail must not be removed.*
Caution: Do not attempt to remove the four high-pressure fuel pipe male unions from the common rail. These parts are not available separately and if disturbed are likely to result in fuel leakage on reassembly.

2.0 litre SOHC engine

10 Disconnect the wiring connectors at the fuel injectors and at the sensor in the middle of the common rail (see illustration).
11 Undo the two nuts securing the plastic wiring harness guide to the cylinder head. Lift the guide off the two mounting studs and move it to one side (see illustration). Disconnect any additional wiring connectors as necessary to enable the harness and guide assembly to be moved further for increased access.
12 Release the retaining clip and disconnect the crankcase ventilation hose from the cylinder head cover. Position it to one side.
13 At the connections above the fuel pump, disconnect the fuel supply and return hose quick-release fittings using a small screwdriver to release the locking clip. Suitably plug or cover the open unions to prevent dirt entry.
14 Similarly disconnect the supply and return hose quick-release fittings at the fuel filter and plug or cover the open unions. Release the fuel hoses from the relevant retaining clips, then undo the fasteners and move the fuel filter support bracket to one side.

15 Disconnect the fuel temperature sensor wiring plug from the left-hand end of the common rail.
16 Thoroughly clean all the high-pressure fuel pipe unions on the common rail, fuel pump and injectors. Using an open-ended spanner, unscrew the union nuts securing the high-pressure fuel pipe to the fuel pump and common rail. Counterhold the unions on the pump and common rail with a second spanner, while unscrewing the union nuts. Withdraw the high-pressure fuel pipe and plug or cover the open unions to prevent dirt entry.
17 Again using two spanners, hold the unions and unscrew the union nuts securing the high-pressure fuel pipes to the fuel injectors and common rail (see illustrations). Withdraw the high-pressure fuel pipes and plug or cover the open unions to prevent dirt entry.
18 Undo the three bolts securing the common rail to the cylinder head and withdraw the rail from its location (see illustration).
Caution: Do not attempt to remove the four high-pressure fuel pipe male unions from the common rail. These parts are not available separately and if disturbed are likely to result in fuel leakage on reassembly.

2.0 litre DOHC engine

19 Disconnect the engine breather hose from the cylinder head cover.
20 Remove the air filter as described in Section 4.
21 Remove the inlet manifold as described in Section 14.
22 Move the oil filler neck to one side.

23 Thoroughly clean all the high-pressure fuel pipe unions on the common rail, fuel pump and injectors. Using an open-ended spanner, unscrew the union nuts securing the high-pressure fuel pipe to the fuel pump and common rail. Counterhold the unions on the pump and common rail with a second spanner, while unscrewing the union nuts. Withdraw the high-pressure fuel pipe and plug or cover the open unions to prevent dirt entry.
24 Again using two spanners, hold the unions and unscrew the union nuts securing the high-pressure fuel pipes to the fuel injectors and common rail (see illustrations 11.17a and 11.17b). Withdraw the high-pressure fuel pipes and plug or cover the open unions to prevent dirt entry.
25 Undo the 2 mounting nuts and manoeuvre the common rail from position. Recover the mounting spacers. Disconnect the sensor wiring plug(s) as the common rail is withdrawn.

Refitting

26 Locate the common rail in position, refit and finger-tighten the mounting bolts/nuts.
27 Reconnect the common rail wiring plug(s).
28 Fit the new pump-to-rail high-pressure pipe, and only finger-tighten the unions at first, then tighten the unions to the specified torque setting. Use a second spanner to counterhold the union screwed into the pump body.
29 Fit the new set of rail-to-injector high pressure pipes, and finger tighten the unions. If it's not possible to fit the new pipes to the injector unions, remove and refit the injectors as described in Section 12. and try again.

11.17a Using two spanners, unscrew the fuel pipe unions at the common rail . . .

11.17b . . . and at each injector

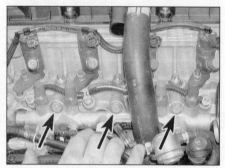

11.18 Common rail mounting bolts (arrowed)

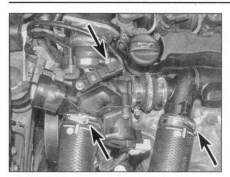

12.3a Inlet ducting clamps (arrowed) . . .

12.3b . . . and bolts (arrowed)

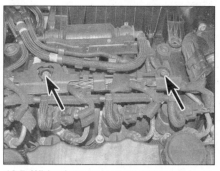

12.5 Wiring harness support bracket bolts (arrowed)

30 Tighten the common rail mounting bolts/nuts to the specified torque.

31 Tighten the rail-to-injector pipe unions to the specified torque setting. Use a second spanner to counterhold the injector unions.

32 The remainder of refitting is a reversal of removal, noting the following points:
 a) Ensure all wiring connectors and harnesses are correctly refitting and secured.
 b) Reconnect the battery as described in Chapter 5A.
 c) Observing the precautions listed in Section 2, start the engine and allow it to idle. Check for leaks at the high-pressure fuel pipe unions with the engine idling. If satisfactory, increase the engine speed to 3000 rpm and check again for leaks. Take the car for a short road test and check for leaks once again on return. If any leaks are detected, obtain and fit additional new high-pressure fuel pipes as required. Do not attempt to cure even the slightest leak by further tightening of the pipe unions.

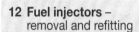

12 Fuel injectors – removal and refitting

⚠ *Warning: Refer to the information contained in Section 2 before proceeding.*

Removal

1 Remove the plastic cover from the top of the engine, and disconnect the battery negative lead as described in Chapter 5A.

1.6 litre engine

Note: *The following procedure describes the removal and refitting of the injectors as a complete set, however each injector may be removed individually if required. New copper washers, upper seals, and a high-pressure fuel pipe will be required for each disturbed injector when refitting.*

2 Remove the EGR cooler as described in Chapter 4C.

3 Undo the bolts, slacken the clamps and remove the air inlet ducting assembly from between the turbocharger and the inlet manifold. Note their fitted positions, and

disconnect the various wiring plugs as the assembly is withdrawn **(see illustrations)**.

4 Disconnect the injector wiring plugs.

5 Undo the bolts and move aside the wiring harness support bracket **(see illustration)**.

6 Release the manual fuel priming pump and its support.

7 Extract the retaining circlip and disconnect the leak-off pipe from each fuel injector **(see illustration)**.

8 Clean the area around the high-pressure fuel pipes between the injectors and the common rail, then unscrew the pipe unions. Use a second spanner to counterhold the union screwed into the injector body **(see illustration)**. The injectors screwed-in unions must not be allowed to move. Remove the bracket above the common rail unions, then remove the pipes. Plug the openings in the common rail and injectors to prevent dirt ingress.

12.7 Prise out the clip and pull the return pipe from each injector

12.9a Injector retaining nuts (arrowed)

9 Unscrew the injector retaining nuts, and carefully pull or lever the injector from place. If necessary, use an open-ended spanner and twist the injector to free it from position **(see illustrations)**. Do not lever against or pull on the solenoid housing at the top of the injector. Note down the injectors position – if the injectors are to be refitted, they must be refitted to their original locations. If improved access is required, undo the bolts and remove the oil separator housing from the front of the cylinder head cover.

10 Remove the copper washer and the upper seal from each injector, or from the cylinder head if they remained in place during injector removal. New copper washers and upper seals will be required for refitting. Cover the injector hole in the cylinder head to prevent dirt ingress.

11 Examine each injector visually for any signs of obvious damage or deterioration.

12.8 Use a second spanner to counterhold the high-pressure pipe union nuts

12.9b Use a spanner to twist the injector and free it from position

12.11 Note the injector classification number

12.12 Disconnect the injector wiring plugs

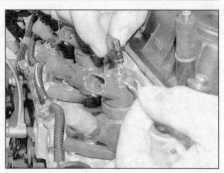

12.14 Extract the clip and disconnect the leak-off pipes

If any defects are apparent, renew the injector(s). Note down the 8-digit injector classification number – this may be needed during the refitting procedure if the ECM has been renewed **(see illustration)**.

Caution: The injectors are manufactured to extremely close tolerances and must not be dismantled in any way. Do not unscrew the fuel pipe union on the side of the injector, or separate any parts of the injector body. Do not attempt to clean carbon deposits from the injector nozzle or carry out any form of ultrasonic or pressure testing.

2.0 litre SOHC engine

Note: *The following procedure describes the removal and refitting of the injectors as a complete set, however each injector may be removed individually if required. New copper washers, upper seals, clamp bolt/nut, and a high-pressure fuel pipe will be required for each disturbed injector when refitting.*

12 Disconnect the wiring connectors at the fuel injectors **(see illustration)**.

13 Undo the two nuts securing the plastic wiring harness guide to the cylinder head. Lift the guide off the two mounting studs and move it clear. Disconnect any additional wiring connectors as necessary to enable the harness and guide assembly to be moved to one side.

14 Extract the retaining circlip and disconnect the leak-off pipe from each fuel injector **(see illustration)**.

15 Thoroughly clean all the high-pressure fuel pipe unions on the fuel injectors and common rail. Using two open-ended spanners, unscrew the union nuts securing the high-pressure fuel pipes to the fuel injectors and common rail **(see illustrations 11.17a and 11.17b)**. Withdraw the high-pressure fuel pipes and plug or cover the open unions on the injectors and common rail to prevent dirt entry. Note

that a new high-pressure fuel pipe will be required for each removed injector when refitting.

16 Unscrew the bolt/nut securing each injector clamp to its cylinder head **(see illustrations)**. Note that new clamp bolt/nut will be required for refitting.

17 Withdraw the injectors, together with their clamps, from the cylinder head. Slide the clamp off the injector once it is clear of the mounting stud. If the injectors are a tight fit in the cylinder head and cannot be released, two screwdrivers may be used to carefully lever them out **(see illustration)**. Alternatively, unscrew one mounting stud (where fitted) using a stud extractor and slide off the injector clamp. Using an open-ended spanner engaged with the clamp locating slot on the injector body, free the injector by twisting it and at the same time lifting it upwards.

18 Recover the injector clamp locating dowel from the cylinder head **(see illustration)**.

19 Remove the copper washer and the upper seal from each injector, or from the cylinder head if they remained in place during injector removal. New copper washers and upper seals will be required for refitting.

20 Examine each injector visually for any signs of obvious damage or deterioration. If any defects are apparent, renew the injector(s).

Caution: The injectors are manufactured to extremely close tolerances and must not be dismantled in any way. Do not unscrew the fuel pipe union on the side of the injector, or separate any parts of the injector body. Do not attempt to clean carbon deposits from the injector nozzle or carry out any form of ultrasonic or pressure testing.

21 If the injectors are in a satisfactory condition, plug the fuel pipe union (if not already done) and suitably cover the electrical element and the injector nozzle.

2.0 litre DOHC engine

Note: *New copper washers, upper seals, and a high-pressure fuel pipe will be required for each disturbed injector when refitting.*

22 Remove the inlet manifold as described in Section 14.

23 Disconnect the wiring plugs from the injectors.

24 Thoroughly clean all the high-pressure fuel

12.16a Undo the injector retaining nut . . .

12.16b . . . and remove the washer

12.17 Withdrawn the injectors, complete with the clamps

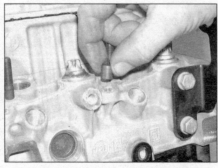

12.18 Recover the clamp locating dowel from the cylinder head

12.24 Use a second spanner to counterhold the injector port when slackening the union nut

12.25a Prise down the lower edge of the retaining clip (shown with the leak-off hose disconnected for clarity) . . .

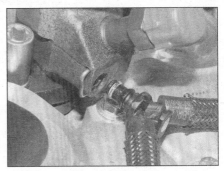

12.25b . . . then pull the hose from the injector

pipe unions on the fuel injectors and common rail. Using two open-ended spanners, unscrew the union nuts securing the high-pressure fuel pipes to the fuel injectors and common rail **(see illustration)**. Withdraw the high-pressure fuel pipes and plug or cover the open unions on the injectors and common rail to prevent dirt entry. Note that a new high-pressure fuel pipe will be required for each removed injector when refitting.

25 Release the retaining clip and disconnect the leak-off pipe from each fuel injector **(see illustrations)**.

26 Progressively and evenly slacken and remove the injector retaining nuts **(see illustration)**.

27 Carefully pull the injectors upwards from the cylinder head. Note down the injectors' position – if the injectors are to be refitted, they must be refitting to their original locations.

28 Remove the lower copper washer and upper seal from each injector.

29 Examine each injector visually for any signs of obvious damage or deterioration. If any defects are apparent, renew the injector(s). Note down the 8-digit injector classification number – this may be needed during the refitting procedure if the ECM has been renewed **(see illustration 12.11)**.

Caution: The injectors are manufactured to extremely close tolerances and must not be dismantled in any way. Do not unscrew the fuel pipe union on the side of the injector, or separate any parts of the injector body. Do not attempt to clean carbon deposits from the injector nozzle or carry out any form of ultrasonic or pressure testing.

30 If the injectors are in a satisfactory condition, plug the fuel pipe union (if not already done) and suitably cover the electrical element and the injector nozzle.

Refitting

31 Locate a new upper seal on the body of each injector, and place a new copper washer on the injector nozzle **(see illustrations)**.

32 Refit the injector clamp locating dowels (where fitted) to the cylinder head.

2.0 litre SOHC engine

33 Place the injector clamp in the slot on each injector body and refit the injectors to

the cylinder head. Guide the clamp over the mounting stud and onto the locating dowel as each injector is inserted. Ensure the upper injector seals are correctly located in the cylinder head.

34 Fit the washer and a new injector clamp retaining nut to each mounting stud. Tighten the nuts finger-tight only at this stage.

1.6 litre and 2.0 litre DOHC engines

35 Ensure the injector clamps are in place over their respective circlips on the injector bodies, then fit the injectors into place in the cylinder head. If the original injectors are being refitted, ensure they are fitted into their original positions **(see illustration)**.

36 Fit the injector retaining bolts/nuts, but only finger-tighten them at this stage. When tightening the nuts/bolts, ensure the clamps stay horizontal.

12.26 Injector clamp nuts (arrowed)

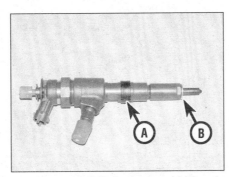

12.31b . . . then fit the upper seal (A) and copper washer (B)

All engines

37 Working on one fuel injector at a time, remove the blanking plugs from the fuel pipe unions on the common rail and the relevant injector. Locate a new high-pressure fuel pipe over the unions and screw on the union nuts. Take care not to cross-thread the nuts or strain the fuel pipes as they are fitted. Once the union nut threads have started, finger-tighten the nuts to the ends of the threads.

38 When all the fuel pipes are in place, tighten the injector clamp retaining nuts/bolts to the specified torque (and angle where applicable).

39 Using an open-ended spanner, hold each fuel pipe union in turn and tighten the union nut to the specified torque using a torque wrench and crow-foot adaptor **(see illustration)**. Tighten all the disturbed union nuts in the same way.

12.31a Ensure the circlip (arrowed) is in place on the 1.6 litre engine injectors . . .

12.35 Fit the injectors into their original locations

40 On 1.6 litre and 2.0 litre DOHC engines, if new injectors have been fitted, their classification numbers must be programmed into the engine management ECM using dedicated diagnostic equipment/scanner. If this equipment is not available, entrust this task to a Citroën dealer or suitably-equipped repairer. Note that it should be possible to drive the vehicle, albeit with reduced performance/increased emissions, to a repairer for the numbers to be programmed.

41 The remainder of refitting is a reversal of removal, following the points listed in Paragraph 32 of the previous Section.

13 Electronic control system components – testing, removal and refitting

Testing

1 If a fault is suspected in the electronic control side of the system, first ensure that all the wiring connectors are securely connected and free of corrosion. Ensure that the suspected problem is not of a mechanical nature, or due to poor maintenance; ie, check that the air cleaner filter element is clean, the engine breather hoses are clear and undamaged, and that the cylinder compression pressures are correct, referring to Chapters 1B and 2C, D or E for further information.

2 If these checks fail to reveal the cause of the problem, the vehicle should be taken to a Citroën dealer or suitably-equipped garage for testing. A diagnostic socket is located beside

12.39 Tighten the high-pressure pipe union nuts using a 'crow-foot' adaptor

the passenger's compartment fusebox, behind the panel in the glovebox **(see illustration)**, to which a fault code reader or other suitable test equipment can be connected. By using the code reader or test equipment, the engine management ECM (and the various other vehicle system ECMs) can be interrogated, and any stored fault codes can be retrieved. This will allow the fault to be quickly and simply traced, alleviating the need to test all the system components individually, which is a time-consuming operation that carries a risk of damaging the ECM.

Removal and refitting

3 Before carrying out any of the following procedures, disconnect the battery (refer to Chapter 5A). Reconnect the battery on completion of refitting.

Electronic control module (ECM)

Note: *If a new ECM is to be fitted, this work*

must be entrusted to a Citroën dealer or suitably-equipped specialist. It is necessary to initialise the new ECM after installation, which requires the use of dedicated Citroën diagnostic equipment.

4 The ECM is located in a plastic box which is mounted on the left-hand front wheel arch.

5 Undo the fasteners and lift off the ECM module box lid **(see illustration)**.

6 Undo the 2 Torx bolts and lift the ECM upwards and remove it from its location **(see illustration)**.

7 Release the wiring connector(s) by depressing the tab and moving the locking lever on top of the connector. Carefully withdraw the connectors from the ECM pins **(see illustration)**

8 To remove the ECM module box, release the clips, disconnect the positive feed connection, and lift the fusebox from place. Undo the screw securing the glow plug relay unit, then undo the mounting bolts, and remove the module box **(see illustrations)**. Release any wiring harness retaining clips as the box is withdrawn.

9 Refitting is a reversal of removal.

Crankshaft speed/position sensor – 1.6 litre and 2.0 litre DOHC engines

10 The crankshaft position sensor is located adjacent to the crankshaft pulley on the right-hand end of the engine. Slacken the right-hand front roadwheel bolts, then jack the front of the vehicle up and support it on axle stands (see *Jacking and vehicle support*). Remove the right-hand front roadwheel.

11 Push in the centre pins a little, then prise out the rivets and remove the wheel arch liner.

13.2 The diagnostic plug (arrowed) is located beside the passenger compartment fusebox

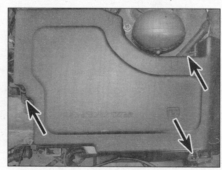

13.5 ECM module box lid fasteners (arrowed)

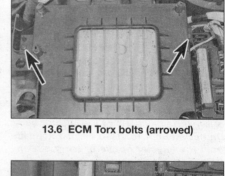

13.6 ECM Torx bolts (arrowed)

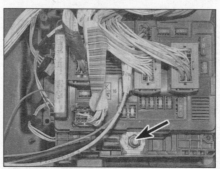

13.7 Lever over the locking catches and disconnect the wiring plugs

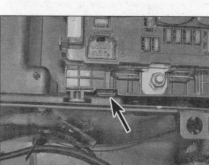

13.8a Undo the nut (arrowed) securing the battery connection

13.8b Release the clip at the front and rear of the fusebox (front clip arrowed) . . .

13.8c . . . and lift out the fusebox

13.8d Undo the screw (arrowed) and remove the glow plug relay . . .

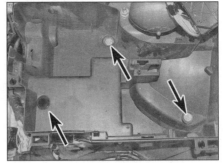

13.8e . . . then undo the 3 mounting bolts (arrowed) . . .

13.8f . . . and remove the module box

13.12 Crankshaft position sensor (arrowed) – 1.6 litre and 2.0 litre DOHC engines

13.18 Slacken the bolt securing the sensor to the bellhousing . . .

12 Disconnect the sensor wiring plug **(see illustration)**.

13 Undo the bolt and remove the sensor.

14 Refitting is a reversal of removal, tightening the sensor retaining bolt securely.

Crankshaft speed/position sensor – 2.0 litre SOHC engine

15 The crankshaft speed/position sensor is located at the top of the transmission bellhousing, directly above the engine flywheel. To gain access, remove the air cleaner assembly as described in Section 4, then remove the battery and battery tray as described in Chapter 5A.

16 Undo the retaining nuts and bolts and release the plastic wiring harness guide from its mountings.

17 Working below the thermostat housing, disconnect the wiring connector from the crankshaft speed/position sensor.

18 Slacken the bolt securing the sensor to the bellhousing **(see illustration)**. It is not necessary to remove the bolt completely as the sensor mounting flange is slotted.

19 Turn the sensor body to clear the mounting bolt, then withdraw the sensor from the bellhousing **(see illustration)**.

20 Refitting is reverse of the removal procedure ensuring the sensor retaining bolt is securely tightened.

Camshaft position sensor – 1.6 litre engine

21 The camshaft position sensor is mounted on the right-hand end of the cylinder head cover, directly behind the camshaft sprocket.

22 Remove the upper timing belt cover, as described in Chapter 2C.

23 Unplug the sensor wiring connector.

24 Undo the bolt and pull the sensor from position **(see illustration)**.

25 Upon refitting, position the sensor so that the air gap between the sensor end and the webs of the signal wheel is 1.2 mm,

13.19 . . . then turn the sensor body to clear the bolt and withdraw it from position

13.25a The gap between the sensor and the signal wheel (arrowed) . . .

measured with feeler gauges **(see illustrations)**. If a new sensor is being fitted, position it so the nipple of the sensor is just in contact with the camshaft signal wheel. Tighten the sensor retaining bolt to the specified torque.

13.24 Undo the camshaft sensor retaining bolt (arrowed) – 1.6 litre engine

13.25b . . . must be 1.2 mm measured with a feeler gauge

13.29 Remove the camshaft position sensor

13.31 Insert a feeler gauge through the sprocket to measure the sensor air gap

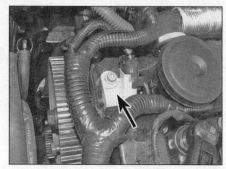

13.35 Camshaft position sensor (arrowed)

26 The remainder of refitting is a reversal of removal.

Camshaft position sensor – 2.0 litre SOHC engine

Note: *The camshaft position sensor is mounted on the right-hand end of the cylinder head cover, directly behind the camshaft sprocket.*

27 Remove the timing belt upper covers as described in Chapter 2D.

28 Disconnect the sensor wiring connector.

29 Undo the retaining bolt and lift the sensor off the cylinder head cover **(see illustration)**.

30 To refit and adjust the sensor position, locate the sensor on the cylinder head cover and loosely refit the retaining bolt.

31 The air gap between the tip of the sensor and the signal wheel at the rear of the camshaft sprocket hub must be set to 1.2 mm, using feeler blades. Clearance for the feeler

blades is limited with the timing belt and camshaft sprocket in place, but it is just possible if the feeler blades are bent through 90° so they can be inserted through the holes in the sprocket to rest against the inner face of the signal wheel. Note that if a new sensor is being fitted, position it so the nipple on the end of the sensor is just in contact with the signal wheel **(see illustration)**.

32 Hold the sensor in this position and tighten the retaining bolt.

33 With the gap correctly adjusted, reconnect the sensor wiring connector, then refit the timing belt upper and intermediate covers as described in Chapter 2D.

Camshaft position sensor – 2.0 litre DOHC engine

Note: *The camshaft position sensor is mounted on the right-hand end of the cylinder head cover, directly behind the camshaft sprocket.*

34 Remove the plastic cover from the top of the engine.

35 Disconnect the sensor wiring plug **(see illustration)**.

36 Undo the retaining bolt and remove the sensor.

37 To refit and adjust the sensor position, locate the sensor on the cylinder head cover and loosely refit the retaining bolt.

38 When refitting a used sensor, position it against the camshaft sprocket spoke, then pull it back 1.2 mm **(see illustrations)**. Tighten the retaining bolt securely.

39 When fitting a new sensor, position the sensor so the nipple on the tip is just in contact with the signal wheel. Tighten the retaining bolt securely.

Accelerator pedal position sensor – models without accelerator cable

40 On these models, the pedal sensor is integral with the accelerator pedal assembly. Refer to the relevant Section of Chapter 4A for the pedal removal procedure.

Accelerator pedal position sensor – models with accelerator cable

41 The accelerator pedal position sensor is located adjacent to the left-hand transmission mounting **(see illustration)**.

42 Remove the ECM and module box as described in this Section.

43 Undo the two bolts and remove the sensor complete with bracket **(see illustration)**.

44 Refitting is reverse of the removal procedure.

Coolant temperature sensor

45 Refer to Chapter 3.

Fuel temperature sensor – 1.6 litre engine

⚠️ *Warning: Refer to the information contained in Section 2 before proceeding.*

46 The sensor is clipped in to the plastic fuel manifold at the right-hand rear end of the cylinder head. To remove the sensor, disconnect the wiring plug, then unclip the sensor from the manifold. Be prepared for fuel spillage **(see illustration)**.

47 Refitting is a reversal of removal. Observing the precautions listed in Section 2, start the engine and allow it to idle. Check for leaks at

13.38a Position the sensor against the camshaft sprocket spoke . . .

13.38b . . . then pull it back 1.2 mm

13.41 Accelerator pedal position sensor

13.43 Pedal position sensor bolts (arrowed)

the fuel temperature sensor with the engine idling. If satisfactory, increase the engine speed to 4000 rpm and check again for leaks. Take the car for a short road test and check for leaks once again on return. If any leaks are detected, obtain and fit a new sensor.

Fuel temperature sensor – 2.0 litre engines

 Warning: Refer to the information contained in Section 2 before proceeding.

48 The fuel temperature sensor is located in the fuel supply pipe between the fuel filter and the high-pressure pump, in the vicinity of the common rail.
49 Disconnect the fuel temperature sensor wiring connector.
50 Thoroughly clean the area around the sensor and its location.
51 Suitably protect the components below the sensor and have plenty of clean rags handy. Be prepared for considerable fuel spillage.
52 Release the retaining clips and detach the sensor from the fuel pipes.
53 Refit the sensor to the fuel pipes, ensuring the clips fully engage.
54 Reconnect the sensor wiring plug.
55 Observing the precautions listed in Section 2, start the engine and allow it to idle. Check for leaks at the fuel temperature sensor with the engine idling. If satisfactory, increase the engine speed to 4000 rpm and check again for leaks. Take the car for a short road test and check for leaks once again on return. If any leaks are detected, obtain and fit a new sensor.

Airflow meter

56 The airflow meter is located in the inlet ducting from the air cleaner housing.
57 Disconnect the meter wiring plug **(see illustrations)**.
58 Slacken the retaining clips and disconnect the air inlet ducting from either side of the airflow meter. Suitably plug or cover the turbocharger inlet duct, using clean rag to prevent any dirt or foreign material from entering. The airflow meter is bolted to the air cleaner cover.
59 Refitting is reverse of the removal procedure.

Fuel pressure sensor

60 The fuel pressure sensor is integral with the common rail, and is not available separately. Citroën insist that the sensor is not removed from the rail.

Fuel pressure control valve

61 The fuel pressure control valve is integral with the high-pressure fuel pump and cannot be separated.

Preheating system control unit

62 Refer to Chapter 5A.

EGR solenoid valve

63 Refer to Chapter 4C, Section 2.

13.46 Fuel temperature sensor (arrowed)

13.57b . . . 2.0 litre SOHC engines . . .

Vehicle speed sensor

64 The engine management ECM receives the vehicle speed signal from the wheel speed sensors via the ABS ECM. Refer to Chapter 9 for wheel speed sensor removal.

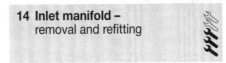
14 Inlet manifold – removal and refitting

1.6 litre engine

1 The inlet manifold is integral with the cylinder head cover. Refer to Chapter 2C.

2.0 litre engines

SOHC

2 The inlet manifold is located on the rear of the cylinder head together with the exhaust

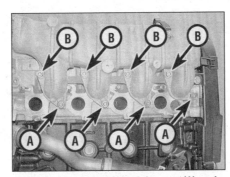

14.3 Inlet manifold retaining nut (A) and bolts (B)

13.57a Airflow meter wiring plug (arrowed) – 1.6 litre engines . . .

13.57c . . . and 2.0 litre DOHC engines

manifold. First, remove the exhaust manifold as described in Section 15.
3 Undo the four bolts and four nuts securing the inlet manifold's flanges to the cylinder head **(see illustration)** and recover the washers. If preferred, the lower mounting nuts may be loosened and not removed, as the lower inlet manifold holes are slotted to allow the manifold to be lifted upwards once the upper bolts have been removed.
4 Lift the manifold off the cylinder head studs and recover the gasket.
5 Refitting is reverse of the removal procedure, bearing in mind the following points.
  a) Ensure that the manifold and cylinder head mating faces are clean, with all traces of old gasket removed.
  b) Use a new gasket when refitting the manifold.
  c) Ensure that all fixings and attachments are securely tightened.
  d) Refit the exhaust manifold as described in Section 15.

DOHC

6 The inlet manifold is integral with the cylinder head cover. Refer to Chapter 2E.

15 Exhaust manifold – removal and refitting

Removal

1 Remove the turbocharger as described in Section 17.
2 Undo the retaining nuts, recover the spacers

15.2a Exhaust manifold –
1.6 litre engines . . .

15.2b . . . 2.0 litre SOHC engines . . .

15.2c . . . 2.0 litre DOHC engines

(where fitted), and remove the manifold. Recover the gasket **(see illustrations)**.

Refitting

3 Refitting is a reverse of the removal procedure, bearing in mind the following points:
  a) *Ensure that the manifold and cylinder head mating faces are clean, with all traces of old gasket removed.*
  b) *Use new gaskets when refitting the manifold to the cylinder head.*
  c) *Tighten the exhaust manifold retaining nuts to the specified torque.*

16 Turbocharger –
description and precautions

Description

1 A turbocharger is fitted to increase engine efficiency by raising the pressure in the inlet manifold above atmospheric pressure. Instead of the air simply being sucked into the cylinders, it is forced in.
2 Energy for the operation of the turbocharger comes from the exhaust gas. The gas flows through a specially-shaped housing (the turbine housing) and, in so doing, spins the turbine wheel. The turbine wheel is attached to a shaft, at the end of which is another vaned wheel known as the compressor wheel. The compressor wheel spins in its own housing, and compresses the inlet air on the way to the inlet manifold.
3 Boost pressure (the pressure in the inlet

manifold) is limited by a wastegate, which diverts the exhaust gas away from the turbine wheel in response to a pressure-sensitive actuator. On 1.6 litre and 2.0 litre DOHC engines, the turbocharger incorporates a variable inlet nozzle to improve boost pressure at low engine speeds.
4 The turbo shaft is pressure-lubricated by an oil feed pipe from the main oil gallery. The shaft 'floats' on a cushion of oil. A drain pipe returns the oil to the sump.

Precautions

5 The turbocharger operates at extremely high speeds and temperatures. Certain precautions must be observed, to avoid premature failure of the turbo, or injury to the operator.
6 Do not operate the turbo with any of its parts exposed, or with any of its hoses removed. Foreign objects falling onto the rotating vanes could cause excessive damage, and (if ejected) personal injury.
7 Do not race the engine immediately after start-up, especially if it is cold. Give the oil a few seconds to circulate.
8 Always allow the engine to return to idle speed before switching it off – do not blip the throttle and switch off, as this will leave the turbo spinning without lubrication.
9 Allow the engine to idle for several minutes before switching off after a high-speed run.
10 Observe the recommended intervals for oil and filter changing, and use a reputable oil of the specified quality. Neglect of oil changing, or use of inferior oil, can cause carbon formation on the turbo shaft, leading to subsequent failure.

17 Turbocharger –
removal, inspection and refitting

Removal

1 Chock the rear wheels then jack up the front of the vehicle and support it on axle stands (see *Jacking and vehicle support*). Undo the screws and remove the engine undershield.
2 Disconnect the battery negative lead as described in Chapter 5A.

1.6 litre engine

3 Place a sheet of thick cardboard over the rear of the radiator to protect it from accidental damage.
4 Slacken the clamps, undo the bolts, and remove the air ducts to and from the turbocharger and inlet manifold **(see illustrations 12.3a and 12.3b)**. Note their fitted positions and disconnect the various wiring plugs as the assembly is withdrawn.
5 Disconnect the vacuum hose from the turbocharger wastegate control assembly **(see illustration)**.
6 Undo the mounting bolts **(see illustration)**, and remove the heat shield from above turbocharger.
7 Remove the catalytic converter/particle filter (where applicable) as described in Section 19.
8 Undo the oil supply pipe banjo bolts and recover the sealing washers **(see illustration)**.
9 Slacken the retaining clip and disconnect the oil return pipe from the turbocharger and cylinder block.

17.5 Disconnect the vacuum pipe from the wastegate control assembly (arrowed)

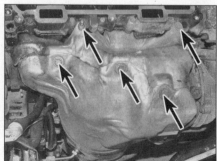

17.6 Undo the bolts and remove the turbocharger heat shield (arrowed)

17.8 Turbocharger oil supply and return pipes (arrowed)

17.10 Undo the 3 nuts (arrowed – one hidden) and remove the support bracket (arrowed)

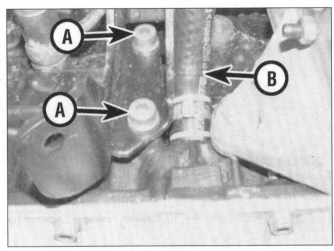

17.13 Turbocharger lower mounting bracket bolts (A) and oil return pipe (B)

10 Unscrew the four nuts, and the nut securing the support bracket, then remove the turbocharger from the exhaust manifold **(see illustration)**.

2.0 litre SOHC engine

11 Remove the front subframe as described in Chapter 10.

12 Disconnect the turbocharger inlet duct and move it to one side.

13 Undo the bolts securing the turbocharger support bracket to the cylinder block **(see illustration)**.

14 Unscrew the union bolts and disconnect the oil supply and return pipes from the turbocharger and engine cylinder block **(see illustration)**. Tape over the openings.

15 Disconnect the vacuum hose from the turbocharger control valve.

16 On models without an intercooler, unscrew the three retaining nuts and withdraw the turbocharger from the exhaust manifold studs.

17 Undo the three nuts securing the turbocharger to the exhaust manifold, then remove the turbocharger down through the exhaust tunnel **(see illustration)**. If the turbocharger is reluctant to separate from the manifold, remove the manifold along with the turbocharger, and separate them on the work bench.

2.0 litre DOHC engine

18 Remove the air filter assembly as described in Section 4.

19 Remove the front subframe as described in Chapter 10.

20 Remove the right-hand driveshaft as described in Chapter 8.

21 Move the EGR valve and cooler assembly to one side without disconnecting the coolant hoses (refer to Chapter 4C).

22 Undo the bolts and remove the heat shield over the turbocharger.

23 Detach the right-hand driveshaft intermediate bearing housing from the cylinder block.

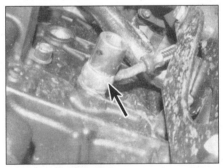

17.14 Turbocharger oil supply pipe banjo on the rear of the cylinder block (arrowed)

24 Remove the heat shields over the pre-catalyst, then undo the fasteners, remove the pre-catalyst support bracket at the right-hand end, undo the mounting bolt at the left-hand end, slacken the clamp securing the pre-catalyst to the turbocharger, and remove the pre-catalyst **(see illustrations)**.

25 Disconnect the turbocharger air inlet and outlet ducts.

26 Remove the support bracket beneath the turbocharger.

27 Disconnect the vacuum pipe and wiring plug from the turbocharger control **(see illustration)**.

28 Disconnect the oil supply and return

17.17 Turbocharger-to-manifold nuts (arrowed – one hidden)

17.24a Remove the pre-catalyst heat shield

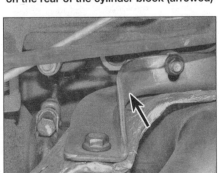

17.24b Remove the support bracket at the right-hand end (arrowed) . . .

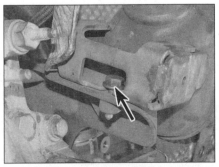

17.24c . . . and undo the bolt at the left-hand end of the pre-catalyst (arrowed)

17.24d Slacken the clamp (arrowed) securing the pre-catalyst to the turbocharger

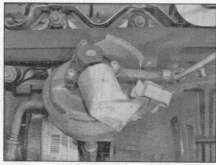

17.27 Disconnect the vacuum pipe and wiring plug from the turbocharger control

17.28a Disconnect the turbocharger oil supply pipe (arrowed) . . .

17.28b . . . and return pipe (arrowed)

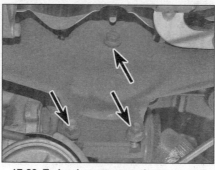

17.29 Turbocharger mounting nuts and bolt (arrowed)

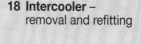

18 Intercooler –
removal and refitting

Note: *No intercooler is fitted to the 2.0 litre DW10TD engine.*

Removal

1 The intercooler is located at the front of the engine compartment, on the left-hand side of the radiator. Chock the rear wheels then jack up the front of the vehicle and support it on axle stands (see *Jacking and vehicle support*). Undo the screws and remove the engine undershield.
2 Remove the engine top cover.
3 On 2.0 litre models, remove the air filter assembly as described in Section 4. On 1.6 litre models, remove the air inlet ducting from the front of the engine compartment to the air filter housing.
4 Loosen the clip and disconnect the outlet air duct from the intercooler.
5 Working under the car, loosen the clip and disconnect the inlet air duct from the inter-cooler **(see illustration)**.
6 Release the clips and pull the top mounting from the crossmember **(see illustrations)**.
7 Lift the intercooler from its lower mountings and remove from the vehicle.

Refitting

8 Refitting is a reversal of removal.

pipes from the engine cylinder block **(see illustrations)**. Tape over the openings.
29 Undo the nuts/bolt securing the turbocharger to the exhaust manifold, lift the assembly slightly, then lower the turbocharger downwards from position **(see illustration)**.

Inspection

30 With the turbocharger removed, inspect the housing for cracks or other visible damage.
31 Spin the turbine or the compressor wheel to verify that the shaft is intact and to feel for excessive shake or roughness. Some play is normal, since in use the shaft is 'floating' on a film of oil. Check that the wheel vanes are undamaged.
32 If oil contamination of the exhaust or induction passages is apparent, it is likely that turbo shaft oil seals have failed.

33 No DIY repair of the turbo is possible and none of the internal or external parts are available separately. If the turbocharger is suspect in any way a complete new unit must be obtained. Do not attempt to dismantle the turbocharger control assemblies.

Refitting

34 Refitting is a reverse of the removal pro-cedure, bearing in mind the following points:
a) *Renew the turbocharger retaining nuts and gaskets.*
b) *If a new turbocharger is being fitted, change the engine oil and filter. Also renew the filter in the oil feed pipe.*
c) *Prime the turbocharger by injecting clean engine oil through the oil feed pipe union before reconnecting the union.*

18.5 Slacken the clamp (arrowed) and disconnect the inlet duct from the intercooler

18.6a Insert a small screwdriver to release the clip each side (arrowed) . . .

18.6b . . . then remove the intercooler

19.7a Unscrew the pressure take-off union from the side of the catalyst/filter . . .

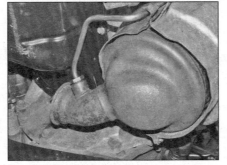

19.7b . . . and the one at the base

19.10 Exhaust pipe-to-catalyst/filter clamp (arrowed)

19 Exhaust system – general information and component renewal

General information

1 According to model, the exhaust system consists of either two, three or four sections. Three-section systems consist of a catalytic converter, an intermediate pipe, and a tailpipe. The DW10ATED and DV6TED system consists of a pre-catalyst after the turbocharger, followed by a catalytic converter, particulate filter (not all models), intermediate pipe, and tailpipe. On two-section systems, the catalytic converter and intermediate pipe are combined to form a single section.

2 The exhaust joints are of either the spring-loaded ball type (to allow for movement in the exhaust system) or clamp-ring type.

3 The system is suspended throughout its entire length by rubber mountings.

Removal

4 Each exhaust section can be removed individually, or alternatively, the complete system can be removed as a unit. Even if only one part of the system needs attention, it is often easier to remove the whole system and separate the sections on the bench.

5 To remove the system or part of the system, first jack up the front or rear of the car, and support it on axle stands (see *Jacking and vehicle support*). Alternatively, position the car over an inspection pit, or on car ramps.

Catalytic converter/particulate filter – 1.6 litre engine

6 Undo the screws and remove the engine undershield.

7 Unscrew the pressure take off unions from the side and base of the assembly (see illustrations).

8 Disconnect the sensor wiring plug on the side of the catalytic converter.

9 Undo the bolts and remove the heat shield from the catalytic converter/particulate filter.

10 Slacken the retaining clamps joining the catalytic converter to the turbocharger, and exhaust pipe. Take care not to damage the

flexible section of the front exhaust pipe (see illustration).

11 Slacken the clamp securing the catalytic converter to the turbocharger.

12 Undo the 2 nuts securing the catalytic converter to the cylinder block and manoeuvre it down and out of the engine compartment (see illustration).

13 If required, note its fitted position, then slacken the clamp and detach the particulate filter from the base of the catalytic converter (see illustration).

Catalytic converter – 2.0 litre SOHC engine

14 The catalytic converter is integral with the front section of the exhaust pipe. Undo the screws and remove the engine undershield.

15 Slacken the retaining clamps securing the front pipe to the manifold and intermediate pipe.

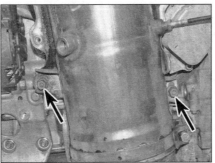

19.12 Catalytic converter/particulate filter retaining nuts (arrowed)

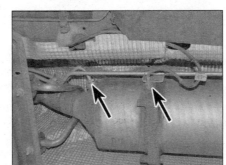

19.18a Front pressure take-off and temperature sensor (arrowed) . . .

16 Release the pipe from the rubber mountings and manoeuvre is from under the vehicle.

Catalytic converter/particulate filter – 2.0 litre DOHC engine

17 Disconnect the wiring connector from the particulate filter.

18 Mark or label the pressure pipes to aid refitting, then disconnect them at the connectors (see illustrations). Be prepared for fluid spillage.

19 Unscrew the temperature sensor from the assembly. Take care not to damage the sensor probe during removal.

20 Unscrew the assembly front and rear clamp bolts, and carefully lower it from the vehicle.

21 It is possible to separate the particle filter from the catalytic converter. With the assembly on a bench undo the four bolts/nuts and separate the two halves. Recover the gasket.

19.13 Undo the clamp (arrowed) and slide the particulate filter from the catalytic converter

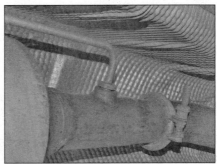

19.18b . . . rear pressure take-off

Pre-catalytic converter – 2.0 litre DOHC engine

22 The pre-catalyst removal procedure is described within the turbocharger removal procedure – see Section 18.

Intermediate pipe

23 Slacken the clamping ring bolts, and disengage both clamps from the flange joints.
24 Release the pipe from its mounting rubber and remove it from underneath the vehicle. Alternatively, undo the nuts/bolts securing the mountings to the vehicle body.

Tailpipe

25 Slacken the tailpipe clamping ring bolts, and disengage the clamp from the flange joint.
26 Unhook the tailpipe from its mounting rubbers, and remove it from the vehicle. Alternatively, undo the nuts/bolts securing the mountings to the vehicle body.

Complete system

27 Unscrew the front clamp ring bolt and release the catalytic converter or front pipe from the turbocharger. On models with a particulate filter, note their fitted positions, and disconnect the various pipes/sensors from the system. Free the system from its mounting rubbers and remove it from underneath the vehicle. Alternatively, undo the nuts/bolts securing the mountings to the vehicle body.

Heat shield(s)

28 The heat shields are secured to the underside of the body by various nuts and bolts. Each shield can be removed once the relevant exhaust section has been removed. If a shield is being removed to gain access to a component located behind it, it may prove sufficient in some cases to remove the retaining nuts and/or bolts, and simply lower the shield, without disturbing the exhaust system.

Refitting

29 Each section is refitted by reversing the removal sequence, noting the following points:
  a) *Ensure that all traces of corrosion have been removed from the flanges, and renew all necessary gaskets.*
  b) *Inspect the rubber mountings for signs of damage or deterioration, and renew as necessary.*
  c) *On joints secured together by a clamping ring, apply a smear of exhaust system jointing paste to the flange joint, to ensure a gas-tight seal. Tighten the clamping ring nuts evenly and progressively, so that the clearance between the clamp halves remains equal on either side.*
  d) *Prior to tightening the exhaust system fasteners, ensure that all rubber mountings are correctly located, and that there is adequate clearance between the exhaust system and vehicle underbody.*

Chapter 4 Part C:
Emission control systems

Contents

Degrees of difficulty

Easy, suitable for novice with little experience		**Fairly easy,** suitable for beginner with some experience		**Fairly difficult,** suitable for competent DIY mechanic		**Difficult,** suitable for experienced DIY mechanic		**Very difficult,** suitable for expert DIY or professional	

Specifications

Engine identification

Petrol engines

Indirect injection:
  Designation:
    1.8 litre EW7J4
    2.0 litre EW10J4
  Engine code:
    1.8 litre 6FZ
    2.0 litre . . . . RFN
Direct injection:
  Designation:
    2.0 litre EW10D
  Engine code . . . . RLZ

Diesel engines

1.6 litre:
  Designation. DV6TED4
  Engine codes . . . . 9HY or 9HZ
2.0 litre SOHC:
  Designation. . . . . DW10TD or DW10ATED
  Engine codes:
    DW10TD . . . . RHY
    DW10ATED . . . . RHZ
2.0 litre DOHC:
  Designation. DW10BTED4
  Engine code . . . . RHR

1 General information

All petrol engines use unleaded petrol and also have various other features built into the fuel system to help minimise harmful emissions. In addition, all engines are equipped with the crankcase emission control system described below. All engines are also equipped with a catalytic converter, exhaust gas recirculation system, and an evaporative emission control system. Some EW10J4 and EW7J4 petrol engines equipped to emission standard EEC2000 Depoll also utilise a secondary air injection system to quickly bring the catalytic converter up to normal working temperature.

All diesel engines are also designed to meet the strict emission requirements and are equipped with a crankcase emission control system and a catalytic converter. To further reduce exhaust emissions, all diesel engines are also fitted with an exhaust gas recirculation (EGR) system. Additionally, diesel models may be equipped with a particulate emission filter which uses porous silicon carbide substrate to trap particulates of carbon as the exhaust gases pass through.

The emission control systems function as follows.

Petrol engines

Crankcase emission control

To reduce the emission of unburned hydrocarbons from the crankcase into the atmosphere, the engine is sealed and the blow-by gases and oil vapour are drawn from inside the crankcase, through a wire mesh oil separator, into the inlet tract to be burned by the engine during normal combustion.

Under all conditions the gases are forced out of the crankcase by the (relatively) higher crankcase pressure; if the engine is worn, the raised crankcase pressure (due to increased blow-by) will cause some of the flow to return under all manifold conditions.

Exhaust emission control

To minimise the amount of pollutants which escape into the atmosphere, a catalytic converter is fitted in the exhaust system. On all models where a catalytic converter is fitted, the system is of the closed-loop type, in which lambda (oxygen) sensors in the exhaust system provides the fuel injection/ignition system ECM with constant feedback, enabling the ECM to adjust the mixture to provide the best possible conditions for the converter to operate.

The lambda sensors have a heating element built-in that is controlled by the ECM through the lambda sensor relay to quickly bring the sensor's tip to an efficient operating temperature. The sensor's tip is sensitive to oxygen and sends the ECM a varying voltage depending on the amount of oxygen in the exhaust gases; if the inlet air/fuel mixture is too rich, the exhaust gases are low in oxygen so the sensor sends a low-voltage signal, the voltage rising as the mixture weakens and the amount of oxygen rises in the exhaust gases.

Evaporative emission control

To minimise the escape into the atmosphere of unburned hydrocarbons, an evaporative emission control system is fitted to models equipped with a catalytic converter. The fuel tank filler cap is sealed and a charcoal canister is mounted behind the wheel arch liner under the left-hand side rear wing to collect the petrol vapours generated in the tank when the car is parked. It stores them until they can be cleared from the canister (under the control of the fuel-injection/ignition system ECM) via the purge valve into the inlet tract to be burned by the engine during normal combustion.

To ensure that the engine runs correctly when it is cold and/or idling and to protect the catalytic converter from the effects of an over-rich mixture, the purge control valve is not opened by the ECM until the engine has warmed-up, and the engine is under load; the valve solenoid is then modulated on and off to allow the stored vapour to pass into the inlet tract.

Secondary air injection

Some EW10J4 and EW7J4 petrol engines are also equipped with a secondary air injection system. This system is designed to reduce exhaust emissions in the period between first starting the engine and until the catalytic converter reaches operating (functioning) temperature. Introduction of air into the exhaust system during the initial start-up period creates an 'afterburner' effect which quickly increases the temperature in the exhaust system front pipe, thus bringing the catalytic converter up to normal operating temperatures very quickly.

The system consists of an air pump, mounted at the front left-hand side of the car, an air injection valve, mounted on a bracket at the front of the cylinder head, a connecting pipe linking the valve to the exhaust manifold, and interconnecting air hoses.

The system operates for between 10 and 45 seconds after engine start-up, depending on coolant temperature.

Exhaust gas recirculation system

Refer to the description for diesel engines.

Diesel models

Crankcase emission control

Refer to the description for petrol engines.

Exhaust emission control

To minimise the level of exhaust pollutants released into the atmosphere, a catalytic converter is fitted in the exhaust system of all models.

The catalytic converter consists of a canister containing a fine mesh impregnated with a catalyst material, over which the hot exhaust gases pass. The catalyst speeds up the oxidation of harmful carbon monoxide, unburnt hydrocarbons and soot, effectively reducing the quantity of harmful products released into the atmosphere via the exhaust gases.

Exhaust gas recirculation system

This system is designed to recirculate small quantities of exhaust gas into the inlet tract, and therefore into the combustion process. This process reduces the level of oxides of nitrogen present in the final exhaust gas which is released into the atmosphere.

The volume of exhaust gas recirculated is controlled by the system electronic control module.

A vacuum-operated valve is fitted to the exhaust manifold to regulate the quantity of exhaust gas recirculated. The valve is operated by the vacuum supplied by the solenoid valve.

Particulate filter system

The particulate filter is combined with the catalytic converter in the exhaust system, and its purpose it to trap particulates of carbon (soot) as the exhaust gases pass through, in order to comply with latest emission regulations.

The filter can be automatically regenerated (cleaned) by the system's ECM on-board the vehicle. The engine's high pressure injection system is utilised to inject fuel into the exhaust gases during the post-injection period; this causes the filter temperature to increase sufficiently to oxidise the particulates, leaving an ash residue. The regeneration period is automatically controlled by the on-board ECM, located to the left of the heater blower motor behind the facia. Subsequently, at the correct service interval the filter must be removed from the exhaust system, and renewed.

To assist the combustion of the trapped carbon (soot) during the regeneration process, a fuel additive (cerium-based Eolys) is automatically mixed with the diesel fuel in the fuel tank. The additive is stored in a 5 litre container attached to the bottom of the fuel tank, and the ECM regulates the amount of additive to send to the fuel tank by means of an additive injector located on the top of the fuel tank.

2 Emission control systems
– testing and component renewal

Petrol models

Crankcase emission control

1 The components of this system require no attention other than to check that the hose(s) are clear and undamaged at regular intervals.

Evaporative emission control

2 If the system is thought to be faulty, disconnect the hoses from the charcoal

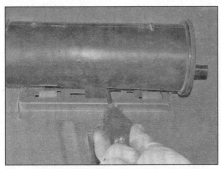

2.4 Depress the clip and slide the canister forwards

2.5 Depress the release button and disconnect the hoses

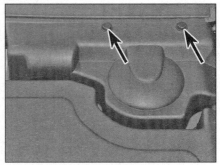

2.7 Prise up the centre pins a little (arrowed) and lever out the plastic expansion rivets

canister and purge control valve and check that they are clear by blowing through them. If the purge control valve or charcoal canister are thought to be faulty, they must be renewed.

Charcoal canister renewal

3 The charcoal canister is located under the rear wheel arch on the left-hand side. To gain access, slacken the left-hand rear roadwheel bolts, jack up the rear of the car and support it on axle stands. Remove the roadwheel, then remove the various fasteners and manoeuvre the wheel arch liner from place.

4 Depress the clip and slide the canister forwards from its mountings **(see illustration)**.

5 Identify the location of the two hoses then depress the quick-release button and disconnect the hoses from the canister **(see illustration)**.

6 Refitting is a reverse of the removal procedure ensuring that the hoses are correctly reconnected.

Purge valve renewal

7 The purge valve is located in the left-hand rear corner of the engine compartment. Prise up the centre pins, lever out the plastic expansion rivets and remove the plastic cover over the right-hand front suspension sphere **(see illustration)**.

8 Disconnect the wiring plug, and hoses, then ease the valve upwards from its rubber mounting **(see illustration)**.

9 Refitting is a reversal of removal.

Exhaust emission control

10 The performance of the catalytic converter can be checked only by measuring the exhaust gases using a good-quality, carefully-calibrated exhaust gas analyser.

11 If the CO level at the tailpipe is too high, the vehicle should be taken to a Citroën dealer or specialist so that the complete fuel injection and ignition systems, including the lambda sensor, can be thoroughly checked using the special diagnostic equipment. Once these have been checked and are known to be free from faults, the fault must be in the catalytic converter, which must be renewed as described in Part A of this Chapter.

Catalytic converter renewal

12 Refer to Part A of this Chapter.

Lambda (oxygen) sensor renewal

Note: *The lambda sensor is delicate and will not work if it is dropped or knocked, if its power supply is disrupted, or if any cleaning materials are used on it.*

13 Trace the wiring back from the lambda sensor(s), which are located before and after the catalytic converters. Disconnect both wiring connectors and free the wiring from any relevant retaining clips or ties. Note that the wiring may be clipped to the inside of the heat shield – undo the fasteners, lower the heat shield and unclip the wiring **(see illustration)**.

14 Unscrew the sensor from the exhaust system front pipe/pre-catalyser and remove it along with its sealing washer **(see illustration)**.

15 Refitting is a reverse of the removal procedure using a new sealing washer. Prior to installing the sensor apply a smear of high-temperature grease to the sensor threads. Ensure that the sensor is securely tightened and that the wiring is correctly routed and in no danger of contacting either the exhaust system or engine.

Testing secondary air injection

16 The components of this system require no attention other than to check that the hose(s) are clear and undamaged at regular intervals.

17 Accurate testing of the system operation entails the use of diagnostic test equipment and should be entrusted to a Citroën dealer or specialist.

Air pump renewal

18 The air pump is located at the front right-hand corner of the engine. Remove the air filter housing as described in Chapter 4A.

19 Slacken and remove the nuts and withdraw the pump from the mounting bracket.

20 Disconnect the air hoses and wiring connector and remove the pump.

21 Refitting is a reverse of the removal procedure, ensuring that the hoses are correctly reconnected.

Air injection valve renewal

22 Disconnect the battery (see Chapter 5A).

23 Slacken and remove the retaining screws, and remove the shroud from the top of the exhaust manifold.

24 Undo the two bolts securing the

2.8 The purge valve is located behind the engine compartment electrical box (arrowed)

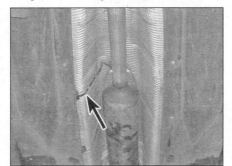

2.13 Post-catalyst lambda sensor (arrowed) – the wiring is clipped to the heat shield

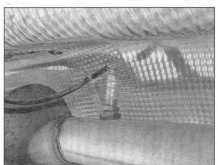

2.14 Unscrew the sensor from the exhaust pipe

2.25 Undo the two bolts and carefully remove the air injection valve from the cylinder head

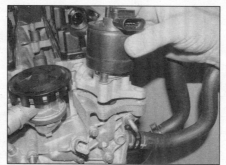

2.33a EGR valve – EW7J4 and EW10J4 engines

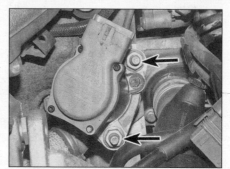

2.33b EGR valve mounting nuts (arrowed) – EW10D engines

connecting pipe flange to the exhaust manifold.

25 Undo the two bolts securing the valve mounting bracket to the cylinder head **(see illustration)**.

26 Withdraw the valve and connecting pipe, disconnect the air hose and remove the air injection valve and connecting pipe as an assembly.

27 If necessary, the air pipe can be removed from the valve and the valve removed from the mounting bracket after undoing the two retaining nuts. Collect the flange gasket after removal.

28 Refitting is a reverse of the removal procedure, but use a new gasket between the valve and mounting bracket.

Exhaust gas recirculation system

29 Testing of the system should ideally be entrusted to a Citroën dealer since a vacuum pump and vacuum gauges are required.

EGR valve renewal

30 The EGR valve is located on the front, left-hand side of the cylinder head. Remove the plastic cover from the top of the engine.

31 Disconnect the valve wiring plug.

32 Release the EGR valve-to-inlet manifold pipe clamp.

33 Undo the 2 nuts and pull the valve from place **(see illustrations)**. Recover the gasket.

34 Refitting is a reversal of removal, using a new gasket.

Diesel models

Crankcase emission control

35 The components of this system require no attention other than to check that the hose(s) are clear and undamaged at regular intervals.

Exhaust emission control

36 The performance of the catalytic converter can be checked only by measuring the exhaust gases using a good-quality, carefully-calibrated exhaust gas analyser.

37 If the catalytic converter is thought to be faulty, before assuming the catalytic converter is faulty, it is worth checking the problem is not due to a faulty injector(s). Refer to your Citroën dealer for further information.

Catalytic converter renewal

38 Refer to Part B of this Chapter.

Exhaust gas recirculation system

39 Testing of the system should ideally be entrusted to a Citroën dealer since a vacuum pump and vacuum gauge are required.

EGR valve renewal – 1.6 litre engine

40 Disconnect the battery negative lead as described in Chapter 5A.

41 Remove the air cleaner housing as described in Chapter 4B.

42 Release the clamps securing the EGR pipe to the EGR cooler, and the EGR cooler to the EGR valve **(see illustrations)**.

43 Disconnect the EGR valve wiring plug.

44 Undo the 2 EGR valve mounting bolts, move the EGR cooler to one side, and manoeuvre the valve from position **(see illustration)**. Recover the gasket/seal. If required, then CLIC-type clamps can be updated with normal worm-drive clips.

45 Refitting is a reversal of removal.

EGR valve renewal – 2.0 litre engines

46 Remove the plastic cover from the top of the engine. The EGR valve is located at the rear of the cylinder head.

47 Note their fitted positions, and disconnect the vacuum pipe(s)/wiring plugs from the EGR valve.

48 Slacken the collar/undo the retaining bolts securing the EGR valve to the EGR cooler.

49 Undo the nuts securing the EGR valve to the cylinder head, and lift the valve from position **(see illustration)**.

50 Refitting is a reversal of removal.

EGR heat exchanger (cooler) renewal

51 Fit hose clamps to the hoses connected to the EGR heat exchanger.

2.42a EGR cooler-to-valve clamp (arrowed) . . .

2.42b . . . EGR cooler-to-pipe clamp (arrowed)

2.44 EGR valve mounting bolts (arrowed – one hidden)

2.49 The EGR valve is secured by 2 screws to the cylinder head, and one Allen screw on its underside (arrowed)

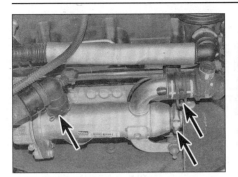
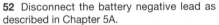

2.55 EGR heat exchanger pipe clamp and coolant hoses (arrowed)

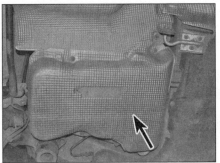
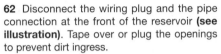

2.60 Remove the heat shield beneath the additive reservoir (arrowed)

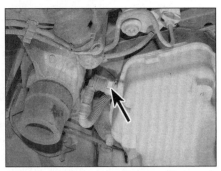

2.61 Depress the release button (arrowed) and disconnect the breather hose

52 Disconnect the battery negative lead as described in Chapter 5A.

53 Remove the air cleaner housing as described in Chapter 4B.

54 Remove the heat shield over the EGR pipe (where applicable).

55 Undo the 2 bolts securing the EGR pipe, and release the clamp securing the pipe to the EGR cooler (see illustration).

56 Release the clamps and disconnect the coolant hoses from the cooler, then undo the mounting bolts/nuts, remove the bracket, and manoeuvre it from place. On the 1.6 litre engine, undo the 2 bolts and remove the EGR valve along with the cooler.

57 Refitting is a reversal of removal.

Fuel additive system (vehicles equipped with particle filter)

58 It is possible to check the fuel additive system. However, this should be made by a Citroën dealer or suitably-equipped specialist due to the requirement for specialised diagnostic test equipment. A fuel cap presence sensor is fitted to the fuel filler neck, which informs the ECM when the filler cap is removed, to enable it to calculate the amount of fuel added so that the correct amount of additive can be injected. A permanent magnet is fitted to the filler cap, which changes the resistance of the sensor when it's fitted. Bear this in mind should a filler cap be lost and a temporary replacement considered.

Fuel additive reservoir renewal

Note: *Ideally, the additive reservoir should be empty before removing it, otherwise take precautions against spillage.*

 Warning: Wear protective gloves and eye protection when handling the reservoir.

59 To remove the fuel additive reservoir, chock the front wheels then jack up the rear of the vehicle and support on axle stands (see *Jacking and vehicle support*). The reservoir is attached to the left-hand side of the fuel tank.

60 Undo the fasteners and remove the heat shield from beneath the reservoir (see illustration).

61 Disconnect the breather pipe at the connection to the left of the reservoir (see illustration).

62 Disconnect the wiring plug and the pipe connection at the front of the reservoir (see illustration). Tape over or plug the openings to prevent dirt ingress.

63 Undo the mounting bolt, release the retaining clip and slide the reservoir to the left-hand side and remove it (see illustration).

64 Refitting is a reversal of removal.

65 Have the reservoir refilled by a Citroën dealer or suitably equipped specialist.

Particulate filter

66 Renewal of the particulate filter is described in part B of this Chapter.

Pressure differential sensor

67 This sensor measures the pressure at the entrance and exit of the particulate filter, and is located in the engine compartment (see illustrations).

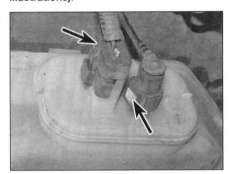

2.62 Unclip the wiring plug and depress the hose release button (arrowed)

2.67a The pressure differential sensor is located at the top, right-hand corner of the radiator – 1.6 litre models

68 Note their fitted positions, then disconnect the rubber hoses and wiring plug from the sensor.

69 Undo the mounting bolts and remove the sensor.

3 Catalytic converter – general information and precautions

1 The catalytic converter is a reliable and simple device which needs no maintenance in itself, but there are some facts of which an owner should be aware if the converter is to function properly for its full service life.

Petrol models

a) *DO NOT use leaded petrol in a car equipped with a catalytic converter – the*

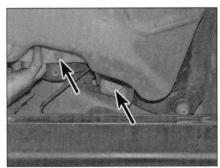

2.63 Release the clip, undo the bolt and slide the reservoir to the left (arrowed)

2.67b On 2.0 litre models, the pressure differential sensor is located at the engine compartment bulkhead

lead will coat the precious metals, and will eventually destroy the converter.

b) Always keep the ignition and fuel systems well-maintained to the service schedule.

c) If the engine develops a misfire, do not drive the car at all (or at least as little as possible) until the fault is cured.

d) DO NOT push- or tow-start the car – this will soak the catalytic converter in unburned fuel, causing it to overheat when the engine does start.

e) DO NOT switch off the ignition at high engine speeds.

f) DO NOT use fuel or engine oil additives – these may contain substances harmful to the catalytic converter.

g) DO NOT continue to use the car if the engine burns oil to the extent of leaving a visible trail of blue smoke.

h) Remember that the catalytic converter operates at very high temperatures. DO NOT, therefore, park the car in dry undergrowth, over long grass or piles of dead leaves after a long run.

i) Remember that the catalytic converter is FRAGILE – do not strike it with tools.

j) In some cases a sulphurous smell (like that of rotten eggs) may be noticed from the exhaust. This is common to many catalytic converter-equipped cars and once the car has covered a few thousand miles the problem should disappear.

k) If the converter is no longer effective it must be renewed.

Diesel models

2 Refer to parts f, g, h and i of the petrol models information given above.

Chapter 5 Part A:
Starting and charging systems

Contents

Degrees of difficulty

Easy, suitable for novice with little experience	**Fairly easy,** suitable for beginner with some experience	**Fairly difficult,** suitable for competent DIY mechanic	**Difficult,** suitable for experienced DIY mechanic	**Very difficult,** suitable for expert DIY or professional

Specifications

Engine identification

Petrol engines

Indirect injection:
  Designation:
    1.8 litre EW7J4
    2.0 litre EW10J4
  Engine code:
    1.8 litre 6FZ
    2.0 litre .... RFN
Direct injection:
  Designation:
    2.0 litre EW10D
  Engine code .... RLZ

Diesel engines

1.6 litre:
  Designation... DV6TED4
  Engine codes .... 9HY or 9HZ
2.0 litre SOHC:
  Designation... DW10TD or DW10ATED
  Engine codes:
    DW10TD.. RHY
    DW10ATED... RHZ
2.0 litre DOHC:
  Designation... DW10BTED4
  Engine code .... RHR

System type.. 12 volt, negative earth

Battery

Type .... Low maintenance or 'maintenance-free' sealed for life
Charge condition:
  Poor .... 12.5 volts
  Normal .... 12.6 volts
  Good .... 12.7 volts

Alternator

Type . . . . Denso, Bosch, Magneti Marelli or Valeo or Mitsubishi (depending on model)

Rating:
1.8 litre petrol engine . . . . 80, 90 or 120 amp
2.0 litre petrol engine . . . . 120 or 150 amp
Diesel engines . . . . 150 or 180 amp

Starter motor

Type . . . . Mitsubishi, Valeo, Denso, Paris-Rhone, or Bosch (depending on model)

Preheating system

Preheating period at ambient temperatures of (approximate values):
-30°C . . . . 20 seconds
-10°C . . . . 5 seconds
0°C . . . . 0.5 seconds
18°C . . . . 0 seconds

Post-heating system

Post-heating period at ambient temperatures of (approximate values):
-30°C . . . . 3 minutes
-10°C . . . . 3 minutes
0°C . . . . 1 minute
18° . . . . 30 seconds
40° . . . . 0 seconds

Torque wrench settings

	Nm	lbf ft
Alternator mounting bolts	40	30
Auxiliary drivebelt eccentric tensioner (2.0 litre SOHC diesel engine)	43	31
Glow plugs:		
1.6 litre engine	10	7
2.0 litre engines	22	16
Oil pressure switch	30	22
Starter motor:		
1.6 litre diesel engine	20	15
All other engines	35	26

1 General information and precautions

General information

The engine electrical system consists mainly of the charging and starting systems. Because of their engine-related functions, these components are covered separately from the body electrical devices such as the lights, instruments, etc (which are covered in Chapter 12). On petrol engine models refer to Part B for information on the ignition system.

The electrical system is of the 12 volt negative earth type.

The battery is of the low maintenance or 'maintenance-free' (sealed for life) type and is charged by the alternator, which is belt-driven from the crankshaft pulley.

The starter motor is of the pre-engaged type incorporating an integral solenoid. On starting, the solenoid moves the drive pinion into engagement with the flywheel ring gear before the starter motor is energised. Once the engine has started, a one-way clutch prevents the motor armature being driven by the engine until the pinion disengages from the flywheel.

Precautions

Further details of the various systems are given in the relevant Sections of this Chapter. While some repair procedures are given, the usual course of action is to renew the component concerned.

It is necessary to take extra care when working on the electrical system to avoid damage to semi-conductor devices (diodes and transistors), and to avoid the risk of personal injury. In addition to the precautions given in *Safety first!* at the beginning of this manual, observe the following when working on the system:

• Always remove rings, watches, etc, before working on the electrical system. Even with the battery disconnected, capacitive discharge could occur if a component's live terminal is earthed through a metal object. This could cause a shock or nasty burn.

• Do not reverse the battery connections. Components such as the alternator, electronic control units, or any other components having semi-conductor circuitry could be irreparably damaged.

• If the engine is being started using jump leads and a slave battery, connect the batteries positive-to-positive and negative-to-negative (see *Jump starting*). This also applies when connecting a battery charger.

• Never disconnect the battery terminals, the alternator, any electrical wiring or any test instruments when the engine is running.

• Do not allow the engine to turn the alternator when the alternator is not connected.

• Never 'test' for alternator output by 'flashing' the output lead to earth.

• Never use an ohmmeter of the type incorporating a hand-cranked generator for circuit or continuity testing.

• Always ensure that the battery negative lead is disconnected when working on the electrical system.

• Before using electric-arc welding equipment on the car, disconnect the battery, alternator and components such as the fuel injection/ignition electronic control module to protect them from the risk of damage.

2 Electrical fault finding – general information

Refer to Chapter 12.

3 Battery –
testing and charging

Testing

Standard and low maintenance battery

1 If the vehicle covers a small annual mileage, it is worthwhile checking the specific gravity of the electrolyte every three months to determine the state of charge of the battery. Use a hydrometer to make the check and compare the results with the following table. Note that the specific gravity readings assume an electrolyte temperature of 15°C; for every 10°C below 15°C subtract 0.007. For every 10°C above 15°C add 0.007.

	Ambient temperature	
	Above 25°C	Below 25°C
Fully-charged	1.210 to 1.230	1.270 to 1.290
70% charged	1.170 to 1.190	1.230 to 1.250
Discharged	1.050 to 1.070	1.110 to 1.130

2 If the battery condition is suspect, first check the specific gravity of electrolyte in each cell. A variation of 0.040 or more between any cells indicates loss of electrolyte or deterioration of the internal plates.

3 If the specific gravity variation is 0.040 or more, the battery should be renewed. If the cell variation is satisfactory but the battery is discharged, it should be charged as described later in this Section.

Maintenance-free battery

4 In cases where a 'sealed for life' maintenance-free battery is fitted, topping-up and testing of the electrolyte in each cell is not possible. The condition of the battery can therefore only be tested using a battery condition indicator or a voltmeter.

5 Certain models may be fitted with a 'Delco' type maintenance-free battery, with a built-in charge condition indicator. The indicator is located in the top of the battery casing, and indicates the condition of the battery from its colour. If the indicator shows green, then the battery is in a good state of charge. If the indicator shows black, then the battery requires charging, as described later in this Section. If the indicator shows blue, then the electrolyte level in the battery is too low to allow further use, and the battery should be renewed.

Caution: Do not attempt to charge, load or jump start a battery when the indicator shows clear/yellow.

All battery tyres

6 If testing the battery using a voltmeter, connect the voltmeter across the battery and compare the result with those given in the Specifications under 'charge condition'. The test is only accurate if the battery has not been subjected to any kind of charge for the previous six hours. If this is not the case, switch on the headlights for 30 seconds, then

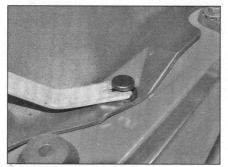

4.3a Prise up the centre pin and remove the plastic rivet from the battery cover . . .

wait four to five minutes before testing the battery after switching off the headlights. All other electrical circuits must be switched off, so check that the doors, boot and/or tailgate are fully shut when making the test.

7 If the voltage reading is less than 12.2 volts, then the battery is discharged, whilst a reading of 12.2 to 12.4 volts indicates a partially discharged condition.

8 If the battery is to be charged, remove it from the vehicle (Section 4) and charge it as described later in this Section.

Charging

Note: *The following is intended as a guide only. Always refer to the manufacturer's recommendations (often printed on a label attached to the battery) before charging a battery.*

Standard and low maintenance battery

9 Charge the battery at a rate of 3.5 to 4 amps and continue to charge the battery at this rate until no further rise in specific gravity is noted over a four hour period.

10 Alternatively, a trickle charger charging at the rate of 1.5 amps can safely be used overnight.

11 Specially rapid 'boost' charges which are claimed to restore the power of the battery in 1 to 2 hours are not recommended, as they can cause serious damage to the battery plates through overheating.

12 While charging the battery, note that the temperature of the electrolyte should never exceed 38°C.

Maintenance-free battery

13 This battery type takes considerably longer to fully recharge than the standard type, the time taken being dependent on the extent of discharge, but it can take anything up to three days.

14 A constant voltage type charger is required to be set, when connected, to 13.9 to 14.9 volts with a charger current below 25 amps. Using this method, the battery should be usable within three hours, giving a voltage reading of 12.5 volts, but this is for a partially-discharged battery and, as mentioned, full-charging can take considerably longer.

15 If the battery is to be charged from a fully

4.3b . . . then release the clips and remove the cover

discharged state (condition reading less than 12.2 volts), have it recharged by your Citroën dealer or local automotive electrician, as the charge rate is higher and constant supervision during charging is necessary.

4 Battery –
removal and refitting

Note: *The audio unit fitted as standard equipment by Citroën may be equipped with an anti-theft system, to deter thieves. If the power source is disconnected, the audio unit may need the security code re-entering upon battery reconnection. Check in the Owners Handbook, or with your local dealer.*

Note: *Prior to disconnecting the battery, wait at least 15 minutes after switching off the ignition to guarantee the ECM initialisations are stored.*

Removal

1 Prior to disconnecting the battery, close all windows and the sunroof, and ensure that the vehicle alarm system is deactivated (see Owners Handbook).

2 The battery is located on the left-hand side of the engine compartment.

3 Prise up the centre pin followed by the plastic rivet, then release the clips and remove the cover from the battery (see illustrations).

4 Lift the clamp arm and lift the negative (-) clamp from the battery terminal (see illustration).

4.4 Lift up the arm and disconnect the battery negative clamp . . .

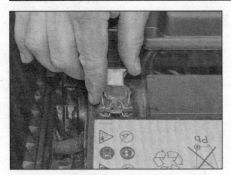

4.5 . . . followed by the positive clamp

5 Disconnect the positive (+) terminal clamp in the same way **(see illustration)**.

6 Unscrew the bolt 90° and slide back the battery retaining clamp **(see illustration)**.

7 Lift the battery out of the engine compartment.

8 Te remove the battery tray, remove the air cleaner assembly (Chapter 4A or 4B) (only applies to models where the air cleaner assembly is adjacent to the battery), then undo the 3 bolts and remove the battery tray **(see illustration)**. Release any wiring harness clips as the tray is removed.

9 Carefully move aside all cables and hoses, then lift the battery box out of the engine compartment.

Refitting

10 Refitting is a reversal of removal, but smear petroleum jelly on the terminals after reconnecting the leads, and always reconnect the positive lead first, and the negative lead last.

11 With the battery reconnected, switch on the ignition and wait at least 1 minute before starting the engine. This will allow the vehicle electronic systems and control units to stabilise.

12 After reconnecting the battery, it may be necessary to carry out the following re-initialisation/reset procedures:

a) *Lock, then unlock the tailgate (Estate models).*
b) *Reprogramme the 'overspeed' control settings (Owners Handbook).*
c) *Lower the electric windows completely, then fully raise them – perform this on each window in turn.*
d) *Re-initialise the sunroof: Press the switch to place the sunroof in the 'maximum tilt' position (keep the switch pressed for at least one second after the movement is completed). Release the switch, then press the switch again within 5 seconds (keep the switch pressed until the movement is completed).*
e) *Reset the multifunction screen display language.*

5 Charging system – testing

Note: *Refer to the warnings given in 'Safety first!' and in Section 1 of this Chapter before starting work.*

1 If the ignition warning light fails to illuminate when the ignition is switched on, first check the alternator wiring connections for security. If satisfactory, check that the warning light bulb has not blown, and that the bulbholder is secure in its location in the instrument panel. If the light still fails to illuminate, check the continuity of the warning light feed wire from the alternator to the bulbholder. If all is satisfactory, the alternator is at fault and should be renewed or taken to an auto-electrician for testing and repair.

2 If the ignition warning light illuminates when the engine is running, stop the engine and check that the drivebelt is correctly fitted and tensioned (see Section 6) and that the alternator connections are secure. If all is so far satisfactory, have the alternator checked by an auto-electrician for testing and repair.

3 If the alternator output is suspect even though the warning light functions correctly, the regulated voltage may be checked as follows.

4 Connect a voltmeter across the battery terminals and start the engine.

5 Increase the engine speed until the voltmeter reading remains steady; the reading should be approximately 12 to 13 volts, and no more than 14 volts.

6 Switch on as many electrical accessories (eg, the headlights, heated rear window and heater blower) as possible, and check that the alternator maintains the regulated voltage at around 13 to 14 volts.

7 If the regulated voltage is not as stated, the fault may be due to worn brushes, weak brush springs, a faulty voltage regulator, a faulty diode, a severed phase winding, or worn or damaged slip-rings. The brushes and slip-rings may be checked (see Section 8), but if the fault persists, the alternator should be taken to an auto-electrician for testing and repair, or else renewed.

6 Auxiliary drivebelt – renewal

Renewal

1 Chock the rear wheels, raise the front of the vehicle and support it securely on axle stands (see *Jacking and vehicle support*). Remove the right-hand front roadwheel.

2 Undo the fasteners and remove the right-hand front wheel arch liner **(see illustrations)**. Note the rear of the liner is retained by an expanding plastic river, accessible once the mudlfap (where fitted) has been removed. If the belt is to be refitted, mark its direction of normal rotation with a pen.

Petrol engines

3 Using a spanner on the centre nut/bolt, rotate the tensioner pulley anti-clockwise, and detension the belt **(see illustration)**.

4.6 Rotate the bolt 90° anti-clockwise to retract the battery clamp

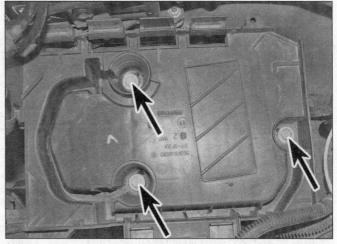

4.8 Undo the 3 bolts (arrowed) and remove the battery tray

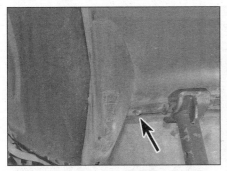

6.2a Remove the front mudflap (fastener arrowed) to access the liner fasteners

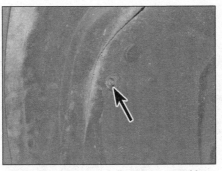

6.2b The wheel arch liner is secured by plastic nuts (arrowed) . . .

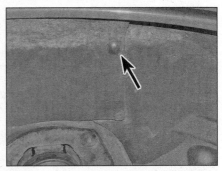

6.2c . . . plastic push-in clips (arrowed) . . .

4 Manoeuvre the belt from the pulleys. Take the opportunity to check the tensioner and idler pulleys spin freely, with no signs of roughness or slack.

5 Begin refitting by placing the belt on the pulleys, ensuring it's correctly located in grooves of the pulleys. Rotate the tensioner anti-clockwise again, and feed the belt under the tensioner pulley **(see illustrations)**.

6 Slowly allow the tensioner pulley to rotate clockwise, and act against the belt.

7 Refit the wheel arch liner and roadwheel, then lower the vehicle to the ground.

1.6 litre diesel engine

8 Using a spanner on the centre bolt, rotate the tensioner pulley clockwise, and detension the belt **(see illustration)**.

9 Lock the tensioner in this position using

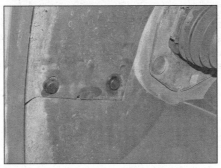

6.2d . . . and plastic rivets (prise up the centre pins)

a 4.0 mm drill bit through the holes in the tensioner **(see illustration)**.

10 Manoeuvre the belt from the pulleys.

6.3 Using a spanner on the centre bolt (arrowed) rotate the tensioner anti-clockwise

Take the opportunity to check the tensioner and idler pulleys spin freely, with no signs of roughness or slack.

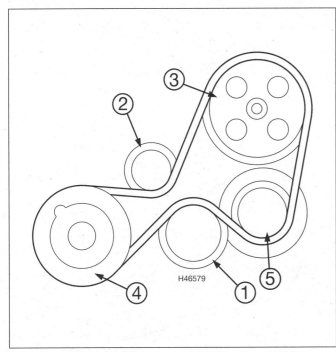

6.5a Belt routing – petrol models without air conditioning

1 Idler pulley
2 Tensioner pulley
3 Power steering pump pulley
4 Crankshaft pulley
5 Alternator pulley

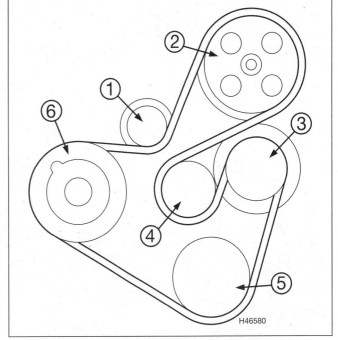

6.5b Belt routing – petrol model with air conditioning

1 Tensioner pulley
2 Power steering pump pulley
3 Alternator pulley
4 Idler pulley
5 Air conditioning compressor pulley
6 Crankshaft pulley

6.8 Rotate the tensioner clockwise with a spanner on the centre bolt (arrowed – shown with the belt removed for clarity)

6.9 Insert a 4.0 mm drill bit/rod through the holes in the tensioner (arrowed)

11 Begin refitting by placing the belt on the pulleys, ensuring it's correctly located in grooves of the pulleys (see illustrations).

12 Hold the tensioner in place with the spanner, remove the locking drill bit, and slowly allow the tensioner pulley to rotate anti-clockwise and act against the belt.

13 Refit the wheel arch liner and roadwheel, then lower the vehicle to the ground.

2.0 litre SOHC diesel engine

14 Using a suitable spanner on the stud/bolt in the centre of the automatic tensioner pulley, move the pulley anti-clockwise to detension the belt, then slip the belt from the pulleys. Take the opportunity to check the tensioner and idler pulleys spin freely, with no signs of roughness or slack.

15 Using a spanner, rotate the automatic tensioner pulley anti-clockwise until the hole in the pulley arm is aligned with the hole in the mounting bracket behind. When the holes are aligned, slide a suitable locking tool (a bolt or cranked length of bar of approximately 4.0 mm diameter) through the holes (see illustration).

16 Slacken the bolt located in the centre of the eccentric tensioner pulley (see illustration).

17 If the belt is being renewed, ensure the correct type is used. Fit the belt around the pulleys, ensuring that the ribs on the belt are engaging correctly with the grooves in the pulleys, and the belt is correctly routed (see illustrations).

18 Turn the eccentric tensioner pulley to apply tension to the belt, until the load is

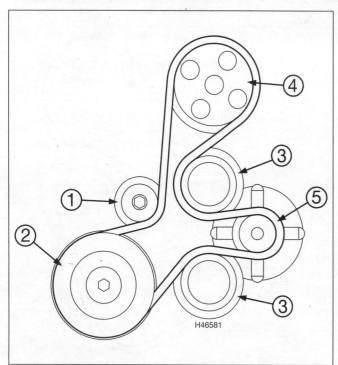

6.11a Belt routing – 1.6 litre diesel models without air conditioning

1	Tensioner pulley bolt	4	Power steering pump
2	Crankshaft pulley		pulley
3	Idler pulleys	5	Alternator pulley

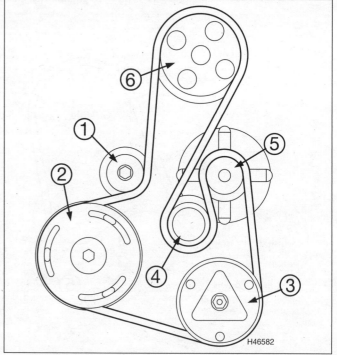

6.11b Belt routing – 1.6 litre diesel models with air conditioning

1	Tensioner pulley bolt	4	Idler pulley
2	Crankshaft pulley	5	Alternator pulley
3	Air conditioning	6	Power steering pump
	compressor pulley		pulley

6.15 Align the hole (arrowed) and insert the locking tool

6.16 Slacken the eccentric tensioner pulley retaining bolt (arrowed)

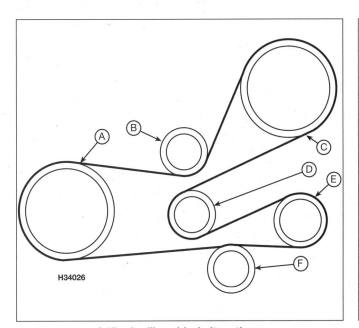

**6.17a Auxiliary drivebelt routing –
2.0 litre SOHC diesel without air conditioning**

A Crankshaft pulley
B Automatic tensioner pulley
C Power steering pump pulley
D Eccentric tensioner pulley
E Alternator pulley
F Idler pulley

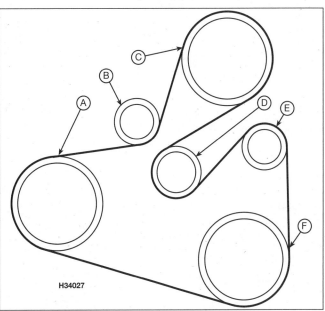

**6.17b Auxiliary drivebelt routing –
2.0 litre SOHC diesel with air conditioning**

A Crankshaft pulley
B Automatic tensioner pulley
C Power steering pump
  pulley
D Eccentric tensioner pulley
E Alternator pulley
F Air conditioning
  compressor pulley

released from the locking tool in the automatic tensioner. Without altering the position of the eccentric tensioner pulley, tighten its retaining bolt to the specified torque.

19 Remove the locking tool from the automatic tensioner, then rotate the crankshaft through 4 complete revolutions clockwise.

20 Check that the holes in the automatic tensioner and the bracket are still aligned, and that it's now possible to insert a 2.0 mm diameter setting tool through both holes. If the setting tool will not slide in easily, slacken the eccentric tensioner pulley retaining bolt and repeat the entire tensioning procedure.

21 Refit the wheel arch liner and roadwheel, then lower the vehicle to the ground.

2.0 litre DOHC diesel engine

22 Using a spanner on the centre bolt, rotate the tensioner pulley anti-clockwise, and detension the belt **(see illustration)**.

23 Lock the tensioner in this position using a 4.0 mm drill bit through the holes in the tensioner pulley **(see illustration)**.

24 Manoeuvre the belt from the pulleys. Take the opportunity to check the tensioner pulley spins freely, with no signs of roughness or slack.

25 Begin refitting by placing the belt on the

6.22 Use a spanner (arrowed) on the centre bolt to rotate the tensioner pulley anti-clockwise . . .

6.23 . . . then insert a 4.0 mm drill bit/rod through the aligned holes (arrowed)

pulleys, ensuring it's correctly located in the grooves of the pulleys **(see illustration)**.
26 Hold the tensioner in place with the spanner, remove the locking drill bit, and slowly allow the tensioner to rotate and act upon the belt.
27 Refit the wheel arch liner and roadwheel, then lower the vehicle to the ground.

7 Alternator – removal and refitting

Removal

1 Disconnect the battery positive lead (see Section 4).
2 Raise the front of the vehicle and support it securely on axle stands (see *Jacking and vehicle support*). Remove the auxiliary drivebelt as described in Section 6.

7.3 Prise out the rubber cover (arrowed), unscrew the nut, then disconnect the wiring plug (arrowed)

7.10 Alternator mounting bolts (arrowed)

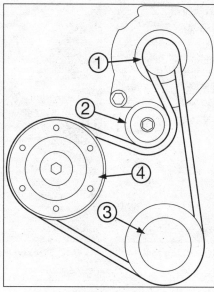

6.25 Belt routing – 2.0 litre DOHC diesel engine

1 *Alternator pulley*
2 *Tensioner centre bolt*
3 *Air conditioning compressor pulley*
4 *Crankshaft pulley*

1.6 litre diesel engine – without air conditioning

3 Remove the rubber cover from the alternator terminal, then unscrew the retaining nut and disconnect the wiring from the rear of the alternator **(see illustration)**. Release the harness from any retaining clips.

7.9 Unscrew the guide roller screw and upper alternator mounting bolt (arrowed)

7.12 Prise out the rubber cover and disconnect the alternator wiring (arrowed)

4 Remove the oil level dipstick, then prise out the centre caps and undo the bolts securing the two guide rollers adjacent to the alternator.
5 Unscrew the three alternator mounting bolts, and manoeuvre the alternator from position.
6 Manoeuvre the alternator away from its mounting brackets and out from the engine compartment.

1.6 litre diesel engine – with air conditioning

7 Disconnect the compressor wiring plug, then undo the mounting bolts and move the compressor to one side. Suspend the compressor from the vehicle bodywork using wire/string etc. Do not disconnect the refrigerant pipes.
8 Remove the rubber cover from the alternator terminal, then unscrew the retaining nut and disconnect the wiring from the rear of the alternator **(see illustration 7.3)**. Release the harness from any retaining clips.
9 Remove the oil level dipstick, prise out the centre cap (where fitted) and undo the bolts securing the lower guide roller/alternator mounting **(see illustration)**.
10 Undo the remaining alternator securing bolts **(see illustration)**, and manoeuvre the alternator from position.
11 Manoeuvre the alternator away from its mounting brackets and out from the engine compartment.

All other engines

12 Remove the rubber covers (where fitted) from the alternator terminals, then unscrew the retaining nuts and disconnect the wiring from the rear of the alternator **(see illustration)**. Prise out the retaining clip to release the wiring harness routed around the left-hand end of the alternator.
13 On 2.0 litre DOHC diesel engines, disconnect the fuel supply and return pipes, then undo the fasteners and move the fuel filter and mounting bracket assembly to one side. Plug or cover the openings to prevent contamination.
14 Unscrew the lower nut(s) and/or mounting bolt(s). Note that, where a long through-bolt is used to secure the alternator in position, the bolt does not need to be fully removed; the alternator can be disengaged from the bolt once it has been slackened sufficiently. On some models, it may be necessary to remove the drivebelt idler/tensioner pulley to gain access to the alternator mounting nuts and bolts (depending on specification). On 2.0 litre diesel models without air conditioning, the lower front mounting bolt also carries the auxiliary drivebelt idler pulley **(see illustrations)**.
15 Manoeuvre the alternator away from its mounting brackets and out from the engine compartment.

Refitting

16 Refitting is a reversal of removal,

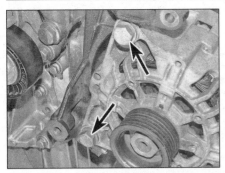

7.14a Alternator mounting bolts (arrowed)

7.14b The rear bolt acts as a centraliser

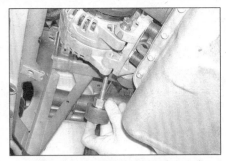

7.14c On some 2.0 litre diesel models, the lower mounting bolt also carrier the auxiliary drivebelt pulley

8.2 Undo the screws/nuts and remove the cover from the alternator (arrowed)

8.4 Undo the screws and remove the regulator/brush holder (arrowed)

tensioning the auxiliary drivebelt as described in Section 6, and ensuring that the alternator mountings are securely tightened. Note that the bolt that acts as a centraliser and should be tightened first.

8 Alternator brushes, regulator and drive pulley – inspection and renewal

Brushes and regulator

1 Remove the alternator as described in Section 1.

2 Unscrew the nuts/screws securing the cover to the rear of the alternator (see illustration).

3 Using a screwdriver, lever off the cover, and remove it from the rear of the alternator.

4 Unscrew and remove the three retaining screws, and remove the regulator/brush holder from the rear of the alternator (see illustration).

5 Check the brushes for excessive wear and damage. No specifications for brush length are given by Citroën. If the brushes are suspect, renew them along with the regulator as a complete assembly.

6 If the brushes are in good condition, clean them and check that they move freely in their holders.

7 Wipe clean the alternator slip-rings, and check them for signs of scoring or burning (see illustration). It may be possible to have the slip-rings renovated by an electrical specialist.

8 Use a paper clip to restrain the brushes, then refit the regulator/brush holder assembly and securely tighten the retaining screws (see illustration).

9 Refit the cover, then insert and tighten the retaining screws/nuts.

10 Refit the alternator with reference to Section 7.

Drive pulley

11 On diesel models, the alternator drive pulley is fitted with a one-way clutch to reduced wear and stress on the auxiliary drivebelt. In order to remove the pulley, a special tool will be required to hold the alternator shaft whilst unscrewing the pulley. This tool should be available from auto electrical specialists/automotive tool specialists.

12 Prise the plastic cap from the pulley.

13 Insert the special tool into the splines of the pulley, engaging the central Torx bit with the alternator shaft (see illustrations).

8.7 Check the condition of the alternator slip-rings

8.8 Use a screwdriver to push back the brushes against the springs, then insert a paper clip as shown to hold them in place (arrowed)

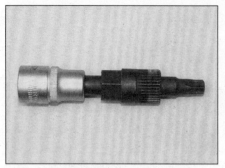

8.13a A special tool is required to remove the alternator pulley

8.13b Insert the central Torx bit into the end of the alternator shaft, unscrew the pulley . . .

8.13c . . . and remove it from the shaft

Unscrew the pulley anti-clockwise whilst holding the shaft with the Torx bit, and remove the pulley.

14 Fit the pulley to the alternator shaft, and tighten it securely using the special tool.

9 Starting system – testing

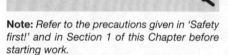

Note: *Refer to the precautions given in 'Safety first!' and in Section 1 of this Chapter before starting work.*

1 If the starter motor fails to operate when the ignition key is turned to the appropriate position, the following possible causes may be to blame.

a) *The engine immobiliser is faulty.*
b) *The battery is faulty.*
c) *The electrical connections between the switch, solenoid, battery and starter motor are somewhere failing to pass the necessary current from the battery through the starter to earth.*
d) *The solenoid is faulty.*
e) *The starter motor is mechanically or electrically defective.*

2 To check the battery, switch on the headlights. If they dim after a few seconds, this indicates that the battery is discharged – recharge (see Section 3) or renew the battery. If the headlights glow brightly, operate the ignition switch and observe the lights. If they dim, then this indicates that current is reaching the starter motor, therefore the fault must lie in the starter motor. If the lights continue to glow

brightly (and no clicking sound can be heard from the starter motor solenoid), this indicates that there is a fault in the circuit or solenoid – see following paragraphs. If the starter motor turns slowly when operated, but the battery is in good condition, then this indicates that either the starter motor is faulty, or there is considerable resistance somewhere in the circuit.

3 If a fault in the circuit is suspected, disconnect the battery leads (including the earth connection to the body), the starter/solenoid wiring and the engine/transmission earth strap – located on the top of the transmission housing **(see illustration)**. Thoroughly clean the connections, and reconnect the leads and wiring, then use a voltmeter or test lamp to check that full battery voltage is available at the battery positive lead connection to the solenoid, and that the earth is sound. Smear petroleum jelly around the battery terminals to prevent corrosion – corroded connections are amongst the most frequent causes of electrical system faults.

4 If the battery and all connections are in good condition, check the circuit by disconnecting the wire from the solenoid blade terminal. Connect a voltmeter or test lamp between the wire end and a good earth (such as the battery negative terminal), and check that the wire is live when the ignition switch is turned to the 'start' position. If it is, then the circuit is sound – if not the circuit wiring can be checked as described in Chapter 12.

5 The solenoid contacts can be checked by connecting a voltmeter or test lamp between

the battery positive feed connection on the starter side of the solenoid, and earth. When the ignition switch is turned to the 'start' position, there should be a reading or lighted bulb, as applicable. If there is no reading or lighted bulb, the solenoid is faulty and should be renewed.

6 If the circuit and solenoid are proved sound, the fault must lie in the starter motor. In this event, it may be possible to have the starter motor overhauled by a specialist, but check on the cost of spares before proceeding, as it may prove more economical to obtain a new or exchange motor.

10 Starter motor – removal and refitting

Removal

1 Disconnect the battery (see Section 4), and remove the plastic cover from the top of the engine (where fitted).

2 So that access to the motor can be gained both from above and below, chock the rear wheels then jack up the front of the vehicle and support it on axle stands (see *Jacking and vehicle support*). Release the screws and remove the engine undershield (where fitted).

3 On 1.6 litre diesel engines, remove the air inlet ducting from the left-hand rear of the engine compartment. Undo the bolt and move aside the vacuum reservoir at the rear of the cylinder block **(see illustration)**.

4 On petrol and 2.0 litre diesel models, remove the air cleaner assembly (see Chapter 4A or 4B).

5 On some models, the clutch slave cylinder obstructs the lower starter motor bolt. So where necessary undo the bolts and move aside the clutch slave cylinder, without disconnecting the fluid pipe **(see illustration)**.

6 Slacken and remove the two retaining nuts and disconnect the wiring from the starter motor solenoid. Recover the washers under the nuts. Release the wiring loom from any retaining clips **(see illustration)**.

7 Undo the three mounting bolts (two at the rear of the motor, and one which comes through from the top of the transmission

9.3 Check the earth strap on the top of the transmission (arrowed)

10.3 Vacuum reservoir retaining bolt (arrowed) – 1.6 litre diesel engines

10.5 The clutch slave cylinder obstructs the starter motor lower bolt (arrowed)

10.6 Disconnect the starter motor wiring (arrowed)

housing), supporting the motor as the bolts are withdrawn. Recover the washers from under the bolt heads and note the locations of any wiring or hose brackets secured by the bolts.

8 Manoeuvre the starter motor out from underneath the engine and recover the locating dowel(s) from the engine/transmission (as applicable).

Refitting

9 Refitting is a reversal of removal, ensuring that the locating dowel(s) are correctly positioned. Also make sure that any wiring or hose brackets are in place under the bolt heads as noted prior to removal.

11 Starter motor –
testing and overhaul

If the starter motor is thought to be suspect, it should be removed from the vehicle and taken to an auto-electrician for testing. Most auto-electricians will be able to supply and fit brushes at a reasonable cost. However, check on the cost of repairs before proceeding as it may prove more economical to obtain a new or exchange motor.

12 Ignition switch –
removal and refitting

The ignition switch is integral with the steering column lock, and can be removed as described in Chapter 10.

13 Oil pressure
warning light switch –
removal and refitting

Removal

1 The switch is fitted at the front of the cylinder block, in the following locations:
Petrol engines:
  Screwed into the base of the oil filter housing.
1.6 litre diesel engine:
  Adjacent to the oil dipstick guide tube
2.0 litre SOHC diesel engine:
  Above the oil filter mounting.
2.0 litre DOHC diesel engine:
  Screwed into the oil filter housing.
Note that on some models access to the switch may be improved if the vehicle is jacked up and supported on axle stands,

and the engine undershield removed (where fitted), so that the switch can be reached from underneath (see *Jacking and vehicle support*).
2 Remove the protective sleeve from the wiring plug (where applicable), then disconnect the wiring from the switch.
3 Unscrew the switch from the cylinder block, and recover the sealing washer **(see illustrations)**. Be prepared for oil spillage, and if the switch is to be left removed from the engine for any length of time, plug the hole in the cylinder block.

Refitting

4 Examine the sealing washer for signs of damage or deterioration and if necessary renew.
5 Refit the switch, complete with washer, and tighten it securely. Reconnect the wiring connector.
6 Lower the vehicle to the ground then check and, if necessary, top-up the engine oil as described in *Weekly Checks*.

14 Oil level sensor –
removal and refitting

1 The sensor is fitted in the following locations:

13.3a The oil pressure switch is located above the oil filter housing (arrowed) . . .

13.3b . . . adjacent to the oil cooler (arrowed) . . .

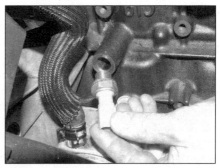

13.3c . . . or at the front, right-hand end of the cylinder block

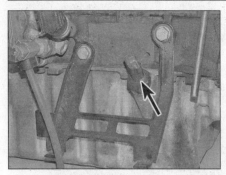

**14.2 Oil level sensor –
2.0 litre diesel engine**

Petrol engines:
Rear side of the cylinder block at the sump-to-block joint.
1.6 litre diesel engine:
Rear side of the cylinder block, between cylinders 2 and 3.
2.0 litre SOHC diesel engine:
Rear side of the cylinder block, adjacent to the transmission housing.
2.0 litre DOHC diesel engine:
Front side of the cylinder block, adjacent to the transmission housing.

2 The removal and refitting procedure is as described for the oil pressure switch in Section 13. Access is most easily obtained from underneath the vehicle **(see illustration)**. Be prepared for fluid spillage.

15 Pre-post heating system – description and testing

Description

1 To assist cold starting, diesel engines are fitted with a preheating system, which consists of four of glow plugs (one per cylinder), a glow plug relay unit, a facia-mounted warning lamp, the engine management ECM, and the associated electrical wiring.
2 The glow plugs are miniature electric heating elements, encapsulated in a metal case with a probe at one end and electrical connection at the other. Each combustion chamber has one glow plug threaded into it,

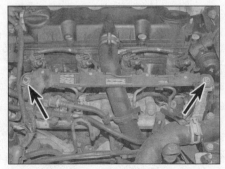

15.11 Undo the 2 nuts (arrowed) and move the wiring harness tray to one side

with the tip of the glow plug probe positioned directly in line with incoming spray of fuel from the injectors. When the glow plug is energised, it heats up rapidly, causing the fuel passing over the glow plug probe to be heated to its optimum combustion temperature, ready for combustion. In addition, some of the fuel passing over the glow plugs is ignited and this helps to trigger the combustion process.
3 The preheating system begins to operate as soon as the ignition key is switched to the second position, but only if the engine coolant temperature is below 20°C and the engine is turned at more than 70 rpm for 0.2 seconds. A facia-mounted warning lamp informs the driver that preheating is taking place. The lamp extinguishes when sufficient preheating has taken place to allow the engine to be started, but power will still be supplied to the glow plugs for a further period until the engine is started. If no attempt is made to start the engine, the power supply to the glow plugs is switched off after 10 seconds, to prevent battery drain and glow plug burn-out.
4 With the electronically-controlled diesel injection systems fitted to models in this manual, the glow plug relay unit is controlled by the engine management system ECM, which determines the necessary preheating time based on inputs from the various system sensors. The system monitors the temperature of the inlet air, then alters the preheating time (the length for which the glow plugs are supplied with current) to suit the conditions.
5 Post-heating takes place after the ignition key has been released from the 'Start' position, but only if the engine coolant temperature is below 20°C, the injected fuel flow is less than a certain rate, and the engine speed is less than 2000 rpm. The glow plugs continue to operate for a maximum of 60 seconds, helping to improve fuel combustion whilst the engine is warming-up, resulting in quieter, smoother running and reduced exhaust emissions.

Testing

6 If the system malfunctions, testing is ultimately by substitution of known good units, but some preliminary checks may be made as follows.
7 Connect a voltmeter or 12 volt test lamp between the glow plug supply cable and earth (engine or vehicle metal). Make sure that the live connection is kept clear of the engine and bodywork.
8 Have an assistant switch on the ignition, and check that voltage is applied to the glow plugs. Note the time for which the warning light is lit, and the total time for which voltage is applied before the system cuts out. Switch off the ignition.
9 Compare the results with the information given in the Specifications. Warning light time will increase with lower temperatures and

decrease with higher temperatures.
10 If there is no supply at all, the control unit or associated wiring is at fault.
11 To gain access to the glow plugs for further testing, remove the following components, according to model:
1.6 litre engine – Remove the cylinder head cover/air filter assembly as described in Chapter 2C.
*2.0 litre SOHC engine – Undo the four plastic fasteners and remove the engine cover from the top of the engine. Disconnect the injector wiring plugs and move the wiring harness tray to one side after undoing the two retaining nuts **(see illustration)**. For access to No 4 glow plug, undo the three bolts and move the fuel pipe support bracket to one side.*
2.0 litre DOHC engine – working as described in Chapter 4C, undo the bolts and move the EGR cooler and valve assembly to one side. There's no need to disconnect the coolant hoses, so no need to drain the cooling system.
12 Disconnect the main supply cable and the interconnecting wire or strap from the top of the glow plugs. Be careful not to drop the nuts and washers.
13 Use a continuity tester, or a 12 volt test lamp connected to the battery positive terminal, to check for continuity between each glow plug terminal and earth. The resistance of a glow plug in good condition is very low (less than 1 ohm), so if the test lamp does not light or the continuity tester shows a high resistance, the glow plug is certainly defective.
14 If an ammeter is available, the current draw of each glow plug can be checked. After an initial surge of 15 to 20 amps, each plug should draw 12 amps. Any plug which draws much more or less than this is probably defective.
15 As a final check, the glow plugs can be removed and inspected as described in the following Section. On completion, refit any components removed for access.

16 Glow plugs – removal, inspection and refitting

Caution: If the preheating system has just been energised, or if the engine has been running, the glow plugs will be very hot.

Removal

1 Ensure the ignition is turned off. To gain access to the glow plugs, remove the components described in Section 15, according to engine.
2 Unscrew the nuts from the glow plug terminals, and recover the washers. Note that on some models, an interconnecting wire/shunt is fitted between the four plugs **(see illustration)**.

16.2 Undo the nut securing the wiring to the top of the glow plug (arrowed) – 2.0 litre SOHC engine

16.4a Unscrew the glow plugs (arrowed) from the cylinder head – 1.6 litre engine . . .

16.4b . . . 2.0 litre SOHC engines . . .

16.4c . . . and 2.0 litre DOHC engine

17.3 Undo the Torx bolt (arrowed) and lift out the relay unit

3 Where applicable, carefully move any obstructing pipes or wires to one side to enable access to the relevant glow plug(s).

4 Unscrew the glow plug(s) and remove from the cylinder head **(see illustrations)**.

Inspection

5 Inspect each glow plug for physical damage. Burnt or eroded glow plug tips can be caused by a bad injector spray pattern. Have the injectors checked if this sort of damage is found.

6 If the glow plugs are in good physical condition, check them electrically using a 12 volt test lamp or continuity tester as described in the previous Section.

7 The glow plugs can be energised by applying 12 volts to them to verify that they heat up evenly and in the required time. Observe the following precautions:

a) *Support the glow plug by clamping it carefully in a vice or self-locking pliers. Remember it will become red-hot.*

b) *Make sure that the power supply or test lead incorporates a fuse or overload trip to protect against damage from a short-circuit.*

c) *After testing, allow the glow plug to cool for several minutes before attempting to handle it.*

8 A glow plug in good condition will start to glow red at the tip after drawing current for 5 seconds or so. Any plug which takes much longer to start glowing, or which starts glowing in the middle instead of at the tip, is defective.

Refitting

9 Refit by reversing the removal operations. Apply a smear of copper-based anti-seize compound to the plug threads and tighten the glow plugs to the specified torque. Do not overtighten, as this can damage the glow plug element.

10 Refit any components removed for access.

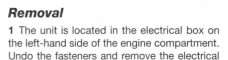

17 Glow plug relay unit – removal and refitting

Removal

1 The unit is located in the electrical box on the left-hand side of the engine compartment. Undo the fasteners and remove the electrical box lid.

2 Undo the 2 Torx bolts and remove the ECM to one side. Note there is no need to disconnect the ECM wiring plugs.

3 Unscrew the retaining Torx bolt securing the unit to the electrical box **(see illustration)**.

4 Lift out the unit and disconnect the wiring plugs.

Refitting

5 Refitting is a reversal of removal, ensuring that the wiring connectors are correctly connected.

Notes

Chapter 5 Part B:
Ignition system (petrol engines)

Contents

Degrees of difficulty

Easy, suitable for novice with little experience	Fairly easy, suitable for beginner with some experience	Fairly difficult, suitable for competent DIY mechanic	Difficult, suitable for experienced DIY mechanic	Very difficult, suitable for expert DIY or professional

Specifications

General

System type	Static (distributorless) ignition system controlled by engine management ECM
Firing order.	1-3-4-2 (No 1 cylinder at transmission end)
Spark plugs	See Chapter 1A Specifications
Ignition timing.	Controlled by engine management ECM

Torque wrench setting

	Nm	lbf ft
Knock sensor bolt	20	15

1 Ignition system –
general information

The ignition system is integrated with the fuel injection system to form a combined engine management system under the control of one ECM (see Chapter 4A for further information). The ignition side of the system is of the static (distributorless) type, consisting of the ignition coils and spark plugs. The ignition coils are housed in a single unit mounted directly above the spark plugs. The coils are integral with the spark plug caps and are pushed directly onto the spark plugs. This removes the need for any HT leads connecting the coils to the plugs.

The ECM uses its inputs from the various sensors to calculate the required ignition advance setting and coil charging time, depending on engine temperature, load and speed. At idle speeds, the ECM varies the ignition timing to alter the torque characteristic of the engine, enabling the idle speed to be controlled. This system operates in conjunction with the idle speed control motor – see Chapter 4A for additional details.

A knock sensor is also incorporated into the ignition system. Mounted onto the cylinder block, the sensor detects the high-frequency vibrations caused when the engine starts to pre-ignite, or 'pink'. Under these conditions, the knock sensor sends an electrical signal to the ECM which in turn retards the ignition advance setting in small steps until the 'pinking' ceases.

3.2a Disconnect the coil pack wiring plug . . .

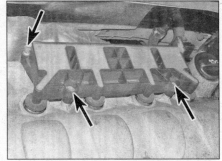

3.2b . . . undo the bolts (arrowed) – EW10D engine . . .

3.2c . . . and EW7/EW10J4 engines . . .

3.2d . . . and pull the coil pack upwards

2 Ignition system – testing

> ⚠ **Warning: Voltages produced by an electronic ignition system are considerably higher than those produced by conventional ignition systems. Extreme care must be taken when working on the system with the ignition switched on. Persons with surgically-implanted cardiac pacemaker devices should keep well clear of the ignition circuits, components and test equipment.**

If a fault appears in the engine management (fuel injection/ignition) system, first ensure that the fault is not due to a poor electrical connection or poor maintenance: ie, check that the air cleaner filter element is clean, the spark plugs are in good condition and

5.1 The knock sensor (arrowed) is locate on the front face of the cylinder block

correctly gapped, and that the engine breather hoses are clear and undamaged, referring to Chapter 1A for further information. Also check that the accelerator cable (where fitted) is correctly adjusted as described in Chapter 4A. If the engine is running very roughly, check the compression pressures as described in Chapter 2A or 2B, where applicable.

If these checks fail to reveal the cause of the problem the vehicle should be taken to a suitably-equipped Citroën dealer or specialist for testing. A wiring block diagnostic connector is incorporated in the engine management circuit into which a special electronic diagnostic tester can be plugged. The tester will locate the fault quickly and simply alleviating the need to test all the system components individually which is a time-consuming operation that carries a high risk of damaging the ECM.

The only ignition system checks which can be carried out by the home mechanic are those described in Chapter 1A relating to the spark plugs.

3 Ignition coil unit – removal, testing and refitting

Removal

1 Rotate the fasteners 90° anti-clockwise and lift up the plastic cover on the top of the engine (EW7J4 or EW10J4 engines), or pull the plastic cover on the top of the engine

straight up from its rubber mountings (EW10D engines).
2 Disconnect the wiring connector at the end of the ignition coil unit. Undo the retaining bolts and lift the coil unit upwards, off the spark plugs **(see illustrations)**.

Testing

3 The circuitry arrangement of the ignition coil unit on these engines is such that testing of an individual coil in isolation from the remainder of the engine management system is unlikely to prove effective in diagnosing a particular fault. Should there be any reason to suspect a faulty individual coil, the engine management system should be tested by a Citroën dealer or specialist using diagnostic test equipment (see Section 2).

Refitting

4 Refitting is a reversal of the relevant removal procedure ensuring the wiring connectors are securely reconnected.

4 Ignition timing – checking and adjustment

1 There are no timing marks on the flywheel or crankshaft pulley. The timing is constantly being monitored and adjusted by the engine management ECM, and nominal values cannot be given. Therefore, it is not possible for the home mechanic to check the ignition timing.
2 The only way in which the ignition timing can be checked is using special electronic test equipment, connected to the engine management system diagnostic connector (refer to Chapter 4A for further information).

5 Knock sensor – removal and refitting

Removal

1 On all engines, the sensor is mounted on to the front face of the cylinder block **(see illustration)**.
2 Chock the rear wheels then jack up the front of the vehicle and support it securely on axle stands (see *Jacking and vehicle support*). Undo the screws and remove the engine undershield (where fitted).
3 Trace the wiring back from the sensor to its wiring connector, and disconnect it from the main loom.
4 Undo the sensor securing bolt and remove the sensor from the cylinder block.

Refitting

6 Refitting is a reversal of the removal procedure, ensuring that the sensor securing bolt is tightened to the specified torque.

Chapter 6
Clutch

Contents

Degrees of difficulty

Easy, suitable for novice with little experience	**Fairly easy,** suitable for beginner with some experience	**Fairly difficult,** suitable for competent DIY mechanic	**Difficult,** suitable for experienced DIY mechanic	**Very difficult,** suitable for expert DIY or professional

Specifications

Engine identification

Petrol engines

Indirect injection:
  Designation:
    1.8 litre EW7J4
    2.0 litre EW10J4
  Engine code:
    1.8 litre 6FZ
    2.0 litre . . . .   RFN
Direct injection:
  Designation:
    2.0 litre EW10D
  Engine code . . . .   RLZ

Diesel engines

1.6 litre:
  Designation. DV6TED4
  Engine codes . . . .   9HY or 9HZ
2.0 litre SOHC:
  Designation. . . . .   DW10TD or DW10ATED
  Engine codes:
    DW10TD . . . .   RHY
    DW10ATED . . . .   RHZ
2.0 litre DOHC:
  Designation. DW10BTED4
  Engine code . . . .   RHR

Type . . . .   Single dry plate with diaphragm spring, hydraulic operation

Friction disc diameter

Petrol engines:
  1.8 litre . . . .   228.6 mm
  2.0 litre . . . .   228.6 mm
Diesel engines:
  1.6 litre . . . .   225 mm
  2.0 litre SOHC. . . . .   225 mm
  2.0 litre DOHC . . . .   235 mm

Torque wrench settings

	Nm	lbf ft
Clutch slave cylinder	20	15
Pressure plate retaining bolts.	20	15

2.2 Prise the clutch master cylinder pushrod from the pedal

1 General information

The clutch consists of a friction disc, a pressure plate assembly, a release bearing and the release mechanism, all of these components being contained in the transmission bellhousing, sandwiched between the engine and the transmission. The release mechanism is mechanical, and is operated hydraulically by means of a master and slave cylinder together with interconnecting hydraulic pipework.

The friction disc is fitted between the engine flywheel and the clutch pressure plate, and is free to slide along the transmission input shaft splines.

The pressure plate assembly is bolted to the engine flywheel. When the engine is running, drive is transmitted from the crankshaft, through the flywheel, to the friction disc (these components being clamped securely together by the pressure plate assembly) and from the friction disc to the transmission input shaft.

The disc is held in position between the flywheel and the pressure plate by the pressure of the diaphragm spring. Friction lining material is riveted to the disc which, on all petrol engines and the non-intercooled DW10TD diesel engine, has a spring-cushioned hub to absorb transmission shocks and help ensure a smooth take-up of the drive. There is no spring-cushioned hub on the other diesel engines, however, the flywheel is designed in two sections with an internal cushion to take up transmission shocks – dual mass.

2.6 Refit the pedal assist spring assembly

2.3 Undo the nut (arrowed) and slide out the pivot bolt

Two different types of clutch release mechanism are used. The first is a conventional 'push-type' mechanism, where an independent clutch release bearing, fitted concentrically around the transmission input shaft, is pushed onto the pressure plate assembly; this type is fitted to all petrol engines and the 2.0 litre DW10TD (non-intercooled) diesel engine. The second is a 'pull-type' mechanism, where the clutch release bearing is an integral part of the pressure plate assembly, and is lifted away from the friction disc.

On models with the conventional 'push-type' mechanism, the clutch release mechanism consists of a release fork and bearing which are in permanent contact with the fingers of the diaphragm spring. Depressing the clutch pedal actuates the release arm by means of the hydraulic master and slave cylinders, and the release bearing is pushed against the diaphragm fingers, so moving the centre of the diaphragm spring inwards. As the centre of the spring is pushed in, the outside of the spring pivots out, so moving the pressure plate backwards and disengaging its grip on the friction disc.

On models with the 'pull-type' mechanism, the clutch release mechanism consists of a release fork which pivots on a spindle inside the gearbox bellhousing. Depressing the clutch pedal rotates the release fork on its spindle, and lifts the release bearing, which is attached to the pressure plate springs, away from the friction disc, and releases the clamping force exerted at the pressure plate periphery.

Adjustment of the clutch to compensate for

3.3 Disconnect the clutch fluid supply hose (arrowed)

wear of the friction disc linings is automatically taken up by the self-adjusting hydraulic clutch components. On some models, a self-adjusting clutch (SAC) is fitted, where an adjustment ring rotates in the pressure plate assembly, adjusting the diaphragm spring fingers pivot points as the friction disc wears. This maintains the clutch pedal 'bite point'.

2 Clutch pedal – removal and refitting

Removal

1 Remove the brake pedal as described in Chapter 9.
2 Release the clip and disconnect the master cylinder pushrod from the pedal **(see illustration)**.
3 Slacken and remove the pivot bolt and nut, and remove the clutch pedal from the vehicle **(see illustration)**. Slide the spacer out from the pedal pivot. Examine all components for signs of wear or damage, renewing them as necessary.

Refitting

4 Apply a smear of multipurpose grease to the spacer, and insert it into the pedal pivot bore.
5 Manoeuvre the pedal into position, and insert the pivot bolt. Refit the nut to the pivot bolt and tighten it securely.
6 Reconnect the master cylinder pushrod to the pedal. Refit the pedal assist spring assembly **(see illustration)**.
7 Depress and release the clutch pedal several times and check for correct operation.
8 Refit the brake pedal as described in Chapter 9.

3 Clutch hydraulic system components – removal and refitting

Clutch master cylinder

Removal

1 Remove the sound insulation material/heat shield from the right-hand side of the engine compartment.
2 Disconnect the clutch master cylinder pushrod from the pedal as described in the previous Section.
3 Working in the engine compartment, syphon out the hydraulic fluid from the brake/clutch fluid reservoir. Disconnect the clutch hydraulic fluid supply hose from the master cylinder then tape over or plug the hose and aperture **(see illustration)**.
4 Unclip the slave cylinder hydraulic line from the clutch master cylinder **(see illustration)**.
5 Turn the clutch master cylinder clockwise to release it from the bulkhead attachment. If necessary, make up a tool from metal tube to

3.4 Prise out the clip (arrowed)

3.16 Prise out the pipe clip

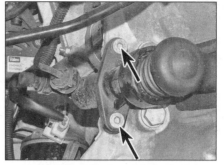

3.17 Slave cylinder retaining bolts (arrowed)

engage the master cylinder, so that it can be turned easily.

Refitting

6 Locate the master cylinder in position. Push and turn the cylinder anti-clockwise to secure.

7 Refit the slave cylinder hydraulic line to the clutch master cylinder.

8 On right-hand drive models, lower the car to the ground. On left-hand drive models, refit the brake vacuum servo unit and the master cylinder with reference to Chapter 9.

9 Reconnect the clutch hydraulic supply hose to the fluid reservoir.

10 Working inside the car, lubricate the master cylinder pushrod balljoint, then lift the clutch pedal and connect the pushrod.

11 Top-up the hydraulic fluid in the reservoir, then bleed the clutch hydraulic system as described in Section 4.

12 Refit the lower facia panels.

13 Refit the air cleaner housing.

Clutch slave cylinder

Removal

14 Remove the air cleaner housing and intake duct components as described in the relevant Part of Chapter 4.

15 Place a clamp on the slave cylinder fluid pressure hose, or plug/seal the hose once it's been disconnected.

16 Unclip the hydraulic pipe from the clutch slave cylinder and move it to one side **(see illustration)**. Be prepared for fluid spillage, and plug/seal the openings to prevent contamination.

17 On BE4R gearboxes, the slave cylinder is retained by 2 bolts. Undo the two bolts and pull the cylinder from position **(see illustration)**.

18 On other gearboxes, release the slave cylinder from the transmission by pushing it in by hand and at the same time turning it 90° anti-clockwise **(see illustrations)**. Withdraw the cylinder from the engine compartment.

Refitting

Note: *On a new assembly, the slave cylinder pushrod is retained in the cylinder by a plastic collar which will automatically break off when the clutch pedal is depressed for the first time. Do not attempt to release this collar manually prior to fitting or the pushrod may be ejected.*

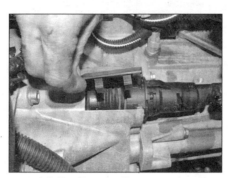

3.18a Remove the cover . . .

19 Lubricate the end of the slave cylinder pushrod with molybdenum disulphide grease then locate the slave cylinder in the transmission. Push it in by hand and at the same time turn it 90° clockwise to secure, or secure it with the retaining bolts as applicable.

20 Reconnect the hydraulic pipe to the slave cylinder.

21 Top-up the hydraulic fluid in the reservoir, then bleed the clutch hydraulic system as described in Section 4.

22 Refit the air cleaner housing with reference to the relevant Part of Chapter 4.

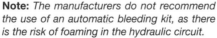

4 Clutch hydraulic system – bleeding

Note: *The manufacturers do not recommend the use of an automatic bleeding kit, as there is the risk of foaming in the hydraulic circuit.*

1 Bleeding of the clutch hydraulic system is carried out in the same manner as bleeding the brake hydraulic system (see Chapter 9). First top up the brake/clutch fluid reservoir.

2 Remove the air cleaner housing and intake duct components as described in the relevant Part of Chapter 4.

3 Connect a bleed tube to the bleed screw on the clutch slave cylinder, and place the free end of the tube in a suitable jar with sufficient hydraulic fluid to cover the end of the tube **(see illustration)**.

4 Loosen the bleed screw, then have an assistant depress and release the clutch pedal fully 7 times. On the last stroke, have the

3.18b . . . then twist and remove the clutch slave cylinder

assistant hold the pedal depressed. Tighten the bleed screw and have the pedal released.

5 Top-up the hydraulic fluid, then repeat the procedure described in paragraph 4.

6 Top-up the fluid again, then operate the clutch pedal 40 times at the rate of 1 forward and backward movement per second.

7 With the handbrake applied, start the engine and engage a gear. Check that the start of friction of the clutch pedal occurs at a distance of at least 35 mm from the floor. If it occurs at less than 35 mm from the floor, air must still be present in the hydraulic system and it will be necessary to bleed the system again. An alternative method of checking the operation of the clutch pedal is to place a 35 mm thick spacer beneath the pedal on the floor, and check that all gears can be engaged normally when the pedal is depressed onto the spacer.

8 On completion, refit the air cleaner housing.

4.3 Prise off the rubber cap (arrowed) and attach a bleed tube

5.2 Mark the relationship of the flywheel to the pressure plate assembly

5 Clutch assembly –
removal, inspection and refitting

⚠️ **Warning: Dust created by clutch wear and deposited on the clutch components may contain asbestos, which is a health hazard. DO NOT blow it out with compressed air, or inhale any of it. DO NOT use petrol or petroleum-based solvents to clean off the dust. Brake system cleaner or methylated spirit should be used to flush the dust into a suitable receptacle. After the clutch components are wiped clean with rags, dispose of the contaminated rags and cleaner in a sealed, marked container.**

Note: *Although some friction materials may no longer contain asbestos, it is safest to assume that they do, and to take precautions accordingly.*

5.5a Press down on the pressure plate . . .

5.5c . . . and remove the release bearing from the pressure plate diaphragm

Removal

1 Unless the complete engine/transmission is to be removed from the car and separated for major overhaul (see Chapter 2F), the clutch can be reached by removing the transmission as described in Chapter 7A.

2 Before disturbing the clutch, mark the relationship of the pressure plate assembly to the flywheel, using a marker pen or similar **(see illustration)**.

3 Working in a diagonal sequence, slacken the pressure plate bolts by half a turn at a time, until spring pressure is released and the bolts can be unscrewed by hand.

4 Prise the pressure plate assembly off its locating dowels, and collect the friction disc, noting which way round the friction disc is fitted.

5 On models with the 'pull-type' release mechanism, first press down the pressure plate on the bench, then use a screwdriver to prise out the circlip and remove the release bearing from the pressure plate diaphragm spring **(see illustrations)**. Take care not to deform the circlip, and after removing the bearing, refit the circlip in its groove.

Inspection

Note: *Due to the amount of work necessary to remove and refit clutch components, it is usually considered good practice to renew the clutch friction disc, pressure plate assembly and release bearing as a matched set, even if only one of these is actually worn enough to require renewal. It is also worth considering the renewal of the clutch components on*

5.5b . . . then prise out the circlip . . .

5.14a Fit the friction disc with the sprung hub facing away from the flywheel . . .

a preventative basis if the engine and/or transmission have been removed for some other reason.

6 When cleaning clutch components, read first the warning at the beginning of this Section; remove dust using a clean, dry cloth, and working in a well-ventilated atmosphere.

7 Check the friction disc facings for signs of wear, damage or oil contamination. If the friction material is cracked, burnt, scored or damaged, or if it is contaminated with oil or grease (shown by shiny black patches), the friction disc must be renewed.

8 If the friction material is still serviceable, check that the centre boss splines are unworn, that the torsion springs (where fitted) are in good condition and securely fastened, and that all the rivets are tight. If any wear or damage is found, the friction disc must be renewed.

9 If the friction material is fouled with oil, this must be due to an oil leak from the crankshaft left-hand oil seal, from the sump-to-cylinder block joint, or from the transmission input shaft. Renew the seal or repair the joint, as appropriate, as described in the relevant Part of Chapter 2 or 7, before installing the new friction disc.

10 Check the pressure plate assembly for obvious signs of wear or damage; shake it to check for loose rivets or worn or damaged fulcrum rings, and check that the drive straps securing the pressure plate to the cover do not show signs of overheating (such as a deep yellow or blue discoloration). If the diaphragm spring is worn or damaged, or if its pressure is in any way suspect, the pressure plate assembly should be renewed.

11 Examine the machined bearing surfaces of the pressure plate and flywheel; they should be clean, completely flat, and free from scratches or scoring. If either is discoloured from excessive heat, or shows signs of cracks, it should be renewed – although minor damage of this nature can sometimes be polished away using emery paper.

12 Check that the release bearing contact surface rotates smoothly and easily, with no sign of noise or roughness. Also check that the surface itself is smooth and unworn, with no signs of cracks, pitting or scoring. If there is any doubt about its condition, the bearing must be renewed. On clutches with a 'pull-type' release mechanism, check that the retaining circlip is in good condition, and renew it if necessary.

Refitting

13 On reassembly, ensure that the bearing surfaces of the flywheel and pressure plate are completely clean, smooth, and free from oil or grease. Use solvent to remove any protective grease from new components.

14 Fit the friction disc so its spring hub (where applicable) faces away from the flywheel; there may also be a marking to show which way round the plate is to be refitted **(see illustration)**. On most models, the thickness of the spring hub makes it impossible to fit it with the hub against the flywheel. On models without a sprung hub, fit the disc with the hub away from the flywheel **(see illustration)**.

Models with self-adjusting clutch

15 On these models, the clutch pressure plate is unusual, as there is a pre-adjustment mechanism to compensate for wear in the friction disc (this is termed by Citroën as a self-adjusting clutch (SAC), which is slightly ambiguous as all clutches fitted to these models are essentially self-adjusting). However, this mechanism must be reset before refitting the pressure plate. A new plate may be supplied preset, in which case this procedure can be ignored.

16 A large diameter bolt (M14 at least) long enough to pass through the pressure plate, a matching nut, and several large diameter washers, will be needed for this procedure. Mount the bolt head in the jaws of a sturdy bench vice, with one large washer fitted.

17 Offer the plate over the bolt, friction disc surface facing down, and locate it centrally over the bolt and washer – the washer should bear on the centre hub **(see illustration)**.

18 Fit several further large washers over the bolt, so that they bear on the ends of the spring fingers, then add the nut and tighten by hand to locate the washers.

19 The purpose of the procedure is to turn the plate's internal adjuster disc so that the three small coil springs visible on the plate's outer surface are fully compressed. Tighten the nut just fitted until the adjuster disc is free to turn. Using a pair of thin-nosed, or circlip, pliers in one of the two windows in the top surface, open the jaws of the pliers to turn the adjuster disc anti-clockwise, so that the springs are fully compressed **(see illustration)**.

20 Hold the pliers in this position, then unscrew the centre nut. Once the nut is released, the adjuster disc will be gripped in position, and the pliers can be removed. Take the pressure plate from the vice, and it is ready to fit.

All models

21 Refit the pressure plate assembly, aligning the marks made on dismantling (if the original pressure plate is re-used), and locating the pressure plate on its locating dowels. Fit the pressure plate bolts, but tighten them only finger-tight, so that the friction disc can still be moved.

22 The friction disc must now be centralised, so that when the transmission is refitted, its input shaft will pass through the splines at the centre of the friction disc.

23 Centralisation can be achieved by passing a screwdriver or other long bar through the friction disc and into the hole in the crankshaft; the friction disc can then be moved around until it is centred on the crankshaft hole. Alternatively, a clutch-aligning tool can be used to eliminate the guesswork; these can be obtained from most accessory shops **(see illustration)**. A home-made alignment tool

5.14b . . . or the protruding hub away from the flywheel

5.19 . . . then move the adjusting ring (arrowed) anti-clockwise to the stop

can be fabricated from a length of metal rod or wooden dowel which fits closely inside the crankshaft hole, and has insulating tape wound around it to match the diameter of the friction disc splined hole.

24 When the friction disc is centralised, tighten the pressure plate bolts evenly and in a diagonal sequence to the specified torque setting.

25 Refit the transmission as described in Chapter 7A. On models with the 'pull-type' release mechanism, use the tool described in Chapter 7A, Section 8, to engage the release bearing with the pressure plate diaphragm spring before refitting the slave cylinder.

6 Clutch release mechanism – removal, inspection and refitting

Note: *Refer to the warning concerning the*

6.2 Slide the release bearing from the input shaft

5.17 Using some threaded rod, washers and 2 nuts, compress the diaphragm spring and the pressure plate together . . .

5.23 Centralise the friction plate on the flywheel using a clutch aligning tool

dangers of asbestos dust at the beginning of Section 5.

Removal

1 Unless the complete engine/transmission is to be removed from the car and separated for major overhaul (see Chapter 2F), the clutch release mechanism can be reached by removing the transmission only, as described in Chapter 7A.

Push-type release mechanism

2 Unhook the release bearing from the fork, and slide it off the input shaft **(see illustration)**.

3 Squeeze together the clips, and pull the fork from the pivot stud **(see illustrations)**.

Pull-type release mechanism

4 Access to the inner end of the release fork shaft is not possible, and the shaft must be pulled or levered out from the outside of the

6.3a Squeeze together the tabs of the retaining clips and remove the release fork . . .

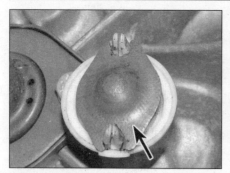

6.3b ... recover the shim (arrowed) ...

6.3c ... and unscrew the pivot ball-stud

6.4a Use a lever to remove the release fork shaft

6.4b Remove the release fork shaft ...

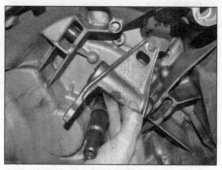

6.5 ... and withdraw the release fork from the bellhousing

6.13 Drive the release shaft into the casing

bellhousing. A slide hammer may be attached to the groove in the end of the shaft, or alternatively a lever may be used taking care not to damage the transmission casing (see illustrations).

5 With the shaft removed, withdraw the release fork from the bellhousing, noting which way round it is fitted (see illustration).

Inspection

6 Check the release mechanism, renewing any component which is worn or damaged. Carefully check all bearing surfaces and points of contact.

7 When checking the release bearing itself, note that it is often considered worthwhile to renew it as a matter of course. Check that the contact surface rotates smoothly and easily, with no sign of noise or roughness, and that the surface itself is smooth and unworn, with no signs of cracks, pitting or scoring. If there is any doubt about its condition, the bearing must be renewed.

Refitting

Push-type release mechanism

8 Apply a smear of molybdenum disulphide grease to the pivot stud face.

9 Locate the fork reinforcement plate on the pivot stud, then push the fork over the retaining clips.

10 Slide the release bearing onto the input shaft, and engage it with the release fork.

Pull-type release mechanism

11 Apply a smear of molybdenum disulphide grease to the shaft and contact surfaces of the release fork.

12 Insert the shaft through the transmission casing then locate the release fork inside the bellhousing and insert the shaft through it into the inner location hole. Make sure that the slave cylinder contact point is facing the correct direction.

13 Using a soft-metal drift, drive the shaft fully into the casing, taking care not to damage the inner blind hole (see illustration).

All models

14 Refit the transmission as described in Chapter 7A.

Chapter 7 Part A:
Manual transmission

Contents

Degrees of difficulty

Easy, suitable for novice with little experience	Fairly easy, suitable for beginner with some experience	Fairly difficult, suitable for competent DIY mechanic	Difficult, suitable for experienced DIY mechanic	Very difficult, suitable for expert DIY or professional

Specifications

General

Type . . . .   Manual, five or six forward speeds and reverse. Synchromesh on all forward speeds

Designation:
  Petrol engines. BE4R
  1.6 litre diesel engine BE4R
  2.0 litre diesel engine:
    DW10TD BE4R
    DW10ATED . . . .   ML5T or ML5C
    DW10BTED4 . . . .   ML6C

Lubrication

Recommended oil . . . .   See *Lubricants and fluids*
Capacity:
  BE4R transmission. . . . .   1.8 litres
  ML5T and ML5C transmissions . . . .   2.1 litres
  ML6C transmission:
    Without cooling fins on the gearbox casing. . . . .   1.9 litres
    With cooling fins on the gearbox casing . . . .   2.6 litres

Torque wrench settings

	Nm	lbf ft
BE4R transmissions		
Clutch release bearing guide sleeve bolts	12	9
Engine movement limiter to driveshaft intermediate bearing housing . .	45	33
Engine movement limiter to subframe	85	63
Engine-to-transmission fixing bolts	60	44
Left-hand engine/transmission mounting:		
Centre nut.	65	48
Mounting stud bracket to transmission	60	44
Mounting stud to transmission.	50	37
Rubber mounting-to-bracket bolts.	30	22
Oil drain plug	30	22
Oil filler/level plug.	20	15
Reversing light switch	25	18
Right-hand driveshaft intermediate bearing retaining bolt nuts.	10	7
Roadwheel bolts.	90	66
ML5 and ML6C transmissions		
Clutch release bearing guide sleeve bolts:		
ML6C	10	7
ML5T.	12	9
ML5C	20	15
Engine movement limiter to subframe	65	48
Engine-to-transmission fixing bolts	60	44
Gearchange lever housing bolts.	7	5
Left-hand engine/transmission mounting:		
Mounting bracket to transmission	45	33
Mounting to bracket.	45	33
Mounting to vehicle body (ML5C and ML6C only).	27	20
Oil drain plug	30	22
Oil filler/level plug:		
ML5T.	20	15
ML5C	30	22
Reversing light switch:		
ML5T and ML6C.	25	18
ML5C	30	22
Roadwheel bolts.	90	66

1 General information

The transmission is contained in a cast-aluminium alloy casing bolted to the engine's left-hand end, and consists of the gearbox and final drive differential. Three transmission types are fitted according to model, the types being BE4R, ML5T, ML5C and ML6C. The transmissions have 5 or 6 forward gears and 1 reverse gear, and are similar in operation. The ML6C transmission was specially developed to cope with the high torque output of the later 2.0 litre diesel engines. With 6 forward speeds and capable of handling 350 Nm of torque, the transmission is 'filled for life' with fluid – there's no recommended interval for changing the fluid, although it may be prudent to do so at some stage in the vehicle's life.

Drive is transmitted from the crankshaft through the clutch to the input shaft, which has a splined extension to accept the clutch friction disc, and which rotates in sealed ball-bearings. From the input shaft, drive is transmitted to the output shaft, which rotates in a roller bearing at its right-hand end, and a sealed ball-bearing at its left-hand end. From the output shaft, the drive is transmitted to the differential crown wheel, which rotates with the differential case and planetary gears, thus driving the sun gears and driveshafts. The rotation of the planetary gears on their shaft allows the inner roadwheel to rotate at a slower speed than the outer roadwheel when the car is cornering.

The input and output shafts are arranged side-by-side, parallel to the crankshaft and driveshafts, so that their gear pinion teeth are in constant mesh. In the neutral position, the relevant input shaft and output shaft gear pinions rotate freely, so that drive cannot be transmitted to the output shaft and crown wheel.

Gear selection is by a floor-mounted lever actuating a selector cable mechanism. The selector cables cause the appropriate selector fork to move its respective synchro sleeve along the shaft, to lock the gear pinion to the synchro-hub. Since the synchro-hubs are splined to the input and output shafts, this locks the pinion to the shaft, so that drive can be transmitted. To ensure that gearchanging can be made quickly and quietly, a synchromesh system is fitted to all forward gears, consisting of baulk rings and spring-loaded fingers, together with the gear pinions and synchro-hubs. The synchromesh cones are formed on the mating faces of the baulk rings and gear pinions.

2 Manual transmission – draining and refilling

Note: *A suitable square section wrench may be required to undo the transmission filler/level and drain plugs. These wrenches can be obtained from most motor factors or your Citroën dealer.*

1 This operation is much quicker and more efficient if the car is first taken on a journey of sufficient length to warm the engine/transmission up to operating temperature.

2 Park the car on level ground, switch off the ignition and apply the handbrake firmly. To ensure that the car remains level when refilling, jack up the front and rear of the car and support it securely on axle stands.

3 On models equipped with the BE4R transmission, remove the left-hand front roadwheel then release the screws and clips and remove the wheel arch liner from under the wing for access to the filler/level plug. On all models, remove the engine undershield.

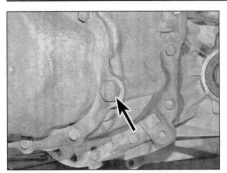

2.4 Oil filler/level plug (arrowed) – BE4R transmission shown

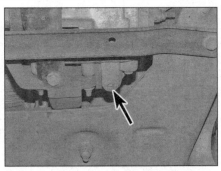

2.5 Transmission oil drain plug (arrowed)

2.9 On BE4R transmissions, top up the oil through the wheel arch

4 Wipe clean the area around the filler/level plug. On the BE4R transmission, the filler/level plug is the largest bolt among those securing the end cover to the transmission; on the ML5 transmission, the filler/level plug is located on the rear face of the differential housing, and a hexagon key will be required to unscrew the plug. Remove the filler/level plug from the transmission and recover the sealing washer **(see illustration)**. On ML6C transmissions, fluid is added through the breather valve on the top face of the transmission.

5 Position a suitable container under the drain plug (situated on the final drive casing at the rear of the transmission) and unscrew the plug **(see illustration)**.

6 Allow the oil to drain completely into the container. If the oil is hot, take precautions against scalding. Clean both the filler/level and the drain plugs, being especially careful to wipe any metallic particles off the magnetic inserts. Discard the original sealing washers; they should be renewed whenever they are disturbed.

7 When the oil has finished draining, clean the drain plug threads and those of the transmission casing, fit a new sealing washer and refit the drain plug, tightening it to the specified torque wrench setting.

8 Refilling the transmission is an extremely awkward operation. Above all, allow plenty of time for the oil level to settle properly before checking it. Note that the car must be level when checking the oil level.

BE4R and ML5 transmissions

9 Refill the transmission with the exact amount of the specified type of oil **(see illustration)** then check the oil level as described in the relevant Part of Chapter 1; if the correct amount was poured into the transmission and a large amount flows out on checking the level, refit the filler/level plug and take the car on a short journey so that the new oil is distributed fully around the transmission components, then check the level again on your return.

10 When the level is correct, fit a new sealing washer to the filler/level plug. Tighten the plug to the specified torque wrench setting. Wash off any spilt oil. Where necessary, refit the wheel arch liner and splash guard, and secure with the retaining screws and clips. Refit the

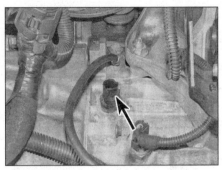

2.12a Prise off the breather cap (arrowed) . . .

roadwheel where removed then lower the car to the ground.

ML6C transmissions

11 Remove the air cleaner assembly as described in Chapter 4B.

12 Carefully prise off the breather from the top of the transmission casing, and add the exact amount specified **(see illustrations)**.

13 Refit the breather cap.

14 Refit the air cleaner assembly, and the engine/transmission undershield, and lower the vehicle to the ground.

3 Gearchange cables – removal and refitting

Removal

1 Chock the rear wheels then jack up the front

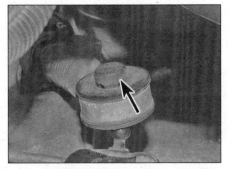

3.3a Depress the release button on the end of the cable (arrowed)

2.12b . . . and add the exact amount of fluid specified

of the vehicle and support it on axle stands (see Jacking and vehicle support). Remove the engine/transmission undershield.

2 Remove the air cleaner assembly and air inlet ducts as described in the relevant Part of Chapter 4.

3 Note their fitted positions, then press down the centre buttons (where applicable), and detach the ends of the selector cables from the lever balljoints at the transmission end. Where no release buttons are fitted, the ends are prised from the balljoints. Release the outer cables from the bracket on the transmission. On some models, the cables are retained by a clip – the ends of which must be squeezed together, whilst on others, the plastic sleeve must be pulled rearwards, or the ends of the clips compressed and the cable lifted from the bracket **(see illustrations)**.

4 Remove the left-hand front roadwheel, then remove the wheel arch liner.

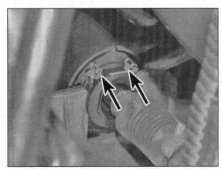

3.3b Squeeze together the ends of the clip (arrowed) or . . .

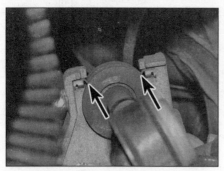

3.3c ... press the ends of the clip outwards (arrowed) and lift the outer cable

5 Remove the front section of the exhaust pipe as described in Chapter 4A or 4B, then remove the heat shield beneath the gearchange lever location. Note that in order to remove the heat shield, the edges of the

3.8 Remove the foam/rubber trim piece to expose the 4 mounting nuts and the retaining clip (arrowed)

3.10a Pull out the retaining clip ...

3.10c Prise out the clips securing the outer cable

3.5 Rotate the fasteners 90° anti-clockwise to remove it

underbody panels must be released **(see illustration)**.

ML5C and ML6C transmissions

6 Undo the bolt and remove the reverse

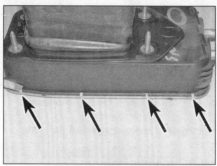

3.9 Fold back the baseplate clips (arrowed)

3.10b ... and pull the cable and bush from the lever

3.11a Prise the inner cable fitting from the collar ...

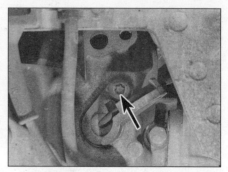

3.6 Working through the wheel arch aperture, undo the Torx bolt and remove the reverse gear locking device from the transmission (arrowed)

gear unlocking device from the left-hand rear upper edge of the transmission housing **(see illustration)**. Unclip the cable from the support bracket. Discard the O-ring seal, a new one must be fitted.

All transmissions

7 Remove the centre console (see Chapter 11).
8 Remove the rubber/foam trim piece around the top of the gearchange lever housing, then undo the 4 nuts, release the clip, and remove the lever housing and gearchange cables as an assembly from under the car **(see illustration)**.
9 Cut through/fold back the clips securing the baseplate to the lever housing, and prise the plate from place **(see illustration)**.
10 Note their fitted positions, then carefully prise the end of the gear engagement control cables from the lever, then on 5-speed gearboxes, pull out the pin, remove the bush and detach the end of the gear selection cable from its lever. On ML5 and ML6 gearboxes, prise both cables from the levers. Prise out the retaining clip and pull the cables from the housing **(see illustrations)**.

ML5C and ML6C transmissions

11 To remove the reverse gear unlocking cable, disengage the inner cable end fitting from the lifting collar, and pull the outer cable from the bracket on the lever **(see illustrations)**.
12 Release the retaining clip and pull the outer cable grommet from the lever housing, then withdrawn the cable from the housing **(see illustration)**.

3.11b ... and pull the outer cable from the bracket

Refitting

13 Refitting is a reversal of the removal procedure, noting the following points:

a) *Ensure that the sound-proofing foam is correctly positioned when refitting the lever housing.*

b) *Ensure that the cables are fitted to the correct selector levers on the transmission.*

c) *Apply a bead of silicone sealant to the base of the lever housing, and refit the plate (see illustration).*

d) *On ML5C and ML6C transmissions, renew the reverse gear unlocking device O-ring.*

e) *Adjust the cables as described in Section 4, prior to refitting the centre console.*

f) *Refit the heat shields, exhaust components, air cleaner assembly, and the centre console.*

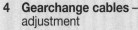
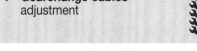

4 Gearchange cables – adjustment

1 Remove the air cleaner assembly as described in Chapter 4, to access the gearchange cables at the top of the transmission.

2 If not already done so, remove the centre console as described in Chapter 11.

3 Ensure the transmission is in neutral.

4 Disconnect the ends of the gearchange cables from the levers on the transmission as described in Section 3.

5 The gearchange lever must be secured in the neutral position. Citroën tool (No 8605-T) may be available for this task, or it is possible to fabricate a home-made equivalent **(see illustration)**.

6 Insert the tool into the side of the gearchange lever housing, and then rotate it 90° anti-clockwise to lock the lever in neutral **(see illustrations)**

BE4R transmission

7 Carefully prise out the yellow catch to release the end fitting locking sleeve on the gearchange cable **(see illustration)**.

8 Using 2 small screwdrivers, depress the security pawls, and rotate the selector cable outer sleeve in the opposite direction to the arrow on the sleeve body **(see illustration)**.

9 Check the gearchange lever is still in the neutral position, then press the ends of the cables on the balljoints at the transmission.

10 Press the yellow locking catch into place, and secure the gearchange cable, then rotate the sleeve in the direction of the arrow and secure the gear selector cable.

ML5 and ML6C transmissions

Up to RPO 09985

11 Carefully prise out the catch to release the end fitting locking sleeve on each gear change cable **(see illustration 4.7)**.

12 Check the gearchange lever is still in the

3.12 Squeeze together the sides of the clip to release the outer cable

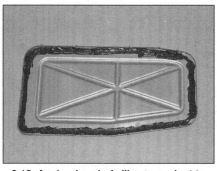

3.13 Apply a bead of silicone sealant to the baseplate

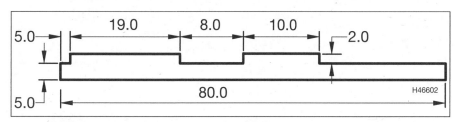

4.5 Fabricate a gear lever setting tool from 2.0 mm thick wood or metal to the dimensions shown

All dimensions are in mm   *Drawing not to scale*

neutral position, then press the ends of the cables on the balljoints at the transmission.

13 Press in the locking catches to secure the cables locking sleeves.

From RPO 09986

14 On these transmissions, only the gear selection control cable can be adjusted. Pull

4.6 Insert the tool through the right-hand side of the housing to hold the lever in the neutral position

4.8 Depress the security pawl (arrowed) and rotate the plastic collar clockwise (viewed from the front of the vehicle)

the locking sleeve on the transmission end of the cable, towards the end, and prise up the locking catch **(see illustration)**.

15 Check the gearchange lever is still in the neutral position, then press the ends of the cables on the balljoints at the transmission.

16 Press-down the locking catch to secure the cables locking sleeve.

4.7 Prise up the yellow locking catch (arrowed)

4.14 Pull the collar forwards and prise up the locking catch (arrowed)

5.2 Prise the driveshaft oil seal from place

5.3 Drive the oil seal into place using a tube or socket

5.5a Pull the release bearing from the actuating arm . . .

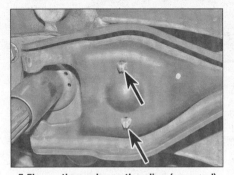

5.5b . . . then release the clips (arrowed) and remove the arm

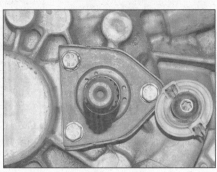

5.6a Undo the bolts and remove the guide sleeve . . .

5.6b . . . and note any shims

All transmissions

17 Check the operation of the gearchange lever. If all is satisfactory, refit the centre console and air cleaner assembly.

5 Oil seals – renewal

Driveshaft oil seals

1 Remove the relevant driveshaft as described in Chapter 8.
2 Carefully prise the oil seal out of the transmission, using a large flat-bladed screwdriver **(see illustration)**.
3 Remove all traces of dirt from the area around the oil seal aperture, then fill the space between the lips of the new oil seal with grease. Fit the new seal into its aperture, and drive it squarely into position using a suitable tubular drift (such as a socket) which bears only on the hard outer edge of the seal, until it abuts its locating shoulder. If the seal was supplied with a plastic protector sleeve, leave this in position until the driveshaft has been refitted **(see illustration)**.
4 Refit the driveshaft(s) as described in Chapter 8.

Input shaft oil seal

5 Remove the transmission as described in Section 7, then remove the release bearing and unclip the actuating arm **(see illustrations)**.
6 Undo the bolts securing the clutch release bearing guide sleeve in position, and slide the guide off the input shaft, along with its O-ring or gasket (where fitted) **(see illustrations)**. Recover any shims or thrustwashers which have stuck to the rear of the guide sleeve, and refit them to the input shaft. Note that on ML5 and ML6C transmissions, the oil seal appears to be integral with the guide sleeve. Check with your Citroën parts specialist.

BE4R transmission

7 Carefully lever the oil seal out of the guide using a suitable flat-bladed screwdriver **(see illustration)**.
8 Before fitting a new seal, check the input shaft's seal rubbing surface for signs of burrs, scratches or other damage, which may have caused the seal to fail in the first place. It may be possible to polish away minor faults of this sort using fine abrasive paper; however, more serious defects will require the renewal of the input shaft. Ensure the input shaft is clean and greased, to protect the seal lips on refitting.
9 Dip the new seal in clean oil, and fit it to the guide sleeve.
10 Refit any shims removed between the sleeve and the input shaft bearing, then carefully slide the sleeve into position over the input shaft. Refit the retaining bolts and tighten them to the specified torque.

ML5 and ML6C transmissions

11 Lubricate the lips of the new seal within the guide tube, then position the tube over the input shaft, and tighten the retaining bolts securely **(see illustration)**.

All transmissions

12 Take the opportunity to inspect the clutch components if not already done (Chapter 6). Finally, refit the transmission (Section 7).

5.7 Lever the old oil seal from the sleeve

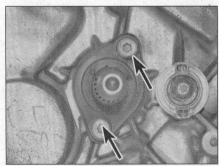

5.11 Guide sleeve Torx bolts (arrowed) – ML6C transmission

6 Reversing light switch – testing, removal and refitting

Testing

1 The reversing light circuit is controlled by a plunger-type switch that is screwed into the top of the transmission casing. If a fault develops in the circuit, first ensure that the circuit fuse has not blown.

2 To test the switch, remove the air cleaner components as required for access (see the relevant Part of Chapter 4) then disconnect the wiring connector, and use a multimeter (set to the resistance function) or a battery-and-bulb test circuit to check that there is continuity between the switch terminals only when reverse gear is selected. If this is not the case, and there are no obvious breaks or other damage to the wires, the switch is faulty, and must be renewed.

Removal

3 Remove the air cleaner components as described in the relevant Part of Chapter 4.

4 Disconnect the wiring connector, then unscrew it from the transmission casing along with its sealing washer (if fitted) **(see illustrations)**.

Refitting

5 Fit a new sealing washer (where applicable) to the switch, then screw it back into position in the top of the transmission housing and tighten it to the specified torque setting. Reconnect the wiring connector, and test the operation of the circuit. Refit any components removed for access.

7 Manual transmission – removal and refitting

Removal

1 Remove the battery as described in Chapter 5A.

2 Chock the rear wheels then jack up the front of the vehicle and support it on axle stands (see *Jacking and vehicle support*). Remove both front roadwheels, then release the screws and clips and remove the wheel arch liner from under the left- and right-hand wings. Remove the engine undershield.

3 Drain the transmission oil as described in Section 2, then refit the drain and filler plugs, and tighten them to their specified torque settings.

4 Remove the air cleaner assembly and intake ducting (see Chapter 4A or 4B, as applicable).

5 Remove both driveshafts as described in Chapter 8.

6 Remove the engine management ECM and module box as described in Chapter 4A or 4B, as applicable.

7 Remove the clutch slave cylinder as described in Chapter 6, and support to one side without disconnecting the hydraulic line.

6.4a The reversing light switch is on the front of the transmission casing (arrowed) . . .

8 From under the car, undo the bolts securing the rear torque rod to the right-hand driveshaft intermediate bearing housing and subframe. Manipulate the torque rod from its location **(see illustration)**.

9 On diesel models, slacken the clamps, undo the retaining screws and remove the charge air pipe under the engine **(see illustration)**.

10 Note their fitted positions, and disconnect the various wiring plugs from the transmission. Release the wiring harness from and retaining clips.

11 Disconnect the front exhaust pipe from the pre-catalyser/exhaust manifold/turbocharger, as applicable – refer to Chapter 4A or 4B, as applicable.

12 Disconnect the gearchange cables from the transmission as described in Section 3. On ML5C and ML6C transmissions, also disconnect the reverse gear locking device as described in Section 3.

7.8 Remove the rear torque rod

7.13 Disconnect the earth cable from the transmission (arrowed)

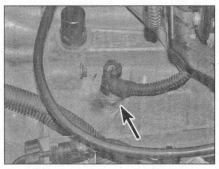

6.4b . . . or on the top (arrowed)

13 Disconnect the earth cable from the transmission casing **(see illustration)**.

14 Remove the starter motor as described in Chapter 5A.

15 Remove the flywheel lower cover plate (where applicable).

16 Attach a hoist or support bar to the engine left-hand lifting eye and just take the engine weight.

17 Place a jack and block of wood beneath the transmission, and raise the jack to take the weight of the transmission.

18 On ML5 and ML6C transmissions, undo the 3 nuts/1 bolt and remove the gearbox impact absorber from the end of the transmission casing, then undo the bolt, prise apart the balljoint, and remove the counterweight from the transmission.

19 On BE4R transmissions, undo the bolts/nuts and remove the brace from under the transmission **(see illustration)**.

7.9 Remove the charge air pipe under the engine

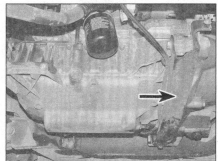

7.19 Remove the brace (arrowed) from under the transmission

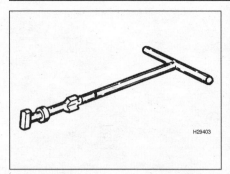

7.25 Citroen tool for securing the release bearing to the clutch pressure plate

20 Undo the nuts/bolts and remove the left-hand transmission mounting assembly.

21 With the jack positioned beneath the transmission taking the weight, slacken and remove the remaining bolts securing the transmission housing to the engine. Note the correct fitted positions of each bolt, and the necessary brackets as they are removed, to use as a reference on refitting. Make a final check that all components have been disconnected, and are positioned clear of the transmission so that they will not hinder the removal procedure.

22 With the bolts removed, lower the engine and move the trolley jack and transmission to the left, to free it from its locating dowels. Once the transmission is free, lower the jack and manoeuvre the unit out from under the car. Remove the locating dowels from the transmission or engine if they are loose, and keep them in a safe place.

Refitting

BE4R, ML5C and ML6C transmissions

23 The transmission is refitted by a reversal of the removal procedure, bearing in mind the following points:

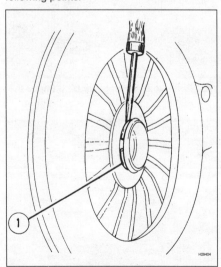

7.28 Remove the release bearing retaining circlip (1) from the inside of the pressure plate diaphragm spring . . .

7.26 Use a screwdriver to lever the release fork and engage the release bearing with the pressure plate

a) *Check the clutch release bearing and fork with reference to Chapter 6.*
b) *Renew the driveshaft oil seals, as described in Section 5, prior to refitting the transmission.*
c) *Ensure that the locating dowels are correctly positioned prior to installation.*
d) *Apply thread-locking fluid to the left-hand engine/transmission mounting bolt threads, prior to refitting. Tighten the nuts/bolts to the specified torque.*
e) *Tighten all nuts and bolts to the specified torque (where given).*
f) *Refit the driveshafts as described in Chapter 8.*
g) *On completion, refill the transmission with the specified type and quantity of lubricant, as described in Section 2.*

ML5T transmission

24 The design of the clutch release bearing and clutch release fork is unusual on this type of transmission in that it is necessary to remove the 'pull-type' release bearing from the clutch pressure plate, and reposition it on the transmission before the transmission is re-attached to the engine. With the transmission refitted, the release bearing is then secured back on the pressure plate by means of a special tool. If the following procedure is not followed exactly, it will be impossible to operate the clutch on completion.

25 The Citroën special tool (9047-T.M) for securing the release bearing in place, consists of a T-shaped rod with a rectangular end **(see illustration)**. The rod is inserted through the slave cylinder aperture in the transmission bellhousing so that the rectangular end engages through the slot in the clutch release fork. When the tool is turned through 90° the rectangular end locks in the release fork slot. Pulling the tool sharply rearwards pivots the release fork and forces the release bearing hard against the pressure plate, causing a snap-ring on the bearing to lock into the pressure plate.

26 Before proceeding, either obtain the Citroën special tool, or fabricate an alternative on the same pattern that will operate as described above. Note, however, on later models, a cut-out (with plastic cover) is

provided in the clutch bellhousing, and it is possible to lever the release fork with a screwdriver **(see illustration)**.

27 Begin by removing the clutch assembly as described in Chapter 6.

28 Using a screwdriver, carefully remove the release bearing retaining snap-ring from the inside of the pressure plate diaphragm spring **(see illustration)**. The snap-ring may not be immediately visible, in which case it will be necessary to press down on the pressure plate to push out the inner end of the release bearing. Take care not to deform the snap-ring as it is removed.

29 Remove the release bearing from the pressure plate, then refit the snap-ring back into the groove in the release bearing boss **(see illustration)**.

30 Refit the clutch assembly (see Chapter 6).

31 Slide the release bearing onto the guide tube on the transmission input shaft, while at the same time engaging the release fork between the contact lugs on the release bearing. Check that the release fork and bearing operate smoothly and that the fork ends are correctly engaged between the bearing lugs.

32 Using the Citroën tool or the home-made alternative, check that the tool will enter the release fork slot and lock when turned through 90°, enabling the fork to be pulled away from the bellhousing end of the transmission by means of the tool. If all is satisfactory, remove the tool.

33 Renew the driveshaft oil seals as described in Section 5 before refitting the transmission. The transmission can now be refitted.

34 The transmission is refitted by a reversal of the removal procedure, bearing in mind the following points:

a) *Ensure the release bearing is in position on the transmission as previously described.*
b) *Ensure that the locating dowels are correctly positioned prior to installation.*
c) *Once the transmission is bolted to the engine, engage the Citroën tool, or the home-made alternative as described previously, and pull on the tool so that*

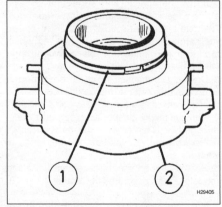

7.29 . . . then refit the circlip (1) back into the release bearing (2)

the release bearing snap-ring engages with the clutch pressure plate. Check for correct engagement by attempting to push the release fork back towards the engine with a screwdriver; there should be slight play but no appreciable travel.

d) Refit the front suspension subframe as described in Chapter 10.

e) Tighten all nuts and bolts to the specified torque (where given).

f) When refitting the clutch slave cylinder, remove the tie used to retain the pushrod, and lubricate the pushrod end with molybdenum disulphide grease. Locate the slave cylinder in the transmission, push it in by hand, and at the same time turn it 90° clockwise to secure. With the cylinder installed, slowly depress the clutch pedal to the floor, then slowly lift it again by hand. Wait for ten seconds and repeat this procedure. Depress the pedal again, release it and check that it rises correctly after being released.

g) Ensure that the gearchange cables are fitted to the correct selector levers on the transmission as described in Section 3.

h) On completion, refill the transmission with the specified type and quantity of lubricant, as described in Chapter 1B.

8 Manual transmission overhaul – general information

Overhauling a manual transmission is a difficult and involved job for the DIY home mechanic. In addition to dismantling and reassembling many small parts, clearances must be precisely measured and, if necessary, changed by selecting shims and spacers. Internal transmission components are also often difficult to obtain, and in many instances, extremely expensive. Because of this, if the transmission develops a fault or becomes noisy, the best course of action is to have the unit overhauled by a specialist repairer, or to obtain an exchange reconditioned unit.

Nevertheless, it is not impossible for the more experienced mechanic to overhaul the transmission, provided the special tools are available, and the job is done in a deliberate step-by-step manner, so nothing is overlooked.

The tools necessary for an overhaul include internal and external circlip pliers, bearing pullers, a slide hammer, a set of pin punches, a dial test indicator, and possibly a hydraulic press. In addition, a large, sturdy workbench and a vice will be required.

During dismantling of the transmission, make careful notes of how each component is fitted, to make reassembly easier and more accurate.

Before dismantling the transmission, it will help if you have some idea what area is malfunctioning. Certain problems can be closely related to specific areas in the transmission, which can make component examination and renewal easier. Refer to the *Fault finding* Section at the rear of this manual for more information.

Notes

Chapter 7 Part B:
Automatic transmission

Contents

Degrees of difficulty

Easy, suitable for novice with little experience	**Fairly easy,** suitable for beginner with some experience	**Fairly difficult,** suitable for competent DIY mechanic	**Difficult,** suitable for experienced DIY mechanic	**Very difficult,** suitable for expert DIY or professional

Specifications

Engine identification

Petrol engines

Indirect injection:
  Designation:
    1.8 litre EW7J4
    2.0 litre EW10J4
  Engine code:
    1.8 litre 6FZ
    2.0 litre . . . . RFN
Direct injection:
  Designation:
    2.0 litre EW10D
  Engine code . . . . RLZ

Diesel engines

2.0 litre SOHC:
  Designation. DW10ATED
  Engine code . . . . RHZ
2.0 litre DOHC:
  Designation. DW10BTED4
  Engine code . . . . RHR

General

Type . . . . Automatic, four or five forward speeds and reverse
Applications:
  EW7J4, EW10J4, EW10D and DW10ATED engines. AL4
  DW10BTED engine. AM6

Lubrication

Recommended fluid. . . . . Refer to *Lubricants and fluids*
Capacity (approximate):
  AL4:
    Drain and refill. . . . . 4.5 litres
    Total capacity (including torque converter). . . . . 6.0 litres
  AM6:
    Drain and refill. . . . . 3.0 litres
    Total capacity (including torque converter). . . . . 7.0 litres

Torque wrench settings

	Nm	lbf ft
AL4 transmission		
Engine/transmission left-hand mounting:		
Mounting bracket to transmission	60	44
Rubber mounting centre nut	65	48
Rubber mounting to body	27	20
Engine-to-transmission securing bolts	52	38
Fluid cooler centre bolt	50	37
Input speed sensor	10	7
Oil drain plug	33	24
Oil filler and level plugs	24	18
Output speed sensor	10	7
Selector lever position switch bolts	15	11
Torque converter-to-driveplate bolts*:		
Stage 1	10	7
Stage 2	30	22
Transmission selector shaft lever clamp bolt and nut	15	11
AM6 transmission		
Engine/transmission left-hand mounting:		
Mounting to transmission	55	41
Engine to transmission bolts	60	44
Fluid drain plug	10	7
Fluid filler plug	40	30
Fluid level plug	24	18
Heat exchanger centre bolt	42	31
Torque converter bolts*:		
Stage 1	20	15
Stage 2	Slacken 100°	
Stage 3	60	44

Do not re-use

1 General information

AL4 transmission

The AL4 transmission, available on cars with petrol engines as well as the SOHC diesel engine model, incorporates electronic control; the automatic gearchanges are electronically-controlled, rather than hydraulically. The advantage of electronic management is to provide a faster gearchange response. A kickdown facility is also provided, to enable a faster acceleration response when required.

The torque converter incorporates an automatic lock-up feature which eliminates any possibility of converter slip in the top two gears; this aids performance and economy. In addition to the normal alternative of manual change, the three-position mode switch on the centre console (adjacent to the selector lever) provides Normal, Sport or Snow settings, as required. In Sport mode, upshifts are delayed longer, to make full use of engine power. In Snow mode, either 2nd or 3rd gear is used to pull away from rest, maximising traction in slippery conditions.

Another feature of this transmission is the Park Lock, which is partly a safety and partly a security feature. Moving the lever out of the P position requires the ignition to be on, and the brake pedal must be depressed.

The gear selector cable has an automatic adjuster mechanism, meaning that cable adjustment should not be required. The AL4 transmission is also regarded as being 'lubricated for life', with routine fluid changes not featuring in the manufacturer's maintenance schedule.

In the event of a problem developing with the transmission, the transmission ECM may select one of two emergency back-up modes, to enable the car to continue being driven. When operating in this back-up mode, shifting out of N or R will become more jerky, or the transmission will only select 3rd gear (no gearchanges). If a fault is suspected, your Citroën dealer will be able to download fault codes from the transmission ECM memory, to speed-up diagnosis.

AM6 transmission

The AM6 transmission is available on DOHC diesel engined models. The transmission is electronically controlled, with an ECM mounted on the upper face of the transmission casing. This transmission offers 6 forward speeds, with manual or automatic gear selection, and three driving modes: Normal, Sport, and Snow. In function, the transmission is very similar to the AL4 unit, with the transmission ECM communicating with the engine management ECM to provide smooth gearchanges, with minimum fuel consumption and exhaust emissions. Citroën insist that the transmission is 'lubricated for life', with no requirement for routine changes.

If a fault occurs with the transmission, have the ECM's self-diagnosis facility interrogated by a Citroën dealer or suitably-equipped specialist, before considering any removal or investigative procedures.

All transmission types

Due to the complexity of the automatic transmission, any repair or overhaul work must be left to a Citroën dealer or specialist with the necessary special equipment for fault diagnosis and repair. The contents of the following Sections are therefore confined to supplying general information, and any service information and instructions that can be used by the owner.

2 Automatic transmission fluid – draining and refilling

Note: *Transmission fluid renewal on the AL4 and AM6 transmissions is not a service requirement and the following operations will normally only be necessary to allow transmission repair work to be carried out.*

1 Take the vehicle on a short run, to warm the transmission up to normal operating temperature.

2 Park the vehicle on level ground, switch off the ignition and apply the handbrake firmly. For improved access, chock the rear wheels then jack up the front of the vehicle and support it on axle stands (see *Jacking and vehicle support*). Remove the engine undershield if fitted. Note that the vehicle must be lowered

2.4 Unscrew the transmission drain plug (arrowed)

to the ground and be level to ensure accuracy when refilling and checking the fluid level.

3 Remove the dipstick (where applicable), then position a suitable container under the transmission drain plug. The drain plug is located in the centre of the transmission casing.

4 Unscrew the drain plug and allow the fluid to drain completely into the container. Note that the inner oil level plug is screwed into the outer drain plug, and both must be removed to drain the fluid **(see illustration)**. Also note that it is not possible to completely drain the torque converter. If the fluid is hot, take precautions against scalding. Clean the drain plug, being especially careful to wipe any metallic particles off the magnetic insert. Discard the original sealing washer which should be renewed whenever it is disturbed.

5 When the fluid has finished draining, clean the drain plug threads and those of the transmission casing, fit a new sealing washer to the drain plug and refit it to the transmission, tightening securely. Only fit the drain plug and do not fit the centre level plug. If the vehicle was raised for the draining operation, lower it to the ground.

6 Refilling the transmission with fluid is through the fluid filler plug **(see illustrations)**.

7 Position a container beneath the level plug, then add the specified type of fluid through the filler plug aperture until it starts to flow from the level plug. Note that the vehicle must be parked on flat level ground when checking the fluid level.

8 Refit and tighten the filler and level plugs, then start the engine and allow it to idle for a few minutes. Switch the engine off and recheck

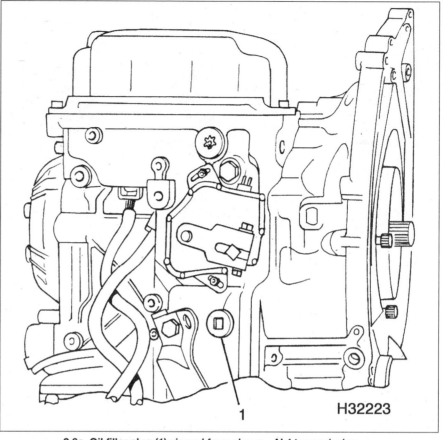

2.6a Oil filler plug (1) viewed from above – AL4 transmission . . .

the level, topping-up if necessary. Take the vehicle on a short run to fully distribute the new fluid around the transmission, then recheck the fluid level with reference to the relevant Part of Chapter 1.

3 Selector cable – removal and refitting

Removal

1 Apply the handbrake, switch on the ignition, depress the brake pedal and place the selector lever in position N. Switch off the ignition.

2 Remove the plastic cover from the top of

the engine (where fitted), then remove the air cleaner assembly as described in the relevant Part of Chapter 4.

3 Remove the battery cover.

4 Working in the engine compartment, carefully prise the selector cable balljoint from the selector lever on the transmission lever arm.

5 Pull back the outer cable sleeve and pull the cable upwards from the bracket (AL4 transmission) or press out the catch, squeeze together the clips and pull the cable from the bracket (AM6 transmission) **(see illustrations)**

6 Chock the rear wheels, then jack up the front of the car and support it on axle stands.

7 Refer to the relevant Part of Chapter 4 and remove the exhaust system and heat shields,

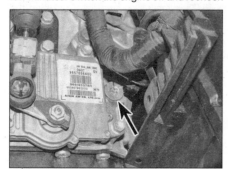

2.6b . . . and AM6 transmission (arrowed)

3.5a Push the catch (arrowed) rearwards . . .

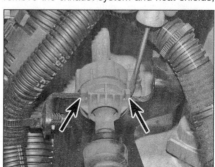

3.5b . . . then squeeze together the clips (arrowed) and pull the outer cable upwards

3.12a Prise up the cable locking catch (arrowed)

as necessary, for access to the cable and gear selector lever housing.

8 Pull the selector lever knob upwards from place, then carefully prise up and remove the lever surround trim.

9 Remove the centre console (Chapter 11).

10 Work back along the selector cable, releasing it from any relevant retaining clips, and noting its correct routing.

11 From inside the car, remove the selector lever soundproofing gaiter. Unscrew the nuts securing the selector lever housing to the floor. Release any remaining clips or ties, then remove the selector lever housing and cable as an assembly from under the car.

Refitting

12 Refitting is the reverse of removal, ensuring that the selector lever is in the P position and the cable is correctly routed and retained with any relevant clips and ties. To adjust the cable, pull out the locking catch, ensure the selector lever and transmission levers are in position N, then press the locking catch down **(see illustrations)**.

4 Oil seals – renewal

Driveshaft oil seals

1 Refer to Chapter 7A.

Selector shaft oil seal (AM6 transmission only)

2 Remove the ECM as described in Section 6 for access to the oil seal.

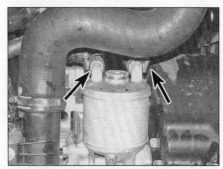

5.4 Fluid cooler hose clips (arrowed)

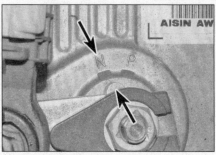

3.12b Ensure the transmission lever shaft lug is aligned with the N on the casing (arrowed)

3 Punch or drill two small holes opposite each other in the seal. Screw a self-tapping screw into each, and pull on the screws with pliers to extract the seal.

4 Clean the seal housing, and polish off any burrs or raised edges, which may have caused the seal to fail in the first place. Small imperfections can be removed using emery paper, but larger defects will require the renewal of the selector shaft.

5 Lubricate the lips of the new seal with clean engine oil, and carefully ease the seal into position over the end of the shaft, taking great care not to damage its sealing lip. Tap the seal into position until it is flush with the transmission casing, using a suitable tubular drift (such as a socket) which bears only on the hard outer edge of the seal. Note that the seal lips should face inwards.

6 Refit the selector lever position switch/ECM as described in Section 6.

5 Fluid cooler – removal and refitting

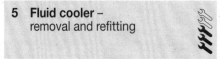

Removal

1 The fluid cooler is mounted on the transmission housing.

2 To gain access to the fluid cooler, chock the rear wheels jack up the front of the vehicle and support it on axle stands (see *Jacking and vehicle support*). Remove the left-hand front wheel and the engine undershield (where fitted).

3 Using hose clamps or similar, clamp both

6.7 Squeeze together the sides of the clip and pull the cable from the balljoint (arrowed)

of the fluid cooler coolant hoses to minimise coolant loss during subsequent operations.

4 Disconnect both coolant hoses from the fluid cooler, being prepared for some coolant spillage **(see illustration)**. Wash off any spilt coolant immediately with cold water, and dry the surrounding area before proceeding further.

5 Slacken and remove the fluid cooler mounting bolt(s), and remove the cooler from the transmission. Remove the mounting bolt seal(s), and the two seals fitted to the base of the cooler, and discard them; new ones must be used on refitting.

Refitting

6 Lubricate the new seals with clean automatic transmission fluid, then fit the two new seals to the base of the fluid cooler, and a new seal to the mounting bolt(s).

7 Locate the fluid cooler on the transmission housing, then refit the mounting bolt(s), and tighten to the specified torque setting, where given. Note that on AM6 transmission, the tab on the cooler must align between the two notches on the transmission casing.

8 Reconnect the coolant hoses to the fluid cooler and remove the hose clamps.

9 Refit the intake duct/air cleaner or support bracket components, engine undershield/ roadwheel as applicable.

10 On completion, top-up the cooling system and check the automatic transmission fluid level as described in the relevant Part of Chapter 1.

6 Electronic control module (ECM) – removal and refitting

Removal

AL4 transmissions

1 Disconnect the battery as described in Chapter 5A.

2 The automatic transmission ECM, together with the engine management ECM, is located in the ECM box, situated at the front right-hand side of the engine compartment, behind the battery. Undo the screws, and lift off the ECM box lid. The automatic transmission ECM is the unit nearest to the side of the car.

3 Release the wiring connector by lifting the locking lever on top of the connector. Lift the connector at the rear, disengage the tag at the front and carefully withdraw the connector from the ECM pins.

4 Undo the screws and lift the ECM upwards and remove it from its location.

AM6 transmission

5 Fully apply the handbrake, then turn on the ignition and place the selector lever in position N. Turn off the ignition.

6 Remove the air cleaner housing as described in the relevant part of Chapter 4.

7 Squeeze together the side of the clip and pull the end of the selector cable from

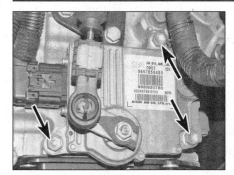

6.10 Transmission ECM mounting bolts (arrowed)

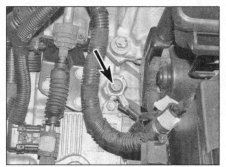

7.10 Transmission earth lead (arrowed)

7.12 Remove the tie-bar (arrowed)

the balljoint on the transmission lever **(see illustration)**.
8 Undo the nut and remove the lever from the top of the selector shaft.
9 Disconnect the ECM wiring plug.
10 Undo the 3 retaining bolts, and lift the ECM straight upwards and over the end of the shaft, disconnecting the ECM from the transmission internal connections as it's withdrawn **(see illustration)**.

Refitting

AL4 transmissions

11 Refitting is a reversal of removal. Note that if a new ECM has been fitted, it must be programmed and matched to the engine management ECM using Citroën diagnostic equipment. Entrust this task to a Citroën dealer or suitably-equipped specialist. Even after reprogramming/matching, the vehicle should be taken on an extensive road test, on a route which will allow numerous gearchanges and full use of the transmission mode settings. Initially, transmission response and gearchange quality may be less than acceptable, but should improve as the ECM control circuitry adapts to the transmission parameters.

AM6 transmission

12 Ensure the lug on the selector lever shaft is still in position N **(see illustration 3.12b)**.
13 Lower the ECM over the shaft, and position it on the transmission casing, ensure the locating notch fits over the lug on the casing. Tighten the ECM retaining bolts securely.
14 The refitting is a reversal of removal. Note that if a new ECM has been fitted, it must be programmed and matched to the engine management ECM using Citroën diagnostic equipment. Entrust this task to a Citroën dealer or suitably-equipped specialist. Even after reprogramming/matching, the vehicle should be taken on an extensive road test, on a route which will allow numerous gearchanges and full use of the transmission mode settings. Initially, transmission response and gearchange quality may be less than acceptable, but should improve as the ECM control circuitry adapts to the transmission parameters.

7 Automatic transmission – removal and refitting

Removal

1 Remove the battery and battery box as described in Chapter 5A.
2 Remove the air cleaner assembly and intake ducting as described in the relevant Part of Chapter 4.
3 Remove the engine management ECM and housing as described in the relevant Part of Chapter 4.
4 Chock the rear wheels, then jack up the front of the vehicle, and securely support it on axle stands. Remove both front roadwheels, then release the screws and clips and remove the wheel arch liner from under the left-hand wing. Remove the engine undershield.
5 Disconnect the selector cable from the transmission as descried in Section 3.
6 Note their fitted positions, then disconnect the various wiring connectors from the transmission. Release the wiring harnesses from any retaining clips.
7 Using hose clamps or similar, clamp both the fluid cooler coolant hoses to minimise coolant loss during subsequent operations.
8 Remove the fluid cooler as described in Section 5. Plug of cover the openings to prevent contamination.
9 Remove both driveshafts as described in Chapter 8.
10 Disconnect the earth lead from the top of the transmission casing **(see illustration)**.
11 On turbo diesel engines, slacken the clamps, undo the retaining bolts and remove the charge air pipe from under the engine.
12 Remove the metal tie bar from behind the engine oil sump, between the two halves of the subframe **(see illustration)**.
13 Remove the pre-catalyser or catalytic converter from the manifold/turbocharger as applicable, as described in the relevant Part of Chapter 4.
14 Undo the starter motor mounting bolts and move the starter clear without disconnecting the wiring.
15 From under the car, undo the bolts securing the lower torque rod to the right-hand

driveshaft intermediate bearing housing and subframe. Manipulate the torque rod from its location.
16 Undo the bolts securing the power steering pipes to the transmission/subframe.
17 Attach a hoist or support bar to the engine left-hand lifting eye and just take the engine weight.
18 Attach a second hoist to the transmission lifting eye located next to the fluid cooler.
19 Locate the access hole (remove the driveplate lower cover plate, where fitted) at the lower rear of the cylinder block, then turn the crankshaft, by means of a socket on the crankshaft pulley bolt, until one of the torque converter retaining bolts is accessible through the access hole.
20 Undo the accessible torque converter bolt then turn the crankshaft as necessary and undo the remaining two bolts. Discard the bolts, new ones must be fitted.
21 With the transmission securely supported, undo the bolts/nuts and remove the left-hand transmission mounting assembly.
22 Slacken and remove the bolts securing the transmission housing to the engine. Note the correct fitted positions of each bolt, and the necessary brackets as they are removed to use as a reference on refitting. Make a final check that all components have been disconnected, and are positioned clear of the transmission so that they will not hinder the removal procedure.
23 With the bolts removed, pull the transmission to the left, to free it from its locating dowels. Ensure the torque converter stays with the transmission, and is not pulled from the input shaft.
24 On AM6 transmissions, once the transmission is free, and sufficient clearance exists, insert a bolt with a suitable washer through the RPM sensor hole in the transmission bell-housing to retain the torque converter on the transmission. It's essential the torque converter stays on the transmission input shaft.
25 On other transmissions, as the transmission casing is withdrawn, ensure the torque converter stays with the transmission, and is not pulled from the input shaft.
26 On all transmissions, lower the engine and transmission hoists and manoeuvre the transmission out from under the car. Remove

the locating dowels from the transmission or engine if they are loose, and keep them in a safe place.

27 With the transmission removed make sure that the torque converter is held securely in place using a bracket across the bellhousing, etc.

Refitting

28 Both transmission types are refitted using a reversal of the removal procedure, bearing in mind the following points:

a) *Ensure that the bush fitted to the centre of the crankshaft is in good condition, and apply a little Molykote G1 grease to the torque converter centring pin. Do not apply too much, otherwise there is a possibility of the grease contaminating the torque converter.*

b) *On the AL4 transmission, turn the torque converter so that one of the mounting studs is positioned opposite the right-hand driveshaft output shaft (approximately the 9 o'clock position). Turn the engine crankshaft so that the corresponding mounting hole in the driveplate is in the same position. The torque converter mounting studs and the corresponding holes in the driveplate should then be in alignment when the transmission is fitted.*

c) *Ensure that the engine/transmission locating dowels are correctly positioned prior to installation.*

d) *Once the transmission and engine are correctly joined, refit the securing bolts, tightening them to the specified torque setting, then remove the metal strip used to retain the torque converter.*

e) *Tighten all nuts and bolts to the specified torque (where given).*

f) *Renew the driveshaft oil seals with reference to Chapter 7A.*

g) *Refit the driveshafts to the transmission as described in Chapter 8.*

h) *Citroën insist that if a new transmission is fitted, the fluid cooler must also be renewed.*

i) *On completion, top-up the cooling system, then refill the transmission with the specified type and quantity of fluid as described in Section 2.*

j) *If a new transmission has been fitted, it will be necessary to reprogramme the transmission ECM using dedicated Citroën diagnostic equipment. Entrust this task to a Citroën dealer or suitably-equipped specialist.*

8 Automatic transmission overhaul – general information

In the event of a fault occurring with the transmission, it is first necessary to determine whether it is of an electrical, mechanical or hydraulic nature, and to do this, special test equipment is required. It is therefore essential to have the work carried out by a Citroën dealer or suitably-equipped specialist, if a transmission fault is suspected.

Do not remove the transmission from the car for possible repair before professional fault diagnosis has been carried out, since most tests require the transmission to be in the vehicle.

Chapter 8
Driveshafts

Contents

Degrees of difficulty

Easy, suitable for novice with little experience	**Fairly easy,** suitable for beginner with some experience	**Fairly difficult,** suitable for competent DIY mechanic	**Difficult,** suitable for experienced DIY mechanic	**Very difficult,** suitable for expert DIY or professional

Specifications

Lubrication (overhaul only – see text)

Lubricant type/specification . . . . Use only special grease supplied in sachets with gaiter kits – joints are otherwise pre-packed with grease and sealed

Torque wrench settings

	Nm	lbf ft
Driveshaft retaining nut	325	240
Lower suspension arm balljoint retaining nuts	45	33
Right-hand driveshaft intermediate bearing retaining bolts/nuts	20	15
Roadwheel bolts	90	66

1 General information

Drive is transmitted from the differential to the front wheels by means of two solid-steel driveshafts of unequal length.

Both driveshafts are splined at their outer ends, to accept the wheel hubs, and are threaded so that each hub can be fastened by a large nut. The inner end of each driveshaft is splined, to accept the differential sun gear.

Constant velocity (CV) joints are fitted to each end of the driveshafts, to ensure that the smooth and efficient transmission of power at all suspension and steering angles. The outer constant velocity joints are of the ball-and-cage type, and the inner constant velocity joints are of the tripod type.

On the right-hand side, due to the length of the driveshaft, the inner constant velocity joint is situated approximately halfway along the shaft's length, and an intermediate support bearing is mounted in the engine/transmission rear mounting bracket. The inner end of the driveshaft passes through the bearing (which prevents any lateral movement of the driveshaft inner end) and the inner constant velocity joint outer member.

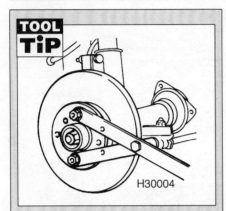

TOOL TiP

H30004

Use a fabricated tool to hold the front hub stationary whilst slackening the driveshaft nut.

2 Driveshafts – removal and refitting

Note: *A new suspension lower balljoint nut will be required on refitting.*

Removal

1 Chock the rear wheels of the car, firmly apply the handbrake, then jack up the front of the car and support it on axle stands (see *Jacking and vehicle support*). Remove the appropriate front roadwheel.
2 Prise out the R-clip and remove the locking

2.5a Pull the hub assembly outwards . . .

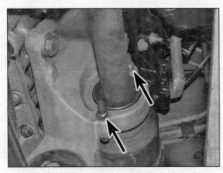

2.7a Slacken the intermediate bearing retaining nuts (arrowed) and rotate the bolts 90° on some models . . .

2.4 Use an Allen key to counterhold the balljoint shank whilst slackening the nut

cap from the driveshaft nut. In order to slacken the nut, the wheel hub must be prevented from rotating. This can be achieved by attaching a locking tool to the hub, or having an assistant firmly depress the foot brake pedal **(see Tool Tip)**. Slacken the driveshaft nut.
3 On manual transmission models drain the transmission oil as described in Chapter 7A.
4 Slacken and remove the nut securing the front suspension lower balljoint to the hub carrier, and free the balljoint from the lower arm, using a balljoint separator tool **(see illustration)**. Discard the nut and remove the protector plate (if loose).

Left-hand driveshaft

5 Release the wiring harness from the retaining bracket on the inner wing, then carefully pull the hub carrier assembly outwards, and withdraw the driveshaft outer constant velocity joint from the hub assembly **(see illustrations)**.

2.5b . . . then manoeuvre the driveshaft from the hub

2.7b . . . whilst on others the Torx bolts are slackened and the retaining plate swung rearwards

If necessary, the shaft can be tapped out of the hub using a soft-faced mallet.
6 Support the driveshaft, then withdraw the inner constant velocity joint from the transmission, taking care not to damage the driveshaft oil seal. Remove the driveshaft from the vehicle. **Note:** *Do not allow the vehicle to rest on its wheels with one or both driveshafts removed, as damage to the wheel bearing(s) may result. If moving the vehicle is unavoidable, temporarily insert the outer end of the driveshaft(s) in the hub(s) and tighten the driveshaft nut(s). Support the inner end(s) of the driveshaft(s) to avoid damage.*

Right-hand driveshaft

7 On some models, it's necessary to loosen the two intermediate bearing retaining bolt nuts, then rotate the bolts through 90°, so that their offset heads are clear of the bearing outer race, whilst on others slacken the retaining bolts several turns and swing the retaining plate rearwards **(see illustrations)**.
8 Release the wiring harness from the retaining bracket on the inner wing, then carefully pull the hub carrier assembly outwards, and withdraw the driveshaft outer constant velocity joint from the hub assembly. If necessary, the shaft can be tapped out of the hub using a soft-faced mallet.
9 Support the outer end of the driveshaft, then pull on the inner end of the shaft to free the intermediate bearing from its mounting bracket.
10 Once the driveshaft end is free from the transmission, slide the dust seal (where fitted) off the inner end of the shaft, noting which way around it is fitted, and remove the driveshaft from the vehicle. **Note:** *Do not allow the vehicle to rest on its wheels with one or both driveshafts removed, as damage to the wheel bearing(s) may result. If moving the vehicle is unavoidable, temporarily insert the outer end of the driveshaft(s) in the hub(s) and tighten the driveshaft nut(s). Support the inner end(s) of the driveshaft(s) to avoid damage.*

Refitting

11 Before installing the driveshaft, examine the driveshaft oil seal in the transmission for signs of damage or deterioration and, if necessary, renew it as described in the relevant part of Chapter 7. It is highly recommended that the seal is renewed, regardless of its apparent condition.
12 Thoroughly clean the driveshaft splines, and the apertures in the transmission and hub assembly. Apply a thin film of grease to the oil seal lips, and to the driveshaft splines and shoulders. Check that all gaiter clips are securely fastened.

Left-hand driveshaft

13 Offer up the driveshaft, and locate the joint splines with those of the differential sun gear, taking great care not to damage the oil seal. Push the joint fully into position.
14 Locate the outer constant velocity joint splines with those of the hub carrier, and slide the joint back into position in the hub.

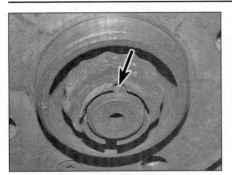

2.16a Fit the locking cap to the nut so the holes align (arrowed) . . .

2.16b . . . then insert the R-clip

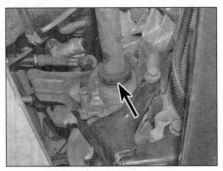

2.21 Right-hand driveshaft dust seal (arrowed)

15 Refit the protector plate (where removed) to the lower balljoint, then align the balljoint with the lower arm. Fit the new balljoint nut and tighten it to the specified torque setting.
16 Lubricate the inner face and threads of the driveshaft nut with clean engine oil, and refit it to the end of the driveshaft. Use the method employed on removal to prevent the hub from rotating (see paragraph 2), and tighten the driveshaft retaining nut to the specified torque. Check that the hub rotates freely, then engage the locking cap with the driveshaft nut, so that one of its cut-outs is aligned with the driveshaft hole, and secure the cap in position with the R-clip **(see illustrations)**.
17 Refit the roadwheel, then lower the vehicle to the ground and tighten the roadwheel bolts to the specified torque.
18 Refill the manual transmission with the specified type and amount of fluid/oil, and check the level using the information given in Chapter 7A.

Right-hand driveshaft

19 Check that the intermediate bearing rotates smoothly, without any sign of roughness or undue free play between its inner and outer races. If necessary, renew the bearing as described in Section 5. Examine the dust seal for signs of damage or deterioration, and renew if necessary.
20 Apply a smear of grease to the outer race of the intermediate bearing, and to the inner lip of the dust seal (where fitted).
21 Pass the inner end of the shaft through the bearing mounting bracket then, where necessary, carefully slide the dust seal into

position on the driveshaft, ensuring that its flat surface is facing the transmission **(see illustration)**.
22 Carefully locate the inner driveshaft splines with those of the differential sun gear, taking care not to damage the oil seal. Align the intermediate bearing with its mounting bracket, and push the driveshaft fully into position. If necessary, use a soft-faced mallet to tap the outer race of the bearing into position in the mounting bracket.
23 Locate the outer constant velocity joint splines with those of the hub carrier, and slide the joint back into position in the hub.
24 Ensure that the intermediate bearing is correctly seated, then either rotate its retaining bolts back through 90°, so that their offset heads are resting against the bearing outer race, and tighten the retaining nuts to the specified torque, or swing the retaining plate back into position and tighten the bolts securely (as applicable – dependant on the type of fixing – see paragraph 7).
25 Carry out the operations described above in paragraphs 14 to 18.

3 Driveshaft rubber gaiters – renewal

Outer joint

1 Remove the driveshaft from the vehicle as described in Section 2.
2 Secure the driveshaft in a vice equipped with soft jaws, and release the two outer

gaiter retaining clips. If necessary, the gaiter retaining clips can be cut to release them **(see illustration)**.
3 Slide the rubber gaiter down the shaft, to expose the outer constant velocity joint. Scoop out the excess grease.
4 Using a hammer and suitable soft metal drift, sharply strike the inner member of the outer joint to drive it off the end of the shaft **(see illustration)**. The joint is retained on the driveshaft by a circlip, and striking the joint in this manner forces the circlip into its groove, so allowing the joint to slide off.
5 Once the joint assembly has been removed, remove the circlip from the groove in the driveshaft splines, and discard it **(see illustration)**. A new circlip must be fitted on reassembly.
6 Withdraw the rubber gaiter from the driveshaft.
7 With the constant velocity joint removed from the driveshaft, thoroughly clean the joint using paraffin, or a suitable solvent, and dry it thoroughly. Carry out a visual inspection of the joint.
8 Move the inner splined driving member from side-to-side, to expose each ball in turn at the top of its track. Examine the balls for cracks, flat spots, or signs of surface pitting.
9 Inspect the ball tracks on the inner and outer members. If the tracks have widened, the balls will no longer be a tight fit. At the same time, check the ball cage windows for wear or cracking between the windows.
10 If on inspection, any of the constant velocity joint components are found to be worn or damaged, it will be necessary to renew the

3.2 If necessary, cut through the gaiter clips

3.4 Use a punch to drive the inner member of the outer joint from the shaft

3.5 Prise the old circlip from the shaft

3.11a Fit the small diameter clip to the new gaiter, and slide it over the end of the driveshaft . . .

3.11b . . . fit a new circlip into the groove on the end of the shaft . . .

3.11c . . . align the outer joint inner member with the splines on the shaft . . .

3.11d . . . and tap the outer joint into place with a soft-faced hammer. Ensure the joint is securely retained by the circlip . . .

3.11e . . . pack the joint with the contents of the grease sachet supplied with the kit. Work the grease well into the joint . . .

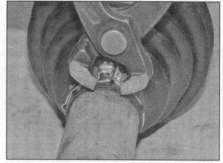

3.11f . . . locate the small diameter of the gaiter in the groove on the shaft, and crimp the retaining clip . . .

complete joint assembly (where available), or even the complete driveshaft (where no joint components are available separately). Refer to your Citroën dealer or parts specialist for further information on parts availability. If the joint is in satisfactory condition, obtain a repair kit consisting of a new gaiter, circlip, retaining clips, and the correct type and quantity of grease.

11 To install the new gaiter, perform the operations shown **(see illustrations)**. Be sure to stay in order, and follow the captions carefully. Note that the gaiter retaining clips supplied with the repair kit may be different to those shown in the sequence. To secure this other type of clip in position, lock the ends of the clip together, then remove any slack in the clip by carefully compressing the raised section of the clip using a pair of side-cutters.

Note: *If the inner gaiter is to be renewed, carry out the procedure before fitting the new outer gaiter.*

12 Check that the constant velocity joint moves freely in all directions, then refit the driveshaft to the vehicle as described in Section 2.

Inner joint

13 Remove the driveshaft from the vehicle as described in Section 2.
14 Remove the outer constant velocity joint as described above in paragraphs 1 to 5.
15 Tape over the splines on the driveshaft, and carefully remove the outer constant velocity joint rubber gaiter, and (where fitted) the gaiter inner end plastic bush. It is recommended that the outer joint gaiter is also renewed, regardless of its apparent condition.

16 Make alignment marks between the inner joint housing and the outer shaft, so it can be refitted into its original position.
17 Release the retaining clips, then slide the inner gaiter off the shaft and (where fitted) remove its plastic bush. As the gaiter is released, the joint outer member will also be freed from the end of the shaft.
18 Thoroughly clean the joint using paraffin, or a suitable solvent, and dry it thoroughly. Check the tripod joint bearings and joint outer member for signs of wear, pitting or scuffing on their bearing surfaces. Check that the bearing rollers rotate smoothly and easily around the tripod joint, with no traces of roughness.
19 If on inspection, the tripod joint or outer member reveal signs of wear or damage, it will be necessary to renew the complete driveshaft assembly, since the joint is not available separately. If the joint is in satisfactory condition, obtain a repair kit consisting of a new gaiter, retaining clips, and the correct type and quantity of grease. Although not strictly necessary, it is also recommended that the outer constant velocity joint gaiter is renewed, regardless of its apparent condition.
20 On reassembly, pack the inner joint with the grease supplied in the gaiter kit **(see illustration)**. Work the grease well into the bearing tracks and rollers, while twisting the joint.
21 Clean the shaft, using emery cloth to remove any rust or sharp edges which may damage the gaiter, then slide the plastic bush (where fitted) and inner joint gaiter along

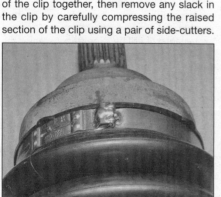

3.11g . . . with the large diameter of the gaiter located on the outside of the outer joint, crimp the retaining clip

3.20 Pack the inner joint with the grease supplied in the kit

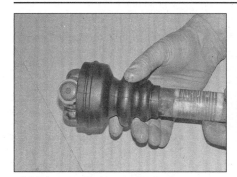

3.21 Locate the new gaiter in the groove on the shaft

3.22 Fit the new clips and crimp them into place

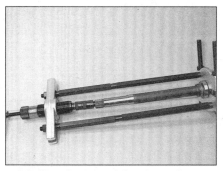

5.3 Use a long-reach bearing puller to remove the intermediate bearing from the right-hand driveshaft

the driveshaft. Locate the plastic bush in its recess on the shaft, and seat the inner end of the gaiter on top of the bush; where no bush is fitted, seat the small end of the gaiter in the recess on the shaft **(see illustration)**.

22 Fit the outer member over the end of the shaft, and locate the gaiter in the groove on the joint outer member. Push the outer member onto the joint, so that its spring-loaded plunger is compressed, then lift the outer edge of the gaiter to equalise air pressure in the gaiter. Fit both the inner and outer retaining clips, securing them in position using the information given in paragraph 11 **(see illustration)**. Ensure that the gaiter retaining clips are securely tightened, then check that the joint moves freely in all directions.

23 Refit the outer constant velocity joint components using the information given in paragraph 11.

4 Driveshaft overhaul – general information

1 If any of the checks described in Chapter 1A or 1B reveal wear in any driveshaft joint, first remove the roadwheel trim or centre cap (as appropriate).

2 If the R-clip is still in position, the driveshaft nut should be correctly tightened; if in doubt, remove the R-clip and locking cap, and use a torque wrench to check that the nut is securely fastened. Once tightened, refit the locking cap and R-clip, then refit the centre cap or trim. Repeat this check on the remaining driveshaft nut.

3 Road test the vehicle, and listen for a metallic clicking from the front as the vehicle is driven slowly in a circle on full-lock. If a clicking noise is heard, this indicates wear in the outer constant velocity joint. This means that the joint must be renewed; reconditioning is not possible.

4 If vibration, consistent with roadspeed, is felt through the car when accelerating, there is a possibility of wear in the inner constant velocity joints.

5 To check the joints for wear, remove the driveshafts, then dismantle them as described in Section 3; if any wear or free play is found, the affected joint must be renewed. In the case of the inner joints (and on some models, the outer joints), this means that the complete driveshaft assembly must be renewed, as the joints are not available separately. Refer to your Citroën dealer or parts specialist for latest information on the availability of driveshaft components.

5 Right-hand driveshaft intermediate bearing – renewal

Note: *A suitable bearing puller will be required, to draw the bearing and collar off the driveshaft end.*

1 Remove the right-hand driveshaft as described in Section 2 of this Chapter.

2 Check that the bearing outer race rotates smoothly and easily, without any signs of roughness or undue free play between the inner and outer races. If necessary, renew the bearing as follows.

3 Using a long-reach universal bearing puller, carefully draw the collar and intermediate bearing off the driveshaft inner end **(see illustration)**. Apply a smear of grease to the inner race of the new bearing, then fit the bearing over the end of the driveshaft. Using a hammer and suitable piece of tubing which bears only on the bearing inner race, tap the new bearing into position on the driveshaft, until it abuts the constant velocity joint outer member. Once the bearing is correctly positioned, tap the bearing collar onto the shaft until it contacts the bearing inner race.

4 Check that the bearing rotates freely, then refit the driveshaft as described in Section 2.

Chapter 9
Braking system

Contents

Degrees of difficulty

Easy, suitable for novice with little experience	**Fairly easy,** suitable for beginner with some experience	**Fairly difficult,** suitable for competent DIY mechanic	**Difficult,** suitable for experienced DIY mechanic	**Very difficult,** suitable for expert DIY or professional

Specifications

General

System type	Dual hydraulic circuit diagonally split. Anti-lock braking system standard on all models. Front and rear disc brakes fitted to all models. Servo assisted. Cable-operated handbrake operating on front wheels

Front brakes

Type	Ventilated disc, with single-piston sliding caliper
Disc diameter:	
1.6 and 2.0 litre models	283.0 mm
1.8 litre models:	
Hatchback	266.0 mm
Estate	283.0 mm
Disc thickness:	
1.6, 1.8 Estate and 2.0 litre models:	
New	26.0 mm
Minimum	24.0 mm
1.8 litre Hatchback models:	
New	22.0 mm
Minimum	20.0 mm
Maximum variation in disc thickness between sides	0.1 mm
Maximum disc run-out	0.05 mm
Minimum disc pad friction material	2.5 mm
ABS sensor air gap (non-adjustable)	0.2 to 1.5 mm

Rear brakes

Type	Solid disc, with twin-piston fixed calipers
Disc diameter	276.0 mm
Disc thickness:	
New	14.0 mm
Minimum thickness	12.0 mm
Maximum variation in thickness between sides	0.1 mm
Maximum disc run-out	0.05 mm
Minimum disc pad friction material thickness	3.0 mm
ABS sensor air gap (non-adjustable)	0.15 to 1.5 mm

Torque wrench settings

	Nm	lbf ft
ABS hydraulic valve block securing nuts.........................	22	16
ABS wheel sensor securing bolts/studs.........................	8	6
Brake pedal assembly-to-bulkhead bolts	18	13
Brake pipe unions	8	6
Front caliper bracket-to-hub carrier bolts	120	89
Front caliper guide bolts......................................	31	23
Master cylinder nuts..	20	15
Rear caliper securing bolts*...................................	70	52
Roadwheel bolts..	90	66
Servo bolts/nuts..	21	15

* Do not re-use – see text

---

1 General information and precautions

General information

The braking system of the servo-assisted, dual-circuit hydraulic type. The arrangement of the hydraulic circuit is such that each circuit operates one front and one rear brake from a tandem master cylinder. Under normal circumstances, both circuits operate in unison. However, in the even of hydraulic failure in one circuit, full braking force will still be available at two wheels.

The front brake calipers are of single-piston floating type, operating on ventilated discs, while the rear brake calipers are of twin-piston fixed type, operating on solid discs.

On diesel engines, there is insufficient vacuum in the intake manifold to operate the braking system effectively at all times. To overcome this, a vacuum pump is mounted on the end of the cylinder head, and is driven directly from the end of the camshaft.

The mechanical handbrake mechanism is operated by a floor-mounted lever, and acts on the front calipers via flexible cables.

An anti-lock braking system (ABS) is fitted as standard on all models. The system is described in more detail in Section 15.

All models are available with CBC (Cornering Brake Control) and ESP (Electronic Stability Program). These systems are designed to maintain the stability of the vehicle during extreme braking/cornering manoeuvres by operating the wheel brakes independently on each other. Theses systems utilise the same wheel speed sensor/brake operating components as the ABS/TCS system, with the addition of a lateral acceleration sensor (Yaw rate) and a steering angle sensor.

Precautions

Cleanliness is of the utmost importance when working on the hydraulic system and its components. Clean all adjacent areas before disconnecting components. After removal, blank off all orifices, and ensure that components, pipes and hoses do not get contaminated.

When servicing any of this system, work carefully and methodically; also observe scrupulous cleanliness when overhauling any of the hydraulic system. Always renew components (in axle sets – where applicable) if in doubt about their condition, and use only genuine Citroën parts, or at least those of known good quality.

2 Hydraulic system – bleeding

Warning: Hydraulic fluid is poisonous; wash off immediately and thoroughly in the case of skin contact, and seek immediate medical advice if any fluid is swallowed or gets into the eyes. Certain types of hydraulic fluid are inflammable, and may ignite when brought into contact with hot components; when servicing any hydraulic system, it is safest to assume that the fluid is inflammable, and to take precautions against the risk of fire as though it is petrol that is being handled. Hydraulic fluid is also an effective paint stripper, and will attack plastics; if any is spilt, it should be washed off immediately, using copious quantities of fresh water. Finally, it is hygroscopic (it absorbs moisture from the air) – old fluid may be contaminated and unfit for further use. When topping-up or renewing the fluid, always use the recommended type, and ensure that it comes from a freshly-opened sealed container.

General

1 The correct operation of any hydraulic system is only possible after removing all air from the components and circuit; this is achieved by bleeding the system.

2 During the bleeding procedure, add only clean, unused hydraulic fluid of the recommended type; never re-use fluid that has already been bled from the system. Ensure that sufficient fluid is available before starting work.

3 If there is any possibility of incorrect fluid being already in the system, the brake components and circuit must be flushed completely with uncontaminated, correct fluid, and new seals should be fitted to the various components.

4 If hydraulic fluid has been lost from the system, or air has entered because of a leak, ensure that the fault is cured before proceeding further.

5 Park the vehicle over an inspection pit or on car ramps. Alternatively, apply the handbrake then jack up the front and rear of the vehicle and support it on axle stands (see *Jacking and vehicle support*). For improved access with the vehicle jacked up, remove the roadwheels.

6 Check that all pipes and hoses are secure, unions tight and bleed screws closed. Clean any dirt from around the bleed screws.

7 Unscrew the master cylinder reservoir cap, and top the master cylinder reservoir up to the MAX level line; refit the cap loosely, and remember to maintain the fluid level at least above the MIN level line throughout the procedure, otherwise there is a risk of further air entering the system.

8 There is a number of one-man, do-it-yourself brake bleeding kits currently available from motor accessory shops. It is recommended that one of these kits is used whenever possible, as they greatly simplify the bleeding operation, and also reduce the risk of expelled air and fluid being drawn back into the system. If such a kit is not available, the basic (two-man) method must be used, which is described in detail below.

9 If a kit is to be used, prepare the vehicle as described previously, and follow the kit manufacturer's instructions, as the procedure may vary slightly according to the type being used; generally, they are as outlined below in the relevant sub-section.

10 Whichever method is used, the same sequence must be followed (paragraphs 11 and 12) to ensure the removal of all air from the system.

Bleeding sequence

11 If the system has been only partially disconnected, and suitable precautions were taken to minimise fluid loss, it should only be necessary to bleed that part of the system (ie, the primary or secondary circuit).

12 If the complete system is to be bled, then it should be done working in the following sequence:
   a) Left-hand front brake.
   b) Right-hand rear brake.
   c) Left-hand rear brake.
   d) Right-hand front brake.

Bleeding

Basic (two-man) method

13 Collect together a clean glass jar, a suitable length of plastic or rubber tubing which is a tight fit over the bleed screw, and a ring spanner to fit the screw. The help of an assistant will also be required.

14 Remove the dust cap from the first bleed screw in the sequence. Fit the spanner and tube to the screw, place the other end of the tube in the jar, and pour in sufficient fluid to cover the end of the tube **(see illustration)**.

15 Ensure that the master cylinder reservoir fluid level is maintained at least above the MIN level mark throughout the procedure.

16 Have the assistant fully depress and release the brake pedal several times to build-up initial pressure in the system.

17 Unscrew the bleed screw approximately half a turn then have the assistant slowly depress the brake pedal down to the floor and hold it there. Tighten the bleed screw and have the assistant slowly release the pedal to its rest position.

18 Repeat the procedure given in paragraph 17 until the fluid emerging from the bleed screw is free from air bubbles. After every two or three depressions of the pedal, check the level of fluid in the reservoir and top-up if necessary.

19 When no more air bubbles appear, securely tighten the bleed screw, remove the tube and spanner, and refit the dust cap. Do not overtighten the bleed screw.

20 Repeat the procedure on the remaining screws in the sequence, until all air is removed from the system and the brake pedal feels firm again.

Using a one-way valve kit

21 As the name implies, these kits consist of a length of tubing with a one-way valve fitted, to prevent expelled air and fluid being drawn back into the system; some kits include a translucent container, which can be positioned so that the air bubbles can be more easily seen flowing from the end of the tube.

22 The kit is connected to the bleed screw, which is then opened. The user returns to the driver's seat, depresses the brake pedal with a smooth, steady stroke, and slowly releases it; this is repeated until the expelled fluid is clear of air bubbles.

23 Note that these kits simplify work so much that it is easy to forget the master cylinder reservoir fluid level; ensure that this is maintained at least above the MIN level line at all times.

Using a pressure-bleeding kit

24 These kits are usually operated by a reservoir of pressurised air contained in the spare tyre. However, note that it will probably be necessary to reduce the pressure to a lower level than normal; refer to the instructions supplied with the kit.

25 By connecting a pressurised, fluid-filled container to the master cylinder reservoir, bleeding can be carried out simply by opening each screw in turn (in the specified sequence), and allowing the fluid to flow out until no more air bubbles can be seen in the expelled fluid.

26 This method has the advantage that the large reservoir of fluid provides an additional safeguard against air being drawn into the system during bleeding.

27 Pressure-bleeding is particularly effective when bleeding 'difficult' systems, or when bleeding the complete system at the time of routine fluid renewal.

All methods

28 When bleeding is complete, and firm pedal feel is restored, wipe off any spilt fluid, securely tighten the bleed screws, and refit the dust caps.

29 Check the hydraulic fluid level in the master cylinder reservoir, and top-up if necessary (see *Weekly checks*).

30 Discard any hydraulic fluid that has been bled from the system; it will not be fit for re-use.

31 Check the feel of the brake pedal. If it feels at all spongy, air must still be present in the system, and further bleeding is required. Failure to bleed satisfactorily after a reasonable repetition of the bleeding procedure may be due to worn master cylinder seals, or air trapped in the ABS modulator. In which case either the master cylinder must be renewed, or the system bled using Citroën dedicated diagnostic equipment.

3 Hydraulic pipes and hoses – renewal

1 If any pipe or hose is to be renewed, minimise fluid loss by first removing the master cylinder reservoir cap, then tightening it down onto a piece of polythene to obtain an airtight seal. The cap incorporates a level warning float so, alternatively, hose clamps can be fitted to flexible hoses to isolate sections of the circuit; metal brake pipe unions can be plugged (if care is taken not to allow dirt into the system) or capped immediately they are disconnected. Place a wad of rag under any union that is to be disconnected, to catch any spilt fluid.

2 If a flexible hose is to be disconnected, unscrew the brake pipe union nut before removing the spring clip which secures the hose to its mounting bracket **(see illustration)**. Where applicable, unscrew the banjo union bolt securing the hose to the caliper and recover the copper washers.

3 To unscrew union nuts, it is preferable to obtain a 'split' brake pipe spanner of the correct size; these are available from most motor accessory shops. Failing this, a close-fitting open-ended spanner will be required, though if the nuts are tight or corroded, their flats may be rounded-off if the spanner slips. In such a case, a self-locking wrench is often the only way to unscrew a stubborn union, but it follows that the pipe and the damaged nuts must be renewed on reassembly. Always clean a union and surrounding area before disconnecting it. If disconnecting a component with more

2.14 Bleeding a rear brake caliper

than one union, make a careful note of the connections before disturbing any of them.

4 If a brake pipe is to be renewed, it can be obtained, cut to length and with the union nuts and end flares in place, from a dealer's parts shop. All that is then necessary is to bend it to shape, following the line of the original, before fitting it to the car. Alternatively, most motor accessory shops can make up brake pipes from kits, but this requires very careful measurement of the original, to ensure that the new one is of the correct length. The safest answer is usually to take the original to the shop as a pattern.

5 On refitting, do not overtighten the union nuts.

6 When refitting hoses to the calipers, always use new copper washers and tighten the banjo union bolts to the specified torque. Make sure that the hoses are positioned so that they will not touch surrounding bodywork or the roadwheels.

7 Ensure that the pipes and hoses are correctly routed, with no kinks, and that they are secured in the clips or brackets provided. After fitting, remove the polythene from the reservoir, and bleed the hydraulic system as described in Section 2. Wash off any spilt fluid, and check carefully for fluid leaks.

4 Front brake pads – renewal

⚠️ *Warning: Renew both sets of front brake pads at the same time – never renew the pads on*

3.2 Undo the union nut and remove the spring clip

only one wheel, as uneven braking may result. Note that the dust created by wear of the pads may contain asbestos, which is a health hazard. Never blow it out with compressed air, and don't inhale any of it. An approved filtering mask should be worn when working on the brakes. DO NOT use petrol or petroleum-based solvents to clean brake parts; use brake cleaner or methylated spirit only.

1 Chock the rear wheels then slacken the front roadwheel bolts. Jack up the front of the vehicle and support it on axle stands (see *Jacking and vehicle support*). Remove both front roadwheels.

2 Follow the accompanying photos **(illustrations 4.2a to 4.2w)** for the actual pad renewal procedure. Be sure to stay in order and read the caption under each illustration, and note the following points:

a) New pads may have an adhesive foil on the backplates. Remove this foil prior to installation.

b) Thoroughly clean the caliper guide surfaces, and apply a little brake assembly (Molykote P37 or Copperslip) grease.

c) If new pads are to be fitted, use a piston retraction tool to push the piston back *and* twist it at the same time; **anti-clockwise** for the right-hand caliper, and **clockwise** for the left-hand caliper – keep an eye on the fluid level in the reservoir whilst retracting the piston. Do not allow the rubber gaiter around the piston to revolve as the piston is rotated.

3 Depress the brake pedal repeatedly, until the pads are pressed into firm contact with the brake disc, and normal (non-assisted) pedal pressure is restored.

4 Repeat the above procedure on the remaining front brake caliper.

5 Check the handbrake adjustment as described in Section 11.

6 Refit the roadwheels, then lower the vehicle to the ground and tighten the roadwheel bolts to the specified torque.

7 Check the hydraulic fluid level as described in *Weekly checks*.

Caution: New pads will not give full braking efficiency until they have bedded-in. Be prepared for this, and avoid hard braking as far as possible for the first hundred miles or so after pad renewal.

4.2a Disconnect the brake pad wear sensors wiring plugs from the bracket on the top of the caliper (arrowed)

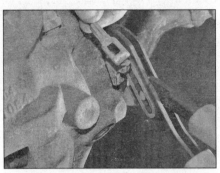
4.2b Rotate the handbrake operating lever on the caliper with a pair of pliers and disengage the cable end fitting. Pull the outer cable from the caliper

4.2c Pull the brake hose from the bracket above the caliper

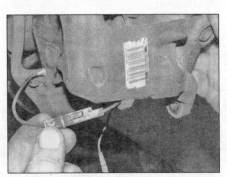
4.2d Pull the lower wear indicator sensor from the caliper

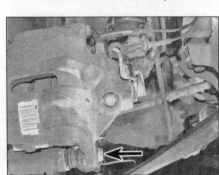
4.2e Undo the lower caliper guide bolt (arrowed) . . .

4.2f . . . and pivot the caliper up and around to expose the brake pads

4.2g Remove the outer pad . . .

4.2h . . . and the inner pad

4.2i Clean the pad mounting surfaces in the caliper mounting bracket

4.2j Take the opportunity to measure the thickness of the discs, and compare with the dimensions given in the Specifications

4.2k Fit the new inner pad (friction material against the disc) . . .

4.2l . . . and the outer pad

4.2m Push the inner pad wear sensor into the hole in the pad backplate . . .

4.2n . . . followed by the outer pad sensor

4.2o If new pads have been fitted, the piston must be forced back into the caliper housing to provide the necessary clearance. See text for direction. Keep an eye on the fluid level in the reservoir!

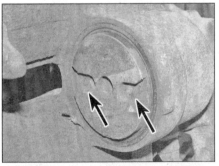

4.2p When the piston has been forced back enough, position the slots (arrowed) horizontally to align with the pins on the back of the pads

4.2q Lower the caliper back down into place . . .

4.2r . . . and feed the lower wear sensor wire back through the bracket on the caliper

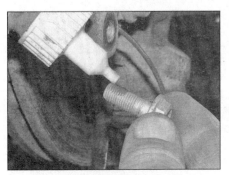

4.2s Apply a little thread-locking compound . . .

4.2t . . . then refit the caliper guide bolt (arrowed) and tighten it to the specified torque

4.2u Refit the brake hose to the bracket

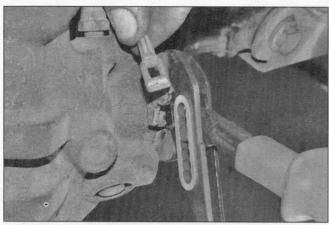

4.2v Insert the handbrake cable into the bracket and reconnect the end fitting to the operating lever

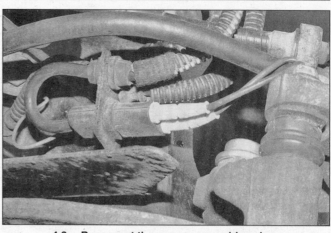

4.2w Reconnect the wear sensor wiring plugs

5 Rear brake pads – renewal

⚠ **Warning: Renew both sets of rear brake pads at the same time – never renew the pads on only one wheel, as uneven braking may result. Note that the dust created by wear of the pads may contain asbestos, which is a health hazard. Never blow it out with compressed air, and don't inhale any of it. An approved filtering mask should be worn when working on the brakes. DO NOT use petrol or petroleum-based solvents to clean brake parts; use brake cleaner or methylated spirit only.**

1 Chock the front wheels, slacken the rear road-wheel bolts, then jack up the rear of the vehicle and support it on axle stands (see *Jacking and vehicle support*). Remove the rear wheels.

2 With the handbrake lever fully released, follow the accompanying photos **(see illustrations 5.2a to 5.2r)** for the actual pad renewal procedure. Be sure to stay in order and read the caption under each illustration, and note the following points:

a) If re-installing the original pads, ensure they are fitted to their original positions.

b) Thoroughly clean the caliper guide surfaces, and apply a little brake assembly (Molykote P37 or Copperslip) grease.

3 Depress the brake pedal repeatedly, until the pads are pressed into firm contact with the brake disc, and normal (non-assisted) pedal pressure is restored.

4 Repeat the above procedure on the remaining brake caliper.

5 Refit the roadwheels, then lower the vehicle to the ground and tighten the roadwheel bolts to the specified torque.

6 Check the hydraulic fluid level as described in *Weekly checks*.

Caution: New pads will not give full braking efficiency until they have bedded-in. Be prepared for this, and avoid hard braking as far as possible for the first hundred miles or so after pad renewal.

5.2a Slacken the pad retaining bolt nut . . .

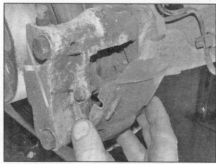

5.2b . . . and remove the cover

5.2c Remove the retaining bolt . . .

5.2d . . . and the spring

5.2e Remove the inner pad and anti-rattle shim . . .

5.2f . . . and use a screwdriver to push the piston back into the caliper. Keep an eye on the fluid level in the reservoir!

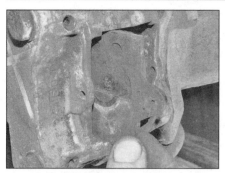

5.2g Remove the outer pad and anti-rattle shim

5.2h Use a wire brush to clean the pad mounting surfaces in the caliper

5.2i Apply a little high-temperature grease to the backing plate of the new pad . . .

5.2j . . . the position the new anti-rattle shim on the backing plate . . .

5.2k . . . apply a little of the grease to the shim . . .

5.2l . . . and insert the pad into the caliper. Ensure the friction material is against the disc!

5.2m Use a screwdriver to force back the outer piston into the caliper. Keep an eye on the fluid level in the reservoir!

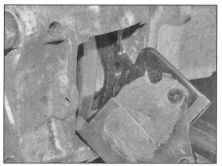

5.2n Apply a little grease to the outer pad backing plate and shim (as described for the inner pad), then slide them into the caliper

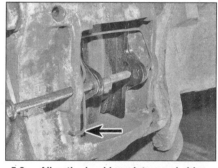

5.2o Align the backing plates and shims refit the spring (arrowed), then apply a little grease to the retaining bolt and insert it into position

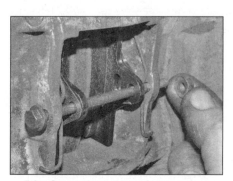

5.2p Screw the nut on a few turns . . .

5.2q . . . refit the cover . . .

5.2r . . . and tighten the nut and bolt securely

6.7 Caliper mounting bracket Torx bolts (arrowed)

6.8 Front brake disc mounting Torx bolts (arrowed)

6.18 Rear brake disc mounting Torx bolts (arrowed)

6 Brake discs –
inspection, removal and refitting

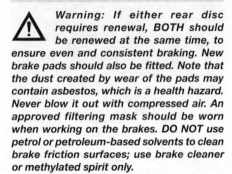

⚠ *Warning: If either rear disc requires renewal, BOTH should be renewed at the same time, to ensure even and consistent braking. New brake pads should also be fitted. Note that the dust created by wear of the pads may contain asbestos, which is a health hazard. Never blow it out with compressed air. An approved filtering mask should be worn when working on the brakes. DO NOT use petrol or petroleum-based solvents to clean brake friction surfaces; use brake cleaner or methylated spirit only.*

Front brake disc

Inspection

1 Chock the rear wheels, then jack up the front of the car and support it on axle stands (see *Jacking and vehicle support*). Remove the appropriate front roadwheel.

2 Slowly rotate the brake disc so that the full area of both sides can be checked; remove the brake pads if better access is required to the inboard surface (see Section 4). Light scoring is normal in the area swept by the brake pads, but if heavy scoring or cracks are found, the disc must be renewed.

3 It is normal to find a lip of rust and brake dust around the disc's perimeter; this can be scraped off if required. If, however, a lip has formed due to excessive wear of the brake pad swept area, then the disc's thickness must be measured using a micrometer **(see illustration 4.2j)**. Take measurements at several places around the disc, at the inside and outside of the pad swept area; if the disc has worn at any point to the specified minimum thickness or less, the disc must be renewed.

4 If the disc is thought to be warped, it can be checked for run-out. Either use a dial gauge mounted on any convenient fixed point, while the disc is slowly rotated, or use feeler gauges to measure (at several points all around the disc) the clearance between the disc and a fixed point, such as the caliper mounting bracket. If the measurements obtained are at the specified maximum or beyond, the disc

is excessively warped and must be renewed; however, it is worth checking first that the hub bearing is in good condition (Chapters 1 and/ or 10). Also try the effect of removing the disc and turning it through 180°, to reposition it on the hub; if the run-out is still excessive, the disc must be renewed.

5 Check the disc for cracks, especially around the wheel bolt holes, and any other wear or damage, and renew if necessary.

Removal

6 Remove the front brake pads (Section 4), then undo the remaining caliper guide bolt and move the caliper to one side, taking care not to strain the fluid hose. Suspend the caliper to one side using wire or string.

7 Unscrew the two bolts securing the caliper bracket to the hub carrier. Note that on some models, the brake air cooling duct is retained by the caliper bracket bolts **(see illustration)**.

8 Unscrew the two brake disc securing Torx bolts, then withdraw the disc from the hub **(see illustration)**.

Refitting

9 Ensure that the mating faces of the disc and the hub are absolutely clean, then fit the disc to the hub.

10 Refit and tighten the disc securing screws.

11 Refit the caliper mounting bracket, and tighten the securing bolts to the specified torque.

12 Refit the brake pads as described in Section 4.

Rear brake disc

Inspection

13 Apply the handbrake and chock the front wheels, then jack up the rear of the car and support it securely on axle stands (see *Jacking and vehicle support*).

14 Proceed as described for the front brake disc in paragraphs 2 to 5, but refer to Section 5 if the brake pads are to be removed.

Removal

15 Jack up the vehicle and support it securely on axle stands with the wheels clear of the ground (see *Jacking and vehicle support*).

16 Remove the relevant roadwheel.

17 Remove the brake caliper as described in Section 8.

18 Remove the disc securing Torx bolts, then withdraw the disc from the hub **(see illustration)**.

Refitting

19 Where applicable, remove the caliper upper securing bolt, and move the caliper to one side to facilitate refitting of the disc.

20 Ensure that the mating faces of the disc and the hub are absolutely clean, then fit the disc to the hub. Refit and tighten the disc securing screw.

21 Refit the caliper as described in Section 8, and the brake pads as described in Section 5.

7 Front brake caliper –
removal, overhaul and refitting

Note: *Refer to the precautions at the end of Section 1 before proceeding.*

Removal

1 Remove the brake pads (see Section 4).

2 Place a suitable container under the fluid hose union on the caliper, to catch any escaping hydraulic fluid. Unscrew the union and disconnect the hose from the caliper. Plug the open ends of the hose and caliper to prevent dirt ingress and further fluid loss.

3 Remove the remaining guide bolt, and withdraw the caliper assembly from the mounting bracket.

Overhaul

4 The caliper can be overhauled after obtaining the relevant repair kit from a Citroën dealer. Ensure the correct repair kit is obtained for the caliper being worked on. Note the locations of all components to ensure correct refitting, and lubricate the new seals using clean brake fluid. Follow the assembly instructions supplied with the repair kit. **Note:** *At the time of writing, it would appear that only the guide pins rubber sleeves and the piston dust seal are available as a kit with the various screws – check with your parts supplier.*

Refitting

5 Offer the caliper into position, then refit the guide bolt and tighten it to the specified torque.

6 Reconnect the fluid hose, and tighten the union.

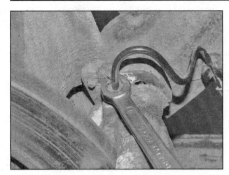

8.5 Undo the union and disconnect the fluid pipe from the rear caliper

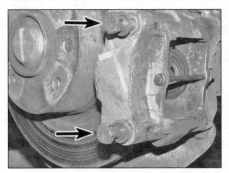

8.6 Undo the caliper mounting bolts (arrowed)

8.12 Clean out the mounting holes in the caliper body using a 10 mm drill bit held in a bench vice

7 Refit the brake pads as described in Section 4.
8 Bleed the brakes with reference to Section 2.
9 Refit the roadwheels and lower the vehicle to the ground.

8 Rear brake caliper –
removal, overhaul and refitting

Note: *Refer to the precautions at the end of Section 1 before proceeding. A new fluid pipe seal will be required on refitting.*

Removal

1 Jack up the vehicle and support it securely on axle stands with the wheels clear of the ground (see *Jacking and vehicle support*).
2 Remove the relevant roadwheel.
3 Remove the brake pads (see Section 5).
4 Refit the pad retaining pin to the caliper, then refit and tighten the pin securing nut to hold the two halves of the caliper together.
5 Place a suitable container under the fluid pipe union on the caliper to catch any escaping hydraulic fluid. Unscrew the union and disconnect the pipe from the caliper. Plug the open ends of the pipe and caliper, or clamp the flexible fluid hose to prevent dirt ingress and further fluid loss **(see illustration)**.
6 Unscrew the two securing bolts and withdraw the caliper **(see illustration)**.

Overhaul

7 The caliper can be overhauled after obtaining the relevant repair kit from a Citroën dealer. Ensure that the correct repair kit is obtained for the caliper being worked on. Note the locations of all components to ensure correct refitting, and lubricate the new seals using clean brake fluid. Follow the assembly instructions supplied with the repair kit.

Refitting

Note: *There are two types of rear calipers fitted to the C5. At first glance they look identical, but the type fitted to later vehicles (from RPO No 08879) are identified by four holes drilled in the caliper castings. The refitting procedure for the two types is different. Follow the procedure given for your type of caliper.*

Vehicles up to RPO No 08878

8 Lubricate the threads of the caliper securing bolts, then refit the caliper and tighten the bolts to the specified torque.
9 Reconnect the fluid pipe to the caliper, using a new seal, and tighten the union.
10 Unscrew the securing nut, and remove the pad retaining pin from the caliper.

Vehicles from RPO No 00879

11 Remove the caliper mounting bolts from the caliper. On our vehicle, it was necessary to force the bolts from the caliper using a hydraulic press. Discard the mounting bolts, new ones must be fitted.
12 Clean out the mounting bolt holes in the caliper body using a 10 mm drill bit. Take great care to only clean out the sealant, and

8.13 Use a drill bit to clean out sealant from the drilled holes leading to the mounting holes

8.15a Apply sealant to the caliper mounting face . . .

not to touch the caliper body with the drill **(see illustration)**.
13 Remove any sealant residue from the drilled holes at the top and bottom of the casting **(see illustration)**.
14 Ensure the mating surfaces between the caliper and the suspension arm is clean and free from grease and corrosion **(see illustration)**.
15 Apply a little sealant to the caliper and suspension arm mating surfaces (Citroën recommend FORMAJOINT 510, but any anaerobic sealant with a temperature resistance of 200°C will suffice) **(see illustrations)**.
16 Position the caliper, coat the new bolts with Loctite 7649 activator, and tighten them to the specified torque. Don't forget to place the washers on the bolts before inserting them **(see illustration)**.

8.14 Ensure the caliper and suspension arm mounting faces are free from corrosion

8.15b . . . and spread it over the whole of the mounting face to prevent corrosion from forming

8.16 Ensure the washers are in place before fitting the new bolts

17 Inject Loctite 270 thread-locking compound through the outer holes in the caliper body, until it can be seen emerging though the inner holes, then spray Loctite 7649 activator over the holes to seal them **(see illustration)**.
18 Reconnect the fluid pipe to the caliper, using a new seal, and tighten the union.

All vehicles
19 Refit the brake pads (see Section 5).
20 Bleed the brakes with reference to Section 2.
21 Refit the roadwheel and lower the vehicle to the ground.

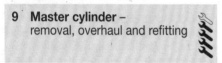

9 Master cylinder – removal, overhaul and refitting

Removal

1 Disconnect the battery negative lead as described in Chapter 5A.

9.3 Brake fluid level sensor wiring plug, and clutch fluid hose (arrowed)

9.8 Disconnect the fluid pipes and pressure sensor wiring plug (where fitted)

8.17 Inject thread-locking compound into the outer holes

2 Exhaust the vacuum present in the brake servo unit by repeatedly depressing the brake pedal.
3 Disconnect the wiring from the brake fluid warning switch **(see illustration)**.
4 Syphon out the fluid from the reservoir. Alternatively, open any convenient bleed screw in the system, and gently pump the brake pedal to expel the fluid through a plastic tube connected to the bleed screw (see Section 2). Do not allow the level of the fluid to fall below the base of the reservoir.

 Warning: Do not syphon the fluid by mouth, as it is poisonous; use a syringe or an old poultry baster.

5 Place cloth rags beneath the master cylinder to catch spilt fluid.
6 On manual transmission models, disconnect the clutch hydraulic hose from the brake fluid reservoir.
7 Release the clip each side, and pull the fluid

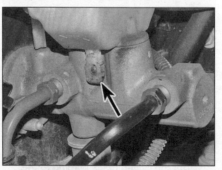

9.7 Release the clip each side (arrowed) and remove the reservoir

9.9 Master cylinder mounting nuts (arrowed)

reservoir upwards to release it from the rubber sealing grommets **(see illustration)**.
8 Note the position of the brake lines, then unscrew the union nuts and move the lines to one side so that they are just clear of the master cylinder **(see illustration)**. Do not bend the brake lines excessively. If available, use a split spanner to unscrew the nuts, as they can be very tight. Tape over or plug the outlets of the brake lines and master cylinder. Discard the sealing washers (where fitted) – new ones must be used.
9 Unscrew the mounting nuts and withdraw the master cylinder from the front of the vacuum servo **(see illustration)**. Wrap the master cylinder in cloth rags and remove it from the engine compartment. Take care not to spill fluid on the vehicle paintwork.

Overhaul
10 At the time of writing, no overhaul parts were available for the master cylinder, with the exception of the reservoir mounting grommets. If the cylinder is faulty, it may have to be renewed as a complete unit – check with a Citroën dealer or parts specialist.

Refitting
11 Refitting is a reversal of removal, noting the following points:
a) *Always use new brake fluid.*
b) *Tighten all fasteners to the specified torque where given.*
c) *Bleed the system as described in Section 2.*
d) *Reconnect the battery as described in Chapter 5A.*
e) *Thoroughly check the operation of the braking system prior to using the vehicle on the road.*

10 Brake pedal – removal and refitting

Removal

1 Disconnect the battery negative lead as described in Chapter 5A.
2 Remove the facia as described in Chapter 11.
3 Remove the retaining clip, and pull out the pin securing the servo cross-shaft pushrod to the brake pedal **(see illustration)**.

10.3 Prise the retaining clip from the pushrod pin

10.4 Brake pedal pivot bolt nut (arrowed)

11.8 Undo the Torx bolts (arrowed) and lift up the rear section of the console

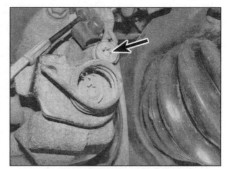

11.10a Ensure the operating lever is against the stop screw (arrowed)

4 Undo the retaining nut, and pull out the pedal pivot bolt to the right-hand side **(see illustration)**.
5 Lower the pedal from place, and if necessary withdrawn the pivot bush.

Refitting

6 Refitting is a reversal of removal.

11 Handbrake – adjustment

Automatic wear adjustment

1 The front brake calipers incorporate an automatic adjustment mechanism, which compensates for the clearance in the handbrake operating mechanism created by brake pad wear. The adjustment mechanism is operated by hydraulic pressure as the brakes are applied.
2 The following operation should be carried out if the front brake pads have been removed, or if work has been carried out on the front calipers, in order to initially set the adjustment mechanism.
3 Start the engine, and allow it to run at idle.
4 Ensure that the handbrake lever is in the 'released' position.
5 Depress the brake pedal several times to operate the adjustment mechanism.
6 Fully apply and release the handbrake lever 5 times.
7 Release the brake pedal, and check that the handbrake can be fully applied by moving the lever 5 clicks. If necessary, adjust the handbrake cables as described in the following paragraphs.

Cable adjustment

8 Fully release the handbrake, then lift out the centre console rear ashtray, undo the 2 Torx bolts and remove the rear section of the centre console **(see illustration)**.
9 Depress and release the brake pedal 5 times, then apply and release the handbrake lever 5 times.
10 Working on one of the calipers, check that the caliper lever is on the stop screw, and the clearance between the end of the cable and the lever is 0.1 to 1.0 mm **(see illustrations)**.

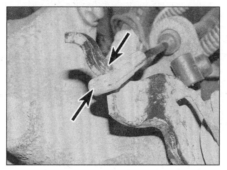

11.10b The clearance between the lever and the cable end fitting must be 0.1 to 1.0 mm (arrowed)

11 Repeat the procedure on the remaining caliper.
12 With the lever in the released position, adjust the cable nut until all clearance between the nut and the bracket is eliminated **(see illustration)**.
13 Operate the handbrake several times, and check that the handbrake can be fully applied by moving the lever 5 clicks, and the front wheels are able to spin freely with the handbrake released.

12 Handbrake lever – removal and refitting

Removal

1 Disconnect the battery negative lead as described in Chapter 5A.
2 Remove the centre console (Chapter 11).

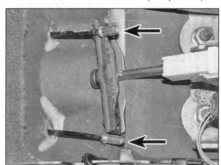

12.3 Detach the cables (arrowed) from the equaliser plate

11.12 Handbrake cable adjustment nut (arrowed)

3 Slacken the handbrake cable adjusting nut sufficiently, then disconnect the cables from the equaliser plate **(see illustration)**.
4 Disconnect the handbrake 'on' warning light switch wiring plug.
5 Unscrew the 4 securing nuts, and withdraw the lever assembly **(see illustration)**.

Refitting

6 Refitting is a reversal of removal, but on completion, check the handbrake adjustment as described in Section 11.

13 Handbrake cables – removal and refitting

Removal

1 The handbrake mechanism is operated by

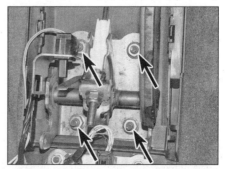

12.5 Handbrake lever assembly mounting nuts (arrowed)

14.3 Wriggle the stop-light switch whilst pulling it rearwards

14.4 Rotate the switch 90° anti-clockwise and pull it from the bracket

14.5 Prise the old clip from the bracket (arrowed)

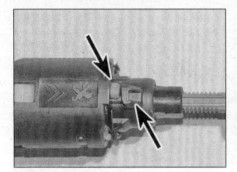

14.10 Align the red locking catch with the centring lug (arrowed) . . .

two cables – one for each side of the vehicle. Begin by disconnecting the battery negative lead as described in Chapter 5A.

2 Jack up the vehicle and support it securely on axle stands with the wheels clear of the ground (see *Jacking and vehicle support*). Remove the front roadwheels.

3 Remove the centre console as described in Chapter 11.

4 Slacken the adjusting nut, and disengage the cable end fittings from the handbrake equaliser plate **(see illustration 12.3)**.

5 Disengage the cables from the calipers **(see illustration 4.2b)**.

6 Pull the cables from the cable guides.

Refitting

7 Refitting is a reversal of removal, remembering to adjust the cables as described in Section 11.

14 Stop-light switch – removal and refitting

Removal

1 On RHD models, remove the passenger's side lower facia panel as described in Chapter 11. On LHD models, remove the driver's side lower facia panel.

Pre-facelift models (up to September 2004)

2 Disconnect the light switch wiring plug. Note that 2 switches may be fitted. The white switch illuminates the stop-light, whilst the

14.11 . . . and pull the pushrod out a little (arrowed)

red or brown switch is for the cruise control system.

3 Grasp the switch, gently wriggle it from side-to-side whilst pulling it rearwards **(see illustration)**.

Post-facelift models (from September 2004)

4 Disconnect the wiring plug, rotate the switch 90° anti-clockwise and remove it **(see illustration)**.

Refitting

Pre-facelift models

5 Citroën insist that a new switch retaining clip is fitted. Prise the old clip from the bracket **(see illustration)**.

6 Fit the new clip, then reconnect the wiring plug to the brake light switch (white in colour).

7 Turn on the ignition. The brake lights should illuminate.

8 Insert the switch into the clip and push it forward notch-by-notch, until the brake lights extinguish.

9 Measure the distance from the bracket face to the mounting face of the switch, then insert the cruise control switch (where fitted) to the same dimension.

Post-facelift models

10 Ensure the red locking catch is aligned with the switch centring lug **(see illustration)**.

11 Pull out the switch pushrod a little **(see illustration)**.

12 Insert the switch into the bracket, and push it firmly until the base of the switch is in contact with the bracket.

13 Rotate the switch 90° clockwise to lock it in position.

14 If the switch is correctly fitted, the pushrod support should be flush with the body of the switch, and the end of the pushrod is in contact with the brake pedal/cross-shaft lever.

All models

15 The remainder of refitting is a reversal of removal.

15 Anti-lock braking system (ABS) – general information and fault finding

General information

1 To prevent wheel locking, the system provides pressure modulation in the braking circuits. To achieve this, sensors fitted to each wheel monitor the rotational speeds of the wheels and are able to detect when there is a risk of wheel locking (low rotational speed). Solenoid valves are positioned in the brake circuits to each wheel, and the solenoid valves are incorporated in a modulator assembly, which is controlled by an electronic control module (ECM). The ECM controls modulation of the braking effort applied to each wheel, according to the information supplied by the wheel sensors.

2 The ECM has the capacity to monitor the status and condition of all the components in the system, including itself. If the ECM detects a fault, it responds by shutting down the ABS and illuminating the dashboard-mounted ABS warning light. Under these circumstances, conventional non-ABS braking is maintained. Note also that the warning light will be illuminated if the power supply to the ABS ECM is disconnected (eg, if the supply fuse blows).

3 If the ABS warning lights indicate a fault, it is very difficult to diagnose problems without the equipment and expertise to electronically 'interrogate' the ECM for fault codes. Therefore, this Section is limited firstly to a list of the basic checks that should be carried out to establish the integrity of the system.

4 If the cause of the fault cannot be immediately identified using the check list described, the *only* course of action open is to take the vehicle to a Citroën dealer or specialist for examination. Dedicated test equipment is needed to interrogate the ABS ECM to determine the nature of the fault.

Basic fault finding checks

Brake fluid level

5 Check the brake fluid level (see *Weekly checks*). If the level is low, check the complete braking system for signs of leaks. Refer to Chapter 1A or 1B and carry out a check of the brake hoses and pipes throughout the vehicle. If no leaks are apparent, remove each roadwheel in turn, and check for leaks at the brake caliper pistons.

Fuses

6 The main fuses for the ABS/TCS/ESP are located in the engine compartment electrical centre. Remove the cover and pull out the fuses. Visually check the fuse filaments; if it is difficult to see whether or not it has blown, use a multimeter to check the continuity of the fuse. If any of the fuses are blown, determine the cause before fitting a new one – if necessary, have the vehicle inspected by a Citroën dealer or specialist.

Electrical connections

7 The engine bay is a hostile environment for electrical connections, and even the best seals can sometimes be penetrated. Water, chemicals and air will induce corrosion on the connector's contacts and prevent good continuity, sometimes intermittently. Disconnect the battery negative cable, then check the security and condition of all connectors at the ABS hydraulic unit, situated on the left-hand side of the engine bay.

8 Unplug each connector, and examine the contacts inside. Clean any contacts that are found to be dirty or corroded. Avoid scraping the contacts clean with a blade, as this will accelerate corrosion later. Use a piece of lint-free cloth in conjunction with a proprietary cleaning solvent to produce a clean, shiny contact surface.

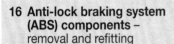

16 Anti-lock braking system (ABS) components – removal and refitting

Hydraulic valve block/ modulator/ECM

Removal

1 Disconnect the battery negative lead as described in Chapter 5A.
2 Remove the engine management ECM and module box as described in the relevant part of Chapter 4.
3 Use a brake pedal depressor tool, or length of wood jammed between the steering wheel and the pedal to firmly depress the brake pedal. This will minimise the amount of fluid loss.

16.4 Lift the locking catch (arrowed) and disconnect the wiring plug

4 Disconnect the wiring plug from the ABS ECM **(see illustration)**.
5 Note their fitted positions, then loosen the unions, and disconnect the fluid pipes from the valve block **(see illustration)**. Be prepared for fluid spillage, and plug the open ends of the pipes and valve block to avoid further fluid spillage and dirt ingress.
6 Remove the three securing nuts, then lift out the hydraulic valve block, complete with the electronic control module. No further dismantling of the modulator assembly is recommended.

Refitting

7 Refitting is a reversal of removal, bearing in mind the following points:
 a) *New valve blocks/modulator are supplied prefilled with fluid – remove the plugs prior to connecting the fluid pipes.*
 b) *New ECMs must be initialised and programmed using Citroën dedicated diagnostic equipment. Entrust this task to a Citroën dealer or suitably-equipped specialist.*
 c) *On completion, bleed the brake hydraulic system as described in Section 2.*

Front wheel sensor

Removal

8 Chock the rear wheels, then jack up the front of the vehicle, and support it securely on axle stands (see *Jacking and vehicle support*). Remove the relevant roadwheel.
9 Unclip the wiring from the brackets.
10 Trace the wiring back from the sensor, and

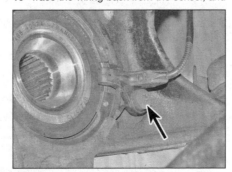

16.11 ABS wheel speed sensor retaining Torx bolt (arrowed) – driveshaft removed for clarity

16.5 Disconnect the pipes from the valve block

separate the two halves of the wiring connector (in the engine compartment). Note the routing of the wiring to aid correct refitting.
11 Unscrew the securing bolt, and withdraw the sensor **(see illustration)**. Take care not to damage the sensor – they're fragile.

Refitting

12 Refitting is a reversal of removal, noting the following points:
 a) *Ensure that the mating faces of the sensor and the hub carrier are clean.*
 b) *Coat the threads of the sensor securing bolt with thread-locking compound before refitting.*
 c) *Check the air gap between the end of the sensor and the hub/seal, and compare with that given in the Specifications, to ensure the sensor is correctly fitted.*
 d) *Route the wiring as noted before removal.*

Rear wheel sensor

Removal

13 Working as described in the relevant part of Chapter 4, lower the fuel tank sufficiently to gain access to the ABS sensor wiring harness clips on the top of the tank, and the clips on the rear suspension arm **(see illustration)**.
14 Trace the wiring back from the sensor, and separate the two halves of the wiring connector.
15 Tie a length of string to the end of the sensor wiring harness.
16 Unscrew the securing bolt, and withdraw the sensor **(see illustration)**. Take care not to damage the sensor – they're fragile.

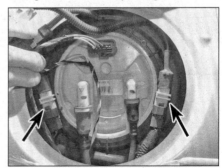

16.13 Rear ABS wheel speed sensor connections (arrowed)

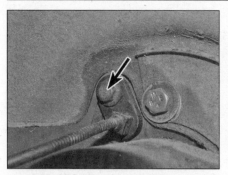

16.16 ABS rear wheel speed sensor retaining bolt (arrowed)

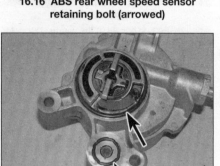

17.4b Renew the pump O-ring seals (arrowed)

Refitting

17 Refitting is a reversal of removal, bearing in mind the following points:

a) *Ensure that the sensor protector plate is correctly refitted.*

b) *Make sure that the mating faces of the sensor and the suspension arms are clean.*

c) *Check the air gap between the end of the sensor and the hub/seal, and compare with that given in the Specifications, to ensure the sensor is correctly fitted.*

18.5 Prise off the servo pushrod pin retaining clip (arrowed)

17.4a Vacuum pump retaining bolt (arrowed)

17.4c Ensure the drive lugs engage with the slot in the end of the camshaft (arrowed)

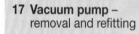

d) *Apply a little thread-locking compound to the sensor bolt.*

17 Vacuum pump –
removed and refitting

Removal

1 Remove the plastic cover on the top of the engine.

18.6 Disconnect the vacuum hose and sensor wiring plug (arrowed)

2 Remove the air ducting at the left-hand end of the cylinder head.

3 Note their fitted positions, and disconnect the vacuum pipe(s) from the vacuum pump at the left-hand end of the cylinder head.

4 Undo the retaining screws and remove the vacuum pump. Recover the O-ring seals **(see illustrations)**.

Refitting

5 Refitting is a reversal of removal.

18 Servo unit –
removal and refitting

Removal

1 Remove the brake master cylinder as described in Section 9.

2 Undo the unions and remove the rigid brake fluid pipes from the master cylinder to the ABS modulator.

3 Undo the nut securing the suspension fluid hose bracket to the inner wing and move the hose to one side.

4 Working inside the car, remove the passenger's side glovebox as described in Chapter 11.

5 Release the clip securing the servo pushrod to the brake pedal cross-shaft **(see illustration)**.

6 Disconnect the vacuum hose and the servo pressure sensor wiring plug **(see illustration)**.

7 Undo the nuts securing the servo unit to the bulkhead bracket in the engine compartment, and pull the servo from place **(see illustration)**.

Refitting

8 Refitting is a reversal of removal.

18.7 Servo mounting nuts (arrowed)

Chapter 10
Suspension and steering

Contents

Degrees of difficulty

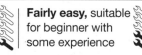

Easy, suitable for novice with little experience	Fairly easy, suitable for beginner with some experience	Fairly difficult, suitable for competent DIY mechanic	Difficult, suitable for experienced DIY mechanic	Very difficult, suitable for expert DIY or professional

Specifications

Front wheel alignment and steering angles

Front wheel toe setting . . . . 0 to 3.0 mm (0°00' to 0°25') toe-out
Front wheel castor (not adjustable) . . . . 3° ± 30'
Front wheel camber (not adjustable) . . . . 0°00' ± 30'
King pin inclination (not adjustable) . . . . 12°56' ± 30'

Rear wheel alignment

Rear wheel toe setting (not adjustable) . . . . 4.5 ± 1.3 mm (0°38' ± 11') toe-in
Rear wheel camber . . . . -1° ± 20'

Suspension fluid

Type . . . . See *Lubricants and fluids*
Capacity:
  Hydractive 3 system:
    RHD . . . . 4.7 litres
    LHD . . . . 4.5 litres
  Hydractive 3+ system . . . . 5.4 litres

Torque wrench settings

	Nm	lbf ft
Front suspension		
Anti-roll bar clamp	42	31
Anti-roll bar drop link securing nuts*	64	47
Driveshaft retaining nut	325	240
Firmness regulator bolts.	10	7
Front subframe rear brackets to body	100	74
Front subframe tie-bar bolts.	66	49
Front subframe to body	140	103
Hub carrier-to-suspension strut clamp nut and bolt	55	41
Hydraulic regulator securing screws	10	7
Lower arm balljoint to hub carrier	250	185
Lower arm front pivot nut*	130	96
Lower arm rear securing bolts	105	77
Lower balljoint-to-lower arm nut*	45	33
Suspension sphere.	27	20
Suspension strut upper fixing nut:		
Stage 1	50	37
Stage 2	Angle-tighten a further 65°	
Suspension upper mounting to body nuts	43	32
Rear suspension		
Anti-roll bar bolts	130	96
Firmness regulator bolts.	10	7
Hydraulic regulator securing screws	10	7
Rear hub nut*	250	185
Rear subframe mounting bolts.	111	82
Rear subframe rubber mountings to body	90	66
Suspension sphere.	27	20
Suspension strut retaining bolts.	16	12
Trailing arm pivot shaft nut*	150	111
Steering		
Steering column mounting nuts/bolts	23	17
Steering column universal joint pinch-bolt.	23	17
Steering rack-to-subframe nuts	80	59
Steering wheel bolt.	20	15
Track rod balljoint locknut	60	44
Track rod balljoint nut*	35	26
Track rod-to-steering rack balljoint	90	66
Roadwheels		
Roadwheel bolts.	90	66

Do not re-use

1 General information

The suspension is of an independent hydropneumatic type, exclusive to Citroën.

The front suspension comprises a vertically-mounted hydraulic suspension strut unit, a lower arm, and an anti-roll bar. The lower arms and the anti-roll bar are mounted on the front subframe. The front suspension sphere hydraulic units are supplied with hydraulic fluid under pressure, supplied by the BHI (Built-in Hydro-electronic Interface) unit located in the front, right-hand corner of the engine compartment. The BHI unit comprises of an electric pump, an ECM, and the associated valves and wiring. The pressure of fluid to and from the spheres is controlled by the ECM based on information received from the electronic height sensors, vehicle speed (from the engine management ECM), steering angle sensor, and the manually-adjustable height setting controls on the centre console. An anti-roll bar is attached to the front subframe to limit body roll during cornering, and the ends of the anti-roll bar are attached to the suspension strut by drop links.

A trailing arm rear suspension is used, and the rear suspension sphere hydraulic units are supplied with hydraulic fluid from the BHI. Rear suspension height sensors are fitted, as is a rear anti-roll bar.

Two different suspension systems are available: Hydractive 3 and Hydractive 3+ **(see illustration)**. From the owner's point of view, the difference between the two is small. Hydractive 3+ allows the vehicle to be raised and lowered automatically at different vehicles speeds, and the 'firmness' adjusted to further improve roadholding, with a pressure accumulator/regulator at the front and rear. Automatic damping is incorporated in the suspension sphere hydraulic units, which take the place of the coil springs and dampers found in a conventional suspension system.

The steering is of rack-and-pinion type, mounted on the front subframe. The steering column incorporates a universal joint and coupling. Power assisted steering is fitted to all models, although two different systems maybe encountered. The first is a traditional system where fluid pressure is supplied from a pump driven by the auxiliary drivebelt – the same belt that drives the alternator. However, fluid for the pump is supplied from the reservoir above the suspension BHI unit – the suspension and the steering us the same LDS fluid. The second type, fitted to some facelifted C5s, is an electro-hydraulic system where a combined electric motor/pump/ECM unit is fitted under the right-hand front wing, with fluid provided again by the suspension fluid reservoir as on the previous system. The advantages of the electro-hydraulic system is that assistance, and therefore fluid pressure, is only provided when needed, and can be varied in relation to vehicle speed, steering wheel angle rate-of-change, etc, resulting in reduced fuel consumption and exhaust emissions.

Precautions

The fluid used in the C5 hydraulic system is LDS fluid, which is orange in colour. The use of any other type of fluid will damage the system rubber seals and hoses. Keep the fluid carefully sealed in its original container.

2 Suspension system depressurisation

1 Start the engine and set the suspension height to the 'Low' position. Stop the engine. Wait at least 15 minutes before proceeding. **Note:** *Access to the bleed screws is extremely limited once the vehicle is lowered. It's*

recommended that the vehicle be jacked up and supported on axle stands (see 'Jacking and vehicle support'), prior to depressurising the system.
2 Attach a pipe to the front bleed screw, and position the other end of the pipe into a container. Undo the screw by one turn **(see illustrations)**. Wait for the system to fully depressurise, and tighten the screw. To improve access on 2.0 litre petrol engines with Hydractive 3+, undo the 2 outer nuts and remove the short crossmember/heat shield immediately behind the front subframe **(see illustration)**.

2.2a The front bleed screw (arrowed) is located on the top of the firmness regulator – Hydractive 3+

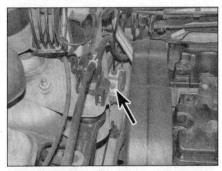

2.2b Front bleed screw (arrowed) on the right-hand side of the engine compartment – Hydractive 3

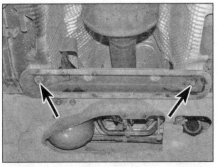

2.2c On 2.0 litre petrol engines with Hydractive 3+, undo the nuts and remove the crossmember and heat shield assembly (arrowed)

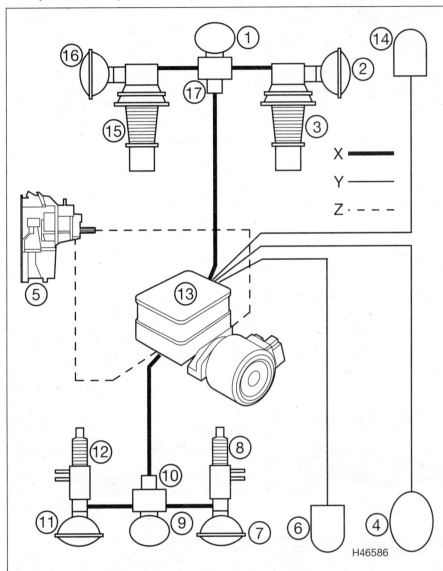

X ▬▬
Y ───
Z ·—·—·

H46586

1.4 Hydractive system layout

1 *Front stiffener regulator accumulator (Hydractive 3+)*
2 *Front suspension sphere*
3 *Front suspension strut*
4 *One-touch suspension control unit*
5 *LDS fluid reservoir*
6 *Rear height sensor*
7 *Rear suspension sphere*
8 *Rear suspension strut*
9 *Rear stiffener regulator accumulator (Hydractive 3+)*
10 *Rear firmness regulator (Hydractive 3+)*
11 *Rear suspension sphere*
12 *Rear suspension strut*
13 *BHI unit*
14 *Front height sensor*
15 *Front suspension strut*
16 *Front suspension sphere*
17 *Front firmness regulator (Hydractive 3+)*

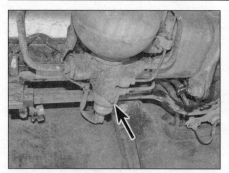

2.3a The rear bleed screw (arrowed) is on the underside or the firmness regulator – Hydractive 3+

2.3b The rear bleed screw (arrowed) in the centre of the rear axle – Hydractive 3

balljoint nut (unscrew the nut to the end of the threads on the balljoint to prevent damage as the joint is released). Release the balljoint using a balljoint separator and remove the nut **(see illustration 24.2)**.

4 Unbolt the wiring/hose bracket from the hub carrier, and move it to one side **(see illustration)**.

5 Unscrew the retaining bolt and remove the wheel speed sensor (see Chapter 9).

6 Remove the brake disc (see Chapter 9), but do not disconnect the brake fluid hose from the caliper. Suspend the caliper from the vehicle body using string, wire, etc.

7 Slacken and partially unscrew the hub carrier-to-lower arm balljoint nut (unscrew the nut to the end of the threads on the balljoint to prevent damage as the joint is released). Release the balljoint using a balljoint separator and remove the nut **(see illustration)**.

8 Unscrew and remove the clamp nut and bolt securing the hub carrier to the suspension strut **(see illustration)**.

9 Engage an Allen key or hexagon bit in the slot in the hub carrier, and turn the key/bit through a quarter turn to spread the slot **(see illustration)**. Simultaneously pull the hub carrier down to release it from the strut.

10 Pull the hub carrier from the driveshaft, leaving the driveshaft in the transmission. Do not disconnect the inboard end of the driveshaft from the transmission, and when working on the right-hand driveshaft, there is no need to release the intermediate bearing. Support the free, outboard end of the driveshaft by suspending it using wire or string – do not allow the end of the driveshaft to hang under its own weight.

3 Attach a pipe to the rear bleed screw, and position the other end of the pipe into a container. Undo the screw by one turn **(see illustrations)**. Wait for the system to fully depressurise, and tighten the screw.

3.2a Pull out the R-clip . . .

3 Front hub carrier assembly – removal and refitting

Note: *A balljoint separator tool will be required for this operation. A new suspension lower balljoint nut and a new track rod balljoint nut will be required on refitting.*

Removal

1 Chock the rear wheels, then jack up the front of the car and support it on axle stands (see *Jacking and vehicle support*). Remove the appropriate front roadwheel

2 Withdraw the R-clip, remove the locking cap, then slacken the driveshaft nut **(see illustrations)**. Have an assistant fully apply the footbrake to prevent the hub from rotating.

3 Slacken and partially unscrew the track rod

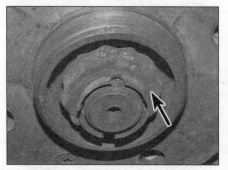

3.2b . . . remove the locking cap (arrowed) . . .

3.2c . . . and unscrew the driveshaft nut

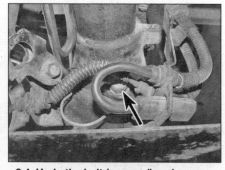

3.4 Undo the bolt (arrowed) and remove the wiring/hose bracket

3.7 Use an Allen key to prevent the balljoint shank from rotating whilst slackening the balljoint nut

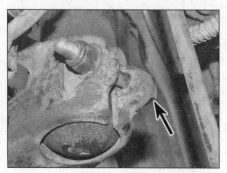

3.8 Remove the strut-to-hub carrier bolt (arrowed)

3.9 Insert an Allen key and rotate it to spread the gap a little

Refitting

11 Commence refitting by using the Allen key to spread the slot in the hub carrier, as during removal, if not already done.

12 Engage the hub carrier with the strut, noting that the raised positioning boss on the strut must engage with the hub carrier slot **(see illustration)**.

13 Push the hub carrier onto the strut until the top surface of the hub carrier rests against the shoulder on the strut.

14 Insert the end of the driveshaft into the hub.

15 Refit the hub carrier clamp bolt, noting that it fits from the front. Fit a new nut, tightening it to the specified torque.

16 Refit the brake disc and the caliper, and reconnect and adjust the handbrake cable, as described in Chapter 9.

17 Tighten the driveshaft retaining nut, as described in Chapter 8.

18 Refit the ABS wheel speed sensor as described in Chapter 9.

19 Refit the wiring/hose bracket to the hub carrier, and secure with the bolt. Where applicable, reconnect the ABS wheel sensor wiring plug.

20 Reconnect the track rod end to the hub carrier, and secure using a new balljoint nut, tightened to the specified torque.

21 Refit the roadwheel, and lower the vehicle to the ground.

22 On completion, have the front wheel alignment checked (see Section 25).

4 Front hub bearings – renewal

Note 1: *The bearing is a sealed, pre-adjusted and pre-lubricated, double-row roller type, and is intended to last the car's entire service life without maintenance or attention. Never overtighten the driveshaft nut beyond the specified torque wrench setting in an attempt to 'adjust' the bearing.*

Note 2: *A press will be required to dismantle and rebuild the assembly; if such a tool is not available, a large bench vice and spacers (such as large sockets) will serve as an adequate substitute. The bearing's inner races are an interference fit on the hub; if the inner race remains on the hub when it is pressed out of the hub carrier, a knife-edged bearing puller will be required to remove it.*

1 Remove the hub carrier assembly as described in Section 3.

2 Support the hub carrier securely on blocks or in a vice. Using a tubular spacer which bears only on the inner end of the hub flange, press the hub flange out of the bearing. If the bearing's outboard inner race remains on the hub, remove it using a bearing puller (see note above) **(see illustration)**.

3 Extract the bearing retaining circlip from the inner end of the hub carrier assembly **(see illustration)**.

3.12 The raised boss (arrowed) must align with the hub carrier slot

4 Where necessary, refit the inner race back in position over the ball cage, and securely support the inner face of the hub carrier. Using a tubular spacer which bears only on the inner race, press the complete bearing assembly out of the hub carrier.

5 Thoroughly clean the hub and hub carrier, removing all traces of dirt and grease, and polish away any burrs or raised edges which might hinder reassembly. Check both for cracks or any other signs of wear or damage, and renew them if necessary. Renew the circlip, regardless of its apparent condition.

6 On reassembly, apply a light film of oil to the bearing outer race and hub flange shaft, to aid installation of the bearing.

7 Securely support the hub carrier, and locate the bearing in the hub. **Note:** *The bearing incorporates a magnetic wheel integral with one of the oil seals. The bearing side with this oil seal must face towards the driveshaft.*

4.2 Remove the bearing inner race from the hub using a bearing puller

4.7 Ensure the bearing oil seal with the magnetic signal wheel faces the driveshaft side

Press the bearing fully into position, ensuring that it enters the hub squarely, using a tubular spacer which bears only on the bearing outer race **(see illustration)**. Take great care not to damage the oil seal and magnetic wheel.

8 Once the bearing is correctly seated, secure the bearing in position with the new circlip, ensuring that it is correctly located in the groove in the hub carrier. **Note:** *The circlip must be fitted exactly as shown, or the wheel speed sensor may not function correctly* **(see illustration)**.

9 Securely support the outer face of the hub flange, and locate the hub carrier bearing inner race over the end of the hub flange. Press the bearing onto the hub, using a tubular spacer which bears only on the inner race of the hub bearing, until it seats against the hub shoulder. Check that the hub flange rotates freely, and wipe off any excess of oil or grease.

10 Refit the hub carrier assembly as described in Section 3.

5 Front suspension lower arm – removal, overhaul and refitting

Note: *A balljoint separator tool will be required for this operation. New lower arm securing nuts, and a new lower balljoint nut must be used on refitting.*

Removal

1 Chock the rear wheels, then jack up the front of the vehicle and support it securely on axle stands (see *Jacking and vehicle support*). Remove the relevant roadwheel.

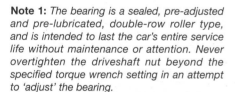

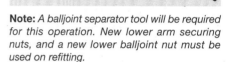

4.3 Use circlip pliers to extract the bearing circlip

4.8 The bearing circlip must be positioned so that its ends are equal distance each side of the ABS wheel speed sensor when fitted

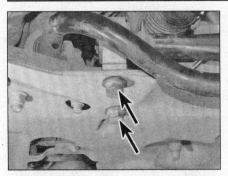

5.3 Undo the lower arm rear mounting bolts (arrowed) . . .

5.4 . . . and front mounting bolt

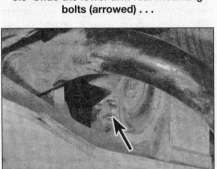

5.5 Undo the nut (arrowed) securing the pipe bracket to the rear mounting

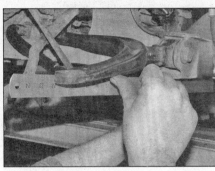

5.10 Position the end of the lower arm approximately 10 mm below the level of the subframe

9 Refit the two lower arm rear securing bolts.

10 Before tightening the front securing nut, the lower edge of the outboard end of the lower arm should be positioned approximately 10.0 mm below the lower surface of the suspension subframe (see illustration).

11 With the arm positioned as described in the previous paragraph, tighten the securing nuts/bolts to the specified torque.

12 Reconnect the suspension lower balljoint, then fit a new securing nut, and tighten to the specified torque.

13 Refit the roadwheel and lower the vehicle to the ground.

6 Front suspension lower balljoint – removal and refitting

Note: *Citroën special tool 7103-T, or an equivalent, and an impact wrench (such as a 'Facom Dynapact' wrench) will be required to unscrew and tighten the balljoint. If these tools are not available, the task should be entrusted to a Citroën dealer.* **Do not** *attempt the work using improvised tools. A new balljoint nut must be used on refitting.*

Removal

1 Chock the rear wheels, then jack up the front of the vehicle and support it securely on axle stands (see *Jacking and vehicle support*). Remove the relevant roadwheel.

2 Slacken and partially unscrew the suspension lower balljoint nut (unscrew the nut as far as the end of the threads on the balljoint to prevent damage to the threads as the joint is released), then release the balljoint using a balljoint separator tool. Remove the nut. Use a 6 mm Allen key to counterhold the balljoint shank if required.

3 Tap the dust shield from the balljoint, using a drift (see illustration).

4 Fit the special tool 7103-T to the balljoint, engaging the tool with the cut-outs in the balljoint, and secure it by screwing the tool locknut onto the threaded section of the balljoint (see illustration). Engage the impact wrench with the tool, and unscrew the balljoint.

Refitting

5 Refitting is a reversal of removal, bearing in mind the following points:
  a) *Tighten the balljoint as far as possible by hand before finally tightening it to the specified torque using the special tools.*
  b) *Take care not to damage the balljoint rubber gaiter during fitting.*
  c) *Lock the dust shield in position by staking it in the cut-outs in the bottom of the hub carrier.*

2 Slacken and partially unscrew the suspension lower balljoint nut (unscrew the nut as far as the end of the threads on the balljoint to prevent damage to the threads as the joint is released), then release the balljoint using a balljoint separator tool. If required, use a 6 mm Allen key to counterhold the balljoint shank (see illustration 3.7). Remove the nut.

3 Unscrew and remove the two lower arm rear securing bolts (see illustration).

4 Unscrew the nut and front pivot bolt securing the front of the lower arm to the subframe, then withdraw the lower arm from the chassis leg (see illustration).

5 Pull the arm forward a little, then undo the nut securing the pipe bracket to the rear arm mounting. Detach the mounting from the bracket, and remove the arm (see illustration).

Overhaul

6 Thoroughly clean the lower arm and the area around the arm mountings, removing all traces of dirt and underseal if necessary, then check carefully for cracks, distortion or any other signs of wear or damage, paying particular attention to the pivot bushes, and renew components as necessary. Check with a Citroën dealer regarding the availability of spares including reconditioned lower arms.

7 Examine the shank of the pivot bolt for signs of wear or scoring, and renew if necessary.

Refitting

8 Offer the lower arm into position, refit the pipe bracket to the rear mounting, then loosely refit the front pivot bolt, and a new nut. Do not fully tighten the nut and bolt at this stage.

6.3 Tap the dust shield from the balljoint

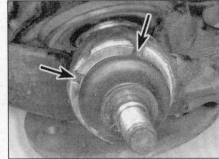

6.4 Engage the special tool with the cut-outs (arrowed) in the balljoint

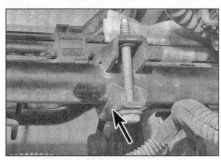

7.3 Make alignment marks between the height sensor clamp and the anti-roll bar (arrowed)

7.4 Undo the anti-roll bar-to-link nuts. Use an Allen key to counterhold the nut

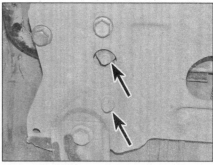

7.5 Undo the nuts (arrowed) securing the anti-roll bar to the subframe

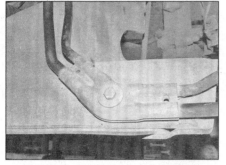

7.6 Undo the pipe support nut/bolt

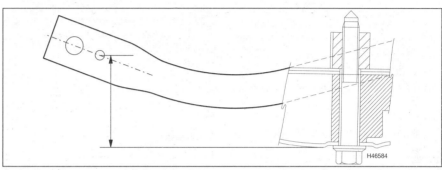

7.11 The distance between the anti-roll bar drop link hole and the lower surface of the subframe must be 50 ± 5 mm

7 Anti-roll bars – removal and refitting

Note: *All Nyloc self-locking nuts must be renewed on refitting.*

Front anti-roll bar

Removal

1 Jack up the vehicle, and support it securely on axle stands, with the roadwheels clear of the ground (see *Jacking and vehicle support*). Remove the front roadwheels.

2 Working inside the vehicle, undo the nut, remove the pinch-bolt from the universal joint, and separate the steering column from the steering rack pinion.

3 Mark the fitted position of the height sensor collar on the anti-roll bar, then undo the bolt and remove clamping collar **(see illustration)**.

4 Undo the nut securing the drop links to the ends of the anti-roll bar **(see illustration)**.

5 Undo the nuts securing the anti-roll bar clamps to the subframe **(see illustration)**.

6 On models with Hydractive 3+, undo the nuts and detach the pipe from the supports **(see illustration)**.

7 Undo the nuts and remove the exhaust mounting crossmember. Support the exhaust pipe to prevent damage to the flexible section.

8 Support the subframe using a trolley jack and interposed block of wood.

9 Remove the 8 subframe securing bolts, and lower the subframe slightly.

10 Remove the anti-roll bar. If required, remove the clamps and rubbers from the bar.

Refitting

11 Refitting is a reversal of removal, bearing in mind the following points:

a) Position the anti-roll bar to give 50 ± 5 mm between the centre of the drop link mounting holes and the lower surface of the subframe, then tighten the anti-roll bar bolts **(see illustration)**.

b) Refit the anti-roll bar bushes with the split facing forwards.

c) All Nyloc self-locking nuts must be renewed.

d) Tighten all fixings to the specified torque.

e) Ensure that all pipes, hoses and wires are correctly routed as noted before removal. Where applicable, use new seals when reconnecting the hydraulic pipes.

f) Check and if necessary top-up the hydraulic fluid level (see Section 16).

Rear anti-roll bar

Removal

12 Raise the rear of the vehicle and support it securely on axle stands (see *Jacking and vehicle support*).

13 Make alignment marks between the anti-roll bar and the suspension height sensor clamp, then undo the bolt and detach the clamp from the bar **(see illustration)**.

14 Undo the 2 Torx bolts at each end and remove the anti-roll bar **(see illustration)**.

Refitting

15 Refitting is a reversal of removal, noting the following points:

a) Tighten the anti-roll bar retaining bolts to their specified torque.

b) Align the height sensor clamp with the previously-made marks.

c) If a new anti-roll bar has been fitted, the suspension height sensor clamp

7.13 Make alignment marks between the rear height sensor clamp and the anti-roll bar

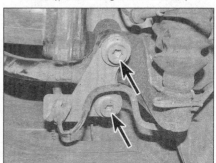

7.14 Undo the 2 Torx bolts (arrowed) at each end of the rear anti-roll bar

8.9 Undo the union and disconnect the fluid feed pipe from the top of the strut

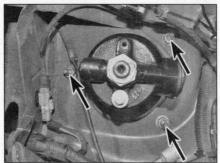

8.10 Undo the 3 nuts (arrowed) and lower the suspension unit

position must be set using Citroën diagnostic equipment. Entrust this task to a Citroën dealer or suitably-equipped specialist.

Drop links

Note: *New securing nuts must be used on refitting.*

Removal

16 Chock the rear wheels, then jack up the front of the vehicle, and support it on axle stands (see *Jacking and vehicle support*). Remove the relevant front roadwheel.

17 Partially unscrew the nut securing the anti-roll bar drop link to the end of the anti-roll bar, then separate the end of the bar from the drop link using a balljoint separator tool. Remove the nut. Counterhold the end of the drop link pin using a 6.0 mm Allen key whilst unscrewing the nut.

18 Unscrew the securing nut, and disconnect the anti-roll bar drop link from the suspension strut. Again, a 6.0 mm Allen key can be used to hold the drop link pin **(see illustration 7.4)**. If necessary, use a balljoint separator tool to free the drop link from the strut, but in this case, screw the nut onto the end of the drop link, to prevent damage to the thread.

19 Withdraw the drop link.

Refitting

20 Refitting is a reversal of removal, but use new securing nuts, and tighten them to the specified torque.

8 Front suspension sphere hydraulic unit/strut assembly – removal and refitting

Note: *All Nyloc self-locking nuts must be renewed on refitting. Where applicable, use new seals when reconnecting the hydraulic fluid pipes.*

Removal

1 Jack up the vehicle, and support it securely on axle stands, with the roadwheels clear of the ground (see *Jacking and vehicle support*). Remove the relevant front roadwheel.

2 Depressurise the hydraulic system as described in Section 2.

3 Unscrew the securing nut, and disconnect the anti-roll bar drop link from the suspension strut. Counterhold the end of the drop link pin using a 5.0 mm Allen key whilst unscrewing the nut. If necessary, use a balljoint separator tool to free the drop link from the strut, but in this case screw the nut onto the end of the drop link to prevent damage to the thread.

4 Unscrew and remove the clamp nut and bolt securing the hub carrier to the suspension strut **(see illustration 3.8)**.

5 Engage an 8.0 mm Allen key in the slot in the hub carrier, and turn the Allen key through a quarter-turn to spread the slot. Simultaneously pull the hub carrier down to release it from the strut **(see illustration 3.9)**.

6 Disconnect the hydraulic fluid return pipe

from the suspension strut where the flexible rubber pipe joins the rigid plastic pipe at the top of the wheel arch. Be prepared for fluid spillage, and plug the open ends of the pipe and strut to prevent dirt ingress.

7 Proceed as follows according to whether the complete suspension hydraulic unit/strut assembly, or just the strut is to be removed.

Hydraulic unit/strut assembly

8 Remove the suspension sphere as described in Section 14.

9 Working in the engine compartment, unscrew the union and disconnect the hydraulic fluid feed pipe from the suspension sphere hydraulic unit **(see illustration)**. Plug the open ends of the pipe and hydraulic unit to prevent dirt ingress and reduce fluid loss. Unbolt the pipe bracket(s) from the hydraulic unit.

10 Unscrew the 3 nuts securing the hydraulic unit to the body **(see illustration)**.

11 Lower the suspension unit from position.

Suspension strut

12 Working under the wheel arch, prise the suspension strut gaiter from the base of the suspension sphere hydraulic unit **(see illustration)**.

13 Prise off the plastic cover, then slacken the nut securing the top of the strut to the hydraulic unit. If necessary, counterhold the strut piston using a 6.0 mm Allen key **(see illustration)**.

14 Spray penetrating oil, or a lubricating fluid, onto the top of the suspension strut cone (below the nut), to help to free the strut from the suspension sphere hydraulic unit.

15 Remove the nut, and withdraw the unit downwards and remove from under the wheel arch.

Refitting

Hydraulic unit/strut assembly

16 Offer the assembly into position, taking care not to trap the hydraulic fluid return pipe, then refit the suspension sphere hydraulic unit securing bolts, and tighten them to the specified torque.

17 Reconnect the hydraulic fluid feed pipe to the suspension sphere hydraulic unit, using a new seal where applicable, and tighten the union.

18 Refit the suspension sphere as described in Section 14.

19 Proceed to paragraph 23.

Suspension strut

20 Check a condition of the O-ring seals in the bore of the hydraulic unit, and renew them if necessary **(see illustrations)**. Lubricate the top of the strut cone and the sealing surfaces with clean LDS fluid.

21 Coat the threads at the top of the strut with thread-locking compound, then offer the assembly into position from under the wheel arch. Refit the securing nut, and tighten it to the specified torque.

8.12 Prise the gaiter from place (arrowed)

8.13 Undo the retaining nut, counterholding it with an Allen key in the top of the strut (arrowed)

8.20a Use a small screwdriver to carefully prise out . . .

8.20b . . . and renew the 2 O-rings in the hydraulic unit (arrowed)

8.20c Ensure the gaiter is correctly located at the top of the strut . . .

22 Secure the strut gaiter to the base of the suspension sphere hydraulic unit.

All procedures

23 Commence refitting by using the Allen key to spread the slot in the hub carrier, as during removal, if not already done.
24 Engage the hub carrier with the strut, noting that the raised positioning boss on the strut must engage with the hub carrier slot.
25 Push the hub carrier onto the strut until the top surface of the hub carrier rests against the shoulder on the strut.
26 Refit the clamp bolt, noting that the bolt fits from the front of the strut, then fit a new nut, and tighten it to the specified torque.
27 Reconnect the anti-roll bar drop link to the suspension strut, and tighten a new nut to the specified torque.
28 Refit the wiring/hose bracket to the strut, and secure with the bolt.
29 Reconnect the hydraulic fluid return pipe to the suspension strut, using a new seal where applicable, and secure it with a new clip.
30 Refit the roadwheel, and lower the vehicle to the ground.
31 Bleed the hydraulic system as described in Section 16.
32 Close the hydraulic pressure regulator screw, then set the suspension height control to the 'Maximum' position.
33 Check and if necessary top-up the hydraulic fluid level (see Section 16).

8.20d . . . then slide on the bump stop . . .

8.20e . . . and washer

9 Front and rear suspension height sensors – removal and refitting

Note: *Where applicable, use new seals when reconnecting the hydraulic fluid pipes.*

Removal

1 Disconnect the battery negative lead as described in Chapter 5A.
2 Jack up the vehicle and support it securely on axle stands (see *Jacking and vehicle support*).
3 Disconnect the sensor wiring plug.
4 Prise the linkage rod from the sensor arm **(see illustration)**.
5 Lock the sensor arm in place using a 5.0 mm diameter rod/drill bit **(see illustration)**.
6 Undo the retaining bolt and remove the sensor **(see illustration)**.

Refitting

7 Refitting is a reversal of removal, bearing in mind the following points:
a) *Remove the locking rod before reconnecting the linkage rod.*
b) *On completion, if a new sensor has been fitted, have the vehicle's ride height checked by a Citroën dealer or suitably-equipped specialist.*

10 Front suspension subframe – removal and refitting

Note: *A balljoint separator tool will be required for this operation. All Nyloc self-locking nuts must be renewed on refitting.*

Removal

1 Jack up the vehicle, and support it securely

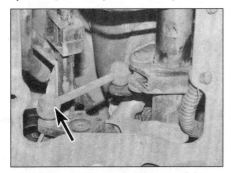

9.4 Prise the linkage rod (arrowed) from the balljoint on the sensor arm – front sensor shown

9.5 Lock the sensor arm using a 5.0 mm drill bit (arrowed) – rear sensor shown

9.6 Sensor retaining bolt (arrowed)

10.5 Undo the bolts/nuts and remove the torque arm between the subframe and the bracket

10.11a Front subframe rear mounting bolts (arrowed) . . .

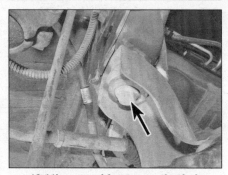

10.11b . . . and front mounting bolt (right-hand side bolt arrowed)

on axle stands with the wheels clear of the ground (see *Jacking and vehicle support*). Remove the front roadwheels.

2 Depressurise the hydraulic system as described in Section 2.

3 Working on each side of the vehicle in turn, slacken and partially unscrew the suspension lower balljoint nut (unscrew the nut as far as the end of the threads on the balljoint to prevent damage to the threads as the joint is released), then release the balljoint using a balljoint separator tool. Remove the nut. If necessary, counterhold the balljoint shank with a 6.0 mm Allen key.

4 Similarly, working on each side of the vehicle in turn, partially unscrew the nut securing the anti-roll bar drop link to the end of the anti-roll bar, then separate the end of the bar from the drop link using a balljoint separator tool. Counterhold the end of the drop link pin using a 5.0 mm Allen key whilst unscrewing the nut.

5 Undo the bolt securing the rear torque arm to the subframe **(see illustration)**.

6 Undo the bolts securing the pipes to the support brackets **(see illustration 7.6)**.

7 Undo the nuts securing the exhaust front mounting crossmember. Support the exhaust to prevent damage to the flexible section.

8 Disconnect the steering rack wiring plugs, then unclip the wiring harness from the subframe.

9 Undo the 2 nuts securing the steering rack to the subframe, then suspend the rack from the exhaust manifold using wire, string, etc **(see illustration 21.13a)**.

10 Support the subframe using a trolley jack and interposed block of wood.

11 Remove the 8 subframe securing bolts **(see illustrations)**.

12 Remove the retaining bolt and move the front suspension height sensor to one side.

13 Undo the bolts securing the hydraulic regulator to the subframe, then attach the regulator to the handbrake cable guide using wire, string, etc.

14 Lower the subframe a little, then undo the 2 bolts each side securing the anti-roll bar clamps to the subframe.

15 Lower the subframe and remove it from under the vehicle.

Refitting

16 Refitting is a reversal of removal, bearing in mind the following points:

a) *Where applicable, refit the lower arms and the anti-roll bar as described in Sections 5 and 7 respectively, noting that the final tightening of the fixings must be carried out when the subframe has been refitted.*

b) *Where applicable, use new seals when reconnecting the hydraulic pipes.*

c) *Renew all Nyloc self-locking nuts, and tighten all fixings to the specified torque.*

d) *Ensure that all pipes, hoses and wires are correctly routed as noted before removal.*

e) *Check the front wheel alignment as described in Section 25.*

f) *After lowering the vehicle to the ground, close the hydraulic pressure regulator screw, then set the suspension height control to the 'Maximum' position.*

g) *On completion, have the vehicle ride height checked by a Citroën dealer or suitably-equipped specialist.*

11 Rear hub/bearing assembly – removal and refitting

Note: *Do not remove the hub assembly unless it is absolutely necessary. A puller will be required to draw the hub assembly off the stub axle, and the hub bearing will almost certainly be damaged by the removal procedure. A new hub nut and hub cap will be required on refitting.*

Removal

1 Remove the rear brake disc as described in Chapter 9.

2 Undo the bolt and remove the ABS wheel speed sensor.

3 Using a hammer and a large flat-bladed screwdriver, carefully tap and prise the cap out of the centre of the hub. Discard the cap – a new one must be used on refitting. Using a hammer and a chisel-nosed tool, tap up the staking securing the hub retaining nut to the groove in the stub axle **(see illustration)**.

4 Using a 40 mm socket and long bar, slacken and remove the rear hub nut. Discard the hub nut – a new nut must be used on refitting.

5 Using a puller, draw the hub assembly off the stub axle, along with the outer bearing race **(see illustration)**. With the hub removed, use the puller to draw the inner bearing race off the stub axle.

6 Note that the complete hub/bearing assembly must be renewed as one.

7 With the hub removed, examine the stub axle shaft for signs of wear or damage, and if necessary renew it. The stub axle is retained by a circlip, and can either be tapped out of position, using a hammer and a soft-metal drift, or pushed out using a heavy-duty bearing puller. When installing the new stub axle, align its splines with those of the trailing arm, and drift or press it fully into position in the arm. Use a new circlip to secure the stub axle.

Refitting

8 Lubricate the stub axle shaft with multipurpose grease, then slide on the spacer, ensuring it is fitted the correct way round.

9 Slide the hub/bearing assembly onto the

11.3 Prise the cap out from the centre of the hub

11.5 Use a puller to draw the hub from the stub axle

11.10a Fit and tighten the new nut . . .

11.10b . . . then 'stake' the new nut into the groove on the stub axle using a punch . . .

11.10c . . . and tap a new cap into the centre of the hub

stub axle. If necessary, tap it into position using the tubular drift.

10 Fit the new hub nut, and tighten it to the specified torque. Stake the nut firmly into the groove on the stub axle to secure it in position, then tap the new hub cap into place in the centre of the hub **(see illustrations)**.

11 Refit the ABS wheel speed sensor and tighten the retaining bolt to the specified torque.

12 Refit the rear brake disc as described in Chapter 10.

12 Rear suspension trailing arm – removal and refitting

Note: *A new trailing arm pivot shaft nut must be used on refitting.*

Removal

1 Chock the front wheels and apply the handbrake, then jack up the rear of the vehicle, and support it securely on axle stands with the rear wheels clear of the ground (see *Jacking and vehicle support*). Remove the relevant roadwheel.

2 Depressurise the hydraulic system as described in Section 2.

3 Undo the retaining screw and withdraw the ABS wheel speed sensor from the rear hub.

4 Unscrew the union, and disconnect the fluid pipe from the brake caliper. Plug the open ends of the pipe and the caliper to prevent dirt ingress. Release the brake pipe from the clips on the trailing arm.

5 Mark the position of the height sensor clamp on the anti-roll bar, then undo the bolt and remove the clamp **(see illustration 7.13)**.

6 Undo the 2 bolts each side and remove the rear anti-roll bar **(see illustration 7.14)**.

7 Remove the clip securing the end of the suspension strut to the trailing arm. If the end of the strut is reluctant to move, carefully pull back the rubber gaiter, and use a pair of pliers to lever it from the trailing arm **(see illustrations)**.

8 Unscrew the nut from the end of the trailing arm pivot shaft **(see illustrations)**.

9 Withdraw the trailing arm pivot shaft, then manipulate the arm out from under the vehicle.

10 Renewal of the trailing arm pivot bearings requires numerous Citroën special tools. Consequently, it's recommended that this task is entrusted to a Citroën dealer or suitably-equipped specialist. Check to see if reconditioned, exchange trailing arms are available.

Refitting

11 Refitting is a reversal of removal, bearing in mind the following points:
a) *Grease the entire length of the trailing arm pivot shaft.*
b) *Use a new pivot shaft nut, and tighten all fixings to the specified torque.*
c) *Apply grease to the end of the suspension strut where it locates in the trailing arm.*
d) *Bleed the brake hydraulic system as described in Chapter 9.*

13 Rear suspension strut – removal, overhaul and refitting

Removal

1 Remove the rear suspension sphere as described in Section 14

2 Disconnect the hydraulic fluid supply pipe from the suspension hydraulic unit. Plug the open ends of the hydraulic unit and the pipe to prevent dirt ingress. Be prepared for fluid spillage.

3 Remove the clip securing the strut to the trailing arm **(see illustration 12.7a and 12.7b)**.

4 Disconnect the hydraulic fluid return pipe and the vent pipe **(see illustration)**.

5 Undo the 2 retaining bolts and manoeuvre the strut from position **(see illustration)**.

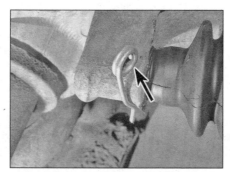

12.7a Pull the clip (arrowed) from place . . .

12.7b . . . and lever the end of the strut from the trailing arm

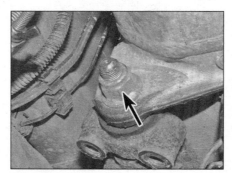

12.8a Undo the nut (arrowed) . . .

12.8b . . . and pull out the pivot shaft

13.4 Pull the vent pipe and the fluid return pipe from the fittings on the gaiter

13.5 Undo the 2 Torx bolts (arrowed) and remove the strut

13.7 Use water pump pliers to release the gaiter clip

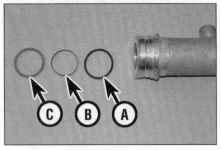

13.10a Strut seals

A Rubber seal   C O-ring seal
B Sliding seal

13.10b Fit the new rubber seal into the lowest groove . . .

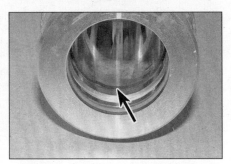

13.10c . . . then fit the thin sliding seal (arrowed) into the inside of the rubber seal . . .

Overhaul

6 The only parts available for the strut are the sphere, the rubber gaiter and the piston seals. Renewal of the sphere is described in Sec-tion 14. Renew the gaiter and seals as follows. Note that this can be carried out with the strut fitted to the vehicle, after the removing the clip securing it to the trailing arm (paragraph 3), and the pipes are disconnected (paragraph 4).

7 Pull the piston rod from the gaiter, then release the clip and pull the gaiter from the strut (see illustration).

8 Remove the mounting plate from the cylinder.

9 Pull the piston from the strut, and extract the seals from the strut. Be prepared for fluid spillage.

10 Fit the new rubber seal, sliding seal and O-ring seal to the strut (see illustrations). Note that the sliding seal fits inside the rubber seal.

11 Lubricate the seals with clean LDS fluid, then carefully insert the piston into the strut using a gentle twisting motion (see illustration).

12 Fit the mounting plate to the cylinder (see illustration).

13 Fit the piston rod into the gaiter, then fit the new gaiter to the strut as shown. Secure the gaiter with the clip (see illustrations)

13.10d . . . then fit the O-ring seal into the upper groove

13.11 Insert the piston into the strut using a gentle twisting motion

13.12 Fit the mounting plate to the strut

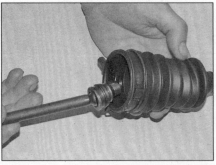

13.13a Fit the piston rod into the gaiter . . .

13.13b . . . ensuring the end is correctly located . . .

13.13c . . . then fit the gaiter and piston rod . . .

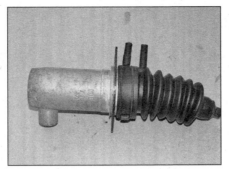

13.13d . . . onto the strut

13.14 Use a syringe to inject 25 cc of LDS fluid through the vent aperture

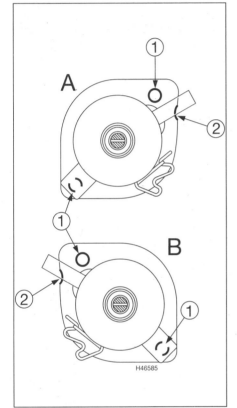

13.15 The suspension struts are left- and right-handed

A Right-hand strut   1 Mounting holes
B Left-hand strut   2 Locating notch

Refitting

14 Pour 25 cc of new LDS fluid through the air vent aperture into the strut gaiter **(see illustration)**.

15 Fit the strut into position, reconnecting the vent and return hoses as it's fitted. Note that the struts are handed **(see illustration)**. Refit the retaining bolts but don't tighten them at this stage.

16 Refit the clip securing the strut to the trailing arm.

17 Reconnect the fluid supply pipe union, using a new seal **(see illustration)**, then tighten then strut retaining bolts to the specified torque.

18 Refit the suspension sphere as described in Section 14.

19 Bleed the hydraulic system as described in Section 16.

14 Suspension spheres – removal and refitting

Note: *A strap wrench will be required to unscrew the suspension sphere from the hydraulic unit. A new sphere-to-strut seal will be required on refitting.*

Removal

1 If removing a rear sphere, jack up the vehicle, and support it on axle stands with the roadwheels clear of the ground (see *Jacking and vehicle support*). Remove the relevant roadwheel.

13.17 Reconnect the fluid pressure pipe with a new seal

2 Depressurise the hydraulic system as described in Section 2.

3 If removing a front sphere, open the bonnet. Where applicable, prise up the centre pins, remove the plastic rivets, and lift away the plastic trim panels above the spheres.

4 Use a strap wrench to loosen the suspension sphere, then unscrew the sphere from the strut **(see illustrations)**. Note that the spheres can be extremely tight to unscrew. In order to prevent the strap wrench from slipping, position a length of coarse emery paper between the sphere and the wrench.

Refitting

5 Grease the contact face of the suspension sphere, and refit the sphere using a new seal **(see illustration)**. Tighten the sphere to the specified torque if possible, or securely using a strap wrench.

6 The remainder of refitting is a reversal of removal.

14.4a Unscrew the sphere using a strap wrench . . .

14.4b . . . or large pair of water pump pliers

14.5 Fit the sphere using a new seal

15.6 Undo the firmness regulator fluid pipe unions

15.10a Rear firmness regulator fluid pipes

15.10b Counterhold the port with a second spanner whilst slackening the fluid pipe union

15 Firmness regulators –
removal and refitting

Note: *These procedures apply only to models with Hydractive 3+ suspension.*

Removal

1 Depressurise the hydraulic system as described in Section 2.

Front regulator

2 Chock the rear wheels, then jack up the front of the vehicle and support it securely on axle stands (see *Jacking and vehicle support*).

3 Unclip the wiring harness, then undo the nuts and remove the exhaust pipe front mounting crossmember. Support the exhaust pipe to prevent damage to the flexible section.

4 Using a strap wrench, or large pair of water pump pliers, unscrew the sphere from the regulator **(see illustration 14.4b)**. Remove the mounting bolts, and move the regulator rearwards a little, then manoeuvre the sphere from position.

5 Disconnect the wiring plug from the regulator.

6 Undo the unions and disconnect the fluid pipes from the regulator **(see illustration)**. Be prepared for fluid spillage. Plug the regulator and pipe openings to prevent contamination.

7 Move the pipes aside and manoeuvre the regulator from place. It's essential that the fluid pipes are not distorted during this procedure. If necessary, unclip the pipes and slacken the unions at the ends of the pipes to be able to move them aside.

Rear regulator

8 Chock the front wheels, then jack up the rear of the vehicle and support it securely on axle stands (see *Jacking and vehicle support*).

9 Disconnect the wiring plug from the regulator.

10 Undo the unions and disconnect the fluid pipes from the regulator **(see illustrations)**. Be prepared for fluid spillage. Plug the regulator and pipe openings to prevent contamination. Detach the pipe support brackets from the regulator mounting bracket. It's essential that the fluid pipes are not distorted during this procedure. If necessary, unclip the pipes and slacken the unions at the ends of the pipes to be able to move them aside.

11 Remove the height sensor as described in Section 9.

12 Undo the mounting retaining screws, move the pipes aside and manoeuvre the regulator from place.

Refitting

13 Refitting is a reversal of removal, noting the following points:

a) *Renew the union/sphere seals where applicable.*

b) *Tighten all fasteners to the specified torque where given.*

c) *Bleed the hydraulic system as described in Section 16.*

16 LDS fluid –
draining, refilling and bleeding

Draining

1 Start the engine, place the suspension height control in the 'Low' position, and stop the engine.

2 Raise the vehicle and support it securely on axle stands (see *Jacking and vehicle support*).

3 Prise up the centre pins, lever out the plastic rivets, and remove the plastic trim panel over the LDS fluid reservoir on the right-hand side of the engine compartment **(see illustration)**. Slowly release the LDS reservoir cap. ***Caution: The LDS reservoir may contain some pressure. Wrap a rag around the cap, and release it very slowly, allowing the pressure to dissipate before removing the cap.***

4 Remove the right-hand front roadwheel, then undo the fasteners and remove the right-hand wheel arch liner.

5 Cut off the clip securing the hose to the base of the reservoir, pull the hose from the union and allow the LDS fluid to drain into a container **(see illustration)**. **Note:** *LDS fluid must not be re-used.*

6 Reconnect the hose to the base of the reservoir, and secure it with a new clip.

7 Refit the wheel arch liner, and the road-wheel.

8 Lower the vehicle to the ground.

Refilling

9 Unscrew the LDS reservoir cap, if not already done so.

10 Add new LDS fluid to the reservoir, until the level is between the minimum and maximum marks (Hydractive 3 system) or the HYD mark (Hydractive 3+ system) **(see illustrations)**.

Bleeding

11 With the suspension in the 'Low' position, ensure the ignition is turned off, then slowly remove the LDS fluid reservoir cap, as described in paragraph 3.

12 If necessary, add new LDS fluid to the level specified in paragraph 10.

13 Apply 0.5 bar of air pressure to the LDS fluid reservoir. This can be achieved using

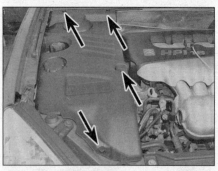

16.3 Prise out the fasteners (arrowed) and remove the plastic cover over the LDS fluid reservoir

16.5 Disconnect the hose (arrowed) from the base of the reservoir

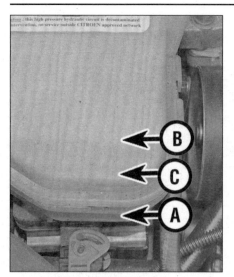

**16.10a LDS fluid levels –
up to RPO No 09064**

A *Minimum*
B *Maximum – Hydractive 3+*
C *Maximum – Hydractive 3*

a special tool, eg. Facom 920, or by using a generic brake pressure bleeding kit **(see illustration)**.
Caution: Ensure the brake pressure bleeding vessel is clean and free from brake fluid.
14 Start the engine, and set the suspension height to the 'High' position. Once the vehicle has settled at this height, set it to the 'Low' position.

Auxiliary drivebelt driven pump

15 Turn the steering wheel from lock-to-lock in each direction. Stop the engine.

Electropump

16 Turn the steering from lock-to-lock 10 times.
17 Start the engine, and wait approximately 3 minutes.
18 Turn the steering from lock-to-lock until there are no points of resistance, then stop the engine.

All models

19 Remove the pressure bleed kit/Facom tool, check the fluid level. If necessary, add fluid to the level specified in paragraph 10.

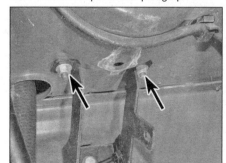

17.5 Undo the 2 nuts (arrowed) at the base of the BHI unit

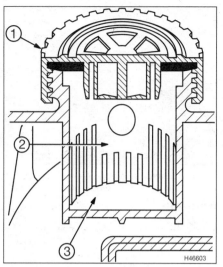

**16.10b LDS fluid levels –
from RPO No 09065**

1 *Reservoir cap*
2 *Maximum level*
3 *Minimum level*

20 Refit the plastic cover over the LDS fluid reservoir, and secure it with the plastic clips.

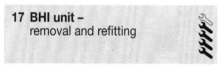

17 BHI unit –
removal and refitting

Removal

1 Chock the rear wheels, then raise the front of the vehicle and support it securely on axle stands (see *Jacking and vehicle support*). Remove the right-hand roadwheel and wheel arch liner.
2 Depressurise the hydraulic system as described in Section 2.
3 Disconnect the battery negative lead as described in Chapter 5A.
4 Cut off the clip securing the hose to the base of the LDS fluid reservoir, pull the hose from the union and allow the LDS fluid to drain into a container **(see illustration 16.5)**. **Note:** *LDS fluid must not be re-used.*
5 Working through the wheel arch, undo the 2 nuts at the base of the BHI unit **(see illustration)**.

17.6 LDS fluid reservoir retaining nuts (arrowed)

16.13 Pressurise the LDS fluid reservoir with 0.5 bar of air using Facom 920 tool, or a generic brake pressure bleeding kit

6 Remove the plastic cover over the top of the reservoir, then undo the 2 reservoir retaining nuts **(see illustration)**.
7 Move the reservoir to one side, then note their fitted positions and disconnect the supply and return hose(s) from the BHI unit.
8 Note their fitted positions, and disconnect the wiring plugs from the BHI unit.
9 Undo the unions, and disconnect the high-pressure pipes from the BHI unit, without distorting the pipes **(see illustration)**.
10 Slide the BHI unit to the left and manoeuvre it from position.

Refitting

11 Refitting is a reversal of removal, noting the following points:
a) *Refill and bleed the hydraulic system as described in Section 16.*
b) *Always use new LDS fluid.*
c) *Attach the hose to the base of the fluid reservoir using a new clip.*
d) *If a new BHI unit has been fitted, it must be initialised using Citroën diagnostic equipment. Entrust this task to a Citroën dealer or suitably-equipped specialist.*

18 Steering wheel –
removal and refitting

Removal

1 Remove the driver's airbag unit as described in Chapter 12.

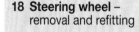

17.9 Disconnect the pipes from the BHI unit

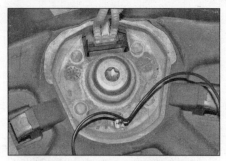

18.2 Disconnect the steering wheel controls wiring plug, then undo the retaining Torx bolt

2 Disconnect the steering wheel controls wiring plug **(see illustration)**.

3 Unscrew the steering wheel securing bolt using a Torx bit, and withdraw the steering wheel. Feed the wiring through the centre of the steering wheel as it is withdrawn.

19.3 Release the clip and slide the audio control (right-hand) switch stalk from the steering column module

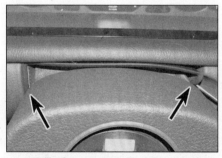

19.4b Squeeze together the sides (arrowed) and detach the gaiter frame from the facia

19.6c ... the lower clip (arrowed) ...

19.2 Lower steering column screws (arrowed)

Refitting

4 Refit the steering wheel to the column shaft. Ensure the master spline on the shaft aligns with the corresponding groove in the wheel centre. Feed the wires through the wheel as it's refitted.

19.4a Release the upper steering column shroud clips (arrowed)

19.6a Slacken the clamp screw (arrowed) ...

19.6d ... and slide the steering column switch assembly/module from the column

5 Tighten the wheel retaining bolt to the specified torque.
6 Refit the airbag unit as described in Chapter 12.

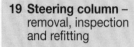

19 Steering column –
removal, inspection and refitting

Removal

1 Remove the steering wheel as described in Section 18.
2 Undo the 2 screws and remove the column lower shroud **(see illustration)**.
3 Depress the clip and slide the audio control switch stalk out from the module **(see illustration)**.
4 Release the 2 clips and lift the column upper shroud upwards, then squeeze together the sides of the gaiter frame and release it from the facia **(see illustrations)**.
5 Secure the airbag contact unit in position using tape.
6 Note their fitted positions, disconnect the switch assembly wiring plugs, slacken the clamp screw, prise out the clips and slide the switch assembly over the end of the steering column **(see illustrations)**.
7 Remove the driver's knee airbag as described in Chapter 12 (where applicable). On models not equipped with a driver's knee airbag, remove the trim panel beneath the steering column, then undo the scrivet, release the clip and remove the soundproofing panels under the driver's side of the facia **(see illustration)**.

19.6b ... prise up the upper clip (arrowed) ...

19.7 Lift out the trim panel beneath the steering column

19.9 Undo the nut and remove the pinch-bolt (arrowed)

19.10a Undo the 2 bolts at the top (arrowed) . . .

19.10b . . . and the cross-bolt halfway down the steering column (arrowed)

Disconnect the footwell light wiring plug as the soundproofing is removed.

8 Trace the wiring back from the ignition switch, then note their fitted positions, and disconnect the wiring plugs from the ignition switch. Release the wiring harness from the various retaining clips.

9 Working at the lower end of the column, unscrew the steering column universal joint pinch-bolt **(see illustration)**.

10 Unscrew the 3 steering column securing bolts, and withdraw the steering column upwards from place **(see illustrations)**.

Inspection

11 The steering column incorporates a telescopic safety feature. In the event of a front-end crash, the shaft collapses and prevents the steering wheel injuring the driver. Before refitting the steering column, examine the column and mountings for signs of damage and deformation, and renew as necessary.

12 Check the steering shaft for signs of free play in the column bushes, and check the universal joints for signs of damage or roughness in the joint bearings. If any damage or wear is found on the steering column universal joints or shaft bushes, the column must be renewed as an assembly.

Refitting

13 Refitting is a reversal of removal, bearing in mind the following points:
a) Ensure that the roadwheels are in the straight-ahead position before refitting.
b) Tighten all fixings to the specified torque.

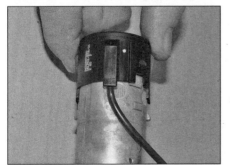

20.3 Unclip the transponder ring from the ignition switch

20 Ignition switch/ steering column lock – removal and refitting

Removal

1 Proceed as described in Section 19, paragraphs 1 and 2.

2 Working under the steering column, locate the two ignition switch wiring connectors, and separate the two halves of each connector (pre-facelift models), or disconnect the single connector from the rear of the switch (post-facelift models). Release the wiring from any clips.

3 Unclip the immobiliser transponder ring from the end of the ignition switch **(see illustration)**.

4 Move the wiring harness to one side, then remove the lock retaining bolt. This is a shear-type bolt, designed that the head of the bolts shears off when it's tightened to make removal of switch difficult for car thieves, etc. To remove the bolt, use sharp punch and a hammer to rotate the bolt anti-clockwise, or if access permits, use an electric drill to remove the head of the bolt **(see illustration)**. Obviously, a new bolt will be needed upon refitting.

5 Insert the ignition key, and turn it to the first position.

6 Using a small flat-bladed screwdriver, depress the lock retaining lug, and pull the lock from the housing using the key **(see illustration)**.

20.4 Drill out the shear bolt (arrowed) or use a hammer and punch

Refitting

7 Refitting is a reversal of removal, bearing in mind the following points:
a) Ensure that the lock retaining lug is correctly engaged.
b) Check the operation of the steering lock before refitting the column shrouds.
c) Refit the steering wheel as described in Section 18.

21 Steering rack assembly – removal, overhaul and refitting

Note: A balljoint separator tool will be required for this operation. New track rod balljoint nuts, and a new intermediate shaft-to-steering rack pinion pinch-bolt will be required on refitting. New hydraulic fluid pipe seals will be required.

Removal

1 Disconnect the battery negative lead as described in Chapter 5A.

2 Use a hose clamp to pinch the fluid supply hose to the power steering pump **(see illustration)**. Note this only applies to non-electropump steering.

3 Ensure the front wheels are in the 'straight-ahead' position, then chock the rear wheels, raise the front of the vehicle and support it securely on axle stands (see *Jacking and vehicle support*). Remove the front roadwheels.

4 Remove the trim panel above the pedals, then undo the nut and withdrawn the

20.6 Depress the lock retaining lug

21.2 Clamp the fluid supply hose to the power steering pump

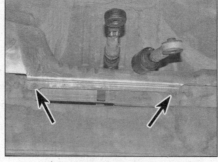

21.6 Undo the 2 screws (arrowed) and remove the heat shield

21.12 Disconnect the fluid pipes from the steering rack

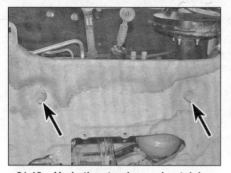

21.13a Undo the steering rack retaining nuts (arrowed) . . .

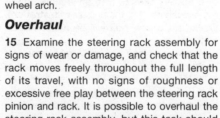

21.13b . . . then unscrew the mounting studs

steering column universal joint pinch-bolt **(see illustration 19.9)**. Move the security clip and slide the joint up from the steering rack pinion.

5 Detach both the track rod ends from the hub carriers as described in Section 24.

6 Undo the 2 screws and remove the heat shield from the steering rack **(see illustration)**.

7 Undo the bolts securing the various power steering pipes to their support brackets.

8 Undo the nuts securing the exhaust front mounting crossmember. Support the exhaust to prevent damage to the flexible section.

9 Support the subframe using a trolley jack and interposed block of wood.

10 Undo the bolts securing the hydraulic regulator to the subframe, then attach the regulator to the handbrake cable guide using wire, string, etc.

11 Remove the 8 subframe securing bolts **(see illustration 10.11a and 10.11b)**.

12 Undo the retaining bolts, and detach the power steering pipes from the rack **(see illustration)**. Discard the O-ring seals, new ones must be fitted. Plug the openings to prevent contamination.

13 Undo the 2 nuts, remove the washers, and use a Torx bit to remove the 2 studs securing the rack to the subframe **(see illustrations)**. Recover the toothed washers.

14 Lower the subframe a little, and manoeuvre the steering rack out through the right-hand wheel arch.

Overhaul

15 Examine the steering rack assembly for signs of wear or damage, and check that the rack moves freely throughout the full length of its travel, with no signs of roughness or excessive free play between the steering rack pinion and rack. It is possible to overhaul the steering rack assembly, but this task should

be entrusted to a Citroën dealer. The only components which can be renewed easily by the home mechanic are the rubber gaiters (see Section 22), and the track rod balljoints (see Section 24).

Refitting

16 Refitting is a reversal of removal, bearing in mind the following points:
a) Centralise the rack so that the steering is effectively in the straight-ahead position before refitting the steering rack.
b) Use new nuts when reconnecting the track rod balljoints, and use a new nut when refitting the steering universal joint pinch-bolt.
c) Use new seals when reconnecting the fluid pipes to the steering rack.
d) Ensure that the steering wheel is in the straight-ahead position, and that the steering rack is centralised before reconnecting the intermediate shaft to the steering rack.
e) Bleed the hydraulic system as described in Section 16.
f) On completion, check and if necessary adjust the front wheel alignment as described in Section 25.

22 Steering rack rubber gaiters – renewal

1 Remove the track rod end on the relevant side as described in Section 24.

2 Remove the track rod locknut, counting the threads to aid accurate refitting.

3 Release the inner and outer gaiter retaining clips, and pull the old gaiter from the rack **(see illustrations)**. Note that access to the inner clip is limited. The only way to improve access is to remove the steering rack assembly as described in Section 21.

4 Pull the air balance pipe from the gaiter(s) as they are withdrawn.

5 Slide the new gaiter into place, and secure it with the clips supplied in the repair kit.

6 Refit the air balance pipe below the gaiters.

7 Refit the locknuts and the track rod ends as described in Section 24.

22.3a Release the gaiter inner clip (arrowed) . . .

22.3b . . . and outer clip (arrowed)

23.4 Clamp the fluid supply hose to the pump

23.5 Undo the pressure pipe union (arrowed)

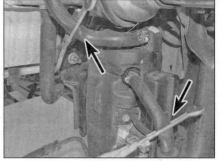

23.9 Clamp the hoses to the pump (arrowed)

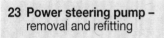

23 Power steering pump – removal and refitting

Removal

1 Note that 2 types of power steering pumps maybe fitted. The first type is the traditional mechanical pump driven by the auxiliary drivebelt, the second type is an electropump assembly, fitted in front of the right-hand roadwheel, behind the wing. Proceed as described under the relevant heading.

Auxiliary drivebelt driven pump

2 Remove the auxiliary drivebelt as described in Chapter 5A.
3 Remove the plastic cover on the top of the engine (where fitted).
4 Use hose clamps to pinch the fluid supply and return hoses to the pump, then slacken the clip and disconnect the hoses **(see illustration)**. Be prepared for fluid spillage.
5 Undo the union and disconnect the pressure pipe from the pump **(see illustration)**. Plug the openings to prevent contamination.
6 Undo the mounting bolts/nuts and remove the pump.

Electropump

7 Chock the rear wheels, raise the front of the vehicle and support it securely on axle stands (see *Jacking and vehicle support*). Remove the right-hand roadwheel and wheel arch liner.
8 Disconnect the battery negative lead as described in Chapter 5A.
9 Pinch the fluid supply and return hoses using hose clamps, cut through the clips and disconnect the hoses from the electropump assembly **(see illustration)**. Be prepared for fluid spillage. Plug the openings to prevent contamination.
10 Undo the Torx retaining bolt, and disconnect the pressure pipe from the assembly **(see illustration)**. Plug the openings to prevent contamination. Discard the O-ring seal, a new one must be fitted.
11 Unclip the hose at the base of the assembly.
12 Undo the 3 retaining bolts and manoeuvre the electropump assembly from position **(see illustration)**.

23.10 Undo the Torx bolt (arrowed) and disconnect the pressure pipe

13 Undo the 2 Torx bolts, remove the cover, then disconnect the wiring plugs from the electropump.
14 No further dismantling of the electropump assembly is recommended. At the time of writing, the electropump was only available as a complete assembly – consult a Citroën dealer or parts specialist.

Refitting

15 Refitting is a reversal of removal, noting the following points:
a) Renew the pressure pipe O-ring seals.
b) Tighten the fasteners to the specified torque where given.
c) Bleed the hydraulic system as described in Section 16.
d) Ensure the steering system functions correctly before taking the vehicle onto the road.

24 Track rod balljoint – removal and refitting

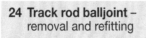

Note: *A new balljoint-to-hub carrier nut will be required on refitting.*

Removal

1 Chock the rear wheels, then jack up the front of the vehicle, and support it securely on axle stands (see *Jacking and vehicle support*). Remove the relevant roadwheel.
2 Slacken and partially unscrew the track rod balljoint nut (unscrew the nut as far as the end of the threads on the balljoint to prevent

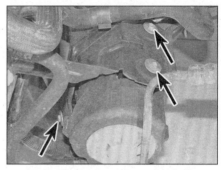

23.12 Electropump mounting bolts (arrowed)

damage to the threads as the joint is released), then release the balljoint using a balljoint separator tool **(see illustration)**. Remove the nut.
3 If the balljoint is to be re-used, use a straight-edge and a scriber, or similar, to mark its relationship to the track rod.
4 Hold the track rod, and unscrew the balljoint locknut by a quarter of a turn. Do not move the locknut from this position, as it will serve as a handy reference mark on refitting.
5 Counting the **exact** number of turns necessary to do so, unscrew the balljoint from the track rod end.
6 Count the number of exposed threads between the end of the balljoint and the locknut, and record this figure. If a new balljoint is to be fitted, unscrew the locknut from the old balljoint.
7 Carefully clean the balljoint and the threads. Renew the balljoint if its movement is sloppy

24.2 Release the balljoint using a separator tool

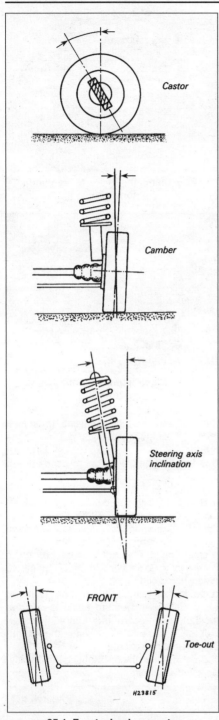

25.1 Front wheel geometry

or too stiff, if excessively worn, or if damaged in any way; carefully check the stud taper and threads. If the balljoint gaiter is damaged, the complete balljoint assembly must be renewed; it is not possible to obtain the gaiter separately.

Refitting

8 If a new balljoint is to be fitted, screw the locknut onto its threads, and position it so that the same number of exposed threads are visible, as was noted prior to removal.

9 Screw the balljoint into the track rod by the number of turns noted on removal. This should bring the balljoint locknut to within a quarter of a turn from the locknut, with the alignment marks that were made on removal (if applicable) lined up.

10 Reconnect the balljoint to the hub carrier, then fit a new nut and tighten it to the specified torque.

11 Refit the roadwheel, then lower the vehicle to the ground and tighten the roadwheel bolts to the specified torque.

12 Check and, if necessary, adjust the front wheel alignment as described in Section 25, then securely tighten the balljoint locknut.

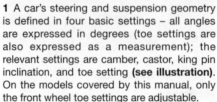

25 Wheel alignment and steering angles – general information

1 A car's steering and suspension geometry is defined in four basic settings – all angles are expressed in degrees (toe settings are also expressed as a measurement); the relevant settings are camber, castor, king pin inclination, and toe setting **(see illustration)**. On the models covered by this manual, only the front wheel toe settings are adjustable.

2 Camber is the angle at which the front wheels are set from the vertical when viewed from the front or rear of the car. Negative camber is the amount (in degrees) that the wheels are tilted inward at the top from the vertical.

3 The front camber angle is adjusted by slackening the steering knuckle-to-suspension strut mounting bolts and repositioning the hub carrier assemblies as necessary.

4 Castor is the angle between the steering axis and a vertical line when viewed from each side of the car. Positive castor is when the steering axis is inclined rearward at the top.

5 Steering axis (king pin) inclination is the angle (when viewed from the front of the vehicle) between the vertical and an imaginary line drawn through the front suspension strut upper mounting and the control arm balljoint.

6 Toe setting is the amount by which the distance between the front inside edges of the roadwheels (measured at hub height) differs from the diametrically opposite distance measured between the rear inside edges of the roadwheels. Toe-in is when the roadwheels point inwards, towards each other at the front, while toe-out is when they splay outwards from each other at the front.

7 The front wheel toe setting is adjusted by altering the length of the steering track rods on both sides. This adjustment is normally referred to as the tracking.

8 All other suspension and steering angles are set during manufacture, and no adjustment is possible. It can be assumed, therefore, that unless the vehicle has suffered accident damage, all the preset angles will be correct.

9 Special optical measuring equipment is necessary to accurately check and adjust the front and rear toe settings and front camber angles, and this work should be carried out by a Citroën dealer or similar expert. Most tyre-fitting centres have the expertise and equipment to carry out at least a front wheel toe setting (tracking) check for a nominal charge.

Chapter 11
Bodywork and fittings

Contents

Degrees of difficulty

Easy, suitable for novice with little experience	**Fairly easy,** suitable for beginner with some experience	**Fairly difficult,** suitable for competent DIY mechanic	**Difficult,** suitable for experienced DIY mechanic	**Very difficult,** suitable for expert DIY or professional

Specifications

Torque wrench settings

	Nm	lbf ft
Front seat belt inertia reel.	30	22
Front seat belt upper/lower anchorage	30	22
Rear seat belt inertia reel nut	35	26
Rear seat belt lower anchorages	35	26

1 General information

The bodyshell is made of pressed-steel sections, and is available in five-door Hatchback or Estate versions. Most components are welded together, but some use is made of structural adhesives.

A number of structural components and body panels are made of galvanised steel to provide a high level of protection against corrosion. Extensive use is also made of plastic materials, mainly in the interior, but also in exterior components. The front and rear bumpers are moulded from a synthetic material that is very strong and yet light. Plastic components such as wheel arch liners are fitted to the underside of the vehicle to further improve corrosion resistance.

2 Maintenance – bodywork and underframe

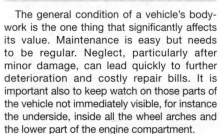

The general condition of a vehicle's bodywork is the one thing that significantly affects its value. Maintenance is easy but needs to be regular. Neglect, particularly after minor damage, can lead quickly to further deterioration and costly repair bills. It is important also to keep watch on those parts of the vehicle not immediately visible, for instance the underside, inside all the wheel arches and the lower part of the engine compartment.

The basic maintenance routine for the bodywork is washing preferably with a lot of water, from a hose. This will remove all the loose solids which may have stuck to the vehicle. It is important to flush these off in such a way as to prevent grit from scratching the finish. The wheel arches and underframe need washing in the same way to remove any accumulated mud which will retain moisture and tend to encourage rust. Oddly enough, the best time to clean the underframe and wheel arches is in wet weather when the mud is thoroughly wet and soft. In very wet weather the underframe is usually cleaned of large accumulations automatically and this is a good time for inspection.

Periodically, except on vehicles with a wax-based underbody protective coating, it is a good idea to have the whole of the underframe of the vehicle steam-cleaned, engine compartment included, so that a thorough inspection can be carried out to see what minor repairs and renovations are necessary. Steam-cleaning is available at many garages, and is necessary for removal of the accumulation of oily grime which sometimes is allowed to become thick in certain areas. If steam-cleaning facilities are not available, there are one or two excellent grease solvents available which can be brush applied; the dirt can then be simply hosed off. Note that these methods should not be used on vehicles with wax-based underbody protective coating, or the coating will be removed. Such vehicles should be inspected annually, preferably just prior to winter, when the underbody should be washed down and any damage to the wax coating repaired using underseal. Ideally, a completely fresh coat should be applied. It would also be worth considering the use of such wax-based protection for injection into door panels, sills, box sections, etc, as an additional safeguard against rust damage where such protection is not provided by the vehicle manufacturer.

After washing paintwork, wipe off with a chamois leather to give an unspotted clear finish. A coat of clear protective wax polish will give added protection against chemical pollutants in the air. If the paintwork sheen has dulled or oxidised, use a cleaner/polisher combination to restore the brilliance of the shine. This requires a little effort, but such dulling is usually caused because regular washing has been neglected. Care needs to be taken with metallic paintwork, as special non-abrasive cleaner/polisher is required to avoid damage to the finish.

Always check that the door and ventilator opening drain holes and pipes are completely clear, so that water can be drained out. Brightwork should be treated in the same way as paintwork. Windscreens and windows can be kept clear of the smeary film which often appears by the use of a proprietary glass cleaner. Never use any form of wax or other body or chromium polish on glass, especially not on the windscreen or tailgate.

3 Maintenance – upholstery and carpets

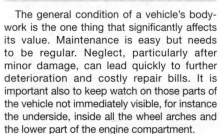

Mats and carpets should be brushed or vacuum cleaned regularly to keep them free of grit. If they are badly stained, remove them from the vehicle for scrubbing or sponging, and make quite sure they are dry before refitting. Seats and interior trim panels can be kept clean by wiping with a damp cloth and a proprietary upholstery cleaner. If they do become stained (which can be more apparent on light-coloured upholstery) use a little liquid detergent and a soft nail brush to scour the grime out of the grain of the material. Do not forget to keep the headlining clean in the same way as the upholstery. When using liquid cleaners inside the vehicle, do not over-wet the surfaces being cleaned. Excessive damp could get into the seams and padded interior causing stains, offensive odours or even rot.

HAYNES HiNT *If the inside of the vehicle gets wet accidentally, it is worthwhile taking some trouble to dry it out properly, particularly where carpets are involved. Do not leave oil or electric heaters inside the vehicle for this purpose.*

4 Minor body damage – repair

Minor scratches

If the scratch is very superficial, and does not penetrate to the metal of the bodywork, repair is very simple. Lightly rub the area of the scratch with a paintwork renovator, or a very fine cutting paste, to remove loose paint from the scratch, and to clear the surrounding bodywork of wax polish. Rinse the area with clean water.

In the case of metallic paint, the most commonly-found 'scratches' are not in the paint, but in the lacquer top coat, and appear white. If care is taken, these can sometimes be rendered less obvious by very careful use of paintwork renovator (which would otherwise not be used on metallic paintwork); otherwise, repair of these scratches can be achieved by applying lacquer with a fine brush.

Apply touch-up paint to the scratch using a fine paint brush; continue to apply fine layers of paint until the surface of the paint in the scratch is level with the surrounding paintwork. Allow the new paint at least two weeks to harden: then blend it into the surrounding paintwork by rubbing the scratch area with a paintwork renovator or a very fine cutting paste. Finally, apply wax polish.

Where the scratch has penetrated right through to the metal of the bodywork, causing the metal to rust, a different repair technique is required. Remove any loose rust from the bottom of the scratch with a penknife, then apply rust-inhibiting paint, to prevent the formation of rust in the future. Using a rubber or nylon applicator fill the scratch with bodystopper paste. If required, this paste can be mixed with cellulose thinners, to provide a very thin paste which is ideal for filling narrow scratches. Before the stopper-paste in the scratch hardens, wrap a piece of smooth cotton rag around the top of a finger. Dip the finger in cellulose thinners, and then quickly sweep it across the surface of the stopper-paste in the scratch; this will ensure that the surface of the stopper-paste is slightly hollowed. The scratch can now be painted over as described earlier in this Section.

Dents

When deep denting of the vehicle's bodywork has taken place, the first task is to pull the dent out, until the affected bodywork almost attains its original shape. There is little point in trying to restore the original shape completely, as the metal in the damaged area will have stretched on impact, and cannot be reshaped fully to its original contour. It is better to bring the level of the dent up to a point which is about 3 mm below the level of the surrounding bodywork. In cases where the dent is very shallow anyway, it is not worth trying to pull it out at all. If the underside of the dent is accessible, it can be hammered out gently from behind, using a mallet with a wooden or plastic head. Whilst doing this, hold a suitable block of wood firmly against the outside of the panel to absorb the impact from the hammer blows and thus prevent a large area of the bodywork from being 'belled-out'.

Should the dent be in a section of the bodywork which has a double skin or some other factor making it inaccessible from behind, a different technique is called for. Drill several small holes through the metal inside the area – particularly in the deeper section. Then screw long self-tapping screws into the holes just sufficiently for them to gain a good purchase in the metal. Now the dent can be pulled out by pulling on the protruding heads of the screws with a pair of pliers.

The next stage of the repair is the removal of the paint from the damaged area, and from an inch or so of the surrounding 'sound' bodywork. This is accomplished most easily by using a wire brush or abrasive pad on a power drill, although it can be done just as effectively by hand using sheets of abrasive paper. To complete the preparation for filling, score the surface of the bare metal with a screwdriver or the tang of a file, or alternatively, drill small holes in the affected area. This will provide a really good 'key' for the filler paste.

To complete the repair, see the Section on filling and re-spraying.

Rust holes or gashes

Remove all paint from the affected area, and from an inch or so of the surrounding 'sound' bodywork, using an abrasive pad or a wire brush on a power drill. If these are not available, a few sheets of abrasive paper will do the job just as effectively. With the paint removed, you will be able to gauge the severity of the corrosion, and therefore decide whether to renew the whole panel (if this is possible) or to repair the affected area. New body panels are not as expensive as most people think, and it is often quicker and more satisfactory to fit a new panel than to attempt to repair large areas of corrosion.

Remove all fittings from the affected area, except those which will act as a guide to the original shape of the damaged bodywork. Then, using tin snips or a hacksaw blade, remove all loose metal and any other metal badly affected by corrosion. Hammer the edges of the hole inwards in order to create a slight depression for the filler paste.

Wire-brush the affected area to remove the powdery rust from the surface of the remaining metal. Paint the affected area with rust-inhibiting paint; if the back of the rusted area is accessible treat this also.

Before filling can take place, it will be necessary to block the hole in some way. This can be achieved by the use of aluminium or plastic mesh, or aluminium tape.

Aluminium or plastic mesh or glass fibre matting is probably the best material to use for a large hole. Cut a piece to the approximate size and shape of the hole to be filled, then position it in the hole so that its edges are below the level of the surrounding bodywork. It can be retained in position by several blobs of filler paste around its periphery.

Aluminium tape should be used for small or very narrow holes. Pull a piece off the roll and trim it to the approximate size and shape required, then pull off the backing paper (if used) and stick the tape over the hole; it can be overlapped if the thickness of one piece is insufficient. Burnish down the edges of the tape with the handle of a screwdriver or similar, to ensure that the tape is securely attached to the metal underneath.

Filling and re-spraying

Before using this Section, see the Sections on dent, deep scratch, rust holes and gash repairs.

Many types of bodyfiller are available, but generally speaking those proprietary kits which contain a tin of filler paste and a tube of resin hardener are best for this type of repair; some can be used directly from the tube. A wide, flexible plastic or nylon applicator will be found invaluable for imparting a smooth and well contoured finish to the surface of the filler.

Mix up a little filler on a clean piece of card or board – measure the hardener carefully (follow the maker's instructions on the pack) otherwise the filler will set too rapidly or too slowly. Using the applicator, apply the filler paste to the prepared area; draw the applicator across the surface of the filler to achieve the correct contour and to level the filler surface. As soon as a contour that approximates to the correct one is achieved, stop working the paste – if you carry on too long the paste will become sticky and begin to 'pick up' on the applicator. Continue to add thin layers of filler paste at twenty-minute intervals until the level of the filler is just proud of the surrounding bodywork.

Once the filler has hardened, excess can be removed using a metal plane or file. From then on, progressively finer grades of abrasive paper should be used, starting with a 40-grade production paper and finishing with 400-grade wet-and-dry paper. Always wrap the abrasive paper around a flat rubber, cork, or wooden block – otherwise the surface of the filler will not be completely flat. During the smoothing of the filler surface the wet-and-dry paper should be periodically rinsed in water. This will ensure that a very smooth finish is imparted to the filler at the final stage.

At this stage the 'dent' should be surrounded by a ring of bare metal, which in turn should be encircled by the finely 'feathered' edge of the good paintwork. Rinse the repair area with clean water, until all of the dust produced by the rubbing-down operation has gone.

Spray the whole repair area with a light coat of primer – this will show up any imperfections in the surface of the filler. Repair these imperfections with fresh filler paste or bodystopper, and once more smooth the surface with abrasive paper. If bodystopper is used, it can be mixed with cellulose thinners to form a really thin paste which is ideal for filling small holes. Repeat this spray and repair procedure until you are satisfied that the surface of the filler, and the feathered edge of the paintwork are perfect. Clean the repair area with clean water and allow to dry fully.

The repair area is now ready for final spraying. Paint spraying must be carried out in a warm, dry, windless and dust free atmosphere. This condition can be created artificially if you have access to a large indoor working area, but if you are forced to work in the open, you will have to pick your day very carefully. If you are working indoors, dousing the floor in the work area with water will help to settle the dust which would otherwise be in the atmosphere. If the repair area is confined to one body panel, mask off the surrounding panels; this will help to minimise the effects of a slight mis-match in paint colours. Bodywork fittings (eg chrome strips, door handles etc) will also need to be masked off. Use genuine masking tape and several thicknesses of newspaper for the masking operations.

Before commencing to spray, agitate the aerosol can thoroughly, then spray a test area (an old tin, or similar) until the technique is mastered. Cover the repair area with a thick coat of primer; the thickness should be built up using several thin layers of paint rather than one thick one. Using 400 grade wet-and-dry paper, rub down the surface of the primer until it is really smooth. While doing this, the work area should be thoroughly doused with water, and the wet-and-dry paper periodically rinsed in water. Allow to dry before spraying on more paint.

Spray on the top coat, again building up the thickness by using several thin layers of paint. Start spraying in the centre of the repair area and then, with a single side-to-side motion, work outwards until the whole repair area and about 50 mm of the surrounding original paintwork is covered. Remove all masking material 10 to 15 minutes after spraying on the final coat of paint.

Allow the new paint at least two weeks to harden, then, using a paintwork renovator or a very fine cutting paste, blend the edges of the paint into the existing paintwork. Finally, apply wax polish.

Plastic components

With the use of more and more plastic body components by the vehicle manufacturers (eg bumpers, spoilers, and in some cases major body panels), rectification of more serious damage to such items has become a matter of either entrusting repair work to a specialist in this field, or renewing complete components. Repair of such damage by the DIY owner is not really feasible owing to the cost of the equipment and materials required for effecting such repairs. The basic technique involves making a groove along the line of the

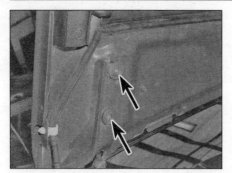

6.3 Slacken the upper bolt, and unscrew the lower one (arrowed)

crack in the plastic using a rotary burr in a power drill. The damaged part is then welded back together by using a hot-air gun to heat up and fuse a plastic filler rod into the groove. Any excess plastic is then removed and the area rubbed down to a smooth finish. It is important that a filler rod of the correct plastic is used, as body components can be made of a variety of different types (eg polycarbonate, ABS, polypropylene).

Damage of a less serious nature (abrasions, minor cracks etc) can be repaired by the DIY owner using a two-part epoxy filler repair material. Once mixed in equal proportions, this is used in similar fashion to the bodywork filler used on metal panels. The filler is usually cured in twenty to thirty minutes, ready for sanding and painting.

If the owner is renewing a complete component himself, or if he has repaired it with epoxy filler, he will be left with the

problem of finding a suitable paint for finishing which is compatible with the type of plastic used. At one time the use of a universal paint was not possible owing to the complex range of plastics encountered in body component applications. Standard paints, generally speaking, will not bond to plastic or rubber satisfactorily. However, it is now possible to obtain a plastic body parts finishing kit which consists of a pre-primer treatment, a primer and coloured top coat. Full instructions are normally supplied with a kit, but basically the method of use is to first apply the pre-primer to the component concerned and allow it to dry for up to 30 minutes. Then the primer is applied and left to dry for about an hour before finally applying the special coloured top coat. The result is a correctly-coloured component where the paint will flex with the plastic or rubber, a property that standard paint does not normally possess.

5 Major body damage – repair

Where serious damage has occurred or large areas need renewal due to neglect, completely new sections or panels will need welding in – this is best left to professionals. If the damage is due to impact, it will also be necessary to check completely the alignment of the body shell structure. Due to the principle of construction, the strength and shape of the whole can be affected by damage to a part. In such instances, the services of a Citroën agent

with specialist checking jigs are essential. If a body is left misaligned, it is first of all dangerous as the car will not handle properly and secondly uneven stresses will be imposed on the steering, engine and transmission, causing abnormal wear or complete failure. Tyre wear may also be excessive.

6 Bonnet – removal, refitting and adjustment

Removal

1 Open the bonnet, and disconnect the washer tube adjacent to the hinge. On post-facelift models, undo the Torx bolt each side securing the plastic hinge trim to the bonnet.
2 Mark around the hinge bracket on the underside of the bonnet with a felt tip pen for reference when refitting.
3 With the aid of an assistant, support the bonnet, prise off the support strut clips and pull the struts from place, then slacken the upper hinge bolts, and remove the lower ones **(see illustration)**. Lift off the bonnet and store it in a safe place.

Refitting and adjustment

4 Before refitting, place pads of rags under the corners of the bonnet near the hinges to protect the paintwork from damage.
5 Fit the bonnet and insert the hinge bolts. Just nip the bolts up in their previously-marked positions, then refit the support struts.
6 Reconnect the washer tube.
7 Shut the bonnet and check its fit. If necessary slacken the bolts and reposition the bonnet.
8 Tighten the hinge bolts securely when adjustment is correct.

7 Bonnet release cable – removal and refitting

Removal

1 Remove the front bumper as described in Section 19.
2 Remove the panel above the driver's pedals (pre-facelift models) or the passenger's footwell (post-facelift models), then pull away the rubber weatherstrip, undo the Torx bolt, and pull the driver's door sill trim panel upwards from place **(see illustration)**.
3 Undo the 2 bolts securing the handle to the vehicle body. Recover the spacers **(see illustration)**. Note that the cable is integral with the handle.
4 Pull out the retaining clips, pull the cable outer from the bracket on the front cross-member, and disengage the end of the cable from the bonnet lock **(see illustrations)**.
5 Trace the cable back and release it from any retaining clips.

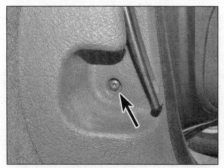

7.2 Undo the Torx bolt and remove the trim panel (arrowed)

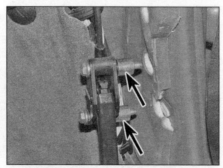

7.3 Undo the bolt securing the handle and recover the spacers (arrowed)

7.4a Release the clip securing the outer cable . . .

7.4b . . . and disengage the end of the cable

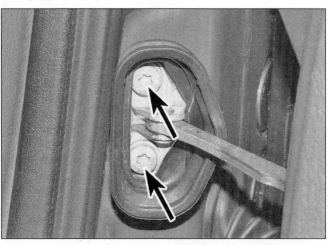

8.3 Bonnet lock retaining bolts (arrowed)

9.3 Undo the check strap Torx bolts (arrowed)

6 Tie a length of string to the end of the cable, and pull the cable into the passenger's cabin, then untie the string and leave it in place to aid refitting.

Refitting

7 Refit by reversing the removal operations.

8 Bonnet lock – removal and refitting

Removal

1 Remove the front bumper as described in Section 19.
2 Detach the release cable (see previous Section), then trace the wiring back and disconnect the plug.
3 Undo the two lock retaining bolts and remove the lock **(see illustration)**.

Refitting

4 Refitting is a reversal of removal. Only finger-tighten the lock retaining bolts, then shut the bonnet to centralise the catch. Tighten the retaining bolts securely.

9 Doors – removal and refitting

Removal

1 Disconnect the battery negative lead (see Chapter 5A).
2 Open the door and support it with a jack or axle stand, using rags to protect the paintwork.
3 Release the door check strap by undoing the 2 Torx bolts securing it to the pillar bracket **(see illustration)**.
4 Have an assistant steady the door, then prise out the clips, and pull out the hinge pins **(see illustration)**.
5 As the door is withdrawn, disconnect the door electrical wiring by releasing the convoluted sleeve from the door pillar, pull

the connector from the pillar, slide up the red locking catch and separate the two halves of the connector **(see illustration)**.
6 Carry the door from the vehicle.

Refitting

7 Refit the door by reversing the removal operations. Note that it will be necessary to re-attach the plastic collar to the wiring harness convoluted sleeve before clipping it to the pillar.
8 Once the door is fitted, adjust the striker plate so that the door opens and closes easily but firmly. With the door handle pulled out, shut the door and check that the lock slides over the striker plate without scraping.

9.4 Prise out the pin retaining clip (arrowed)

10 Door interior trim panel – removal and refitting

Removal

1 Ensure the ignition is switched off. Wait at least one minute for any stored electrical energy to dissipate before commencing work.

Front door

2 Prise out the plastic plug, undo the Torx bolt, and remove the interior release handle surround trim **(see illustrations)**.
3 Prise off the trim on the outside of the door grab handle, then prise up the switch

9.5 Slide up the red locking catch (arrowed) and disconnect the door wiring loom connector

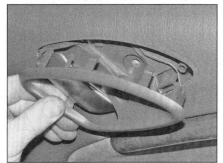

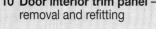

10.2a Prise out the plastic cap, undo the Torx bolt . . .

10.2b . . . and prise away the interior release handle surround trim

10.3a Prise away the grab handle outer trim

10.3b Starting from the rear, prise up the door switch panel

10.4 Pull the trim panel over the mirror mounting from the door

10.5a Undo the grab handle Torx bolts – driver's side . . .

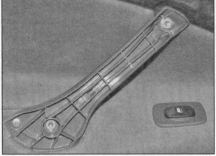
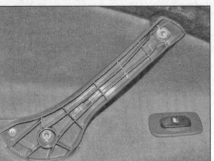

10.5b . . . and passenger's side

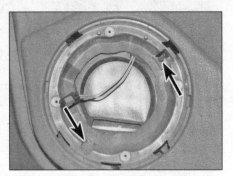

10.7 Undo the Torx bolts (arrowed) in the speaker aperture

assembly **(see illustrations)**. Disconnect the wiring plug as the switch is withdrawn.

4 Carefully prise away the mirror trim panel **(see illustration)**.

5 Undo the Torx bolts in the handle aperture **(see illustrations)**.

6 Prise off the speaker panel, undo the screws and remove the speaker. Disconnect the wiring plug as the speaker is removed.

7 Undo the 2 bolts in the speaker aperture **(see illustration)**.

8 Prise down the light unit from the lower

edge of the door trim, and disconnect the wiring plug **(see illustration)**.

9 Remove the plastic cap from the rear edge of the door trim, and undo the Torx bolt **(see illustration)**.

10 The door trim panel is further secured by plastic clips around the base and front/rear/top edges of the panel. Use a flat-bladed tool to carefully prise the panel from the door frame

11 Lift the panel to detach it from the window seal, then pull the panel away from the door sufficiently to gain access to the various wiring plugs/cables behind it. Noting their locations, and disconnect the plugs.

Rear door

12 Carefully prise away the triangular trim panel from the corner of the window **(see illustration)**.

13 Prise up the electric window switch, and disconnect the wiring plug, or pull the window regulator handle from place (as applicable) **(see illustrations)**.

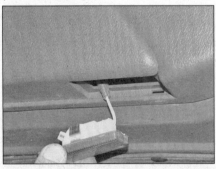

10.8 Prise down the light and disconnect the wiring plug

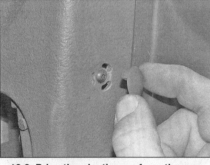

10.9 Prise the plastic cap from the rear edge of the trim panel

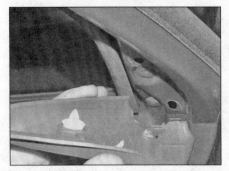

10.12 Pull the triangular trim from the corner of the window

10.13a Prise up the window switch . . .

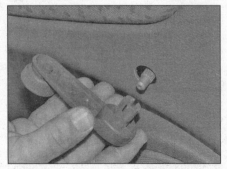

10.13b . . . or pull the window winder handle from the spindle

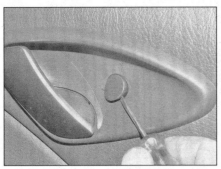

10.14 Prise out the cap to expose the Torx bolt

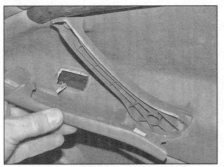

10.15 Prise away the grab handle trim

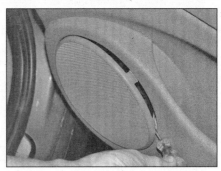

10.16 Prise away the speaker grille

14 Prise out the plastic cap, undo the Torx bolt and remove the interior release handle surround trim **(see illustration)**.

15 Starting at the top, prise off the trim on the outside of the door grab handle, and undo the 2 Torx bolts **(see illustration)**.

16 Prise away the speaker grille, undo the 4 retaining Torx bolts, and remove the speaker from the door **(see illustration)**.

17 Undo the 2 Torx bolts in the speaker aperture **(see illustration)**.

18 The door trim panel is further secured by plastic clips around the base and front/rear/ top edges of the panel. Use a flat-bladed tool to carefully prise the panel from the door frame **(see illustration)**.

19 Lift the panel to detach it from the window seal, then pull the panel away from the door sufficiently to gain access to any wiring plugs/ cables behind it. Noting their locations, and disconnect the plugs.

Refitting

20 Refitting is a reversal of removal. Obtain and fit new fasteners for the base/edges of the panel if any were broken during removal. Check the operation of all switches before finally fitting the trim panel into place.

---

11 Door handle and lock components –
removal and refitting

Outer handle

Front door

1 Remove the door lock assembly as described later in this Section. Note that there is no need to remove the lock from the door – lay it in the base of the door.

2 Undo the 2 nuts and remove the aluminium cover from the rear of the handle, complete with the lock cylinder **(see illustration)**.

3 Manoeuvre the handle from the door **(see illustration)**.

4 Refitting is a reversal of removal.

Rear door

5 Remove the door lock as described later in this Section. Undo the inner cover retaining nut, then using a screwdriver through the

10.17 With the speaker removed, undo the Torx bolts (arrowed)

lock aperture, slide the aluminium inner cover forwards, and manoeuvre the handle assembly from the door **(see illustrations)**.

6 Refitting is a reversal of removal.

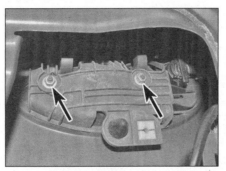

11.2 Undo the 2 nuts (arrowed) and remove the cover with the lock cylinder

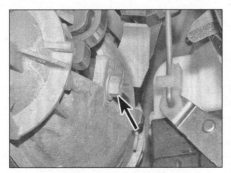

11.5a Undo the nut (arrowed) . . .

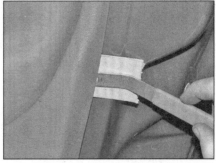

10.18 Use a piece of card between the tool and the door paint

Front door lock cylinder

7 Remove the outer door handle as described in this Section.

11.3 Manoeuvre the handle from the door

11.5b . . . insert a screwdriver through the lock aperture . . .

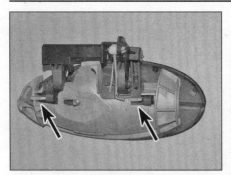

11.5c . . . and slide the cover forwards to release the catches (arrowed) . . .

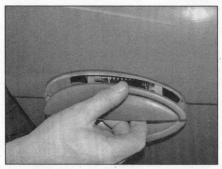

11.5d . . . then manoeuvre the handle from the door

11.8 Prise out the clip (arrowed) to release the lock cylinder

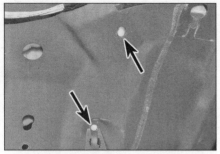
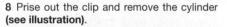

11.12 Use a pair of pliers to squeeze together the sides and release the damping block clips (arrowed)

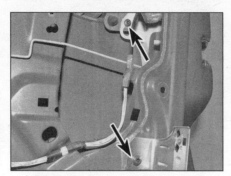

11.13a Undo the 2 rear window guide screws on the inner face (arrowed) . . .

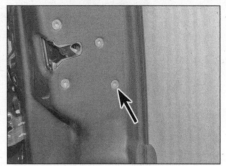

11.13b . . . and one at the rear face (arrowed)

8 Prise out the clip and remove the cylinder **(see illustration)**.

9 Refitting is a reversal of removal.

Front door lock assembly

10 Ensure the window is fully raised, then

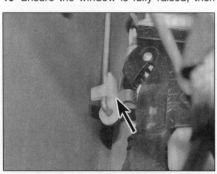

11.14 Rotate the clip (arrowed) anti-clockwise to release the lock cylinder rod

11.15 Undo the 3 Torx bolts securing the lock at the rear face of the door

remove the door inner trim panel as described in Section 10.

11 Carefully peel away the weatherproof membrane in the area behind the door lock. Use a sharp knife to cut through the sealant.

12 Release the 2 clips and remove the damping block **(see illustration)**.

13 Undo the 3 screws and remove the rear window guide **(see illustrations)**.

14 Release the lock cylinder operating rod from the lock lever (where applicable) **(see illustration)**.

15 Undo the 3 Torx bolts securing the lock to the door frame **(see illustration)**.

16 Pull the lock away from the door frame a little, and unclip the exterior handle operating rod.

17 Manoeuvre the lock from the door, disconnecting the wiring plug as it's withdrawn.

18 Refitting is a reversal of the removal procedure. Check for correct operation before refitting the door trim.

Rear door lock assembly

19 Remove the door window as described in Section 12. However, instead of removing the window, slide it fully upwards and tape it in position.

20 Unclip the exterior handle rod from the lock **(see illustration)**.

21 Remove the 3 Torx bolts at the rear end of the door securing the lock mechanism **(see illustration)**.

22 Manoeuvre the lock assembly from the door, disconnecting the wiring plug as it's withdrawn.

23 Refitting is a reversal of the removal procedure. Check for correct operation before refitting the door trim.

Interior handles

24 Remove the interior door trim panel as described in Section 10.

11.20 Rotate the clip (arrowed) anti-clockwise to release the exterior handle rod

11.21 Undo the 3 Torx bolts securing the lock at the rear face of the door

25 Lift the handle assembly upwards to disengage the clips, then unclip the operating rod **(see illustration)**.

26 Refitting is a reversal of removal.

12 Door window regulator, motor and glass – removal and refitting

Front door window regulator

Removal

1 Remove the door window as described in this Section. However, instead of removing the window, slide it fully upwards and tape it in position.

2 Use a 6.0 mm drill to remove the 4 rivets securing the regulator **(see illustration)**.

3 Release the 3 clips securing the regulator motor support **(see illustration)**.

4 Release the cable clips and manoeuvre the regulator assembly from the door **(see illustration)**.

Refitting

5 Refitting is a reversal of the removal procedure.

11.25 Lift the door interior handle from position

Rear door window regulator

Removal

6 Remove the door window as described in this Section. However, instead of removing the window slide it fully upwards and tape it in position.

7 Use a 5.0 mm drill bit to remove the 5 rivets (manual window), or 3 rivets (electric window) securing the regulator to the door frame **(see illustration)**.

8 Manoeuvre the regulator from the door. Disconnect the motor wiring plug as the regulator is withdrawn (where applicable).

Refitting

9 Refitting is a reversal of the removal procedure.

Front door window glass

Removal

10 Lower the window approximately 250 mm, then disconnect the battery negative lead as described in Chapter 5A.

11 Remove the door inner trim panel as described in Section 10.

12 Undo the 3 Torx bolts, disconnect the wiring plug and remove the window electric motor **(see illustration 12.30)**.

13 Lift the interior handle assembly upwards to disengage the lugs, and detach the operating rod.

14 Carefully peel away the weatherproof membrane from the door frame. Use a sharp knife to cut through the sealant **(see illustration)**.

15 Prise up and remove the interior window weatherstrip **(see illustration)**.

16 Release the window retaining clips **(see illustrations)**. Note that both the clips must be released before the window can be lifted.

17 Starting at the rear, pull the window

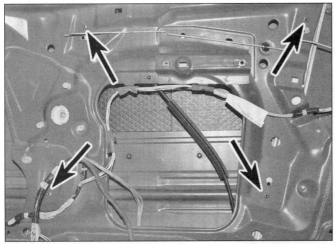

12.2 Drill out the 4 rivets securing the window regulator (arrowed)

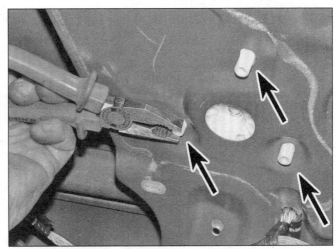

12.3 Use a pair of pliers to squeeze together the sides and release the motor support clips (arrowed)

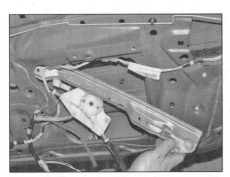

12.4 Manoeuvre the regulator through the door aperture

12.7 Drill out the rivets securing the regulator

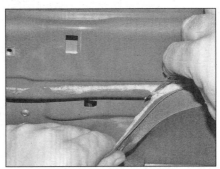

12.14 Use a sharp knife to cut through the membrane sealant

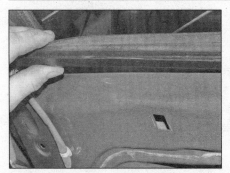

12.15 Prise up the rubber weatherstrip from the inside of the door

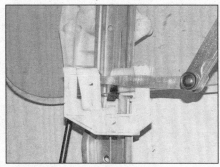

12.16a Lever the clip outwards to release the window

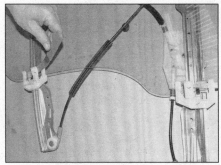

12.16b Use a tool to wedge one clip outwards whilst the other is being released (shown with the window removed for clarity) . . .

12.17 . . . then lift the rear edge of the window and manoeuvre it from the door

upwards, and manoeuvre it from the door **(see illustration)**.

Refitting

18 Refitting is a reversal of removal. **Note:** *If the weatherproof membrane is damaged, renew it.*

12.23 Prise up the interior weatherstrip

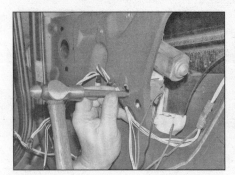

12.26b . . . use a punch to drive the centre of the pin from position

12.22 Drill out the 3 rivets (arrowed)

Rear door window glass

Removal

19 Lower the window approximately 300 mm.
20 Remove the door inner trim panel as described in Section 10.

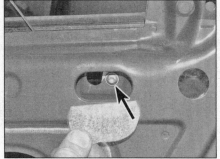

12.24 Prise out the front runner guide

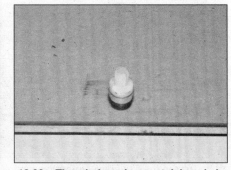

21 Lift up the interior door handle assembly, and disengage the control rod.
22 Drill out the 3 rivets (5.0 mm drill bit) and remove the 'anti-intrusion' cover from the door frame **(see illustration)**.
23 Prise up and remove the window interior weatherstrip **(see illustration)**.
24 Carefully remove the window front runner guide **(see illustration)**.
25 Carefully peel away the weatherproof membrane from the door frame. Use a sharp knife to cut through the sealant **(see illustration 12.14)**.
26 Drive out the 2 parts of the clamp retaining pin and lift the window upwards into the top of the guide **(see illustrations)**.
27 Undo the 2 retaining Torx bolts and remove the rear window guide, then manoeuvre the window from the door **(see illustrations)**.

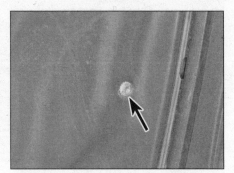

12.26a The window clamp retaining pin is in 2 parts . . .

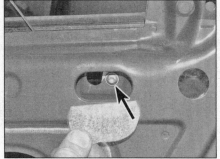

12.27a Undo the Torx bolt at the top (arrowed) . . .

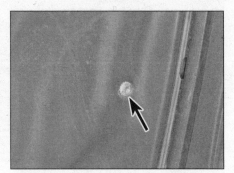

12.27b . . . and the one at the bottom securing the rear window guide (arrowed)

Refitting

28 Press the 2 parts of the window retaining pin into place in the window clamp, then manoeuvre the window into position. The pin engages with the regulator by pressing the window down into place **(see illustration)**.
29 The remainder of refitting is a reversal of removal. **Note:** *If the weatherproof membrane is damaged, renew it.*

Front window electric motor

Removal

30 Remove the door inner trim panel as described in Section 10.
31 Note their fitted positions, then disconnect the wiring plug(s) from the motor.
32 Undo the 3 Torx retaining bolts and pull the motor assembly from the regulator **(see illustration)**.

Refitting

33 Refitting is a reversal of removal.

Rear window electric motor

34 The electric motor is integral with the regulator assembly.

---

13 Tailgate interior trim panel – removal and refitting

Removal

Hatchback

1 Open the tailgate, push in the centre pin, and prise out the parcel shelf support posts **(see illustrations)**.
2 Carefully pull the tailgate window side trims inwards to release the retaining clips, and remove them. Note that the upper trims will come away with the side trims **(see illustration)**.
3 On pre-facelift models, prise out the plastic rivets (4 on the upper edge, 4 on the lower, and 2 each side) **(see illustration)**, on post-facelift models, undo the Torx bolt in each handle recess, and pull the trim panel from the tailgate to release the push-in clips.
4 On pre-facelift models, the lower panel is now secured by 1 push-in clip in the handle recess each side **(see illustration)**.

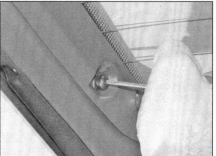

12.28 With the clamp pin refitted, press the window down into the clamp (arrowed)

Estate

5 Prise out the plastic rivets (6 on the upper edge, 6 on the lower, 3 each side, and 2 in each handle recess), remove the plastic pull-down

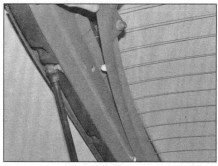

13.1a Push in the centre pins . . .

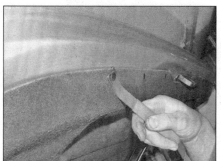

13.2 Pull the window side trims inwards to release the clips

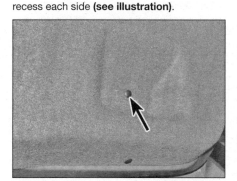

13.4 . . . and a plastic rivet or Torx bolt in the handle recess each side (arrowed)

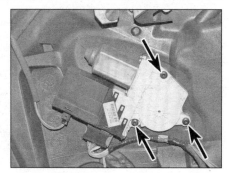

12.32 Window motor retaining Torx bolts (arrowed)

handles, then remove the lower trim panel **(see illustration)**.
6 Use a flat-bladed tool to release the push-on clips and remove the window side trims **(see illustration)**.

13.1b . . . and pull out the support posts

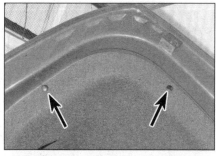

13.3 The lower tailgate panel is secured by plastic rivets around the circumference (arrowed) . . .

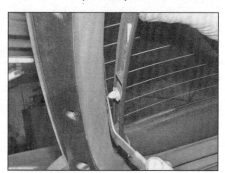

13.6 Prise inwards the side trim panels

13.5 Prise out the plastic rivets securing the lower tailgate panel

13.7a Release the clips on the underside of the plastic trim panel . . .

7 Release the push-on clips and remove the trim panel under the rear window **(see illustrations)**. Disconnect the rear window switch wiring plug as the panel is removed.

Refitting

8 Refitting is a reversal of removal.

14 Tailgate –
removal and refitting

Removal

1 Remove the tailgate trim panels as described in Section 13.

Hatchback

2 Remove the left-hand side C-pillar trim panel as described in Section 22, then disconnect

14.2 Disconnect the tailgate wiring loom plug (arrowed)

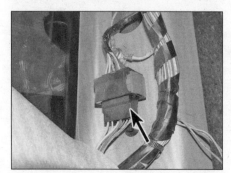

14.6 Tailgate loom wiring plug (arrowed)

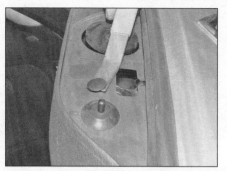

13.7b . . . and prise up the clip on the top

the tailgate gate loom wiring plug **(see illustration)**.
3 Have an assistant support the tailgate, then disconnect the tailgate struts as described in Section 15.
4 Make alignment marks between the tailgate hinges and the vehicle bodywork to aid refitting, then undo the hinge bolts and remove the tailgate. Feed the harness through the tailgate as it is withdrawn.

Estate

5 Pull out the plastic trim panel behind the hinges **(see illustration)**.
6 Remove the right-hand side D-pillar trim as described in Section 22, then disconnect the tailgate loom wiring plug **(see illustration)**.
7 Prise out the clip and detach the tailgate balancers on each side **(see illustration)**.
8 Lower the tailgate, and raise the rear windscreen glass.
8 Make alignment marks between the tailgate

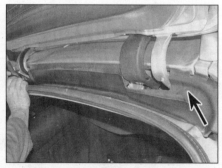

14.5 Pull out the trim panel behind the hinges (arrowed)

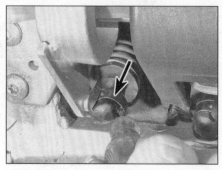

14.7 Prise out the retaining clip (arrowed)

hinges and the vehicle bodywork to aid refitting, then undo the hinge Torx bolts and remove the tailgate. Feed the harness through the tailgate as it is withdrawn.

Refitting

9 Refitting is a reversal of removal.

15 Tailgate/bonnet
support struts –
removal and refitting

Note: *On Estate models, removal of the tailgate struts requires the headlining to be lowered. This is an involved task, requiring patience and dexterity. Consequently, we recommend this task is entrusted to a dealer or upholstery specialist.*
1 Open the tailgate/bonnet, then prise off the retaining clips at each end, then detach the strut from the mounting balljoints **(see illustration)**.

⚠ *Warning: The tailgate is extremely heavy. Have an assistant support it before detaching the struts.*

2 Refitting is a reversal of removal.

16 Tailgate components –
removal and refitting

Lock assembly removal

1 Remove the tailgate interior lower trim panel as described in Section 13. On Estate models, carefully remove the waterproof panel from the inside of the tailgate panel.
2 Undo the 2 bolts securing the lock assembly to the tailgate, then depress the clip each side of the plastic cover **(see illustration)**.
3 Disconnect the lock wiring plug.
4 Withdraw the lock from the tailgate.

Exterior handle removal

5 Remove the tailgate interior lower trim panel as described in Section 13.

Hatchback

6 Carefully peel away the waterproof plastic panels from the tailgate.

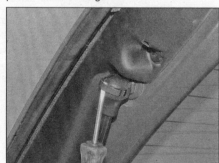

15.1 Prise out the clip and detach the support strut

16.2 With the bolts removed, depress the clip each side an push the lock upwards into the tailgate

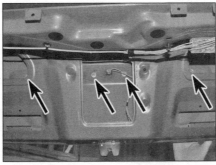

16.7a Hatchback tailgate handle mounting nuts (arrowed) – pre-facelift models

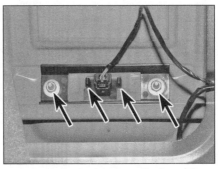

16.7b Undo the 2 nuts, and release the clips (arrowed) – post-facelift models

7 Undo the 4 nuts (pre-facelift), or 2 nuts, remove the retaining plate, release the 2 clips (post-facelift), and pull the handle assembly from position **(see illustrations)**.
8 Disconnect the wiring plug as the handle is withdrawn.

Estate

9 Undo the 4 nuts and pull the handle assembly from position **(see illustrations)**.
10 Disconnect the wiring plug as the handle is withdrawn.

Tailgate window removal

Note: *Estate only.*
11 Open the tailgate window, undo the 4 spoiler retaining Torx bolts, and pull the rear spoiler away from the glass **(see illustration)**.
12 Disconnect the high-level stop-light wiring plug, and the washer jet tube.
13 Remove the rear spoiler.
14 Make alignment marks between the mounting washers and the window **(see illustration)**.
15 Undo the 2 retaining nuts, lift off the metal washer, and remove the tailgate window along with the rubber grommets.

Tailgate window lock removal

Note: *Estate only.*
16 Remove the tailgate lower panels as described in Section 13.
17 Disconnect the lock wiring plug, then undo the 2 nuts and remove the lock assembly from the tailgate **(see illustration)** Unclip the wiring harness as the lock is withdrawn.

Refitting

18 Refitting is a reversal of the relevant removal procedure.

17 Windscreen and other fixed glass – removal and refitting

Special equipment and techniques are needed for successful removal and refitting of the windscreen, rear window and side windows. Have the work carried out by a Citroën dealer or a windscreen specialist.

16.9a On Estate models, there are 2 nuts in the centre (arrowed) . . .

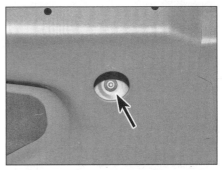

16.9b . . . and one each side (arrowed)

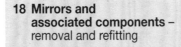

18 Mirrors and associated components – removal and refitting

⚠ *Warning: If the mirror glass is broken, wear gloves to protect your hands. This is good advice, in fact, even if the glass is not broken, due to the risk of glass breakage.*

Removal

Door mirror glass

1 Pivot the mirror glass into the mirror housing as far as possible on the upper edge.
2 Insert a thin flat-bladed tool between the lower edge of the glass and the mirror housing, and carefully release the glass retaining clip **(see illustration)**.
3 Pull the mirror glass out of the housing,

16.14 Use masking tape to make alignment marks around the rear window mounting washers

and disconnect the heating element wiring. Before refitting the glass, ensure the retaining clip is correctly located around the outside of the locating lugs **(see illustration)**.

16.11 The spoiler is secured by 4 Torx bolts (right-hand bolts arrowed)

16.17 Undo the 2 nuts (arrowed) and remove the tailgate window lock

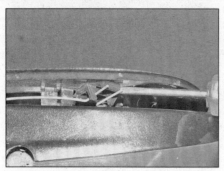

18.2 Release the mirror glass retaining clip

18.3 Ensure the retaining clip is located around the outside of the lugs

Door mirror motor

4 Remove the mirror glass as described.
5 Undo the 3 Torx bolts, and release the motor **(see illustration)**. Disconnect the wiring plug from the rear of the unit as it's withdrawn.

Door mirror cover

6 Remove the mirror glass as previously described in this Section.
7 Release the 4 retaining clips and press the cover forwards **(see illustration)**. Note that it is extremely likely that the clips will be damaged during removal, necessitating the renewal of the cover.

Door mirror (complete unit)

8 Remove the door inner trim panel as described in Section 10.
9 Disconnect the motor wiring at the connector inside the door, and release it from the retaining clips.
10 Support the mirror, then undo the 3 Torx retaining bolts, remove the rubber trim strip at the front and withdraw the mirror from the door **(see illustrations)**. Release the rubber seal from the door as the mirror is withdrawn. Check the condition of the seal and renew if necessary.

Interior mirror

11 Grasp the mirror base/sensor cover and slide it sharply downwards **(see illustration)**.

Refitting

12 Refitting is a reversal of the relevant removal procedure. Where applicable, ensure that the rubber grommet is correctly located in its hole in the door.

19 Bumpers – removal and refitting

Note: *The bumpers consist of several sections, and once the bumper assembly has been removed as described below, the outer cover can be unclipped and the bumper dismantled. It is unclear at the time of writing whether the individual sections that make up the bumper are available separately.*

Front bumper

Pre-facelift models (before September 2004)

1 Open the bonnet and undo the 4 Torx bolts at the top of the front grille **(see illustration)**.

18.5 Mirror motor bolts (arrowed)

18.7 Release the 4 clips (arrowed) and pull the mirror cover forwards

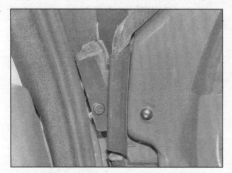

18.10a Pull away the rubber strip . . .

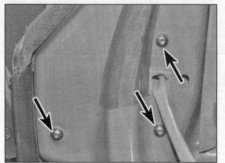

18.10b . . . then undo the mirror mounting Torx bolts (arrowed)

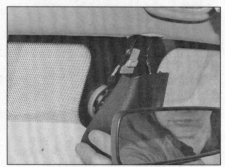

18.11 Pull the mirror base/sensor cover sharply downwards

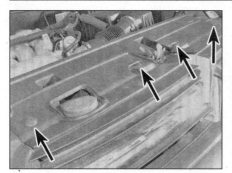

19.1 Undo the 4 Torx bolts across the top of the bumper (arrowed)

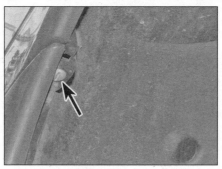

19.2a Undo the bumper-to-wing screw (arrowed) . . .

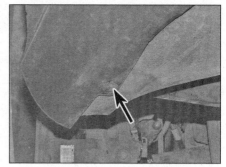

19.2b . . . and the wheel arch liner-to-bumper screws (arrowed)

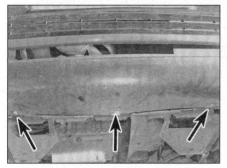

19.3 Rotate the fasteners 90° anti-clockwise (arrowed)

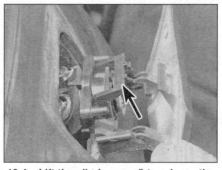

19.4a Lift the clip (arrowed) to release the washer jet cover

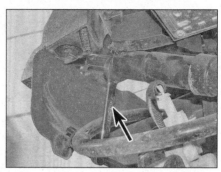

19.4b To aid refitment, pull out the washer jet and hold it in position using a 13 mm spanner

2 Undo the screw each side in the wheel arch where the bumper edge meets the wing, and the screws securing the wheel arch liner to the bumper **(see illustrations)**.
3 The bumper is now secured by 3 fasteners in the centre, underside. Rotate the fasteners 90° to remove them **(see illustration)**.
4 Carefully pull the headlight washer jet covers from the bumper, then lift the black plastic clip at the top and remove the covers (where fitted) **(see illustrations)**. Note that the covers are very fragile and easily damaged.
5 With the help of an assistant, pull the rear edges of the bumper sides outwards slightly to release the clips, then pull it forward and remove it from the vehicle. Note their fitted positions and disconnect the various wiring plugs as the bumper is withdrawn.
6 Refitting is a reversal of removal. Take care when offering the bumper into position that the side mounting slides engage correctly (where applicable).

Post-facelift models (from September 2004)

7 Undo the 3 Torx bolts each side securing the bumper to the engine/radiator undershields **(see illustrations)**.
8 Undo the 2 screws each side in the wheel arch where the bumper edge meets the wing, and the bumper meets the wheel arch liner **(see illustration)**.
9 Undo the 3 Torx bolts at the top of the rear edge of the bumper, above the bonnet slam panel **(see illustration)**.
10 Pull the bumper slightly forwards, then

release the clips each side beneath the headlights. With the help of an assistant, pull the bumper forward and remove it from the vehicle. Note their fitted positions and

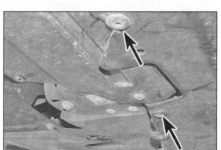

19.7a Undo the 2 Torx bolts at the front edge each side (arrowed) . . .

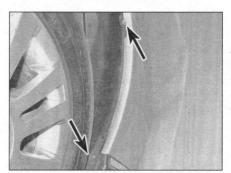

19.8 Undo the 2 Torx bolts (arrowed) in the wheel arch aperture

disconnect the various wiring plugs as the bumper is withdrawn **(see illustrations)**.
11 Refitting is a reversal of removal. Take care when offering the bumper into position

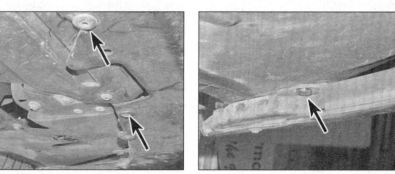

19.7b . . . and the one at the side (arrowed)

19.9 Undo the Torx bolts at the top of the bumper (arrowed)

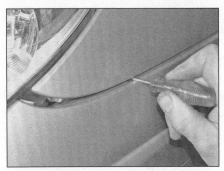

19.10a Insert a screwdriver through the gap . . .

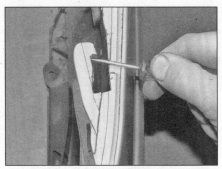

19.10b . . . to push in and release the retaining clip

19.13a Undo the bumper-to-wing screw (arrowed) . . .

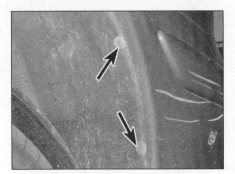

19.13b . . . and the wheel arch liner-to-bumper bolts (arrowed)

that the side mounting slides engage correctly (where applicable).

Rear bumper – Hatchback

12 Remove the wing-mounted rear light units as described in Chapter 12.

19.16a Undo the nut each side in the light unit aperture

19.18a Undo the screw securing the bumper to the rear wing . . .

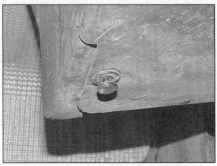

19.14 Prise out the centre pin, then pull out the plastic rivet each side

Pre-facelift models (before September 2004)

13 Slacken the screw each side in the wheel arch where the bumper meets the rear wing, and the 2 Torx bolts securing the wheel arch liner to the bumper (see illustrations).

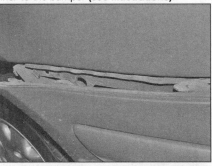

19.16b Pull the bumper rearwards and outwards to release the clips

19.18b . . . and the 2 securing the bumper to the wheel arch liner (arrowed)

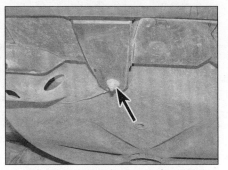

19.15 Undo the nut (arrowed) on the bumper underside

14 Prise out the centre pin, the lever out the plastic expansion rivet each side at the front, lower edge of the bumper (see illustration).
15 Slacken the nut on the underside of the bumper adjacent to the spare wheel well (see illustration).
16 Undo the nut each side at the lower edge of the rear light apertures, then release the clips at the upper edge and, with the help of as assistant, manoeuvre the bumper rearwards (see illustrations). Disconnect any wiring plugs as the bumper is withdrawn.
17 Refitting is a reversal of removal. Take care when offering the bumper into position that the side mounting slides engage correctly (where applicable).

Post-facelift models (from September 2004)

18 Undo the 3 screws each side securing the wheel arch liner to the rear bumper (see illustrations).
19 Prise out the centre pins, and lever out the 2 plastic expansion rivets each side on underside of the bumper, slacken the 2 Torx bolts and slacken the nut adjacent to the spare wheel well (see illustrations).
20 Working in the luggage compartment area, remove the rear light access panels, and undo the 2 nuts each side (see illustration).
21 With the help of an assistant, pull the bumper rearwards and remove it from the vehicle. Note their fitted positions and disconnect any wiring plugs as the bumper is withdrawn.
22 Refitting is a reversal of removal. Take care when offering the bumper into position

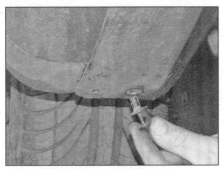

19.19a Prise out the centre pins, and remove the 2 plastic expansion rivets each side

19.19b Slacken the Torx bolt underneath the bumper each side at the rear (right-hand screw arrowed) . . .

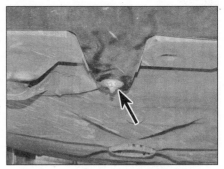

19.19c . . . and the nut adjacent to the spare wheel well (arrowed)

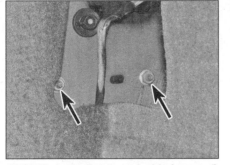

19.20 Undo the 2 nuts each side (arrowed) below the rear lights

19.23 Undo the 3 screws (arrowed) securing the wheel arch liner to the bumper

19.24a Prise out the centre pin and remove the single plastic rivet – pre-facelift models . . .

19.24b . . . or 2 rivets – post-facelift models

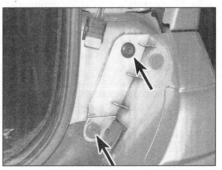

19.26 Undo the 2 Torx bolts each side (arrowed)

19.27 Pull the bumper rearwards and outwards

that the side mounting slides engage correctly (where applicable).

Rear bumper – Estate

23 Undo the 3 screws each side securing the wheel arch liner to the bumper **(see illustration)**.
24 Prise down the centre pin, then lever out the plastic expansion rivet(s) each side securing the lower front edge of the bumper to the wheel arch liner **(see illustrations)**.
25 Remove the lower rear light units as described in Chapter 12.
26 Undo the 2 Torx bolts each side at the base of the light unit apertures **(see illustration)**.
27 With the help of an assistant, pull the bumper rearwards and remove it from the vehicle **(see illustration)**. Note their fitted positions and disconnect any wiring plugs as the bumper is withdrawn.

28 Refitting is a reversal of removal. Take care when offering the bumper into position that the side mounting slides engage correctly (where applicable).

20 Front grille panel – removal and refitting

Note: *Pre-facelift models only (before September 2004).*

Removal

1 Remove the front bumper as described in Section 19.
2 Release the 4 retaining screws and remove the grille **(see illustration)**.

Refitting

3 Refit by reversing the removal operations.

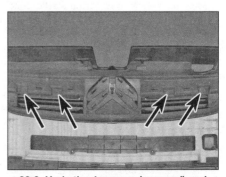

20.2 Undo the 4 screws (arrowed) and remove the grille

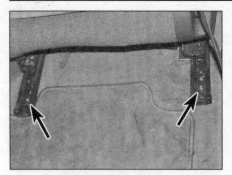

21.1 Undo the Torx bolts at the rear of the runners (arrowed)

21.4a Prise up the clip and lift up the plastic panel

21.4b Disconnect the seat wiring plug on the underside of the panel

21.7 Pull the mounting rods to one side to disengage them

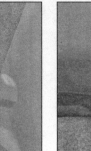

21.8 Undo the 2 bolts at the outer hinge (arrowed) . . .

21.10 . . . and the 2 nuts at the centre hinge (arrowed)

21 Seats –
removal and refitting

Note: *All models are equipped with a airbag fitted into the side of the front seat backrest. Refer to Chapter 12 for further information on the SRS systems.*

Front seat

1 Slide the seat fully forward, then undo the Torx bolt at the rear end of each seat runner **(see illustration)**.
2 Slide the seat fully rearward, then undo the Torx bolt at the front end of each seat runner.
3 Ensure that the ignition is switched off, then disconnect the battery negative lead as described in Chapter 5A. Wait at least 5 minutes for any residual electrical energy to dissipate before proceeding.
4 Prise up the clip and lift the plastic panel from the floor. Note their fitted positions, then release the clips and disconnect the seat wiring plug(s) **(see illustrations)**.
5 Lift the seat and manoeuvre it through the front door. As the seats are very heavy, the help of an assistant would be a good idea.
6 Refitting is a reversal of removal. Make sure that no-one is inside the car, then reconnect the battery negative lead as described in Chapter 5A.

Rear seat

7 Pivot the seat cushion forwards, then pull the mounting rods to one side to release them from the brackets **(see illustration)**.

8 Tilt the backrest forward, lift the front edge of the luggage compartment carpet, and undo the 2 bolts at the outer edges securing the seat hinge to the body **(see illustration)**.
9 Undo the bolt securing the centre seat belt lower anchorage.
10 Undo the upper nut and lower bolt securing the central hinge bracket, and manoeuvre the backrest from the vehicle **(see illustration)**. Note that on models equipped with '60/40' backrests, the '40' must be removed first.
11 Refitting is a reversal of removal.

22 Interior trim –
removal and refitting

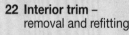
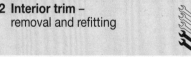

Note: *Refer to earlier Sections of this Chapter for specific procedures covering door and tailgate interior trim panels.*

General

1 The interior trim panels are secured using either screws or various types of trim fasteners, usually studs or clips.
2 Check that there are no other panels overlapping the one to be removed, or other components hindering removal; usually there is a sequence that has to be followed, and this will only become obvious on close inspection.
3 Some of the interior panels will additionally be retained by the screws which are used to secure other items, such as the grab handles.
4 Remove all visible retainers such as screws, noting that these may be hidden under small plastic caps. If the panel will not come free, it

is held by internal clips or fasteners. These are usually situated around the edges of the panel, and can be prised up to release them; note, however that they can break quite easily, so new ones should be available. The best way of releasing such clips is to use a large flat-bladed screwdriver or other wide-bladed tool. Note that in many cases, the adjacent sealing strip must be prised back to release a panel.
5 When removing a panel, **never** use excessive force or the panel may be damaged; always check carefully that all fasteners or other relevant components have been removed or released before attempting to withdraw a panel.
6 Refitting is a reversal of removal; secure the fasteners by pressing them firmly into place and ensure that all disturbed components are correctly secured to prevent rattles.

Carpets

7 The passenger compartment floor carpet is in one large section, and is secured at the sides by the front and rear sill trim panels.
8 Carpet removal and refitting is reasonably straightforward, but is very time-consuming because all adjoining trim panels must be removed first, as must components such as the seats, centre console and seat belt lower anchorages.

Headlining

9 The headlining is stuck to the roof using double-sided tape, and can be withdrawn only once all fittings such as grab handles, sunvisors, sunroof (if fitted), fixed window glass, and related trim panels have been

22.12 Pull the A-pillar trim panel inwards to release the clips

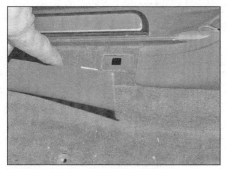

22.15 Pull the door sill trim panel upwards to release the clips

22.16 Undo the seal belt lower anchorage bolt

removed and the relevant sealing strips have been prised clear.

10 Note that headlining removal and refitting requires considerable skill and experience if it is to be carried out without damage, and is therefore best entrusted to a dealer or automotive upholstery specialist.

A-pillar trims

11 Pull the rubber weatherstrip from the door aperture adjacent to the A-pillar.
12 Starting at the top edge, pull the A-pillar trim inwards towards the centre of the passenger cabin to release the clips **(see illustration)**.
13 Refitting is a reversal of removal.

B-pillar trims

14 Move the front seat as far forward as possible, then pull the rubber weatherstrips from the door apertures adjacent to the B-pillar.
15 Pull the front door sill trim panel straight up to release it from the retaining clips. Repeat the procedure on the rear door sill trim panel **(see illustration)**.
16 Prise off the rubber cap, undo the bolt and disconnect the seat belt lower anchorage **(see illustration)**. **Note:** *On the passenger's side of post-facelift models (from September 2004), if the trim is to be completely removed, it will be necessary to unscrew the lower anchorage point belt retractor once the lower trim is completely removed.*
17 Pull the upper edge of the lower B-pillar trim in towards the centre of the cabin to release the clips, and lift it from place, then pull the upper trim inwards/downwards to release the clips **(see illustrations)**. Feed the seat belt through the panel as it's withdrawn.
18 Refitting is a reversal of removal.

C-pillar trims

Hatchback

19 Pull the rubber weatherstrip from the door aperture and tailgate aperture adjacent to the pillar trim panel.
20 Undo the 3 screws and remove the parcel shelf tray support **(see illustration)**. Note that the support is clipped to the C-pillar trim – pull the support inwards to release the clip.
21 Prise out the AIRBAG emblem, then pull the C-pillar trim panel inwards and release the 3 push-on clips **(see illustrations)**.

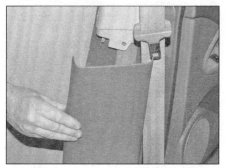

22.17a Pull the top of the lower B-pillar trim panel inwards . . .

22 Refitting is a reversal of removal.

Estate

23 Pull the rubber weatherstrip from the door aperture adjacent to the pillar trim panel.

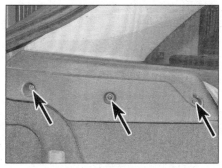

22.20 Parcel shelf support screws (arrowed) – Hatchback models

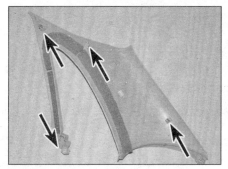

22.21b C-pillar trim panel retaining clips (arrowed)

22.17b . . . and pull the upper B-pillar trim panel inwards/downwards to disengage the upper lugs

24 Undo the 2 retaining screws, pull the parcel shelf support inwards to release the retaining clip **(see illustration)**.
25 Release the clip at the base of the pillar

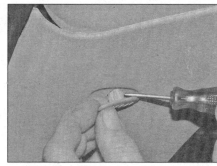

22.21a Prise out the AIRBAG emblem

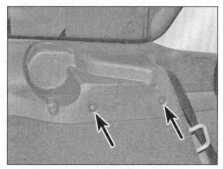

22.24 Parcel shelf support screws (arrowed) – Estate models

22.25a Release the clip . . .

22.25b . . . and pull the C-pillar trim panel inwards to release the clips

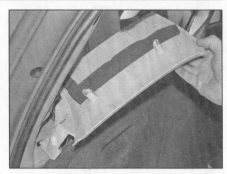

22.28 Pull the top of the D-pillar trim panel inwards to release the clips

trim, then pull it inwards to release the push-in clips **(see illustrations)**.

26 Refitting is a reversal of removal.

D-pillar trims

Estate

27 Undo the 2 retaining screws, and remove the parcel shelf support **(see illustration 22.24)**.

28 Pull the top D-pillar trim panel in towards the centre of the vehicle **(see illustration)**.

29 Refitting is a reversal of removal.

Luggage area side panel

Hatchback

30 Pull the rubber weatherstrip from the tailgate aperture adjacent to the luggage compartment side panel.

31 Undo the 3 screws and remove the parcel shelf support **(see illustration 22.20)**. Note that the support is clipped to the C-pillar trim – pull the support inwards to release the clip.

32 Unclip the rear light unit bulbholder.

33 Prise out the luggage compartment light, and disconnect the wiring plug.

34 Disconnect the wiring plugs, undo the mounting screws, and remove the audio amplifier (where fitted) from the side panel.

35 Unclip the floor netting, and lift out the luggage compartment floor panel.

36 Prise out the clips and remove the tailgate sill trim panel **(see illustrations)**.

37 Prise out the clip at the rear, then starting at the rear edge, pull the panel inwards, and manoeuvre it from the luggage compartment **(see illustration)**.

38 Refitting is a reversal of removal.

Estate

39 Lift out the floor panel, then undo the screws and remove the tailgate sill trim panel **(see illustration)**.

40 Undo the 2 screws and remove the parcel shelf support **(see illustration 22.24)**.

41 Prise out the luggage compartment light and disconnect the wiring plug. Carefully remove the rear loading height adjustment switch (where applicable) by depressing the clips on the upper and lower edges of the switch. Disconnect the wiring plug. Pull the panel inwards to displace the power outlet socket.

42 Pull the panel inwards to release the retaining clips **(see illustration)**. If necessary, pull the top part of the door sill trim panel from the C-pillar, to manoeuvre the side panel over the seat bracket. Disconnect any wiring plugs as the panel is withdrawn.

43 Refitting is a reversal of removal.

Glovebox

Passenger's side

44 Rotate the fasteners anti-clockwise, release the scrivet and remove the trim panel between the front edge of the glovebox and the bulkhead **(see illustration)**.

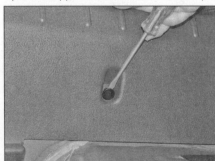

22.36a Prise out the clips each side . . .

22.36b . . . then pull up the tailgate sill trim panel

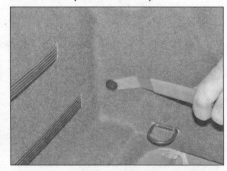

22.37 Prise out the clip at the rear of the side panel

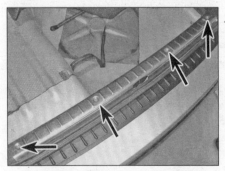

22.39 Undo the screws (arrowed) and remove the tailgate sill trim panel

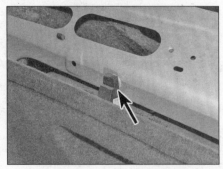

22.42 Pull the side panel inwards to release the clips (arrowed)

22.44 Remove the scrivet and the fastener (arrowed)

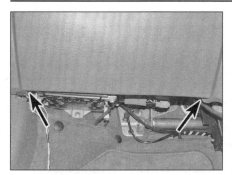

22.45 Undo the Torx bolt each side inserted from the front (arrowed)

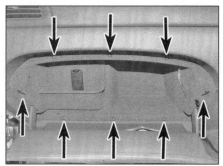

22.46 Glovebox securing Torx bolts (arrowed)

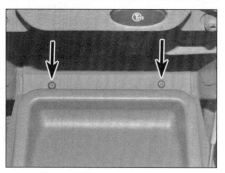

22.51 Driver's side glovebox lid Torx bolts (arrowed)

45 Undo the 2 Torx bolts at the lower, outer edges of the glovebox inserted from the front **(see illustration)**.
46 Open the glovebox lid, then undo the 8 Torx bolts securing it to the facia **(see illustration)**.
47 Prise out the glovebox light, and disconnect the wiring plug.
48 Remove the glovebox from the facia.
49 Refitting is a reversal of removal.

Driver's side

50 Open the glovebox, release the clip and allow the lid to fully open downwards.
51 Undo the 2 bolts at the hinge and remove the glovebox lid **(see illustration)**. To completely remove the glovebox, the facia must be removed as described in Section 25.
52 Refitting is a reversal of removal.

Sunvisor

53 Undo the outer mounting retaining Torx

bolt and remove the sunvisor **(see illustration)**. Feed the wiring out from the headlining and disconnect the wiring plug.
54 To remove the inner mounting, undo the retaining Torx bolt **(see illustration)**.
55 Refitting is a reversal of removal.

Driver's side lower facia panel

56 Prise out the centre pins and lever out the plastic expansion rivets securing the panel **(see illustration)**.
57 Pull the lower facia panel downwards and manoeuvre it from the cabin. Disconnect the light unit wiring plug as the panel is withdrawn.
58 Refitting is a reversal of removal.

Grab handles

59 Prise up the covers and undo the retaining Torx bolts **(see illustration)**.
60 Refitting is a reversal of removal.

Door storage compartments

61 To remove the compartments, open the lid, press down on the ends of the springs/clips each side and fold the lid out from the trim panel **(see illustration)**.
62 If the storage compartment lid spring retainers have weakened, allowing the lid to open when the door is closed, they can be adjusted by removing them from the storage compartment, and bending them to their original shape **(see illustration)**.
63 Refitting is a reversal of removal.

23 Seat belts – general information, removal and refitting

1 All models are equipped with pyrotechnical front seat belt tensioners as part of the Supplemental Restraint System (SRS). The

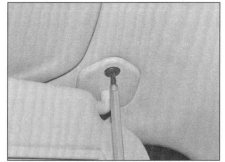

22.53 Undo the sunvisor outer mounting Torx bolt . . .

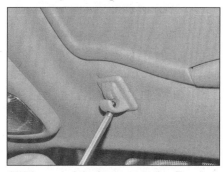

22.54 . . . and the inner mounting Torx bolt

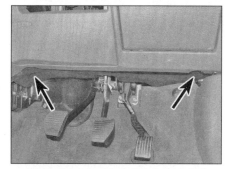

22.56 Driver's side lower facia panel plastic expansion rivets (arrowed)

22.59 Prise up the covers and undo the grab handle Torx bolts (arrowed)

22.61 Press the end of the spring downwards and pull out the storage compartment

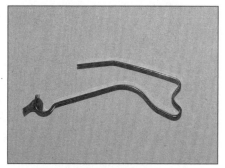

22.62 Carefully bend the spring to its original shape

23.6 Seat belt retractor securing bolt (arrowed)

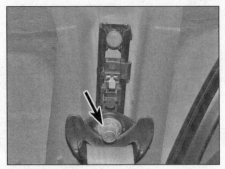

23.7 Front seat belt upper anchorage bolt (arrowed)

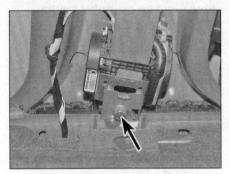

23.8 Front seat belt inertia reel bolt (arrowed)

23.11 Outer seat belt inertia reel securing nut (arrowed) – Hatchback models

system is designed to instantaneously take up any slack in the seat belt in the case of a sudden frontal impact, therefore reducing the possibility of injury to the front seat occupants. Each front seat is fitted with the system, the tensioner being situated behind the B-pillar trim panel. Note that on post-facelift models (from September 2004), an additional pyrotechnic retractor is fitted to the lower anchorage end of the passenger's front seatbelt.

2 The seat belt tensioner is triggered, with the driver's and passenger's airbag, by a frontal impact above a predetermined force. Lesser impacts, including impacts from behind, will not trigger the system.

3 When the system is triggered, the explosive gas in the tensioner mechanism retracts and locks the seat belt through a cable which acts on the inertia reel. This prevents the seat belt moving, and keeps the occupant firmly in position in the seat. Once the tensioner

has been triggered, the seat belt will be permanently locked and the assembly must be renewed. If any abnormal rattling noises are heard when pulling out or retracting the belt, this also indicates that the tensioner has been triggered.

4 There is a risk of injury if the system is triggered inadvertently when working on the vehicle, and it is therefore strongly recommended that any work involving the seat belt tensioner system is entrusted to a Citroën dealer. Note the following warnings before contemplating any work on the front seat belts.

⚠️ **Warning: Switch off the ignition, disconnect the battery negative lead, and wait for at least 5 minutes** for any residual electrical energy to dissipate before starting work involving the front seat belts.

• Do not expose the tensioner mechanism to temperatures in excess of 100°C.

• If the tensioner mechanism is dropped, it must be renewed, even it has suffered no apparent damage.
• Do not allow any solvents to come into contact with the tensioner mechanism.
• Do not attempt to open the tensioner mechanism, as it contains explosive gas.
• Tensioners from other vehicles, even from the same model and year, must not be fitted.
• Tensioners must be discharged before they are disposed of, but this task should be entrusted to a Citroën dealer or specialist.

Front seat belt removal

5 Switch off the ignition, then disconnect the battery negative lead as described in Chapter 5A. Wait for at least 5 minutes before proceeding.
6 Remove the B-pillar trim as described in Section 22. If removing the passenger's seat belt on post-facelift models (from September 2004), pull away the carpet, and unclip the plastic cover over the seat belt retractor. Undo the bolt, disconnect the wiring plug and remove the retractor **(see illustration)**.
7 Undo the seat belt upper anchorage bolt **(see illustration)**.
8 Disconnect the wiring plug, then undo the bolt and remove the inertia reel **(see illustration)**.

Outer rear seat belts removal

9 Switch off the ignition, then disconnect the battery negative lead as described in Chapter 5A. Wait for at least 5 minutes before proceeding.

Hatchback

10 Fold down the rear seat backrest, undo the 3 screws and remove the parcel shelf support **(see illustration 22.20)**.
11 Slacken and remove the inertia reel retaining nut **(see illustration)**.
12 Undo the seat belt lower anchorage bolt, feed the belt through the parcel shelf, and remove it from the cabin.

Estate

13 Undo the 2 Torx bolts and remove the parcel shelf support **(see illustration 22.24)**.
14 Disconnect the pretensioner wiring plug, then undo the retaining nut and lift the inertia reel from place **(see illustration)**. If required, undo the floor anchor bolt and feed the seat belt through the parcel shelf support.

Centre rear seat belt removal

Note: Removing the centre rear seat belt inertia reel involves removal of the seat cover. Patience and dexterity are required to successfully remove and refit the cover.
9 Switch off the ignition, then disconnect the battery negative lead as described in Chapter 5A. Wait for at least 5 minutes before proceeding.
15 Access to the buckles and floor anchorages is gained by tipping the seat cushion forwards **(see illustration)**.

23.14 Outer seat belt inertia reel securing nut (arrowed) – Estate models

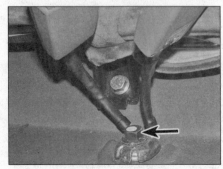

23.15 Tip the seat cushion forwards to access the seat belt stalk bolt(s) (arrowed)

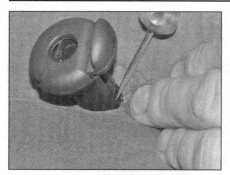

23.18a Depress the clip each side . . .

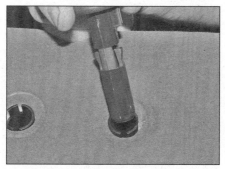

23.18b . . . and pull the headrest mounting
tubes from the seat back

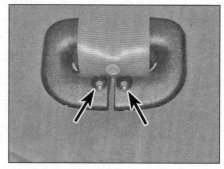

23.19 Seat belt guide Torx bolts (arrowed)

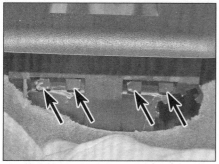

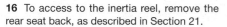

23.20a Squeeze together the pairs of clips
(arrowed) . . .

16 To access to the inertia reel, remove the
rear seat back, as described in Section 21.
17 Press in the headrest release button, and
pull the headrests from the backrest.
18 Compress the seat foam, depress the
clips each side and slide out the headrest
mounting tubes **(see illustrations)**.
19 Undo the 2 Torx bolts, prise up and seat
belt guide and disengage it from the seat belt
(see illustration).
20 Squeeze together the clips each side
and remove the seat backrest release button
surround **(see illustrations)**.
21 Carefully prise the seat covering beading
from the top and outer edge of the backrest
(see illustrations).
22 Undo the retaining nut and manoeuvre the
inertia reel from place **(see illustration)**

Refitting

23 In all cases, refit by reversing the removal
operations. Tighten the seat belt mountings to
the specified torque. Make sure that no-one
is inside the car. Switch on the ignition, then
reconnect the battery negative lead. Switch
the ignition off, then on again, and check that
the SRS warning light comes on, then goes
out after a few seconds.

24 Centre console –
removal and refitting

Removal

1 Fully apply the handbrake, then move the

gear or selector lever to neutral – note that it
may be necessary to move the gear or selector
lever as the console is removed.
2 Ensure the front seats are in the fully
lowered, rearmost position.
3 Using a flat-bladed plastic or wooden tool,

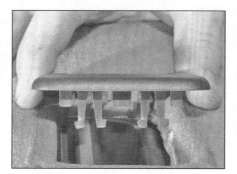

23.20b . . . and remove the release button
surround

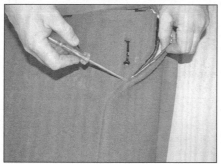

23.21b . . . and outer edges of the backrest

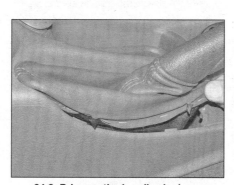

24.3 Prise up the handbrake lever
gaiter . . .

carefully prise up the handbrake lever gaiter
from the console, and pull it over the lever
(see illustration).
4 In the same manner, on manual transmission
models, carefully prise up and remove the gear
lever gaiter from the console **(see illustration)**.

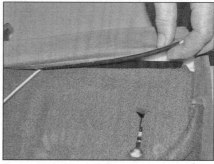

23.21a Prise out the beading at the top . . .

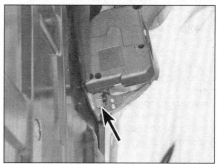

23.22 Seat belt inertia reel retaining nut
(arrowed)

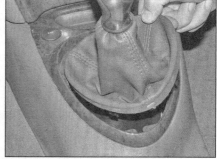

24.4 . . . and the gear lever gaiter

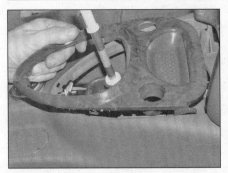

24.5a Prise up the gear lever surround . . .

24.5b . . . or the selector lever surround

24.6 Remove the trim in front of the handbrake lever

24.8 Undo the 2 Torx bolts and lift up the rear section of the console (arrowed)

24.9a Undo the nuts at the rear of the console (arrowed) . . .

24.9b . . . then manoeuvre the console over the gear/selector and handbrake levers

Pull the gaiter up around the lever – there's no need to remove it from the lever.
5 Carefully prise the gear/selector lever surround from place **(see illustrations)**.
6 Remove the plastic trim in front of the handbrake lever **(see illustration)**.
7 Lift the rear ashtray from place.
8 Undo the 2 bolts in the rear ashtray aperture and remove the rear section of the console **(see illustration)**.
9 Undo the 2 nuts at the rear, slide the console rearwards a little, then lift the rear of the console, manoeuvring it over the handbrake and gearchange/selector levers, and out from the vehicle **(see illustrations)**. Note their fitted positions and disconnect the wiring plugs as the console is removed.

Refitting

10 Refitting is a reversal of removal, taking care not to overtighten any retaining screws

as the console and its associated panels are fragile and at risk from cracking.

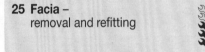

25 Facia –
removal and refitting

Removal

1 Ensure the front seats are in the rearmost positions, then disconnect the battery negative lead (see Chapter 5A), and wait at least 5 minutes before proceeding to allow any residual electrical energy to dissipate.
2 Remove the steering wheel and steering column as described in Chapter 10.
3 Remove the centre console as described in Section 24.
4 Remove the front windscreen wiper motor and linkage as described in Chapter 12.

5 Working in the engine compartment, undo the 2 bolts securing the facia to the bulkhead **(see illustration)**.
6 Undo the Torx retaining bolt, pull to release the clip at the front edge and remove the vent cover each side of the heater assembly in the cabin **(see illustration)**. Note that the right-hand cover is also secured by an additional Torx bolt at the front edge.
7 Undo the bolts and remove the facia support bracket on the driver's side of the heater assembly **(see illustration)**.
8 Carefully prise the trim panel from each end of the facia, then undo the 2 facia retaining bolts in the panel aperture **(see illustrations)**.
9 Reach through the facia end aperture on the driver's side and push the passenger's airbag de-activation switch from place, and disconnect the wiring plug.

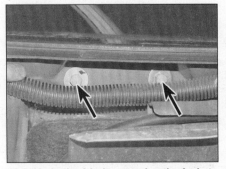

25.5 Undo the 2 bolts securing the facia to the bulkhead (arrowed)

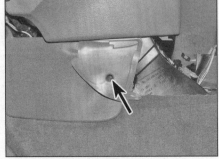

25.6 Undo the Torx bolt(s) and remove the vent cover each side (arrowed)

25.7 Undo the bolts and remove the facia support bracket

25.8a Prise away the trim panel . . .

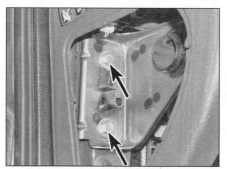

25.8b . . . and undo the bolts (arrowed) at each end of the facia

25.11 Push the switches from the facia and disconnect the wiring plugs

25.12a Undo the 2 Torx bolts (arrowed) . . .

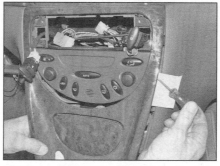

25.12b . . . and prise the panel from the facia – note the cardboard to prevent damage

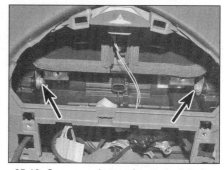

25.13 Crossmember-to-heater unit bolts (arrowed)

Pre-facelift models (before September 2004)

10 Remove the facia-mounted audio unit, and instrument panel as described in Chapter 12.

11 Reach through and push the switches from the facia each side of the audio unit aperture (see illustration). Disconnect the wiring plugs and remove the switches.

12 Undo the 2 Torx retaining screws at the lower edge, then unclip and remove the centre panel from the facia (see illustrations). Disconnect the upper vent control wiring plug, and pull the ashtray bulbholder out as the panel is withdrawn.

13 Undo the 2 bolts securing the facia cross-member to the heater unit (see illustrations).

14 Undo the 6 bolts in the central aperture (see illustrations). Note that 4 of these bolts secure the air conditioning panel. Release the clip each side and push the panel forwards, then manoeuvre it from the facia, disconnecting the wiring plugs as it's withdrawn.

Post-facelift models (from September 2004)

15 Using a blunt, flat-bladed tool, carefully prise off the trim moulding above the facia-mounted audio unit (see illustration).

16 Remove the facia-mounted audio unit as described in Chapter 12.

17 Pull the air conditioning panel from place (see illustration). Disconnect the wiring plugs as the panel is withdrawn.

18 Undo the 2 bolts in the moulding aperture (see illustration).

19 Undo the 2 Torx bolts at the lower edge, then unclip and remove the central panel (see illustrations).

20 Undo the 2 bolts in the central aperture securing the facia to the heater assembly (see illustration 25.13).

21 Undo the 2 bolts in the lower part of the central aperture.

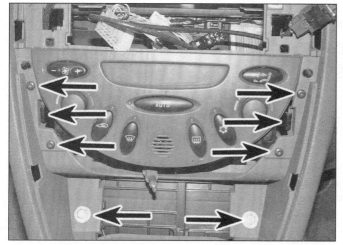

25.14 Undo the 6 bolts, release the two clips, push the control panel into the facia, then manoeuvre it from place (arrowed)

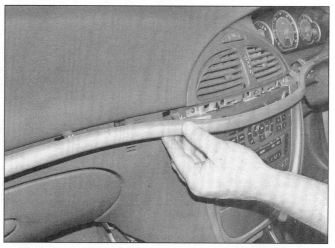

25.15 Use a blunt, flat-bladed tool to carefully prise the trim moulding from place

25.17 Pull the air conditioning panel from place

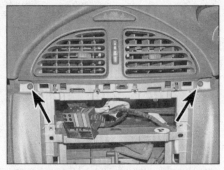

25.18 Undo the 2 Torx bolts at the top of the panel . . .

25.19a . . . the 2 at the base . . .

25.19b . . . then carefully prise the panel rearwards

All models

22 Note their fitted positions and disconnect the various facia wiring plugs. Undo the earth connection behind the gear lever (see illustrations).

23 Pull the facia rearwards a little, and release the wiring harness from the clips on the heater assembly.

24 With the help of an assistant, pull the facia rearwards and manoeuvre it through the passenger's door opening.

Refitting

25 Refitting is a reversal of removal.

26 Upon completion, make sure that no-one is inside the car. Switch on the ignition, then reconnect the battery negative lead as

described in Chapter 5A. Switch the ignition off, then on again, and check that the SRS warning light comes on, then goes out after a few seconds.

26 Sunroof – general information, panel renewal and adjustment

General information

An electrically-operated sunroof is available as standard or optional equipment, according to model.

The sunroof is maintenance-free, but any removal and refitting of the component parts (apart from the glass panel) should be

entrusted to a dealer or specialist, due to the complexity of the unit and the need to remove much of the interior trim and headlining to gain access. The latter operation is involved, and requires care and specialist knowledge to avoid damage.

If the sunroof action becomes sluggish, the slides and/or cables may need lubricating – consult a Citroën dealer or specialist for advice on a suitable product to use. Further checks in the event of non-operation are limited to checking the fuse and wiring, with reference to the wiring diagrams at the end of Chapter 12.

Removal

1 Position the sunroof in the full tilt position.

2 Carefully unclip the upper and lower parts of the apron trim.

3 Undo the 4 retaining bolts and remove the glass panel.

Refitting

4 Refitting is a reversal of removal, noting the following points:

a) If a new rubber weatherstrip has been fitted, position the weatherstrip join in the centre of the panel's rear edge.

b) Adjust the position of the panel, as described in this Section prior to refitting the apron trim.

Adjustment

5 Remove the sunroof apron trim as described in paragraph 2 of this Section.

6 With the sunroof in the closed position, the panel should be flush with the roof panel at the front and rear.

7 If adjustment is needed, slacken the 4 sunroof glass panel retaining bolts.

8 Adjust the position of the panel so the front and rear edges of the rubber seal are approximately 2.0 mm above the roof panel. This should position the panel flush with the roof. Tighten the rear panel retaining bolts securely.

9 Check for correct operation, then refit the apron trim.

25.22a Disconnect the facia wiring looms from the various connectors, including the BSI unit . . .

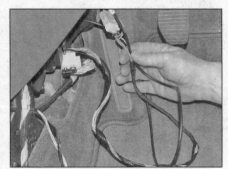

25.22b . . . alongside the heater unit . . .

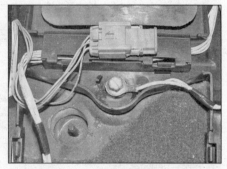

25.22c . . . and the earth connection behind the gear lever

Chapter 12
Body electrical system

Contents

Degrees of difficulty

Easy, suitable for novice with little experience 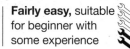	Fairly easy, suitable for beginner with some experience	Fairly difficult, suitable for competent DIY mechanic	Difficult, suitable for experienced DIY mechanic	Very difficult, suitable for expert DIY or professional

Specifications

System type .... 12 volt, negative earth

Bulbs — Power rating (watts)

Direction indicators	21 PY amber
Direction indicator side repeaters	5 capless
Front foglight after September 2004 (post-facelift)	55 H11
Headlight (Halogen):	
Dipped	55 H7
Main:	
With foglights up to September 2004 (pre-facelift).............	60/55 H4
Without foglights up to September 2004 (pre-facelift)	55 H1
From September 2004 (post-facelift)	55 H1
Xenon headlights:	
Dipped:	
Up to September 2004 (pre-facelift)......................	D2R
From September 2004 (post-facelift)	D1S
Main	55 H1
Glovebox light	5 capless
Heater control panel (pre-facelift)............................	1.2 capless
High-level brake light	LEDs
Interior light	5 capless
Number plate light	5 capless
Luggage compartment light...................................	5 capless
Reading light	5 capless
Rear foglight/tail light.......................................	21/5
Reversing light	21
Sidelights	5 capless or 5 bayonet (see text)
Stop-light	21
Vanity mirror	2 festoon

Torque wrench settings

	Nm	lbf ft
Airbag control unit nuts	8	6
Crash sensor bolts..	8	6
Driver's knee airbag nuts	4	3

1 General information and precautions

⚠️ **Warning: Before carrying out any work on the electrical system, read through the precautions given in 'Safety first!' at the beginning of this manual, and in Chapter 5A.**

1 The electrical system is of 12 volt negative earth type. Power for the lights and all electrical accessories is supplied by a lead-acid type battery which is charged by the alternator.

2 This Chapter covers repair and service procedures for the various electrical components not associated with the engine. Information on the battery, alternator and starter motor can be found in Chapter 5A.

3 It should be noted that prior to working on any component in the electrical system, the battery negative terminal should first be disconnected to prevent the possibility of electrical short-circuits and/or fires. **Note:** *If the vehicle has a security-coded radio, check that you have a copy of the code number before disconnecting the battery. Refer to your Citroën dealer if in doubt.*

2 Electrical fault finding – general information

Note: *Refer to the precautions given in 'Safety first!' and in Chapter 5A before starting work. The following tests relate to testing of the main electrical circuits, and should not be used to test delicate electronic circuits (such as anti-lock braking systems), particularly where an electronic control module is used.*

Caution: *The Citroën C5 electrical system is extremely complex. All of the ECMs/ECUs are connected via a 'Databus' (Multiplex) system, where they are able to share information from the various sensors, and communicate with each other. For instance, as the automatic gearbox approaches a gear ratio shift point, it signals the engine management ECM via the Databus. As the gearchange is made by the transmission ECM, the engine management ECM retards the ignition timing, momentarily reducing engine output, to ensure a smoother transition from one gear ratio to the next. Many of the electrical components are operated via a multiplex system, identified by 2 wires twisted together. Due to the design of the Databus/Multiplex system, it is not advisable to backprobe the ECMs/ECUs with a multimeter in the traditional manner. Instead, the electrical systems are equipped with a sophisticated self-diagnosis system, which can interrogate the various ECMs/ECUs to reveal stored fault codes, and help pin-point faults. In order to access the self-diagnosis system, specialist test equipment (fault code reader/scanner) is required.*

General

1 Typically, an electrical circuit consists of an electrical component, any switches, relays, motors, fuses, fusible links or circuit breakers related to that component, and the wiring and connectors which link the component to both the battery and the chassis. To help to pin-point a problem in an electrical circuit, wiring diagrams are included at the end of this Chapter.

2 Have a good look at the appropriate wiring diagram before attempting to diagnose an electrical fault, to obtain a complete understanding of the components included in the particular circuit concerned. The possible sources of a fault can be narrowed down by noting if other components related to the circuit are operating properly. If several components or circuits fail at one time, the problem is likely to be related to a shared fuse or earth connection.

3 An electrical problem will usually stem from simple cause, such as loose or corroded connections, a faulty earth connection, a blown fuse, a melted fusible link, or a faulty relay (refer to Section 3 for details of testing relays). Visually inspect the condition of all fuses, wires and connections in a problem circuit before testing the components. Use the wiring diagrams to determine which terminal connections will need to be checked in order to pin-point the trouble-spot.

4 The basic tools required for electrical fault finding include a circuit tester or voltmeter (a 12 volt bulb with a set of test leads can also be used for certain tests); a self-powered test light (sometimes known as a continuity tester); an ohmmeter (to measure resistance); a battery and set of test leads; and a jumper wire, preferably with a circuit breaker or fuse incorporated, which can be used to bypass suspect wires or electrical components. Before attempting to locate a problem with test instruments, use the wiring diagram to determine where to make the connections.

5 Sometimes, an intermittent wiring fault (usually caused to a poor or dirty connection, or damaged wiring insulation) can be pin-pointed by performing a wiggle test on the wiring. This involves wiggling the wiring by hand to see if the fault occurs as the wiring is moved. It should be possible to narrow down the source of the fault to a particular section of wiring. This method of testing can be used in conjunction with any of the tests described in the following sub-Sections.

6 Apart from problems due to poor connections, two basic types of fault can occur in an electrical circuit: open-circuit, or short-circuit.

7 Largely, open-circuit faults are caused by a break somewhere in the circuit, which prevents current from flowing. An open-circuit fault will prevent a component from working, but will not cause the relevant circuit fuse to blow.

8 Low resistance or short-circuit faults are caused by a 'short'; a failure point which allows the current flowing in the circuit to 'escape' along an alternative route, somewhere in the circuit. This typically occurs when a positive supply wire touches either an earth wire, or an earthed component such as the bodyshell. Such faults are normally caused by a breakdown in wiring insulation, A short circuit fault will normally cause the relevant circuit fuse to blow.

9 Fuses are designed to protect a circuit from being overloaded. A blown fuse indicates that there may be problem in that particular circuit and it is important to identify and rectify the problem before renewing the fuse. Always renew a blown fuse with one of the correct current rating; fitting a fuse of a different rating may cause an overloaded circuit to overheat and even catch fire.

Finding an open-circuit

10 One of the most straightforward ways of finding an open-circuit fault is by using a circuit test meter or voltmeter. Connect one lead of the meter to either the negative battery terminal or a known good earth. Connect the other lead to a connector in the circuit being tested, preferably nearest to the battery or fuse. Switch on the circuit, bearing in mind that some circuits are live only when the ignition switch is moved to a particular position. If voltage is present (indicated either by the tester bulb lighting or a voltmeter reading, as applicable), this means that the section of the circuit between the relevant connector and the battery is problem-free. Continue to check the remainder of the circuit in the same fashion. When a point is reached at which no voltage is present, the problem must lie between that point and the previous test point with voltage. Most problems can be traced to a broken, corroded or loose connection.

⚠️ **Warning: Under no circumstances may live measuring instruments such as ohmmeters, voltmeters or a bulb and test leads be used to test any of the airbag circuitry. Any testing of these components must be left to a Citroën dealer or specialist, as there is a danger of activating the system if the correct procedures are not followed.**

Finding a short-circuit

11 Loading the circuit during testing will produce false results and may damage your test equipment, so all electrical loads must be disconnected from the circuit before it can be checked for short circuits. Loads are the components which draw current from a circuit, such as bulbs, motors, heating elements, etc.

12 Keep both the ignition and the circuit under test switched off, then remove the relevant fuse from the circuit, and connect a circuit test meter or voltmeter to the fuse connections.

13 Switch on the circuit, bearing in mind that some circuits are live only when the ignition switch is moved to a particular position. If voltage is present (indicated either by the

tester bulb lighting or a voltmeter reading, as applicable), this means that there is a short-circuit. If no voltage is present, but the fuse still blows with the load(s) connected, this indicates an internal fault in the load(s).

Finding an earth fault

14 The battery negative terminal is connected to 'earth': the metal of the engine/transmission and the car body – and most systems are wired so that they only receive a positive feed, the current returning through the metal of the car body. This means that the component mounting and the body form part of that circuit. Loose or corroded mountings can therefore cause a range of electrical faults, ranging from total failure of a circuit, to a puzzling partial fault. In particular, lights may shine dimly (especially when another circuit sharing the same earth point is in operation), motors (eg, wiper motors or the radiator auxiliary cooling fan motor) may run slowly, and the operation of one circuit may have an apparently unrelated effect on another. Note that on many vehicles, earth straps are used between certain components, such as the engine/transmission and the body, usually where there is no metal-to-metal contact between components due to flexible rubber mountings, etc **(see illustrations)**.

15 To check whether a component is properly earthed, disconnect the battery and connect one lead of an ohmmeter to a known good earth point. Connect the other lead to the wire or earth connection being tested. The resistance reading should be zero; if not, check the connection as follows.

16 If an earth connection is thought to be faulty, dismantle the connection and clean back to bare metal both the bodyshell and the wire terminal or the component earth connection mating surface. Be careful to remove all traces of dirt and corrosion, then use a knife to trim away any paint, so that a clean metal-to-metal joint is made. On reassembly, tighten the joint fasteners securely; if a wire terminal is being refitted, use serrated washers between the terminal and the bodyshell to ensure a clean and secure connection. When the connection is remade, prevent the onset of corrosion in the future by applying a coat of petroleum jelly or silicone-based grease or by spraying on (at regular intervals) a proprietary ignition sealer or a water dispersant lubricant.

3 Fuses and relays – general information

Main fuses

1 The fuses are located behind a panel in the passenger's side glovebox, and in a fusebox on the left-hand side of the engine compartment.

2 Access to the passenger cabin fuses is gained by opening the passenger's glovebox,

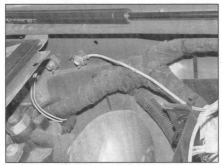

2.14a Earth connections at the left-hand rear corner of the engine compartment . . .

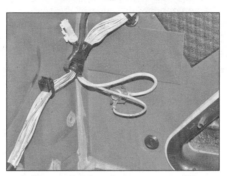

2.14c . . . left-hand rear corner of the luggage compartment . . .

and pulling open the cover to expose the fusebox **(see illustration)**.

3 To access the engine compartment fusebox, open the bonnet, release the fasteners and open the fusebox cover **(see illustration)**.

4 Each fuse is numbered; the fuses' ratings and circuits they protect are listed on the rear face of the cover panel. A list of fuses is given with the wiring diagrams.

5 To remove a fuse, first switch off the circuit concerned (or the ignition), then pull the fuse out of its terminals – a pair of tweezers provided specifically for this purpose are fitted on the cover of the passenger's compartment fusebox cover. The wire within the fuse should be visible; if the fuse is blown the wire will have a break in it, which will be visible through the plastic casing.

6 Always renew a fuse with one of an identical rating; never use a fuse with a different rating from the original or substitute anything else.

3.2 Open the passenger's glovebox, and pull down the cover

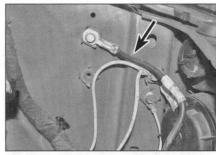

2.14b . . . the front left-hand corner of the engine compartment. Note the strap to the top of the transmission casing (arrowed) . . .

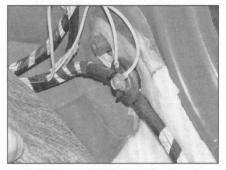

2.14d . . . and both the driver's and passenger's side footwells

Never renew a fuse more than once without tracing the source of the trouble. The fuse rating is stamped on top of the fuse; note that the fuses are also colour-coded for easy recognition.

7 If a new fuse blows immediately, find the cause before renewing it again; a short to earth as a result of faulty insulation is most likely. Where a fuse protects more than one circuit, try to isolate the defect by switching on each circuit in turn (if possible) until the fuse blows again. Always carry a supply of spare fuses of each relevant rating on the vehicle, a spare of each rating should be clipped into the base of the fusebox.

8 Note that some circuits are protected by 'maxi' fuses fitted in the engine compartment fusebox. These fuses are physically much bigger than the normal fuses, and have correspondingly higher ratings. Should one of these fuses fail, have the circuit examined a

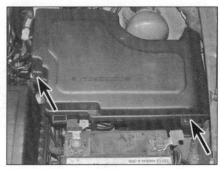

3.3 Engine compartment fusebox cover fasteners (arrowed)

5.5a Undo the lower shroud screws (arrowed)

5.5b Release the lower shroud clips (arrowed)

5.5c Depress the clip and slide the right-hand control stalk from the switch module a little

Citroën dealer or specialist prior to renewing the fuse.

9 Two fusible links are fitted to the battery positive lead. These are designed to protect the starter motor and alternator wiring harnesses from damage resulting from a major fault. If either of these two links should fail, do not renew them until the circuit concerned has been examined.

Relays

10 The main relays are located in the passenger compartment fuse box. Note that many of the traditional functions of the relays are controlled by the BSI unit (which incorporates the fusebox), eg, direction indicator flasher relay. The location and function of the relays is given on the underside of the fusebox lid.

11 The relays are of sealed construction, and cannot be repaired if faulty. The relays are of the plug-in type, and may be removed by pulling directly from their terminals. In some cases, it will be necessary to prise the two plastic clips outwards before removing the relay.

12 If a circuit or system controlled by a relay develops a fault and the relay is suspect, operate the system; if the relay is functioning, it should be possible to hear it click as it is energised. If this is the case, the fault lies with

the components or wiring of the system. If the relay is not being energised, then either the relay is not receiving a main supply or a switching voltage, or the relay itself is faulty. Testing is by the substitution of a known good unit, but be careful; while some relays are identical in appearance and in operation, others look similar but perform different functions.

13 To renew a relay, first ensure that the ignition switch is off. The relay can then simply be pulled out from the socket and the new relay pressed in.

4 Ignition switch – removal and refitting

Removal of the ignition switch is described in Chapter 10, along with the steering lock removal.

5 Steering column switch/ module – general information, removal and refitting

General information

1 The steering wheel module is fitted to the

top of the steering column, and is the man/ machine interface for the cruise control, wipers, audio controls and lighting. The unit also contains the steering angle sensor.

2 The steering wheel module is in constant communication with the vehicle's other control modules via an information network, known as a 'Databus'.

3 Should a fault occur, the module is equipped with a sophisticated self-diagnosis facility, which can be interrogated via the vehicle's diagnostic connector located under the driver's side of the facia, using a fault code reader.

Removal

4 Ensure the front wheels are in the straight-ahead position, then refer to Chapter 10 and remove the steering wheel. Secure the airbag rotary contact unit in place using adhesive tape.

5 Undo the 2 screws and remove the steering column lower shroud, then release the clips and remove the upper shroud **(see illustrations)**.

6 Depress the clip each side, and slide the lower switches from the module **(see illustration 5.5c)**. Note that in order to completely remove the right-hand switch, it's necessary to release the clips and slide the immobiliser ring from the end of the ignition switch.

5.5d Release the clips (arrowed)

5.5e Squeeze together the sides (arrowed) and detach the shroud gaiter from the facia

5.8a Slacken the clamp bolt (arrowed) . . .

5.8b . . . prise up the upper clip (arrowed) . . .

5.8c . . . and lower clip (arrowed) . . .

5.8d . . . then slide the switch module from the column

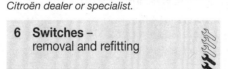

5.10 Align the arrow mark with the indicator – pre-facelift models

5.11 Align the arrow with the aperture (arrowed) – post-facelift models

7 Note their fitted positions, then disconnect the wiring plugs from the module.
8 Slacken the retaining clamp bolt, prise out the clips and slide the module upwards, over the end of the column shaft **(see illustrations)**. No further dismantling of the assembly is recommended. Only the two lower switches are available separately.

Refitting

9 Refitting is a reversal of removal. If the airbag rotary contact unit's position has been disturbed, proceed as follows:

Pre-facelift models (up to September 2004)

10 Depress the centre steering wheel locating boss, then gently rotate the front face of the contact unit until the arrow mark aligns with the indicator, and the pin is in the centre groove on the side of the unit **(see illustration)**.

Post-facelift models (from September 2004)

11 Gently rotate the front face of the unit until the aperture aligns with the arrow mark **(see illustration)**. If the symbol in the aperture is O, then the contact unit is set in the straight-ahead position. If any other symbol is displayed, rotate the unit as given in the following table:

Symbol	Rotate the switch
D	One turn to the left
DD	Two turns to the left
G	One turn to the right
GG	Two turns to the right

Note: *If a new steering wheel module has been fitted, it must be programmed and initialised*

using Citroën diagnostic equipment. Consult a Citroën dealer or specialist.

6 Switches – removal and refitting

Glovebox light switch

1 The switch is integral with the light unit.
2 Carefully prise the light unit from place **(see illustration)**.
3 Disconnect the wiring plug as the unit is withdrawn.
4 Refitting is a reversal of removal.

Door mirror adjuster

5 The door mirror adjusters are integral with the window switch assemblies fitted to the door panels.
6 To remove the switch assemblies, using

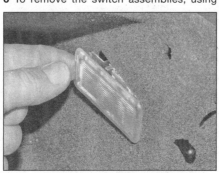

6.2 Carefully prise the light unit from the side of the glovebox

a flat-bladed, blunt tool, carefully prise the switch panel straight up from the door trim panel **(see illustration)**.
7 Detach the wiring connector.
8 Refit in the reverse order of removal.

Sunroof control switch

9 Carefully prise the interior light lens/cover from place, then undo the single screw and detach the light console from the headlining.
10 Carefully prise the interior light console from downwards from the headlining.
11 Press-out the retaining clips and pull the switch from the console.
12 Refit in the reverse order of removal.

Window switches

13 To remove the switch assemblies, using a flat-bladed, blunt tool, carefully prise the switch/panel straight up from the door trim panel **(see illustrations 6.6)**.

6.6 Starting at the rear, prise up the switch panel, and compress the retaining clips

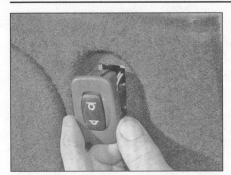

6.17 Prise the loading assistance switch from the side panel

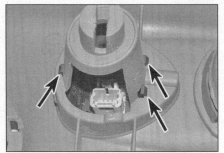

6.20 Release the clips (arrowed) and push the suspension height control switch from the console

6.23 Depress the clips (arrowed) and remove the handbrake warning switch

14 Detach the wiring connector.
15 Refit in the reverse order of removal.

Courtesy light switches

16 The courtesy lights are controlled by microswitches incorporated into the door locks. The switches are not available separately. If defective, the door lock assembly must be renewed (see Chapter 11).

Loading assistance switch

17 Open the tailgate, and carefully prise the switch from the luggage compartment side panel by compressing the retaining clip at the upper and lower edge (see illustration). Disconnect the wiring plug as the switch is withdrawn.
18 Refitting is a reversal of removal.

Suspension height control switch

19 Remove the centre console as described in Chapter 11.

20 Release the 3 clips and push the switch from the console (see illustration).
21 Refitting is a reversal of removal.

Handbrake warning switch

22 Remove the centre console as described in Chapter 11.
23 Depress the 2 clips and remove the switch (see illustration).
24 Detach the wiring connector from the switch.
25 Refit in the reverse order of removal.

Stop-light switch

26 Refer to Chapter 9.

Hazard warning switch

Pre-facelift models (before September 2004)

27 Remove the facia-mounted audio unit as

described in Section 19, then prise up the gear lever/selector lever surround trim (see illustration).
28 Prise out the switches, undo the 2 Torx bolts, and remove the central facia panel (see illustrations).
29 Reach through the aperture and push the hazard warning switch from place (see illustration). Disconnect the wiring plug as the switch is withdrawn.
30 Refitting is a reversal of removal.

Post-facelift models (from September 2004)

31 Remove the air conditioning/heater control panel as described in Chapter 3.
32 Release the clips and detach the front panel from the control panel (see illustration).
33 Turn the panel over and remove the loose switch buttons. Note their fitted positions to aid refitting.

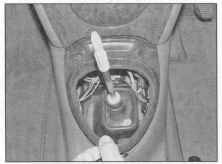

6.27 Prise up the gear lever surround trim

6.28a Prise out the switch each side . . .

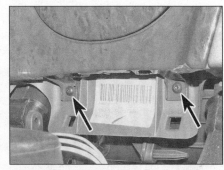

6.28b . . . undo the 2 Torx bolts (arrowed) . . .

6.28c . . . then prise the centre panel from place

6.29 Push the hazard warning switch from the facia

6.32 Release the clips and detach the front panel

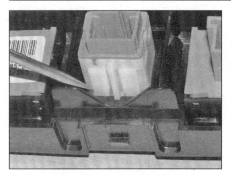

6.34 Release the clips and push the hazard warning switch from place

34 Depress the clips and push the switch from position **(see illustration)**.
35 Refitting is a reversal of removal.

Central locking/volumetric sensor/ Hatchback release switches

Pre-facelift models (up to September 2004)

36 Carefully prise up the flap at the relevant side of the facia-mounted audio unit **(see illustration 19.2)**.
37 Using small screwdrivers, carefully prise the switch from position **(see illustration)**. Disconnect the wiring plug as the switch is withdrawn.
38 Refitting is a reversal of removal.

Post-facelift models (from September 2004)

39 Remove the air conditioning/heater control panel as described in Chapter 3.
40 Release the clips and detach the front panel from the control panel **(see illustration 6.32)**.
41 Turn the panel over and remove the loose switch buttons. Note their fitted positions to aid refitting.
42 Depress the clips and push the switch from position **(see illustration)**.
43 Refitting is a reversal of removal.

ESP control switch

Pre-facelift models (up to September 2004)

34 Remove the centre console as described in Chapter 11.
45 Release the clips and push the switch from the console.
46 Refitting is a reversal of removal.

Post-facelift models (from September 2004)

47 Remove the ESP switch as described for the central locking/volumetric sensor switches in paragraph 38 onwards.

7 Exterior light bulbs – renewal

1 Whenever a bulb is renewed, note the following points:
  a) *Remember that if the light has just been in use, the bulb may be extremely hot.*

6.37 Prise the switch from place

  b) ***Do not*** *touch the bulb glass with the fingers, as the small deposits can cause the bulb to cloud over.*
  c) *Always check the bulb contacts and holder, ensuring that there is clean metal-to-metal contact. Clean off any corrosion or dirt before fitting a new bulb.*
  d) *Wherever bayonet-type bulbs are fitted, ensure that the live contacts bear firmly against the bulb contact.*
  e) *Always ensure that the new bulb is of the correct rating and that it is completely clean before fitting it.*

Headlight

Note: *This section does not cover bulb renewal on models fitted with gas discharge headlights (Xenon); refer to Section 10 for renewal details.*

Main and/or dipped beam

2 Remove the headlight unit as described in

7.3 Pull the rubber cap from the rear of the headlight unit

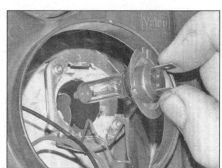

7.4b . . . and pull the bulb from place

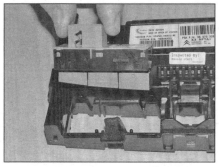

6.42 Depress the clips and remove the switch block from the panel

Section 9. **Note:** *It is possible to renew the bulbs with the headlight in place, but access is quite limited.*
3 Rotate the plastic cover anti-clockwise and remove it from the rear of the headlight, or pull away the rubber cap (as applicable) **(see illustration)**.
4 Pull the wiring connector from the rear of the bulb, then release the retaining clip and pull the bulb from the headlight **(see illustrations)**. If the bulb is to be refitted, do not touch the glass with the fingers. If the glass is accidentally touched, clean it with methylated spirit.
5 Fit the new bulb using a reversal of the removal procedure.

Sidelight

6 Rotate the plastic cover anti-clockwise and remove it from the rear of the headlight **(see illustration)**. Note that on pre-facelifted models, the sidelight is accessed through the

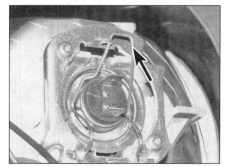

7.4a Move the clip to one side to release it (arrowed) . . .

7.6 Rotate the plastic cover anti-clockwise to access the sidelight bulb on post-facelift models

7.7a On pre-facelift models, the sidelight is alongside the main beam bulb

7.7b Use pliers to rotate the bulbholder anti-clockwise and pull it from place – post-facelift models

7.13 Rotate the foglight bulbholder anti-clockwise and remove it with the integral bulb

main beam cover, whilst on post-facelifted models, the sidelight has its own cover.

7 Rotate the bulbholder anti-clockwise and pull it from the headlight **(see illustrations)**.

8 Remove the bulb from the bulbholder. Capless bulbs on pre-facelift models, bayonet fitting bulbs on post-facelift models.

9 Fit the new bulb using a reversal of the removal procedure.

Front foglight

Pre-facelift models (up to September 2004)

10 The fog light beam is integral with the main beam bulb (double element bulb). Refer to main beam bulb renewal in this Section.

Post-facelift models (from September 2004)

11 Remove the engine undershield.

12 Disconnect the wiring from the bulb-holder.

13 Rotate the bulbholder anti-clockwise and pull it from the foglight **(see illustration)**. Note that the bulb is integral with the bulbholder.

14 Fit the new bulb using a reversal of the removal procedure.

Front direction indicator

15 Rotate the bulbholder anti-clockwise and pull it from the headlight **(see illustration)**.

16 Depress and twist the bulb to remove it from the bulbholder **(see illustration)**.

17 Fit the new bulb using a reversal of the removal procedure.

Direction indicator side repeater

18 Push the repeater rearwards, pull out the front edge and pull the unit from the wing **(see illustration)**

19 Rotate the bulbholder anti-clockwise and pull it from the lens **(see illustration)**.

20 Pull the capless bulb from the bulb-holder.

21 Fit the new bulb using a reversal of the removal procedure.

Rear combination light

Pre-facelift Hatchback models (up to September 2004)

22 Release the plastic clips and withdraw the bulbholder from the rear light unit **(see illustration)**.

23 Press and twist the relevant bulb anti-clockwise, and withdraw it from the bulbholder **(see illustration)**.

24 Fit the new bulb using a reversal of the removal procedure.

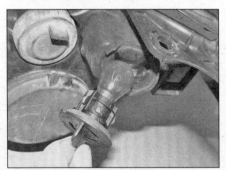

7.15 Rotate the front direction indicator bulbholder anti-clockwise . . .

7.16 . . . then depress and twist the bulb to remove it

7.18 Push the side repeater lens rearwards and pull out the front edge

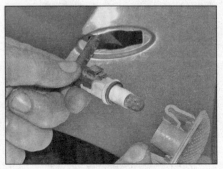

7.19 Rotate the bulbholder anti-clockwise and pull it from the lens

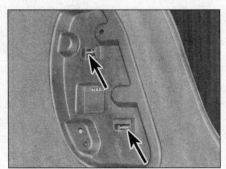

7.22 Release the clips (arrowed) and remove the bulbholder panel

7.23 Press and twist to remove the relevant bulb

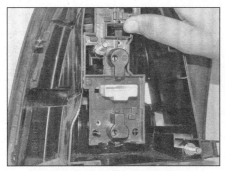

7.26a Lift the clip and remove the wing-mounted rear light bulbholder assembly

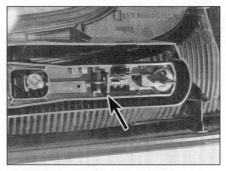

7.26b Release the clip (arrowed) and pull the bulbholder from the tailgate-mounted rear lights

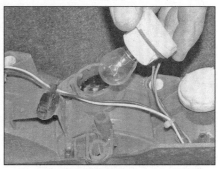

7.27 Rotate the bulbholder anti-clockwise – Estate models

Post-facelift Hatchback models (from September 2004)

25 Remove the relevant light unit (tailgate or wing-mounted) as described in Section 9, then remove the foam seal.
26 Unclip the bulbholder, then press and twist the relevant bulb anti-clockwise, and withdraw it from the bulbholder **(see illustrations)**.
27 Fit the new bulb using a reversal of the removal procedure. Ensure the seal is in place.

Estate models

28 Remove the light units as described in Section 9.
29 Rotate the relevant bulbholder anti-clockwise and pull it from the light **(see illustration)**.
30 Press and twist the bulb anti-clockwise, and withdraw it from the bulbholder.
31 Fit a new bulb using a reversal of the removal procedure.

Number plate light

32 The number plate lights are located in the tailgate, just above the number plate. For better access to the retaining screws, open the tailgate.
33 On some models, the lens is retained by a single screw, whilst on others, the lens is clipped into place. Undo the retaining screw and prise down the lens, or prise down the lens as applicable **(see illustration)**.
34 Pull the capless bulb from the holder.
35 Fit the new bulb using a reversal of the removal procedure.

High-level stop-light

Hatchback models

36 Open the tailgate, press-in the release tabs and remove the plastic cover **(see illustration)**.
37 Disconnect the wiring plug, then release the 2 clips and pull the bulbholder from the light unit. Pull the capless bulb from the holder **(see illustrations)**.
38 Fit the new bulb using a reversal of the removal procedure.

Estate models

39 The high-level stop-light is illuminated by non-renewable LEDs (Light Emitting Diodes). If faulty, the complete stop-light assembly must be renewed as described in Section 9.

7.33 Carefully prise the number plate lens from place

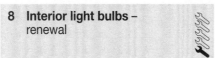

7.37a Release the 2 clips, remove the bulbholder assembly . . .

8 Interior light bulbs – renewal

1 Whenever a bulb is renewed, note the following points:
a) Remember that if the light has just been in use, the bulb may be extremely hot.
b) Always check the bulb contacts and holder, ensuring that there is clean metal-to-metal contact between the bulb and its live and earth. Clean off any corrosion or dirt before fitting a new bulb.
c) Wherever bayonet-type bulbs are fitted, ensure that the live contact(s) bear firmly against the bulb contact.
d) Always ensure that the new bulb is of the correct rating and that it is completely clean before fitting it.

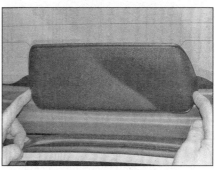

7.36 Press-in the tabs and remove the high level stop-light cover

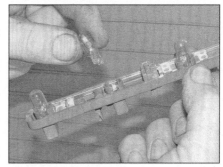

7.37b . . . then pull the capless bulb(s) from the holder

Interior/reading lights

2 Carefully unclip the lens **(see illustration)**.
3 Pull the capless bulb from the holder **(see illustration)**.

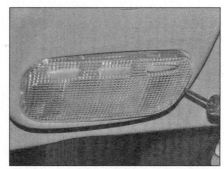

8.2 Carefully prise the interior light lens from the overhead console

8.3 Pull the capless bulb from the holder

8.5 Prise the glovebox light from place

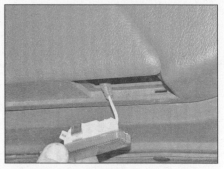

8.8 Prise the light from the base of the door

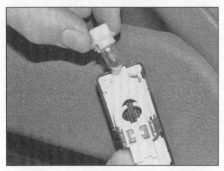

8.9 Twist the bulbholder anti-clockwise

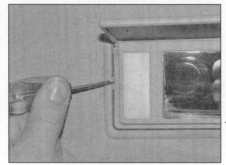

8.11 Prise the vanity light mirror/cover from place . . .

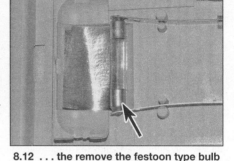

8.12 . . . the remove the festoon type bulb (arrowed)

4 Fit the new bulb using a reversal of the removal procedure.

Glovebox/footwell lights

5 Insert a flat-bladed screwdriver behind the end of the lens, and prise it free (see illustration).
6 Pull the capless bulb from its holder.
7 Fit the new bulb using a reversal of the removal procedure. Note that the lens will only fit one-way round.

Door sill light

8 Carefully prise the lens from the base of the door (see illustration).
9 Twist the bulbholder anti-clockwise and remove it from the light. Pull the capless bulb from the holder (see illustration).
10 Fit a new bulb using a reversal of the removal procedure.

Sunvisor/vanity mirror light

11 Carefully prise out the mirror/cover from

the sunvisor, using a small screwdriver (see illustration).
12 Pull the festoon-type bulb from the contacts (see illustration).
13 Fit the new bulb using a reversal of the removal procedure.

Instrument panel bulbs

14 On all models covered by this Manual, it is not possible to renew the instrument panel bulbs individually as they are of LED design and soldered to a printed circuit board. It is not possible to renew a single LED. Where an LED is not functioning, the complete instrument panel must be renewed.

Luggage compartment light

15 Insert a flat-bladed screwdriver behind the end of the lens, depress the retaining clip and prise free the light lens/unit (see illustration).

16 Unclip the cover, then pull the capless from its holder (see illustration).
17 Fit the new bulb using a reversal of the removal procedure.

Switch illumination

18 The switches are illuminated by integral LEDs. If faulty, the complete switch must be renewed.

Heater/air conditioning control panel illumination

Manual air conditioned and non-air conditioned models

19 Remove the control panel as described in Chapter 3.
20 Rotate the bulbholder anti-clockwise and remove it from the panel (see illustrations). Pull the capless bulb from the holder.
21 Fit the new bulb using a reversal of the removal procedure.

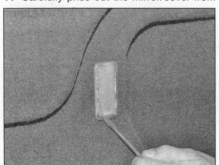

8.15 Prise the luggage compartment light from place . . .

8.16 . . . then unclip the cover

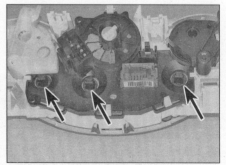

8.20a Twist the bulbholder(s) (arrowed) anti-clockwise . . .

Automatic air conditioned (climate control) models

22 The control panel is illuminated by non-renewable LEDs. If defective, the control panel may need to be renewed.

Multifunction display unit illumination

23 Remove the multifunction display as described in Section 11.
24 Rotate the bulbholder(s) anti-clockwise and remove them from the rear of the screen **(see illustration)**. Note that the bulb is integral with the bulbholder.
25 Fit the new bulb/holder using a reversal of the removal procedure.

9 Exterior light units –
removal, refitting and beam adjustment

Headlight unit

Caution: On models equipped with gas discharge headlights (Xenon), disconnect the battery negative lead as described in Chapter 5A prior to working on the headlights.

1 Remove the front bumper as described in Chapter 11.
2 Undo the 3 headlight retaining bolts, then unclip the headlight washer (where fitted) from the base of the headlight **(see illustrations)**.
3 Manoeuvre the headlight from position. Disconnect the wiring plug as the headlight is withdrawn **(see illustration)**.
4 Refitting is a reversal of the removal procedure. On completion check for satisfactory operation, and have the headlight beam adjustment checked as soon as possible.

Front foglight

Post-facelift models (from September 2004)

5 Using a screwdriver, prise out the inner edge of the foglight surround trim from the bumper **(see illustration)**.
6 Undo the 2 mounting screws, withdraw the foglight from the front bumper, and disconnect the wiring **(see illustration)**.

8.20b . . . and remove them

7 Refitting is a reversal of removal, but have the foglight beam setting checked at the earliest opportunity. An approximate adjustment can be made by positioning the car 10 metres in front of a wall marked with the centre point

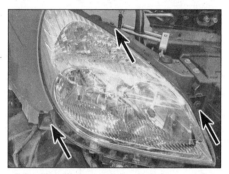

9.2a Headlight retaining bolt (arrowed) – pre-facelift models

9.2c Headlight upper mounting bolt (arrowed) – post-facelift models

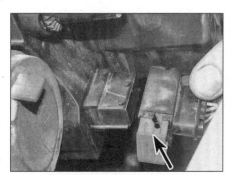

9.3 Slide out the red locking catch (arrowed) and disconnect the wiring plug

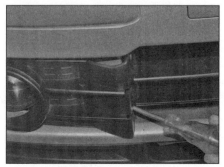

9.5 Starting at the inner edge, prise out the foglight surround

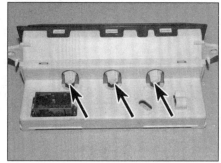

8.24 Rotate the multifunction display unit bulbholder(s) (arrowed) anti-clockwise

of the foglight lens. Unclip the panel behind the foglight, and turn the adjustment screw as required **(see illustration)**. Note that only height adjustment is possible – there is no lateral adjustment.

9.2b Headlight lower mounting bolts (arrowed) – post-facelift models

9.2d Depress the clip (arrowed) and slide the headlight washer from place

9.6 Foglight mounting screws (arrowed)

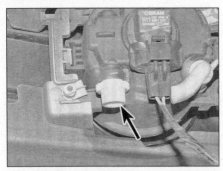

9.7 Foglight adjustment screw (arrowed)

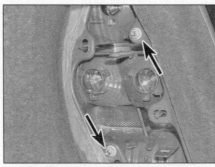

9.10 Rear light retaining nuts (arrowed)

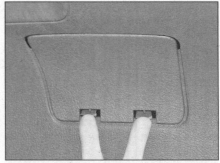

9.12a Lift the retaining clips and open the access flap

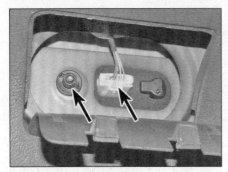

9.12b Depress the clip, disconnect the wiring plug, then undo the retaining nut (arrowed)

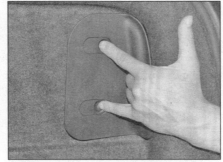

9.15a Slide across the release clip and remove the access flap

9.15b Depress the clip, disconnect the wiring plug, and undo the retaining nuts (arrowed)

Direction indicator side repeater

8 The procedure is as described for bulb renewal in Section 7.

Rear combination light – pre-facelift Hatchback models (up to September 2004)

9 Release the clips and remove the bulbholder from the light (see illustration 7.22).
10 Undo the 2 retaining nuts and pull the light unit from position (see illustration).
11 Refitting is a reversal of removal. Ensure that the seal is correctly positioned.

Rear combination light – post-facelift Hatchback models (from September 2004)

Tailgate-mounted lights

12 Open the access flap, peel away the foam pad and disconnect the wiring connector from the light (see illustrations).
13 Undo the retaining nut, and lift the light from place, releasing the ball-stud from the clip as it's withdrawn.
14 Refitting is a reversal of removal.

Wing-mounted lights

15 Open the access flap, and disconnect the wiring connector from the light (see illustrations).
16 Undo the 2 nuts and remove the light.
17 Refitting is a reversal of removal.

Rear combination light – Estate models

18 Open the tailgate, prise out the lower

plastic cover and unscrew the retaining nut securing the lower light unit (see illustrations).
19 Pull the lower light unit rearwards to release the clips. Disconnect the wiring plug as the light unit is withdrawn.

9.18a Prise out the plastic cover . . .

9.20a Prise out the plastic cover . . .

20 Prise out the plastic cover, undo the retaining nut, and pull the upper light unit rearwards to remove it (see illustrations). Disconnect the wiring plug as the light unit is withdrawn.

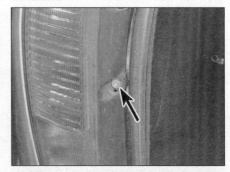

9.18b . . . and unscrew the retaining nut (arrowed)

9.20b . . . and unscrew the upper light unit retaining nut (arrowed)

21 Refitting is a reversal of removal. Note that the upper light unit must be refitted first. Ensure the locating clips engage correctly (see illustration).

Number plate light

Pre-facelift Hatchback (up to September 2004) and Estate models

22 Remove the tailgate lower trim panel as described in Chapter 11. Carefully peel away the waterproof plastic panels from the centre of the tailgate.
23 Squeeze together the retaining clips and pull the light from the tailgate. Disconnect the wiring plug as the light is withdrawn.
24 Refitting is a reversal of removal.

Post-facelift Hatchback models (from September 2004)

25 Push the light to one side to compress the clip, and pull the other end from the tailgate.
26 Disconnect the wiring plug as the light is withdrawn.
27 Refitting is a reversal of removal.

High-level stop-light

Hatchback models

28 Press together the release tabs and remove the plastic cover from the light (see illustration 7.36).
29 Undo the 2 retaining screws, disconnect the wiring plug, and remove the light unit from position (see illustration).
30 Refitting is a reversal of removal.

Estate models

31 Undo the 4 Torx bolts securing the rear spoiler to the tailgate (see illustration).
32 Disconnect the wiring plug and the washer jet tube, then remove the rear spoiler (see illustration).
33 Undo the 2 bolts and remove the high-level stop-light (see illustration).
34 Refitting is a reversal of removal.

Beam adjustment

Note: *Models fitted with Xenon gas-discharge headlight are equipped with self adjusting/ levelling systems. If faulty, have the system inspected by a Citroën dealer or specialist.*

Halogen headlights only

35 Accurate adjustment of the headlight beam is only possible using optical beam setting equipment, and this work should therefore be carried out by a Citroën dealer or suitably-equipped workshop.
36 For reference, the headlights can be adjusted using the adjuster screws, accessible via the rear of each light unit (see illustration).
37 Some models are equipped with an electrically-operated headlight beam adjustment system which is controlled through the switch in the facia. On these models, ensure that the switch is set to the basic O position before adjusting the headlight aim.

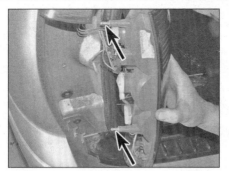

9.21 Ensure the lugs engage correctly (arrowed)

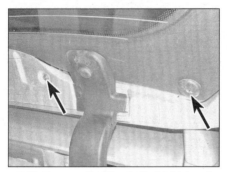

9.31 Rear spoiler Torx bolts (right-hand bolts arrowed)

10 Xenon gas discharge headlights – component removal, refitting and adjustment

General information

1 Xenon gas discharge headlights were available as an optional extra on all models covered in this manual. The headlights are fitted with dipped beam bulbs that produce light by means of an electric arc, rather than by heating a metal filament as in conventional halogen bulbs. The arc is generated by a control circuit which operates at voltages of above 28 000 volts. The intensity of the emitted light means that the headlight beam has to be controlled dynamically to avoid dazzling other road users. An electronic control unit monitors the vehicle's pitch and overall ride height by using the information from the Hydractive 3+

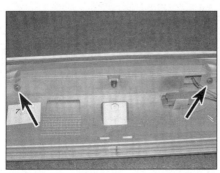

9.33 High-level stop-light bolts (arrowed)

9.29 High-level stop-light retaining screws (arrowed) – Hatchback models

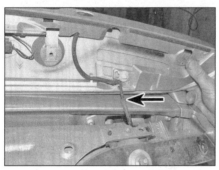

9.32 Disconnect the tailgate washer tube (arrowed)

ride height sensors mounted on the front and rear anti-roll bars, and adjusts the beam range accordingly, using the range control motors built into the headlight units.

 Warning: The discharge bulb starter circuitry operates at extremely high voltages. To avoid the risk of electric shock, ensure that the battery negative cable is disconnected before working on the headlight units (see Chapter 5A), then additionally switch the dipped beam on and off to discharge any residual voltage.

Bulb renewal

Headlight main beam

2 Remove the headlight as described in Section 9.
3 Rotate the plastic cover anti-clockwise and remove it from the rear of the headlight (see illustration 7.3).

9.36 Headlight aim adjustment screw (arrowed)

10.7 Rotate the plastic cover anti-clockwise

10.8 Rotate the igniter anti-clockwise (arrowed)

10.9a Press the clip (arrowed) down and move it to the right to release it

10.9b Note the locating lug at the top of the bulb (arrowed)

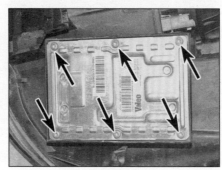

10.17 The ballast unit is secured by 6 Torx bolts (arrowed)

4 Disconnect the wiring plug from the rear of the bulb, then release the retaining clip and pull the bulb from the reflector **(see illustration 7.4a and 7.4b)**. Note how the lugs on the bulb engage with the slots in the reflector. If the bulb is to be refitted, do not touch the glass with the fingers. If the glass is accidentally touched, clean it with methylated spirit.

5 Fit the new bulb using a reversal of the removal procedure.

Headlight dipped beam

Caution: The dipped beam bulb is under gas pressure of at least 10 bars, therefore it is recommended that protective glasses are worn during this procedure.

6 Remove the headlight as described in Section 9.

7 Rotate the plastic cover anti-clockwise and remove it from the rear of the light unit **(see illustration)**.

8 Rotate the igniter unit anti-clockwise and pull it from the rear of the bulb **(see illustration)**.

9 Release the retaining clip and pull the bulb from the headlight **(see illustrations)**. If the glass is accidentally touched, clean it with methylated spirit.

10 Fit the new bulb using a reversal of the removal procedure, ensuring the lug at the top of the bulb engages correctly with the corresponding slot in the reflector.

Sidelight

11 Remove the headlight unit as described in Section 9.

12 Unscrew the main beam plastic cover,

then squeeze together the clips, and pull the bulbholder from the headlight unit **(see illustration 7.7a)**. Pull only on the bulbholder – not the cable.

13 Pull the wedge-type bulb directly from the bulbholder.

14 Fit the new bulb using a reversal of the removal procedure.

Gas discharge light ballast

15 Two ballast units are fitted – one for each headlight. The units communicate with the BSI electronic module (integral with the passenger's cabin fusebox) via a LIN (Local Interconnect Network). The ballast units are responsible for converting the current from DC to AC, and regulating the voltage to the bulb. The voltage required to start the bulb is approximately 1000 V, and about 100 V to maintain the arc between the bulb's electrodes.

11.3 Release the 2 clips at the lower edge of the instrument panel

16 Remove the headlight as described in Section 9.

17 Undo the 6 screws and remove the ballast assembly from the base of the headlight **(see illustration)**.

18 Disconnect the wiring plugs and remove the ballast unit.

19 Refitting is a reversal of removal.

Beam adjustment

20 The basic alignment procedure of the headlights is the same as normal halogen headlights (see Section 9). However, before the procedure is attempted, the ride height sensors must be calibrated using dedicated Citroën test equipment. Therefore this task should be entrusted to a Citroën dealer or suitably-equipped specialist.

Range control positioning motor

21 The range control motors are integral with the headlights, and cannot be renewed separately. If faulty, the complete headlight must be renewed.

11 Instrument panel and multifunction display unit – removal and refitting

Note: *The instrument panel and multifunction displays units function is included in the vehicle's self-diagnosis program. If the instrument panel has a fault, it would be prudent to have the vehicle's fault code memory interrogated by a Citroën dealer or specialist prior to removing the panel.*

Instrument panel

Removal

1 Disconnect the battery negative lead as described in Chapter 5A.

2 Fully extend the steering column, and move it to its lowest position.

3 Using 2 blunt, flat-bladed tools, release the 2 clips at the lower edge of the panel, and pull it from place **(see illustration)**.

4 Disconnect the wiring plugs as the panel is withdrawn.

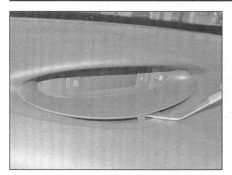

11.7 Carefully prise up the lower edge of the cover

12.3a Undo the wiper spindle nut

12.3b If necessary, use a puller to remove the wiper arm

Refitting

5 Refitting is a reversal of removal.

Multifunction display unit

Removal

6 Disconnect the battery negative lead as described in Chapter 5A.
7 Using a blunt, flat-bladed tool, carefully prise up lower edge of the cover, and pull it rearwards **(see illustration)**.
8 Undo the retaining screws and remove the display unit. Disconnect the wiring plugs as the unit is withdrawn.

Refitting

9 Refitting is a reversal of removal.

12 Windscreen wiper components –
removal and refitting

Wiper blades

1 Refer to *Weekly checks*.

Wiper arms

2 If the wipers are not in their parked position, switch on the ignition, and allow the motor to automatically park.
3 Before removing an arm, mark its parked position on the glass with a strip of adhesive tape. Prise off the cover (where fitted) and unscrew the spindle nut. Ease the arm from the spindle by rocking it slowly from side-to-side. If the arm is reluctant to release, use a puller **(see illustrations)**.
4 Refitting is a reversal of removal, but before tightening the spindle nuts, position the wiper blades as marked before removal. If the position of the blades has been lost, or the windscreen renewed, position the blades so that the end of the uppermost blade is 10 mm above the lower blade.

Wiper motor

5 Remove the wiper arms as described in the previous sub-Section.
6 Prise up the cover, then undo the Torx bolt securing the windscreen lower finisher trim each side. Prise away the top edge, then pull the trim rearwards to release it **(see illustrations)**.

12.6a Prise up the cover . . .

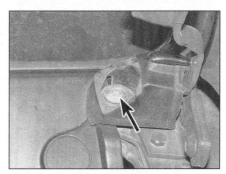

12.6b . . . undo the Torx bolt (arrowed) . . .

7 Undo the 4 Torx bolts and remove the scuttle panel grille by pulling upwards from the base of the windscreen **(see illustration)**.
8 Undo the 3 screws and remove the right-hand (RHD) or left-hand (LHD) scuttle closing panel **(see illustration)**.

9 Undo the 3 Torx bolts, disconnect the wiring plug, and manoeuvre the wiper motor linkage from position **(see illustration)**.
10 Undo the nut securing the linkage to the motor spindle, then note its fitted position and detach the linkage from the spindle.

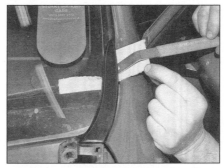

12.6c . . . prise the cover from the pillar, and pull it rearwards

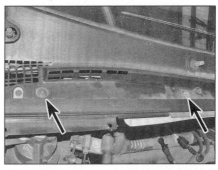

12.7 The scuttle panel grille is secured by 4 Torx bolts (right-hand screws arrowed)

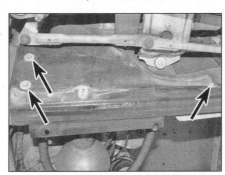

12.8 Undo the 3 screws (arrowed) and remove the scuttle closing panel

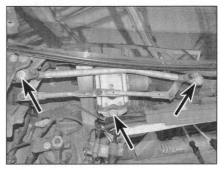

12.9 Undo the wiper linkage mounting bolts (arrowed)

11 Undo the 3 bolts and detach the motor from the bracket **(see illustration)**.
12 Refitting is a reversal of removal.

13 Washer system – general

1 All models are fitted with a windscreen washer system and a tailgate washer, and some models are fitted with headlight washers.
2 The fluid reservoir for the windscreen/ headlight washer is located behind the right-hand side inner wing, behind the wheel arch liner. The windscreen washer fluid pump is attached to the side of the reservoir body, as is the level sensor **(see illustrations)** and where headlight washers are fitted, a lift cylinder/accumulator is located in the supply

12.11 Undo the 3 Torx bolts (arrowed) and remove the motor from the bracket

tube, behind the front bumper. The headlight washers have their own pump. Access to the reservoir, pump and lift cylinders is achieved by removing either the right-hand front wheel arch liner or front bumper.

13.2a The washer fluid reservoir is located behind the right-hand front inner wing

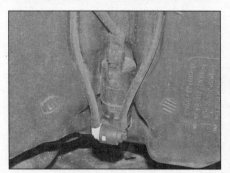

13.3 Washer fluid pump

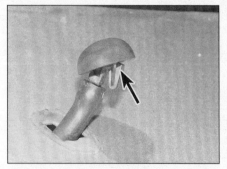

13.8 Press the clip (arrowed) and push the jet from place

13.2b Washer fluid level sensor

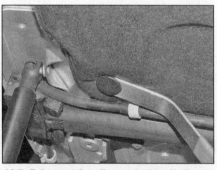

13.7 Prise out the clips securing the lower section of the bonnet insulation material

13.10a Prise the tailgate jet from place . . .

3 The tailgate washer is fed by the same reservoir, with a dual output pump. The pump rotates in one direction to supply the windscreen washer jets, and reverses direction to supply the tailgate washer jet **(see illustration)**.
4 The reservoir fluid level must be regularly topped-up with windscreen washer fluid containing an antifreeze agent, but not cooling system antifreeze – see *Weekly checks*.
5 The supply hoses are attached by rubber couplings to their various connections, and if required, can be detached by simply pulling them free from the appropriate connector.
6 The windscreen washer jets can be adjusted by inserting a pin into the jet and altering the aim as required.
7 To remove a washer jet, open the bonnet, prise out the clips and remove the lower section of the bonnet sound insulation panel **(see illustration)**.
8 Reach through the aperture, compress the retaining clip, and pull the jet from the bonnet **(see illustration)**.
9 Disconnect the washer hose from the base of the jet.
10 To remove a tailgate washer jet, prise out the outer edge. Pull the jet from the spoiler, and disconnect the hose **(see illustrations)**. Take care not to allow the hose to disappear into the spoiler.
11 The headlight washer jets are best adjusted using the Citroën tool, and should therefore be entrusted to a Citroën dealer or specialist to set.

14 Tailgate wiper motor – removal and refitting

Removal

1 Make sure the tailgate wiper is switched off and in its rest position, then remove the tailgate trim panel as described in Chapter 11.
2 On Estate models, unclip the plastic cover using a small screwdriver, then undo the wiper arm spindle nut **(see illustration)**.
3 Remove the wiper arm and blade as described in Section 12.
4 Detach the wiring connector from the wiper motor.

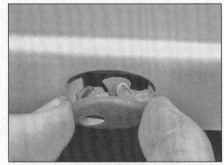

13.10b . . . and disconnect the hose

14.2 Insert a small screwdriver into the slot, and release the cover clip

5 Undo the 3 mounting nuts/drill out the 3 rivets and remove the wiper motor from the tailgate **(see illustrations)**. Check the condition of the spindle rubber grommet in the tailgate, and if necessary, renew it.

Refitting

6 Refit in the reverse order of removal. Refit the wiper arm and blade so that the arm is parked correctly.

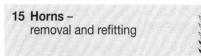

15 Horns – removal and refitting

Removal

1 The horns are located at the front end of the vehicle. Access to the horns is achieved by removing the front bumper (see Chapter 11).
2 Disconnect the horn wiring plug, undo the mounting nut/bolt and remove the horn from the vehicle **(see illustration)**.

Refitting

3 Refit in the reverse order of removal. Check for satisfactory operation on completion.

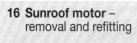

16 Sunroof motor – removal and refitting

Removal

1 Removal of the motor is an involved task. Access to the mounting bolts is gained by

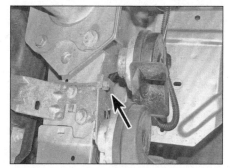

15.2 Horn assembly mounting nut (arrowed)

14.5a Tailgate motor mounting nuts (arrowed) – Estate models

lowering the front of the headlining, after having removed the sunvisors, grab handles, A-pillar trims, roof console, sunroof finishing strip and the sunroof glass panel (see Chapter 11). Extreme care must be exercised to avoid creasing/damage the headlining during the removal and refitting procedure. If in any doubt, have the repair carried out by a Citroën dealer or specialist.
2 With the front of the headlining lowered, position two foam spacers approximately 100 mm thick to hold the headlining down and allow access to the motor.
3 Disconnect the motor wiring plug, then undo the 3 bolts and remove the motor.

Refitting

4 Set the sunroof mechanism to the 'zero' position, by pulling the runner forward against the stop, positioning the carriage so the holes align, and locking them in position by inserting a 3 mm rod through the holes **(see illustration)**. Repeat this procedure on the remaining side.
5 Refit the motor, withdraw the aligning rods, and tighten the retaining bolts securely.
6 Reconnect the wiring plug and check the operation of the motor/mechanism.
7 The remainder of refitting is a reversal of removal.

14.5b Drill out the 3 rivets (arrowed) – Hatchback models

Emergency closing

8 In the event of a motor/control module malfunction/failure, the sunroof can be closed manually. Remove the interior light console and frame.
9 Insert an Allen key into the screw in the centre of the motor gear housing.
10 Rotate the screw in the appropriate direction to close the sunroof.

17 Central locking system – general information

1 All models are equipped with a central door locking system, which automatically locks all doors and the tailgate in unison with the manual locking of the driver's front door. The system is operated electronically with motors/switches incorporated into the door/tailgate lock assemblies. The system is controlled by the Built-in Sytems Interface (BSI), incorporated into the passenger's cabin fusebox. The BSI communicates with the vehicles other control modules via an information network known as a databus.
2 The vehicle's locks can be operated using

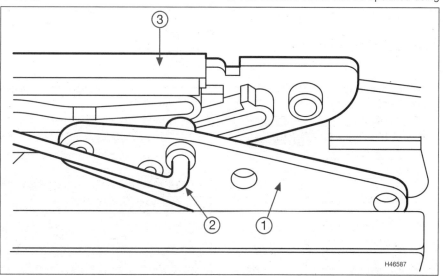

16.4 Position the carriage (1) so a 3 mm rod (2) can be inserted into the corresponding hole in the runner (3)

19.2 Prise up the lower edge of the switch trims . . .

19.3 . . . and undo the 3 Torx bolts (arrowed)

19.4 The left-hand switch block comes out as one unit (arrowed)

the vehicle's remote control key fob. When the remote control is used, a coded message is transmitted to the vehicle's receiver, which relays the code to the BSI, and carries out the request. After every time the remote is used, the BSI changes the code and updates the remote control. To allow the system to continue to function even when the remote has not been updated, the BSI will accept an incorrect code within certain tolerance limits. Once these limits have been exceeded (eg, the remote is operated many times outside the range of the receiver), the remote control must be resynchronised as follows:

a) Insert the key whose remote is to be resynchronised into the ignition switch.

b) Turn on the ignition and press one of the remote buttons within 10 seconds.

3 The BSI is equipped with a self-diagnosis capability. Should the system develop a fault, have the BSI interrogated by a Citroën dealer or suitably-equipped specialist. Once the fault has been established, refer to the relevant Section of Chapter 11 to renew a door or tailgate lock as applicable.

18 Parking aid components –
general, removal and refitting

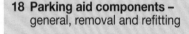

General information

1 The parking aid system is available on all models. Four ultrasound sensors located in the bumpers measure the distance to the closest object behind or in front the car, and

inform the driver using acoustic signals from a buzzer located under the rear luggage compartment trim. The nearer the object, the more frequent the acoustic signals.

2 The system includes a control module and self-diagnosis program, and therefore, in the event of a fault, the vehicle should be taken to a Citroën dealer or suitably-equipped specialist who will be able to interrogate the system.

Electronic control module

Removal

3 The control module is located behind the right-hand luggage compartment side trim panel. Remove the luggage compartment side panel trim as described in Chapter 11.

4 Undo the 2 retaining screws, and remove the ECM. As the unit is removed, disconnect the wiring plugs.

5 On Estate models, undo the 3 screws and remove the base retainer.

6 On all models, disconnect the control unit wiring plugs, then undo the 2 screws and remove the control unit.

Refitting

7 Refitting is a reversal of removal.

Range/distance sensor

Removal

8 Remove the relevant bumper as described in Chapter 11.

9 Disconnect the sensor wiring plug, then push the retaining clips apart, and pull the sensor from position.

Refitting

10 Refitting is a reversal of removal. Press the sensor firmly into position until the retaining clips engage.

19 Audio units –
removal and refitting

Note: *This Section applies only to standard-fit audio equipment.*

Removal

1 Disconnect the battery negative lead as described in Chapter 5A.

Facia-mounted audio unit –
pre-facelift models
(up to September 2004)

2 Using a blunt, flat-bladed tool, carefully prise up the lower edge of the switch trims each side of the audio unit **(see illustration)**.

3 Undo the 2 retaining screws and pull the unit from the facia **(see illustration)**.

4 Note their fitted positions and disconnect the wiring connectors as the unit is withdrawn **(see illustrations)**.

Facia-mounted audio unit –
post-facelift models
(from September 2004)

5 Undo the 2 Torx retaining bolts and pull the audio unit from the facia **(see illustration)**.

6 Note the fitted positions and disconnect the wiring connectors as the unit is withdrawn.

CD autochanger

7 Remove the driver's seat as described in Chapter 11.

8 Undo the 2 Torx bolts securing the mounting bracket to the seat frame and pull the autochanger from position **(see illustration)**. Release the wiring plug from the plastic panel.

Power amplifier

9 The power amplifier is located in the luggage compartment on the left-hand side. To remove the amplifier, remove the luggage compartment side panel trim as described in Chapter 11.

10 Disconnect the wiring plugs, then undo the fasteners and remove the amplifier.

19.5 Undo the Torx bolts (arrowed) and pull the audio unit from place

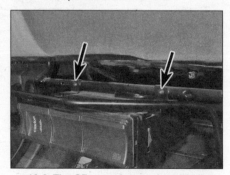

19.8 The CD autochanger bracket is secured by 2 Torx bolts (arrowed)

20.1 Prise away the speaker grille . . .

20.2 . . . then undo the retaining screws (arrowed)

20.5 Prise the speaker from the facia

Refitting

11 Refitting is a reversal of removal, but if a new unit has been fitted, it must be configured using Citroën diagnostic equipment. This also applies to the activation/deactivation of the automatic vehicle speed/audio unit volume function. Entrust these tasks to a Citroën dealer or suitably-equipped specialist.

20 Speakers – removal and refitting

Door speakers

1 To remove a door-mounted speaker, prise away the plastic speaker grille **(see illustration)**.
2 Undo the screws securing the speaker to the door **(see illustration)**.
3 Disconnect the wiring plugs as the speaker is withdrawn.
4 Refit in the reverse order of removal.

Facia speaker

5 Carefully prise up the speaker from the facia **(see illustration)**. Disconnect the speaker wiring plug as it's withdrawn.
6 Refitting is a reversal of removal.

21 Airbag system – general information and precautions

⚠️ **Warning: Before carrying out any operations on the airbag system, disconnect the battery negative terminal (see Chapter 5A). When operations are complete, make sure no one is inside the vehicle when the battery is reconnected.**
• **Note that the airbag(s) must not be subjected to temperatures in excess of 90°C. When the airbag is removed, ensure that it is stored with the pad up to prevent possible inflation.**
• **Do not allow any solvents or cleaning agents to contact the airbag assemblies. They must be cleaned using only a damp cloth.**

• **The airbags and control unit are both sensitive to impact. If either is dropped or damaged they should be renewed.**
• **Disconnect the airbag control unit wiring plug prior to using arc-welding equipment on the vehicle.**

Both a driver's and passenger's airbags are fitted as standard equipment to models in the Citroën C5 range. One driver's airbag is fitted to the centre of the steering wheel, whilst another may be fitted at knee height (post-facelift models only). The passenger's airbag is fitted to the upper surface of the facia, above the glovebox. The airbag system comprises the airbag unit(s) (complete with gas generators), impact sensors, the control unit (with integral crash sensor) and a warning light in the instrument panel. Seat-mounted side airbags and overhead curtain airbags are also fitted on certain models, and seat belt tensioners are incorporated into the seat belt reels.

The airbag system is triggered in the event of a direct or offset frontal impact above a predetermined force. The airbag is inflated within milliseconds, and forms a safety cushion between the driver and the steering wheel or (where applicable) the passenger and the facia. This prevents contact between the upper body and the steering wheel, column and facia, and therefore greatly reduces the risk of injury. The airbag then deflates almost immediately through vents in the side of the airbag.

Every time the ignition is switched on, the airbag control unit performs a self-test. The

22.3 Insert a screwdriver into the hole and lift it to release the airbag clip

self-test takes a approximately 6 seconds, and during this time the airbag warning light on the facia is illuminated. After the self-test has been completed, the warning light should go out. If the warning light fails to come on, remains illuminated after the initial period, or comes on at any time when the vehicle is being driven, there is a fault in the airbag system. The vehicle should then be taken to a Citroën dealer or specialist for examination at the earliest possible opportunity.

22 Airbag system components – removal and refitting

Note: Refer to the warnings in Section 21 before carrying out the following operations.
1 Disconnect the battery negative terminal (see Chapter 5A). Wait at least 5 minutes for any residual electrical energy to dissipate before commencing work. **Note:** If removing the driver's airbag, turn the steering wheel 90° from straight-ahead before disconnecting the battery, otherwise the steering lock will engage.

Driver's airbag

2 Release the steering column adjustment lever, and pull the wheel out and down as far as possible.
3 Locate the access hole in the reverse side of the steering wheel, and insert a flat-bladed screwdriver into the hole, then pull the screwdriver upwards to release the retaining clip **(see illustration)**. Turn the airbag 180° and release the clip on the other side.
4 Temporarily touch the striker plate of the front door to discharge any electrostatic electricity. Return the steering wheel to the straight-ahead position, then carefully lift the airbag assembly away from the steering wheel, lift the locking catches and disconnect the wiring connectors from the rear of the unit **(see illustration)**. Note that the airbag must not be knocked or dropped, and should be stored the correct way up with its padded surface uppermost.
5 On refitting, reconnect the wiring connectors and locate the airbag unit in the steering wheel, making sure the wire does not become

22.4 Prise up the locking catches and disconnect the wiring plugs

22.7 Lift up the locking catch (arrowed) then disconnect the passenger's airbag wiring plugs

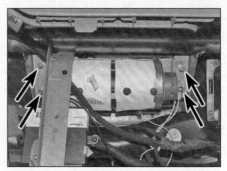

22.8 Passenger's airbag nuts (arrowed)

trapped, and push the airbag into place to engage the retaining clips. Reconnect the battery negative lead (see Chapter 5A). Ensure no-one is in the vehicle when the battery is reconnected.

Passenger's airbag

6 Remove the passenger's glovebox as described in Chapter 11.
7 Temporarily touch the striker plate of the front door to discharge any electrostatic electricity. Disconnect the airbag wiring plugs **(see illustration)**.
8 Undo the 4 nuts and remove the airbag **(see illustration)**. Note that the airbag must not be knocked or dropped, and should be stored the correct way up with its padded surface uppermost.
9 Refitting is a reversal of removal. Ensure that the wiring connector is securely reconnected. Ensure that no-one is inside the vehicle.

Reconnect the battery lead as described in Chapter 5A.

Curtain airbag

10 Renewal of the curtain airbag involves removal of the headlining. This is an involved task, beyond the scope of this manual. Consequently, we recommend this task be entrusted to a Citroën dealer or specialist.

Seat airbag

11 Renewal of the seat airbag involves removal of the seat covering. This is an involved task, beyond the scope of this manual. Consequently, we recommend this task be entrusted to a Citroën dealer or specialist.

Driver's knee airbag

12 Remove the trim panel above the pedals as described in Chapter 11.

13 Temporarily touch the striker plate of the front door to discharge any electrostatic electricity. Undo the 2 retaining nuts, disconnect the wiring plug and remove the airbag **(see illustrations)**. Note that the airbag must not be knocked or dropped, and should be stored the correct way up with its padded surface uppermost.

Airbag wiring contact unit

14 The contact unit is integral with the steering column switch/module. Removal and refitting of the unit is described in Section 5 of this Chapter.

Electronic Control Module

15 Refer to Chapter 11 and remove the centre console.
16 Release the locking devices and disconnect the wiring plugs for the control unit.
17 Undo the 3 retaining nuts and remove the control module **(see illustration)**.
18 Refitting is a reversal of removal, ensuring the module is refitted with the arrow mark on the top pointing forwards. Note that if a new module has been fitted, it may need to be initialised and configured using Citroën diagnostic equipment. Entrust this task to a Citroën dealer or suitably-equipped specialist.

Side crash sensors

19 Remove the relevant front seat and B-pillar trim panel as described in Chapter 11.
20 Lift the carpet outer edge to access the sensor.
21 Release the retaining tab and disconnect the sensor wiring plug.
22 Undo the nut(s)s and remove the sensor **(see illustration)**. Note that the sensor must be handled carefully. Do not refit a sensor that has been dropped or knocked.
23 Refitting is a reversal of removal, noting the following points:
  a) *Reconnect the battery negative lead (see Chapter 5A), and check the operation of the airbag warning light.*
  b) *It is possible that when the battery is reconnected, the airbag warning light may indicate that a fault has been stored. Have the fault erased, and see if it re-occurs – consult a Citroën dealer or specialist if it does.*

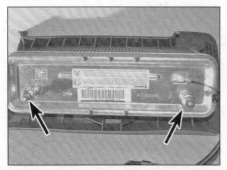

22.13a Undo the knee airbag retaining nuts (arrowed) . . .

22.13b . . . and remove the airbag

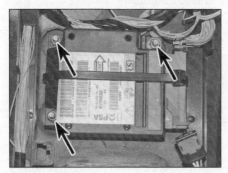

22.17 SRS ECM mounting nuts (arrowed)

22.22 Side crash sensor mounting nuts (arrowed)

23 Lane wandering warning system – information, removal and refitting

Information

1 Some models may be equipped with a warning system that is designed to alert the driver if the vehicle wanders across a solid, or broken white line without operating the directional indicators first. Intended for use on dual carriageways and motorways, the system is only operative above 50 mph. The system comprises of 3 sensors fitted each side beneath the front bumper, a central control module (ECM), a warning light in the central facia panel, and two vibrating devices on the underside of the driver's seat. The sensors function by sending and receiving infrared signals onto the road surface.

Removal and refitting

2 Disconnect the battery negative lead as described in Chapter 5A.

Sensors

Note: *The sensors can be cleaned without removing them. Use clean soapy water, and a soft sponge. Take care not to scratch the lenses. Dry the sensors with soft, clean, lint-free cloth.*

3 Raise the front of the vehicle and support it securely with axle stands (see *Jacking and vehicle support*).

4 Undo the screws and remove the undershield beneath the bumper.

5 Undo the bolt in the centre of the sensor, then release the clip each side and remove it from the bracket. Disconnect the wiring plug as the sensor is withdrawn. **Note:** *Label the sensor to indicates its fitted position. If it's to be refitted, It's essential that if it's returned to it's original position.*

6 Refitting is a reversal of removal. If a new sensor is fitted, it will need to be programmed using Citroën diagnostic equipment. Entrust this task to a Citroën dealer or suitably-equipped specialist.

Seat vibrators

7 Remove the driver's seat as described in Chapter 11.

8 Unclip the vibrator(s) from the seat frame.

Note: *If both vibrators are to be removed, label them to indicate their fitted positions. It's essential that they're fitted into their original positions.*

9 Disconnect the wiring plugs as the vibrators are withdrawn.

10 Refitting is a reversal of removal.

Electronic Control Module (ECM)

11 The ECM is located on the underside of the BSI unit, under the passenger's side of the facia. Undo the bolt, remove the 2 clips and remove the trim panel under the passenger's side of the facia **(see illustration)**. Pull back the carpet a little.

12 Unclip the electrical harness, then unclip the ECM support from the underside of the BSI.

13 Disconnect the 2 wiring plugs, undo the 2 screws and remove the ECM.

14 Refitting is a reversal of removal. If a new ECM has been fitted, it will need to be configured using Citroën diagnostic equipment. Entrust this task to a Citroën dealer or suitably-equipped specialist.

24 Anti-theft alarm system – general information

An anti-theft alarm and immobiliser system is fitted as standard equipment. Should the system become faulty, the vehicle should be taken to a Citroën dealer or specialist for examination. They will have access to a special diagnostic tester which will quickly trace any fault present in the system.

25 BSI unit – information, removal and refitting

Information

1 The BSI unit (Built-in Systems Interface) is responsible for the control of the exterior lights, horn, headlight levelling control, and interior lights, as well as functioning as the central junction for the vehicle's databus/multiplexing system. The BSI is located under the left-hand side of the facia, and is integral with the fusebox. No repairs are possible on the unit. Should a fault occur, have the

23.11 Undo the fasteners (arrowed) and remove the panel above the passenger's footwell

systems self-diagnosis facility interrogated using a fault code reader/Citroën diagnostic equipment (Lexia or Proxia)

Removal

1 Disconnect the battery negative lead as described in Chapter 5A.

2 Rotate the fastener 90° anti-clockwise, undo the scrivet, and lower the trim panel under the passenger's side of the facia. Disconnect the footwell illumination light as the panel is withdrawn.

3 Remove the passenger's side glovebox as described in Chapter 11.

Pre-facelift models (up to September 2004)

4 Undo the 2 bolts at the front, underside of the unit, then release the clips lift the rear, and lower the front whilst gently pulling the unit rearwards **(see illustrations)**.

Post-facelift models (from September 2004)

5 Release the clip each side and lift up the top half of the BSI plastic box.

6 Slide the rear of the BSI unit upwards, then pull it forwards from position **(see illustration)**.

All models

7 Note their fitted positions, then disconnect the wiring plugs and remove the BSI.

Refitting

8 Refitting is a reversal of removal. If a new BSI has been fitted, it will need to be initialised and configured using Citroën diagnostic equipment. Entrust this task to a Citroën dealer or suitably-equipped specialist.

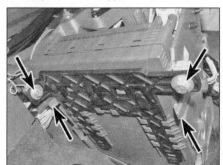

25.4a Undo the bolts and release the clips (arrowed) . . .

25.4b . . . then lower the front of the BSI and pull it rearwards

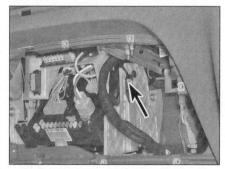

25.6 Slide the rear of the BSI upwards to disengage the mounting lugs (arrowed)

Citroën C5 wiring diagrams

Diagram 1

 WARNING: *This vehicle is fitted with a supplemental restraint system (SRS) consisting of a combination of driver (and passenger) airbag(s), side impact protection airbags and seatbelt pre-tensioners. The use of electrical test equipment on any SRS wiring systems may cause the seatbelt pre-tensioners to abruptly retract and airbags to explosively deploy, resulting in potentially severe personal injury. Extreme care should be taken to correctly identify any circuits to be tested to avoid choosing any of the SRS wiring in error.*
For further information see airbag system precautions in body electrical systems chapter.
Note: The SRS wiring harness can normally be identified by yellow and/or orange harness or harness connectors.

The prime method of wire identification is by the colour of the wire (each wire on the diagrams being colour coded – see key). Additionally, the wires can be identified by using the terminal pin numbers (moulded into each component or connector and shown in the diagrams) together with the number code printed on each wire. To relate each diagram to the vehicle wiring, locate the relevant component or connector illustrated and find the wire(s) connected to the terminal pin(s) as shown in the diagram.
Caution: Whilst a number (indicating the function of that wire) may be printed on each wire, this is not always the case, and in such instances, this is reflected by the absence of such wire numbering on our diagrams. Similarly, numbering of the connector/component terminal pins is not always available from the manufacturers' source information and may also be missing from our diagrams.

Key to symbols

Solenoid actuator		Bulb	Wire splice, soldered joint, or unspecified connector
Earth point	E7	Switch	Connecting wires
Multiplexed network	XE004(BA)	Fuse **F26**	Diode
Wire identification and colour	100A(BE)	Maxifuse fusible link **MF1**	Light-emitting diode
		Resistor	Item number **12**
Dashed outline denotes part of a larger item, containing in this case an electronic or solid state device.	16GR 5 9 K	Variable resistor	Motor/pump (M)
16GR - 16 pin grey connector, pins 5 & 9		Variable resistor	Heating element

Engine fusebox ④

Fuse	Rating	Circuit protected
F1	10A	Reversing lights
F2	30A	Fuel pump
F3	10A	ECU (ABS, suspension)
F4	7.5A	ECU (drive control, auto. transmission)
F5	2A	Diesel particle filter
F6	15A	Front foglights
F7	20A	Headlight washer
F8	20A	Engine control relay
F9	15A	LH dipped beam
F10	15A	RH dipped beam
F11	10A	LH main beam
F12	10A	RH main beam
F13	15A	Horn
F14	10A	Windscreen washer
F15	15A	Engine management
F16	30A	Air pump
F17	30A	Windscreen wiper
F18	40A	Heater blower

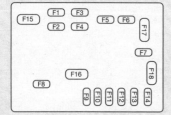

Built-in systems interface ⑥

Fuse	Rating	Circuit protected
F1	10A	Foglight
F2	15A	Rear screen wiper
F3	-	Spare
F4	15A	Diesel additive, driver's door control unit, alarm
F5	15A	LH stoplight
F6	-	Spare
F7	20A	Front accessory socket
F8	-	Spare
F9	30A	Front electric windows, sun roof, luggage compartment accessory socket
F10	15A	Battery+
F11	15A	Display, alarm, navigation, air conditioning, car phone
F12	10A	RH front sidelight, RH tail light
F13	-	Spare
F14	30A	Central locking, deadlocking
F15	30A	Rear electric windows
F16	5A	Steering wheel controls, airbag control unit, engine compartment fusebox
F17	10A	RH stop light
F18	10A	Flywheel angle sensor, automatic gearbox lever switch, diagnostic connector
F19	-	
F20	10A	Navigation system, audio system
F21	-	Spare
F22	10A	Front LH sidelight, LH tail light
F23	15A	Supply to engine management, ABS & suspension control units
F24	15A	Air conditioning, car phone, parking assistance, instrument cluster
F25	-	
F26	40A	Heated rear screen
G36	30A	Audio amplifier
G37	30A	Front RH electric seat
G38	30A	Front LH electric seat
G39	30A	Front RH heated seat
G40	30A	Front LH heated seat

H33786

Colour codes

BA	White	OR	Orange
BE	Blue	RG	Red
BG	Beige	RS	Pink
GR	Grey	VE	Green
JN	Yellow	VI	Mauve
MR	Brown	VJ	Green/
NR	Black		Yellow

Key to items

1 Battery
2 Starter motor
3 Alternator
4 Engine fusebox
5 Ignition switch
6 Built-in systems interface
7 Instrument cluster
   a = alternator warning light
8 Low tone horn
9 High tone horn
10 Steering wheel control unit
   a = horn switch
11 Diagnostic connector

Diagram 2

H33787

Typical starting & charging

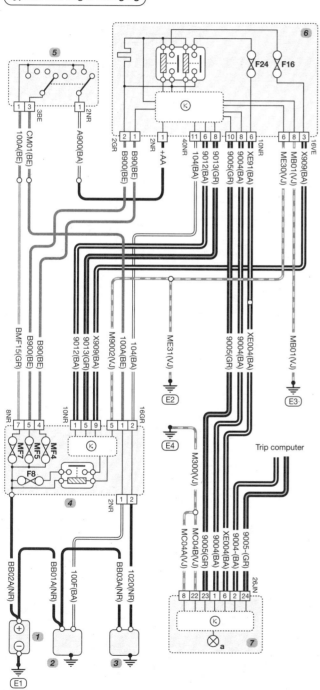

Typical horn

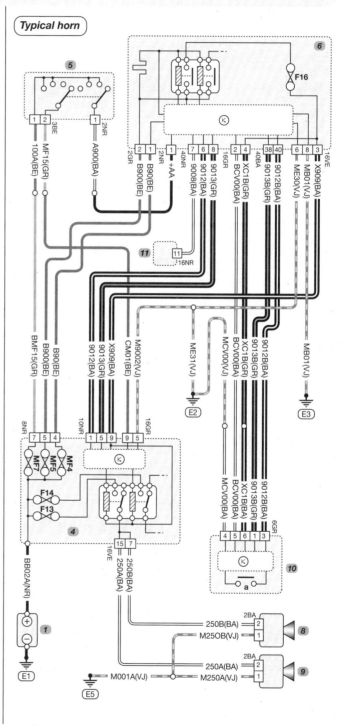

Colour codes

BA	White	**OR**	Orange
BE	Blue	**RG**	Red
BG	Beige	**RS**	Pink
GR	Grey	**VE**	Green
JN	Yellow	**VI**	Mauve
MR	Brown	**VJ**	Green/
NR	Black		Yellow

Key to items

1 Battery
4 Engine fusebox
5 Ignition switch
6 Built-in systems interface
11 Diagnostic connector
15 Engine management control unit
16 Coolant temperature sensor
17 Engine cooling fan
18 Engine cooling fan resistor
19 Low speed fan supply relay
20 Mid speed cooling fan relay
21 High speed coling fan relay
22 Stop light switch
23 Reversing light switch
24 LH rear light unit
  a = stop light
  b = reversing light
25 RH rear light unit
  a = stop light
  b = reversing light
26 High level stop light

Diagram 3

H33788

Typical engine cooling fan

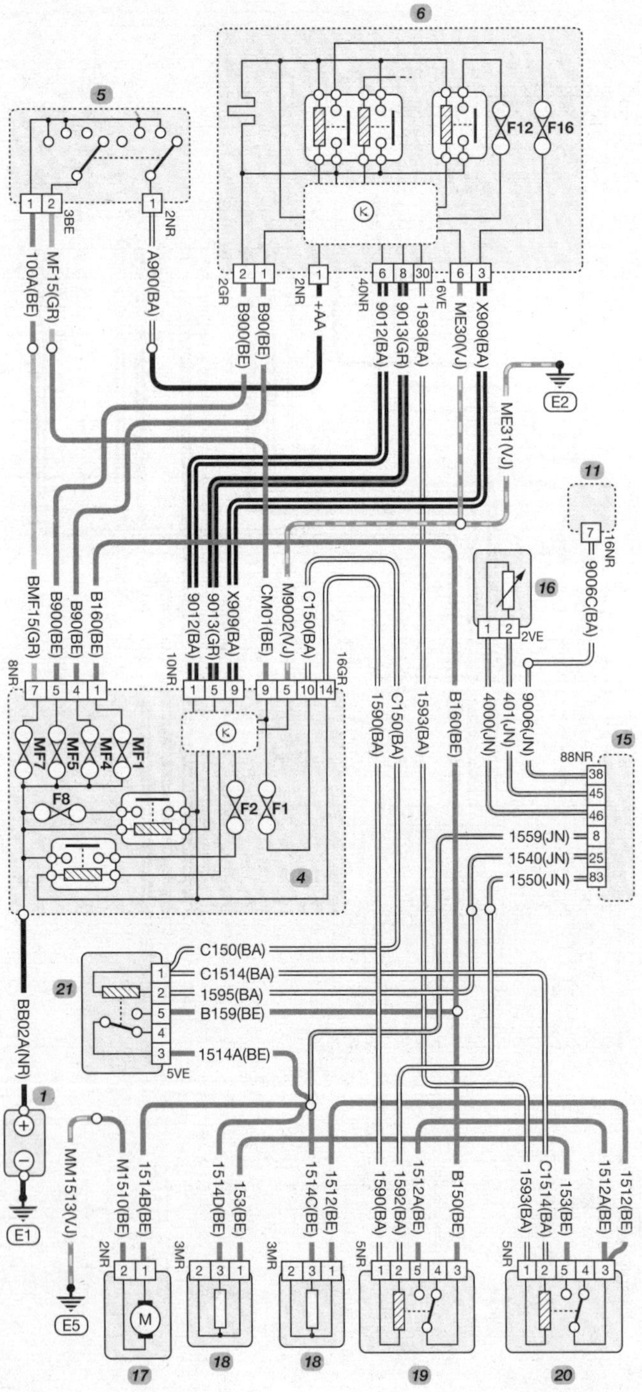

Typical stop & reversing lights

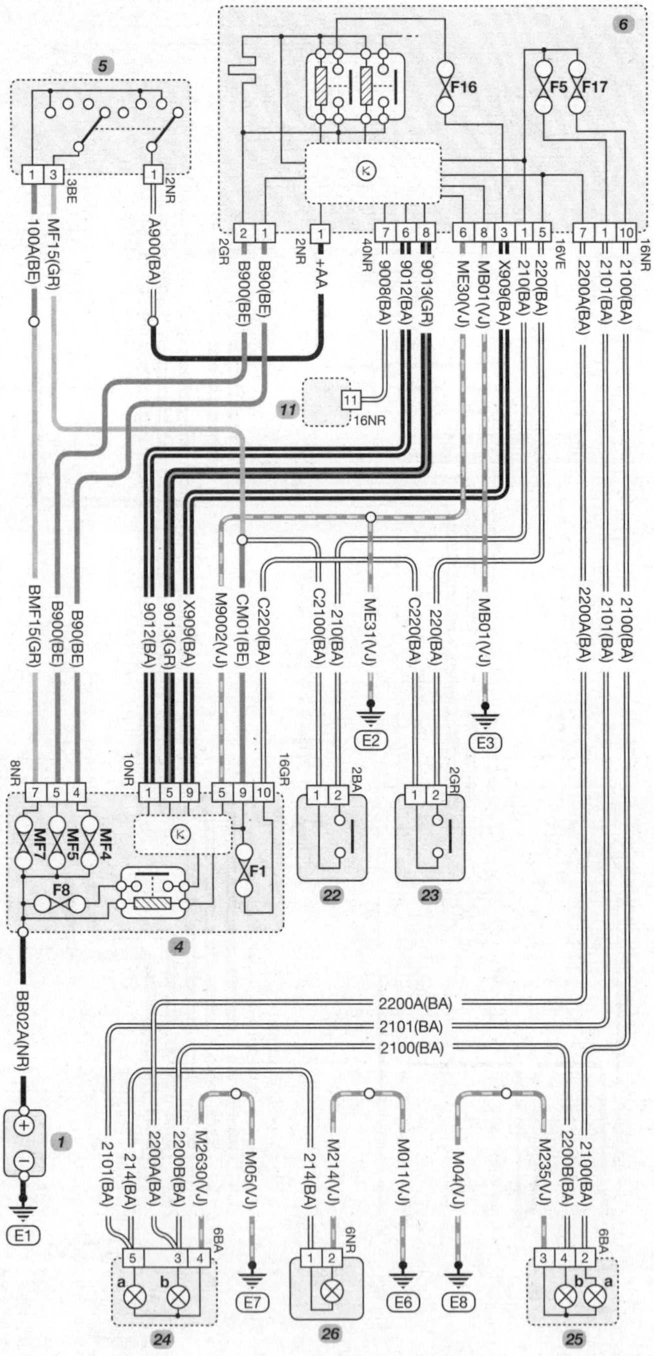

Colour codes

BA	White	**OR**	Orange
BE	Blue	**RG**	Red
BG	Beige	**RS**	Pink
GR	Grey	**VE**	Green
JN	Yellow	**VI**	Mauve
MR	Brown	**VJ**	Green/
NR	Black		Yellow

Key to items

1 Battery
4 Engine fusebox
5 Ignition switch
6 Built-in systems interface
7 Instrument cluster
10 Steering wheel control unit
11 Diagnostic connector
24 LH rear light unit
  c = tail light

25 RH rear light unit
  c = tail light
29 Daylight sensor
30 Rain sensor
31 Number plate light
32 LH headlight unit
  a = dip beam
  b = main beam
  c = side light

33 RH headlight unit
  a = dip beam
  b = main beam
  c = side light

Diagram 4

H33789

Typical side & headlights lights

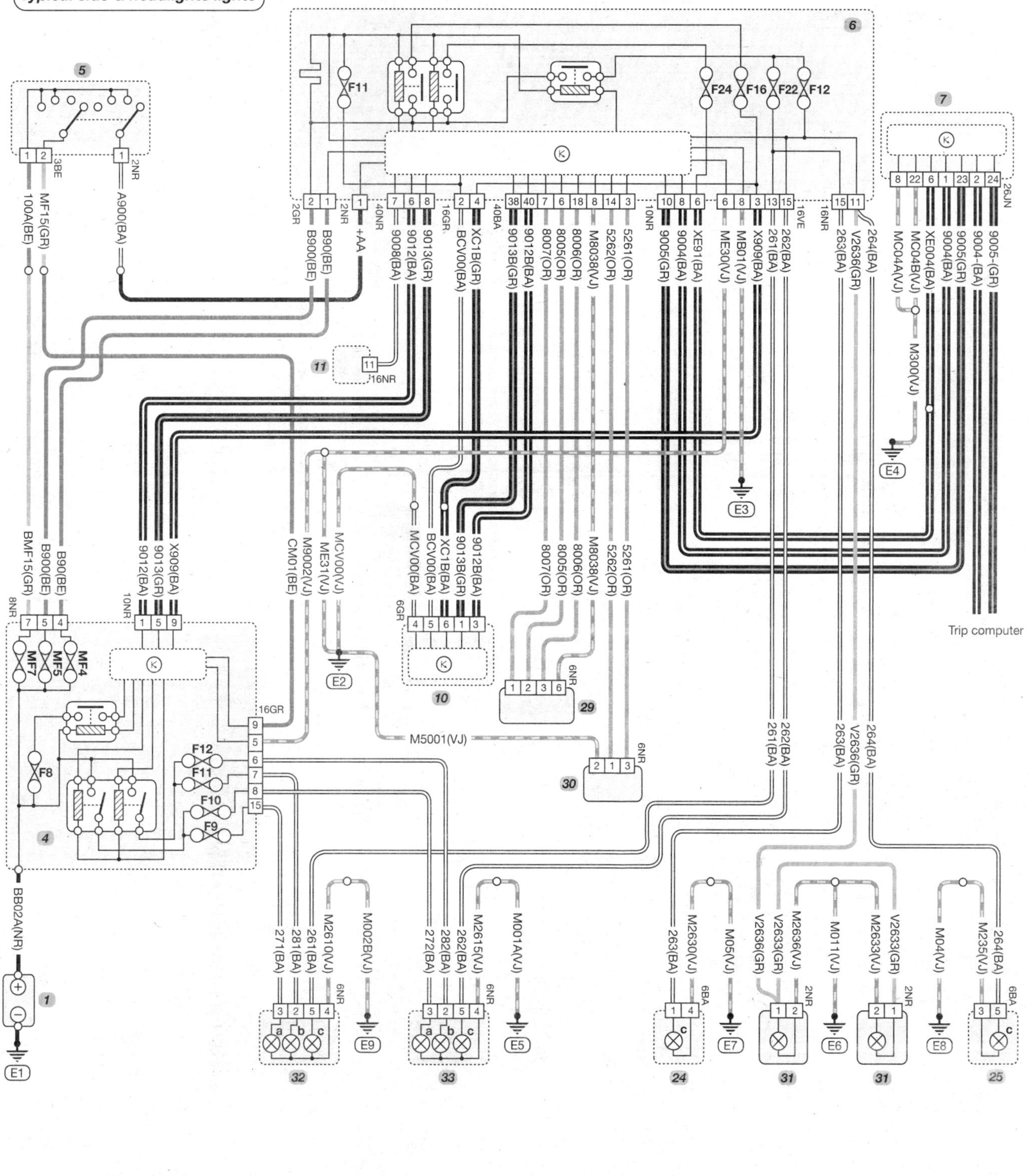

Trip computer

Colour codes

BA	White	OR	Orange
BE	Blue	RG	Red
BG	Beige	RS	Pink
GR	Grey	VE	Green
JN	Yellow	VI	Mauve
MR	Brown	VJ	Green/
NR	Black		Yellow

Key to items

1 Battery
4 Engine fusebox
5 Ignition switch
6 Built-in systems interface
7 Instrument cluster
  b = LH direction indicator
  c = RH direction indicator
10 Steering wheel control unit
11 Diagnostic connector

24 LH rear light unit
  d = direction indicator
25 RH rear light unit
  d = direction indicator
32 LH headlight unit
  d = direction indicator
33 RH headlight unit
  d = direction indicator
36 Hazard warning light switch

37 Airbag control unit
38 LH indicator side repeater
39 RH indicator side repeater

Diagram 5

H33790

Typical direction indicators & hazard warning lights

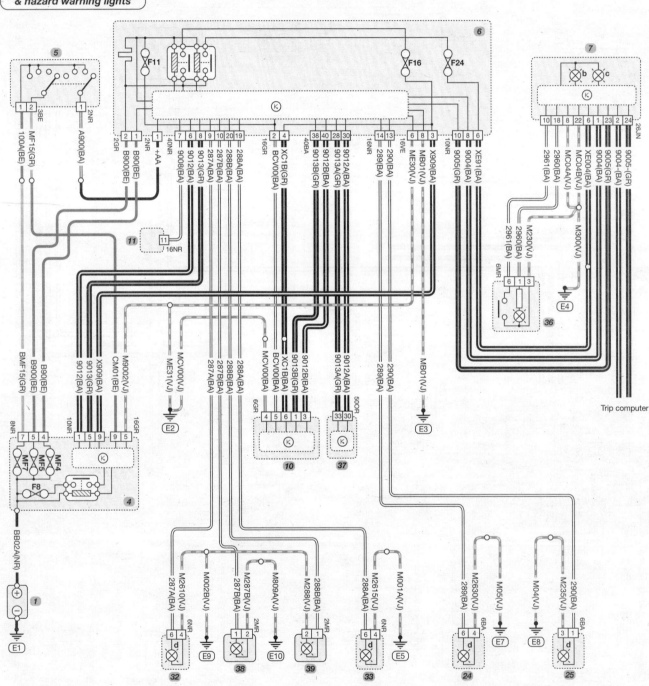

Trip computer

Colour codes

BA	White	OR	Orange
BE	Blue	RG	Red
BG	Beige	RS	Pink
GR	Grey	VE	Green
JN	Yellow	VI	Mauve
MR	Brown	VJ	Green/
NR	Black		Yellow

Key to items

1 Battery
4 Engine fusebox
5 Ignition switch
6 Built-in systems interface
7 Instrument cluster
   d = front foglight indicator
   e = rear foglight indicator
10 Steering wheel control unit
11 Diagnostic connector

24 LH rear light unit
   e = foglight
25 RH rear light unit
   e = foglight
32 LH headlight unit
   e = foglight
33 RH headlight unit
   e = foglight

Diagram 6

H33791

Typical front & rear foglights

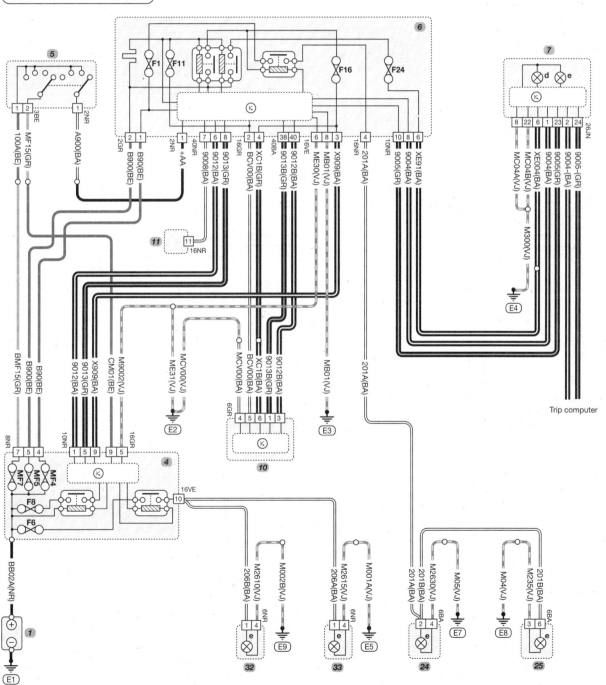

Trip computer

Colour codes

BA	White	**OR**	Orange
BE	Blue	**RG**	Red
BG	Beige	**RS**	Pink
GR	Grey	**VE**	Green
JN	Yellow	**VI**	Mauve
MR	Brown	**VJ**	Green/
NR	Black		Yellow

Key to items

1 Battery
4 Engine fusebox
5 Ignition switch
6 Built-in systems interface
7 Instrument cluster
   f = lighting rheostat
11 Diagnostic connector
45 Suspension control unit
46 LH headlight levelling motor

47 RH headlight levelling motor
48 Front body height sensor
49 Rear body height sensor
50 Front interior light
51 Rear interior light
52 LH luggage compartment light
53 RH luggage compartment light
54 Glovebox light/switch
55 Central air vent illumination

56 LH air vent illumination
57 RH air vent illumination
58 Ashtray illumination

Diagram 7

H33792

Typical headlight levelling

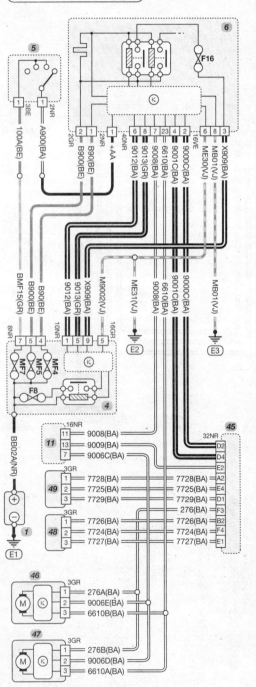

Typical interior lighting

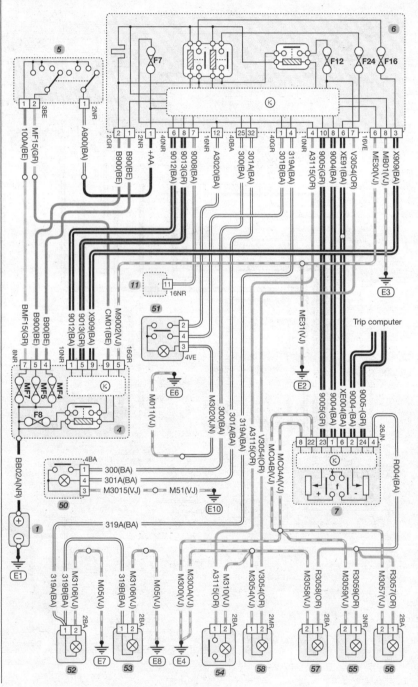

Colour codes

BA	White	OR	Orange
BE	Blue	RG	Red
BG	Beige	RS	Pink
GR	Grey	VE	Green
JN	Yellow	VI	Mauve
MR	Brown	VJ	Green/
NR	Black		Yellow

Key to items

1 Battery
4 Engine fusebox
5 Ignition switch
6 Built-in systems interface
7 Instrument cluster
10 Steering wheel control unit
11 Diagnostic connector

30 Rain sensor
60 Front windscreen wiper
61 Rear screen wiper
62 Front/rear washer pump
63 Headlight washer pump
64 Washer fluid level sensor

Diagram 8

H33793

Typical wash/wipe & headlight washer

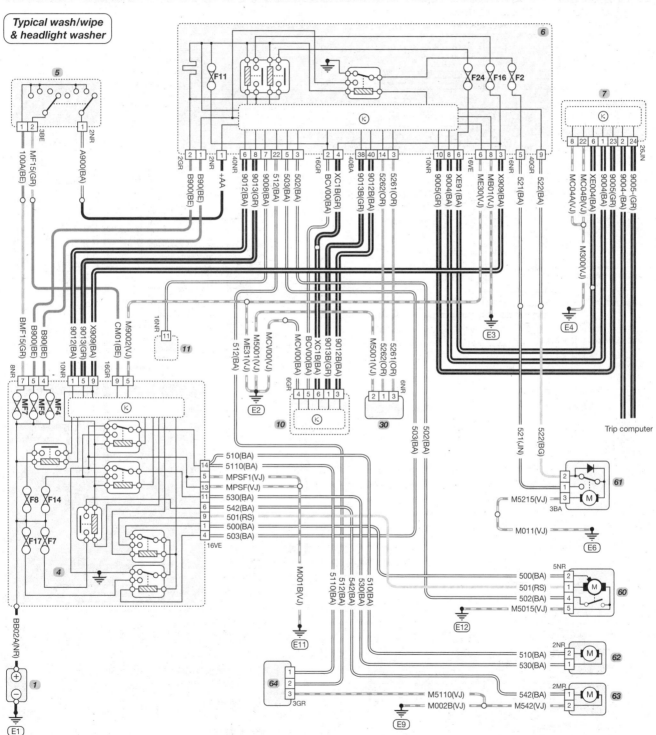

Trip computer

Colour codes

BA	White	OR	Orange
BE	Blue	RG	Red
BG	Beige	RS	Pink
GR	Grey	VE	Green
JN	Yellow	VI	Mauve
MR	Brown	VJ	Green/
NR	Black		Yellow

Key to items

1 Battery
4 Engine fusebox
5 Ignition switch
6 Built-in systems interface
7 Instrument cluster
11 Diagnostic connector
65 Front accessory socket
66 Rear accessory socket
67 Cigar lighter
68 Heater control panel
69 Recirculation motor
70 Heater blower motor
71 Heater blower resistors

Diagram 9

H33794

Typical cigar lighter & accessory socket

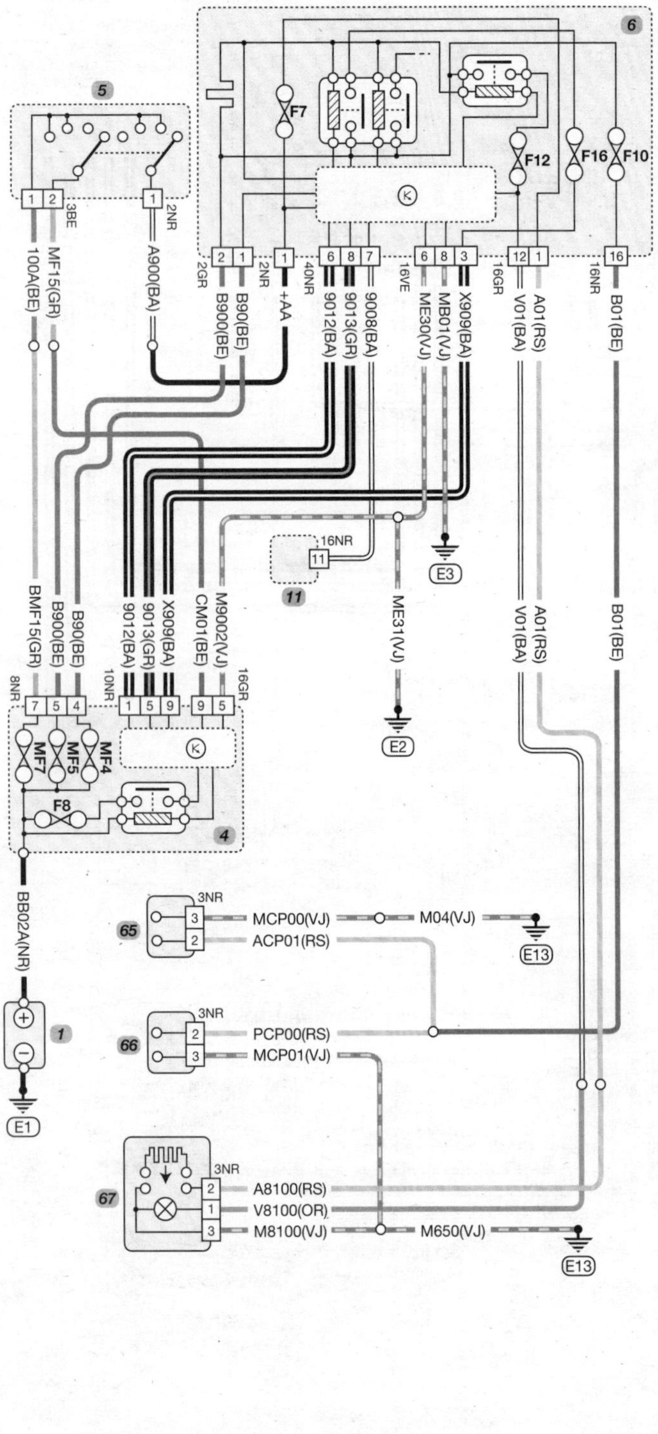

Typical heater blower

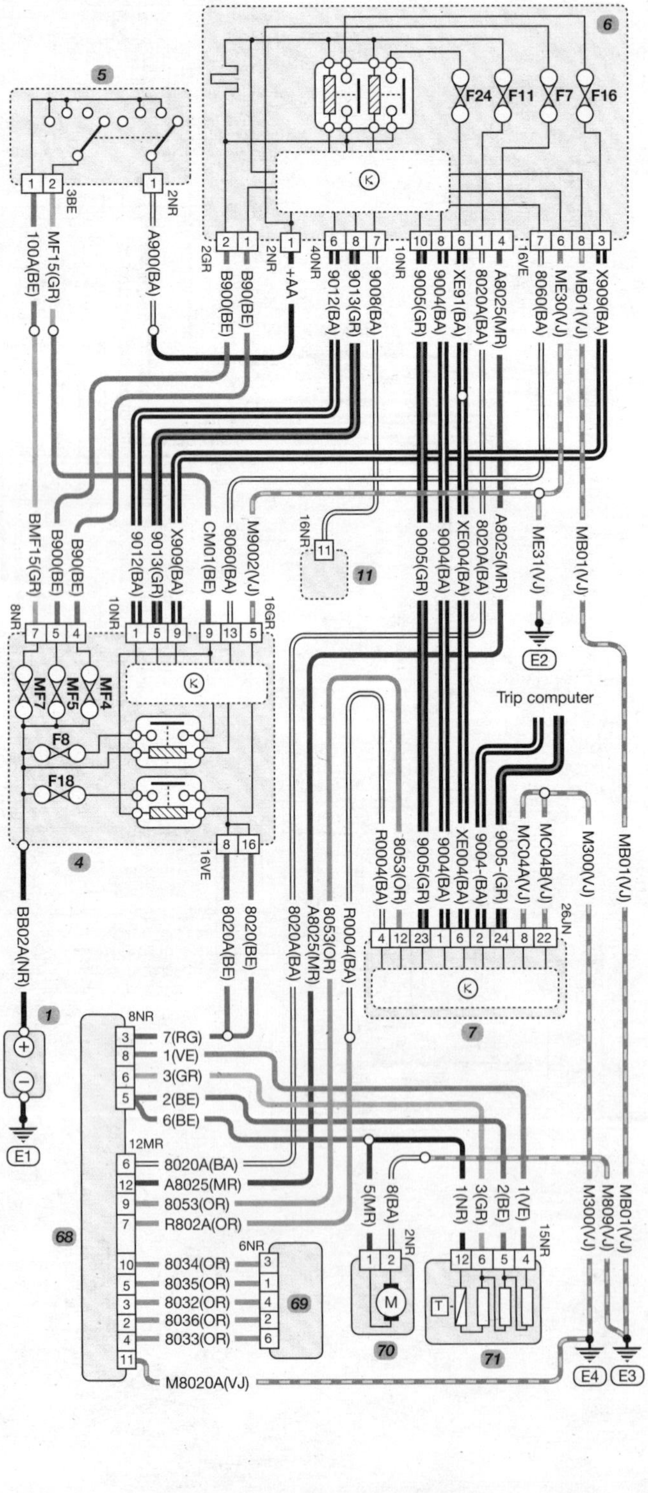

Colour codes

BA	White	**OR**	Orange
BE	Blue	**RG**	Red
BG	Beige	**RS**	Pink
GR	Grey	**VE**	Green
JN	Yellow	**VI**	Mauve
MR	Brown	**VJ**	Green/
NR	Black		Yellow

Key to items

1 Battery
4 Engine fusebox
5 Ignition switch
6 Built-in systems interface
7 Instrument cluster
11 Diagnostic connector
68 Heater control panel

75 Heated rear window
76 LH front door control unit
77 RH front door control unit
78 LH door mirror assembly
79 RH door mirror assembly

Diagram 10

H33795

**Typical heated rear window
& heated mirrors**

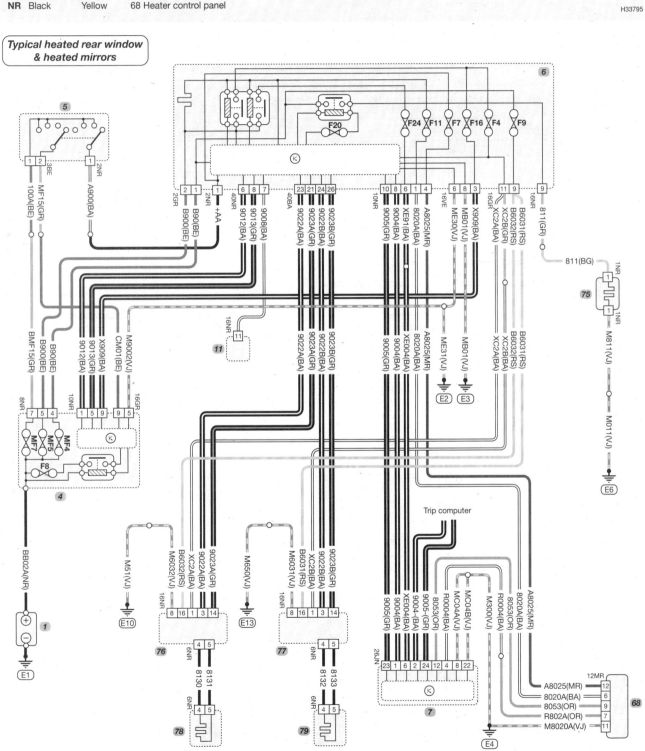

Colour codes

BA	White	OR	Orange
BE	Blue	RG	Red
BG	Beige	RS	Pink
GR	Grey	VE	Green
JN	Yellow	VI	Mauve
MR	Brown	VJ	Green/
NR	Black		Yellow

Key to items

1 Battery
4 Engine fusebox
5 Ignition switch
6 Built-in systems interface
7 Instrument cluster
10 Steering wheel control unit
11 Diagnostic connector

45 Suspension control unit
83 ABS control unit
84 Aerial amplifier
85 Audio unit
86 CD player
87 Telephone microphone
88 LH rear speaker

89 RH rear speaker
90 LH front tweeter
91 RH front tweeter
92 LH front door speaker
93 RH front door speaker

Diagram 11

H33796

Typical audio system

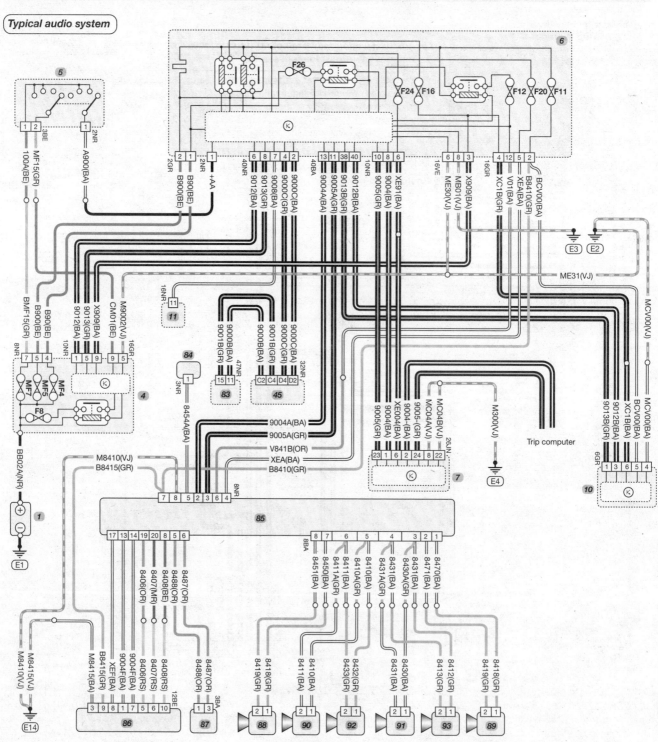

Colour codes

BA	White	**OR**	Orange
BE	Blue	**RG**	Red
BG	Beige	**RS**	Pink
GR	Grey	**VE**	Green
JN	Yellow	**VI**	Mauve
MR	Brown	**VJ**	Green/
NR	Black		Yellow

Key to items

1 Battery
4 Engine fusebox
5 Ignition switch
6 Built-in systems interface
7 Instrument cluster
10 Steering wheel control unit
11 Diagnostic connector

15 Engine management control unit
37 Airbag control unit
38 LH indicator side repeater
39 RH indicator side repeater
45 Suspension control unit
83 ABS control unit
95 Vehicle speed sensor

96 Central locking switch
97 Luggage compartment lock motor
98 Luggage compartment lock switch
99 LH front door lock assembly
100 RH front door lock assembly
101 LH rear door lock assembly
102 RH rear door lock assembly

Diagram 12

H33797

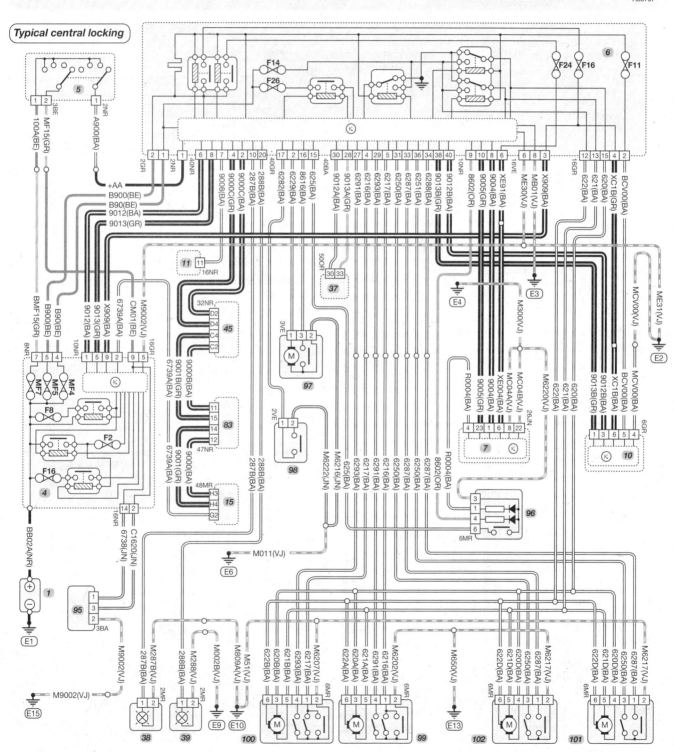

Typical central locking

Colour codes

BA	White	**OR**	Orange
BE	Blue	**RG**	Red
BG	Beige	**RS**	Pink
GR	Grey	**VE**	Green
JN	Yellow	**VI**	Mauve
MR	Brown	**VJ**	Green/
NR	Black		Yellow

Key to items

1 Battery
4 Engine fusebox
5 Ignition switch
6 Built-in systems interface
10 Steering wheel control unit
11 Diagnostic connector
76 LH front door control unit
77 RH front door control unit
105 LH front door electric window/mirror switch
106 RH front door electric window switch
107 LH rear door electric window switch
108 RH rear door electric window switch
109 LH rear window motor
110 RH rear window motor

Diagram 13

H33798

Typical electric windows

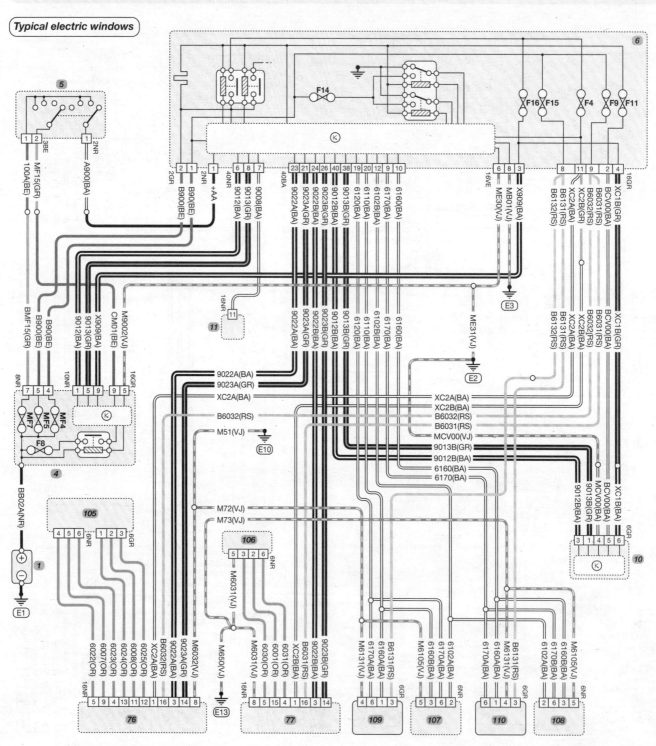

Colour codes

BA	White	**OR**	Orange
BE	Blue	**RG**	Red
BG	Beige	**RS**	Pink
GR	Grey	**VE**	Green
JN	Yellow	**VI**	Mauve
MR	Brown	**VJ**	Green/
NR	Black		Yellow

Key to items

1 Battery
4 Engine fusebox
5 Ignition switch
6 Built-in systems interface
10 Steering wheel control unit
11 Diagnostic connector
23 Reversing light switch
76 LH front door control unit
77 RH front door control unit
78 LH door mirror assembly
79 RH door mirror assembly
105 LH front door electric window/mirror switch

Diagram 14

H33799

Typical electric mirrors

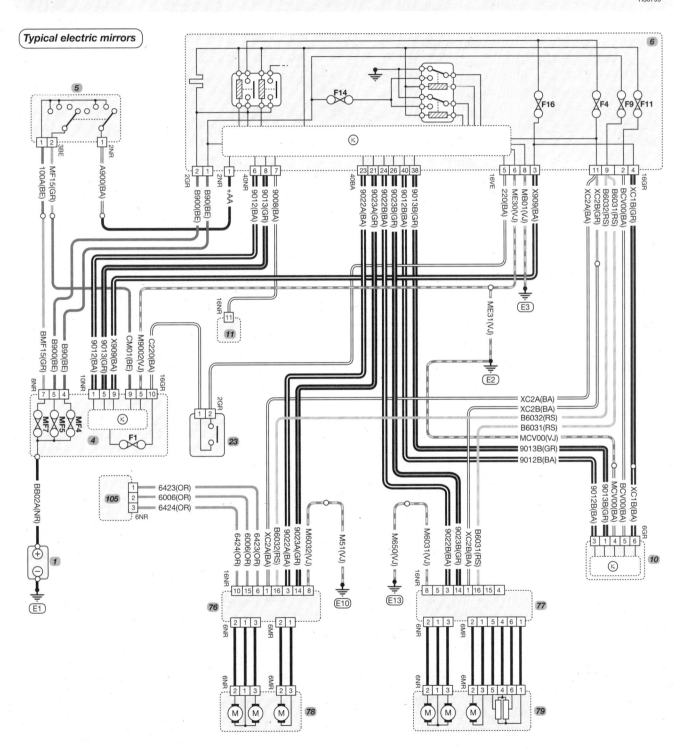

Reference REF•1

Dimensions and weights

Note: *All figures are approximate, and may vary according to model. Refer to manufacturer's data for exact figures.*

Dimensions

Overall length:
  Pre-facelift models (up to September 2004)
    Hatchback . . . . 4620 mm
    Estate . . . . 4760 mm
  Post-facelift models (from September 2004)
    Hatchback . . . . 4740 mm
    Estate . . . . 4840 mm
Overall width . . . . 2100 mm
Wheelbase . . . . 2750 mm
Height (without roof bars):
  Hatchback . . . . 1480 mm
  Estate . . . . 1510 mm

Weights

Gross vehicle weight . . . . 1810 to 2078 kg*
Maximum towing weight:
  Trailer without brakes . . . . 680 to 750 kg*
  Trailer with brakes . . . . 1500 to 2000 kg*
Maximum roof rack load . . . . 75 kg
Dependent on model – see Owners Handbook

Fuel economy

Although depreciation is still the biggest part of the cost of motoring for most car owners, the cost of fuel is more immediately noticeable. These pages give some tips on how to get the best fuel economy.

Working it out

Manufacturer's figures

Car manufacturers are required by law to provide fuel consumption information on all new vehicles sold. These 'official' figures are obtained by simulating various driving conditions on a rolling road or a test track. Real life conditions are different, so the fuel consumption actually achieved may not bear much resemblance to the quoted figures.

How to calculate it

Many cars now have trip computers which will

display fuel consumption, both instantaneous and average. Refer to the owner's handbook for details of how to use these.

To calculate consumption yourself (and maybe to check that the trip computer is accurate), proceed as follows.

1. Fill up with fuel and note the mileage, or zero the trip recorder.
2. Drive as usual until you need to fill up again.
3. Note the amount of fuel required to refill the tank, and the mileage covered since the previous fill-up.
4. Divide the mileage by the amount of fuel used to obtain the consumption figure.

For example:

Mileage at first fill-up (a) = 27,903
Mileage at second fill-up (b) = 28,346
Mileage covered (b - a) = 443
Fuel required at second fill-up = 48.6 litres

The half-completed changeover to metric units in the UK means that we buy our fuel

in litres, measure distances in miles and talk about fuel consumption in miles per gallon. There are two ways round this: the first is to convert the litres to gallons before doing the calculation (by dividing by 4.546, or see Table 1). So in the example:

48.6 litres ÷ 4.546 = 10.69 gallons
443 miles ÷ 10.69 gallons = 41.4 mpg

The second way is to calculate the consumption in miles per litre, then multiply that figure by 4.546 (or see Table 2).

So in the example, fuel consumption is:

443 miles ÷ 48.6 litres = 9.1 mpl
9.1 mpl x 4.546 = 41.4 mpg

The rest of Europe expresses fuel consumption in litres of fuel required to travel 100 km (l/100 km). For interest, the conversions are given in Table 3. In practice it doesn't matter what units you use, provided you know what your normal consumption is and can spot if it's getting better or worse.

Table 1: conversion of litres to Imperial gallons

litres	1	2	3	4	5	10	20	30	40	50	60	70
gallons	0.22	0.44	0.66	0.88	1.10	2.24	4.49	6.73	8.98	11.22	13.47	15.71

Table 2: conversion of miles per litre to miles per gallon

miles per litre	5	6	7	8	9	10	11	12	13	14
miles per gallon	23	27	32	36	41	46	50	55	59	64

Table 3: conversion of litres per 100 km to miles per gallon

litres per 100 km	4	4.5	5	5.5	6	6.5	7	8	9	10
miles per gallon	71	63	56	51	47	43	40	35	31	28

Maintenance

A well-maintained car uses less fuel and creates less pollution. In particular:

Filters

Change air and fuel filters at the specified intervals.

Oil

Use a good quality oil of the lowest viscosity specified by the vehicle manufacturer (see *Lubricants and fluids*). Check the level often and be careful not to overfill.

Spark plugs

When applicable, renew at the specified intervals.

Tyres

Check tyre pressures regularly. Under-inflated tyres have an increased rolling resistance. It is generally safe to use the higher pressures specified for full load conditions even when not fully laden, but keep an eye on the centre band of tread for signs of wear due to over-inflation.

When buying new tyres, consider the 'fuel saving' models which most manufacturers include in their ranges.

Driving style

Acceleration

Acceleration uses more fuel than driving at a steady speed. The best technique with modern cars is to accelerate reasonably briskly to the desired speed, changing up through the gears as soon as possible without making the engine labour.

Air conditioning

Air conditioning absorbs quite a bit of energy from the engine – typically 3 kW (4 hp) or so. The effect on fuel consumption is at its worst in slow traffic. Switch it off when not required.

Anticipation

Drive smoothly and try to read the traffic flow so as to avoid unnecessary acceleration and braking.

Automatic transmission

When accelerating in an automatic, avoid depressing the throttle so far as to make the transmission hold onto lower gears at higher speeds. Don't use the 'Sport' setting, if applicable.

When stationary with the engine running, select 'N' or 'P'. When moving, keep your left foot away from the brake.

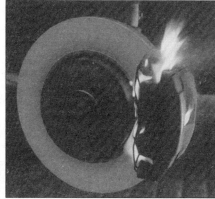

Braking

Braking converts the car's energy of motion into heat – essentially, it is wasted. Obviously some braking is always going to be necessary, but with good anticipation it is surprising how much can be avoided, especially on routes that you know well.

Carshare

Consider sharing lifts to work or to the shops. Even once a week will make a difference.

Electrical loads

Electricity is 'fuel' too; the alternator which charges the battery does so by converting some of the engine's energy of motion into electrical energy. The more electrical accessories are in use, the greater the load on the alternator. Switch off big consumers like the heated rear window when not required.

Freewheeling

Freewheeling (coasting) in neutral with the engine switched off is dangerous. The effort required to operate power-assisted brakes and steering increases when the engine is not running, with a potential lack of control in emergency situations.

In any case, modern fuel injection systems automatically cut off the engine's fuel supply on the overrun (moving and in gear, but with the accelerator pedal released).

Gadgets

Bolt-on devices claiming to save fuel have been around for nearly as long as the motor car itself. Those which worked were rapidly adopted as standard equipment by the vehicle manufacturers. Others worked only in certain situations, or saved fuel only at the expense of unacceptable effects on performance, driveability or the life of engine components.

The most effective fuel saving gadget is the driver's right foot.

Journey planning

Combine (eg) a trip to the supermarket with a visit to the recycling centre and the DIY store, rather than making separate journeys.

When possible choose a travelling time outside rush hours.

Load

The more heavily a car is laden, the greater the energy required to accelerate it to a given speed. Remove heavy items which you don't need to carry.

One load which is often overlooked is the contents of the fuel tank. A tankful of fuel (55 litres / 12 gallons) weighs 45 kg (100 lb) or so. Just half filling it may be worthwhile.

Lost?

At the risk of stating the obvious, if you're going somewhere new, have details of the route to hand. There's not much point in achieving record mpg if you also go miles out of your way.

Parking

If possible, carry out any reversing or turning manoeuvres when you arrive at a parking space so that you can drive straight out when you leave. Manoeuvering when the engine is cold uses a lot more fuel.

Driving around looking for free on-street parking may cost more in fuel than buying a car park ticket.

Premium fuel

Most major oil companies (and some supermarkets) have premium grades of fuel which are several pence a litre dearer than the standard grades. Reports vary, but the consensus seems to be that if these fuels improve economy at all, they do not do so by enough to justify their extra cost.

Roof rack

When loading a roof rack, try to produce a wedge shape with the narrow end at the front. Any cover should be securely fastened – if it flaps it's creating turbulence and absorbing energy.

Remove roof racks and boxes when not in use – they increase air resistance and can create a surprising amount of noise.

Short journeys

The engine is at its least efficient, and wear is highest, during the first few miles after a cold start. Consider walking, cycling or using public transport.

Speed

The engine is at its most efficient when running at a steady speed and load at the rpm where it develops maximum torque. (You can find this figure in the car's handbook.) For most cars this corresponds to between 55 and 65 mph in top gear.

Above the optimum cruising speed, fuel consumption starts to rise quite sharply. A car travelling at 80 mph will typically be using 30% more fuel than at 60 mph.

Supermarket fuel

It may be cheap but is it any good? In the UK all supermarket fuel must meet the relevant British Standard. The major oil companies will say that their branded fuels have better additive packages which may stop carbon and other deposits building up. A reasonable compromise might be to use one tank of branded fuel to three or four from the supermarket.

Switch off when stationary

Switch off the engine if you look like being stationary for more than 30 seconds or so. This is good for the environment as well as for your pocket. Be aware though that frequent restarts are hard on the battery and the starter motor.

Windows

Driving with the windows open increases air turbulence around the vehicle. Closing the windows promotes smooth airflow and

reduced resistance. The faster you go, the more significant this is.

And finally . . .

Driving techniques associated with good fuel economy tend to involve moderate acceleration and low top speeds. Be considerate to the needs of other road users who may need to make brisker progress; even if you do not agree with them this is not an excuse to be obstructive.

Safety must always take precedence over economy, whether it is a question of accelerating hard to complete an overtaking manoeuvre, killing your speed when confronted with a potential hazard or switching the lights on when it starts to get dark.

Conversion factors

Length (distance)

Inches (in)	x 25.4	= Millimetres (mm)	x 0.0394	= Inches (in)
Feet (ft)	x 0.305	= Metres (m)	x 3.281	= Feet (ft)
Miles	x 1.609	= Kilometres (km)	x 0.621	= Miles

Volume (capacity)

Cubic inches (cu in; in³)	x 16.387	= Cubic centimetres (cc; cm³)	x 0.061	= Cubic inches (cu in; in³)
Imperial pints (Imp pt)	x 0.568	= Litres (l)	x 1.76	= Imperial pints (Imp pt)
Imperial quarts (Imp qt)	x 1.137	= Litres (l)	x 0.88	= Imperial quarts (Imp qt)
Imperial quarts (Imp qt)	x 1.201	= US quarts (US qt)	x 0.833	= Imperial quarts (Imp qt)
US quarts (US qt)	x 0.946	= Litres (l)	x 1.057	= US quarts (US qt)
Imperial gallons (Imp gal)	x 4.546	= Litres (l)	x 0.22	= Imperial gallons (Imp gal)
Imperial gallons (Imp gal)	x 1.201	= US gallons (US gal)	x 0.833	= Imperial gallons (Imp gal)
US gallons (US gal)	x 3.785	= Litres (l)	x 0.264	= US gallons (US gal)

Mass (weight)

Ounces (oz)	x 28.35	= Grams (g)	x 0.035	= Ounces (oz)
Pounds (lb)	x 0.454	= Kilograms (kg)	x 2.205	= Pounds (lb)

Force

Ounces-force (ozf; oz)	x 0.278	= Newtons (N)	x 3.6	= Ounces-force (ozf; oz)
Pounds-force (lbf; lb)	x 4.448	= Newtons (N)	x 0.225	= Pounds-force (lbf; lb)
Newtons (N)	x 0.1	= Kilograms-force (kgf; kg)	x 9.81	= Newtons (N)

Pressure

Pounds-force per square inch (psi; lbf/in²; lb/in²)	x 0.070	= Kilograms-force per square centimetre (kgf/cm²; kg/cm²)	x 14.223	= Pounds-force per square inch (psi; lbf/in²; lb/in²)
Pounds-force per square inch (psi; lbf/in²; lb/in²)	x 0.068	= Atmospheres (atm)	x 14.696	= Pounds-force per square inch (psi; lbf/in²; lb/in²)
Pounds-force per square inch (psi; lbf/in²; lb/in²)	x 0.069	= Bars	x 14.5	= Pounds-force per square inch (psi; lbf/in²; lb/in²)
Pounds-force per square inch (psi; lbf/in²; lb/in²)	x 6.895	= Kilopascals (kPa)	x 0.145	= Pounds-force per square inch (psi; lbf/in²; lb/in²)
Kilopascals (kPa)	x 0.01	= Kilograms-force per square centimetre (kgf/cm²; kg/cm²)	x 98.1	= Kilopascals (kPa)
Millibar (mbar)	x 100	= Pascals (Pa)	x 0.01	= Millibar (mbar)
Millibar (mbar)	x 0.0145	= Pounds-force per square inch (psi; lbf/in²; lb/in²)	x 68.947	= Millibar (mbar)
Millibar (mbar)	x 0.75	= Millimetres of mercury (mmHg)	x 1.333	= Millibar (mbar)
Millibar (mbar)	x 0.401	= Inches of water (inH$_2$O)	x 2.491	= Millibar (mbar)
Millimetres of mercury (mmHg)	x 0.535	= Inches of water (inH$_2$O)	x 1.868	= Millimetres of mercury (mmHg)
Inches of water (inH$_2$O)	x 0.036	= Pounds-force per square inch (psi; lbf/in²; lb/in²)	x 27.68	= Inches of water (inH$_2$O)

Torque (moment of force)

Pounds-force inches (lbf in; lb in)	x 1.152	= Kilograms-force centimetre (kgf cm; kg cm)	x 0.868	= Pounds-force inches (lbf in; lb in)
Pounds-force inches (lbf in; lb in)	x 0.113	= Newton metres (Nm)	x 8.85	= Pounds-force inches (lbf in; lb in)
Pounds-force inches (lbf in; lb in)	x 0.083	= Pounds-force feet (lbf ft; lb ft)	x 12	= Pounds-force inches (lbf in; lb in)
Pounds-force feet (lbf ft; lb ft)	x 0.138	= Kilograms-force metres (kgf m; kg m)	x 7.233	= Pounds-force feet (lbf ft; lb ft)
Pounds-force feet (lbf ft; lb ft)	x 1.356	= Newton metres (Nm)	x 0.738	= Pounds-force feet (lbf ft; lb ft)
Newton metres (Nm)	x 0.102	= Kilograms-force metres (kgf m; kg m)	x 9.804	= Newton metres (Nm)

Power

Horsepower (hp)	x 745.7	= Watts (W)	x 0.0013	= Horsepower (hp)

Velocity (speed)

Miles per hour (miles/hr; mph)	x 1.609	= Kilometres per hour (km/hr; kph)	x 0.621	= Miles per hour (miles/hr; mph)

Fuel consumption*

Miles per gallon, Imperial (mpg)	x 0.354	= Kilometres per litre (km/l)	x 2.825	= Miles per gallon, Imperial (mpg)
Miles per gallon, US (mpg)	x 0.425	= Kilometres per litre (km/l)	x 2.352	= Miles per gallon, US (mpg)

Temperature

Degrees Fahrenheit = (°C x 1.8) + 32   Degrees Celsius (Degrees Centigrade; °C) = (°F - 32) x 0.56

It is common practice to convert from miles per gallon (mpg) to litres/100 kilometres (l/100km), where mpg x l/100 km = 282

The jack supplied with the vehicle tool kit should only be used for changing the roadwheels – see *Wheel changing* at the front of this manual. When carrying out any other kind of work, raise the vehicle using a hydraulic trolley jack, and always supplement the jack with axle stands positioned under the vehicle jacking points.

When using a trolley jack or axle stands, position the jack head or axle stand head adjacent to one of the relevant wheel changing jacking points under the sills (see illustration). Use a block of wood between the jack or axle stand and the sill.

Do not attempt to jack the vehicle under the sump, or any of the suspension components. It is permissible to jack the vehicle under the middle of the front subframe, and position axle stands under the rear section of the front subframe. Its also permissible to position the jack head under the reinforced rim of the spare wheel well at the rear (see illustrations).

The jack supplied with the vehicle locates in the jacking points on the underside of the sills – see *Wheel changing* at the front of this manual. Ensure that the jack head is correctly engaged before attempting to raise the vehicle.

Never work under, around, or near a raised vehicle, unless it is adequately supported in at least two places.

Position axle stands adjacent to the wheel changing jacking points under the sills

Position the jack head in the middle of the front subframe crossmember

Position the jack head under the reinforced section of the spare wheel well

Buying spare parts

Spare parts are available from many sources, including maker's appointed garages, accessory shops, and motor factors. To be sure of obtaining the correct parts, it will sometimes be necessary to quote the vehicle identification number. If possible, it can also be useful to take the old parts along for positive identification. Items such as starter motors and alternators may be available under a service exchange scheme – any parts returned should be clean.

Our advice regarding spare parts is as follows.

Officially appointed garages

This is the best source of parts which are peculiar to your car, and which are not otherwise generally available (eg, badges, interior trim, certain body panels, etc). It is also the only place at which you should buy parts if the vehicle is still under warranty.

Accessory shops

These are very good places to buy materials and components needed for the maintenance of your car (oil, air and fuel filters, light bulbs, drivebelts, greases, brake pads, touch-up paint, etc). Components of this nature sold by a reputable shop are usually of the same standard as those used by the car manufacturer.

Besides components, these shops also sell tools and general accessories, usually have convenient opening hours, charge lower prices, and can often be found close to home. Some accessory shops have parts counters where components needed for almost any repair job can be purchased or ordered.

Motor factors

Good factors will stock all the more important components which wear out comparatively quickly, and can sometimes supply individual components needed for the overhaul of a larger assembly (eg, brake seals and hydraulic parts, bearing shells, pistons, valves). They may also handle work such as cylinder block reboring, crankshaft regrinding, etc.

Tyre and exhaust specialists

These outlets may be independent, or members of a local or national chain. They frequently offer competitive prices when compared with a main dealer or local garage, but it will pay to obtain several quotes before making a decision. When researching prices, also ask what extras may be added – for instance fitting a new valve and balancing the wheel are both commonly charged on top of the price of a new tyre.

Other sources

Beware of parts or materials obtained from market stalls, car boot sales or similar outlets. Such items are not invariably sub-standard, but there is little chance of compensation if they do prove unsatisfactory. in the case of safety-critical components such as brake pads, there is the risk not only of financial loss, but also of an accident causing injury or death.

Second-hand components or assemblies obtained from a car breaker can be a good buy in some circumstances, but this sort of purchase is best made by the experienced DIY mechanic.

Whenever servicing, repair or overhaul work is carried out on the car or its components, observe the following procedures and instructions. This will assist in carrying out the operation efficiently and to a professional standard of workmanship.

Joint mating faces and gaskets

When separating components at their mating faces, never insert screwdrivers or similar implements into the joint between the faces in order to prise them apart. This can cause severe damage which results in oil leaks, coolant leaks, etc upon reassembly. Separation is usually achieved by tapping along the joint with a soft-faced hammer in order to break the seal. However, note that this method may not be suitable where dowels are used for component location.

Where a gasket is used between the mating faces of two components, a new one must be fitted on reassembly; fit it dry unless otherwise stated in the repair procedure. Make sure that the mating faces are clean and dry, with all traces of old gasket removed. When cleaning a joint face, use a tool which is unlikely to score or damage the face, and remove any burrs or nicks with an oilstone or fine file.

Make sure that tapped holes are cleaned with a pipe cleaner, and keep them free of jointing compound, if this is being used, unless specifically instructed otherwise.

Ensure that all orifices, channels or pipes are clear, and blow through them, preferably using compressed air.

Oil seals

Oil seals can be removed by levering them out with a wide flat-bladed screwdriver or similar implement. Alternatively, a number of self-tapping screws may be screwed into the seal, and these used as a purchase for pliers or some similar device in order to pull the seal free.

Whenever an oil seal is removed from its working location, either individually or as part of an assembly, it should be renewed.

The very fine sealing lip of the seal is easily damaged, and will not seal if the surface it contacts is not completely clean and free from scratches, nicks or grooves. If the original sealing surface of the component cannot be restored, and the manufacturer has not made provision for slight relocation of the seal relative to the sealing surface, the component should be renewed.

Protect the lips of the seal from any surface which may damage them in the course of fitting. Use tape or a conical sleeve where possible. Where indicated, lubricate the seal lips with oil before fitting and, on dual-lipped seals, fill the space between the lips with grease.

Unless otherwise stated, oil seals must be fitted with their sealing lips toward the lubricant to be sealed.

Use a tubular drift or block of wood of the appropriate size to install the seal and, if the seal housing is shouldered, drive the seal down to the shoulder. If the seal housing is unshouldered, the seal should be fitted with its face flush with the housing top face (unless otherwise instructed).

Screw threads and fastenings

Seized nuts, bolts and screws are quite a common occurrence where corrosion has set in, and the use of penetrating oil or releasing fluid will often overcome this problem if the offending item is soaked for a while before attempting to release it. The use of an impact driver may also provide a means of releasing such stubborn fastening devices, when used in conjunction with the appropriate screwdriver bit or socket. If none of these methods works, it may be necessary to resort to the careful application of heat, or the use of a hacksaw or nut splitter device. Before resorting to extreme methods, check that you are not dealing with a left-hand thread!

Studs are usually removed by locking two nuts together on the threaded part, and then using a spanner on the lower nut to unscrew the stud. Studs or bolts which have broken off below the surface of the component in which they are mounted can sometimes be removed using a stud extractor.

Always ensure that a blind tapped hole is completely free from oil, grease, water or other fluid before installing the bolt or stud. Failure to do this could cause the housing to crack due to the hydraulic action of the bolt or stud as it is screwed in.

For some screw fastenings, notably cylinder head bolts or nuts, torque wrench settings are no longer specified for the latter stages of tightening, "angle-tightening" being called up instead. Typically, a fairly low torque wrench setting will be applied to the bolts/nuts in the correct sequence, followed by one or more stages of tightening through specified angles.

When checking or retightening a nut or bolt to a specified torque setting, slacken the nut or bolt by a quarter of a turn, and then retighten to the specified setting. However, this should not be attempted where angular tightening has been used.

Locknuts, locktabs and washers

Any fastening which will rotate against a component or housing during tightening should always have a washer between it and the relevant component or housing.

Spring or split washers should always be renewed when they are used to lock a critical component such as a big-end bearing retaining bolt or nut. Locktabs which are folded over to retain a nut or bolt should always be renewed.

Self-locking nuts can be re-used in non-critical areas, providing resistance can be felt when the locking portion passes over the bolt or stud thread. However, it should be noted that self-locking stiffnuts tend to lose their effectiveness after long periods of use, and should then be renewed as a matter of course.

Split pins must always be replaced with new ones of the correct size for the hole.

When thread-locking compound is found on the threads of a fastener which is to be re-used, it should be cleaned off with a wire brush and solvent, and fresh compound applied on reassembly.

Special tools

Some repair procedures in this manual entail the use of special tools such as a press, two or three-legged pullers, spring compressors, etc. Wherever possible, suitable readily-available alternatives to the manufacturer's special tools are described, and are shown in use. In some instances, where no alternative is possible, it has been necessary to resort to the use of a manufacturer's tool, and this has been done for reasons of safety as well as the efficient completion of the repair operation. Unless you are highly-skilled and have a thorough understanding of the procedures described, never attempt to bypass the use of any special tool when the procedure described specifies its use. Not only is there a very great risk of personal injury, but expensive damage could be caused to the components involved.

Environmental considerations

When disposing of used engine oil, brake fluid, antifreeze, etc, give due consideration to any detrimental environmental effects. Do not, for instance, pour any of the above liquids down drains into the general sewage system, or onto the ground to soak away. Many local council refuse tips provide a facility for waste oil disposal, as do some garages. You can find your nearest disposal point by calling the Environment Agency on 08708 506 506 or by visiting www.oilbankline.org.uk.

Note: It is illegal and anti-social to dump oil down the drain. To find the location of your local oil recycling bank, call 08708 506 506 or visit www.oilbankline.org.uk.

Modifications are a continuing and unpublicised process in vehicle manufacture, quite apart from major model changes. Spare parts manuals and lists are compiled upon a numerical basis, the individual vehicle identification numbers being essential to correct identification of the component concerned.

When ordering spare parts, always give as much information as possible. Quote the car model, year of manufacture, body and engine numbers as appropriate.

The *vehicle identification plate* is situated under the left-hand rear seat cushion on pre-facelift models (up to September 2004) and on the left-hand centre door pillar on post-facelift models (from September 2004) **(see illustrations)**. The *vehicle identification number* is also repeated in the form of plate visible through the windscreen on the passenger's side and on the right-hand inner wing in the engine compartment **(see illustrations)**. The vehicle RPO (build)

number is located on a sticker attached to the A-pillar in the driver's door aperture **(see illustration)**.

The *engine number and type designation* is located on the front, right-hand end of the engine, and on some vehicles, on the timing belt cover.

Other identification numbers or codes are stamped on major items such as the gearbox, etc.

On pre-facelift models, the vehicle identification plate is under the rear seat

On post-facelift models, the vehicle identification plate is on the left-hand centre door pillar

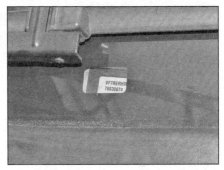

The VIN is visible through the base of the windscreen . . .

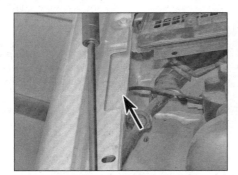

. . . and is repeated in the engine compartment on the right-hand inner wing (arrowed)

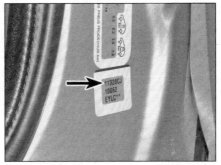

The RPO (build) number (arrowed) is located on a sticker attached to the A-pillar

Engine identification

Petrol engines

Indirect injection

Designation:
  1.8 litre EW7J4
  2.0 litre EW10J4
Engine code:
  1.8 litre 6FZ
  2.0 litre . . . . RFN

Direct injection

Designation:
  2.0 litre EW10D
Engine code . . . . RLZ

Diesel engines

1.6 litre

Designation DV6TED4
Engine codes . . . . .9HY or 9HZ

2.0 litre SOHC

Designation . . . . DW10TD or DW10ATED
Engine codes:
  DW10TD . . . . .RHY
  DW10ATED . . . . .RHZ

2.0 litre DOHC

Designation DW10BTED4
Engine code . . . . RHR

Introduction

A selection of good tools is a fundamental requirement for anyone contemplating the maintenance and repair of a motor vehicle. For the owner who does not possess any, their purchase will prove a considerable expense, offsetting some of the savings made by doing-it-yourself. However, provided that the tools purchased meet the relevant national safety standards and are of good quality, they will last for many years and prove an extremely worthwhile investment.

To help the average owner to decide which tools are needed to carry out the various tasks detailed in this manual, we have compiled three lists of tools under the following headings: *Maintenance and minor repair, Repair and overhaul*, and *Special*. Newcomers to practical mechanics should start off with the *Maintenance and minor repair* tool kit, and confine themselves to the simpler jobs around the vehicle. Then, as confidence and experience grow, more difficult tasks can be undertaken, with extra tools being purchased as, and when, they are needed. In this way, a *Maintenance and minor repair* tool kit can be built up into a *Repair and overhaul* tool kit over a considerable period of time, without any major cash outlays. The experienced do-it-yourselfer will have a tool kit good enough for most repair and overhaul procedures, and will add tools from the *Special* category when it is felt that the expense is justified by the amount of use to which these tools will be put.

Maintenance and minor repair tool kit

The tools given in this list should be considered as a minimum requirement if routine maintenance, servicing and minor repair operations are to be undertaken. We recommend the purchase of combination spanners (ring one end, open-ended the other); although more expensive than open-ended ones, they do give the advantages of both types of spanner.

- ☐ *Combination spanners:*
  Metric - 8 to 19 mm inclusive
- ☐ *Adjustable spanner - 35 mm jaw (approx.)*
- ☐ *Spark plug spanner (with rubber insert) - petrol models*
- ☐ *Spark plug gap adjustment tool - petrol models*
- ☐ *Set of feeler gauges*
- ☐ *Brake bleed nipple spanner*
- ☐ *Screwdrivers:*
  Flat blade - 100 mm long x 6 mm dia
  Cross blade - 100 mm long x 6 mm dia
  Torx - various sizes (not all vehicles)
- ☐ *Combination pliers*
- ☐ *Hacksaw (junior)*
- ☐ *Tyre pump*
- ☐ *Tyre pressure gauge*
- ☐ *Oil can*
- ☐ *Oil filter removal tool (if applicable)*
- ☐ *Fine emery cloth*
- ☐ *Wire brush (small)*
- ☐ *Funnel (medium size)*
- ☐ *Sump drain plug key (not all vehicles)*

Repair and overhaul tool kit

These tools are virtually essential for anyone undertaking any major repairs to a motor vehicle, and are additional to those given in the *Maintenance and minor repair* list. Included in this list is a comprehensive set of sockets. Although these are expensive, they will be found invaluable as they are so versatile - particularly if various drives are included in the set. We recommend the half-inch square-drive type, as this can be used with most proprietary torque wrenches.

The tools in this list will sometimes need to be supplemented by tools from the *Special* list:

- ☐ *Sockets to cover range in previous list (including Torx sockets)*
- ☐ *Reversible ratchet drive (for use with sockets)*
- ☐ *Extension piece, 250 mm (for use with sockets)*
- ☐ *Universal joint (for use with sockets)*
- ☐ *Flexible handle or sliding T "breaker bar" (for use with sockets)*
- ☐ *Torque wrench (for use with sockets)*
- ☐ *Self-locking grips*
- ☐ *Ball pein hammer*
- ☐ *Soft-faced mallet (plastic or rubber)*
- ☐ *Screwdrivers:*
  Flat blade - long & sturdy, short (chubby), and narrow (electrician's) types
  Cross blade – long & sturdy, and short (chubby) types
- ☐ *Pliers:*
  Long-nosed
  Side cutters (electrician's)
  Circlip (internal and external)
- ☐ *Cold chisel - 25 mm*
- ☐ *Scriber*
- ☐ *Scraper*
- ☐ *Centre-punch*
- ☐ *Pin punch*
- ☐ *Hacksaw*
- ☐ *Brake hose clamp*
- ☐ *Brake/clutch bleeding kit*
- ☐ *Selection of twist drills*
- ☐ *Steel rule/straight-edge*
- ☐ *Allen keys (inc. splined/Torx type)*
- ☐ *Selection of files*
- ☐ *Wire brush*
- ☐ *Axle stands*
- ☐ *Jack (strong trolley or hydraulic type)*
- ☐ *Light with extension lead*
- ☐ *Universal electrical multi-meter*

Sockets and reversible ratchet drive

Brake bleeding kit

Torx key, socket and bit

Hose clamp

Angular-tightening gauge

Special tools

The tools in this list are those which are not used regularly, are expensive to buy, or which need to be used in accordance with their manufacturers' instructions. Unless relatively difficult mechanical jobs are undertaken frequently, it will not be economic to buy many of these tools. Where this is the case, you could consider clubbing together with friends (or joining a motorists' club) to make a joint purchase, or borrowing the tools against a deposit from a local garage or tool hire specialist.

The following list contains only those tools and instruments freely available to the public, and not those special tools produced by the vehicle manufacturer specifically for its dealer network. You will find occasional references to these manufacturers' special tools in the text of this manual. Generally, an alternative method of doing the job without the vehicle manufacturers' special tool is given. However, sometimes there is no alternative to using them. Where this is the case and the relevant tool cannot be bought or borrowed, you will have to entrust the work to a dealer.

- ☐ Angular-tightening gauge
- ☐ Valve spring compressor
- ☐ Valve grinding tool
- ☐ Piston ring compressor
- ☐ Piston ring removal/installation tool
- ☐ Cylinder bore hone
- ☐ Balljoint separator
- ☐ Coil spring compressors (where applicable)
- ☐ Two/three-legged hub and bearing puller
- ☐ Impact screwdriver
- ☐ Micrometer and/or vernier calipers
- ☐ Dial gauge
- ☐ Tachometer
- ☐ Fault code reader
- ☐ Cylinder compression gauge
- ☐ Hand-operated vacuum pump and gauge
- ☐ Clutch plate alignment set
- ☐ Brake shoe steady spring cup removal tool
- ☐ Bush and bearing removal/installation set
- ☐ Stud extractors
- ☐ Tap and die set
- ☐ Lifting tackle

Buying tools

Reputable motor accessory shops and superstores often offer excellent quality tools at discount prices, so it pays to shop around.

Remember, you don't have to buy the most expensive items on the shelf, but it is always advisable to steer clear of the very cheap tools. Beware of 'bargains' offered on market stalls, on-line or at car boot sales. There are plenty of good tools around at reasonable prices, but always aim to purchase items which meet the relevant national safety standards. If in doubt, ask the proprietor or manager of the shop for advice before making a purchase.

Care and maintenance of tools

Having purchased a reasonable tool kit, it is necessary to keep the tools in a clean and serviceable condition. After use, always wipe off any dirt, grease and metal particles using a clean, dry cloth, before putting the tools away. Never leave them lying around after they have been used. A simple tool rack on the garage or workshop wall for items such as screwdrivers and pliers is a good idea. Store all normal spanners and sockets in a metal box. Any measuring instruments, gauges, meters, etc, must be carefully stored where they cannot be damaged or become rusty.

Take a little care when tools are used. Hammer heads inevitably become marked, and screwdrivers lose the keen edge on their blades from time to time. A little timely attention with emery cloth or a file will soon restore items like this to a good finish.

Working facilities

Not to be forgotten when discussing tools is the workshop itself. If anything more than routine maintenance is to be carried out, a suitable working area becomes essential.

It is appreciated that many an owner-mechanic is forced by circumstances to remove an engine or similar item without the benefit of a garage or workshop. Having done this, any repairs should always be done under the cover of a roof.

Wherever possible, any dismantling should be done on a clean, flat workbench or table at a suitable working height.

Any workbench needs a vice; one with a jaw opening of 100 mm is suitable for most jobs. As mentioned previously, some clean dry storage space is also required for tools, as well as for any lubricants, cleaning fluids, touch-up paints etc, which become necessary.

Another item which may be required, and which has a much more general usage, is an electric drill with a chuck capacity of at least 8 mm. This, together with a good range of twist drills, is virtually essential for fitting accessories.

Last, but not least, always keep a supply of old newspapers and clean, lint-free rags available, and try to keep any working area as clean as possible.

Micrometers

Dial test indicator ("dial gauge")

Oil filter removal tool (strap wrench type)

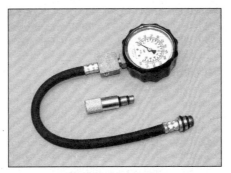
Compression tester

Bearing puller

This is a guide to getting your vehicle through the MOT test. Obviously it will not be possible to examine the vehicle to the same standard as the professional MOT tester. However, working through the following checks will enable you to identify any problem areas before submitting the vehicle for the test.

It has only been possible to summarise the test requirements here, based on the regulations in force at the time of printing. Test standards are becoming increasingly stringent, although there are some exemptions for older vehicles.

An assistant will be needed to help carry out some of these checks.

The checks have been sub-divided into four categories, as follows:

1 Checks carried out **FROM THE DRIVER'S SEAT**

2 Checks carried out **WITH THE VEHICLE ON THE GROUND**

3 Checks carried out **WITH THE VEHICLE RAISED AND THE WHEELS FREE TO TURN**

4 Checks carried out on **YOUR VEHICLE'S EXHAUST EMISSION SYSTEM**

1 Checks carried out **FROM THE DRIVER'S SEAT**

Handbrake (parking brake)

☐ Test the operation of the handbrake. Excessive travel (too many clicks) indicates incorrect brake or cable adjustment.
☐ Check that the handbrake cannot be released by tapping the lever sideways. Check the security of the lever mountings.

☐ If the parking brake is foot-operated, check that the pedal is secure and without excessive travel, and that the release mechanism operates correctly.
☐ Where applicable, test the operation of the electronic handbrake. The brake should engage and disengage without excessive delay. If the warning light does not extinguish when the brake is disengaged, this could indicate a fault which will need further investigation.

Footbrake

☐ Depress the brake pedal and check that it does not creep down to the floor, indicating a master cylinder fault. Release the pedal,

wait a few seconds, then depress it again. If the pedal travels nearly to the floor before firm resistance is felt, brake adjustment or repair is necessary. If the pedal feels spongy, there is air in the hydraulic system which must be removed by bleeding.

☐ Check that the brake pedal is secure and in good condition. Check also for signs of fluid leaks on the pedal, floor or carpets, which would indicate failed seals in the brake master cylinder.
☐ Check the servo unit (when applicable) by operating the brake pedal several times, then keeping the pedal depressed and starting the engine. As the engine starts, the pedal will move down slightly. If not, the vacuum hose or the servo itself may be faulty.

Steering wheel and column

☐ Examine the steering wheel for fractures or looseness of the hub, spokes or rim.
☐ Move the steering wheel from side to side and then up and down. Check that the steering wheel is not loose on the column, indicating wear or a loose retaining nut. Continue moving the steering wheel as before, but also turn it slightly from left to right.

☐ Check that the steering wheel is not loose on the column, and that there is no abnormal movement of the steering wheel, indicating wear in the column support bearings or couplings.
☐ Check that the ignition lock (where fitted) engages and disengages correctly.
☐ Steering column adjustment mechanisms (where fitted) must be able to lock the column securely in place with no play evident.

Windscreen, mirrors and sunvisor

☐ The windscreen must be free of cracks or other significant damage within the driver's field of view. (Small stone chips are acceptable.) Rear view mirrors must be secure, intact, and capable of being adjusted.

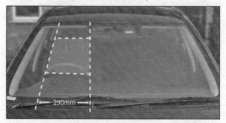

☐ The driver's sunvisor must be capable of being stored in the "up" position.

Seat belts and seats

Note: *The following checks are applicable to all seat belts, front and rear.*

☐ Examine the webbing of all the belts (including rear belts if fitted) for cuts, serious fraying or deterioration. Fasten and unfasten each belt to check the buckles. If applicable, check the retracting mechanism. Check the security of all seat belt mountings accessible from inside the vehicle, ensuring any height adjustable mountings lock securely in place.

☐ Seat belts with pre-tensioners, once activated, have a "flag" or similar showing on the seat belt stalk. This, in itself, is not a reason for test failure.

☐ The front seats themselves must be securely attached and the backrests must lock in the upright position.

Doors

☐ Both front doors must be able to be opened and closed from outside and inside, and must latch securely when closed.

Bonnet and boot/tailgate

☐ The bonnet and boot/tailgate must latch securely when closed.

2 Checks carried out WITH THE VEHICLE ON THE GROUND

Vehicle identification

☐ Number plates must be in good condition, secure and legible, with letters and numbers correctly spaced – spacing at (A) should be 33 mm and at (B) 11 mm. At the front, digits must be black on a white background and at the rear black on a yellow background. Other background designs (such as honeycomb) are not permitted.

☐ The VIN plate and/or homologation plate must be permanently displayed and legible.

Electrical equipment

☐ Switch on the ignition and check the operation of the horn.

☐ Check the windscreen washers and wipers, examining the wiper blades; renew damaged or perished blades. Also check the operation of the stop-lights.

☐ Check the operation of the sidelights and number plate lights. The lenses and reflectors must be secure, clean and undamaged.

☐ Check the operation and alignment of the headlights. The headlight reflectors must not be tarnished and the lenses must be undamaged.

☐ Switch on the ignition and check the operation of the direction indicators (including the instrument panel tell-tale) and the hazard warning lights. Operation of the sidelights and stop-lights must not affect the indicators - if it does, the cause is usually a bad earth at the rear light cluster. Indicators should flash at a rate of between 60 and 120 times per minute – faster or slower than this could indicate a fault with the flasher unit or a bad earth at one of the light units.

☐ Check the operation of the rear foglight(s), including the warning light on the instrument panel or in the switch.

☐ The warning lights must illuminate in accordance with the manufacturer's design. For most vehicles, the ABS and other warning lights should illuminate when the ignition is switched on, and (if the system is operating properly) extinguish after a few seconds. Refer to the owner's handbook.

Footbrake

☐ Examine the master cylinder, brake pipes and servo unit for leaks, loose mountings, corrosion or other damage. If ABS is fitted, this unit should also be examined for signs of leaks or corrosion.

☐ The fluid reservoir must be secure and the fluid level must be between the upper (**A**) and lower (**B**) markings.

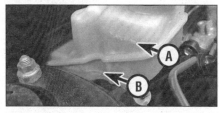

☐ Inspect both front brake flexible hoses for cracks or deterioration of the rubber. Turn the steering from lock to lock, and ensure that the hoses do not contact the wheel, tyre, or any part of the steering or suspension mechanism. With the brake pedal firmly depressed, check the hoses for bulges or leaks under pressure.

Steering and suspension

☐ Have your assistant turn the steering wheel from side to side slightly, up to the point where the steering gear just begins to transmit this movement to the roadwheels. Check for excessive free play between the steering wheel and the steering gear, indicating wear or insecurity of the steering column joints, the column-to-steering gear coupling, or the steering gear itself.

☐ Have your assistant turn the steering wheel more vigorously in each direction, so that the roadwheels just begin to turn. As this is done, examine all the steering joints, linkages, fittings and attachments. Renew any component that shows signs of wear or damage. On vehicles with power steering, check the security and condition of the steering pump, drivebelt and hoses.

☐ Check that the vehicle is standing level, and at approximately the correct ride height.

Shock absorbers

☐ Depress each corner of the vehicle in turn, then release it. The vehicle should rise and then settle in its normal position. If the vehicle continues to rise and fall, the shock absorber is defective. A shock absorber which has seized will also cause the vehicle to fail.

Exhaust system

☐ Start the engine. With your assistant holding a rag over the tailpipe, check the entire system for leaks. Repair or renew leaking sections.

3 Checks carried out
WITH THE VEHICLE RAISED AND THE WHEELS FREE TO TURN

Jack up the front and rear of the vehicle, and securely support it on axle stands. Position the stands clear of the suspension assemblies. Ensure that the wheels are clear of the ground and that the steering can be turned from lock to lock.

Steering mechanism

☐ Have your assistant turn the steering from lock to lock. Check that the steering turns smoothly, and that no part of the steering mechanism, including a wheel or tyre, fouls any brake hose or pipe or any part of the body structure.
☐ Examine the steering rack rubber gaiters for damage or insecurity of the retaining clips. If power steering is fitted, check for signs of damage or leakage of the fluid hoses, pipes or connections. Also check for excessive stiffness or binding of the steering, a missing split pin or locking device, or severe corrosion of the body structure within 30 cm of any steering component attachment point.

Front and rear suspension and wheel bearings

☐ Starting at the front right-hand side, grasp the roadwheel at the 3 o'clock and 9 o'clock positions and rock gently but firmly. Check for free play or insecurity at the wheel bearings, suspension balljoints, or suspension mount-ings, pivots and attachments.
☐ Now grasp the wheel at the 12 o'clock and 6 o'clock positions and repeat the previous inspection. Spin the wheel, and check for roughness or tightness of the front wheel bearing.

☐ If excess free play is suspected at a component pivot point, this can be confirmed by using a large screwdriver or similar tool and levering between the mounting and the component attachment. This will confirm whether the wear is in the pivot bush, its retaining bolt, or in the mounting itself (the bolt holes can often become elongated).

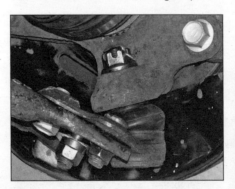

☐ Carry out all the above checks at the other front wheel, and then at both rear wheels.

Springs and shock absorbers

☐ Examine the suspension struts (when applicable) for serious fluid leakage, corrosion, or damage to the casing. Also check the security of the mounting points.
☐ If coil springs are fitted, check that the spring ends locate in their seats, and that the spring is not corroded, cracked or broken.
☐ If leaf springs are fitted, check that all leaves are intact, that the axle is securely attached to each spring, and that there is no deterioration of the spring eye mountings, bushes, and shackles.

☐ The same general checks apply to vehicles fitted with other suspension types, such as torsion bars, hydraulic displacer units, etc. Ensure that all mountings and attachments are secure, that there are no signs of excessive wear, corrosion or damage, and (on hydraulic types) that there are no fluid leaks or damaged pipes.
☐ Inspect the shock absorbers for signs of serious fluid leakage. Check for wear of the mounting bushes or attachments, or damage to the body of the unit.

Driveshafts
(fwd vehicles only)

☐ Rotate each front wheel in turn and inspect the constant velocity joint gaiters for splits or damage. Also check that each driveshaft is straight and undamaged.

Braking system

☐ If possible without dismantling, check brake pad wear and disc condition. Ensure that the friction lining material has not worn excessively, (A) and that the discs are not fractured, pitted, scored or badly worn (B).

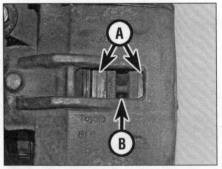

☐ Examine all the rigid brake pipes underneath the vehicle, and the flexible hose(s) at the rear. Look for corrosion, chafing or insecurity of the pipes, and for signs of bulging under pressure, chafing, splits or deterioration of the flexible hoses.
☐ Look for signs of fluid leaks at the brake calipers or on the brake backplates. Repair or renew leaking components.
☐ Slowly spin each wheel, while your assistant depresses and releases the footbrake. Ensure that each brake is operating and does not bind when the pedal is released.

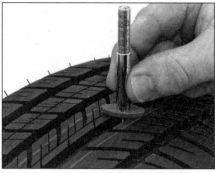

□ Examine the handbrake mechanism, checking for frayed or broken cables, excessive corrosion, or wear or insecurity of the linkage. Check that the mechanism works on each relevant wheel, and releases fully, without binding.

□ It is not possible to test brake efficiency without special equipment, but a road test can be carried out later to check that the vehicle pulls up in a straight line.

Fuel and exhaust systems

□ Inspect the fuel tank (including the filler cap), fuel pipes, hoses and unions. All components must be secure and free from leaks. Locking fuel caps must lock securely and the key must be provided for the MOT test.

□ Examine the exhaust system over its entire length, checking for any damaged, broken or missing mountings, security of the retaining clamps and rust or corrosion.

Wheels and tyres

□ Examine the sidewalls and tread area of each tyre in turn. Check for cuts, tears, lumps, bulges, separation of the tread, and exposure of the ply or cord due to wear or damage. Check that the tyre bead is correctly seated on the wheel rim, that the valve is sound and properly seated, and that the wheel is not distorted or damaged.

□ Check that the tyres are of the correct size for the vehicle, that they are of the same size and type on each axle, and that the pressures are correct.

□ Check the tyre tread depth. The legal minimum at the time of writing is 1.6 mm over the central three-quarters of the tread width. Abnormal tread wear may indicate incorrect front wheel alignment or wear in steering or suspension components.

□ If the spare wheel is fitted externally or in a separate carrier beneath the vehicle, check that mountings are secure and free of excessive corrosion.

Body corrosion

□ Check the condition of the entire vehicle structure for signs of corrosion in load-bearing areas. (These include chassis box sections, side sills, cross-members, pillars, and all suspension, steering, braking system and seat belt mountings and anchorages.) Any corrosion which has seriously reduced the thickness of a load-bearing area (or is within 30 cm of safety-related components such as steering or suspension) is likely to cause the vehicle to fail. In this case professional repairs are likely to be needed.

□ Damage or corrosion which causes sharp or otherwise dangerous edges to be exposed will also cause the vehicle to fail.

Towbars

□ Check the condition of mounting points (both beneath the vehicle and within boot/hatchback areas) for signs of corrosion, ensuring that all fixings are secure and not worn or damaged. There must be no excessive play in detachable tow ball arms or quick-release mechanisms.

4 Checks carried out on **YOUR VEHICLE'S EXHAUST EMISSION SYSTEM**

Petrol models

□ The engine should be warmed up, and running well (ignition system in good order, air filter element clean, etc).

□ Before testing, run the engine at around 2500 rpm for 20 seconds. Let the engine drop to idle, and watch for smoke from the exhaust. If the idle speed is too high, or if dense blue or black smoke emerges for more than 5 seconds, the vehicle will fail. Typically, blue smoke signifies oil burning (engine wear);

black smoke means unburnt fuel (dirty air cleaner element, or other fuel system fault).

□ An exhaust gas analyser for measuring carbon monoxide (CO) and hydrocarbons (HC) is now needed. If one cannot be hired or borrowed, have a local garage perform the check.

CO emissions (mixture)

□ The MOT tester has access to the CO limits for all vehicles. The CO level is measured at idle speed, and at 'fast idle' (2500 to 3000 rpm). The following limits are given as a general guide:

At idle speed – Less than 0.5% CO
At 'fast idle' – Less than 0.3% CO
Lambda reading – 0.97 to 1.03

□ If the CO level is too high, this may point to poor maintenance, a fuel injection system problem, faulty lambda (oxygen) sensor or catalytic converter. Try an injector cleaning treatment, and check the vehicle's ECU for fault codes.

HC emissions

□ The MOT tester has access to HC limits for all vehicles. The HC level is measured at 'fast idle' (2500 to 3000 rpm). The following limits are given as a general guide:

At 'fast idle' – Less then 200 ppm

□ Excessive HC emissions are typically caused by oil being burnt (worn engine), or by a blocked crankcase ventilation system ('breather'). If the engine oil is old and thin, an oil change may help. If the engine is running badly, check the vehicle's ECU for fault codes.

Diesel models

□ The only emission test for diesel engines is measuring exhaust smoke density, using a calibrated smoke meter. The test involves accelerating the engine at least 3 times to its maximum unloaded speed.

Note: *On engines with a timing belt, it is VITAL that the belt is in good condition before the test is carried out.*

□ With the engine warmed up, it is first purged by running at around 2500 rpm for 20 seconds. A governor check is then carried out, by slowly accelerating the engine to its maximum speed. After this, the smoke meter is connected, and the engine is accelerated quickly to maximum speed three times. If the smoke density is less than the limits given below, the vehicle will pass:

Non-turbo vehicles: 2.5m-1
Turbocharged vehicles: 3.0m-1

□ If excess smoke is produced, try fitting a new air cleaner element, or using an injector cleaning treatment. If the engine is running badly, where applicable, check the vehicle's ECU for fault codes. Also check the vehicle's EGR system, where applicable. At high mileages, the injectors may require professional attention.

Engine

- ☐ Engine fails to rotate when attempting to start
- ☐ Engine rotates, but will not start
- ☐ Engine difficult to start when cold
- ☐ Engine difficult to start when hot
- ☐ Starter motor noisy or excessively-rough in engagement
- ☐ Engine starts, but stops immediately
- ☐ Engine idles erratically
- ☐ Engine misfires at idle speed
- ☐ Engine misfires throughout the driving speed range
- ☐ Engine hesitates on acceleration
- ☐ Engine stalls
- ☐ Engine lacks power
- ☐ Engine backfires
- ☐ Oil pressure warning light illuminated with engine running
- ☐ Engine runs-on after switching off
- ☐ Engine noises

Cooling system

- ☐ Overheating
- ☐ Overcooling
- ☐ External coolant leakage
- ☐ Internal coolant leakage
- ☐ Corrosion

Fuel and exhaust systems

- ☐ Excessive fuel consumption
- ☐ Fuel leakage and/or fuel odour
- ☐ Excessive noise or fumes from exhaust system

Clutch

- ☐ Pedal travels to floor – no pressure or very little resistance
- ☐ Clutch fails to disengage (unable to select gears)
- ☐ Clutch slips (engine speed increases, with no increase in vehicle speed)
- ☐ Judder as clutch is engaged
- ☐ Noise when depressing or releasing clutch pedal

Manual transmission

- ☐ Noisy in neutral with engine running
- ☐ Noisy in one particular gear
- ☐ Difficulty engaging gears
- ☐ Jumps out of gear
- ☐ Vibration
- ☐ Lubricant leaks

Automatic transmission

- ☐ Fluid leakage
- ☐ General gear selection problems
- ☐ Transmission will not downshift (kickdown) with accelerator pedal fully depressed
- ☐ Engine will not start in any gear, or starts in gears other than Park or Neutral
- ☐ Transmission slips, shifts roughly, is noisy, or has no drive in forward or reverse gears

Driveshafts

- ☐ Vibration when accelerating or decelerating
- ☐ Clicking or knocking noise on turns (at slow speed on full-lock)

Braking system

- ☐ Vehicle pulls to one side under braking
- ☐ Noise (grinding or high-pitched squeal) when brakes applied
- ☐ Excessive brake pedal travel
- ☐ Brake pedal feels spongy when depressed
- ☐ Excessive brake pedal effort required to stop vehicle
- ☐ Judder felt through brake pedal or steering wheel when braking
- ☐ Pedal pulsates when braking hard
- ☐ Brakes binding
- ☐ Rear wheels locking under normal braking

Steering and suspension

- ☐ Vehicle pulls to one side
- ☐ Wheel wobble and vibration
- ☐ Excessive pitching and/or rolling around corners, or during braking
- ☐ Hard, or over-firm suspension
- ☐ Wandering or general instability
- ☐ Excessively-stiff steering
- ☐ Excessive play in steering
- ☐ Lack of power assistance
- ☐ Tyre wear excessive

Electrical system

- ☐ Battery will not hold a charge for more than a few days
- ☐ Ignition/no-charge warning light remains illuminated with engine running
- ☐ Ignition/no-charge warning light fails to come on
- ☐ Lights inoperative
- ☐ Instrument readings inaccurate or erratic
- ☐ Horn inoperative, or unsatisfactory in operation
- ☐ Windscreen/tailgate wipers inoperative, or unsatisfactory in operation
- ☐ Windscreen washers inoperative, or unsatisfactory in operation
- ☐ Electric windows inoperative, or unsatisfactory in operation

Introduction

The vehicle owner who does his or her own maintenance according to the recommended service schedules should not have to use this section of the manual very often. Modern component reliability is such that, provided those items subject to wear or deterioration are inspected or renewed at the specified intervals, sudden failure is comparatively rare. Faults do not usually just happen as a result of sudden failure, but develop over a period of time. Major mechanical failures in particular are usually preceded by characteristic symptoms over hundreds or even thousands of miles. Those components which do occasionally fail without warning are often small and easily carried in the vehicle.

With any fault-finding, the first step is to decide where to begin investigations. Sometimes this is obvious, but on other occasions, a little detective work will be necessary. The owner who makes half a dozen haphazard adjustments or replacements may be successful in curing a fault (or its symptoms), but will be none the wiser if the fault recurs, and ultimately may have spent more time and money than was necessary.

A calm and logical approach will be found to be more satisfactory in the long run. Always take into account any warning signs or abnormalities that may have been noticed in the period preceding the fault – power loss, high or low gauge readings, unusual smells, etc – and remember that failure of components such as fuses or spark plugs may only be pointers to some underlying fault.

The pages which follow provide an easy-reference guide to the more common problems which may occur during the operation of the vehicle. These problems and their possible causes are grouped under headings denoting various components or systems, such as Engine, Cooling system, etc. The general Chapter which deals with the problem is also shown in brackets; refer to the relevant part of that Chapter for system-specific information. Whatever the fault, certain basic principles apply. These are as follows:

Verify the fault. This is simply a matter of being sure that you know what the symptoms are before starting work. This is particularly important if you are investigating a fault for someone else, who may not have described it very accurately.

Don't overlook the obvious. For example, if the vehicle won't start, is there fuel in the tank? (Don't take anyone else's word on this particular point, and don't trust the fuel gauge either!) If an electrical fault is indicated, look for loose or broken wires before digging out the test gear.

Cure the disease, not the symptom. Substituting a flat battery with a fully-charged one will get you off the hard shoulder, but if the underlying cause is not attended to, the new battery will go the same way. Similarly, changing oil-fouled spark plugs for a new set will get you moving again, but remember that the reason for the fouling (if it wasn't simply an incorrect grade of plug) will have to be established and corrected.

Don't take anything for granted. Particularly, don't forget that a new component may itself be defective (especially if its been rattling around in the boot for months), and don't leave components out of a fault diagnosis sequence just because they are new or recently-fitted. When you do finally diagnose a difficult fault, you'll probably realise that all the evidence was there from the start.

Diesel fault diagnosis

The majority of starting problems on small diesel engines are electrical in origin. The mechanic who is familiar with petrol engines but less so with diesel may be inclined to view the diesel's injectors and pump in the same light as the spark plugs and distributor, but this is generally a mistake.

When investigating complaints of difficult starting for someone else, make sure that the correct starting procedure is understood and is being followed. Some drivers are unaware of the significance of the preheating warning light – many modern engines are sufficiently forgiving for this not to matter in mild weather, but with the onset of winter, problems begin.

As a rule of thumb, if the engine is difficult to start but runs well when it has finally got going, the problem is electrical (battery, starter motor or preheating system). If poor performance is combined with difficult starting, the problem is likely to be in the fuel system. The low-pressure (supply) side of the fuel system should be checked before suspecting the injectors and high-pressure pump. The most common fuel supply problem is air getting into the system, and any pipe from the fuel tank forwards must be scrutinised if air leakage is suspected. Normally the pump is the last item to suspect, since unless it has been tampered with, there is no reason for it to be at fault.

Engine

Engine fails to rotate when attempting to start

- ☐ Battery terminal connections loose or corroded (see *Weekly checks*).
- ☐ Battery discharged or faulty (Chapter 5A).
- ☐ Broken, loose or disconnected wiring in the starting circuit (Chapter 5A).
- ☐ Defective starter solenoid or switch (Chapter 5A).
- ☐ Defective starter motor (Chapter 5A).
- ☐ Starter pinion or flywheel/driveplate ring gear teeth loose or broken (Chapter 2 and 5A).
- ☐ Engine earth strap broken or disconnected (Chapter 5A or 12).

Engine rotates, but will not start

- ☐ Fuel tank empty.
- ☐ Battery discharged (engine rotates slowly) (Chapter 5A).
- ☐ Battery terminal connections loose or corroded (see *Weekly checks*).
- ☐ Ignition components damp or damaged – petrol models (Chapters 1A and 5B).
- ☐ Broken, loose or disconnected wiring in the ignition circuit – petrol models (Chapters 1A and 5B).
- ☐ Worn, faulty or incorrectly-gapped spark plugs – petrol models (Chapter 1A).
- ☐ Preheating system faulty – diesel models (Chapter 5A).
- ☐ Fuel injection system fault – petrol models (Chapter 4A).
- ☐ Air in fuel system – diesel models (Chapter 4B).
- ☐ Major mechanical failure (e.g. timing belt) (Chapter 2).

Engine difficult to start when cold

- ☐ Battery discharged (Chapter 5A).
- ☐ Battery terminal connections loose or corroded (see *Weekly checks*).
- ☐ Worn, faulty or incorrectly-gapped spark plugs – petrol models (Chapter 1A).
- ☐ Preheating system faulty – diesel models (Chapter 5A).
- ☐ Fuel injection system fault – petrol models (Chapter 4A).
- ☐ Other ignition system fault – petrol models (Chapters 1A and 5B).
- ☐ Low cylinder compressions (Chapter 2).

Engine difficult to start when hot

- ☐ Air filter element dirty or clogged (Chapter 1).
- ☐ Fuel injection system fault – petrol models (Chapter 4A).
- ☐ Low cylinder compressions (Chapter 2).

Starter motor noisy or excessively-rough in engagement

- ☐ Starter pinion or flywheel ring gear teeth loose or broken (Chapter 2 and 5A).
- ☐ Starter motor mounting bolts loose or missing (Chapter 5A).
- ☐ Starter motor internal components worn or damaged (Chapter 5A).

Engine starts, but stops immediately

- ☐ Loose or faulty electrical connections in the ignition circuit – petrol models (Chapters 1A and 5B).
- ☐ Vacuum leak at the throttle body or inlet manifold – petrol models (Chapter 4A).
- ☐ Blocked injector/fuel injection system fault – petrol models (Chapter 4A).
- ☐ Poor fuel supply (Chapter 4).

Engine (continued)

Engine idles erratically

- [ ] Air filter element clogged (Chapter 1).
- [ ] Vacuum leak at the throttle body, inlet manifold or associated hoses – petrol models (Chapter 4A).
- [ ] Worn, faulty or incorrectly-gapped spark plugs – petrol models (Chapter 1A).
- [ ] Uneven or low cylinder compressions (Chapter 2).
- [ ] Camshaft lobes worn (Chapter 2).
- [ ] Timing belt incorrectly fitted (Chapter 2).
- [ ] Blocked injector/fuel injection system fault – petrol models (Chapter 4A).
- [ ] Faulty injector(s) – diesel models (Chapter 4B).

Engine misfires at idle speed

- [ ] Worn, faulty or incorrectly-gapped spark plugs – petrol models (Chapter 1A).
- [ ] Vacuum leak at the throttle body, inlet manifold or associated hoses – petrol models (Chapter 4A).
- [ ] Blocked injector/fuel injection system fault – petrol models (Chapter 4A).
- [ ] Faulty injector(s) – diesel models (Chapter 4B).
- [ ] Uneven or low cylinder compressions (Chapter 2).
- [ ] Disconnected, leaking, or perished crankcase ventilation hoses (Chapter 4C).

Engine misfires throughout the driving speed range

- [ ] Fuel filter choked (Chapter 1).
- [ ] Fuel pump faulty, or delivery pressure low – petrol models (Chapter 4A).
- [ ] Fuel tank vent blocked, or fuel pipes restricted (Chapter 4).
- [ ] Vacuum leak at the throttle body, inlet manifold or associated hoses – petrol models (Chapter 4A).
- [ ] Worn, faulty or incorrectly-gapped spark plugs – petrol models (Chapter 1A).
- [ ] Faulty injector(s) – diesel models (Chapter 4B).
- [ ] Faulty ignition coil – petrol models (Chapter 5B).
- [ ] Uneven or low cylinder compressions (Chapter 2).
- [ ] Blocked injector/fuel injection system fault – petrol models (Chapter 4A).

Engine hesitates on acceleration

- [ ] Worn, faulty or incorrectly-gapped spark plugs – petrol models (Chapter 1A).
- [ ] Vacuum leak at the throttle body, inlet manifold or associated hoses – petrol models (Chapter 4A).
- [ ] Blocked injector/fuel injection system fault – petrol models (Chapter 4A).
- [ ] Faulty injector(s) – diesel models (Chapter 4B).

Engine stalls

- [ ] Vacuum leak at the throttle body, inlet manifold or associated hoses – petrol models (Chapter 4A).
- [ ] Fuel filter choked (Chapter 1).
- [ ] Fuel pump faulty, or delivery pressure low – petrol models (Chapter 4A).
- [ ] Fuel tank vent blocked, or fuel pipes restricted (Chapter 4).
- [ ] Blocked injector/fuel injection system fault – petrol models (Chapter 4A).
- [ ] Faulty injector(s) – diesel models (Chapter 4B).

Engine lacks power

- [ ] Timing belt incorrectly fitted or tensioned (Chapter 2).
- [ ] Fuel filter choked (Chapter 1).
- [ ] Fuel pump faulty, or delivery pressure low – petrol models (Chapter 4A).

- [ ] Uneven or low cylinder compressions (Chapter 2).
- [ ] Worn, faulty or incorrectly-gapped spark plugs – petrol models (Chapter 1A).
- [ ] Vacuum leak at the throttle body, inlet manifold or associated hoses – petrol models (Chapter 4A).
- [ ] Blocked injector/fuel injection system fault – petrol models (Chapter 4A).
- [ ] Faulty injector(s) – diesel models (Chapter 4B).
- [ ] Brakes binding (Chapter 9).
- [ ] Clutch slipping (Chapter 6).
- [ ] Air filter element clogged (Chapter 1).

Engine backfires

- [ ] Timing belt incorrectly fitted or tensioned (Chapter 2).
- [ ] Vacuum leak at the throttle body, inlet manifold or associated hoses – petrol models (Chapter 4A).
- [ ] Blocked injector/fuel injection system fault – petrol models (Chapter 4A).

Oil pressure warning light illuminated with engine running

- [ ] Low oil level, or incorrect oil grade (Weekly checks).
- [ ] Faulty oil pressure switch (Chapter 5A).
- [ ] Worn engine bearings and/or oil pump (Chapter 2).
- [ ] High engine operating temperature (Chapter 3).
- [ ] Oil pressure relief valve defective (Chapter 2).
- [ ] Oil pick-up strainer clogged (Chapter 2).

Engine runs-on after switching off

- [ ] Excessive carbon build-up in engine (Chapter 2).
- [ ] High engine operating temperature (Chapter 3).
- [ ] Fuel injection system fault – petrol models (Chapter 4A).

Engine noises

Pre-ignition (pinking) or knocking during acceleration or under load

- [ ] Ignition system fault – petrol models (Chapters 1A and 5B).
- [ ] Defective knock sensor – petrol models (Chapter 5B).
- [ ] Incorrect grade of spark plug – petrol models (Chapter 1A).
- [ ] Vacuum leak at the throttle body, inlet manifold or associated hoses – petrol models (Chapter 4A).
- [ ] Excessive carbon build-up in engine (Chapter 2).
- [ ] Blocked injector/fuel injection system fault – petrol models (Chapter 4A).

Whistling or wheezing noises

- [ ] Leaking inlet manifold or throttle body gasket – petrol models (Chapter 4A).
- [ ] Leaking exhaust manifold gasket or pipe-to-manifold joint (Chapter 4).
- [ ] Leaking vacuum hose (Chapters 4 and 9).
- [ ] Blowing cylinder head gasket (Chapter 2).

Tapping or rattling noises

- [ ] Worn valve gear or camshaft (Chapter 2).
- [ ] Ancillary component fault (coolant pump, alternator, etc) (Chapters 3, 5, etc).

Knocking or thumping noises

- [ ] Worn big-end bearings (regular heavy knocking, perhaps less under load) (Chapter 2).
- [ ] Worn main bearings (rumbling and knocking, perhaps worsening under load) (Chapter 2).
- [ ] Piston slap (most noticeable when cold) (Chapter 2).
- [ ] Ancillary component fault (coolant pump, alternator, etc) (Chapters 3, 5, etc).

Cooling system

Overheating

- [ ] Insufficient coolant in system (*Weekly checks*).
- [ ] Thermostat faulty (Chapter 3).
- [ ] Radiator core blocked, or grille restricted (Chapter 3).
- [ ] Electric cooling fan or thermostatic switch faulty (Chapter 3).
- [ ] Inaccurate temperature gauge sender unit (Chapter 3).
- [ ] Airlock in cooling system (Chapter 1).
- [ ] Expansion tank pressure cap faulty (Chapter 3).

Overcooling

- [ ] Thermostat faulty (Chapter 3).
- [ ] Inaccurate temperature gauge sender unit (Chapter 3).

External coolant leakage

- [ ] Deteriorated or damaged hoses or hose clips (Chapter 1).

- [ ] Radiator core or heater matrix leaking (Chapter 3).
- [ ] Pressure cap faulty (Chapter 3).
- [ ] Coolant pump internal seal leaking (Chapter 3).
- [ ] Coolant pump-to-housing seal leaking (Chapter 3).
- [ ] Boiling due to overheating (Chapter 3).
- [ ] Core plug leaking (Chapter 2).

Internal coolant leakage

- [ ] Leaking cylinder head gasket (Chapter 2).
- [ ] Cracked cylinder head or cylinder block (Chapter 2).

Corrosion

- [ ] Infrequent draining and flushing (Chapter 1).
- [ ] Incorrect coolant mixture or inappropriate coolant type (see *Weekly checks*).

Fuel and exhaust systems

Excessive fuel consumption

- [ ] Air filter element dirty or clogged (Chapter 1).
- [ ] Fuel injection system fault – petrol models (Chapter 4A).
- [ ] Faulty injector(s) – diesel models (Chapter 4B).
- [ ] Ignition system fault – petrol models (Chapters 1A and 5B).
- [ ] Tyres under-inflated (see *Weekly checks*).

Fuel leakage and/or fuel odour

- [ ] Damaged fuel tank, pipes or connections (Chapter 4).

Excessive noise or fumes from exhaust system

- [ ] Leaking exhaust system or manifold joints (Chapters 1 and 4).
- [ ] Leaking, corroded or damaged silencers or pipe (Chapters 1 and 4).
- [ ] Broken mountings causing body or suspension contact (Chapter 1).

Clutch

Pedal travels to floor – no pressure or very little resistance

- [ ] Faulty master or slave cylinder (Chapter 6).
- [ ] Faulty hydraulic release system (Chapter 6).
- [ ] Broken clutch release bearing or arm (Chapter 6).
- [ ] Broken diaphragm spring in clutch pressure plate (Chapter 6).

Clutch fails to disengage (unable to select gears)

- [ ] Faulty master or slave cylinder (Chapter 6).
- [ ] Faulty hydraulic release system (Chapter 6).
- [ ] Clutch disc sticking on gearbox input shaft splines (Chapter 6).
- [ ] Clutch disc sticking to flywheel or pressure plate (Chapter 6).
- [ ] Faulty pressure plate assembly (Chapter 6).
- [ ] Clutch release mechanism worn or incorrectly assembled (Chapter 6).

Clutch slips (engine speed increases, with no increase in vehicle speed)

- [ ] Faulty hydraulic release system (Chapter 6).

- [ ] Clutch disc linings excessively worn (Chapter 6).
- [ ] Clutch disc linings contaminated with oil or grease (Chapter 6).
- [ ] Faulty pressure plate or weak diaphragm spring (Chapter 6).

Judder as clutch is engaged

- [ ] Clutch disc linings contaminated with oil or grease (Chapter 6).
- [ ] Clutch disc linings excessively worn (Chapter 6).
- [ ] Faulty or distorted pressure plate or diaphragm spring (Chapter 6).
- [ ] Worn or loose engine or gearbox mountings (Chapter 2).
- [ ] Clutch disc hub or gearbox input shaft splines worn (Chapter 6).

Noise when depressing or releasing clutch pedal

- [ ] Worn clutch release bearing (Chapter 6).
- [ ] Worn or dry clutch pedal pivot (Chapter 6).
- [ ] Faulty pressure plate assembly (Chapter 6).
- [ ] Pressure plate diaphragm spring broken (Chapter 6).
- [ ] Broken clutch friction plate cushioning springs (Chapter 6).

Manual transmission

Noisy in neutral with engine running

☐ Input shaft bearings worn (noise apparent with clutch pedal released, but not when depressed) (Chapter 7A).*
☐ Clutch release bearing worn (noise apparent with clutch pedal depressed, possibly less when released) (Chapter 6).

Noisy in one particular gear

☐ Worn, damaged or chipped gear teeth (Chapter 7A).*

Difficulty engaging gears

☐ Clutch fault (Chapter 6).
☐ Worn or damaged gear linkage (Chapter 7A).
☐ Worn synchroniser units (Chapter 7A).*

Jumps out of gear

☐ Worn or damaged gear change cables (Chapter 7A).

☐ Worn synchroniser units (Chapter 7A).*
☐ Worn selector forks (Chapter 7A).*

Vibration

☐ Lack of oil (Chapter 1).
☐ Worn bearings (Chapter 7A).*

Lubricant leaks

☐ Leaking oil seal (Chapter 7A).
☐ Leaking housing joint (Chapter 7A).*
☐ Leaking input shaft oil seal (Chapter 7A).

Although the corrective action necessary to remedy the symptoms described is beyond the scope of the home mechanic, the above information should be helpful in isolating the cause of the condition, so that the owner can communicate clearly with a professional mechanic.

Automatic transmission

Note: *Due to the complexity of the automatic transmission, it is difficult for the home mechanic to properly diagnose and service this unit. For problems other than the following, the vehicle should be taken to a dealer service department or automatic transmission specialist. Do not be too hasty in removing the transmission if a fault is suspected, as most of the testing is carried out with the unit still fitted.*

Fluid leakage

☐ Automatic transmission fluid is usually dark in colour. Fluid leaks should not be confused with engine oil, which can easily be blown onto the transmission by airflow.
☐ To determine the source of a leak, first remove all built-up dirt and grime from the transmission housing and surrounding areas using a degreasing agent, or by steam-cleaning. Drive the vehicle at low speed, so airflow will not blow the leak far from its source. Raise and support the vehicle, and determine where the leak is coming from.

General gear selection problems

☐ Chapter 7 deals with checking and adjusting the selector mechanism on automatic transmissions. The following are common problems which may be caused by a poorly-adjusted mechanism:
a) *Engine starting in gears other than Park or Neutral.*
b) *Indicator panel indicating a gear other than the one actually being used.*

c) *Vehicle moves when in Park or Neutral.*
d) *Poor gear shift quality or erratic gear changes.*
☐ Refer to Chapter 7B for the selector mechanism adjustment procedure.

Transmission will not downshift (kickdown) with accelerator pedal fully depressed

☐ Low transmission fluid level (Chapter 1).
☐ Transmission ECM software problem (Chapter 7B).

Engine will not start in any gear, or starts in gears other than Park or Neutral

☐ Faulty transmission electronic component (Chapter 7B).
☐ Incorrect selector cable adjustment (Chapter 7B).

Transmission slips, shifts roughly, is noisy, or has no drive in forward or reverse gears

☐ There are many probable causes for the above problems, but unless there is a very obvious reason (such as a loose or corroded wiring plug connection on or near the transmission), the car should be taken to a franchise dealer or specialist for the fault to be diagnosed. The transmission control unit incorporates a self-diagnosis facility, and any fault codes can quickly be read and interpreted by a dealer with the proper diagnostic equipment.

Driveshafts

Vibration when accelerating or decelerating

☐ Worn inner constant velocity joint (Chapter 8).
☐ Bent or distorted driveshaft (Chapter 8).

Clicking or knocking noise on turns (at slow speed on full-lock)

☐ Worn outer constant velocity joint (Chapter 8).
☐ Lack of constant velocity joint lubricant, possibly due to damaged gaiter (Chapter 8).

Braking system

Note: *Before assuming that a brake problem exists, make sure that the tyres are in good condition and correctly inflated, that the front wheel alignment is correct, and that the vehicle is not loaded with weight in an unequal manner. Apart from checking the condition of all pipe and hose connections, any faults occurring on the anti-lock braking system should be referred to a Citroen dealer for diagnosis.*

Vehicle pulls to one side under braking

☐ Worn, defective, damaged or contaminated front or rear brake pads on one side (Chapters 1 and 9).
☐ Seized or partially-seized front or rear brake caliper (Chapter 9).
☐ A mixture of brake pad lining materials fitted between sides (Chapter 9).
☐ Brake caliper mounting bolts loose (Chapter 9).
☐ Worn or damaged steering or suspension components (Chapters 1 and 10).

Noise (grinding or high-pitched squeal) when brakes applied

☐ Brake pad friction lining material worn down to metal backing (Chapters 1 and 9).
☐ Excessive corrosion of brake disc – may be apparent after the vehicle has been standing for some time (Chapters 1 and 9).
☐ Foreign object (stone chipping, etc) trapped between brake disc and shield (Chapters 1 and 9).

Excessive brake pedal travel

☐ Faulty master cylinder (Chapter 9).
☐ Air in hydraulic system (Chapter 9).
☐ Faulty vacuum servo unit (Chapter 9).
☐ Faulty vacuum pump, where fitted (Chapter 9).

Brake pedal feels spongy when depressed

☐ Air in hydraulic system (Chapter 9).
☐ Deteriorated flexible rubber brake hoses (Chapters 1 and 9).
☐ Master cylinder mountings loose (Chapter 9).
☐ Faulty master cylinder (Chapter 9).

Excessive brake pedal effort required to stop vehicle

☐ Faulty vacuum servo unit (Chapter 9).
☐ Disconnected, damaged or insecure brake servo vacuum hose (Chapters 1 and 9).
☐ Faulty vacuum pump, where fitted (Chapter 9).
☐ Primary or secondary hydraulic circuit failure (Chapter 9).
☐ Seized brake caliper (Chapter 9).
☐ Brake pads incorrectly fitted (Chapter 9).
☐ Incorrect grade of brake pads fitted (Chapter 9).
☐ Brake pads contaminated (Chapter 9).

Judder felt through brake pedal or steering wheel when braking

☐ Excessive run-out or distortion of brake disc(s) (Chapter 9).
☐ Brake pad linings worn (Chapters 1 and 9).
☐ Brake caliper mounting bolts loose (Chapter 9).
☐ Wear in suspension or steering components or mountings (Chapters 1 and 10).

Pedal pulsates when braking hard

☐ Normal feature of ABS – no fault

Brakes binding

☐ Seized brake caliper piston(s) (Chapter 9).
☐ Incorrectly-adjusted handbrake mechanism (Chapter 9).
☐ Faulty master cylinder (Chapter 9).

Rear wheels locking under normal braking

☐ Rear brake pad linings contaminated (Chapters 1 and 9).
☐ Rear brake discs warped (Chapters 1 and 9).
☐ ABS ECM/Modulator fault (Chapter 9).

Steering and suspension

Note: *Before diagnosing suspension or steering faults, be sure that the trouble is not due to incorrect tyre pressures, mixtures of tyre types, or binding brakes.*

Vehicle pulls to one side

☐ Defective tyre (see *Weekly checks*).
☐ Excessive wear in suspension or steering components (Chapters 1 and 10).
☐ Incorrect front wheel alignment (Chapter 10).
☐ Accident damage to steering or suspension components (Chapters 1 and 10).

Wheel wobble and vibration

☐ Front roadwheels out of balance (vibration felt mainly through the steering wheel) (Chapter 10).
☐ Rear roadwheels out of balance (vibration felt throughout the vehicle) (Chapter 10).
☐ Roadwheels damaged or distorted (Chapter 10).
☐ Faulty or damaged tyre (*Weekly checks*).
☐ Worn steering or suspension joints, bushes or components (Chapters 1 and 10).
☐ Wheel nuts loose (Chapter 1 and 10).

Excessive pitching and/or rolling around corners, or during braking

☐ Defective shock absorbers (Chapters 1 and 10).
☐ Broken or weak suspension component (Chapters 1 and 10).
☐ Worn or damaged anti-roll bar or mountings (Chapter 10).

Excessively firm/hard suspension

☐ Defective suspension sphere (Chapter 10)

Wandering or general instability

☐ Incorrect front wheel alignment (Chapter 10).
☐ Worn steering or suspension joints, bushes or components (Chapters 1 and 10).
☐ Roadwheels out of balance (Chapter 10).
☐ Faulty or damaged tyre (*Weekly checks*).
☐ Wheel nuts loose (Chapter 10).
☐ Defective shock absorbers (Chapters 1 and 10).

Excessively-stiff steering

☐ Seized track rod end balljoint or suspension balljoint (Chapters 1 and 10).
☐ Broken or incorrectly adjusted auxiliary drivebelt (Chapter 1).
☐ Incorrect front wheel alignment (Chapter 10).
☐ Steering gear damaged (Chapter 10).

Excessive play in steering

☐ Worn steering column universal joint(s) (Chapter 10).
☐ Worn steering track rod end balljoints (Chapters 1 and 10).
☐ Worn steering rack (Chapter 10).
☐ Worn steering or suspension joints, bushes or components (Chapters 1 and 10).

Lack of power assistance

☐ Broken or incorrectly-adjusted auxiliary drivebelt (Chapter 1).
☐ Incorrect hydraulic fluid level (*Weekly checks*).
☐ Restriction in power steering fluid hoses (Chapter 10).
☐ Faulty power steering pump (Chapter 10).
☐ Faulty steering rack (Chapter 10).

Tyre wear excessive

Tyres worn on inside or outside edges

☐ Incorrect camber or castor angles (Chapter 10).
☐ Worn steering or suspension joints, bushes or components (Chapters 1 and 10).
☐ Excessively-hard cornering.
☐ Accident damage.

Tyre treads exhibit feathered edges

☐ Incorrect toe setting (Chapter 10).

Tyres worn in centre of tread

☐ Tyres over-inflated (*Weekly checks*).

Tyres worn on inside and outside edges

☐ Tyres under-inflated (*Weekly checks*).
☐ Worn shock absorbers (Chapter 10).

Tyres worn unevenly

☐ Tyres/wheels out of balance (*Weekly checks*).
☐ Excessive wheel or tyre run-out (Chapter 10).
☐ Worn shock absorbers (Chapters 1 and 10).
☐ Faulty tyre (*Weekly checks*).

Electrical system

Note: *For problems associated with the starting system, refer to the faults listed under Engine earlier in this Section.*

Battery will not hold a charge more than a few days

☐ Battery defective internally (Chapter 5A).
☐ Battery terminal connections loose or corroded (*Weekly checks*).
☐ Auxiliary drivebelt worn – or incorrectly adjusted, where applicable (Chapter 1).
☐ Alternator not charging at correct output (Chapter 5A).
☐ Alternator or voltage regulator faulty (Chapter 5A).
☐ Short-circuit causing continual battery drain (Chapters 5 and 12).

Ignition/no-charge warning light remains illuminated with engine running

☐ Auxiliary drivebelt broken, worn, or incorrectly adjusted (Chapter 1).
☐ Internal fault in alternator or voltage regulator (Chapter 5A).
☐ Broken, disconnected, or loose wiring in charging circuit (Chapter 5A).

Ignition/no-charge warning light fails to come on

☐ Broken, disconnected, or loose wiring in warning light circuit (Chapter 12).
☐ Alternator faulty (Chapter 5A).

Lights inoperative

☐ Bulb blown (Chapter 12).
☐ Corrosion of bulb or bulbholder contacts (Chapter 12).
☐ Blown fuse (Chapter 12).
☐ Faulty BSI or relay (Chapter 12).
☐ Broken, loose, or disconnected wiring (Chapter 12).
☐ Faulty switch (Chapter 12).

Instrument readings inaccurate or erratic

Fuel or temperature gauges give no reading

☐ Faulty coolant temperature sensor (Chapter 3).
☐ Wiring open-circuit (Chapter 12).
☐ Faulty gauge (Chapter 12).

Fuel or temperature gauges give continuous maximum reading

☐ Faulty coolant temperature sensor (Chapters 3).
☐ Wiring short-circuit (Chapter 12).
☐ Faulty gauge (Chapter 12).

Horn inoperative, or unsatisfactory in operation

Horn operates all the time

☐ Horn contacts permanently bridged or horn push stuck down (Chapter 12).

Horn fails to operate

☐ Blown fuse (Chapter 12).
☐ Cable or cable connections loose, broken or disconnected (Chapter 12).
☐ Faulty horn (Chapter 12).

Horn emits intermittent or unsatisfactory sound

☐ Cable connections loose (Chapter 12).
☐ Horn mountings loose (Chapter 12).
☐ Faulty horn (Chapter 12).

Windscreen/tailgate wipers inoperative, or unsatisfactory in operation

Wipers fail to operate, or operate very slowly

☐ Wiper blades stuck to screen, or linkage seized or binding (*Weekly checks* and Chapter 12).
☐ Blown fuse (Chapter 12).

☐ Cable or cable connections loose, broken or disconnected (Chapter 12).
☐ Faulty BSI/relay (Chapter 12).
☐ Faulty wiper motor (Chapter 12).

Wiper blades sweep over too large or too small an area of the glass

☐ Wiper arms incorrectly positioned on spindles (Chapter 12).
☐ Excessive wear of wiper linkage (Chapter 12).
☐ Wiper motor or linkage mountings loose or insecure (Chapter 12).
☐ Incorrect specification wiper blade fitted.

Wiper blades fail to clean the glass effectively

☐ Wiper blade rubbers worn or perished (*Weekly checks*).
☐ Wiper arm tension springs broken, or arm pivots seized (Chapter 12).
☐ Insufficient windscreen washer additive to adequately remove road film (*Weekly checks*).

Windscreen washers inoperative, or unsatisfactory in operation

One or more washer jets inoperative

☐ Blocked washer jet (Chapter 12).
☐ Disconnected, kinked or restricted fluid hose (Chapter 12).
☐ Insufficient fluid in washer reservoir (*Weekly checks*).

Washer pump fails to operate

☐ Broken or disconnected wiring or connections (Chapter 12).
☐ Blown fuse (Chapter 12).
☐ Faulty washer switch (Chapter 12).
☐ Faulty washer pump (Chapter 12).

Electric windows inoperative, or unsatisfactory in operation

Window glass will only move in one direction

☐ Faulty switch (Chapter 12).

Window glass slow to move

☐ Regulator seized or damaged, or in need of lubrication (Chapter 11).
☐ Door internal components or trim fouling regulator (Chapter 11).
☐ Faulty motor (Chapter 11).

Window glass fails to move

☐ Blown fuse (Chapter 12).
☐ Faulty BSI or relay (Chapter 12).
☐ Broken or disconnected wiring or connections (Chapter 12).
☐ Faulty motor (Chapter 12).

Central locking system inoperative, or unsatisfactory in operation

Complete system failure

☐ Blown fuse (Chapter 12).
☐ Faulty BSI (Chapter 12).
☐ Broken or disconnected wiring or connections (Chapter 12).

Latch locks but will not unlock, or unlocks but will not lock

☐ Faulty switch (Chapter 12).
☐ Broken or disconnected latch operating rods or levers (Chapter 11).
☐ Faulty BSI (Chapter 12).

One lock fails to operate

☐ Broken or disconnected wiring or connections (Chapter 12).
☐ Faulty motor (Chapter 11).
☐ Broken, binding or disconnected lock operating rods or levers (Chapter 11).
☐ Fault in door lock (Chapter 11).

A

ABS (Anti-lock brake system) A system, usually electronically controlled, that senses incipient wheel lockup during braking and relieves hydraulic pressure at wheels that are about to skid.

Air bag An inflatable bag hidden in the steering wheel (driver's side) or the dash or glovebox (passenger side). In a head-on collision, the bags inflate, preventing the driver and front passenger from being thrown forward into the steering wheel or windscreen.

Air cleaner A metal or plastic housing, containing a filter element, which removes dust and dirt from the air being drawn into the engine.

Air filter element The actual filter in an air cleaner system, usually manufactured from pleated paper and requiring renewal at regular intervals.

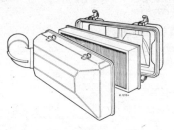

Air filter

Allen key A hexagonal wrench which fits into a recessed hexagonal hole.

Alligator clip A long-nosed spring-loaded metal clip with meshing teeth. Used to make temporary electrical connections.

Alternator A component in the electrical system which converts mechanical energy from a drivebelt into electrical energy to charge the battery and to operate the starting system, ignition system and electrical accessories.

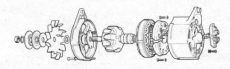

Alternator (exploded view)

Ampere (amp) A unit of measurement for the flow of electric current. One amp is the amount of current produced by one volt acting through a resistance of one ohm.

Anaerobic sealer A substance used to prevent bolts and screws from loosening. Anaerobic means that it does not require oxygen for activation. The Loctite brand is widely used.

Antifreeze A substance (usually ethylene glycol) mixed with water, and added to a vehicle's cooling system, to prevent freezing of the coolant in winter. Antifreeze also contains chemicals to inhibit corrosion and the formation of rust and other deposits that

would tend to clog the radiator and coolant passages and reduce cooling efficiency.

Anti-seize compound A coating that reduces the risk of seizing on fasteners that are subjected to high temperatures, such as exhaust manifold bolts and nuts.

Anti-seize compound

Asbestos A natural fibrous mineral with great heat resistance, commonly used in the composition of brake friction materials. Asbestos is a health hazard and the dust created by brake systems should never be inhaled or ingested.

Axle A shaft on which a wheel revolves, or which revolves with a wheel. Also, a solid beam that connects the two wheels at one end of the vehicle. An axle which also transmits power to the wheels is known as a live axle.

Axle assembly

Axleshaft A single rotating shaft, on either side of the differential, which delivers power from the final drive assembly to the drive wheels. Also called a driveshaft or a halfshaft.

B

Ball bearing An anti-friction bearing consisting of a hardened inner and outer race with hardened steel balls between two races.

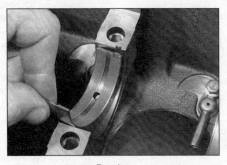

Bearing

Bearing The curved surface on a shaft or in a bore, or the part assembled into either, that permits relative motion between them with minimum wear and friction.

Big-end bearing The bearing in the end of the connecting rod that's attached to the crankshaft.

Bleed nipple A valve on a brake wheel cylinder, caliper or other hydraulic component that is opened to purge the hydraulic system of air. Also called a bleed screw.

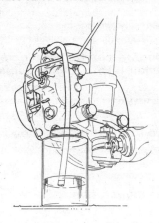

Brake bleeding

Brake bleeding Procedure for removing air from lines of a hydraulic brake system.

Brake disc The component of a disc brake that rotates with the wheels.

Brake drum The component of a drum brake that rotates with the wheels.

Brake linings The friction material which contacts the brake disc or drum to retard the vehicle's speed. The linings are bonded or riveted to the brake pads or shoes.

Brake pads The replaceable friction pads that pinch the brake disc when the brakes are applied. Brake pads consist of a friction material bonded or riveted to a rigid backing plate.

Brake shoe The crescent-shaped carrier to which the brake linings are mounted and which forces the lining against the rotating drum during braking.

Braking systems For more information on braking systems, consult the *Haynes Automotive Brake Manual*.

Breaker bar A long socket wrench handle providing greater leverage.

Bulkhead The insulated partition between the engine and the passenger compartment.

C

Caliper The non-rotating part of a disc-brake assembly that straddles the disc and carries the brake pads. The caliper also contains the hydraulic components that cause the pads to pinch the disc when the brakes are applied. A caliper is also a measuring tool that can be set to measure inside or outside dimensions of an object.

Camshaft A rotating shaft on which a series of cam lobes operate the valve mechanisms. The camshaft may be driven by gears, by sprockets and chain or by sprockets and a belt.

Canister A container in an evaporative emission control system; contains activated charcoal granules to trap vapours from the fuel system.

Canister

Carburettor A device which mixes fuel with air in the proper proportions to provide a desired power output from a spark ignition internal combustion engine.

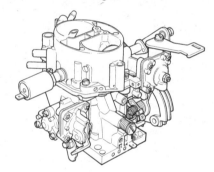

Carburettor

Castellated Resembling the parapets along the top of a castle wall. For example, a castellated balljoint stud nut.

Castellated nut

Castor In wheel alignment, the backward or forward tilt of the steering axis. Castor is positive when the steering axis is inclined rearward at the top.

Catalytic converter A silencer-like device in the exhaust system which converts certain pollutants in the exhaust gases into less harmful substances.

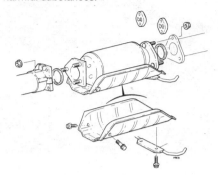

Catalytic converter

Circlip A ring-shaped clip used to prevent endwise movement of cylindrical parts and shafts. An internal circlip is installed in a groove in a housing; an external circlip fits into a groove on the outside of a cylindrical piece such as a shaft.

Clearance The amount of space between two parts. For example, between a piston and a cylinder, between a bearing and a journal, etc.

Coil spring A spiral of elastic steel found in various sizes throughout a vehicle, for example as a springing medium in the suspension and in the valve train.

Compression Reduction in volume, and increase in pressure and temperature, of a gas, caused by squeezing it into a smaller space.

Compression ratio The relationship between cylinder volume when the piston is at top dead centre and cylinder volume when the piston is at bottom dead centre.

Constant velocity (CV) joint A type of universal joint that cancels out vibrations caused by driving power being transmitted through an angle.

Core plug A disc or cup-shaped metal device inserted in a hole in a casting through which core was removed when the casting was formed. Also known as a freeze plug or expansion plug.

Crankcase The lower part of the engine block in which the crankshaft rotates.

Crankshaft The main rotating member, or shaft, running the length of the crankcase, with offset "throws" to which the connecting rods are attached.

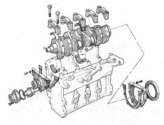

Crankshaft assembly

Crocodile clip See Alligator clip

D

Diagnostic code Code numbers obtained by accessing the diagnostic mode of an engine management computer. This code can be used to determine the area in the system where a malfunction may be located.

Disc brake A brake design incorporating a rotating disc onto which brake pads are squeezed. The resulting friction converts the energy of a moving vehicle into heat.

Double-overhead cam (DOHC) An engine that uses two overhead camshafts, usually one for the intake valves and one for the exhaust valves.

Drivebelt(s) The belt(s) used to drive accessories such as the alternator, water pump, power steering pump, air conditioning compressor, etc. off the crankshaft pulley.

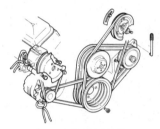

Accessory drivebelts

Driveshaft Any shaft used to transmit motion. Commonly used when referring to the axleshafts on a front wheel drive vehicle.

Driveshaft

Drum brake A type of brake using a drum-shaped metal cylinder attached to the inner surface of the wheel. When the brake pedal is pressed, curved brake shoes with friction linings press against the inside of the drum to slow or stop the vehicle.

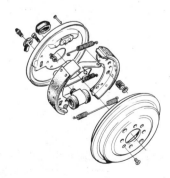

Drum brake assembly

E

EGR valve A valve used to introduce exhaust gases into the intake air stream.

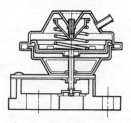

EGR valve

Electronic control unit (ECU) A computer which controls (for instance) ignition and fuel injection systems, or an anti-lock braking system. For more information refer to the *Haynes Automotive Electrical and Electronic Systems Manual*.

Electronic Fuel Injection (EFI) A computer controlled fuel system that distributes fuel through an injector located in each intake port of the engine.

Emergency brake A braking system, independent of the main hydraulic system, that can be used to slow or stop the vehicle if the primary brakes fail, or to hold the vehicle stationary even though the brake pedal isn't depressed. It usually consists of a hand lever that actuates either front or rear brakes mechanically through a series of cables and linkages. Also known as a handbrake or parking brake.

Endfloat The amount of lengthwise movement between two parts. As applied to a crankshaft, the distance that the crankshaft can move forward and back in the cylinder block.

Engine management system (EMS) A computer controlled system which manages the fuel injection and the ignition systems in an integrated fashion.

Exhaust manifold A part with several passages through which exhaust gases leave the engine combustion chambers and enter the exhaust pipe.

Exhaust manifold

F

Fan clutch A viscous (fluid) drive coupling device which permits variable engine fan speeds in relation to engine speeds.

Feeler blade A thin strip or blade of hardened steel, ground to an exact thickness, used to check or measure clearances between parts.

Feeler blade

Firing order The order in which the engine cylinders fire, or deliver their power strokes, beginning with the number one cylinder.

Flywheel A heavy spinning wheel in which energy is absorbed and stored by means of momentum. On cars, the flywheel is attached to the crankshaft to smooth out firing impulses.

Free play The amount of travel before any action takes place. The "looseness" in a linkage, or an assembly of parts, between the initial application of force and actual movement. For example, the distance the brake pedal moves before the pistons in the master cylinder are actuated.

Fuse An electrical device which protects a circuit against accidental overload. The typical fuse contains a soft piece of metal which is calibrated to melt at a predetermined current flow (expressed as amps) and break the circuit.

Fusible link A circuit protection device consisting of a conductor surrounded by heat-resistant insulation. The conductor is smaller than the wire it protects, so it acts as the weakest link in the circuit. Unlike a blown fuse, a failed fusible link must frequently be cut from the wire for replacement.

G

Gap The distance the spark must travel in jumping from the centre electrode to the side

Adjusting spark plug gap

electrode in a spark plug. Also refers to the spacing between the points in a contact breaker assembly in a conventional points-type ignition, or to the distance between the reluctor or rotor and the pickup coil in an electronic ignition.

Gasket Any thin, soft material - usually cork, cardboard, asbestos or soft metal - installed between two metal surfaces to ensure a good seal. For instance, the cylinder head gasket seals the joint between the block and the cylinder head.

Gasket

Gauge An instrument panel display used to monitor engine conditions. A gauge with a movable pointer on a dial or a fixed scale is an analogue gauge. A gauge with a numerical readout is called a digital gauge.

H

Halfshaft A rotating shaft that transmits power from the final drive unit to a drive wheel, usually when referring to a live rear axle.

Harmonic balancer A device designed to reduce torsion or twisting vibration in the crankshaft. May be incorporated in the crankshaft pulley. Also known as a vibration damper.

Hone An abrasive tool for correcting small irregularities or differences in diameter in an engine cylinder, brake cylinder, etc.

Hydraulic tappet A tappet that utilises hydraulic pressure from the engine's lubrication system to maintain zero clearance (constant contact with both camshaft and valve stem). Automatically adjusts to variation in valve stem length. Hydraulic tappets also reduce valve noise.

I

Ignition timing The moment at which the spark plug fires, usually expressed in the number of crankshaft degrees before the piston reaches the top of its stroke.

Inlet manifold A tube or housing with passages through which flows the air-fuel mixture (carburettor vehicles and vehicles with throttle body injection) or air only (port fuel-injected vehicles) to the port openings in the cylinder head.

J

Jump start Starting the engine of a vehicle with a discharged or weak battery by attaching jump leads from the weak battery to a charged or helper battery.

L

Load Sensing Proportioning Valve (LSPV) A brake hydraulic system control valve that works like a proportioning valve, but also takes into consideration the amount of weight carried by the rear axle.

Locknut A nut used to lock an adjustment nut, or other threaded component, in place. For example, a locknut is employed to keep the adjusting nut on the rocker arm in position.

Lockwasher A form of washer designed to prevent an attaching nut from working loose.

M

MacPherson strut A type of front suspension system devised by Earle MacPherson at Ford of England. In its original form, a simple lateral link with the anti-roll bar creates the lower control arm. A long strut - an integral coil spring and shock absorber - is mounted between the body and the steering knuckle. Many modern so-called MacPherson strut systems use a conventional lower A-arm and don't rely on the anti-roll bar for location.

Multimeter An electrical test instrument with the capability to measure voltage, current and resistance.

N

NOx Oxides of Nitrogen. A common toxic pollutant emitted by petrol and diesel engines at higher temperatures.

O

Ohm The unit of electrical resistance. One volt applied to a resistance of one ohm will produce a current of one amp.

Ohmmeter An instrument for measuring electrical resistance.

O-ring A type of sealing ring made of a special rubber-like material; in use, the O-ring is compressed into a groove to provide the sealing action.

O-ring

Overhead cam (ohc) engine An engine with the camshaft(s) located on top of the cylinder head(s).

Overhead valve (ohv) engine An engine with the valves located in the cylinder head, but with the camshaft located in the engine block.

Oxygen sensor A device installed in the engine exhaust manifold, which senses the oxygen content in the exhaust and converts this information into an electric current. Also called a Lambda sensor.

P

Phillips screw A type of screw head having a cross instead of a slot for a corresponding type of screwdriver.

Plastigage A thin strip of plastic thread, available in different sizes, used for measuring clearances. For example, a strip of Plastigage is laid across a bearing journal. The parts are assembled and dismantled; the width of the crushed strip indicates the clearance between journal and bearing.

Plastigage

Propeller shaft The long hollow tube with universal joints at both ends that carries power from the transmission to the differential on front-engined rear wheel drive vehicles.

Proportioning valve A hydraulic control valve which limits the amount of pressure to the rear brakes during panic stops to prevent wheel lock-up.

R

Rack-and-pinion steering A steering system with a pinion gear on the end of the steering shaft that mates with a rack (think of a geared wheel opened up and laid flat). When the steering wheel is turned, the pinion turns, moving the rack to the left or right. This movement is transmitted through the track rods to the steering arms at the wheels.

Radiator A liquid-to-air heat transfer device designed to reduce the temperature of the coolant in an internal combustion engine cooling system.

Refrigerant Any substance used as a heat transfer agent in an air-conditioning system. R-12 has been the principle refrigerant for many years; recently, however, manufacturers have begun using R-134a, a non-CFC substance that is considered less harmful to the ozone in the upper atmosphere.

Rocker arm A lever arm that rocks on a shaft or pivots on a stud. In an overhead valve engine, the rocker arm converts the upward movement of the pushrod into a downward movement to open a valve.

Rotor In a distributor, the rotating device inside the cap that connects the centre electrode and the outer terminals as it turns, distributing the high voltage from the coil secondary winding to the proper spark plug. Also, that part of an alternator which rotates inside the stator. Also, the rotating assembly of a turbocharger, including the compressor wheel, shaft and turbine wheel.

Runout The amount of wobble (in-and-out movement) of a gear or wheel as it's rotated. The amount a shaft rotates "out-of-true." The out-of-round condition of a rotating part.

S

Sealant A liquid or paste used to prevent leakage at a joint. Sometimes used in conjunction with a gasket.

Sealed beam lamp An older headlight design which integrates the reflector, lens and filaments into a hermetically-sealed one-piece unit. When a filament burns out or the lens cracks, the entire unit is simply replaced.

Serpentine drivebelt A single, long, wide accessory drivebelt that's used on some newer vehicles to drive all the accessories, instead of a series of smaller, shorter belts. Serpentine drivebelts are usually tensioned by an automatic tensioner.

Serpentine drivebelt

Shim Thin spacer, commonly used to adjust the clearance or relative positions between two parts. For example, shims inserted into or under bucket tappets control valve clearances. Clearance is adjusted by changing the thickness of the shim.

Slide hammer A special puller that screws into or hooks onto a component such as a shaft or bearing; a heavy sliding handle on the shaft bottoms against the end of the shaft to knock the component free.

Sprocket A tooth or projection on the periphery of a wheel, shaped to engage with a chain or drivebelt. Commonly used to refer to the sprocket wheel itself.

Starter inhibitor switch On vehicles with an automatic transmission, a switch that prevents starting if the vehicle is not in Neutral or Park.

Strut See MacPherson strut.

T

Tappet A cylindrical component which transmits motion from the cam to the valve stem, either directly or via a pushrod and rocker arm. Also called a cam follower.

Thermostat A heat-controlled valve that regulates the flow of coolant between the cylinder block and the radiator, so maintaining optimum engine operating temperature. A thermostat is also used in some air cleaners in which the temperature is regulated.

Thrust bearing The bearing in the clutch assembly that is moved in to the release levers by clutch pedal action to disengage the clutch. Also referred to as a release bearing.

Timing belt A toothed belt which drives the camshaft. Serious engine damage may result if it breaks in service.

Timing chain A chain which drives the camshaft.

Toe-in The amount the front wheels are closer together at the front than at the rear. On rear wheel drive vehicles, a slight amount of toe-in is usually specified to keep the front wheels running parallel on the road by offsetting other forces that tend to spread the wheels apart.

Toe-out The amount the front wheels are closer together at the rear than at the front. On front wheel drive vehicles, a slight amount of toe-out is usually specified.

Tools For full information on choosing and using tools, refer to the *Haynes Automotive Tools Manual*.

Tracer A stripe of a second colour applied to a wire insulator to distinguish that wire from another one with the same colour insulator.

Tune-up A process of accurate and careful adjustments and parts replacement to obtain the best possible engine performance.

Turbocharger A centrifugal device, driven by exhaust gases, that pressurises the intake air. Normally used to increase the power output from a given engine displacement, but can also be used primarily to reduce exhaust emissions (as on VW's "Umwelt" Diesel engine).

U

Universal joint or U-joint A double-pivoted connection for transmitting power from a driving to a driven shaft through an angle. A U-joint consists of two Y-shaped yokes and a cross-shaped member called the spider.

V

Valve A device through which the flow of liquid, gas, vacuum, or loose material in bulk may be started, stopped, or regulated by a movable part that opens, shuts, or partially obstructs one or more ports or passageways. A valve is also the movable part of such a device.

Valve clearance The clearance between the valve tip (the end of the valve stem) and the rocker arm or tappet. The valve clearance is measured when the valve is closed.

Vernier caliper A precision measuring instrument that measures inside and outside dimensions. Not quite as accurate as a micrometer, but more convenient.

Viscosity The thickness of a liquid or its resistance to flow.

Volt A unit for expressing electrical "pressure" in a circuit. One volt that will produce a current of one ampere through a resistance of one ohm.

W

Welding Various processes used to join metal items by heating the areas to be joined to a molten state and fusing them together. For more information refer to the *Haynes Automotive Welding Manual*.

Wiring diagram A drawing portraying the components and wires in a vehicle's electrical system, using standardised symbols. For more information refer to the *Haynes Automotive Electrical and Electronic Systems Manual*.

Note: *References throughout this index are in the form "**Chapter number**" • "**Page number**". So, for example, 2C•15 refers to page 15 of Chapter 2C.*

*Note: References throughout this index are in the form "**Chapter number**" • "**Page number**". So, for example, 2C•15 refers to page 15 of Chapter 2C.*

Note: *References throughout this index are in the form "***Chapter number***" • "***Page number***". So, for example, 2C•15 refers to page 15 of Chapter 2C.*

Note: *References throughout this index are in the form* "**Chapter number**" • "**Page number**". *So, for example, 2C•15 refers to page 15 of Chapter 2C.*

Preserving Our Motoring Heritage

>
The Model J Duesenberg
Derham Tourster.
Only eight of these
magnificent cars were
ever built – this is the
only example to be found
outside the United States
of America

Almost every car you've ever loved, loathed or desired is gathered under one roof at the Haynes Motor
Museum. Over 300 immaculately presented cars and motorbikes represent every aspect of our motoring
heritage, from elegant reminders of bygone days, such as the superb Model J Duesenberg to curiosities like the
bug-eyed BMW Isetta. There are also many old friends and flames. Perhaps you remember the 1959 Ford
Popular that you did your courting in? The magnificent 'Red Collection' is a spectacle of classic sports cars
including AC, Alfa Romeo, Austin Healey, Ferrari, Lamborghini, Maserati, MG, Riley, Porsche and Triumph.

A Perfect Day Out

Each and every vehicle at the Haynes Motor Museum has played its part in the history and culture of
Motoring. Today, they make a wonderful spectacle and a great day out for all the family. Bring the kids, bring
Mum and Dad, but above all bring your camera to capture those golden memories for ever. You will also find
an impressive array of motoring memorabilia, a comfortable 70 seat video cinema and one of the most
extensive transport book shops in Britain. The Pit Stop Cafe serves everything from a cup of tea to
wholesome, home-made meals or, if you prefer, you can enjoy the large picnic area nestled in the beautiful
rural surroundings of Somerset.

>
John Haynes O.B.E.,
Founder and
Chairman of the
museum at the wheel
of a Haynes Light 12.

<
Graham Hill's Lola
Cosworth Formula 1
car next to a 1934
Riley Sports.

The Museum is situated on the A359 Yeovil to Frome road at Sparkford, just off the A303 in Somerset. It is about 40 miles south of Bristol, and
25 minutes drive from the M5 intersection at Taunton.
Open 9.30am - 5.30pm (10.00am - 4.00pm Winter) 7 days a week, *except Christmas Day, Boxing Day and New Years Day*
Special rates available for schools, coach parties and outings Charitable Trust No. 292048